International Economic Regulation

The Library of Essays in International Law
General Editor: Robert McCorquodale

Titles in the Series

International Human Rights Law
Michael Addo

International Law and Indigenous Peoples
S. James Anaya

Law of the Sea
Hugo Caminos

Humanitarian Law
Judith Gardam

International Economic Regulation
Jane Kelsey

Sources of International Law
Martti Koskenniemi

Self-Determination in International Law
Robert McCorquodale

International Dispute Settlement
Mary Ellen O'Connell

International Crimes
Nikos Passas

International Environmental Law, Volumes I and II
Paula M. Pevato

State Responsibility in International Law
René Provost

Jurisdiction in International Law
W. Michael Reisman

Title to Territory
Malcolm Shaw

The Nature of International Law
Gerry Simpson

Collective Security Law
Nigel D. White

International Economic Regulation

Edited by

Jane Kelsey

The University of Auckland, New Zealand

Routledge
Taylor & Francis Group

LONDON AND NEW YORK

First published 2002 by Dartmouth Publishing Company and Ashgate Publishing

Reissued 2018 by Routledge
2 Park Square, Milton Park, Abingdon, Oxon OX14 4RN
711 Third Avenue, New York, NY 10017, USA

Routledge is an imprint of the Taylor & Francis Group, an informa business

Publisher's Note
The publisher has gone to great lengths to ensure the quality of this reprint but points out that some imperfections in the original copies may be apparent.

Disclaimer
The publisher has made every effort to trace copyright holders and welcomes correspondence from those they have been unable to contact.

A Library of Congress record exists under LC control number: 2001022332

ISBN 13: 978-1-138-73511-8 (hbk)
ISBN 13: 978-1-138-73510-1 (pbk)
ISBN 13: 978-1-315-18393-0 (ebk)

Contents

Acknowledgements

The editor and publishers wish to thank the following for permission to use copyright material.

Frederick M. Abbott (1996), 'The WTO Trips Agreement and Global Economic Development', *Chicago-Kent Law Review*, **72**, pp. 385–405. Copyright © Frederick M. Abbott.

American Society of International Law for the essays: Kenneth J. Vandevelde (1998), 'The Political Economy of a Bilateral Investment Treaty', *American Journal of International Law*, **92**, pp. 621–41. Copyright © 1998 The American Society of International Law; John W. Head (1996), 'Evolution of the Governing Law for Loan Agreements of the World Bank and other Multilateral Development Banks', *The American Journal of International Law*, **90**, pp. 214–34. Copyright © 1996 The American Society of International Law.

Blackwell Publishers Limited for the essays: Jagdish Bhagwati (1997), 'The Global Age: From a Sceptical South to a Fearful North', *World Economy*, **20**, pp. 259–83. Copyright © 1997 Blackwell Publishers Limited; Joseph E. Stiglitz (1999), 'The World Bank at the Millennium', *The Economic Journal*, **109**, pp. F577–F597. Copyright © 1999 Royal Economic Society.

Chicago-Kent College of Law for the essay: John Jackson (1996), 'Reflections on Constitutional Changes to the Global Trading System', *Chicago-Kent Law Review*, **72**, pp. 511–20. Reprinted in Jackson, John. H., *The Jurisprudence of GATT & The WTO: Insights on Treaty Law and Economics Relations*, New York: Cambridge University Press, 2000.

Columbia Journal of Transnational Law for the essay: John H. Jackson (1997), 'The Great 1994 Sovereignty Debate: United States Acceptance and Implementation of the Uruguay Round Results', *Columbia Journal of Transnational Law*, **36**, pp. 157–88. Copyright © 1997 John H. Jackson & Columbia Journal of Transnational Law.

Elsevier Science for the essay: Robert Howse and Michael J. Trebilcock (1996), 'The Fair Trade-Free Trade Debate: Trade, Labor, and the Environment', *International Review of Law and Economics*, **16**, pp. 61–79. Copyright © 1996 Elsevier Science. Reprinted with permission from Elsevier Science.

Foreign Policy for the essay: George Soros (1998–99), 'Capitalism's Last Chance?', *Foreign Policy*, **113**, pp. 55–66. Reprinted with permission from Foreign Policy 113 (Winter 1998–1999). Copyright © 1988 The Carnegie Endowment for International Peace.

Gerard Greenfield (2000), 'Putting Worker and Trade Union Rights in the WTO?', Issue 3, *Quanqiuhua Jiancai (Globalisation Monitor)*, **3**, pp. 1–3. Copyright © Gerard Greenfield.

Taylor & Francis Ltd for the essay: Richard Falk (1998), 'Global Civil Society: Perspectives, Initiatives, Movements', *Oxford Development Studies*, **26**, pp. 99–110. http://www.tandf.co.uk/journals

Third World Network for the essay: Martin Khor (2000), 'Rethinking Liberalization and Reforming the WTO', *Third World Economics*, **227**, pp. 11–15, 10.

Part I
Four Contrasting Perspectives

Introduction

Economic globalization has moved from the euphoria of the post-Cold War 1990s into much more turbulent times. Debates about the desirability, feasibility and the appropriate form of international economic regulation are now a heavily contested domain. This selection of recently published essays reflects the diversity of perspectives that are shaping the scope and direction of those debates, from legal formalism and law and economics to Third World legal theories and other critical perspectives.

By its very nature, the study of international economic regulation is also interdisciplinary. The desirability, effectiveness and impact of regulatory options can only be assessed within the broad context in which those economic activities take place. The collection therefore includes contributions from economists, international relations specialists, sociologists and medical academics. Voices from outside the academy also appear, as a reminder to lawyers that the insights and experiences of those within the international institutions, financial community, non-government and workers' organizations are essential to our understanding of these complex and controversial issues.

Since the World Trade Organization (WTO) was established in 1995, debates on international economic regulation have centred around the triumvirate of the International Monetary Fund (IMF), the World Bank group and the WTO. The current operations and future development of those institutions are a major focus of this volume. The diversity of topics it touches upon show how extensively domestic law and policy have been affected, directly or indirectly, by the integration of the world economy and the array of regulatory mechanisms that seek to structure and promote its development. The cross-section of subjects includes constitutional rights, intellectual property, public services, environment law, labour rights, competition law, rights of indigenous peoples, financial transactions, commercial practices and the legal system itself.

The essays in this volume span the early period of the WTO, through the financial crises of 1997 and 1998 and the consequent challenges that confront the World Bank and IMF, to the failure of the WTO ministerial meeting in Seattle in late 1999 to launch a new negotiating round. By the middle of this decade, international economic conditions and the challenges facing the international institutions will have taken another turn. Such turbulence makes it essential to understand the dynamics that are buffeting international economic regimes, as well as their substantive legal frameworks and instruments. This selection of essays seeks to provide that balance. The marked, and sometimes irreconcilable, differences of perspective which they present are more than academic. They reflect the contests of ideology, interests and objectives which make the regulation of economic activity in an internationalized environment so difficult and interesting.

Four Contrasting Perspectives

This collection begins with scene-setting contributions from two international relations specialists and a trade economist, as well as two legal academics from differing perspectives. The themes they address – the distribution of power between and within states; the tension between national sovereignty and international rule-making; and the contrast between normative and critical analyses of globalization – permeate the subject-specific contributions in the remainder of the volume.

Andrew Hurrell and Ngaire Woods, writing on 'Globalisation and Inequality' (Chapter 1), present an image of globalization as inherently dynamic and contested. They accuse liberal theories of failing to address the unequal distribution of power among states that shapes the choices and constraints they face. States with more power have more choices and benefit the most; less powerful states are more subject to coercion. Each dynamic generates a backlash against globalization, which is reflected in the reassertion of sovereignty and alternative economic models. That, in turn, affects the political processes of globalization at both domestic and international levels. Similar dynamics are evident in the increasingly powerful international economic institutions, affecting who sets the agenda, whose rules are applied, and how they are imposed and enforced. These institutions have, in practice, supplanted other international organizations which historically placed primacy on sovereign equality, decolonization, racial equality and economic justice. This displacement, according to Hurrell and Woods, has provoked calls from weaker states for more democracy in the economic institutions and moves to resurrect or develop alternatives.

Jadgish Bhagwati explores the imbalance of power from the perspective of a trade economist who supports the rules-based global trading system. In 'The Global Age: From a Sceptical South to a Fearful North' (Chapter 2), Bhagwati expresses the fear that a renewed North–South divide could derail the trade liberalization agenda and suggests ways to manage the disparity. In particular, he argues that the United National Conference on Trade and Development (UNCTAD) should perform the role for poorer states that the OECD does for richer ones, especially as UNCTAD has now endorsed the liberalization agenda.

United States free trade advocate, John Jackson, takes a more traditional legalist approach in 'Reflections on Constitutional Changes to the Global Trading System' (Chapter 3). Jackson questions how far the rationale for, and forms of, domestic economic regulation apply to international economic activities. He observes that problems of market failure, information asymmetry, public goods and distributive justice exist in both domestic and international spheres. However, domestic responses using taxation, subsidies and altering incentives are impractical at the international level. Regulation is more feasible and appropriate. International institutions aim to provide the structure for clear rule-making processes and effective implementation. Jackson notes that designing such a system involves questions of voting power, institutional capability and legitimation. Although the historic secrecy that surrounds international negotiations has raised issues of legitimacy, he argues that it is often necessary to secure compromises and allow time for education of the citizenry. Writing in 1996 he wondered whether the WTO would be able to meet these requirements and, with some reservations, concluded that the general outlook was promising.

In 'Fragmented States and International Rules of Law' (Chapter 4), Sol Picciotto offers a more critical legal analysis of the relationship between international and national economic regulation. Legal formalism treats states as autonomous and compartmentalized, whereas private economic transactions constantly cross borders and jurisdictions. As shifting patterns of capital accumulation reshape social and economic activities, they prompt the breakdown and restructuring of the relationship between national and international. This response is uneven across states. The result is a fragmented and multilayered patchwork of domestic and international, formal and informal, subject-specific and generalist regulatory regimes. Picciotto suggests that this may produce dissonance, not harmony. Taxation, for example, is a key element of national sovereignty. Despite more sophisticated tax planning by transnational enterprises, and corporate complaints over double taxation, there have been no effective moves to produce a common regulatory regime across jurisdictions because it would threaten state sovereignty. Picciotto concludes that people place more weight on law and legal institutions, domestic and international, than they are able to bear, which undermines their effectiveness and legitimacy.

Regulating International Finance and Investment

Picciotto and Jason Haines expand on the tension between national and international regulation with particular reference to 'Regulating Global Financial Markets' (Chapter 5). The volatility and risks caused by deregulated financial markets and opening of domestic capital markets, and their flow-on effects, raise crucial questions of supervision. These changes have fundamentally weakened the traditional IMF and state-based regulatory mechanisms. Yet attempts at international coordination and harmonization have been hesitant, ad hoc and undermined by the self-interested behaviour of different categories of regulators. The result is a multilayered institutional kaleidoscope that has no clear reference point and operates through informal international networks of professionals and intergovernmental initiatives, including the Basle Committee on Banking Supervision. Picciotto and Haines conclude that the regulation of financial markets may require increasingly global solutions, but it produces only pious generalities. States remain the primary source of regulatory regimes.

From a quite different perspective, the enigmatic George Soros offers an equally ambivalent prognosis in a commentary entitled 'Capitalism's Last Chance?' (Chapter 6). Soros fears that the pathologies inherent in the free movement of capital and deregulated financial markets now threaten the survival of the global capitalist system. While some states have strong systems of government intervention, international mechanisms for crisis management are inadequate. Leaving regulation to individual states, such as Malaysia's imposition of capital controls in 1998, could provoke the withdrawal of capital, followed by political disengagement and domestic repression. Soros's alternative is to revive and stabilize the flow of capital from the centre to the periphery and ensure the political allegiance of those states to the global capitalist system. His suggested vehicle is a credit insurance mechanism operated through the IMF that would guarantee lending to a specified level, although he questions its political feasibility.

In 'The Articles of Agreement of the IMF and the Liberalization of Capital Movements' (Chapter 7) Jacques Polak is more reluctant to extend the IMF's role. Polak examines the IMF's Interim Committee proposal in 1997 to amend the Articles of Agreement of the IMF, making promotion of capital account liberalization one of the Fund's specific purposes and giving it 'appropriate jurisdiction' over capital movements. In the past, creative interpretation has been relied on to extend IMF surveillance, financing, technical assistance and conditionality to tasks not specified in the Articles. He suggests that a similar approach to capital account liberalization would make formal amendment unnecessary, although it might have some symbolic value, and concludes that the proposal to extend the Fund's jurisdiction to capital movements is inappropriate, in part because it would impose a new dogma in an area where the costs and benefits of different approaches are still being explored.

Successive crises in the international regulation of global financial markets have highlighted their fragility. Moves to promote international regulation of foreign investment have been more politically driven. Negotiations on a multilateral agreement on investment (MAI) at the OECD began formally in 1995 and collapsed in 1998. The ambitious project reflected the frustration of investors and major powers at the limited scope of WTO coverage through the General Agreement on Trade in Services (GATS) and the Trade-Related Aspects of Investment Measures (TRIMS) provisions of the GATT, and the uneven quality and fragmented coverage of bilateral investment treaties (BITs). Kenneth Vandevelde in his essay 'The Political Economy of a Bilateral Investment Treaty' (Chapter 8), argues that BITs fall well short of a triumph for economic liberalism. Strong residues of economic nationalism are evident in the generally weak commitments to investor neutrality and minimal support for market facilitation. While relatively strong protections apply to investments, these are generally only available after the investment has been established. He suggests that parties have been more interested in promoting their own investments than in creating a liberal investment regime.

The MAI negotiations promised a more genuinely liberal investment agenda, carrying long-term commitments. Vandervelde acknowledged, however, that the complex undertaking would require compromises and predicted that problems of externalities, tax, labour mobility and public goods could intervene. That proved correct. An equally important obstacle, especially at the national level, was the perceived erosion of state sovereignty. David Schneiderman, writing on 'The Constitutional Strictures of the Multilateral Agreement on Investment' (Chapter 9), observes how pre-commitment strategies in bilateral, regional and transnational agreements can limit the ability of states to regulate market activities and make social policy choices. Increasingly, these supersede and overtake constitutional norms. Using the examples of NAFTA and the draft MAI, Schneiderman describes this as a new form of constitutionalism, where national constitutions are effectively amended through unconstitutional processes and the crucial elements of popular sovereignty and self-government are absent. Such concerns played an important role in derailing the MAI negotiations. They also formed an important foundation for more widespread attacks on the role of international economic regulation and the power of the international institutions.

The Multilateral Development Banks

As the globalization bubble began to burst in the mid-1990s, the future of the Bretton Woods Institutions came under more intensive scrutiny. The IMF remained relatively hardline in response to criticism and even sought to extend its mandate over capital accounts. The World Bank showed more concern to neutralize attacks on its legitimacy. The most frequent source of self-criticism, the Bank's chief economist, Joseph Stiglitz, acknowledged serious deficiencies in the so-called Washington Consensus agenda and in the democratic accountability of the international financial institutions. In his essay 'The World Bank at the Millennium' (Chapter 10) Stiglitz argues that fear of debate has engendered unhealthy and undemocratic levels of secrecy. Imposing technical economic solutions through structural adjustment loans, backed by conditionalities, had proved an ineffective way to change policies, was undemocratic and produced unacceptable social costs. Having recognized this, the Bank was transforming itself into a 'knowledge bank', to focus on building institutional capacity and consensus and leave governments to make the political decisions about policy and law.

Lawrence Tshuma's analysis of 'The Political Economy of the World Bank's Legal Framework for Economic Development' (Chapter 11) casts the Bank's 'good governance and 'capacity building' agenda in a different light. For Tshuma, this is yet another mechanism through which the Bank seeks to dictate a debtor state's system of law. In the past, structural adjustment lending was conditioned on adopting or implementing laws or regulations 'agreed' with the Bank. More recently, policy-based lending and 'good governance' programmes have promoted legal sector institutional reforms that emphasize formal equality and market facilitation. New lending instruments now provide funds for legal and free-standing technical assistance, and institutional capacity-building. Sourced in new institutional economics, these initiatives define a very limited role for the state and continue to circumscribe the choices of debtor states in a more subtle, but equally coercive, way.

John Head provides a lender's perspective on the pressures facing the Banks in this fractious environment in the 'Evolution of the Governing Law for Loan Agreements with the World Bank and other Multilateral Development Banks' (Chapter 12). Head notes that fragile economies and growing dissension in debtor states have created a greater risk of default on debt. With the exception of the European Bank for Reconstruction and Development (EBRD), multilateral development bank loan agreements typically provide for arbitration, but do not state the law to be applied. Although international law applies to agreements directly with states, the legal rules governing agreements with state enterprises remain unclear. Head urges all the banks to follow the EBRD approach which specifies UNCITRAL rules, place, language, law and sources. This, he believes, would prevent disputes, strengthen the banks' position and counter criticisms of their unaccountability.

The World Trade Organization

Parallel arguments about the erosion of state sovereignty and power differentials between members of these international economic organizations have enveloped the WTO since its establishment in 1995. In his essay 'The Great 1994 Sovereignty Debate: United States Acceptance and Implementation of the Uruguay Round Results' (Chapter 13), John Jackson treats the imbalance of power as an enduring reality. He suggests that the degree of constraint on national sovereignty depends on national structures and attitudes, and the effectiveness of enforcement mechanisms. Powerful states such as the United States will resist transferring power to a body dominated by other states with different national goals. Hence, the United States failure to secure *de jure* control of decision-making in the WTO meant limiting the scope of the organization's power and ensuring that the United States enjoyed *de facto* dominance over its decisions. While smaller states face effective constraints through the dispute settlement mechanism, the United States retains the choice whether to endorse formal interpretations of WTO agreements or comply with Appellate Body rulings.

Jackson's analysis implies that this imbalance is sustainable in the long term. Yet the breakdown of the Seattle meeting, and the subsequent outpouring of criticism from poorer Members at the UNCTAD X meeting in Bangkok in February 2000, suggested otherwise. In his essay on 'Rethinking Liberalization and Reforming the WTO' (Chapter 14) the editor of *Third World Economics*, Martin Khor, describes the anger of many poorer states about the refusal to address their concerns and their exclusion from substantive discussions at Seattle. Many poor states have been net losers from the Uruguay Round, some suffering severe losses. Major problems with the agreements on agriculture, textiles and clothing, and anti-dumping have enabled rich states to restrict access to their own markets while demanding that poorer states open their markets. Commitments on services, agriculture, intellectual property and investment, which were little understood at the time they were signed, have been impossible to implement for technical and substantive reasons. As the period of grace given to poorer states expires, enforcement could impose potentially crippling sanctions and the risk of economic collapse, widespread social and political instability and deeper poverty. Echoing the demands of many such states, Khor urges a review of existing Uruguay Round commitments and the refocusing of the WTO on its core role of regulating trade relations within an international trading system that addresses the realities of the majority of its members.

These concerns are reflected in the debate surrounding specific WTO agreements. In his essay 'Assessing the General Agreement on Trade in Services' (Chapter 15), Pierre Sauvé describes the GATS as the first step towards legally binding disciplines that would liberalize trade and investment in services and promote efficiency in the service industries. Because services remain heavily protected through domestic regulatory regimes, rather than through trade barriers, the definition of trade in services had to reach behind the state border to include rights of investment and movement of skilled personnel. Sauvé identifies serious weaknesses in the architecture of the agreement. Its complex matrix, inconsistencies between member's schedules, uneven commitments and unfinished negotiations on important sectors and issues make the implications of the agreement difficult to assess – a problem that is compounded by the lack of reliable data. Belief in its benefits rests on theoretical assumptions about predictability, allocative efficiencies and improved export opportunities. Despite the inbuilt agenda for further negotiations, Sauvé is reserved about the prospects for rapid liberalization and pessimistic about the political will to address the deficiencies in future GATS negotiations.

A major constraining factor is the pressure to address the priorities of poor states which claim that they have suffered the loss of infant services to multinationals under the GATS. Neela Mukherjee in 'GATS and the Millennium Round of Multilateral Negotiations' (Chapter 16) observes that the two main exports from such states are labour, which generates foreign exchange and remittances, and tourism. The most important modes of delivery are the movement of people and consumption of services by foreign firms and individuals abroad. Otherwise, these states are mainly service importers. Tradeable services are dominated by OECD states whose companies are the major beneficiaries of liberalization. Special provisions in the GATS to assist poor states have been virtually ignored. Few such states had the knowledge and capacity to assess the long-term implications of the GATS during the Uruguay Round. A majority now face problems of implementation. Mukherjee proposes extending the free movement of service personnel to all categories of labour; protection of culture and social services; commissioning quality research on the impact of the GATS; and ensuring adequate safeguards against balance of payments vulnerability and abuse by foreign services companies.

Such concerns are not limited to poorer states. The contribution from David Price, Allyson Pollock and Jean Shaoul, entitled 'How the World Trade Organisation is Shaping Domestic Policies in Health Care' and published in *The Lancet* (Chapter 17), examines the consequences of current and future GATS provisions for the importation of public health services into Britain. They view the prospect of opening public services to foreign competition using rules on government procurement and investment, backed by the dispute settlement mechanism, as a threat to universal public provision. In health services, the major beneficiaries would be United States health care providers, the pharmaceutical industry and insurers. While most governments still treat hospitals and public services as part of their national heritage, the authors argue that the restructuring of British funding mechanisms has prepared the ground for a competitive health care market that will have serious consequences for quality, publicly funded health services.

The TRIPS agreement is another major point of contention. Frederick Abbott, writing on 'The WTO Trips Agreement and Global Economic Development' (Chapter 18), observes that intellectual property rights comprise the primary assets of certain industries. Balancing their interests with those of the public is difficult at a domestic level, and more complex internationally. The TRIPS agreement was expected to have negative effects on poorer states through short-term wealth transfers. In return, they were promised longer-term economic returns, trade-offs in areas such as agriculture and textiles, and an effective means of challenging United States unilateralism. Abbott contends that these promises are not supported by empirical evidence. The main benefits accrue to large OECD-based transnationals, creating dangers of stratification between the technology 'haves' and 'have nots' in poorer and rich countries. Such inequalities are likely to cause political antagonisms and may prompt poorer states to revive import substitution and market closure. Recognizing that neither the industries nor major powers are likely to address these concerns, Abbott suggests a range of policy responses that the 'have nots' may adopt at the national, regional and international levels.

Antonio La Viña issues a more fundamental challenge to TRIPS in 'Intellectual Property Rights and Indigenous Knowledge of Biodiversity in Asia' (Chapter 19). He argues that the world-view that treats knowledge as a commercially tradeable commodity is incompatible with the right of indigenous peoples to exercise self-determination over their resources and traditional knowledge. Western legal definitions of intellectual property rights, imposed through colonization, continue to be used for the misappropriation of indigenous resources and knowledge. Resistance to this process, especially in the area of biodiversity, has given rise to an internationally coordinated campaign against the TRIPS agreement.

New Issues

While many poorer WTO members have sought to relitigate the existing agreements, more powerful members are committed to extending the depth and range of its jurisdiction. A particular flashpoint has been the attempt to put new issues of labour, environment, investment and competition law on the WTO agenda. Such moves have provoked criticism from diverse perspectives.

Ignacio De León explains in his essay, ' The Dilemma of Regulating International Competition under the WTO System' (Chapter 20), how the changing nature of trade barriers has created pressure to replace domestic anti-dumping legislation with competition or anti-trust law. Taking a strong public choice position, De León rejects both the anti-dumping and anti-trust law approaches. Even though competition law aims to promote economic efficiency and consumer sovereignty, anti-trust laws actively complement trade protectionism because both are invoked by less efficient producers as a deterrent to competition. Substituting one with the other would simply leave producers vulnerable to new government discretions and arbitrary intervention. Any aggressive behaviour by foreign companies was likely to be considered anti-competitive because it undermined local companies. De León contrasts the ideal of an international order that emerges from the consensus of its participants in the free market with an international regulatory regime that is rife with protectionism and state opportunism and is conducted through complex international negotiations. He argues that both domestic and international rules should reflect the commercial reality that markets are dynamic and in constant disequilibrium. All that parties require from domestic and international law is the clear delineation of individual rights and rules of transmission, and an efficient dispute settlement system.

The most intense controversy about 'new issues' has centred on proposals to enforce labour and environmental standards through the WTO. Bhagwati anticipates this in his essay on 'The Global Age' (Chapter 2), when he warns about the risk of re-creating the traditional North–South divide if rich states sought to moderate the competitive threat from poorer states through a social clause or eco-dumping provisions. He insists that other international forums are more appropriate for addressing such issues. China-based labour activist Gerard Greenfield, in his reflection on 'Putting Worker and Trade Union Rights in the WTO?' (Chapter 21), adopts a similar position to Bhagwati for the very different reason that bringing labour standards under the WTO would do nothing to advance the interests of Asian workers. Given the political nature of WTO disputes, the decision to bring a complaint would be a foreign policy decision, not a defence of workers' rights. A panel of trade experts would then assess whether the violation amounted to unfair trade; the exploitation of the workers would be irrelevant. Trade sanctions could be targeted at totally unconnected products, with no direct impact on the transgressing employer, who might by then have relocated and be exploiting workers in another state.

Robert Howse and Michael Trebilcock in 'The Fair Trade-Free Trade Debate: Trade, Labor, and the Environment' (Chapter 22) approach the same issue from a law and economics perspective. They fear that the dismissive response of free traders to any application of trade sanctions to environmental and labour issues will further undermine support for the rules-based trading system. They seek to distinguish between two kinds of 'fair trade' argument. The use of trade measures to achieve non-trade values, such as human rights and protection of the global commons, as defined by international agreements or norms would, they believe, have an inconclusive welfare effect on the target and sanction-imposing state, and globally. By contrast, fair trade measures that are designed to reduce the competitive advantage of the target state and benefit domestic producers and workers, serve to penalize workers and producers in the target states unfairly and are usually substitutes for politically unpalatable solutions in the sanction-imposing state. Accepting the first approach while rejecting the second would enhance the standing and effect of international treaties, agreements and norms on non-trade issues, and help to deflect challenges to the legitimacy of the WTO.

Legitimacy and Sovereignty

As regulatory regimes reach further behind national borders to govern activities that were previously the realm of domestic law, concerns about sovereignty have intensified. Challenges to the global regulatory regime are commonly expressed in terms of a 'democratic deficit' at the international and domestic levels. Joel Trachtman in his essay 'The Domain of WTO Dispute Resolution' (Chapter 23) offers a technical legal solution to the growing crisis in legitimacy. Using the tools of law and economics, he assesses how the WTO can best deliver a credible and effective rules-based trading system. Trachtman's approach centres on the relative merits of WTO law-making through legislation and adjudication. The thinness of treaty and customary international law means that, even when rules are set out in treaty texts, interpretation problems still arise. The WTO's legislative process makes changes and formal clarification difficult. Trachtman suggests that adopting standards allows more room for flexible and creative interpretation, especially for issues on the margins. Incomplete specification or standard-like provisions imply a political decision to delegate the hard decisions to judicial interpretation within the disputes settlement process. For example, the WTO has preferred not to legislate substantively on trade and environment issues, leaving them to WTO jurisprudence. However, empowering panels to construct WTO law, especially in sensitive cases involving conflicts between WTO and non-WTO treaties, raises issues of legitimacy. Based on a cost–benefit analysis of the Appellate Body's reports in the Shrimp-Turtle and Japanese film cases, Trachtman concludes that their decisions have been conservative and show political sensitivity to the implications for national sovereignty.

That conclusion may not have been shared by critics of the WTO process. Asking 'Is the WTO Open and Transparent?' (Chapter 24), Gabrielle Marceau and Peter Pedersen provide an inside account of recent attempts to defuse accusations of secrecy and unaccountability at the WTO. They outline a range of initiatives taken since 1996 to provide better access to information and increase non-governmental organization (NGO) participation on the periphery of WTO activities. The ability of NGOs to influence WTO decisions still rests with their governments at the national level; the degree of access available to NGOs in different states varies accordingly. Marceau and Pedersen identify two important constraints on extending the role of NGOs in the WTO: how to assess whether they are truly representative and legitimate; and the concern of poorer states that a greater role for predominantly Western NGOs would increase the imbalance of power at the WTO.

In 'Global Civil Society: Perspectives, Initiatives, Movements' (Chapter 25), international lawyer Richard Falk explores the prospects for a broader global polity that might invest the globalization process with a social dimension. Falk argues that the market-oriented and statist direction of globalization-from-above needs to be challenged by a movement promoting globalization-from-below that can effectively address the issues of poverty, social marginalization and environmental decay. He identifies two prerequisites: a coherent ideological and theoretical framework, and a clear critique that can encompass the deep normative concerns about globalization, yet accept its emancipatory potential and the persistence of states and markets. The unity of disparate social forces under the mantle of global civil society, and commitment to these principles, would be achieved through a process of normative democracy. In response to such propositions, Hurrell and Woods (Chapter 1) warn that those who claim to speak for 'civil society' may, in their own way, simply reinforce, and create, new inequalities.

In 'Global Economic Policy-Making: A New Constitutionalism?' (Chapter 26), Jane Kelsey is more sceptical about claims that globalization is inevitable and that the state is becoming impotent as a source of power and locus for resistance. Returning to the conflict between international economic agreements and domestic constitutions raised by Schneiderman (Chapter 9), she draws on practical examples from South Africa, India, Mexico, the Philippines and the

United States to conclude that states are still major players in the regulatory process and have choices about how they respond. Whether they stand firm behind their national constitution and democratically determined priorities or capitulate to the requirements of international regulation will reflect the conjuncture of external and domestic pressures at the time.

In Conclusion

The major institutions and agreements which have been the vehicles for international economic regulation over recent decades are now plagued by contradictions, conflicts and criticisms. Fractures between member states and the instability of global financial markets have slowed and potentially paralysed the formal liberalization process. Vocal, sometimes violent, and increasingly coordinated opposition to the process and outcomes of economic globalization has surfaced around the world and is targeted at both the international institutions and domestic governments. It is impossible to predict what the future might hold. This volume aims to help inform the debate and reflection on the prospects for, and complexities of, international economic regulation in this turbulent environment

Series Preface

Open a newspaper, listen to the radio or watch television any day of the week and you will read or hear of some matter concerning international law. The range of matters include the extent to which issues of trade and human rights should be linked, concerns about refugees and labour conditions, negotiations of treaties and the settlement of disputes, and decisions by the United Nations Security Council concerning actions to ensure compliance with international law. International legal issues have impact on governments, corporations, organisations and people around the world and the process of globalisation has increased this impact. In the global legal environment, knowledge of international law is an indispensable tool for all scholars, legal practitioners, decision-makers and citizens of the 21st century.

The Library of Essays in International Law is designed to provide the essential elements for the development of this knowledge. Each volume contains essays of central importance in the development of international law in a subject area. The proliferation of legal and other specialist journals, the increase in international materials and the use of the internet, has meant that it is increasingly difficult for legal scholars to have access to all the relevant articles on international law and many valuable older articles are now unable to be obtained readily. These problems are addressed by this series, which makes available an extensive range of materials in a manner that is of immeasurable value for both teaching and research at all levels.

Each volume is written by a leading authority in the subject area who selects the articles and provides an informative introduction, which analyses the context of the articles and comments on their significance within the developments in that area. The volumes complement each other to give a clear view of the burgeoning area of international law. It is not an easy task to select, order and place in context essays from the enormous quantity of academic legal writing prublished in journals – in many languages – throughout the world. This task requires professional scholarly judgment and difficult choices. The editors in this series have done an excellent job, for which I thank and congratulate them. It has been a pleasure working with them.

ROBERT McCORQUODALE
General Series Editor
School of Law
University of Nottingham

[1]

Globalisation and Inequality

Andrew Hurrell and Ngaire Woods

Globalisation has become an important part of the rhetoric of contemporary international relations. It survived the end of the Cold War when many of our other ordering or explanatory concepts did not, and is seemingly endlessly capable of reinvention to describe many different types of change in world politics. The term 'globalisation' is often invoked to describe the process of increasing interdependence and global enmeshment which occurs as money, people, images, values, and ideas flow ever more swiftly and smoothly across national boundaries. It is assumed to be a process driven by technological advance which will lead to a more and more homogeneous and interconnected world. In the new globalised world economy, it is argued, states will cooperate more and international institutions will flourish. All of this draws on the 'liberal interpretation of globalisation'.

Neglected in liberal and other writings about globalisation is one particularly important feature of world politics: inequality. Our concern is not to highlight the discontinuities and unevenness of globalisation, which are often noted, but rather to try to unpack the relationship between globalisation and inequality more carefully.[1] Serious analysis of inequality has been neglected behind a number of rhetorical propositions voiced in loud debates between liberals and their critics. The former argue that globalisation ameliorates inequalities, the latter that globalisation exacerbates inequality.[2] Unanswered are the two fundamental questions which link globalisation and inequality. In the first place: how is the *process* of globalisation influenced by inequalities among states? In the second place: how is the *impact* of globalisation affecting inequalities among states?

This article argues that inequality matters not just on grounds of equity, but is also important for understanding the nature of globalisation and its impact on world politics. Inequalities among states both shape the process of globalisation and are affected by it. In the first part of the article, we examine liberal

---

1. We present a critique which differs from those who argue that neither the impact nor the process of globalisation are as complete or as new as is often asserted. For the latter, see Robert Wade, 'Globalisation and its Limits: the Continuing Economic Importance of Nations and Regions', in· Suzanne Berger and Ronald Dore (eds.), *Convergence or Diversity? National Models of Production and Distribution in a Global Economy* (Ithaca, NY: Cornell University Press, forthcoming).
2. For examples of the view that market-driven globalisation exacerbates both political and economic inequalities, see James Petras and Morris Morley (eds.), *US Hegemony under Siege: Class, Politics and Development in Latin America* (London: Verso, 1990), and Barry Gills, Joel Rocamora, and Richard Wilson (eds.), *Low Intensity Democracy: Political Power in the New World Order* (London: Pluto Press, 1993).

© Millennium: Journal of International Studies, 1995. ISSN 0305-8298. Vol. 24, No. 3, pp. 447-470

Millennium

interpretations of globalisation. The term liberal is used to characterise both a market-liberal interpretation of the increasing interconnectedness of world markets, and a broader liberal interpretation of the political and social aspects of globalisation. We start with an examination of this view because its underlying assumptions dominate so much of the literature. Our enquiry both focuses on how and why liberals ignore or downplay inequality, and exposes the unresolved tensions within liberal approaches. This leads us to the second part of the article, in which we present our own reconceptualisation of globalisation, drawing on both an international society view of international relations and a view of the international political economy which emphasises the causes and promulgation of global inequalities. In the third section, we examine four areas which illustrate the linkages between inequality and globalisation: state strength, international institutions, values and norms, and non-state actors.

The Liberal Orthodoxy

Liberalism is a broad church and, as with all churches, has been marked by deep schisms. Yet, three broad propositions, all with deep historical roots, underpin liberal thinking on globalisation and inequality.

In the first place, liberal economists assume that the globalisation of world markets will reduce inequalities among and within states.[3] This strongly optimistic long-run assumption allows liberals to downgrade questions of inequality. The liberal orthodoxy posits a world economy in which a global increase in transactions is driven by technological advance and by self-maximising decisions of private actors. On this view, states and governments are bystanders to globalisation: the real driving forces are markets. Furthermore, the emergence of global markets improves efficiency. In the first place, the free movement of capital and goods across borders produces a more *efficient allocation of resources* around the globe. For example, investment will flow to where it is most profitable to invest it (hence, for example, it flows into developing areas where maximal gains might be made). In the second place, global markets ensure a more *efficient production of goods* in the world economy through the 'gains from trade'. Trade permits countries more effectively to exploit their factor endowments and to gain from specialisation. Furthermore, global investment and the movement of raw materials enhances both effects. Finally, a global world economy with freely exchangeable currencies and open markets ensures an *efficient distribution of goods and services* in a world in which price mechanisms operate globally. There is a real question here as to

---

3. Anne Krueger, 'Global Trade Prospects for the Developing Countries', *The World Economy* (Vol. 15, No. 4, 1992), pp. 457-74; Deepak Lal, *A Liberal International Economic Order: The International Monetary System and Economic Development* (Princeton, NJ: Princeton University International Finance Section, 1980); and John Dunning, *The Globalisation of Business: The Challenge of the 1990s* (London: Routledge, 1993).

Globalisation and Inequality

whether available evidence endorses the improved efficiencies that the liberals hypothesise. We will pick up this point later, but it is worth noting at this stage that modern economists are questioning these theories by opening up other types of investigation into the causes of growth.[4]

A second observation of the liberal view of globalisation is that it will expand not only global markets but also the associated problems of market imperfections, negative externalities, environmental degradation, and, casting the net still wider, refugees, and humanitarian disasters.[5] As a result, globalisation creates a powerful 'demand' for international institutions and cooperation. Political authorities in the new global economy (be they new, emerging authorities or the governments and states for which they are supposed to substitute) will be forced to resolve common problems and to manage the frictions which arise from increasing interdependence. These insights are well highlighted by the liberals. Greater cooperation has become necessary, even if it is no easier to achieve. The prospects of cooperation are said to be enhanced by the fact that states' autonomy is diminishing, and their capacity to regulate and redistribute resources domestically is increasingly limited. Hence, in many areas, governance and regulation at the international level are becoming ever more important. Although such governance predominantly takes the form of inter-state regimes, both formal and informal regimes between private actors are playing an increasingly significant role.[6]

Third, liberals assume that globalisation will tend, in the long-run, to promote societal convergence built around common recognition of the benefits of markets and liberal democracy, and involving the emergence of global values, issues, and institutions. The liberal interpretation of globalisation suggests that the rise of technology and the enmeshment of world markets is bringing about a decrease in states' power and desire for independence. In the first place, the infrastructure of globalisation (global communications and transport systems) and the rise of new technologies (satellites, computer networks, and so forth) make it increasingly difficult for states to stem flows of information. At the same time, it has become increasingly easy for values, knowledge, and ideas to move across national boundaries. Economically, states must now compete actively for foreign investment and technology in global markets and, in order to do so effectively, they are converging on open-market policies. Politically, preferences for particular types of political organisation and values (free elections, sustainable development, human rights, and the like) are spreading. Hence, liberals explain,

---

4. The literature on endogenous growth is one such investigation. See, for example, Paul M. Romer, 'The Origins of Endogenous Growth', *Journal of Economic Perspectives*(Vol. 8, No. 1, 1994), pp. 3-22.
5. See, for example, Richard N. Cooper, *Economic Policy in an Interdependent World: Essays in World Economics* (Cambridge, MA: MIT Press, 1986), Chapter 11, and Robert O. Keohane, *International Institutions and State Power: Essays in International Relations Theory* (Boulder, CO: Westview Press, 1989), Chapter 5.
6. See generally Stephen D. Krasner (ed.), *International Regimes* (Ithaca, NY: Cornell University Press, 1983).

Millennium

there is an increasing homogenisation of economic policies and political organisation caused by globalisation. 'At least in intellectual terms', write John Williamson and Stephan Haggard, 'we today live in one world rather than three'.[7]

At the core of liberal thinking about globalisation lies a set of assumptions about how and why values, norms, and policy ideas converge. It is worth distinguishing two different processes to which liberals allude. In the first place, the convergence of policies across the globe may be attributed to the rationality of the policies and their proponents.[8] It is assumed that policy-makers are increasingly rational, technocratic, and literate in each particular field, be it, for example, environmental policy or economics. These policy-makers can draw on international links to other like-minded technocrats in other countries or in international institutions. One way in which this process is depicted is—following Peter Haas—in terms of epistemic communities consisting of economists or specialists in a field. Haas defines epistemic communities as 'networks of knowledge based communities with an authoritative claim to policy relevant knowledge within their domain of expertise'.[9] On this view, globalisation is facilitating the emergence of transnational governmental coalitions based on technical understanding of particular issues or sets of problems.

In contrast to emerging transnational technocratic coalitions, a second process of convergence involves the flow of ideas and information across borders as a result of increased societal interdependence. Increased communication and travel have facilitated the diffusion of values, knowledge, and ideas, and have enhanced the ability of like-minded groups to organise across national boundaries. From a liberal perspective, the strength of such groups rests on their ability to articulate a powerful set of human values, to harness the growing sense of a cosmopolitan moral awareness, and to respond to the multiple failures of the state system, both locally and globally. Influence does not derive from narrow economic incentives, nor from power political interests, but rather from ideas and values that are felt directly, if still unevenly, by individual human beings. Here, globalisation is leading not merely to instrumental transnational coalitions but to what some call an 'international civil society', or, better, 'global civil society': the 'emergence of a parallel arrangement of political interaction...focused on the

---

7. John Williamson and Stephan Haggard, 'The Political Conditions for Economic Reform', in Williamson and Haggard (eds.), *The Political Economy of Policy Reform* (Washington, DC: International Institute for Economics, 1994), p. 530. See also Robert H. Bates and Anne O. Krueger (eds.), *Political and Economic Interactions in Economic and Policy Reform* (Oxford: Blackwell, 1993), and Haggard and Steven B. Webb (eds.), *Voting for Reform: Democracy, Political Liberalization and Economic Adjustment* (New York, NY: Oxford University Press for the World Bank, 1994).
8. This view is particularly visible in many of the essays in John Williamson (ed.), *The Political Economy of Policy Reform* (Washington, DC: Institute for International Economics, 1993).
9. Peter M. Haas, 'Introduction: Epistemic Communities and International Policy Coordination', *International Organization* (Vol. 46, No. 1, 1992), pp. 1-36. See also Ernst B. Haas, *When Knowledge is Power: Three Models of Change in International Organizations* (Berkeley, CA: University of California Press, 1989).

Globalisation and Inequality

self-conscious construction of networks of knowledge and action, by decentred, local actors....'[10]

Together, these processes lead to the progressive enmeshment of other states and cultures within the liberal system. Globalisation and interdependence help ensure the spread of information, values, and ideas that make non-liberal alternatives decreasingly feasible.[11] In part, the driving mechanism has to do with the rational adaptation on the part of policy-makers to a changing structure of external incentives, which in turn leads to processes of genuine learning and to the internalisation of liberal values. However, more generally, this view develops the Kantian notion of a gradual but progressive diffusion of liberal values, partly as a result of liberal economics and increased economic interdependence, partly as a liberal legal order comes to sustain the autonomy of a global civil society, and partly as a result of the successful example set by the multifaceted liberal capitalist system of states. The problem, as we shall see, is that this kind of view drastically underestimates the role that powerful states and institutions have played in offering incentives to, and applying pressures on, other states to alter their policies.

We might summarise the liberal view of globalisation according to the following argument structure:

(1) the increase in transactions across state boundaries is of great significance to the nature of the international system (in terms of *structure, process*, and *actors*);

(2) the processes of globalisation have a logic and dynamic of their own, driven by technological change, increasing knowledge, and rational decision-making.

(3) As a result, societies across the world are increasingly linked through *markets* and through an increasingly close-knit *transnational civil society*, rather than through the arena of inter-state competition.

(4) Hence, states will no longer form the only or necessarily most important frameworks of political authority (*cf.*, James Rosenau's picture of an

---

10. Ronnie D. Lipschutz, 'Reconstructing World Politics: The Emergence of Global Civil Society', *Millennium: Journal of International Studies* (Vol. 21, No. 3, 1992), p. 390. See also Richard Falk, 'The Global Promise of Social Movements: Explorations at the Edge of Time', *Alternatives* (Vol. 12, No. 2, 1987), pp. 173-96; *Millennium* Special Issue on Social Movements in World Politics (Vol. 23, No. 3, 1994); and Paul Wapner, 'Politics Beyond the State: Environmental Activism and World Civic Politics', *World Politics* (Vol. 47, No. 3, 1995), pp. 311-40. For an example of the broader revival of interest in transnationalism, see Thomas Risse-Kappen (ed.), *Bringing Transnational Relations Back In: Non-State Actors, Domestic Structures and International Institutions* (Cambridge: Cambridge University Press, 1995).

11. See, for example, Daniel Deudney and G. John Ikenberry, 'The International Sources of Soviet Change', *International Security* (Vol. 16, No. 3, 1991/92), pp. 74-118, and the discussion of these ideas in Fred Halliday, *Rethinking International Relations* (London: Macmillan, 1994), especially Chapter 5.

Millennium

autonomous multi-centric system emerging alongside the long-established system of states[12]).

(5) Thus, there is a growing tension between the reality of a globalising world economy and an anachronistic states-system. This tension may be unsettling, but it does not involve any irreconcilable conflicts or contradictions.

(6) In particular, international institutions will grow as states perceive that their interests are better met in a globalising world economy through institutionalised cooperation.

It would be wrong to suggest that contemporary liberalism takes a naively benign view of the impact of globalisation. Although these core propositions continue to underpin much liberal thought, liberals are neither as inflexible nor as unified as the above outline would suggest. Whilst remaining optimistic in the long-run, problems clearly abound. Thus, although efficiency gains will reduce inequalities both among and within states over time, there are two caveats to be made. Liberals accept that, in the short-run, there will be adjustment costs which might exacerbate inequalities. They also accept that the gains from globalisation will not necessarily be evenly spread: whilst every country stands to make an absolute gain from globalisation, some stand to gain relatively more than others. For some, this points to a positive role that government might play in global markets, tilting the playing field towards their own competitors.[13]

In addition, there are the potentially high costs of *political adjustment*. This is the challenge identified and discussed by Robert Reich:

We are living through a transformation that will rearrange the politics and economics of the coming century. There will be no *national* products or technologies, no national corporations, no national industries. There will be no national economies, at least as we have come to understand that concept. All that will remain rooted within national borders are the people who comprise a nation. Each nation's primary assets will be its citizen's skills and insights. Each nation's primary political task will be to cope with the centrifugal forces of the global economy which tear at the ties binding citizens together—bestowing ever greater wealth on the most skilled and insightful, while consigning the less skilled to a declining standard of living.[14]

The issue of adjustment highlighted by Robert Reich, is taken up by Adrian Wood in his work on the impact of globalisation on unskilled workers in the

---

12. James Rosenau, *Turbulence in World Politics* (New York, NY: Harvester Wheatsheaf, 1990).

13. Laura D'Andrea Tyson, *Who's Bashing Whom? Trade Conflict in High-Technology Industries* (Washington, DC: Institute for International Economics, 1992), and Robert Reich, *The Work of Nations: Preparing Ourselves for 21st-Century Capitalism* (London: Simon and Schuster, 1991).

14. Reich, *op. cit.*, in note 13, p. 3, emphasis in original.

Globalisation and Inequality

North.[15] Nevertheless, although the market liberal perspective accepts these problems, ultimately it argues that such developments are a necessary part of wealth creation, and can potentially be managed by rational and enlightened state policies.

The important point, however, is not the recognition of these adjustment problems, but rather the failure to acknowledge that deep, unresolved tensions exist within the liberal view of globalisation. The first concerns the role of the state. At one extreme the anti-statist strand of liberalism has reappeared in strident form, rejecting the state as both a rational institution for effective economic management and as the locus of identity in a world characterised by homogenisation and increasingly complex forms of social communication.[16] As Ohmae puts it: '[t]he nation state has become an unnatural, even dysfunctional, unit for organizing human activity and managing economic endeavor in a borderless world. It represents no genuine, shared community of economic interests; it defines no meaningful flows of economic activity'.[17]

Yet, most contemporary liberals accept the need for the state and for institutional reforms.[18] In this dominant liberal discourse there is a good deal of talk of 'reinventing' government and, increasingly, institutions. The important point here is the fundamentally apolitical and technocratic view of what this 'reinvention' entails. On the technocratic view, it is mostly a matter of 'institutional strengthening' and 'capacity building', sometimes with a dose of decentralisation. The state is certainly the problem for market-minded liberals, but it can also become a central part of the solution, if the right policy-mix is chosen. The real problem here lies in reconciling the reduction of the state, undertaken as part of structural adjustment and economic liberalisation, with the new needs for an effective state to provide the necessary infrastructure in the economy.[19] Managed liberalism requires the state to maintain a high degree of political power and authority, while the liberal interpretation of globalisation suggests that states' political power might well be eroding.

15. Adrian Wood, *North-South Trade, Employment and Inequality: Changing Fortunes in a Skill-Driven World* (Oxford: Oxford University Press, 1994).

16. In this they follow Karl W. Deutsch, *et al.*, *Political Community and the North Atlantic Area: International Organization in the Light of Historical Experience* (New York, NY: Greenwood, 1957, reprinted 1969). For a more detailed treatment of some of the key themes in this debate, see David Long's article in this issue.

17. Kenichi Ohmae, 'The Rise of the Region State', *Foreign Affairs* (Vol. 72, No. 2, 1993), p. 78. Note how closely his words echo those of Norman Angell writing in 1909: 'the very complexity of the division of labour tends to set up cooperation in groups which might thwart political frontiers, so that the political no longer limits or coincides with the economic'. *The Great Illusion* (London: Heinemann, 1933), p. 157.

18. World Bank, *World Bank Development Report 1994* (Washington, DC: World Bank, 1994), and Inter-American Development Bank (IDB), *Economic and Social Progress in Latin America* (Washington, DC: IDB/Johns Hopkins University Press, 1994).

19. A thoughtful contemplation of this problem is Moisés Naím, *Latin America's Journey to the Market: From Macroeconomic Shocks to Institutional Therapy* (San Francisco, CA: International Center for Economic Growth, 1995).

Millennium

A second problem which remains unresolved in the liberal view is the relationship between different parts of the liberal vision: how to balance economic objectives and market liberalisation with liberal political and social goals. This difficulty has been increasingly visible in, for example, the arguments within the World Bank on how to deal with 'new' issues (such as environmental questions and the promotion of 'good governance'),[20] and in discussions of the impact of structural adjustment on poverty.[21] The dominant response is, once again, to see this as a technical problem, and to deal with it, for example, as an issue of 'sequencing'.[22] Yet, as we will argue below, the tensions run far deeper than this and crucially turn on the choice that exists between the effective management of globalisation on the one hand, and the promotion of such liberal values as participation, representation, and legitimacy on the other.

A third tension within liberalism concerns the differential speeds with which the dynamics of liberal progress work themselves out, and how this should be managed. A common theme of recent liberal writing has been to emphasise the increasing divide between a cohesive, prosperous, and peaceful bloc of liberal states and the instability and chaos of the rest of the world. This cleavage between a Grotian core and a Hobbesian periphery has been characterised in various ways: zones of peace *vs.* zones of turmoil;[23] the OECD as something approaching a giant pluralist security community;[24] the 'West' as a cohesive republican order based on economic growth, democratic governance, and liberal tolerance;[25] and the widening gaps on a global scale 'between publics and governments, between haves and have-nots, between nuclear and non-nuclear power', and so forth.[26] Yet, although new divisions in a globalising world are recognised, insufficient attention is given to the subsequent implications of globalisation either for politics on the 'other side of the divide' (outside of the liberal, integrating zone) or for global inequality.

20. See Joan Nelson and Stephanie Eglinton, *Encouraging Democracy: What Role for Conditioned Aid?* (Washington, DC: Overseas Development Council, 1992).

21. This issue was highlighted in the *World Bank Development Report 1990* (Washington, DC: World Bank, 1990).

22. See, for example, Sebastian Edwards, *Macroeconomic Stabilization in Latin America: Recent Experience and Some Sequencing Issues* (Washington, DC: NBER, 1994). For a discussion of other techniques, see Michael Lipton and Jacques Van der Gaag, *Including the Poor* (Washington, DC: World Bank, 1993).

23. Max Singer and Aaron Wildavsky, *The Real World Order: Zones of Peace, Zones of Turmoil* (Chatham, NJ: Chatham House Publishers, 1993).

24. Barry Buzan, *The European Security Order Recast: Scenarios for the Post-Cold War Era* (London: Pinter, 1990).

25. Daniel Deudney and G. John Ikenberry, 'The Logic of the West', *World Policy Journal* (Vol. 10, No. 4, 1993-94), pp. 17-25.

26. James Rosenau and Ernst-Otto Czempiel, *Governance without Government: Order and Change in World Politics* (Cambridge: Cambridge University Press, 1989), Chapter 1.

Globalisation and Inequality

Redefining Globalisation

The liberal orthodoxy highlights the progressive enmeshment of economies and societies that results from globalisation. It emphasises the powerful international and transnational pressures that both constrain the range of viable state policies and influence the complexion of domestic politics. Neglected, however, in the liberal view is an analysis of the unevenness of the process of globalisation and the importance of the hierarchy among the states and actors which drive this process. The core proposition of our critique of the liberal orthodoxy on globalisation is a simple one: inequality among states matters. We explore this proposition in this section, looking first at the ways in which states are unequal and which types of inequality matter. We then move on to examine how these inequalities shape integration into the world economy, and the emergence of institutions, values, and norms associated with globalisation.

We are especially interested, then, in the two-way relationship between state inequality and globalisation. In order to clarify this relationship, we emphasise two aspects of the process of globalisation. One aspect is directly observable: the increase in transactions and interconnectedness among (especially OECD and selected other) states which is driven by both technological change and political choices. These 'observable' changes obviously affect choices and outcomes in world politics. Firms and governments have to rethink their strategies in a world in which the international arena affects an increasing range of decisions. Yet, tracing out the ways in which increased trans-border transactions, changes in technology, and new forms of economic competition have altered incentive structures does not tell us *how* firms, governments, and other actors will reshape their strategies and objectives. Here, another aspect of globalisation is crucial: the way in which it is 'experienced' and the way that experience is rooted within institutions.[27]

Actors across the globe interpret their choices and constraints in very different ways, and these understandings are embedded in very different kinds of domestic institutions and social structures. As a result, the impact of globalisation is nowhere equal and the simple notion of homogenisation conceals a more complex and ambiguous set of processes. Crucially, globalisation affects the political processes within which actors work. For example, governments dealing with issues such as global investment, the environment, human rights, and, to a lesser extent, democratisation, must now face two new sets of political pressures and constraints. At the international level, states must participate in new sets of negotiations and institutions. Within their own political systems, governments now face pressures from domestic actors, empowered or inspired by the international attention given to these issues. Just as technological change may

---

27. For a related, but distinct, emphasis on the importance of subjective understandings of globalisation, see Roland Robertson, *Globalisation: Social Theory and Global Culture* (London: Sage, 1992). It should, however, be noted that Robertson's approach is different from that adopted in this article.

Millennium

drive domestic firms to push for new types of investment regulation, so too conventions on the environment may fuel domestic interest groups to push for changes in domestic environmental standards. Thus, the 'experienced' aspect of globalisation is important because it enables us to look more closely at these political processes that condition the impact of globalisation, both at the international and domestic levels.

This way of understanding the process of globalisation is crucial to examining the impact of inequality on globalisation and vice-versa. Simply put, globalisation affects regions of the world in different ways. In part, this is due to the unevenness of increased flows and interconnectedness, the spread of technology, trade, and communications which is most heavily concentrated among OECD countries. However, the impact of globalisation is also conditioned by political inequalities, at both the international and domestic levels.

In the international realm, some states will have more power (rooted in military as well as political and economic capacity) to influence outcomes of negotiations and decisions. Hence, 'weaker' states face heavily constrained choices or an agenda which they have little influence in defining. Furthermore, their choices will carry powerful political implications; not just because they submit to the will of larger states over a particular issue, but because, over the longer term, weak states' decisions constrain their future options. For example, when weaker states sign up to a human rights convention, or an intellectual property standard, they face a greater prospect than more powerful states of coercive enforcement. Hence, globalisation affects not just their bargaining power at the time of negotiation, but, more widely, their relative power to make choices in the future.

At the domestic level, too, there are important differences among states and governments. Domestically weak governments face much greater difficulties in getting their constituencies to adapt to the changes or agreements worked out in international negotiations and fora. This is less of a problem if the state has power in the international arena, for it can then change the rules to which it agrees to be bound. However, where weak states enter into international undertakings which they cannot alter, they become not only more vulnerable to international pressures, but more susceptible to domestic political weaknesses. In implementing the necessary policies so as to participate in the new global agreements and economy, they can quickly lose domestic support. Such governments frequently become trapped between the so-called 'imperatives of globalisation' (such as economic liberalisation and subscription to a range of international standards on the environment, human rights, and so forth) and a political constituency which refuses to adapt and increasingly rebels against the government.

Overall, our definition of globalisation requires us, in examining its impact, to look at inequality among states at both the international and domestic levels. We might summarise this definition in the following propositions.

Globalisation and Inequality

(1) The observable face of globalisation is an increase in transactions across state boundaries, in part driven by technological change and increasing knowledge, which are mainly developed in large industrialised countries.

(2) The impact of these observable changes is conditioned by the different experiences that states have of increased interconnectedness, depending on variations in their political and economic capacities.

(3) The new interconnectedness is regulated by rules and institutions formulated and enforced mainly by the most powerful actors in the international political arena (especially states and firms).

(4) The benefits of globalisation flow to those states with the greatest capacity to absorb and adapt to the new types of transactions. This capacity includes the domestic political strength of governments.

(5) Increased linkages between societies are effected not just through markets, but also through issues and ideas which give international voice to non-state actors and empower them to be more active in domestic politics (some would refer to this, perhaps exaggeratedly, as the beginnings of a transnational civil society). These transnational linkages can erode the domestic political strength of the government.

Our definition of globalisation requires us to examine the political forces which shape its emergence and impact, and, in doing so, to reconsider the sources and nature of inequality among states. We need to replace the liberal Kantian image of *progressive enmeshment* with the more complex idea of *coercive socialisation*, involving both a range of external pressures (both state-based and market-based) and a variety of transmission mechanisms between the external and the domestic. In defining globalisation in this way, we bring together strands from several different ways of thinking about international relations. Our attention to inter-state power politics suggests something of a realist starting point, but this is heavily diluted: first, by our concern to explain change; second, by our examination of the role of non-state actors; and, third, by our attention to other dimensions of international relations (such as the role of institutions and values). The different strands of thinking are readily apparent in our definition of the core dimensions of state power which assist in examining inequality: the formal status of states (their degree of formally recognised independence); the territory, population, and natural resources of a state· the domestic strength, efficacy, and viability of a state; the distribution of economic wealth, military, and political power among states; the meta-power to make and change the rules of international relations; and the power and relative status of non-state actors. As we will elaborate below, these dimensions of inequality shape the nature and impact of globalisation, and, in turn, globalisation has highly significant effects on inter-state inequalities.

Millennium

Beyond the Liberal View of Inequality and Globalisation

The liberal view of globalisation, as we have already seen in the first section of this paper, highlights the *formal equality of states* which defines the key set of actors in the global market-place. The liberal view also implicitly recognises the uneven *distribution of economic wealth* among states, since this provides one of the conditions for globalisation: the incentive for capital and production to shift to new areas. However, the other dimensions of state power are virtually ignored in the liberal view. Although the role of *non-state actors* (MNCs, foreign investors, global communications conglomerates, and so forth) is recognised, little attention is paid to the political power of these actors. More fundamentally, liberals do not adequately address the *distribution of political power among states*, the capacity of some to set down rules for others, and the relative *domestic strength and viability of the state*. Yet, these other dimensions of inequality among states are crucial to an understanding of the nature and impact of globalisation. This is most simply highlighted by the coincidence between the unevenness of globalisation on the one hand, and the distribution of military and political power and international rule-making authority (or 'meta-power') among states on the other.

State Strength

Reframing one of the points made above, for large and powerful states (either globally or within a region) globalisation is, at least to some extent, a realm of choice. These states have the power to open or close world or regional markets and have discretion over how fast they wish to develop and exploit technological change. Furthermore, the impact of globalisation, because it is a process they influence, is likely to reinforce their position and their relative power (even if it channels it in new ways). For less powerful states in a region or in the world economy, globalisation is a process which is happening to them and to which they must respond. To some degree, they must choose either to accept the rules of the more powerful or not; although in today's world economy, where relative autarchy is punitive and where there is no alternative centre of power (as provided previously by the USSR), some would argue that they have little choice but to accept the rules.

These propositions, however, do not always reflect reality. There are limits to the control and influence of the large and powerful states, and the above arguments underestimate the importance of path dependence and the extent to which the process of globalisation is shaped by ongoing actions and reactions from both sides. For example, over the past four decades, industrialised countries have exhorted less developed countries to integrate into the world economy and to attract more investment. Yet, in each decade, different types of investment from industrialised countries have produced a backlash and a reassertion of state sovereignty. Hence, in the 1970s, developing countries attempted through the United Nations Conference on Trade and Development (UNCTAD), the United

Globalisation and Inequality

Nations General Assembly, and other fora, to control and limit the activities of multinational corporations which had come to be seen as too powerful and exploitative. In the 1980s, Western international commercial banks became the adversary: accused of punishingly high interest rates and imposing stringent adjustment on debtors. After the debt crises of the 1980s, developing countries pushed for new forms of regulation, control, and replacement of international bank loans. In the early 1990s, the backlash is against capital flows into share and bond markets in developing countries. After the crisis in Mexico in 1994 highlighted the volatility and destabilising effects of such investment, the new call from several different regions is for capital controls, as already put in place in Chile and China.[28]

These different forms of 'backlash' against globalisation highlight that the process is a contested one. Yet, it is not the case that the most powerful states in realist power-political terms always win in such contests. Globalisation, and attempts to control it, are shaped by those with power—derived from all of the sources listed above. East Asia provides a particular example of the varied sources of such power. For, although the recent World Bank study of the 'East Asia miracle' points to these countries' integration into world markets,[29] this interpretation is controversial and wrongly ignores, as several economists have pointed out, other political and economic factors.[30]

The debate about East Asia is a crucial one, because it turns on the extent to which governments of small states might control the nature and impact of globalisation on themselves. Crucial to the East Asian countries' success, most analysts agree, were their domestically strong, efficient, and viable state apparatuses.[31] Hence, we see the importance of distinguishing domestically 'strong' and 'weak' states. However, we must also recall that the internal strength of states in East Asia has in turn been due to the security threat that each country faced in the aftermath of the World War II, their strategic importance during the Cold War, and the economic success that they have enjoyed. So, East Asia highlights both that the categories of domestically 'strong' and 'weak' states are crucial, as well as the fact that these domestic

---

28. Critiques of the various stages of globalisation can be followed in UNCTAD, *Trade and Development Report* (New York, NY: United Nations, annually); through issues of the *Cepal Review* (Santiago: Economic Commission for Latin America); and, in respect of money and finance, in the various papers of the Group of Twenty-Four: *International Monetary and Financial Issues for the Developing Countries* (Geneva: UNCTAD, 1987), and *International Monetary and Financial Issues for the 1990s, Volumes I and II* (Geneva: UNCTAD, 1992).
29. The World Bank, *The East Asian Miracle: Economic Growth and Public Policy* (New York, NY: Oxford University Press, 1993).
30. A good survey is Albert Fishlow, *et al.*, *Miracle or Design?: Lessons from the East Asian Experience* (Washington, DC: Overseas Development Council, 1994).
31. Robert Wade, *Governing the Market* (Princeton, NJ: Princeton University Press, 1990); Alice Amsden, *Asia's Next Giant* (New York, NY: Oxford University Press, 1989); Amsden, 'Taiwan's Economic History: A Case of *Etatisme* and a Challenge to Dependency Theory', *Modern China* (Vol. 5, 1979), pp. 341-79; and Stephen Haggard, *Pathways from the Periphery* (Ithaca, NY: Cornell University Press, 1990).

Millennium

characteristics interplay with the international dimensions of state strength we have listed above. The fact that these are small states which have fairly carefully controlled their integration into the world economy—and continue to do so, as Korea's recent clamp-down on foreign investment displays[32]—suggests that any analysis of the nature and impact of globalisation requires a much more careful consideration of state strength and inequality.

Institutions and the Creation of New Structural Power

As we have mentioned above, globalisation is greatly influenced by international institutions established (or adapted) to facilitate and manage new flows of goods, people, ideas, and values across borders. As the liberals highlight, institutions are important in a globalised world as instruments of common purpose. Yet, liberal institutionalist theory has tended to focus on a narrow range of issues, and has paid too much attention to bargaining processes among states. Thus, going back to *Power and Interdependence*, which largely set the agenda for this scholarship, Keohane and Nye write that they 'sought to integrate realism and liberalism *using a conception of interdependence which focused on bargaining*'.[33] In parallel fashion, there has been a growing literature on the importance of linkages between domestic and international factors. Yet, the influential scholarship sparked by Robert Putnam's two-level game analogy has also focused almost entirely on bargaining and negotiation.[34] Missing from the interdependence and bargaining approaches are questions which, in our view, are central to comprehending the process and the impact of globalisation. These are questions as to what and why particular issues are left off the agenda of inter-state politics, who sets the rules of the bargaining game (meta-rules), and whence come the norms and ideas which are used to define issues and within which bargaining takes place.

Institutions are sites of power or dominance. Indeed, the World Bank's interpretation of East Asia's economic success, mentioned above, provides a case study of the struggle for dominance and control within institutions. As Robert Wade has documented, within the World Bank the interpretation of East Asia's success produced a political battle between Japan and the United States, and resulted in a report, the conclusions of which were markedly tilted so as to support the US-favoured, market-oriented approach to policy.[35] The struggles (and silences) within international institutions can only be understood by recognising that institutions do not emerge solely for utilitarian reasons.

---

32. 'New Curbs Hit South Korean Groups', *Financial Times* (12 October 1995), p. 7.
33. Robert O. Keohane and Joseph S. Nye, *Power and Interdependence*, Second Edition (Glenview, IL: Scott, Foresman and Company, 1989), p. 251, emphasis added.
34. Peter Evans, Harold Jacobson, and Robert Putnam (eds.), *Double-Edged Diplomacy* (Berkeley, CA: University of California Press, 1993).
35. Robert Wade, 'The World Bank and the Art of Paradigm Maintenance: the East Asian Miracle as a Response to Japan's Challenge to the Development Consensus', unpublished paper, University of Sussex, 1995.

Globalisation and Inequality

Although international institutions ostensibly arise amongst states concerned with solving common problems and promoting overall welfare, in fact they reflect a pattern of structural power which is central to the management of interdependence.[36] On the one hand, states create institutions because they wish to resolve distributional conflicts and relative gains concerns. Yet, in the end, it is powerful states who will shape the agenda, decide who can play the game, define the rules, and enforce outcomes which are favourable to themselves. Thus, globalisation creates new forms of structural power in which institutions play an important role: ultimately, that which powerful states delegate to them. We return to the point made above that globalisation offers powerful states a realm of choice. Most fundamentally, they can choose whether to favour cooperation in multilateral institutions (of which they often determine the internal structure), or to use bilateral negotiations. Indeed, this has been the pattern of US trade policy over the past two decades.[37]

In summary, the balance between state and market in the process of globalisation is itself an expression and reinforcement of political power. It depends on states' decisions to regulate certain aspects of the international economy and not others. Hence, our attention is drawn again to that dimension of inequality which was expressed above as the power to set the rules and to assert rights in the system.[38]

Institutions also play a critical role in the processes by which 'global' liberal values are transmitted and diffused across the system. Indeed, an important feature of the post-Cold War period has been a revival of the question of stronger enforcement: how to give more effective 'teeth' to the norms of international society.[39] Thus, instead of progressive enmeshment and learning, we need also to recognise the role of conditionality and coercion. The spread of conditionality has become a central element of the globalisation of liberalism.

Although defining conditionality is complicated, the core idea is clear enough: both individual states and multilateral institutions attach formal, specific, and institutionalised sets of conditions to the distribution of economic benefits in order to press (mostly) developing countries to adopt particular kinds of domestic policy. The claim to superior knowledge of how developing countries should manage their affairs, and the implicit use of coercion to try to ensure that that

---

36. Stephen D. Krasner, *Structural Conflict: The Third World Against Global Liberalism* (Berkeley, CA: University of California Press, 1985).
37. I.M. Destler, *American Trade Politics*, Second Edition (Washington, DC: Institute for International Economics, 1992), Chapter 3.
38. See Stephen D. Krasner, 'Global Communications and National Power: Life on the Pareto Frontier', *World Politics* (Vol. 43, No. 3, 1991), pp. 336-66.
39. See, for example, Lori Fisler Damrosch (ed.), *Enforcing Restraint: Collective Intervention in Internal Conflicts* (New York, NY: Council on Foreign Relations Press, 1993); Tom Farer (ed.), *Beyond Sovereignty: Collectively Defending Democracy in the Americas* (Baltimore, MD: Johns Hopkins University Press, 1995); and Philippe Schmitter, 'The Influence of the International Context upon the Choice of National Institutions and Policies in Neo-democracies', in Laurence Whitehead (ed.), *The International Dimensions of Democratization: Europe and the Americas* (Oxford: Oxford University Press, forthcoming).

Millennium

knowledge is acted upon, are, therefore, central to the use of conditionality. Up to the mid-1980s, formal conditionality was mostly limited to IMF-style macro-economic policy conditions.[40] Since then, there has been a very significant expansion within the economic field towards detailed micro-economic reform conditions. There has also been an extension beyond the economic field to include conditions designed to promote good governance, human rights, and democracy; sustainable development; limitations on arms spending; and non-proliferation policies. Here it is important to note, first, the critical move away from conditionality as forming part of a specific economic bargain or contract (as was at least arguably the case with IMF economic conditionality) and towards using conditionality to promote objectives that are wholly unrelated to a specific flow of resources; and second, the entrenchment of political conditionality in the policies of the international financial institutions, and of the OECD development committee.

The trend towards broader and deeper conditionality is not only evident in international institutions. In some ways, conditionality is becoming even more visible at regional levels. It is becoming commonplace for regional groupings to set down formal criteria for admission so that membership of an alliance, economic bloc, or international institution depends on certain kinds of domestic policy. Within regions, the potential levels of coercion rise as the perceived advantages of membership increase. In this respect, the very uneven nature of globalisation is particularly obvious. In both Europe and the Americas, would-be members of existing arrangements (the EU or NAFTA) take their place in a queue. In order to try to move up that queue, aspiring governments attempt to adapt their policies and converge with the required standards. In doing so, however, these future members are taking part in a process which reinforces and perpetuates the power of those who control the conditions and timing of admission. In regions such as the Western Hemisphere, where the distribution of power is already very skewed, this process can easily work to entrench regional hegemony.[41]

Yet, whilst coercion and conditionality are indeed critical features of the ways in which globalisation and liberalism intersect, it is important not to assume that we are dealing simply with external imposition. We need to look very closely at the domestic political processes by which those groups espousing liberal values

---

40. On economic conditionality, see Tony Killick, *The IMF and Stabilization* (London: St Martin's Press, 1984), and Paul Mosley, Jane Harrigan, and John Toye, *Aid and World Power: The World Bank and Policy-based Lending* (London: Routledge, 1990). The academic literature on non-traditional conditionalities remains thin, but see Nelson and Eglinton, *op. cit.*, in note 20.

41. Andrew Hurrell, 'Regionalism in the Americas', in Hurrell and Louise Fawcett (eds.), *Regionalism in World Politics* (Oxford: Oxford University Press, 1995), pp. 250-82, and Victor Bulmer-Thomas, Nikki Craske, and Mónica Serrano (eds.), *Mexico and the North American Free Trade Agreement: Who Will Benefit?* (London: Macmillan, 1994).

Globalisation and Inequality

are either able to achieve predominance or else fail to do so.[42] External pressures and inducements are, of course, likely to be important, but so too are the ways in which these external 'signals' are received and interpreted within the subordinate state. Powerful pressures towards liberalisation come up against equally powerful inherited structures and, in the complex process of break-down and adaptation, the result is highly unlikely to conform to a neat 'liberal' model: a liberalising Brazil is very different from a liberalising India, Mexico, or Poland. Indeed, the successful take-up of, say, market-liberal economic policies, may reinforce illiberal patterns of domestic politics or fuel revisionist and assertive foreign policies. Western institutions have seen this effect most clearly in countries such as Algeria, Tunisia, and Turkey, where stringent programmes of economic liberalisation have inadvertently fuelled rejectionist islamic movements.[43] The overall lesson is that powerful homogenising pressures may not, in fact, produce homogeneity: once again, we see that the processes of globalisation are complex and contested.

Conditionality provides a good illustration of the difficulties of reconciling the promotion of economic and political liberalisation within states with the maintenance of a manifestly unequal and illiberal inter-state order and global economic system. On the one hand, the growth of conditionality threatens to lead to ever greater involvement by the industrialised countries and their agencies in the political, social, and economic life of the developing world. This means that an ever greater range of development priorities are determined not by the governments of developing countries, but by external actors. On the other hand, liberal notions of democratic governance are very centrally about making governments more accountable for their policies and representative of their people. Here lies a real contradiction: governments are to be made increasingly accountable for policies and priorities, and yet they have decreasing control or authority over these policies.

Globalisation supposedly facilitates the transmission of liberal values and policies across the world. Yet, because states are politically and economically unequal, whilst some values are 'transmitted', many others are imposed or coerced. The result is sometimes unintended and often contradictory. Economic liberalisation does not always reinforce democracy. Indeed, many argue that 'insulation' from 'populist' pressures is central to the success of economic reform;[44] or that liberalisation skews political power in favour of a small, enriched group. Similarly, in several cases where international institutions

---

42. A case-study detailing the ways in which the domestic processes and international institutions interact is given in Ngaire Woods, 'The Third Arena: The International Financial Institutions and the Politics of Economic Policy-Making in Mexico 1982-1992', paper presented at the *CIDE*, Mexico City, April 1994, and Oxford Social Studies Faculty Senior Seminar, May 1995.
43. See John Darnton, 'Islamic Fundamentalism is on the Rise in Turkey', *International Herald Tribune* (3 March 1995), p. 2, and David Hirst, 'Egypt: Poised between Control and Chaos', *The Guardian* (11 February 1995), p. 15.
44. Stephan Haggard and Robert Kaufman (eds.), *The Politics of Economic Adjustment* (Princeton, NJ: Princeton University Press, 1992).

Millennium

commit themselves to supporting governments which undertake economic liberalisation, they have found themselves supporting governments which, at the same time, show little regard for human or group rights.

Ultimately, although liberals might be expected to be committed to the 'democratisation' of the international system and its institutions (and some are, such as the Commission on Global Governance), in most cases, the dominant liberal discourse in fact assumes high degrees of global management and enforcement.[45] Global management and institutions of enforcement rely upon inequality among states and reproduce and reinforce existing inequalities. Hence, liberals must ultimately choose between effective management of globalisation on the one hand, and values such as participation, representation, and legitimacy on the other. Those who favour 'effectiveness'—and here the economic liberalisers predominate—will very often end up siding with the realists in seeing the positive virtues of inequality and hierarchy.[46] Globalisation, and its management by institutions, is heavily conditioned by inequality among states, as was also shown by our argument about state strength.

Values, Norms, and International Society

One way in which we might explore and elucidate the contradictions mentioned above is by broadening our conception of international society, so as to analyse the impact of globalisation on conventional thinking about international social norms. We have seen that, for some, globalisation involves promoting a *universal* set of values. Stepping back and surveying the impact on international society, one can readily see that the promotion of a particular set of values will in fact reinforce divisions within international society and create different categories of states: those who do share the values and those who do not. This problem opens up an uncomfortable divide for liberals: on one side there is a long Western tradition of doctrines and ideas that rest on principles of exclusiveness, based on being Christian, European, or 'civilised';[47] on the other hand, there is the powerful counter-current in Western thought that has maintained the existence of a universal community of mankind and that has drawn its primary inspiration from the long tradition of natural law.[48]

---

45. Dharam Ghai, 'Social Policy in a Global Context', paper presented at Queen Elizabeth House, 40th Anniversary Conference, 'The Third World after the Cold War'. See also Richard Falk's review article in this issue on *Our Global Neighbourhood: The Report of the Commission on Global Governance* (Oxford: Oxford University Press, 1995).
46. For an important exception, see Daniele Archibugi and David Held (eds.), *Cosmopolitan Democracy* (Cambridge: Polity Press, 1995).
47. This issue was central to the work of Martin Wight and Hedley Bull. For an overview, see Bull, 'The Emergence of a Universal International Society', in Bull and Adam Watson (eds.), *The Expansion of International Society* (Oxford: Oxford University Press, 1984), pp. 117-26.
48. See Joseph Boyle, 'Natural Law and International Ethics', in Terry Nardin and David Mapel (eds.), *Traditions of International Ethics* (Cambridge: Cambridge University Press, 1992), pp. 112-35.

Globalisation and Inequality

Given this division, the pattern of interaction 'across the divide' becomes critical. At one extreme, realist doctrines have often denied all legal and moral rights to those without the power to force respect for their independence.[49] At the other extreme, revolutionist doctrines have insisted on an absolute equality of rights, both as individuals and as communities, and on a duty to assist their liberation, with versions of these ideas developed in both the French and Russian revolutions.[50] In between, liberals have been deeply divided. One strand has argued for a strong (if never quite absolute) respect for pluralism and equality between communities and cultures, and has laid great emphasis on the norms of sovereignty and non-intervention.[51] The other (far more powerful) strand has accorded only conditional or secondary rights to those outside the inner core, and has argued for intervention (or imperialism) to promote the intrinsically superior values of the inner core.[52]

The dominant trend for most of the twentieth century was to move against this exclusivism and exclusion in the name of greater equality. This was exemplified in the struggle for equal sovereignty, for decolonisation, for racial equality, and for economic justice.[53] Moreover, the dominant norms of international society served to provide a degree of protection, for good and ill, to many extremely fragile political entities ('quasi-states' to use Robert Jackson's phrase[54]). The globalisation of liberalism, however, has begun to pull in the opposite direction, and the resulting process of segmentation may well be working towards greater inequality.

In characterising the increasing inequalities in international society, three questions are of the essence: whose rules govern the society, what is the scope of the rules, and how are the rules enforced? The first question—whose rules—requires us to examine the existing structure of power among states. We are thereby returned to the paradox of universalism already alluded to: the successful promotion of 'universal' or 'global' values, even if they are to some degree genuinely shared, will often depend on the willingness of particularly powerful states to promote them. Furthermore, their successful promotion can all too easily work to reinforce the already marked inequality of power and status.

The second question—what is the scope of the rules—points to an area in which international society is undergoing dramatic change. The range of

---

49. Robert Tucker, *The Inequality of Nations* (New York, NY: Basic Books, 1977).
50. Martin Wight, *International Theory: The Three Traditions* (Leicester: Leicester University Press, 1991).
51. See Andrew Hurrell, 'Vattel: Pluralism and Its Limits', in Ian Clark and Iver Neumann (eds.), *Classical Theories in International Relations* (London: Macmillan, forthcoming). For a powerful contemporary restatement of the pluralist case, see John Rawls, 'The Law of Peoples', in Stephen Shute and Susan Hurley (eds.), *On Human Rights* (New York, NY: Basic Books, 1993), pp. 41-82.
52. On the theoretical underpinning of this view, see Anthony Ellis, 'Utilitarianism and International Ethics', in Nardin and Mapel (eds.), *op. cit.*, in note 48, pp. 158-79.
53. Hedley Bull, *Justice in International Relations, 1983 Hagey Lectures* (Waterloo, ON: University Publications Distribution Service, University of Waterloo, 1984).
54. Robert H. Jackson, *Quasi-States: Sovereignty, International Relations and the Third World* (Cambridge: Cambridge University Press, 1990).

Millennium

objectives that international norms and institutions seek to promote has increased tremendously. This has involved rules that affect the domestic structures and organisation of states, that invest individuals and groups within states with rights and duties, and that seek to embody some notion of a common good (human rights, democratisation, the environment, the construction of more elaborate and intrusive inter-state security orders). The impact on weaker and non-Western states is thus potentially very different from the 'globalisation' of traditional international society, in which the primary goal was minimal coexistence.

The third question which assists us in characterising international society is: how are the new, wider-ranging rules to be enforced? At present, enforcement works through international institutions. These institutions tend to be weak, except where they act as facades for powerful states' actions, or where they are dealing with states which rely upon them for financial assistance (*e.g.*, those states using the resources of the international financial institutions). As strict notions of sovereignty and the norm of non-intervention erode, and as formal schemes of conditionality increase, it has become easier to enforce norms against weaker states. The more powerful target states, however, are able to fend off inclusion (as with China) or to impose 'reverse' conditionalities (as with Malaysia *vs*. Australia and Britain). Furthermore, there is a growing reaction to the imposition of norms in both Asia and in the Middle East, as exemplified by recent controversies over human rights, where official Asian resentment is as much about how human rights are to be implemented as it is over the content of the rights in question.[55] Here, weaker states are reasserting the central defense of state sovereignty, attacking the double standards of powerful states and their conditionalities, and calling for greater democratisation in international institutions.

Contemporary trends suggest that international legitimacy and full membership of international society is increasingly being made conditional on the adoption of certain models of domestic political or economic practice. To some extent, these trends revive an old pattern of hierarchy and superiority. The promotion of 'universal' values and moves towards linking domestic and international legitimacy threaten to re-establish the old pattern of differentiation. Indeed, it is not entirely fanciful to see old, nineteenth-century categories reappearing in the emerging late twentieth-century distinctions between a core zone of liberal states, well-ordered non-liberal societies, and states that have either 'failed' or should be classed as pariahs or outlaws.[56] This prognosis highlights the need for analyses of globalisation to take into account the inequalities which underpin the changing international society.

---

55. See, for example, Bilahari Kausikan, 'Asia's Different Standard', *Foreign Policy* (Vol. 92, 1993), pp. 24-41, and Robert Bartley *et al.*, *Democracy and Capitalism: Asian and American Perspectives* (Singapore: Institute of Southeast Asian Studies, 1993).
56. On the nineteenth-century divisions between civilized, barbarous, and savage humanity, see James Lorimer, *Institutes of the Law of Nations, Volumes I and II* (Edinburgh and London: William Blackwood and Sons, 1883), and Gerrit W. Gong, *The Standard of 'Civilization' in International Society* (Oxford: Clarendon Press, 1984).

Globalisation and Inequality

Transnational Civil Society

Up to this point, we have treated international society as a society of states. Yet, for liberals, globalisation extends the possibilities of global community to a transnational civil society beyond states.[57] The prospect of a transnational civil society is attractive to liberals, who conceive it as enabling and empowering independent self-organised groups to participate politically and to counter the abuses of state power.[58] The use of the word 'society' (and still more 'community') carries with it the idea of some integrated framework of norms and values. Equally, the idea of 'civil society' has long been viewed in liberal thought as something defined in contradistinction to the state and as valuable precisely as a means of checking the power of the state. Confirming this view is the evidence of NGOs which have given voice to the weak and vulnerable and to those who are deemed to be non-members of a particular state or political community, or who fall between the cracks of the state system (*e.g.*, refugees, indigenous peoples, or future generations).

Yet, transnational civil society is itself an arena of power. Relations within transnational civil society, which are not necessarily any more equitable than within the states-system, may work to reinforce and open up new inequalities. In the first place, transnational civil society is pluralistic, encompassing a wide range of social movements, formal political associations, and economic forces and interest groups. It is manifestly wrong to believe that the forces within transnational civil society pull only in one direction. Many actions and actors within transnational civil society are profoundly illiberal and destructive, involving, for example, the privatisation of violence, transnational criminal activity, private trade in weapons, and the increasingly thin line between criminal and social violence. There is a tendency amongst critics of globalisation to take a benign view of transnational civil society and to see 'emerging social forces' as the counterweight both to hegemonic liberal capitalism and to inequalities in the states-system.[59] However, such a black and white image is unhelpful. Transnational civil society can aid the flow of anti-liberal ideas as much as the promotion of justice and equality: religious fundamentalism and Rupert Murdoch are, after all, as much a part of transnational civil society as Amnesty or Greenpeace.

Second, many groups within transnational civil society are the product—direct or indirect—of state action, and cannot be understood outside their relationship

57. See Lipschutz, *op. cit.*, in note 10, and Wapner, *op. cit.*, in note 10.
58. Such thinking is reflected in the increasing emphasis placed on NGO-channelled aid by international financial institutions and bilateral donors. These ideas are developed in such works as John Clark, *Democratizing Development: The Role of Voluntary Organisations* (London: Earthscan, 1991), and David Kroten, *Getting to the 21st Century: Voluntary Action and the Global Agenda* (Hartford, CT: Kumarian Press, 1990).
59. See, for example, Joseph A. Camillieri and Jim Falk, *The End of Sovereignty? The Politics of a Shrinking and Fragmenting World* (London: Edward Elgar, 1992), especially Chapter 8; Paul Ekins, *A New World Order: Grassroots Movements for Global Change* (London: Routledge, 1992); and Falk, *op. cit.*, in note 10.

Millennium

to states. Thus, the politics of transnational civil society is centrally about the way in which certain groups emerge and are legitimised (by governments, institutions, or other groups). As we have seen already, assumptions about the transmission of knowledge and ideas across boundaries are often viewed as the diffusion of knowledge through 'epistemic communities'. Yet, this neglects the issue of whose 'scientific knowledge' becomes critical, through what channels, and with what relationship to states and state power.[60] All too often, the links that exist between influential epistemic communities and particular institutions and particular groups within society are left unexamined.

Third, transnational civil society needs to be viewed as a fragmented and contested arena. Thus, we cannot ignore the unequal political voice and influence accorded to different NGOs: in the international context we might compare the effectiveness of Northern as opposed to Southern NGOs. Even more so than with domestic interest groups, there is a real issue of accountability here. This is usually ignored with respect to NGOs, which are often not accountable to any broad grouping or political process.[61] As some aid-giving states try to bypass governments and channel assistance through NGOs, these questions become all the more important.

Conclusion

Globalisation is profoundly affected by inequalities among states, regions, and non-state actors. This fact is underplayed in liberal interpretations of globalisation, which offer a fairly optimistic account of globalisation and which skate far too quickly over four significant problems: the capacity of states to bear the costs of adjustment to globalisation, the need for institutional reform to manage globalisation, the values which are to underpin the new global system, and the complexity and ambiguity of the emerging transnational civil society.

This article has analysed these four problems with the liberal globalisation thesis. Varying *state strength*, it was argued, affects states' capacities to adapt to, and benefit from, globalisation. On the face of it, the powerful benefit, and the less powerful lose out. For this reason, globalisation has always been a contested process, as illustrated by developing countries' attempts to use political power to limit the activities of foreign investors. Yet, some countries, such as those of East Asia, have succeeded in controlling the impact of globalisation on them, in spite of their size and lack of power in the international arena. Here, a crucial factor in their success has been the *domestic* strength of governments. With a high degree of domestic control, East Asian governments have been able effectively to control and adapt to integration in the global economy. It is

---

60. For one example of work that takes this sort of enquiry seriously, see Karen Litfin, 'Framing Science: Precautionary Discourse and the Ozone Treaties', *Millennium* (Vol. 24, No. 2, 1995), pp. 251-77.
61. For a similar challenge, see Hedley Bull, *The Anarchical Society: A Study of Order in World Politics* (London: Macmillan, 1977), pp. 85-86.

Globalisation and Inequality

important to note that domestic strength is itself not just a function of domestic circumstance. East Asia also provides an example of how it is that domestic political strength has been forged as a result of strategic insecurity and, of course, geostrategic position. The insight here is that domestic and international factors interplay in determining a state's capacity to control its insertion into global economic and political processes.

International institutions are put forward by liberals as the solution to new problems and issues which arise from globalisation. They are viewed as fairly neutral, problem-solving organisations. However, we have stressed that institutions are also arenas of power and influence, in which it is usually the powerful who make and break the rules. Here, we emphasised that globalisation plays into existing power-political relations in the international system. The standards of economic and political reform which are emerging both at the international and regional levels are overwhelmingly formulated by a small group of powerful states. Less powerful states are expected to accept these standards as conditions for their entry into intergovernmental institutions, and access to economic and political favour.

The analysis of international institutions is developed in the paper into a broader view of what globalisation in an unequal global system means for *international society*. Here we posed three questions: whose rules govern the society, what is the scope of the rules, and how are the rules enforced? The answers to these questions suggest that globalisation will not lead to the progressive global enmeshment heralded by liberal analysts. Existing inequalities make it more likely that globalisation will lead to an increasingly sharp division between 'core' states, who share in the values and benefits of a global world economy and polity, and 'marginalised' states, some of which are already branded 'failed states'.

Finally, globalisation, it is often claimed, is creating a new *'transnational civil society'*. The growth in non-state economic, political, and social linkages among societies leads some liberal analysts enthusiastically to point to the empowerment of NGOs and the like. The thesis is attractive to supporters of Greenpeace and Amnesty International, but it overlooks the fact that the activities of other non-state actors—such as terrorist groups—are also facilitated by globalisation. There are two further problems with empowering non-state actors in an uncritical way. In the first place, these groups are not necessarily representative, nor politically accountable. It is unclear how we should square enthusiasm for the rise of NGOs and non-state actors with a concern for democracy. In the second place, the rise of such groups—for example, islamic fundamentalist groups in the Middle East—can swiftly erode the order and political stability of often fragile and tenuous, but *elected*, governments.

In summary, the loss of autonomy associated with globalisation falls unevenly. Powerful states are better able to insulate themselves, by adapting domestic state structures to new constraints (and opportunities), dominating the regimes by which interdependence is managed, competing more effectively within global markets, or developing strong enough state structures to control interdependence.

Millennium

Those states that are able to resist 'internationalisation' will emerge as far more powerful than those that fail to do so. Thus, globalisation is a process the nature and impact of which are vastly influenced by inequalities among states; it is also a process which has profound consequences for the equality of states in the future.

Andrew Hurrell is University Lecturer in International Relations and a Fellow of Nuffield College, Oxford University, Oxford, OX1 1NF

Ngaire Woods is a Fellow of University College, Oxford University, Oxford, OX1 4BH

[2]

The Global Age: From a Sceptical South to a Fearful North

Jagdish Bhagwati

1. INTRODUCTION: PREBISCH AND UNCTAD

IT is an honour and a pleasure to give the Raul Prebisch Lecture. The honour comes from recalling an exceptional man. Prebisch was an eminent scholar and a prominent actor on the policy stage. The honour is the greater because of where the lecture is given. The emergence of the new South Africa under President Mandela, wedded to the rule of law and a commitment to producing racial and ethnic harmony in a world pulling in more dissonant and destructive directions, has been a ray of hope for all of mankind. But it is not geography alone that lends added honour to my lecture. History does as well. Put within the UNCTAD IX programme, it inevitably recalls the glory of UNCTAD under the able leadership of Raul Prebisch at the creation.

My honour goes also with pleasure. The pleasure is immediate and personal. For, as it happens, my very first policy experience on the international stage was at UNCTAD over three decades ago, when Raul Prebisch was the first Secretary General, and I was invited, a young Professor of International Trade in Delhi, at the tender age of 29 to serve on an Expert Group preparing a report on trade liberalisation by and among developing countries. I recall this also because it has many aspects that bear on Raul Prebisch and on UNCTAD itself. The Expert Group, or what we would today call an Eminent Persons' Group in our age of vanity, was chosen by UNCTAD, not nominated by governments, so it had the independence to chase ideas unconstrained by governmental directives. As a result, Raul Prebisch, and UNCTAD under him, were characterised by intellectual curiosity and by a willingness to examine, cross-examine and reject all and even Prebisch's own views. The institution was ahead of the curve: seizing leadership on issues and pronouncing on them with the best intellectual resources then available.

JAGDISH BHAGWATI is Arthur Lehman Professor of Economics and Political Science at Columbia University. This paper is an abbreviated text of the Raul Prebisch Lecture given at UNCTAD IX in Johannesburg on 29 April 1996.

JAGDISH BHAGWATI

In fact, let me recall that issues such as the international migration of skilled manpower and its economic implications for the rights and obligations of migrants, and of the countries of origin and destination, the questions raised by intellectual property protection in a world with growing importance of technology, and trade issues such as tariff escalation and value added protection (now known as effective protection) were first recognised and discussed within UNCTAD and became matters for further analytical contribution in the academe. A personal reminiscence again illustrates the point I am making: it concerns the fact that UNCTAD raised the question of services in world trade long before it got on to the GATT. When, some years ago, I was invited to give the annual Geneva Lecture of the International Insurance Association, I chose the topic of GATT and Trade in Services. Dr Giavini, Secretary of the Association, told me later that when he had told the Chairman of his Council, a leader in Britain's insurance industry and member of the House of Lords, about my subject, he had asked: 'Hmmm; GATT; What is it? Some kind of UNCTAD?'

This is hard to appreciate as the memory of this institution and of Prebisch has faded in the OECD countries, and it has become commonplace in some influential quarters to think of UNCTAD as if it was instead UNWASHED and UNKEMPT. The irony is that, just as this unfortunate view has gained ground, the academic evaluation of the role of more respected agencies, such as the World Bank, as the fountainhead of new ideas has become sceptical. Thus, a much-cited recent study, co-authored by the macroeconomist Michael Gavin, now the principal economist with the Inter-American Development Bank, and one of today's most distinguished young developmental economists Dani Rodrik (who, I might add, started out his career at UNCTAD), has argued that the social rate of return in terms of innovative ideas on the World Bank's massive expenditure to date on research has been negligible.[1]

Nonetheless, there is no smoke without fire. UNCTAD did indeed allow the early openness and stress on expertise to lapse progressively. It also increasingly made the mistake of assuming that intellectually weak argumentation by radical economists on the fringe, just because it was outside the mainstream, was therefore also the appropriate way to think about the developing countries: a *non sequitur* which would be fatal to its health. Instead, UNCTAD should have exploited the enormous diversity of views within the mainstream itself, drawing on a range of

---

[1] See Gavin and Rodrik (1995). These authors do say, however, that the World Bank has done a good job of disseminating (as against creating) good ideas, an area where UNCTAD took the back seat over time. In accounting for the latter, the willingness of the World Bank to draw on mainstream economists and their increasing neglect over the years by UNCTAD (as stated below in the text) must be considered the chief culprit. (Of course, I am describing only the central thrust of each institution's merits and demerits in regard to using and disseminating good ideas. There are important exceptions, especially in regard to UNCTAD's recent work, particularly on so-called 'trade and' issues, such as the interface of trade and the environment.)

GLOBAL AGE: SCEPTICAL SOUTH TO FEARFUL NORTH   261

reputed economists as Prebisch did, to advance the intellectual debate in ways that could have complemented by counterpoint the orthodoxies prevailing in other agencies with agendas defined by their own composition and interests.

The era that lies ahead under Mr Ricupero's leadership is now poised to return UNCTAD to that ambitious role and creative mode that characterised the Prebisch era, as many of us 'friends of UNCTAD' fondly recall it. But the definition of that role cannot be that UNCTAD would reflect a particularistic and unique 'developing country viewpoint' as often in the past. Paradoxically, that approach, if it ever made any sense earlier, certainly makes no sense today, for two contrasting but complementary reasons.

The developing countries are now too *diverse* in their economic and political circumstance and context to make generally possible a unified viewpoint as 'theirs' (i.e. that of the 'South'). This changed reality surely played a principal role in the rapid demise in the 1970s of the Global Negotiations that were predicated on the premise of North–South confrontation.[2]

At the same time, the earlier notion that the developing countries are divided from the developed countries (the 'North') in terms of their economics, justifying Special and Differential Treatment at the GATT etc., has yielded to the view that economics is *universal*, and that ideas and policies such as trade protection, extensive regulation by a bureaucratised state, generic restraints on inward foreign investment and the stifling of markets generally are bad for everyone, whether developing or developed.

In fact, the universalism extends to politics as well, and not just to economics today. Thus, the notion that democracy is fine for the developed countries, but that development requires authoritarian structures of governance, is no longer considered plausible.[3] Since we meet in South Africa, which is a meritorious example of a functioning democracy today as India has been in the postwar decades, let me dwell on this important issue a trifle longer.

I suspect that the defunct claims in support of authoritarianism for the developing countries were a result of the prevalent style of economic thinking when the postwar period of planning began. It was argued, following the influential model of Harrod and Domar, that the rate of growth depends on what you invest and what you get out of it by way of increased income. It thus depends on the savings (and investment) rate as well as on the investment (i.e. 'marginal capital') to output ratio. If one treated the marginal capital–output ratio as more or less a technological parameter, then all policy action was concentrated on

---

[2] So did the recognition that 'commodity power', based on an extension of OPEC's success to several other commodities, was an illusion, even though it had been embraced as a new phenomenon redefining the relationship between developing and developed countries by shrewd politicians such as Henry Kissinger, and by policy intellectuals such as Fred Bergsten, prior to the Nairobi UNCTAD. For a fuller analysis, see Bhagwati and Ruggie (1984, Ch. 2).
[3] I have considered this question in depth in Bhagwati (1995).

raising the average savings rate to increase investment, and hence the growth rate. Moreover, if public sector saving was considered to be the principal agent for raising the savings ratio, as it was at the time, then it was evident that the authoritarian states would be at an advantage over democracies. But, of course, the reality turned out to be otherwise. The variations in growth performance across countries have tended to reflect not just differences in rates of investment, but also dramatic differences in the marginal capital–output ratio. The latter, in turn, reflects the policy framework and its effects on the efficient use of resources.[4] Again, I would argue that the policy framework relevant here includes incentives and democratic processes that both enable and motivate effective participation by the citizenry in the growing economy. And recent arguments further suggest that the combination of economic markets and political democracy is unbeatable as a prescription for sustained, long-run growth.

So, confronted by this new universalism, the intellectual niche that UNCTAD can occupy with success must be embedded within it, instead of being built on the exceptionalism of the developing countries. Within this broad universalism, UNCTAD can nonetheless advance perspectives, informed by scholarly research, that better reflect the *interests* of the developing countries that other institutions are unlikely to offer if past experience and present realities are a guide.[5]

UNCTAD can make its unique contribution to 'trade and development', its original terms of reference and its rationale at the creation in several ways, such as the tasks that Mr Ricupero has been outlining recently: for example, the provision of technical assistance in trade matters to developing countries that lack the capabilities to operate in the increasingly complex trading regime today.[6] But it can do so also by examining these fears of the developed countries, seeking to lay them to rest where they are exaggerated and unwarranted, while also probing the rationale and the wisdom of the measures (such as the proposed Social Clause in the WTO) that these fears have prompted, exposing them to unbiased, scholarly and apolitical scrutiny.

---

[4] We should not forget that the policy framework affects the rate of investment as well. In fact, this played a central role in my view in accounting for East Asia's phenomenal growth in the postwar period, as argued in Bhagwati (1996).

[5] One example might illustrate, lest you might think that I am putting up a straw man. When the question of intellectual property protection (IPP) was being extensively debated at the GATT, the overwhelming view in the scholarly community was that the IPP being demanded in Geneva was being pushed by lobbies in the developed countries to the point where it was far too high. But, to my knowledge, this predominant scholarly view was not forcefully adopted and disseminated by the leading international agencies, whether the OECD or the World Bank. It is doubtful that Prebisch's UNCTAD would have remained so indifferent, abandoning both good economics and the interests of the developing countries, if it had been confronting the IPP question instead. Indeed, the GATT must be complimented for having permitted its staff to pursue precisely the sceptical research, even if in a very small way, that others were unable or unwilling to provide.

[6] The requirements here are enormous, especially as legal fine print has invaded everything concerning trade to a degree where even large and highly-skilled developing countries such as India are handicapped by their lack of trade-legal expertise in looking out for their interests.

GLOBAL AGE: SCEPTICAL SOUTH TO FEARFUL NORTH   263

UNCTAD's history and mission, as an institution focused on the developing countries' problems, should ensure that its perspectives will *complement* those of the OECD, whose history and mission focus its research and agenda so as to reflect more closely the political concerns and the economic interests of the developed countries that constitute its membership.[7] Both should serve to inform and assist, in friendly cooperation, the WTO as it prepares, under Mr Ruggiero's leadership, to extend and strengthen the world trading regime to meet the challenges of the Global Age as we enter the 21st century.[8]

So, I turn to the theme of this lecture: the Global Age and its consequences. I will begin with my central observation and the organising principle of my analysis: the irony of the role reversal that has occurred between the developing and the developed economies on fears of integration into the global economy. I will highlight the fact that these fears of the developed countries are heavily, and destructively, focused on integration with the developing countries, just as the fears of the developing countries in the postwar decades were focused symmetrically on the imagined dangers of integrating with the developed countries.

I will then argue that these fears are, at best, exaggerated and, at worst, ill-informed. In addition, I will suggest that the current, fear-fed demands in the major developed countries for changes in the rules and regimes that govern the world economy are much too often ill-designed. It is time for the leaders of the developed world to defuse these fears and, where the fears have some basis, to act less like politicians lazily compromising with lobbies to accept whatever demands they make, and then forcing the international adoption of their proposed harmful changes in the world economy, and instead to act more like statesmen who recognise these pressures but deflect them into more creative proposals that strengthen, rather than weaken, the architecture of the world economic regime.

---

[7] This view contrasts, I suspect, with that of some OECD governments, chiefly the United States, which would rather emasculate the research capabilities of UNCTAD (and, for that matter, of the WTO) and concentrate them exclusively in the two Bretton Woods institutions, the IMF and the World Bank. The research leadership of these two institutions, one might observe without caricature, has been jealously guarded by the leading developed countries.

[8] Indeed, the redefinition of the UNCTAD role also implies a close working relationship between it and the WTO, putting behind the two institutions the indifference, even hostility at times, that marred their relationship in the early days when the GATT was considered to be the playground of the wealthier nations and UNCTAD the champion of the poorer ones. (The witticism went that the UNCTAD Secretariat was deliberately sited so as to obscure the GATT's view of the lake from its earlier location, in an ultimate act of defiance!)

As the WTO, with the developing countries active players within its own new universalism, now seeks to enlarge its miniscule institutional research capability to support its creative efforts on behalf of the multilateral trading system (in which efforts we can only support), it can also reach out for research cooperation with agencies such as UNCTAD on issues of common concern. Again, under the leadership of Mr Ricupero and Mr Ruggiero, signs of such cooperation can already be found.

2. THE GLOBAL AGE: THE IRONIC ROLE REVERSAL

The dominant feature of the world economy is its increasing globalisation and the growing fear of its consequences in the developed countries. The latter, a consequence of *actual* globalisation or integration into the world economy on several dimensions, is in sharp contrast to the warm embrace of the Global Age by the policy makers in a large number of the developing countries.

It also represents a marked reversal of attitudes in the two sets of countries from the time of Prebisch. At that time, in the early postwar decades, the developing countries were sceptical, even afraid, of *potential* globalisation, shying away from such international integration, while the developed countries were into the Liberal International Economic Order, tearing down trade barriers in successive GATT Rounds, liberalising direct investment flows (despite the occasional protests such as that of Mr Servan-Schreiber of France on *The American Challenge*) and forging ahead on securing currency convertibility.

The developing countries' fear of global integration is best evoked by a celebrated Latin American formulation of the time: 'integration into the world economy leads to disintegration of the national economy'. In place of the agreeable conclusion of conventional economics that international trade, investment, etc. were mutual gain, *benign-impact* phenomena, constituting an opportunity rather than a peril, the developing country intellectuals and policy makers, for the most part, subscribed to a zero-sum view of the integration process which involved what Prebisch called the Centre and the Periphery. Thus, they either had a *malign-impact* view of globalisation, or they believed in *malign-intent* paradigms, where trade and aid were regarded as instruments of neocolonialism.

Today, those attitudes have yielded to the benign-impact views, as developing countries, one after another, have changed their policies to seek fuller integration into the global economy. Three examples should suffice to illustrate. President Cardoso, the dependencia theorist of yesteryear, is today's mastermind of Brazil's economic reforms that take her ever more into the global economy. President Salinas led Mexico into NAFTA, turning on its head former President Porfirio Diaz's famous dictum: 'Poor Mexico: how far from God and how near the United States!' Finally, even India, mired in inward-oriented policies for over a quarter of a century, has begun a deliberate and systemic change of gear to move its economy into the Global Age.[9]

---

[9] The reasons why the developing countries have moved to reforms are the subject of extensive analysis by economists today. Among these reasons, the value of example (i.e. the success of other nations following different policies) and of failure (of one's own policies) is certainly an important factor. In addition, we must reckon with the effect of pro-reform aid conditionality, although the impact of one's policy failures will play a role in turn since such failures are what drive countries into the Bretton Woods institutions that enforce such conditionality.

GLOBAL AGE: SCEPTICAL SOUTH TO FEARFUL NORTH 265

But, as globalisation has proceeded apace on virtually every dimension of international interaction, whether trade or direct investment, or capital flows or migration, the developed countries have witnessed growing alarm from their citizens over its implications for a variety of issues: real wages of workers, economic security, political autonomy and democracy, the ability to maintain high labour standards, etc.

That globalisation has accelerated is hard to dispute. Thus, in both world trade and investment there are greater transactions and flows, often even when adjusted for increased national incomes, suggesting that the economic activities of nations are increasingly in the global arena. But even this index misleads, at least for the implications of globalisation of trade and investment: these averages tell us little about the 'margin' and about what global competition offers in terms of both opportunity and 'vulnerability' to producers.

Let me begin by detailing the changing realities on *trade* flows, as some of the principal fears of the developed countries today and their unfortunate demands follow precisely from this phenomenon. Trade in both goods and services has continued to grow faster relative to national incomes throughout the postwar period, despite the OPEC-induced macro crisis in the 1970s and the deflation during the early 1980s. The successive rounds of reciprocal tariff and NTB reductions under GATT auspices have been a major contributory factor that the Uruguay Round will strengthen as it brings freer markets to new sectors, while opening the doors wider in the old sectors.

But more can be said. In some respects, the rise in the share of trade to GNP has mostly restored world trade to its prewar situation. Thus, for the United States, the share of merchandise trade in national income was 6.1 per cent in 1913 and 7 per cent in 1990: the difference is not compelling. But the shares were 3.6 per cent in 1950 and 3.8 per cent in 1960, so the perceptions today have been defined undoubtedly by the postwar rise, not by the fact that this rise is more or less back to 'normal' levels interrupted by the period between the Great Depression and the end of the Second World War.[10]

More pertinently, this share hides the important reality that the share of trade within the (hugely tradeable) merchandise and primary goods sectors has grown perceptibly compared to both the prewar and the immediate postwar levels. In fact, by the 1980s there was a vast increase in the exposure of tradeable industries to international competition: a situation that was more true of primary industries in the prewar period now characterises most manufactures today. It is not true that these shares continue to increase explosively; in fact, research suggests that they may have stabilised in the last decade. But the reality of substantial exposure to international competition, the fact that few industries today can pretend that they are proof from international competition, and consciousness thereof in defining

---

[10] See Irwin (1996).

266   JAGDISH BHAGWATI

issues and demands for governmental action, are major factors that we ignore at
our peril.

Indeed, the increased integration of the world's financial markets and the
increased transnationalisation of production by multinationals, both phenomena
of globalisation that have run a parallel as well as a supportive course, have
combined with the convergence in technological ability and know-how among
the OECD countries to make competition among firms across nations fairly
fierce. Firms in different countries can access similar technologies, borrow at
similar interest rates and produce where it pays a little more to do so in a manner
which was still difficult a decade ago. The margins of competitive advantage
have therefore become thinner: a small shift in costs somewhere can now be
deadly to your competitiveness.[11] In the old days, we used to call such industries
'footloose': the ability to hold on to them was fragile, as the 'buffer' or margin of
competitive advantage was not substantial. But few considered such industries to
be the norm. Today, because of the factors I have mentioned, they are. I have
called this the phenomenon of *kaleidoscopic comparative advantage*, a concept
that gives meaning to the notion that globalisation of the world economy has led
to fierce competition: slight shifts in costs can now lead to shifting comparative
advantage, which is therefore increasingly volatile.

This argument has the advantage of contributing to the explanation, in a
unified way, of three important phenomena that are in evidence today as the
source of the fears of the Global Age in the developed countries.

(i) The vulnerability of one's competitiveness that has so arisen, reflecting the
newly volatile, kaleidoscopic comparative advantage means that firms are
increasingly tempted to look over their foreign rivals' shoulders to see if
differences in their domestic policies and institutions are giving them that fatal
extra edge in competition which then amounts to *unfair trade*. The proliferation
of 'fair trade' demands in the developed countries to harmonise domestic
institutions and policies as prerequisites for free trade among trading nations
reflects, among other lesser reasons, this growing perception of kaleidoscopic
comparative advantage.[12]

(ii) The globalisation-led kaleidoscopic comparative advantage also
reinforces, albeit in a small way, the substantial sense of *economic insecurity*

---

[11] Economists call this a 'knife-edge' phenomenon, as in the case of Ricardian comparative
advantage, where a small shift in comparative advantage can lead to a substantial shift in
production.
[12] These other reasons include moral ones, as represented by human rights NGOs which seek to
stamp out domestic differences in conformity to universal human rights notions. I have discussed
the different philosophical, economic, structural and political factors variously underlying the many
demands for harmonisation that are breaking out today in Bhagwati and Hudec (1996, Ch. 1),
resulting from a research project under the auspices of the American Society of International Law.

now overtaking the citizens of the developed countries: for it must add to the labour turnover that reflects the increased rate of job displacements and a distinct (though small) reduction in the permanence of jobs that now afflicts even the white-collar workers.

(iii) In the same fashion, it likely contributes in some small way to the *decline in real wages* of the unskilled. For increased labour turnover must mean that workers stay less on average on the job so that they acquire less on-the-job training, and employers also give them less of it as they expect the workers to move on, thus flattening their lifetime earnings curve: just as a rolling stone gathers no moss, a moving worker gains few skills and earns less increments in wages.[13]

Of course, this rise of fierce competition and the attendant sense of economic vulnerability relate to the *globalisation* itself, and are not focused on integration with the *developing countries* as the source of the difficulties in the developed countries. But this is not true if I were to complete the sketch of the developed countries' fears of the Global Age by noting that they have been accentuated by the fact that international capital and labour flows, *vis-à-vis* the developing countries in particular, are also seen as increasingly compounding the problems posed by the expanded trade shares. Let me just outline the principal themes.

Direct foreign investment (DFI) has expanded greatly, with North–North DFI during the 1980s becoming as important as North–South DFI, a phenomenon noticeable in the case of Japan, especially as her DFI partially replaced her exports to the EU and the US in response to protectionist threats in specific sectors such as automobiles, and then later in response to the rising yen. While the Servan-Schreiber variety of anguish at DFI inflows did surface in the United States when Japanese investments began to rise in the late 1980s, the main agitation has arisen from the labour unions, who have always seen the developing countries as their principal foes in the game of economic competition. Long opposed to 'losing jobs' to the developing countries because multinationals move production abroad, unions in the United States have increasingly focused their attacks on the DFI going from the North to the South as a major problem posed by the Global Age.

A matching fear for jobs and wages has arisen from the increased flows of refugee and illegal immigrants from the developing to the developed countries. In a world increasingly of 'borders beyond control', if I might exaggerate for effect, most developed countries are now unable to fully regulate their immigration inflows: illegal immigration (heavily biased in composition towards the

---

[13] I have developed this theory in several recent articles, including Bhagwati and Dehejia (1992). Note that this theory relates to globalisation, not to the allegedly deleterious effect of trade with poor countries which vaguely reflects the conventional Factor Price Equalisation argument.

unskilled, and hence the more resented for its feared economic impact on the real wages of the natives) has been for some time an issue in the United States and other countries.[14]

What is remarkable about these fears of the developed countries is that they mirror so well the fears of the developing countries almost half a century ago. At that time, the countries on the periphery feared the centre. Global integration of countries with unequal power, in that instance integration with the developed countries of greater strength, would lead to predation rather than mutual gain: skilled nationals would leave, multinationals would earn more than they would contribute, free trade would bring about perpetuation of backwardness and destroy nascent industrialisation, income distribution would grow worse, and loss of autonomy and a situation of *dependencia* would follow. Today, the critics of the Global Age equally maintain that continued integration of countries with unequal power, in this instance integration with the developing countries of lesser strength, would cause predation: unskilled migrants would arrive, multinationals would leave to create jobs elsewhere, free trade with countries with lower labour and environmental standards would lead to deindustrialisation and loss of one's own standards, income distribution would worsen, and loss of autonomy to external forces beyond one's control and to institutions such as the WTO, where the Third World has an equal vote, God forbid, would threaten one's sovereignty. Indeed, the world has come full circle!

3. PHANTOMS MORE THAN REALITY: REAL WAGES AND JOBS

But, just as the developing countries have surmounted their fears and learnt that global integration with the developed countries promises more than it threatens, the developed countries need to do the same today in regard to their own global integration with the developing countries. In fact, let me remind you that I plan to argue that these fears are not merely exaggerated, but also do not justify some of the proposed measures to deal with them at the international level. Let me argue this by concentrating on the question of declining wages and rising unemployment.[15]

---

[14] So has the explosion of refugees, some of them leading in turn to an overload on asylum claims in the developed countries even as the fear has arisen that illegal immigration seeks to misuse the asylum route to immigration. The refugee crisis today, as it must be called for it is no less, has been splendidly handled by Madame Ogata as the UNHCR chief, an appointment for which Japan can properly take credit.

[15] Unfortunately, there is not time here to analyse other claims such as the loss of autonomy, the growing sense of alienation, etc. which are also on the Northern scene, and which I equally regard as largely exaggerated and fearful.

GLOBAL AGE: SCEPTICAL SOUTH TO FEARFUL NORTH 269

(i) *The facts:* Consider, for instance, the argument that the decline in real wages of the unskilled in the United States, and alternatively the rise in unemployment in Europe in the 1970s and 1980s, continuing into the 1990s, is a consequence of trading with the South. The demand for protection that follows, then, is not the old and defunct 'pauper-labour' argument which asserted falsely that trade between the South and the North could not be beneficial. Rather, it is the theoretically more defensible income-distributional argument that trade with countries with paupers will produce paupers in one's midst, that trade with the poor countries will produce more poor at home.

It is indeed true that the real wages of the unskilled have fallen significantly in the United States during the previous two decades. In 1973:

real hourly earnings of non-supervisory workers measured in 1982 dollars ... were $8.55. By 1992 they had actually *declined* to $7.43 — a level that had been achieved in the late 1960s. Had earnings increased at their earlier pace, they would have risen by 40 percent to over $12.[16]

The experience in Europe has generally been similar in spirit, with the more 'inflexible' labour markets implying that the adverse impact has been on jobs rather than on real wages.

But the key question is whether the cause of this phenomenon is trade with the South, as unions and many politicians feel, or rapid modern information-based technical change that is increasingly substituting unskilled labour with computers that need skilled rather than unskilled labour. As always, there is debate among economists about the evidence; but the consensus today among the trade experts is that the evidence for linking trade with the South to the observed distress among the unskilled to date is hard to find. In fact, if real wages were to fall for unskilled labour due to trade with the South, a necessary condition is that the goods prices of the unskilled labour-intensive goods would have to have fallen; and subsequent examination of US (and recently of German and Japanese) data on prices of goods shows that the opposite happened to be true in the critical period of the 1980s.[17]

Alongside this is the fear that multinationals will move out to take advantage of cheaper labour in the poor countries as trade becomes freer, thus adding to the pressure which that trade alone, with each nation's capital at home, brings on the real wages of the unskilled. Of course, this is also an unsubstantiated fear: but it has even greater political salience since the loss of jobs to trade is less easily focused on specific competing countries and their characteristics than when a factory shuts down and opens in a foreign country instead. As it happens, I

---

[16] See the many empirical writings of Robert Lawrence on the subject.
[17] This has been widely conceded now by those who were sceptical, including Ed Leamer of UCLA. The only dissident is Jeffrey Sachs whose claim to have overturned this finding is based on debatable adjustments which, even then, produce results which, while cited by the unsuspecting media, are statistically unacceptable. For an evaluation of this question, see my contribution to the forthcoming volume, edited by Susan Collins, for the Brookings Institution, a think-tank in Washington DC.

suspect that, at least in the United States, the flow of capital is also in the wrong direction from the viewpoint of those who are gripped by such fear; because, during the 1980s, the United States received more DFI than it sent out elsewhere, both absolutely and relative to the 1950s and 1960s. Besides, if foreign savings are considered instead, the 1980s saw an influx, corresponding to the current account deficit that has bedevilled US–Japan trade relations.

But regardless of the true realities which make it difficult to assign a significant, if indeed any, role in the present predicament of the Northern unskilled workers to trade and investment in this Global Age with the developing countries, the general feeling persists in many influential quarters that trade with the developing countries is a problem and that the resulting demands on policy change have more political salience than one would care to have but would be foolish to ignore.

(ii) *The demands: isolationism and intrusionism:* These demands take two contrasting forms. *First,* there is the traditional protectionist response. Here there are those who would raise trade barriers against the developing countries: a battle cry of the erstwhile presidential candidate Pat Buchanan in the United States, who wanted an across-the-board 20 per cent tariff on imports from China and an unravelling of NAFTA. Then there are the 'moderates', who would only stop liberalising trade further with the developing countries: here we must count (Sir James Goldsmith among them, I believe) the proponents in the North of free trade areas among 'like-wage' countries as against free trade generally, as the latter would include lower-wage countries.

These protectionist pressures are not that hard for the leaders of the developed countries to resist: the advantages offered by free trade, and the ideological triumph (at least for now) of the open markets alchemy for efficiency and growth in a highly competitive world economy, make it virtually impossible for responsible leadership to embrace such *isolationist* ideas and attendant protectionist pseudo-solutions. But unfortunately, that is not true of the alternative response, no more desirable, than we observe on the part of some of the leading governments in the North.

This *second* alternative is best understood by an analogy. Faced with the prospect of a typhoon, you may move out of its range, shifting from sunny but typhoon-prone Florida to dreary but safe locales: this is the isolationist, withdrawing, protectionist response to the fears (in the developed countries) of the developing countries in the Global Age. But if you have read your Malinowski or Radcliffe Brown, you may also pray to the weather gods and get the typhoons to go elsewhere. This interventionist or *intrusionist* option is one that can be contemplated, as a response to the threats imagined from elsewhere, only by the economically and politically powerful countries, especially hegemons such as the United States: they can aspire to force the developing countries, by using a variety of punishments and inducements, to adopt domestic institutional and policy changes so that the competitive threat is moderated.

This is how we must interpret the chorus of demands that have spread in the US and Europe for inclusion of Environmental and Labour Standards in the WTO, requiring that either they be moved up in the developing countries or that the developed countries should be allowed to countervail the 'implied subsidy' represented by these lower standards.

Several factors, including moral ones, undoubtedly contribute to the emergence of one or more of these 'fair trade' demands. But a principal one among them is surely the desire to raise, in one way or another, the costs of production of your rivals abroad: and what is more easy to do than to say that they are deriving advantage by having lower environmental and labour standards, and therefore free trade with them amounts to 'unfair trade'? This complaint, and attendant agitation for penalising these foreign firms with import taxes if their countries do not raise their standards towards one's own, then has the advantage that, *either* you will be able to get your rivals' costs up and reduce the pressure of their competition by forcing them to raise their environmental and labour standards, *or*, if they do not do so, you will get protection against them as trade barriers are raised against the continuing unfairness of competition. This agitation therefore offers a foolproof method of meeting your foreign rivals' competition: it therefore also accounts for its popularity.

But let me argue that these demands are being properly resisted by the developing countries and are being inappropriately accommodated by some of the governments in the developed countries, as in the recent pressures emanating from the US, and France in particular, in favour of a Social Clause at the WTO.

4. INTRUSIONISM: ENVIRONMENTAL AND LABOUR STANDARDS

These demands are unwisely recreating the North–South divide. To understand the folly of these to developed countries, and the dangers they pose to the developing countries and to the world trading regime, let me now address in succession the parallel but still contrasting issues of eco-dumping (in subsections *a–c*) and of the Social Clause (in subsection *d*) at the WTO.

a. The legitimacy of Diversity and the Folly of Eco-dumping Demands

If we are dealing with 'global' environmental problems when there are transborder externalities, as with the global warming and ozone layer problems, it is now recognised that we need global solutions which avoid free-rider problems and include punishments for defection. The disagreements among countries that universally accept the need for such solutions arise only from differences in their views of what is a 'fair' allocation of the burden of pollution avoidance, especially as there is an understandable tendency on the part of the worst offenders, the developed countries, to shift the burden of adjustment on to the developing countries: a tendency clear in the solutions being devised for dealing with the global warming problem.

The eco-dumping allegation, on the other hand, extends plainly to what economists call 'domestic' environmental problems: as when effluents are discharged into a lake or a river that is entirely within a nation's own borders and there are no transborder spillovers into other jurisdictions.

In this latter set of domestic pollution cases, economists would generally expect to find diversity rather than uniformity of environmental standards in the same industry in different countries. I will call these Cross-country Intra-industry (CCII) differences in standards, typically in the shape of pollution tax rates. This diversity of CCII standards will follow from differences in trade-offs between aggregate pollution and income at different levels of income, as when richer Americans prefer to save dolphins from purse-seine nets, whereas poorer Mexicans prefer to put people first and want to raise the productivity of fishing, and hence accelerate the amelioration of Mexican poverty by using such nets. Again, countries will have natural differences in the priorities attached to which kind of pollution to attack, arising from differences of historical and other circumstances: Mexicans will want to worry more about clean water, as dysentery is a greater problem, than Americans who will want to attach greater priority to spending pollution dollars on clean air. Differences in technological know-how and in endowments can also lead to CCII diversity in pollution tax rates.

The notion, therefore, that the diversity of CCII pollution standards/taxes is illegitimate and constitutes 'unfair trade' or 'unfair competition', to be eliminated or countervailed by eco-dumping duties, is itself illegitimate. It is incorrect, indeed illogical, to assert that competing with foreign firms that do not bear equal pollution tax burdens is unfair. I would add three more observations:

- We should recognise that if we lose competitive advantage because we put a larger negative value on a certain kind of pollution whereas others do not, it is simply the flip side of the differential valuations. To object to that implication of the differential valuation is to object to the differential valuation itself, and hence to our own larger negative valuation.

- Besides, it is worth noting that the attribution of competitive disadvantage to differential pollution tax burdens in the fashion of CCII comparisons for individual industries confuses absolute with comparative advantage. Thus, for instance, in a two-industry world, if both industries abroad have lower pollution tax rates than at home, both will not contract at home. Rather, the industry with the *comparatively* higher tax rate will. The noise that each industry makes on the basis of CCII comparisons, aggregated to total noise by all industries, is then likely to exaggerate seriously the effect of different environmental valuations and CCII differences on the competitiveness of industries in higher-standards nations.

- But the legitimacy of the diversity may be suspect if the governments that are making the decisions on pollution tax rates are unrepresentative. Clearly, one cannot attribute such legitimacy to the Soviet bloc governments which, in fact, polluted wantonly and whose citizens had no voice. But fortunately, democracy has broken out almost everywhere: just a few countries, either the stragglers from the communist era (China, North Korea and Cuba) or the non-ideological one-leader or one-party states (Iraq and Syria), now lie wholly outside the democratic pale.

b. An Unjustified Fear of the 'Race to the Bottom'

One more worry needs to be laid to rest if the demands for upward harmonisation of standards, or eco-dumping duties *in lieu* thereof, are to be effectively dismissed. This is the worry that free trade with countries with lower standards will force down one's higher standards. The most potent of these worries arises from the fear that 'capital and jobs' will move to countries with lower standards, triggering a *race to the bottom* (or, more accurately, a race towards the bottom). So the solution would then lie in coordinating the standard-setting among the nations engaged in freer trade and investment. In turn, this *may* (but is most unlikely to) require harmonisation among countries to the higher standards (though, even then, not necessarily to those in place), or perhaps there might be improvement in welfare from simply setting minimum floors to the standards.

Unlike the argument just rejected that dismisses diversity of standards as illegitimate, and therefore unfair *per se*, this is undoubtedly a theoretically valid argument. The key question for policy, however, is whether the empirical evidence shows, as required by the argument, that: first, capital is in fact responsive to the differences in environmental standards; and second, that different countries/jurisdictions actually play the game of competitive lowering of standards to attract capital. Without both these phenomena holding in a significant fashion in reality, the 'race to the bottom' would be a theoretical curiosity.

As it happens, systematic evidence is available for the former proposition alone, but the finding is that the proposition is not supported by the studies to date: there is very weak evidence, at best, in favour of interjurisdictional mobility in response to CCII differences in environmental standards. There are, in fact, many ways to explain this lack of responsiveness: differences in standards may not be significant and are outweighed by other factors that affect locational decisions; exploiting differences in standards may not be a good strategy relative to not exploiting them; and lower standards may even paradoxically repel, instead of attracting, DFI.

While we do not have similar evidence on the latter proposition, it is hardly likely that, as a systematic tendency, countries would actually be lowering environmental standards in order to attract capital. As it happens, countries, and even state governments in federal countries (e.g. President Bill Clinton when Governor of Arkansas), typically play the game of attracting capital to their jurisdictions: but this game is almost universally played not by inviting firms to pollute freely, but instead through tax breaks and holidays, land grants at throwaway prices, etc., most likely resulting in a 'race to the bottom' on business tax rates which wind up below their optimal levels! It is therefore not surprising that there is little systematic evidence of governments lowering environmental standards in order to attract scarce capital. Contrary to the fears of the environmental groups, the race to the bottom on environmental standards therefore seems to be an unlikely phenomenon in the real world.

I would conclude, then, that both the 'unfair trade' and the 'race to the bottom' arguments for harmonising CCII standards, or else legalising eco-dumping duties at the WTO, are therefore lacking in rationale: the former is theoretically illogical and the latter is empirically unsupported. In addition, such WTO legalisation of eco-dumping will facilitate protectionism without doubt. Anti-dumping processes have become the favoured tool of protectionists today. Is there any doubt that their extension to eco-dumping (and equally to social dumping), where the 'implied subsidy' through lower standards must inevitably be 'constructed' by national agencies such as the Environmental Protection Agency in the same jurisdiction as the complainant industry, will lead to the same results even more surely?

The 'fixing' of the WTO for environmental issues, therefore, should not proceed along the lines of legitimating eco-dumping. However, the political salience of such demands remains a major problem. One may well then ask: are there any 'second-best' approaches, short of the eco-dumping and CCII harmonisation proposals, that may address some of the political concerns at least economic cost?

c. A Proposal to Extend Domestic Standards in High Standard Countries to their Firms in Low Standard Countries, Unilaterally or Preferably through an OECD Code

The political salience of the harmful demands for eco-dumping duties and CCII harmonisation is greatest when *plants are closed* by one's own multinationals and shifted to other countries. The actual shifting of location,

GLOBAL AGE: SCEPTICAL SOUTH TO FEARFUL NORTH 275

and the associated loss of jobs in that plant, greatly magnify the fear of the 'race to the bottom' and the 'impossibility' of competing against low standard countries. Similarly, when investment by one's own firms is seen to go to specific countries which happen to have lower standards, the resentment gets to be focused readily against those countries and their standards. However, when jobs are lost simply because of *trade* competition, it is much harder to locate one's resentment and fear on one specific foreign country and its policies as a source of unfair competition. Hence, a second-best proposal could well be to address this particular fear, however unfounded and often illogical, of outmigration of plants and investment by one's firms abroad to low standard countries.

The proposal that I would like to make, most appropriately in Johannesburg, is to adapt the so-called Sullivan Principles approach to the problem at hand. Under Sullivan, US firms in South Africa were urged to adopt US practices, not the South African apartheid ways, in their operations. If this principle that US firms in Mexico be subject to US environmental policies were adopted by US legislation, that would automatically remove whatever incentive there was to move because of environmental burden differences.

This proposal that one's firms abroad behave as if they were at home can either be legislated unilaterally by any high standard country or by a multilateral binding treaty among different high standard countries. Again, it may be reduced to an exhortation, just as the Sullivan Principles were, by single countries in isolation or by several, as through a non-binding but ethos-defining and policy-encouraging OECD Code.

The disadvantage of this proposal, of course, is that it does violate the diversity-is-legitimate rule (whose desirability was argued by me). Investment flows, like investment of one's own funds, and production and trade therefrom, should reflect this diversity. It therefore reduces the efficiency gains from a freer flow of cross-country investments today. But if environmental tax burden differences are not all that different, or do not figure prominently in firms' locational decisions as the empirical literature seems to stress, the efficiency costs of this proposal could also be minimal, while the gains in allaying fears and therefore moderating the demand for bad proposals could be very large indeed.

Yet another objection may focus on intra-OECD differences in high standards. Since there are differences among the OECD countries in CCII environmental tax burdens in specific industries for specific pollution, this proposal would lead to 'horizontal inequity' among the OECD firms in third countries. If the British burden is higher than the French, British firms would face a bigger burden in Mexico than the French firms. But such differences already exist among firms abroad since tax practices among the OECD countries on taxation of those firms are not harmonised in many respects. Interestingly, the problem of horizontal equity has come up also in relation to the demands of the poor countries (that often find it difficult to enforce import restrictions effectively), that the domestic restrictions on hazardous products be automatically extended to exports by every country. That would put firms in the countries with greater restrictions at an economic disadvantage. But agreement has now been reached to disregard the problem.

Other problems may arise: monitoring of one's firms in a foreign country may be difficult; and the countries with lower standards may object on grounds of 'national sovereignty'. Neither argument seems compelling. It is unlikely that a developing country would object to foreign firms doing better by its citizens in regard to environmental standards. Equally, it would then assist in monitoring the foreign firms.

If I may be cynical, this eminently reasonable proposal, which I made at the time of NAFTA in an article in the *New York Times*, was not received with enthusiasm by the corporate sector, and hence by either the US administration or the Congress, because the well-guarded little secret of the multinationals is that their demands on their governments, and hence on what they want included in the WTO, as with TRIMs and now the more ambitious Multilateral Agreement on Investment, concern the removal of impediments to their expansion, not the imposition of restrictions on their freedom to manoeuvre.

d. The Question of Labour Standards and the Social Clause

The question of labour standards, and making them into prerequisites for market access by introducing a Social Clause in the WTO, has both parallels and contrasts to the environmental questions. The contrast is that labour standards have nothing equivalent to *transborder* environmental externalities. One's labour standards are purely *domestic* in scope; in that regard, the demands for 'social dumping' for lower labour standards that parallel the demands for eco-dumping have the same rationale, and hence must be rejected for the same reasons.

But a different aspect to the whole question results from the fact that labour standards, unlike most environmental standards, are seen in moral terms. Thus, for example, central to much thinking today on the question of the Social Clause is the notion that competitive advantage can sometimes be morally 'illegitimate'. In particular, it is argued that if labour standards elsewhere are different and unacceptable morally, then the resulting competition is morally illegitimate and 'unfair'.

Now when this argument is made about a practice such as slavery, and its other forms such as bonded labour, including the abhorrent practices of mortgaging one's children to *de facto* servitude to employers, and of abusively exploiting prisoners in the labour camps in the *gulag*, there will be nearly universal agreement that if such slavery produces competitive advantage, that advantage is illegitimate and ought to be rejected as posing unfair competition to one's workers in competing industries.

The moral argument, however, may not be merely to consider such slavery-based competition as unfair to our industries and *workers*. It may also be that *we* do not wish to profit from such trade: we will not sup with the devil even though we miss a free meal. Or it may be a consequentialist moral argument that we wish to punish *others* who permit such slavery and, by denying them trade in such slavery-produced goods, we seek to induce them to change such slavery.[18] The insertion of a Social Clause for labour standards in the WTO can then be seen as a way of legitimating a compelling and universally accepted moral exception to the otherwise sensible GATT rule that prohibits the suspension of a contracting party's trading rights concerning a product simply on the ground that another contracting party objects to the process by which that product is produced.

The real problem with the argument, however, is that universally condemned practices such as slavery are indeed rare. The reality is that diversity of labour practices and standards is widespread in practice, and for the most part reflects not necessarily venality and wickedness, but rather diversity of cultural values, economic conditions, and analytical beliefs and theories concerning the economic (and therefore moral) consequences of specific labour standards. The notion that labour standards can be universalised, like human rights such as liberty and *habeas corpus*, simply by calling them 'labour rights', ignores the fact that this easy equation between culture-specific labour standards and universal human rights will have a difficult time surviving deeper scrutiny.

I might illustrate the fundamental difficulties we face by taking the United States (since it is a principal proponent of the Social Clause) and demonstrating immediately that the US logic on the question can lead the US itself into a legitimate demand for a widespread and sustained suspension of its own trading rights if a Social Clause were established.

Thus, for instance, worker participation in decision making on the plant, a measure of true economic democracy for both unionised and non-unionised labour that is surely much more pertinent than the mere unionisation of labour, is far more widespread in Europe than in North America: would we then condemn North America to denial of trading rights by the Europeans? Migrant labour is again ill-treated to the level of brutality and slavery in US agriculture due to grossly inadequate and corrupt enforcement, if investigative shows on US television are a guide; does this mean that other nations should prohibit the import of US agricultural products? Sweatshops exploiting female immigrants with long hours and below minimum wages are endemic in the textile industry, as documented amply by several civil liberties groups and now appreciated widely because of the discovery of an establishment in California that employed virtual slaves, and the subsequent admission by Labour Secretary Reich that monitoring and enforcement were appallingly weak and would remain so because of lack of

---

[18] I have considered the alternative moral arguments in Bhagwati and Hudec (1996, Ch. 1, Vol. 1).

278   JAGDISH BHAGWATI

funds: should the right of the US to export textiles then be suspended by other countries as much as the US seeks a Social Clause to suspend the imports of textiles made by child labour?

Even the right to organise trade unions may be considered inadequate in the US if we go by 'results', as the US favours in judging Japan: only about 12 per cent of the US labour force in the private sector today is unionised. Indeed, it is no secret, except to those who prefer to think that labour standards are inadequate only in developing countries, that unions are actively discouraged in several ways in the United States. Strikes are also circumscribed. Indeed, in essential industries they are restricted: but the definition of such industries also reflects economic structure and political realities, making each country's definition only culture-specific and hence open to objection by others. Should other countries then have suspended US flights because President Reagan had broken the air traffic controllers' strike?

Even the question of child labour is not an easy one. The use of child labour as such is surely not the issue. Few children grow up, even in the US, without working as babysitters or delivering newspapers; many are even paid by parents for housework in the home. The pertinent social question, familiar to anyone with even a nodding acquaintance with Chadwick, Engels and Dickens, and the appalling conditions afflicting children at work in England's factories in the early Industrial Revolution, is rather whether children at work are protected from hazardous and oppressive working conditions.

Whether child labour should be altogether prohibited in a poor country is a matter on which views legitimately differ. Many feel that children's work is unavoidable in the face of poverty and that the alternative to it is starvation, which is a greater calamity; and that eliminating child labour would then be like voting to eliminate abortion without worrying about the needs of the children that are then born.

Then again, insisting on the 'positive rights'-related right to unionise to demand higher wages, for instance, as against the 'negative rights'-related right of freedom to associate for political activity, for example, may also be morally obtuse. In practice, such a right could imply higher wages for the 'insiders' who have jobs, at the expense of the unemployed 'outsiders'. Besides, the unions in developing countries with large populations and much poverty are likely to be in the urban industrial activities, with the industrial proletariat among the better-off sections of the population, whereas the real poverty is among the non-unionised landless labour. Raising the wages of the former will generally hurt, in the opinion of many developing country economists, the prospects of rapid accumulation and growth which alone can pull more of the landless labour eventually into gainful employment. If so, the imposition of the culture-specific developed country union views on poor countries about the rights of unions to push for higher wages will resolve current equity and intergenerational equity problems in ways that are then *morally* unacceptable to these countries.

GLOBAL AGE: SCEPTICAL SOUTH TO FEARFUL NORTH   279

(i) *The Social Clause — a bad idea:* One is then led to conclude that the idea of the Social Clause in the WTO is generally rooted in an ill-considered rejection of the general legitimacy of diversity of labour standards and practices across countries. The alleged claim for the universality of labour standards is (except for a few rare cases such as slavery, and its close variants such as labour in bondage and in the *gulag*) generally unpersuasive. The developing countries cannot, then, be blamed for worrying that the recent escalation of support for such a clause in the WTO in the United States and France, among the leading OECD countries, derives instead from the desire of labour unions to protect their jobs by protecting the industries that face competition from the poor countries. They fear that moral arguments are produced to justify restrictions on such trade since they are so effective in the public domain. In short, 'blue protectionism' is breaking out, masking behind a moral face.

Indeed, this fearful conclusion is reinforced by the fact that none of the major OECD countries pushing for such a Social Clause expect to be the defendants instead of the plaintiffs in Social Clause-generated trade access cases. On the one hand, the standards (such as prohibition of child labour) to be included in the Social Clause to date are invariably presented as those that the developing countries are guilty of violating, even when some transgressions thereof are to be found in the developed countries themselves. Thus, according to a report in *The Financial Times*, a standard example used by the labour movement to garner support for better safety standards is a disastrous fire in a toy factory in Thailand where many died tragically because exits were shut and unusable. Yet when I read this report, I recalled an example just like this (but far more disconcerting when I noted that the fatalities occurred in the richest country in the world) about a chicken plant in North Carolina where the exits were also closed for the same reason. Yet the focus of international agitation has been on the poor, not the rich, country.

At the same time, I must say that the argument that the Social Clause should contain 'core' standards sounds fine, until you realise that this is also tantamount to a choice of standards for attention and sanctions at the WTO that is also clearly biased against the poor countries, in the sense that none of the problems where many of the developed countries themselves would be more likely to be found in significant violation — such as worker participation in management, union rights, rights of migrants and immigrants — are meant to be included in the Social Clause. Symmetry of obligations simply does not exist in the Social Clause, as contemplated currently, in terms of the coverage of the standards.

This theme may be pursued further. The choice of the WTO as the repository of a Social Clause, stacked against the developing countries, is also a way of reducing the probability of being a defendant. This is because the standing to bring cases at the WTO lies with the member governments not with NGOs as in the public interest litigation in India or in the case of human rights if a nation has signed (as the United States has not done) the Optional Protocol on the International Covenant of Civil and Political Rights. India and Egypt, for instance, may be expected to be bamboozled by threats and inducements, political and economic, by major powers into not pursuing Social Clause-led cases against them; but the NGOs would not so easily back away from such a scrap. If indeed the demands are being truly inspired by a moral viewpoint that genuinely seeks symmetric universal rights and their enforcement, the choice of the WTO as the institution of choice for sanctions is hardly credible.

Indeed, both the choice of standards to be included in the Social Clause, and the choice of the institution where the Social Clause will be situated, cannot but leave serious analysts in the developing countries convinced that the movement is a prime example of what I called Intrusionism, inspired by the desire to moderate competition from the developing countries by raising their costs of production. This view is further reinforced when the unions allied to these demands are often seen to be those in industries directly threatened by such competition, or when the morality underlying the demands for a Social Clause is couched in terms of a universalist language that asserts transborder moral concerns by groups that equally support immigration controls that deny the universalism they assert.

(ii) If not a Social Clause, what else? If this analysis is correct, then the idea of a Social Clause in the WTO is not appealing; and the developing countries' opposition to its enactment is totally reasonable. We would not be justified, then, in condemning their objections and unwillingness to go along with such demands as depravity and 'rejectionism'.

But if a Social Clause does not make good sense, is everything lost for those in both developed and developing countries who genuinely wish to advance their views of what are 'good' labour standards in a decent society? Evidently not. It is surely open to them to use other instrumentalities such as non-governmental organisation (NGO)-led educational activities to secure a consensus in favour of their positions. In fact, if your ideas are good, they should spread without coercion. The Spanish Inquisition should not be necessary to spread Christianity; indeed, the Pope has no troops. Mahatma Gandhi's splendid idea of non-violent agitation spread and was picked up by Martin Luther King, and finds strong resonance in the practice and precepts of President Mandela, not because he worked on the Indian government to threaten retribution against others; it happened to be just morally compelling.

I would add that one also has the possibility of recourse to private boycotts, available under national and international law; they are an occasionally effective instrument.[19] They constitute a well-recognised method of protest and consensus creation in favour of one's moral positions.

---

[19] Though, here also, I must add that many NGOs and citizens in the developing countries are rightly concerned by the asymmetric power that can be exerted by private boycotts in countries that are economically more substantial and politically more powerful, thus lending greater weight to the

GLOBAL AGE: SCEPTICAL SOUTH TO FEARFUL NORTH   281

Where, moreover, a nation has unmarketable and culture-specific moral views[20] on the production and import of certain products, and is under domestic political pressure to go alone with official suspension of such imports, it is worth stressing that there is nothing in the current international regime to prevent it from doing so. It can simply suspend the trade of another country and 'pay' for it by making trade concessions, or it can put up with matching retaliation by the other country in the form of its own withdrawal of market access to the punishing country. The latter is, in effect, what the EU did over their politically necessary suspension of the hormone-fed beef trade and the subsequent retaliation by Ambassador Carla Hills of the United States.

5. THE GLOBAL AGE: TRANSCENDING FEARS TO CONSTRUCT A NEW ARCHITECTURE

The new international architecture that we must build to secure the gains from the Global Age must not be founded on faulty foundations inspired by exaggerated fears. It must also not be one that begins by creating a North–South divide when we have just managed to put such dissentions behind us in a common vision reflecting the universalism of both economics and politics that I drew your attention to. What vision, then, should we embrace? Or perhaps, if I may recall Raul Prebisch at the end as I did at the beginning, where would he, simultaneously a visionary and a builder, have led us at this historic juncture?

(i) We need to reject the folly of including a Social Clause and eco-dumping varieties of trade and environmental agendas into the world trading regime: the WTO would surely be handicapped, and the developing countries harmed, by such measures.

(ii) Instead, recognition of the important role of NGOs, careful design of labelling approaches, and encouragement of improved environmental and labour practices by appropriate institutions such as UNEP, UNICEF and the ILO, are among the proper ways to bring these great tasks to attention and fruition today.

(iii) Moreover, instead of moving the world into a foolish straitjacket of 'deep integration' — a shallow concept when it comes to the Social Clause,

---

moral concerns of the citizens of the strong as against those of the weak nations. So the time may well have come to examine whether organised private boycotts should be permitted without restraint when exerted against weaker, foreign nations.

[20] Are the American love for dolphins, the Indian respect for cows and the English affection for dogs universalisable by moral suasion? They are rarely grounded in basic beliefs in animal rights, but seem to reflect notions such as 'cuteness' (dolphins look so human, look at their pretty snouts) or 'loyalty' (a dog is man's best friend) which are surely culture-specific.

282   JAGDISH BHAGWATI

environmental tax burden harmonisation, etc. — and forcing it on the WTO and the developing countries, to whose disadvantage it must work, it is better to finish the task of creating a world of free trade, an essential component of the Global Age that still remains a job unfinished.

(iv) This task is all the more important as the trading system has now been afflicted by a huge and increasing proliferation of free trade areas which are better called by their true name: Preferential Trading Arrangements (PTAs). These PTAs now criss-cross the world economy, creating a 'spaghetti bowl' phenomenon of trade tariffs and NTBs that depend on where products come from: numerous rates apply in the EU and US alone, depending on source, with 'rules of origin': producing a maze messing up the international division of labour in the Global Age.

These PTAs are politically driven: no politician is happy unless he has put his signature on at least one of them. It gives them a place in the sun and, while going preferential, you can still pretend that you are for free trade since no one in the media understands the distinction. We economists now have a CNN theory of regionalism or PTAs: you can get on to world television through an APEC or a Mercosur summit which you cannot at Geneva at the WTO!

So the only way to kill this growing maze of preferences is not through ingenious changes in Article XXIV at the GATT/WTO which sanctions PTAs, or by prohibiting PTAs which simply cannot be suppressed when the political demand for them is so overwhelming, but through going to worldwide free trade (which effectively kills the preferences since a preference relative to zero is zero).

(v) The nations of the world must unite behind such a vision and such a target: worldwide free trade by, say, the year 2010. Mr Renato Ruggiero and Mr Rubens Ricupero can be natural allies in propagating such a target: for it would galvanise both WTO and UNCTAD. Both institutions are at a critical defining moment in their history, the WTO beginning to create it and UNCTAD struggling to survive it.

Mr Ruggiero's task will be to bring the reluctant United States on board: cajoling it away from its current folly of embracing the Social Clause and rejecting an activist further-freeing-of-trade-role for the WTO in the matter of setting its new agenda.[21] On the other hand, remembering that the era of exceptionalism is over, Mr Ricupero must unhesitatingly bring the developing countries on board behind such a target.

---

[21] Indeed, at the QUAD trade talks in Kobe some time ago, the United States managed to bamboozle Canada and Japan into acquiescence on going to the December 1996 Ministerial of the WTO with the demand that the Social Clause be included on that agenda. When a great power is set on a task, no matter how harmful, it is hard to offer continued resistance. I would predict (and hope), however, that this persistence by the United States will produce a major confrontation in Singapore.

GLOBAL AGE: SCEPTICAL SOUTH TO FEARFUL NORTH 283

I am afraid that, ironically, Mr Ruggiero's task is likely to be the more difficult since the US, and indeed France, are in the throes of Intrusionism inspired by the phantom fears of the Global Age. By contrast, Mr Ricupero should find his task much easier as the developing countries now find in the Global Age the virtues that they could not see in the earlier years. But it is my fond hope that the two will be able to lead, hand in hand, in shared partnership, the nations of the world into a truly Golden Age with worldwide free trade. Indeed, one could not hope to find better leadership than what they offer. After all, by a remarkable coincidence, the names of both these men can be initialised to RR: a symbol of exceptional quality to us in the former colonies of Great Britain, where RR stood, of course, for Rolls Royce!

REFERENCES

Bhagwati, J. (1995), 'Democracy and Development: New Thinking on an Old Question', 1994 Rajiv Gandhi Memorial Lecture, published in a slightly abbreviated version in the *Journal of Democracy* (October 1995).

Bhagwati, J. (1996), 'The ''Miracle'' that Did Happen: East Asian Growth in Comparative Perspective', keynote speech to a Cornell University Conference on East Asia (mimeo, Economics Department, Columbia University, May).

Bhagwati, J. and V. Dehejia (1992), in J. Bhagwati and M. Kosters (eds.), *Trade and Wages: Levelling Down?*, (American Enterprise Institute, Washington, DC).

Bhagwati, J. and R. Hudec (ed.) (1996), *Fair Trade and Harmonization: Prerequisites for Free Trade?*, 2 vols (MIT Press, Cambridge, Mass.).

Gavin, M. and D. Rodrik (1995), 'The World Bank in Historical Perspective', *American Economic Review* (May).

Irwin, D. (1996), 'The United States in a Global Economy? A Century's Perspective', *American Economic Review* (May).

[3]

REFLECTIONS ON CONSTITUTIONAL CHANGES TO THE GLOBAL TRADING SYSTEM

John Jackson*

Introduction

My subject includes a "work in progress" of mine, which is designed to step up a level of generality and look at how these issues with which we have struggled, here in some detail, fit into a broader perspective. We have discussed competition policy, telecommunications, and certain other aspects of those; however, there are many subjects that one could think of along the same lines. There are, of course, the very pregnant areas of financial services, and some of the difficulties that have been going on this year, and certain peculiar features of them. In the financial services area, we have to worry much more about problems of fiduciary relationships, prudential protections of consumers, fraud—which bring to mind things such as the *BCCI* case, and so on. Then there is the environment; continuing work on agricultural trade, and the many of the intricacies there; product standards: consumer protection in its broader ramifications; and securities regulation, now moving into a twenty-four-hour market. Around the world there are securities, market operations, telecommunications, airline linkages, and so on. And, if you begin to push the frontier, you also have to think of such things as labor regulations, labor standards, human rights, and how those link. So, how can we begin to think about all this? What I want to do is relate this to the World Trade Organization ("WTO"), and to the broad subject that we are talking about, and ask whether there are some generalizable principles. The broad subject, I think, is the subject of the regulation of economic behavior that crosses borders—international economic regulation.

What I am going to do is present a sort of oversimplified template, or type of analysis, that one could walk through to look at this, basically in two parts. First, I will talk about the policy and economics of international regulation in the context of some of the traditional, almost doctrinal, economics learning about regulation relating to government intervention in the market. Second, I will look at the ques-

* Professor of Law, University of Michigan Law School.

tion of institutions, particularly international institutions, and that is where we move into the questions of some of the very important developments that are going on right now in the world, and in the WTO particularly.

I. MARKET-FAILURE ECONOMICS IN AN INTERDEPENDENT WORLD

The first of these subjects is policy and economics of international economic regulation. The traditional economic learning, the type of things that you get from undergraduate textbooks, tends to let the market work and keep the government out. Government ought not to intervene, it is felt, unless there is some particular reason for intervening.

Immediately, however, there is a reason for intervening sometimes—the so-called question of market failure: let the market work, but when the market fails to work, then there is justification for some kind of intervention. Usually that means government intervention. And so, the question is: when should governments regulate at all?

Now, notice what I am doing. I am moving in a more general way toward some of the issues that have been discussed already, because, I think, there is a tendency to jump immediately to the internationalization. What I am doing with this analysis is starting with the broader question: should you have any government intervention at all? And it is a question that we have faced consistently in domestic economics for many decades, perhaps this century. If the answer to that question is "yes," then we need to ask, "what kind of intervention?"

One of the interesting facets about this is that, in most of the economic texts, these questions are considered in the context of a *domestic* economy. There is very little mention about what the indications of an international economy mean for these conditions. And, what do they tell us?

Regarding the first question and its relation to market failure, the most familiar and the most commonly reiterated in the economics literature are the problems of monopoly (competition policy); the problems of asymmetry of information (for instance, the consumer versus the expert sellers); and the problems of government distortions, for a variety of reasons (and those get very troublesome because there are a lot of different valid policy reasons why governments step in that do not have to do with the functioning of the market, and yet they cause distortions in the market). Also, there is the public goods problem, the problem of where the market cannot, or cannot adequately, give incentive for the creation of something that the public needs, because there is the opportunity for the whole public to use it, or capture it (a subject, of course, that is very close to intellectual property questions). And there is a question which is related to some of the others that I have just mentioned—the question of distributive justice, or other alternative policies of governments.

Here is the point where I think our analysis begins to cut. Suppose you can do that analysis in the context of a domestic economy. Then ask: what difference does it make that we are in the kind of internationally-linked world that we are in? Look first at monopoly or competition policy. In some cases, you are really talking about a world economy; you are not talking about a national economy. And so, that may change entirely your first judgment as to whether government intervention is necessary. For example, perhaps there is a national monopoly but, over time, borders have been thrown open to the product in such a way that the national monopoly is really no longer a market failure, because it has to struggle against the rest of the world. But you can also see the opposite conclusion possible. It may be that things do not look like they are market failures domestically, when you look at a closed economy, or you hypothesize a closed economy. But when you move to the international system, because of various formal or informal linkages of various kinds, you may indeed find that there is market failure. Thus, the international dimension of this creates the potential for different judgments on the question of whether we have a particular market failure, monopoly, or competition policy question.

Asymmetries of information is another case very ripe for difficulties enhanced by the international market. First of all, we have language differences worldwide, which makes it much harder for many persons to be able to understand information. We have deep cultural differences where a "yes" means "no," a "no" means "maybe," etc. We have a whole variety of factors: distance, different legal systems, the ability to enforce contracts in different ways, and so on. So asymmetries of information can really give rise to a lot of different conclusions, based on international activities.

Government distortions, of course, provide many possibilities. Are we beginning to face international government distortions? Are we beginning to face the regulations, for instance, such as General Agreement on Tariffs and Trade's ("GATT") textile system, as an illustration of how the international regulatory system begins to create distortions?

Public goods provide another set of market-failure possibilities. There are a lot of public goods in the international landscape. One is peace and security, for instance, peacekeeping in the United Nations. Another is human rights. There are certain values there, certain broader values than just economic market-oriented values. Thus, again the international landscape leads us to a conclusion that the market is not able to cope the way that we think it ought to be able to.

Distributive justice suggests a variety of policies within the scope of domestic market concerns: progressive taxation, welfare, safety nets, and a social market economy. But, internationally, of course, the developing countries argue for certain preferences. They argue for an international financial safety net, almost the equivalent of international bankruptcy.

So the next question is what the government response to market failure should be. In the economic literature, there are generally several kinds of responses that have been suggested—ways that governments can intervene. The government can tax. The government can subsidize. The government can regulate and create penalties for deviant behavior of various kinds. The government can try to alter various market incentives, for example, by creating a system of permits that are purchased or bid for, to allow certain environmental degradation under certain systems.

What about the international system, then? Now, here is where we begin to see major problems, because the international system is relatively frail and undeveloped and it makes it very hard to take on this whole inventory of responses. It is very hard, or impossible, for the international system to tax, at least under current situations. It is quite hard for the international system to subsidize, because national sovereign governments are not prepared to give enough sums of money to an international body that would be doing the subsidizing, to make it really worthwhile. The focus internationally is really on *regulation*, partly, by second- or third-best-analyses in many cases, because the international system cannot tax very well, or subsidize. The fourth alternative I mentioned, incidentally—altering the market incentives of certain structures—is also difficult for the international system, e.g., to set up an apparatus for selling licenses or auctioning licenses. So, the focus is really on regulation, and in many cases, that seems to be the only available international government intervention.

In this two-part analysis, we look first at where there is a need for intervention and we see how the international system, market, and so on, conditions that. Second, we examine the responses. It is not necessarily the case that, because the international landscape causes a different judgment on market failure, there needs to be an *international* response. It may be that the international landscape, which causes us to make a judgment of market failure and therefore a need for government intervention, could nevertheless lead us to decide that the kind of government intervention ought to be a *national* government intervention, and not necessarily an international one. So, that is part of the analysis also.

And, indeed, then you get into a cost-benefit analysis of choosing institutions to respond. You then have to ask whether it should be international, or whether it should be domestic, or what levels of government are the best for intervention: from the local neighborhood all the way up to global government entities.

In a number of cases, the optimum approach would be some kind of international or global response, but the institution concerned is so weak, or so fraught with the potential abuse that, on a cost-benefit analysis, you decide that you really cannot choose that. You have to fall back on national governments for intervention because of the dangers, or risks, of the international system. Sometimes, because the international system is too rigid—that it is so hard to renegotiate a treaty, for example—that once a measure is in place, it is virtually impossible to amend. We have seen elements of that in the GATT, and maybe now in the WTO. So when we look at the international intervention, let me just remind you that there are a series of different possibilities there. There are also unilateral possibilities in the nation/state acting through extraterritorial measures, or section 301-type measures, of threatened sanctions or threatened retaliation.

II. INSTITUTIONS

Now, let us turn to institutions, particularly international institutions. The first thing we have to ask is: What are some of the goals of the international institutions, or what are some of the goals of having international institutions intervene in markets?

Of course, the prime goal is to facilitate the cooperative mechanisms of many nations. This actually can take you into another kind of economic analysis, sometimes called the prisoner's dilemma, where you look at what governments might do independently, or unilaterally, and you discover that if they all act unilaterally in their own particular interest, the effect is a disaster multilaterally, or a disaster for the world. One country can use tariff increases, for instance, in certain strategic ways to try to gain additional welfare for its population, until other countries start to do the same thing, possibly in retaliation, and then, very soon, you have a spiraling down of the welfare available in the world, even putting aside the question of distribution. The international institution really has to be first and foremost designed to facilitate the cooperative mechanisms that are called for in many cases.

I suggest as another goal that institutions act in a way that allows implementation of goals, which usually means a rule-oriented system because the rule-oriented system allows adequate predictability and becomes a basis of planning for non-governmental organizations ("NGOs"), corporations, private entrepreneurs, and so forth.

By that we mean a system that operates on rules which are negotiated and formulated through some kind of a rule-making process, but once in place, there is a structure to make those rules reasonably effective so that individual entrepreneurs can depend on it and use them for predictability and planning. A reason for this is our desire to have markets work. In other words, this is really tuned to market-oriented economies where you have decentralized decision-making. Millions of entrepreneurs, not the central state agency, are making decisions, and those millions of entrepreneurs need some kind of framework for planning.

For example, if an entrepreneur plans to invest in a shoe plant in Costa Rica, it needs to know several things. It needs to know that its property is reasonably protected. It needs to know something about the intellectual property being protected. It needs to know something about whether that plant will be able sell across borders, because Costa Rica is arguably too small to support an efficient shoe factory. If it does not know these things, then it faces higher risks, and that means it needs a higher return, which in turn means that the lack of a rule orientation raises the "risk premium" of the allocation of capital in the world, and therefore reduces the welfare in the world.

How do you make the rules? Well, you need some kind of an institutional structure that will do that, because you need, first of all, to formulate the initial set of cooperative mechanisms. However, then you need somehow to make it keep up, and that is often the most difficult part of this international system. That is true in a lot of different areas, including arms control, the United Nations Charter, and the worry about the Security Council and its makeup. It is very hard to change treaties, particularly when you have 130 to 180 countries involved with all sorts of constitutional processes. This you do not do lightly, and so the institutions have to be put in place with some of that in mind, and that leads to some subparts of this analysis under rule-making.

You have to figure out how decisions are going to be made. Will you have weighted voting? Will you have a Security Council, a small council-type system, or is it "one-nation, one-vote"? If so, what are the ramifications of that for large, powerful countries in the system, who, de facto, and empirically, are not going to submit to very important decisions on a "one-nation, one-vote" system. You also need the capability at various levels, but probably internationally, to study, gather information, research, analyze, and flag some of the issues coming down the track, so that the system will not be so surprised, as it was, for instance, in the Mexico Peso problem. And, you need legitimation. You need something that seems to be fair in the minds of the world's citizenship, if you will, the world's citizenry.

So that leads to a fourth goal—the goal of oversight and audit, as the way I have phrased this at the moment. You want to keep the institution responsive, moving with the times, but you want to keep it honest. Furthermore, you do not want it to be defrauded all the time, and you do not want special interests taking over portions of the decision-making apparatus. Finally, you want it to be viewed as legitimate, that is, you want, again, the citizens throughout the world to say "yes, they are doing the best they can in looking out for our interests, we know that human institutions are never perfect, but on balance, we need to have that." So what do you do for that?

One response is transparency. This has been an enormous weakness of international organizations and structures, partly from several centuries' history of diplomatic discourse, which has strongly stressed negotiation in a context of secrecy, and, in some cases, secrecy in order to prevent their home constituencies from learning what they are doing. That is not all bad because sometimes what they are doing requires certain compromises, and they do not want to telegraph those compromises too early in a process where there may be some education needed of the citizenry. If there is anything that the environmentalists have taught us in the last five years about international regulation, it is this issue of transparency. It is something, of course, we are struggling with in the context of the WTO.

Participation is important also. This again goes back to the question of international rule-making by elites. We have just begun to develop a worldwide system in some of our institutions where there is much broader public participation, quite often through the formula of NGOs, and certification of NGOs in a variety of contexts. That is something that the new WTO is struggling with right now.

Checks on power, or checks and balances, are necessary to keep the international system from misusing its power. Now, there are a number of interstitial ways that we do that, and some of those have been mentioned yesterday. One of them is limits on decision-making, where we limit the powers of the governing body. There is a lot of this in the WTO charter, and this was a matter of great concern to the U.S. Congress last year, for instance. My own perception and testimony was that the WTO Charter actually had better limits on decision-making, in the sense of checks and balances, than GATT. This raises a counter-problem: are there too many limits on the decision-making and rule-making in the institution? For example, are there too many limits on decisions that relate to voting structure and so forth? The nonself-executing nature of the international decisions and the international treaties are a form of check and balance against overreaching power.

There are limits in the dispute-settlement process also. How far can a panel go, what is its competence, and what should a tribunal do? There have been some specific areas that have been raised in the last few years about this, and we can recognize those as part of a pattern of checks and balances, even if we do not agree in all cases about them. For instance, what should be the standard of review by a panel which is examining a national government executive branch action? Can it review national actions de novo, or should it only look at the law and not the facts? If it looks at the law, is it only the international law, namely the treaty clauses, at which it looks? What are the grounds of interpreting the treaty clauses?

Of course, we have a very interesting clause in the antidumping text, Article 17.6, that in the closing minutes of the Uruguay Round proved to be a possible deal-breaker. The whole round could have collapsed on the basis of this arcane language that I do not think more than about three dozen people in the world understood.

Another example is the legal effect of the result of a panel, or tribunal ruling. Generally, under international law, it is not stare decisis. There is some precedential effect, but it is not stare decisis. That is the approach of the World Court statute, and it is a pattern reaffirmed by some of the preeminent authors of international law. Again, in a sense, that is a form of check, because it is saying: "All right, panelists, you can solve this particular dispute between countries A and B, but you're not going to proclaim a rule that's going to bind the other 138 members of this organization, in all future cases."

Then there is something that distresses some people, what I would call "national oversight and audit" of what the international system is doing. In the United States, we have a lot of it, maybe, some would say, too much of it. We have the Congress holding hearings about the United Nations, refusing to pay its budgetary fees, etc. In the WTO context, we have, on the horizon, something called the "Dole Commission." It is still not legislation, but it tracks a compromise that Senator Dole had with the administration late in 1994, which was absolutely crucial to get approval of the Uruguay Round. The idea calls for a national commission that is supposed to review and advise the Congress on the legitimacy of what a panel does in a decision that relates to the United States. Is this bad? There are certain elements that are pretty benign, although there are one or two elements that are kind of borderline, but I think we could live with them without much trouble.

National constitutions and how they work are necessary to interface the international system with the domestic system. This is a potential check. The question of selecting the officers of the international system will be a check on power. Are there self-perpetuating officers in the system that seem to be able to prolong their tenures, even though there is considerable doubt about their effectiveness as leaders of some of these international organizations? Indeed, this relates even to some allegations of fraudulent behavior.

And then there is this pregnant word that was mentioned once or twice yesterday—"subsidiarity." And, that again, relates to the question of how far up or down the scale of governmental entities should decision-making of government intervention be placed, which is partly a checks-and-balances question, but partly an allocation-of-power question, which are two questions very closely related.

III. WTO

How does the WTO stack up against this? Is the WTO going to be the institution that many of us hope it will be, and will it be an improvement on this very messy, but joyously interesting institution, the GATT of the past? Does it improve on the GATT? I am convinced it does. I think the WTO has many attributes that are far superior to the GATT, along the lines that I have mentioned. The rule-making is much better constrained and checked, for what that is worth. The new WTO dispute-settlement understanding applies a very elaborate set of texts for a dispute-settlement procedure that we all hope is going to work well and improve the system.

The WTO faced an enormous challenge by the United States in May and June in the disastrous Japan/United States auto situation, where I think the United States very shortsightedly thumbed its nose at the system. In the end, however, it appears that the United States backed down, so in doing that, it may have actually strengthened the system.

As indicated above, however, the other side for many of these questions is whether we have gone too far with the checks. Let me just give you several examples. First, in order to amend the dispute-settlement understanding, it takes full consensus. Now, consensus is a delicate word in GATT history and in the new WTO. It is not quite unanimity, but in certain situations, I think it can amount to unanimity, and it can cause a stalemate or the prevention of any progress in evolving the Dispute Settlement Understanding rules. We have to watch and see if we can make the system work nevertheless, using certain custom and practice to try to interpret some of the existing language in a way, for example, to provide for more opportunity for transparency and public citizen understanding.

Another example is whether there will be more opportunity for NGO participation in a way that will enhance the legitimacy of the process. Another example is Annex 4 of the WTO, which contains four international text agreements that are Pluralateral Agreements, which means optional. This is a slight departure from the single-package approach of the Uruguay Round negotiation. This could be a place where you could really make some progress for new upcoming issues. That could be a place, for instance, for competition-policy text, or an environment-policy text. But additions to Annex 4 require full consensus, and thus, can be blocked. We will have to see what the practice will be. That might be an area of dynamicism in which the organization can begin to face many of these new issues, some of them left over from the Uruguay Round and some of them to be faced in the future. On the other hand, it may be a place that will result in more stalemate.

[4]

FRAGMENTED STATES AND INTERNATIONAL RULES OF LAW

SOL PICCIOTTO

Lancaster University, UK

IN 1995, THE UK's Economic and Social Research Council (ESRC) identified and publicized three main 'thematic priorities': globalization; regulation and governance; and social integration and exclusion. Both the selection of these topics and the way in which they have been expressed are very revealing of much current public discussion. The issues themselves are far from new, indeed I myself have been concerned with all three during most of my academic life. However, in current discussions they appear under new and modish guises: now we have the concept of globalization, replacing internationalization; governance, instead of government or the state; and social integration and exclusion, instead of class, race and gender. The newer terms are, I think, rather more fuzzy and elusive about the nature of the social processes to which they refer. The inflection results, I think, partly from changes in the character of those processes but, more significantly, from new ways of perceiving and shaping those processes. Not surprisingly, there is considerable debate and contestation about all three.

GLOBALIZATION AND STATE FRAGMENTATION

Many are ambivalent about the current fashionable discussions of globalization. Has there really been such a transformation of international

SOCIAL & LEGAL STUDIES ISSN 0964 6639 Copyright © 1997 SAGE Publications, London, Thousand Oaks, CA and New Delhi, Vol. 6 (2), 259–279

interactions, resulting in a global homogenization of social and cultural life, as the term suggests? Why has the concept become so popular in both academic and everyday discussions? In some cases, it seems to result from an abrupt awareness that common assumptions about our social world are no longer valid, without too much inquiry about how far they ever were: a realization that we don't just live in and can't just study *a* society, a *single* legal system, or a *national* state, and that the world contains a *multiplicity* of diverse and interacting societies, states and legalities. But if this is the case, why the term *globalization*, which misleadingly suggests an increasing global homogeneity, rather than awareness of diversity or interconnectedness, as I think internationalization does?

In another perspective, globalization debates seem to result from post-Cold War concerns, to envisage and construct a New World Order, which might be more cohesive and coordinated than was previously possible. Yet if globalization is about projects to improve or rationalize world government, actual proposals along these lines do not seem to have much popular resonance. I think that this was shown, for instance, by the resounding silence which met the Report on Global Governance, produced recently by a group of eminent statespeople, which put forward proposals for far-reaching reforms of the United Nations system and international organization generally (Commission on Global Governance, 1995). Equally, we have only to consider the wide-ranging opposition which seems to have grown, at least since the signing at Maastricht of the Treaty on European Union, against any idea that we might need a European super state to govern the Single European Market.

Rather, what seems to have gone global is The Market, or at least ideologies of free trade and open markets. Yet even here things are not quite as they seem. Globalization is generally said to involve an increasing volume or velocity of international flows, in economic terms of trade, investment and finance, in cultural terms of artefacts, signs and symbols. Certainly, globalization could be said to have 'given a cosmopolitan character to production and consumption in every country', so that 'in place of the old local and national seclusion and self-sufficiency, we have intercourse in every direction, universal inter-dependence of nations'. Yet those are quotations from the description of the creation of the world market given almost 150 years ago in 1848 by Karl Marx and Friedrich Engels in *The Manifesto of the Communist Party*. While the nature of the world economy has greatly changed since then, it is not obvious that there has been any substantial increase in the degree of what they already at that time described as 'the universal inter-dependence of nations'. Attempts to quantify the growth of international transactions over the past century or more, at least when calculated in proportion to local or national transactions, do not generally show a significant *relative* increase.[1]

What seems to be more important is the increased *potential* for such flows, resulting from the reduction or elimination of national and local barriers to all kinds of trade and investment. The gradual reduction of tariff barriers and elimination of exchange controls during the 1960s and 1970s widened during the 1980s into a more generalized drive towards national deregulation, opening up all kinds of markets to access from outside. Thus, what has been increasingly created is a network of globally interlinked although still in many ways very locally based markets. However, when looked at more closely, there has been as much re-regulation as de-regulation, and often the new regulatory systems have originated in global arenas and have been imported into national law. A dramatic example is provided by financial markets, where the breaking-down of relatively closed national systems of credit and finance has been accompanied and facilitated by elaborate *new* regulatory arrangements, developed through complex international political processes. The result has been a raft of Brussels directives and Basle guidelines, which have introduced formalized rules and professionalized supervision in place of cosy clubs and informal oversight by central banks and finance ministries (Goldstein et al., 1992; Fishman, 1993; Porter, 1993; Kapstein, 1994). This has involved some intriguing shifts in the *character* of regulation, away from command-and-control through the state, and towards functionalist modes of governance based on the construction of new professional regulatory cultures by accountants, lawyers and managers.

The privatization of the state has been a general global trend: in Britain it now extends beyond utilities, such as water or electricity, and even the raising of money for public projects is being done through the National Lottery (though this idea is not entirely new, even in Britain: historians tell us that William of Orange had an early hit with the Million Lottery of 1694). The new managerialism of the 'audit society' has even spread to venerable institutions, such as universities, as we academics are well aware. These new forms of regulation are designed to enable such social activities and institutions to operate in an environment of global competition, while attempting to define conditions which might ensure both private profit and the fulfilment of public functions (not always very successfully, as seen currently in situations as diverse as the controversy over the National Lottery and the financial crisis of the Channel Tunnel). At the same time, the term *governance* is also used to signify the provision of public order, protection of private property, but not necessarily liberal democracy, to required global standards by countries, especially in eastern Europe and Africa, as a condition of political support and economic investment from the West (Faundez, 1996).

In this perspective, globalization entails a process of fragmentation. In particular, in place of centralized *government* primarily through national states, we have moved to delegated forms of *governance* operating in layers within and across states. Here we find the significance of the second of the ESRC's themes. It is in this context that I believe we should consider the often-cited question of the future of the nation-state and the international state system. By the term *fragmentation*, I would like to suggest a contested process of destabilization and restructuring, involving a search for new forms of synthesis between the economic and political aspects of social relations, rather than a deterministic tendency for economic pressures from an already-existing world market to undermine otherwise stable political structures. In

fact, economic activities are deeply embedded in social, cultural and normative practices.

Here I think we come to the third of the ESRC's priority themes: social
integration and exclusion. Clearly, there has been increasing concern that
global competitive forces tend to exacerbate existing social differences while
creating new forms of exclusion. More broadly, if globalization entails a
process of fragmentation of the public sphere, there must be concern about
its effects on the institutions of liberal democracy. This I think is the subtext
of the fears about the threats to the national democratic state from global free
trade, expressed by commentators and politicians both of the Left and the
Right. But this is to see the threat to our institutions and way of life as coming
from outside, deflecting attention away from internal failures. The term *state
fragmentation* might bring to mind the dramatic breakdowns of *other* states
such as Yugoslavia or Rwanda, but we should not forget that even we in this
United Kingdom have signally failed to resolve the long-running problem of
Northern Ireland. And if we are tempted to attribute such problems to
ancient ethnic rivalries, we should remember that national identities are not
simply inherited but constructed, and that the mythology of national identity in the liberal state depends significantly on acceptance that it can deliver
social justice. Hostility to foreigners is powered by fear that They will take
over Our jobs, Our homes and Our institutions.

RECONSTRUCTING INTERNATIONAL LEGALITY

These changes provide a rich and challenging context for an international
lawyer. In the current period of ferment, reconceptualization and restructuring of the world system, it is not surprising that law is being called upon to
play an increasingly important role in mediating the shifting structures of
power. Too often, however, resort to law seems due to the failure of politics.
In particular, there is increasingly frequent recourse to international law as a
remedy for the failure or inadequacies of the nation-state. Notably, David
Held (1995) outlined a blueprint for a 'cosmopolitan democracy'as a response
to the threats to liberal democracy and the national state posed by globalization. Essentially, this seems to be an argument for a neo-liberal form of
global government, central to which is a stronger role for international law.
Although these are in some ways ambitious proposals, they are surprisingly
uncritical of the capacity of international law to help relieve the pressures on
the state system resulting from the major crises of the global political
economy. In contrast, one of the foremost contemporary critics of international law argues that the international system exists only as a shared
vocabulary and institutional practices, and that 'as long as there is no wide
agreement on what constitutes the good life, the formality of statehood
remains the best guarantee we have against the conquest of modernism's
liberal aspect by modernism's authoritarian impulse' (Koskenniemi, 1991:
397).

International lawyers are familiar enough with the corridors of diplomacy that normally their proposals for a strengthening of world law are tempered with a dose of political realism. This tends, however, to result in a mutually reinforcing formalism. For example, James Crawford (1994) in his inaugural lecture at Cambridge chose the topic 'Democracy and International Law' (cf. Franck, 1992). Interestingly, however, his theme was the extent to which international law contains or should develop some minimum principles for *national* democracy, and not at all what I think is the more important aspect of the issue, the lack of democracy in the *international* sphere and hence the fundamental problem of lack of legitimacy of international law itself.

To understand something of the possibilities and limits of law in the current world system, we need first of all a critical evaluation both of statehood and of international law, and of how they have developed historically. Certainly, the key institution of the international system of liberal capitalism is the national state, yet its character is too often taken for granted. Especially enigmatic is the simultaneously national and international form of the modern state.[2] In what follows I will try to probe some of the contradictions and limits of the present-day process of reconstruction of international legality, within such a broader historical and critical perspective.

SOVEREIGNTY AND STATEHOOD

The central conundrum for international law, as for politics, is state sovereignty. Sovereignty is generally recognized as posing a major obstacle for any general reconceptualization of international law, yet it seems hard to dislodge from its place as the conceptual cornerstone of modern international law, indeed of global law as a whole. Take away state sovereignty and instead of a clear hierarchy of legal orders there would be only a bewildering variety of legalities jostling and competing for acceptance. Thus, it is perhaps not surprising that contemporary international lawyers, even those taking a 'critical' perspective, are deeply divided and ambivalent about the importance of statehood and sovereignty (see Picciotto, 1996). But much depends on how sovereignty itself is understood.

The notion of supreme or untrammelled power embodied in the concept of sovereignty has two aspects, internal and external. In the modern, post-Napoleonic state system, each state claims the monopoly of legitimate power over its subjects, since the overt elements of coercive power have been removed from personal relations and vested in autonomized institutions with a public character. Internally, the state asserts a monopoly on coercive force. Although other normative orders can be tolerated, or even encouraged by delegation to self-regulating associations or institutions, they are subject to the overriding authority of state law, which alone can validate coercive sanctions.[3] State sovereignty can be, and often is, despotic; but within the liberal state it is legitimized by the rule of law. Government through the rule of law claims to guarantee the formal equality and freedom of all legal subjects and to facilitate free economic exchange, through institutions, processes and concepts based on abstract and universalist principles of fairness and justice.

However, much of the work of critical lawyers is concerned to deconstruct this world of formalist law in various ways, and to show that there is a gulf between the formalistic principles and universalist pretensions of law which offer visions of justice based on abstract notions of individual autonomy, equality and freedom and the dense and particular social contexts and experiences of real people. Law at best can provide a framework to test, evaluate and adjudicate competing claims of right. The promise it holds out of governing social relations by providing an independent and neutral basis of predictability and rationality, tends to evaporate when its abstract principles are actually operationalized. At this point we find that the substantive content of decisions must more or less covertly be supplied from political, economic or ethical considerations. Although critics of the liberal conception of the rule of law are sometimes treated as dangerous radicals, I think the aim of a critical approach is to probe the limits of law, so that it can be transcended, not abandoned, and, in particular, to point out, as non-lawyers already know in their hearts, that law alone is incapable of ensuring a fair and just society. Indeed, to move towards such a society we need to develop new understandings, principles, and institutions of legality, and even to transcend our present concepts of legality altogether and integrate them at a higher plane. So much, for now, for the internal aspects of sovereignty and the rule of law.

Externally it is states themselves that are free and equal legal subjects, and this seems at first sight to replicate the internal realm of the state. However, the external aspect of sovereignty means that states themselves are not subject to any higher authority, so they interact formally as equals in a community of a different order and on a higher plane than the national. For some varieties of legal formalism, this creates serious doubt as to whether there can be any international law worth the name. Most people can agree that it is law, but one of a different kind, based on principles and obligations freely accepted as binding by its sovereign state subjects. Thus, international legal obligations are grounded in the mutual self-interest of states, each pursuing what it considers to be its *national interest*, but bound together within an overarching normative order. The lack of centralized institutions with overriding coercive powers is said by some to indicate the 'primitive' nature of the international legal system, while others assert that on the contrary the relatively orderly interaction of states without the need for a higher authority shows the effectiveness of international law as a self-regulatory system.

Yet while the state is clearly an important focus of identity and locus of power, what seems very unsatisfactory is the personification of the state which turns it into the 'subject'of international law, and conceptualizes the international state system as a 'community of states'. By ignoring the social relations on which statehood is built, this makes it hard to understand either the internal or external role of states. It also produces a picture of states as autonomous and compartmentalized units, each governing only its own citizens, whereas even cursory study shows that private economic and social relations cross state boundaries and are therefore governed by multiple and often overlapping *jurisdictions*.

Thus, sovereignty should be seen as a particular way of distributing political power, within and between states. The fiction of unlimited internal sovereignty is complemented and sustained by its corollary, the sovereign equality of states. The exercise of power is legitimated within the state by the generation of consensus around the national common interest. Internationally, formally equal sovereigns bargain on the basis of the national interest of each for reciprocal benefits or to secure mutual or common interests.

Although the principle of state sovereignty appears to establish a clear structure or order in the international system, it rests on a shifting foundation, which continually produces fault lines. The existence and continued dynamic of accumulation through the world market continually reshapes the interdependent or interconnected character of social and economic activities. At the same time, the uneven and unequal patterns of accumulation create substantive political and economic inequalities which undermine the formal principle of sovereign equality. Thus, state sovereignty is not an impermeable barrier but a fluid point of articulation between the international and the domestic sphere. Furthermore, its character shifts and is contested, as can be seen by the controversies among international lawyers and the changes in many of the key principles of international law. If the nineteenth century was the high-water mark of statist conceptions of international law, universalist perspectives have gathered momentum during the twentieth century.

The state-centred view emphasizes the autonomy and sovereignty of the nation-state and, therefore, insists on a strict dualism between international and national law. Statism is reluctant to accept that international legal obligations restrict state autonomy unless very clearly emerging from the 'consent' of sovereign states. It seeks to maintain a strict compartmentalization of legal orders, the borders between national and international law being patrolled by national governments on behalf of the state.

Universalism, on the other hand, sees a continuity between international and national law, which gives individuals and other legal entities more direct access to the international sphere, demoting governments from any position of primacy. It emphasizes, for example, that national courts not only are authoritative in their own sphere but also contribute to the development of international law principles and, equally, that rights and obligations under international law can be invoked in cases under national law where appropriate. Thus, for example, there has been a dilution of principles such as state immunity, which makes it possible for national courts and lawyers to become involved more directly in many issues previously dealt with on an interstate basis. Conversely, rules agreed on an interstate level can become national law, often automatically. The most striking example of this is the direct applicability and direct effect of EC law, developed in the forthright jurisprudence of the European Court of Justice; but in addition, a high proportion of changes in national law result more or less directly from international agreements. Although EC law is generally referred to as 'supranational', it still seems hard to discuss the implications of the greater interpenetration of national and international law without using the term *sovereignty*.

Universalism therefore sees an intermingling of the rights and duties of states and of other legal subjects, both individuals and corporations. From this perspective global legal regimes come into view, covering matters as diverse as human rights, the protection of the natural environment, and international business or commercial activities. These involve an intermingling of public and private actors, in national and international forums. Certainly, many examples can be found demonstrating trends towards what might be called a 'globalization' of legal regimes covering matters of international concern.

However, when looked at more closely these trends are not quite as they are represented in some of the recent globalization debates. First, they have a much longer history than is often appreciated, often going back a century or more. Second, it is generally not a matter of issues previously dealt with nationally somehow bursting their bounds and breaking into the global arena, but rather a process of breakdown and restructuring of the articulation between the national and the international.[4] Third, and most important, the fragmentation of state sovereignty produces a much more complex and layered interaction of regulatory arrangements of various kinds, which may entail dissonance rather than the harmonious coordination suggested by the term *regime*.

In this context of fragmentation, it is not surprising that law and lawyers might play an increased role. Since law links the apparently autonomous spheres of politics and economics, lawyers are accustomed to mediating not only between the public sphere of the state and the private sphere of economic and personal relations but between different public spheres. The lawyer-diplomat has the advantage of having no 'national' allegiance except to the intellectual capital invested in mastering the language and techniques deployed in the fields in which she or he is active, unlike the state official or politician whose duty is to the national interest.[5] Although legal systems are deeply rooted in particular cultural traditions going back over centuries, there has been considerable interaction and mutual influence. Even the staunchly pragmatic common law has had its Romanist influences, and there has been wholesale importation of codes of law not only in colonial contexts, but also by countries such as Japan.

Thus, there is a long historical tradition of the cosmopolitan or comparative lawyer, working at the interface between different legal orders. Moreover, lawyers perhaps have the advantage that although they speak fundamentally the same language of fairness, justice and order, they find that it has many dialects and variations. Thus, the task of the international or comparative lawyer is not to homogenize, or create a legal Esperanto, but to interpret one to the other, evaluate differences, facilitate interactions. Unlike economists, whose aim seems to be to subject us all to the same iron laws of market efficiency, lawyers seem to offer the prospect of preserving particularity while facilitating consensus. Yet, as I have said, this promise may all too often prove illusory. At the end of the day, law is binary: one party is right, the other is wrong; compensation must be paid, punishment administered; the only consistent winner in the game is the lawyer.

THE INTERNATIONALIZATION OF BUSINESS TAXATION

Now, I briefly illustrate some of these issues by taking some examples from my general field of research, the internationalization of business regulation, and especially the area that recently occupied me for several years, international taxation. Although it is commonly regarded as a dry and technical subject, I found the story of how the international arrangements for income taxation were constructed to be a fascinating one, which reveals much about the changing nature of the state in the international system (Picciotto, 1992). Taxation is after all a central nexus in the relation between state and citizen, since without it there would be no collectivity. Taxation has a changing form, reflecting and moulding social changes: thus an important part of the crisis of the nation-state today is its fiscal crisis. A key element of the consolidation of the modern liberal welfare–warfare state, as a national state within an international system, was the shift to a broad basis of taxation based on income, which became generally established in the first decade or two of the twentieth century.[6]

The basis of legitimacy of income taxation is the principle that it applies equally to all citizens, although this still leaves considerable room for dispute about what constitutes fair treatment if incomes are unequal. So there have been recurring debates both about the minimum level of taxable income or tax threshold and about graduated rates on higher levels of income as against a single flat-rate (this has been recently revived, especially in the USA). The income tax became an efficient mass tax in developed capitalist countries with the introduction of deduction at source, especially on employment income, which came at the time of the Second World War. Government revenues in capitalist welfare states became increasingly dependent on employment income, not least because other types of income offer greater opportunities for tax planning or avoidance. Tax planning entails using the flexibility within legal definitions to alter the characterization of an income flow, or to redirect it or shift its timing. Such practices can be legitimized as embodying the right of each individual freely to dispose of property, although in reality they become constituted as an almost routinized game played between accountants, lawyers and government officials.

Taxation is one of the most jealously guarded attributes of national sovereignty, perhaps second only to the maintenance of armed forces. Yet from its inception, income and profits taxation raised questions about national scope and international coordination. The scope of state sovereignty seems clear, since the modern state is defined in terms of territory. However, this still leaves room for considerable extension and produces overlap between the actual *jurisdiction* of states. Thus, taxes on income can be levied when earned and at source, or when received, either by citizens of or residents within the state. States may tax on both these bases, as in fact Britain and some other developed capitalist states have done.[7]

Not surprisingly, as tax rates began to rise early this century, complaints about international double taxation began to be made, most vociferously by those engaged in international business or commerce. They pleaded for equality in the conditions of competition. One of the most vocal in the UK was the Vestey family, who built the biggest private fortune in Britain based on combining cold storage and distribution here with access to cheap sources of food abroad, such as eggs from China and beef from Argentina – they later became familiar as owners of the Dewhursts butcher shops, though the group was recently liquidated. Back at the time of the First World War, the Vestey brothers developed a deep resentment against what they considered to be the unfair double taxation burden created by the British rules of residence. In evidence to the Royal Commission on Income Tax in 1919, Sir William Vestey argued for fairness in taxation of a global business such as his:

> In a business of this nature you cannot say how much is made in one country and how much is made in another. You kill an animal and the product of that animal is sold in 50 different countries. You cannot say how much is made in England and how much is made abroad. . . . It is not my object to escape payment of tax. My object is to get equality of taxation with the foreigner, nothing else.

However, he failed to convince either the Royal Commission or the Prime Minister, Lloyd George, to whom he wrote privately. The official British view was that relief from overlapping taxation would depend on the negotiation of international arrangements, which could take account of the effects on international movements of capital. International negotiations, however, failed to find a comprehensive solution. A diplomatic conference held in 1928 could only agree on the texts of draft treaties, to be used as models for bilateral negotiation between governments, but few treaties were actually concluded during the 1930s.

In the meantime, private wealth-owners and companies devised their own measures. The Vesteys, in particular, resorted to an elaborate international family trust and corporate structure, aimed at reducing their liability to British tax to almost nil. Very briefly, the scheme was for the Union Cold Store company to pay rent for the use of their worldwide assets, allowing most of the global profits to accumulate in a Paris trust, which merely made loans for the personal expenses of the Vestey family in Britain. The scheme eventually resulted in protracted legal battles lasting several decades, in which the Vesteys scored two notable legal victories in the House of Lords. The Vesteys were perhaps exceptional but not unique, and international tax planning developed in the interwar period as a means of mitigating what wealthy families and businesses considered to be an unfair burden, due to the inadequate coordination between states of their national tax jurisdictions. These arrangements were devised by a growing new breed of cosmopolitan business lawyers (Picciotto, 1995).

After 1945, there was a rapid growth of a network of tax treaties, based on the model developed from the prewar drafts. These treaty arrangements were typical of many developed since the late nineteenth century to reconcile national state sovereignty with the development of the world market. No attempt was made to establish a common regulatory regime – each state remained formally free to determine the scope and incidence of its own taxes. However, premised on their mutual interest to stimulate flows of investment between them, the states agreed an allocation of tax jurisdiction.

International investment did indeed gather momentum, but it mainly took the form of direct investment by corporate groups (or transnational corporations, TNCs). Direct investment by TNCs often entailed little actual outflow of money-capital, but relied on local borrowing, capitalization of intangible assets and reinvestment of earnings. There were still complaints about the inadequacy of coordination of tax jurisdiction, but the firms again found their own solutions through international tax planning. Since these firms were organized as international corporate groups, it was relatively easy to route investments through intermediate companies incorporated in convenient jurisdictions. This enabled returns on such investment to be accumulated and reinvested free of home-country tax, unless and until they were actually needed back home, for example to pay dividends. Initially, the home-country tax authorities overlooked or tolerated these arrangements, provided they fell within acceptable limits, which were negotiated relatively informally. However, as the patterns became routinized and much larger in scale, more formal regulations were introduced by the main capital-exporting countries asserting the right to tax the so-called 'passive' income accumulated in intermediary companies in low-tax jurisdictions, or 'tax havens'.

The internationally integrated character of TNCs tended to reveal the inadequacy of international tax arrangements based on allocating jurisdictional rights. This was especially shown in the politicization of transfer pricing . This issue had already been identified by specialists in the 1930s, but surfaced again more publicly in the 1960s. When business is carried on in an integrated way by a corporate group through branches or subsidiaries in different countries, there is often a high flow of transfers between them, involving anything from component parts or subassemblies to intellectual property rights. Since the 1960s there has been a growing awareness that a high proportion of international trade between countries, now amounting to as much as 30 or 40 percent, actually consists of *internal* sales within a *single* international corporate group, such as Ford or Hoffmann LaRoche. The prices fixed for such transfers obviously have a direct bearing on the profits shown in the national accounts of the different affiliates. Legal powers were introduced, for example in the UK as far back as 1915, allowing the national tax authorities to readjust the company's accounts, if they considered that such prices had been manipulated in order to reduce national tax liability.

When related companies operate within a single state, the obvious solution is to permit or require them to submit consolidated accounts. This is rather difficult internationally without severely compromising national sovereignty. The adoption of a global unitary approach to internationally integrated businesses would require at least a comprehensive multilateral agreement between states, defining when a business can be considered unitary, common accounting rules and a common formula for apportioning its taxable profits. Even within the EU such a comprehensive approach is not on the immediate agenda.

The solution adopted, which was first agreed internationally in 1935, is the so-called Arm's Length rule. This enables the subsidiaries of TNCs to be assessed on the basis of their own separate accounts by each state, with intrafirm prices within the group being fixed at what would have been paid had the related entities been independent parties negotiating through the market, at arm's length. It was understood from the beginning that there was a good deal of artificiality in this approach, since the whole *raison d'être* of an internationally integrated firm is that this integration or internalization gives it competitive advantages, so that comparable transactions between independent entities would not be available. This principle was adopted as a second-best solution, but national tax authorities understood from the start that Arm's Length would only defer the problem, since any adjustments to transfer prices by one tax authority would be likely to *create* double taxation unless the authority responsible for taxation of the related firm were willing to accept a '*corresponding adjustment*' to the latter firm's accounts. Thus, the German report to the League of Nations inquiry on the matter in 1932 emphasized that national fiscal authorities would have to give each other reciprocal assistance to facilitate allocation, and anticipated that internationally agreed general principles would gradually emerge. This rather prescient insight has however taken some decades to be proved accurate.

The transfer-pricing question lurked in the shadows until it was illuminated by the growing political concern about the power of 'the multinationals' during the 1960s and 1970s. In response, the tax authorities of the main OECD countries have been trying for two decades to coordinate their approach to transfer price adjustments. They adopted a generally slow and careful bureaucratic approach, but it has been given a good deal more urgency by the growing fiscal crisis of the national state, which I have already mentioned. The revolt of the middle-class taxpayer has led politicians to denounce tax dodgers, and has obliged the Revenue authorities to step up national enforcement. In the USA, for example, a 1990 Congressional study attacked 'unfair competition' from subsidiaries in the USA of Japanese and European firms, claiming that 36 Pacific Rim and European-based multinationals with more than $35 billion in retail sales in the USA in 1986 paid little or no US income tax.[8]

The stepping up of US Internal Revenue Service (IRS) enforcement against TNCs has inevitably led to increased efforts in other countries. Notably Japan's National Tax Administration activated its transfer-price enforcement from 1993, resulting in tax assessments on foreign companies such as Coca-Cola of $145m, Hoechst of $24.9m and Procter & Gamble of $9.5m. Specialist commentators pointed out that the Coca-Cola adjustment was almost exactly the same as the amount the Japanese had been forced to give up following a controversial adjustment made by the IRS on Nissan (Baik and Patton, 1995: 218). Here in Britain also, the Inland Revenue in November 1995 called a press conference to draw attention to figures in its annual report for 1994/5, which showed that its increased compliance effort had netted over £6 billion, the equivalent of 3.5p on the basic rate of income tax. Two-thirds of this apparently came from adjustments on companies, apparently including a transfer price adjustment on one single company, which was not identified, to recover £1,638m (Kelly, 1995).

In fact, although the national tax authorities had long known that transfer-price adjustments could be an extremely cost-effective area of 'compliance' work, they were equally aware that the weakness of the international criteria could lead to tit-for-tat or beggar-my-neighbour competition between states.[9] Thus, the increased pressure on the national state as expressed in its fiscal crisis has also exposed the weaknesses of the international coordination arrangements.

If there is now an 'international tax regime' for TNCs, it consists of an inadequately coordinated, mainly administrative process of negotiation between managers or professionals representing firms and national tax officials of the major developed countries.[10] None of the participants seems to consider it either desirable or politically feasible to envisage a more comprehensive global approach. Just such an approach had been considered, but largely rejected, in the 1930s: so-called worldwide unitary taxation. This would mean consolidating the accounts of all the affiliates within a transnational corporate group, rather than treating them as separate entities, and then allocating the profit between the various business by formula. However, it would increase the risk of 'double taxation' unless there could be broad international agreement both on the basis for consolidation and on the formula for the apportionment of profits between jurisdictions. Tax specialists have considered it impossible to reach political agreement on these difficult political issues, so unitary taxation has been strongly resisted. On the other hand, there is clearly a need for a stronger basis of legitimacy and even an institutional framework to counteract the arbitrariness of the present process, especially when such large sums are involved. In fact, business has argued since the 1930s that there should be a right of access to international arbitration of double taxation claims (especially transfer price adjustments), but governments have long rejected this as involving a limitation on their sovereignty. The possibility of such a procedure has finally been conceded in some recent tax treaties, and there is now a multilateral treaty between the EU states, although the arrangements are secretive and likely to be rarely invoked.

As with taxation, so with many other areas of business and economic activity, state sovereignty has become unravelled, as both its internal and international aspects have come under pressure. Another example, which I do not have space to discuss here in any detail, is intellectual property, for example copyright in literary or artistic works or patents in technology. As with income taxation, legal protection of rights to innovation developed along broadly similar lines in the main capitalist countries in the second half of the nineteenth century; due to the interdependent nature of national economies, intellectual property laws were loosely coordinated through international treaties.[11] As the process of commodification of both science and culture has become much more complex in recent years, the mediation of control over this process through intellectual property rights has become much more contested; and, as with taxation, this has caused a breakdown both of national systems of legitimation and of the international arrangements through which they have been coordinated. Even if the granting of monopoly rights is *economically* justifiable, is it *morally* justified to give such protection, for example, for the genetically engineered onco-mouse or for a rare DNA pattern identified among particular ethnic groups? A computer software firm may be considered entitled to some economic reward for its efforts in compiling a new program, but should this be treated as a literary or artistic work and therefore entitled to copyright, which gives protection for a very long time – the author's life plus 50 or 70 years? And should copyright also protect the design features such as the menu structure of a program, a claim just rejected by an even 4–4 split among the Justices of the US Supreme Court in the dispute between Lotus and Borland over their rival spreadsheets? These are difficult enough questions for a national regulatory system to resolve, yet the world-market scale of the activities calls for global solutions.

GLOBAL GOVERNANCE AND COSMOPOLITAN LEGALISM

I hope that these examples help to illuminate some of the issues posed by what is now referred to as 'global governance'. The growth of the world market and capital accumulation has created increasingly difficult problems of regulation both at national level and of international coordination. The internal fragmentation of the liberal state has been matched by the growth of an increasingly dense network of international coordination arrangements between states. This is not a matter of a sudden collapse of the national state in the face of pressures from the world market. Rather, they are two aspects of the same process, and share much in common. I would like, in this final section, briefly to discuss two features of this process in particular: first, the transformation of politics and the professionalization of governance and, second, the increasingly ubiquitous role of law and, especially in the global context, the implications of the call for a new cosmopolitan legalism.

The first feature, I think, is attributable to the increasingly wide gap between popular social and political expectations and pressures and the capacity of traditional political structures, especially the liberal democratic state, to deliver consensus. Within the state, an increasing cynicism about and disillusionment with parliamentary politics has been accompanied by a broad politicization of everyday life. Lifestyle issues previously considered private have become politicized, through the growth of gender and sexual politics and, more generally, in the highlighting of issues such as the bearing and raising of children; while, conversely, public political questions have been personalized, so that a person's stance towards a foreign government or global issues such as ecology are reflected in the contents of their shopping basket. However, this is a fragmented and dispersed politics, which only sporadically takes form as collective action, although it is in some ways routinized and professionalized through pressure groups and social action organizations. It is hardly surprising that the traditional parliamentary and electoral systems find it hard to respond adequately to this widespread politicization. The corollary, however, can be a growing sense of powerlessness, as popular concerns seem unable to make much impact on public decision-making.

Internationally, it is easier to identify what is generally termed the *democratic deficit* of regional and global arenas. There again, however, I would say that this is due to the politicization of the international sphere and the spotlight that this has thrown on the weaknesses of international political processes. The same broadening of political consciousness that has transformed national politics has also broken into the international arena, as issues such as world poverty, environmental protection and health and disease have become the focus of popular concern in much more direct ways due to the immediacy of global media and communication. As a result, a wide range of activists and organizations have invaded institutions and fields formerly dominated by state officials and diplomats. Non-governmental organizations may not have much power, but they can have considerable influence and are to some extent being incorporated into global governance arrangements (Willetts, 1990; Lipschutz, 1992).[12]

The overall effect is I think of a dispersal of politics away from the centralizing channels which lead to the state, and into a variety of specific functional arenas. This appears to allow particular issues to be regulated in a depoliticized, technocratic manner, by managers or professionals who are directly accountable to their 'customers'. The role of the state can, it seems, be reduced to a bare minimum, which is to provide legitimate coercion and to manage money (though even these could be delegated, as prisons can be contracted out to security firms, and monetary policy to professional central bankers).

Yet, curiously, as the state appears to be withering away, it is being reinvented. The purists who advocate a minimalist role for the state, paradoxically demand that it be a strong state and be based on strict national affiliation and identification. Others accept that there are limits to the market and, therefore, argue for state intervention to make rules which govern market transactions, or to remove some areas from the market, whether to remedy market 'imperfections', to provide a 'social dimension' or to heal social divisions. While political philosophers and practitioners debate the conceptual foundations (the social market, communitarianism, the stakeholder society), the means of *implementation* lie readily to hand: the rule of law. Or rather, *rules* of law, since the appealing advantages of law lie in its pluralism and flexibility, as I have already argued. These are the features which appear to make law apt to handle the increasing problems of diversity and interaction created by the fragmentation which I have described. The difficulty, however, as I have also pointed out, is that law can provide at best a set of techniques or a procedural framework within and through which social power relations must be played out. Indeed, to put forward a legal form of regulation to govern an issue is very often a power play in itself. Much can therefore be learned about the changing dynamics of social power by a careful analysis of the changing forms of law, and the processes of their creation. But law cannot be relied upon by itself to transform relations of power.

It is perhaps not surprising that the widest gap between the expectations that may be aroused by resort to law and its capacity to satisfy them is at the level of international law. Here, as I have tried to show, the dilemmas about the nature of the state and its sovereignty are most acute. There is no shortage of examples of issues that are nowadays identified as requiring global solutions, generally better known than the illustrations from business regulation that I have discussed here. From Stockholm and Rio to New Delhi and Cairo, however, the outcome is generally a grandiose statement of pious generalities, which leaving it up to the state and interstate negotiations to strike the necessary balance between economic imperatives and political acceptability.[13]

Yet, as I have also tried to show, the state and its sovereignty are also an increasingly inadequate basis for resolving governance issues. Hence more weight is put on law and legal institutions, which I doubt they are strong enough to bear. Let me give you a couple more current examples, to conclude. One is Bosnia–Hercegovina, an old state recently reborn and now refounded under a new Constitution, agreed in Dayton, Ohio, signed in Paris, the text of which was made available almost immediately on the World Wide Web. Drawn up by experts in the US State Department, it allows for two 'national entities' each with its own constitution and an unprecedented degree of autonomy, although within a formally unitary state. The armed force necessary to bring the situation on the ground into rough approximation with this blueprint, is under US leadership, NATO coordination and authorized by a Security Council resolution, but has a strict 12-month timetable. What is being relied upon to make this highly innovative structure work? The most advanced machinery of human rights law ever conceived, with a Human Rights Ombudsman, and an international Human Rights Tribunal including judges appointed by Council of Europe states, to be resident in Sarajevo; together with an International War Crimes Tribunal sitting at The Hague. We can only wish it every success.

If that is an example of an international effort to reconstitute a national sovereign state, the contrasting example must be the European Union. Here, law has substituted for the failure or inability to decide whether or how to transcend the national state. The key integrating force of the EEC, now the EU, has been the European Court of Justice (ECJ), which has transformed the Treaty of Rome and its related conventions into a 'constitution for Europe'.[14] Yet this has been 'constitutionalism without a constitution'. The ECJ has been driven forward not only by the fervour of its judges, with the support of the broader network of European lawyers including, very importantly, national court judges, but also by the logic of the economic law it is required to apply. Yet it is now clear that both the fervour and this logic have reached their limits. Clearly, Europe now needs an institutional transformation, and not merely a legal underpinning, to coordinate and sustain the regulatory framework of the Single Market. Of course this does not mean a centralized state, and a range of possibilities can easily be devised by lawyers, whether of a federal or confederal character. Although this should be central to the agenda of the Inter-Governmental Conference which started in March 1996, there seems to be little political basis even to discuss the issues involved.

So of one thing we can be sure: that there will be increased opportunities for creative work for European lawyers – as well as Pan-Asian, Inter-American, international and even cosmopolitan lawyers. This work is inflected by the perspectives and concerns dominant within the private and public institutions and networks of international big business which bestride the globe. However, these perspectives are far from being as homogeneous, internally consistent or rational as they might appear. Even within the heart of these citadels struggles are being waged to combine the relentless drive for economic efficiency with a renewed morality taking into account human rights, and the social and ecological effects of business activities.[15] Furthermore, many others have also had to learn to operate in this new world of intersecting jurisdictions, ranging from social movements, labour and consumer organizations, to migrant workers and street traders.[16] Hence, we should remember that these opportunities are created by the increasing social conflicts and complexities that have put pressure on both national and international state structures and that at best the law and lawyers can mediate – perhaps moderate? – those tensions. Adequate solutions require a more combined effort and, in particular, new mechanisms of political accountability.

NOTES

This is a slightly revised version of my inaugural lecture at Lancaster University, delivered on 31 January 1996. Although I have omitted the anecdotal reminiscences, some of the personal flavour still remains, not as self-indulgence, but to retain the element of reflexiveness which I think has an importance beyond the particular nature of the occasion for which this piece was written. That also accounts for the breadth of issues covered in an all-too short compass. I am particularly grateful to Catherine Hoskyns for her help in preparing this lecture. I am also grateful to Alan Norrie, Peter Fitzpatrick, and two anonymous reviewers for helpful comments.

1. It is frequently pointed out that although trade and international investment

have grown faster than GDP in the 1970s and 1980s, the degree of openness and integration in the world economy has merely returned, in quantitative terms, to the pre-1913 period: see e.g. Krugman, 1994: 258ff; Hirst and Thompson, 1996: 26ff. A similar argument has been made in relation to other measures of global interaction by Thompson and Krasner, 1989. Although there are quantitative counterarguments, the globalization debate is more cogent when it focuses on the qualitative changes in the nature of social and cultural interactions (e.g. Featherstone, 1990).

2. An excellent account, combining theoretical analysis with historical exegesis, has recently been provided by Justin Rosenberg (1994).

3. Thus 'pluralist' perspectives, which stress the multiplicity of interacting legal orders, usually accept that state law claims a dominant position (e.g. Fitzpatrick, 1984), although that position may be seen as contested. It has also been argued that the increasing 'porosity' of legal orders has created a new 'interlegality' amounting to a transition towards postmodern law: Santos, 1987. For a wide-ranging discussion of the effects of globalization on the legal field see Santos, 1995, esp. ch. 4.

4. Thus, Wolfram Hanrieder has argued that 'it is not a new type of international politics which is "dissolving" the traditional nation-state but a new nation-state which is "dissolving" traditional international politics' (1978: 147); but it would be better to say that there is a process of interaction.

5. For a discussion of the particular role of lawyers in constructing an international regulatory arena, see Dezalay, 1996.

6. Although an income tax was introduced in Britain during the Napoleonic Wars, and was reintroduced after the repeal of the Corn laws, it never produced more than 15 percent of government revenues during the nineteenth century. Increased spending during the Boer War led to pressures for a graduated rather than a flat-rate tax, and a super-tax was introduced by Lloyd George's 'people's budget' of 1909, which took effect only after a constitutional conflict with the House of Lords. In the USA, it was only after ratification of the Sixteenth Amendment to the Constitution in 1913 that federal taxation could shift from import duties to a graduated individual income tax, and the 1909 'excise' tax on corporations was redesignated a tax on corporate profits in 1917. In France, despite several attempts after 1871, a general personal income tax was introduced only in 1914, followed in 1917 by schedular taxes on other types of revenue.

7. The British claim to tax *both* the worldwide income of UK residents *and* income earned in the UK even by foreign residents was justified on the basis of territoriality: 'either that from which the taxable income is derived must be situated in the UK, or the person whose income is to be taxed must be resident there' (Lord Herschell, in *Colquhoun v. Brooks* (1899) 14 App Cas 493, at 499). Yet it clearly produces overlapping claims to tax which may be regarded as 'extraterritorial'.

8. This has also involved a shift in US concerns: whereas in the 1970s its enforcement effort focused mainly on combating avoidance by US TNCs of tax on their overseas earnings, with the growth of inward investment attention shifted to avoidance of US taxes by foreign TNCs.

9. A German official stated in 1986 that he had feared for two decades that there would be 'a general open clash between tax authorities in the field of arm's length pricing' (Menck, 1986).

10. Developing countries are largely excluded from international cooperation arrangements. In any case, they themselves are reluctant to create disincentives for inward investment through high taxes on profits. Although corporate taxes

are often a high proportion of state revenues in such countries; this is in many cases due to taxation of natural resource extraction, which is more properly a 'rent' than a tax on income from capital, although it has usually been formulated as an income tax to enable TNCs to credit the foreign taxes paid against their home country liability.

11. In the case of intellectual property, an international campaign to protect the rights of authors and inventors led to the establishment of the Paris and Berne multilateral Unions of 1883 and 1886; however, these provided very loose coordination, as they made little attempt to harmonize the substance of the legal protection to be provided, and only partial coverage (e.g. the USA did not ratify the Berne Convention until 1988); see further Picciotto, 1997.

12. Perhaps the most effective and long-running single-issue activist group has been IBFAN, the International Baby-Food Action Network (for its origins and role see Chetley, 1986), while Greenpeace has been notable for its spectacular, high-risk actions. Coordinated activities by various groups during high-profile international meetings such as the annual IMF/IBRD sessions have helped to put marginalized issues onto the global agenda, and have led those organizations to set up more formal consultative channels to incorporate perspectives projected by activist groups, notably on women and the environment. Nevertheless, such social movements require effective organization to compensate for their lack of economic power. Labour or trade-union organizations, which have a stronger power base, have been hampered by their bureaucratic structures and have been reluctant to join forces with other social movements, which they tend to regard as 'unrepresentative', although this may now be changing (see Munck, 1988). On the other hand, representatives of business organizations tend to get a more respectful hearing, and even formal standing, in global forums, in view of the economic power they wield. Thus, TNCs have been given standing under the complaints procedure of ch.11b of the NAFTA (North Atlantic Free Trade Area), and DeAnn Julius (1994) argued that this should be extended to the important dispute-settlement procedure of the World Trade Organization (WTO), although she sees no need for similar access to be given to NGOs which might have relevant interests to represent, such as those of consumers, or the environment.

13. For example, the principle of 'sustainable development' in the Rio Declaration leaves the balance between economic development and environmental protection to be struck by national states, or by international negotiations.

14. Originally coined by an academic (Stein, 1981), the phrase was taken up by a judge of the Court (Mancini, 1989). Many now argue that the 'neo-functionalist project' (Burley and Mattli, 1993) of integration through law has reached the limits of its legitimacy.

15. I use the term *renewed* advisedly, as a reminder that the emergence of industrial capitalism in the nineteenth century also involved such struggles and that the Anita Roddicks of today have their antecedents, from Robert Owen to Josiah Wedgewood and a whole range of other paternalist and philanthropic capitalists.

16. Thus, Rosemary Coombe points to the 'proliferation of new legalities at the intersection of legal cultures and legal consciousness' (1995: 797), and analyses the example of Songhay traders from West Africa selling counterfeit Malcolm X memorabilia in Manhattan, as an example of the 'multiple frames of cultural reference from which an "interjuridical" consciousness may be forged' (1995: 806).

REFERENCES

Baik, Sunghak Andrew and Andrew Patton (1995) 'Japan Steps up Transfer Price Adjustment: Joins the APA Fray', *Tax Notes International* 13 November: 218.

Burley, Anne-Marie Slaughter and Walter Mattli (1993) 'Europe before the Court: A Political Theory of European Integration', *International Organization* 47(1): 41–76.

Chetley, A. (1986) *The Politics of Baby Foods. Successful Challenges to an International Marketing Strategy.* London: Pinter.

Commission on Global Governance (1995) *Our Global Neighbourhood.* Oxford: Oxford University Press.

Coombe, R. J. (1995) 'The Cultural Life of Things', *American University Journal of International Law and Policy* 10(2): 791–835.

Crawford, James (1994) 'Democracy and International Law', *British Yearbook of International Law* 45: 113–33.

Dezalay, Yves (1996) 'Between the State, Law, and the Market: The Social and Professional Stakes in the Construction and Definition of a Regulatory Arena', ch.2 in W. Bratton, J. McCahery, S. Picciotto and C. Scott (eds) *International Regulatory Competition and Coordination. Perspectives on Economic Regulation in Europe and the United States.* Oxford: Clarendon.

Faundez, Julio (ed.) (1996) *Good Government and Law: Legal and Institutional Reform in Developing Countries.* London: Macmillan.

Featherstone, Mike (ed.) (1990) *Global Culture. Nationalism, Globalization and Modernity.* London: Sage.

Fishman, J. J. (1993) *The Transformation of Threadneedle St. The Deregulation and Reregulation of Britian's Financial Services.* Durham, NC: Carolina Academic Press.

Fitzpatrick, Peter (1984) 'Law and Societies', *Osgoode Hall Law Journal* 22: 115–38.

Franck, T. (1992) 'The Emerging Right to Democratic Governance', *American Journal of International Law* 86: 46.

Goldstein, M., D. Folkerts-Landau, Mohamed El-Erian, Steven Fries and Liliana Rojas-Suarez (1992) *International Capital Markets. Developments, Prospects, and Policy Issues.* Washington, DC: International Monetary Fund.

Hanrieder, W. F. (1978) 'Dissolving International Politics: Reflections on the Nation-State', *The American Political Science Review* 72(4): 1276–87.

Held, D. (1995) *Democracy and the Global Order. From the Modern State to Cosmopolitan Governance.* Cambridge: Polity.

Hirst, Paul and Grahame Thompson (1996) *Globalization in Question. The International Economy and the Possibilities of Governance.* Cambridge: Polity.

Julius, DeAnn (1994) 'International Direct Investment: Strengthening the Policy Regime', pp. 269–86 in Peter B. Kenen (ed.) *Managing the World Economy. Fifty Years after Bretton Woods.* Washington, DC: Institute for International Economics.

Kapstein, E. B. (1994) *Governing the Global Economy. International Finance and the State.* Cambridge, MA: Harvard University Press.

Kelly, Jim (1995) 'Transfer Pricing Comes out of the Shadows', *Financial Times* 23 November.

Knightley, Phillip (1993) *The Rise and Fall of the House of Vestey.* London: Warner.

Koskenniemi, M. (1991) 'The Future of Statehood', *Harvard International Law Journal* 32: 397–410.

Krugman, Paul (1994) *Peddling Prosperity. Economic Sense and Nonsense in the Age of Diminished Expectations.* New York: Norton.

Lipschutz, R. D. (1992) 'Reconstructing World Politics: The Emergence of Global Civil Society', *Millenium* 21(3): 389–420.

Mancini, G. Federico (1989) 'The Making of a Constitution for Europe', *Common Market Law Review* 26: 595–614.

Menck, T. (1986) 'International Taxation: Competent Authorities Share Their Concerns', *Tax Notes* 11 August: 573.

Munck, R. (1988) *The New International Labour Studies. An Introduction.* London: Zed Press.

Picciotto, Sol (1992) *International Business Taxation.* London: Weidenfeld.

Picciotto, Sol (1995) 'The Construction of International Taxation', pp. 25–50 in Y. Dezalay and D. Sugarman (eds) *Professional Competition and Professional Power.* London: Routledge.

Picciotto, Sol (1996) 'International Law in a Changing World', ch. 13 in G. P. Wilson (ed.) *Frontiers of Legal Scholarship.* Chichester, Wiley.

Picciotto, Sol (1997) 'Networks in International Economic Integration', *Northwestern University Journal of International Business Law* 17(2): 800–43.

Porter, T. (1993) *States, Markets, and Regimes in Global Finance.* Basingstoke: Macmillan.

Rosenberg, Justin (1994) *The Empire of Civil Society. A Critique of the Realist Theory of International Relations.* London: Verso.

Santos, Boaventura de Sousa (1987) 'Law, a Map of Misreading: Towards a Postmodern Conception of Law', *Journal of Law and Society* 14: 279–302.

Santos, Boaventura de Sousa (1995) *Towards a New Common Sense.* New York: Routledge.

Stein, Eric (1981) 'Lawyers, Judges, and the Making of a Transnational Constitution', *American Journal of International Law* 75: 1–27.

Thomson, Janice E. and Stephen D. Krasner (1989) 'Global Transactions and the Consolidation of Sovereignty', in Ernst-Otto Czempiel and James N. Rosenau (eds) *Global Changes and Theoretical Challenges.* Lexington, MA: Lexington Books.

Willetts, Peter (1990) 'Transactions, Networks and Systems', in A. J. R. Groom and P. Taylor (eds) *Frameworks for International Cooperation.* London: Pinter.

Part II
Regulating International Finance and Investment

[5]

Regulating Global Financial Markets

Sol Picciotto* and Jason Haines**

This paper discusses the role of regulation in the emergence of a global system of linked financial markets. It traces the origins of the internationalization of financial markets to the emergence of new competitive pressures, rooted in changes in the social structures of savings and investment, breaking down both national systems of financial control and international arrangements for monetary and financial co-ordination. These changes have been accompanied and facilitated by a process of international re-regulation, through informal specialist networks. Although these have facilitated the international diffusion of regulatory standards and practices, and attempted to co-ordinate them, they are greatly hampered by espousing the perspectives of the various markets and firms which it is their task to supervise. Together with their minimalist view of the aims of public legitimation and oversight of financial markets, they have proved inadequate to prevent the destabilizing effects of the new global finance on the world economy.

* Professor of Law, Department of Law, Lancaster University, Lancaster LA1 4YN, England
** Research Fellow, Institute of Advanced Legal Studies, 17 Russell Square, London WC1B 5DR, England

This paper greatly benefited from a grant from the Leverhulme Trust to fund research by the authors into Regulation of Globalized Futures Markets. Earlier papers exploring these issues were presented to the Second Consortium on Globalization, Law and Social Sciences, University of Glasgow, June 1996; and the Third Consortium on Globalization, Law and Social Sciences, Institute for Law and Society, New York University, United States of America, April 1997. A draft of this paper was delivered at the W. G. Hart Workshop on Transnational (Corporate) Finance and the Challenge to the Law, Institute for Advanced Legal Studies, University of London, July 1998. We are grateful to the organizers and participants at these workshops for the opportunity to debate the issues, and especially to David Campbell, Kevin Dowd, and Dede Boden for many helpful comments and fruitful discussions, and to the journal's referees for specific suggestions. We would also like to thank the many financial market participants and regulators who have spared some of their valuable time to participate in our continuing research.

351

INTRODUCTION

There can be few issues of greater public importance than the regulation of global financial markets. The international liberalization of financial markets which gathered momentum in the 1980s has involved a qualitative jump in financial volatility and risk, as well as in the complexity and cost of the devices which are supposed to manage those risks. Consequently, the 1990s have been marked by a series of highly publicized financial disasters of various kinds. The 1994–5 Mexican peso crisis, due to a rapid inflow and even quicker outflow of short-term capital (mainly from United States mutual funds), was responded to by a $50 billion bail-out. Yet within less than eighteen months came the 1997 Asian crisis, triggered by the withdrawal of short-term loans channelled through an international chain of financial intermediaries, resulting in an International Monetary Fund (IMF)-led package of over $117 billion to Thailand, Indonesia, and Korea.[1] In both these cases, financial disasters due to volatile, short-term, international capital flows have led to a more general economic crisis, requiring multilateral rescue measures to avert global repercussions as contagion threatened other countries: the Asian crisis also engulfed Russia and damaged Brazil. Both the Mexican and Asian crises resulted from inadequately monitored large-scale flows of private, short-term capital.[2] In addition to these major events, the opening up of national capital markets to global competition has also resulted in financial sector crises in many countries: research for the IMF has estimated the costs of such crises at between 3 per cent and 25 per cent of GDP.[3]

---

1 Bank for International Settlements (BIS), Basle, *68th Annual Report* (1998).
2 Attention has mainly been focused on the inadequacy of monitoring by the capital-importing countries of the scale and uses made of foreign borrowing, and the inadequacy of their prudential supervision arrangements. However, already in mid-1996 the BIS noted the rapid growth of lending to 'emerging markets', especially in Asia and by European banks, with a predominance of short-term loans and a shift to lending to the non-bank private sector, partly to circumvent host country restrictions on bank borrowing. This should have alerted home country supervisors, although their fears may have been lulled by the apparently low exposures to particular country risk (C.M. Miles, 'The Asian Crisis: Experiences and Lessons for a Home and Host Supervisor', paper for conference on *The Asian Financial Crisis and its Regulatory Implications*, LSE/ESRC Financial Markets Group, London, May 1998). However, it seems that the inter-bank market was used to channel loans to other destinations: in particular, banks in Korea (which became classified as Zone A for the purposes of the Basle capital adequacy requirements once admitted to the OECD in 1996) apparently on-lent to other countries, such as Russia.
3 The United States Savings and Loan disasters of 1984–91 cost 3 per cent of GDP, and the continuing Japanese bad loans crisis will have very high absolute costs, but the impact on smaller economies is even higher: recent cases include Venezuela 18 per cent; Bulgaria, 14 per cent; Mexico, 12–15 per cent; Hungary, 10 per cent; several cases (Argentina, Chile, Côte d'Ivoire) have cost over 25 per cent of GDP: see M. Goldstein and P. Turner, *Banking Crises in Emerging Economies: Origins and Policy Options*, BIS Economic Papers no. 46 (1996), citing research by Caprio and Klingebiel.

352

The inadequacy of efforts at public supervision leads some to argue that not only reform but a radical new approach is needed.[4] Others argue that public intervention is merely counter-productive, and 'the markets' should be left alone, self-regulation by the participants being the only desideratum. Yet many of the financial techniques devised over the past twenty years and justified as mechanisms for the management of financial risk, especially derivatives, have themselves led to enormous losses. Although in some of the highly-publicized cases, such as Barings and Sumitomo, the direct blame has been attached to an inexperienced 'rogue trader', the underlying factor has been the managerial problems of supervising esoteric financial practices, often involving distant and specialized markets. This is greatly exacerbated in the case of exchange-traded derivatives, since their highly-leveraged nature means that mishandled trading quickly runs up large losses.

Indeed, in a speech delivered some four months before the Barings collapse, Sir Andrew Large presciently drew attention to this danger:

> The fact is that over the past five years to ten years, the institutional deregulation initiatives in different countries have combined with huge advances in computing power and communications technology, to create a totally new breed of financial intermediary. You can call these firms international investment banks or global securities businesses or proprietary trading operations. The terminology is not important. What matters is that they have embraced the theory of financial risk management which applies portfolio theory to the range of risks associated with the securities business. I might term this the 'Greek Alphabet' or 'Derivatives' approach to financial markets. The key characteristic of this approach is that it seeks out the common elements of risk wherever they may lie in a portfolio and manages them centrally. These firms no longer respect the traditional boundaries between markets or the old institutional boundaries between banking, securities and insurance. They are in the risk management business pure and simple, and they operate on a large scale and on a truly global basis.[5]

He pointed out that one of this new breed of firms could run into difficulties 'in any market anywhere in the world' due to its trading rather than banking activities.

This was again dramatized by the collapse and rescue in September 1998 of the inaptly-named Long-Term Capital Management (LTCM), an arbitrage hedge fund run by Wall Street's top financial rocket-scientists whose advisers included Nobel laureates who had pioneered the 'science' of financial economics. Unlike Barings and other fiascos, this could not be blamed on a 'rogue trader', but the fund's managers and their backers were nevertheless shielded from the consequences of their mistakes by a rescue facilitated by the New York Federal Reserve Bank, on the grounds that its failure could have had such serious repercussions on other market participants as to threaten the economies of major nations including the United

4 D.I. Campbell, and S. Picciotto, 'The Justification for Financial Futures Exchanges', paper delivered to W. G. Hart Workshop on Transnational (Corporate) Finance and the Challenge to the Law, Institute for Advanced Legal Studies, University of London, July 1998.
5 A. Large, 'Financial Markets and World Economic Growth: Perspectives Towards the 21st Century', speech at the XIX annual conference of IOSCO, Tokyo, 19 October 1994.

States of America.[6] This rescue has two possible, and equally disturbing, implications.[7] One possibility is that the Fed, the world's key financial watchdog, erred in helping to shield the world's most sophisticated financial market participants from the consequences of their activities in the markets they themselves had created. These included not only LTCM itself and its Nobel laureate advisers and financial rocket-scientists, but also the investment banks which knowingly advanced loans enabling LTCM to build up enormous potential losses from a relatively low capital base. LTCM's equity was some $5 billion which was leveraged through loans to over $125 billion of balance-sheet assets; but these funds were being used, as the banks well knew, to take positions in derivatives for which only a small 'margin' is required to be advanced, so that the total off-balance sheet exposure was later valued at over $1 trillion.[8] The alternative explanation is that a potentially deadly threat was created for the world's economy by activities the justification for which is that they help manage risk and smooth out turbulence. What is more, in justifying the action, Federal Reserve Chairman Alan Greenspan stated that such defaults are inevitable in 'dynamic markets', although the systemic threat posed by the collapse of LTCM was apparently exceptional.[9]

The competitive pressures resulting from the shift to new forms of financial trading have also been identified as a major factor behind the rash expansion and stampeding contraction of credit which caused the Mexican and Asian crises. The liberalization of controls over cross-border flows, and the ending of many restrictions which had segmented national capital markets, created competition among a wider range of financial institutions, and inter-connections between multiple financial markets. Even experienced financial regulators have found it hard to keep pace with the complexity and international ramifications of the activities they attempt to supervise, as shown by the difficulties of the Bank of England in relation to BCCI and Barings. Although the techniques and procedures for the supervision of financial markets have undergone major changes in the past twenty years, and much of the impetus for these changes has come from international arenas and in reaction to dramatic crises, the arrangements for international regulatory co-ordination and co-operation still seem to lag well behind the dynamic of the transformations of finance.

6 A. Greenspan, statement before the Committee on Banking and Financial Services, US House of Representatives, 1 October 1998.

7 H.T.C. Hu, Testimony to the Committee on Banking and Financial Services, US House of Representatives, 1 October 1998.

8 J. Treanor and M. Tran, 'Markets in Turmoil: Rescued Hedge Fund was "Leveraged 250 Times"' *Guardian*, 10 October 1998.

9 Greenspan, op. cit., n. 6.

THE COMPETITIVE TRANSFORMATION OF INTERNATIONAL FINANCE

What has been learned about the nature of these transformations, and what are their regulatory implications? First, it has become clear that far from dealing with a single global financial market, globalized finance consists of local markets, rooted in different socio-economic structures, patterns of savings and investment, and regulatory traditions. These have become linked internationally by a relatively small number of global firms which have the organizational and technical capacity to trade on a global basis. At the same time a far larger number of financial intermediaries of various kinds now participate in cross-border financial trading. Some aspire to become full-service global financial firms (not always successfully, as seen in the experience of the British commercial and merchant banks), but the vast majority are relatively small vessels whose once-tranquil domestic financial waters have now become vulnerable to the immense tides and potential storms of international financial flows.

Such cross-border flows followed from the relaxation of a wide variety of national controls on foreign currency transactions and regulations affecting investment. This has taken place in three main stages. The first was the introduction of convertibility for current account payments, which was the aim of the IMF under the Bretton Woods agreement, and was implemented from 1958. Current account convertibility ultimately led to the demise of the fixed exchange rate system in 1971–3, since it proved impossible for national central banks to defend currency parities, as was shown in the sterling crisis of 1967, against enormous hot money flows through the largely unregulated eurodollar market created by transnational corporations (TNCs) and their banks.[10] The ability of such internationally-organized firms to manage their internal payments effectively undermined the distinction on which the Bretton Woods system was based, between current and capital accounts.[11] Thus, currency floating led to the second stage, the ending of general exchange controls, with the United Kingdom leading the way in 1979. Nevertheless, many restrictions and obstacles have remained, both to the ability of residents to borrow from foreign capital markets, and conversely the right of foreign borrowers to tap domestic markets or of domestic savings to be invested abroad. In the third stage, which has been taking place since the mid-1980s, there has been a gradual removal of such restrictions. This is by no means complete, since it entails often substantial revision of regulatory requirements which act as effective obstacles, perhaps most importantly the stringent regulatory regime operated by the Securities and Exchange Commission (SEC) and other United States authorities gov-

---

10 Bank of England, 'Multinational Enterprises', text of an address by the Governor given at the Colloquium organized by the Société Universitaire Européenne de Recherches Financières, (1973) 13 *Bank of England Q. Bull.* 184–92.
11 J. Williamson, *The Failure of World Monetary Reform, 1971–74* (1977).

355

erning access to United States capital markets. Thus, regulatory co-ordination, or even harmonization, is an important element in facilitating cross-border financial movements.

Secondly, a key element of this transformation, indeed its driving force, has been the shift from relational to market-based financial intermediation, sometimes described as the 'financial services revolution'.[12] The roots of this process also lie in the economic boom of the 1950s and 1960s in the developed capitalist countries, based on sharply rising labour productivity and growing world markets, which generated vast sums of financial-capital in new forms of private and corporate savings. The struggles to control and direct these new forms of social savings and investment have shaped the changes in financial structures over the past quarter-century. The three major factors behind the changes in the patterns of financial intermediation have been:

(i)   the financial strength of giant firms especially TNCs, enabling them to fund their activities internally, or by accessing global financial markets directly, rather than borrowing from banks;

(ii) the growth of private savings and the increasingly important role of institutional investors in channelling them; and

(iii) the growing role of social expenditures (for example, for healthcare, education, social security), coupled with the increasing political difficulty of funding them through the state from taxation. This has further augmented the role of private savings by the affluent middle classes, as well as turning the state (in its many institutional forms) into a supplicant in the financial markets, a borrower to be assessed by the lending institutions and specialised agencies which evaluate creditworthiness.

In the capital markets, the financial strength of large industrial firms and of the new investment institutions gave them great power *vis-à-vis* the various types of intermediaries (banks and brokers) who acted as the gatekeepers to these markets, and the ability to by-pass them or play one off against the other.[13] This challenged the restrictions which gave protected positions in the financial markets to these traditional financial intermediaries: the commercial and investment banks, and the stock exchange brokers and market-makers. Competitive pressures created challenges to existing

---

12 M. Moran, *The Politics of the Financial Services Revolution. The USA, the UK, Japan* (1991).

13 For example, in 1982 the SEC introduced Rule 415, allowing corporations to register in advance all the securities they planned to issue over a 2-year period, ending the need for individual filings for each underwriting, and thus relaxing their ties to individual underwriters. This facilitated off-the-shelf issues, which allowed borrowers to make the banks bid against each other for the business: P. Ferris, *Gentlemen of Fortune. The World's Merchant and Investment Bankers* (1984) 83.

market structures, which were embedded in various legal, administrative, and institutional forms, and generated pressures to change these forms. Thus, it was the interaction of internal shifts in patterns of savings and investment, with international pressures due to exploitation of the increased opportunities for capital mobility, that undermined the existing institutional structures of finance. These shifts took place first and most strongly in the United States of America and the United Kingdom, spreading more slowly to other developed countries.

The main dynamic in this process has been the interaction between changes in the United States, the epicentre of money and finance, and London, which was reinvented as the key global financial market-place.[14] The key element in this interaction was the creation of the system of 'offshore' finance, centering on the development of the Eurodollar market, which exploited the opportunities for avoidance of tax as well as banking and financial regulatory requirements, to provide a low-cost source of finance.[15] This received its main impetus with the setting up in London and other centres such as Nassau of branches of United States commercial banks, escaping from the Federal Reserve's interest rate controls. They were followed by the investment banks, who began to tap this market for dollar bond issues, especially after 1968 when new rules required United States TNCs to raise funds abroad for foreign direct investment.[16] The growth of the euromarkets increased the competitive pressures on domestic financial markets, since investors and issuers could arbitrage between the two, based on the effects on yields of interacting fluctuations in rates of interest and of foreign exchange.[17] At the same time, the offshore financial centres, especially London, also became market-places for new financial products and techniques. Firms acquiring this know-how through a base in such centres would seek to deploy it in their own domestic markets.

The patterns and timing of changes in each country also owed much to the specificities of its institutional structures, and of the social and political

14 Moran, op. cit., n. 12.
15 M.P. Hampton, *The Offshore Interface. Tax Havens in the Global Economy* (1996).
16 The eurobond market began in 1963 when the Interest Equalisation Tax blocked access by non-US issuers to the domestic dollar-bond market, and US investment banks (many of whom already had London offices for selling US equities) started trading dollar bonds and issuing them for non-US borrowers. When US firms began also to tap this market, issues could be prepared in the United States and merely completed offshore (see B. Scott-Quinn, 'US Investment Banks as Multinationals' in *Banks as Multinationals*, ed. G. Jones (1990) 280). The euromarkets offered low-cost funds to borrowers as well as attractive returns to investors mainly because of the tax advantages: eurobonds can be bearer bonds and the interest can be paid free of withholding tax to nonresidents, thus offering opportunities for tax avoidance or evasion. Initially, freedom from withholding tax on interest payments was available only in tax havens, but in 1984 the United States and the United Kingdom introduced the same exemption, subject to some controls, aiming to reduce tax evasion by their own residents, although effectively conniving in avoidance/evasion of other countries' taxes (see S. Picciotto, *International Business Taxation* (1992) 123–5, 168–9).
17 Scott-Quinn, id., p. 281.

357

roles of the key groups and factions involved. These included not only the corporate and institutional managers, state officials, and various kinds of financial specialists, but also the professionals who began to play an increasing role in mediating these institutional changes, especially lawyers and accountants. These professionals operate at the interface between the public sphere of the state and the private sphere of market relations, and derive their authority from the major academic disciplines of economics and law, which underpin the major forms of mediation of the public-private interaction, money and the law. The new competitive environment also stimulated, and was further enhanced by, competition amongst various professional groups and fractions emerging within and between the law and economics: accountants, actuaries, financial analysts, tax specialists, and so on.

The new competitive pressures led to a shift from traditional forms of relationship-based financial intermediation to transaction-based or marketplace finance. This meant that banking became more like trading, and trading became transformed from a relatively sedate to an increasingly frenetic process. For example, commercial banks, finding themselves competing for funds with other deposit-takers, and being by-passed by large borrowers in search of cheaper funds, invented Certificates of Deposit (CDs) and other tradeable money-market instruments. Brokerage firms hit by loss of income due to the ending of fixed commissions on share trading turned their attention to the bond markets, which began to boom as monetary policy allowed interest rates to fluctuate, and they invented new instruments such as mortgage bonds.

Thus, the decade 1975–85 was marked by a spate of innovation, involving the devising of a wide range of new types of financial instrument. Many of the innovative financial formats aimed to take advantage of the low-cost funds available by routing transactions through 'offshore' centres, due ultimately to avoidance of tax and other costs such as bank reserve requirements. New ways were devised for high-rated borrowers to tap into the offshore euromarkets, such as note issuance facilities and convertible eurobonds. Improved liquidity and reduced financing costs could also result from securitization (the transformation of an illiquid asset such as a mortgage into a tradeable security with a secondary market). A major feature has been the emergence of 'derivatives', contracts involving a transfer of an element of the risk in an underlying cash asset (for example, agreeing a present price for the delivery at a future date of a block of foreign currency or government bonds). These aimed to deal with fluctuations in inflation, interest rates, and foreign exchange rates, and their interaction. Interest rate and currency risks were managed by new types of swaps and options, as well as forward rate agreements.[18] The trading of many of these instruments in a more public form has become institutionalized, as a result of initiatives by the old commodity futures exchanges, and some stock

18 Bank for International Settlements (BIS), Basle, *Recent Innovations in International Banking* (1986).

358

exchanges, to facilitate trading in financial futures. Thus, the derivatives markets are broadly divided between OTC (over-the-counter) transactions in tailor-made contracts (although often standardized and subject to industry-agreed rules), and exchange-traded futures and options. The institutional arrangements established by the exchanges offer greater transparency and security and attract speculative finance, which provides liquidity but may also generate destabilizing volatility.

The emergence of this market-based international financial system undermined the post-war institutional framework agreed at Bretton Woods. This attempted to facilitate the liberalization of international trade and long-term investment, while leaving macro-economic management, and the political compromises it entailed, to national state authorities and political processes.[19] However, the very process of liberalization, interacting with new competitive forces generated by the patterns of capital accumulation, fatally weakened state-based monetary management and finance. Under the previous system of national, segmented capital markets and restrictions on short-term capital flows, the fixed exchange rates imposed strict limits on the destabilizing effects of short-run changes in sentiment, isolated disturbances, and curbed the tendency of financial markets to exhibit lemming-like panic behaviour.[20]

The new market-based system now puts a heavy premium on the ability of dispersed market agents to process information efficiently, and take decisions based on dispassionate evaluation of long-run economic fundamentals. The markets in which they operate do not exist in a vacuum, but require an institutional and regulatory underpinning. Indeed, the analysis in the next section will show that the construction of the market-based system has been in many ways encouraged and facilitated by a process of international diffusion of institutional and regulatory models and practices.

However, the disintegration of the arrangements for monetary and macro-economic management based on national states and co-ordinated by the IMF has left institutional disorder. A variety of international bodies perform diverse public functions in a fragmented way, and they are undermined both in the performance of those functions, and in their horizontal and vertical co-ordination, by the inadequate understanding of the nature of the state-market relation and the role of regulation shown by economic theory based on neo-classical assumptions.[21]

THE NEW FORMS OF GLOBAL REGULATION

The construction of the new international financial system, as the account in the previous section has shown, has been a process of international interaction

19 J.G. Ruggie, 'International Regimes, Transactions and Change: Embedded Liberalism in the Postwar Economic Order' (1982) 36 *International Organization* 379–415.
20 T. Padoa-Schioppa and F. Saccomanni, 'Managing a Market-Led Global Financial System' in *Managing the World Economy. Fifty Years after Bretton Woods*, ed. P.B. Kenen (1994) 235–68.
21 D.I. Campbell and S. Picciotto, 'Exploring the Interactions between Law and Economics: The Limits of Formalism' (1998) 18 *Legal Studies* 249–78.

between locally-based national financial markets, as their institutional and regulatory structures have responded to and attempted to control the changes in the social structures of savings and investment. The interaction of national and international political and economic processes has fundamentally transformed monetary regulation and financial intermediation. The breaking-down of relatively closed national systems of credit and finance has been accompanied and facilitated by often elaborate new regulatory arrangements, developed through complex international political processes. This has introduced formalized rules and professionalized supervision in place of cosy clubs and informal oversight by central banks and finance ministries.[22] Thus, although there has been national deregulation, in the sense of a dismantling of structural controls and informal oversight, there has also been an international process of re-regulation. This has involved a shift to more formalism and legalisation, based both on state law and state-authorized self-regulation.

Regulatory internationalization has operated through international networks of officials, professionals, and managers, attempting to co-ordinate the performance of specific public functions essential to the management of money and finance. This is part of a more general process of restructuring of state-market relations on a global scale, in which increasingly fragmented public functions are now formally legitimized far less through the political processes of national states.[23] Instead, there has been a growing role for the professional practices of various kinds of specialists: economists, accountants, scientists, and lawyers. The emergence generally of such 'epistemic communities'[24] may be identified as a characteristic feature of the emerging new forms of global governance. However, the term is misleading if it suggests that they are depoliticized, global, homogenous formations. Rather, these professional and ideological fields are themselves the sites of conflict and contestation,[25] involving the renegotiation and redefinition of

22 Moran, op. cit., n. 12; T. Porter, *States, Markets, and Régimes in Global Finance* (1993); E.B. Kapstein, *Governing the Global Economy. International Finance and the State* (1994); M. Goldstein, D. Folkerts-Landau, et al., *International Capital Markets. Developments, Prospects, and Policy Issues* (1992).

23 S. Picciotto, 'Fragmented States and International Rules of Law' (1997) 6 *Social and Legal Studies* 259–79.

24 P.M. Haas, 'Introduction: Epistemic Communities and International Policy Co-ordination' (1992) 46 *International Organization* (special issue on Knowledge, Power and International Policy Co-ordination) 1–36.

25 Thus, although Ethan Kapstein contributed an essay analysing the emergence of the Basle Committee and its capital adequacy standards to the special issue (Haas, id.), he took the view that it was not the product of an 'epistemic community', although it remained possible that central bankers could become such. The capital adequacy standard, he argued, did not originate from a common technical approach, but from judgements by central bankers of what was desirable and possible in the international and domestic politics of the debt crisis of the early 1980s. Thus, they were not acting from pure technical considerations, but making a political calculation in 'attempting to serve several conflicting public and private sector interests in an effort to maintain if not enhance their positional power in their domestic political structures' (E.B. Kapstein, 'Between Power and Purpose: Central Bankers and the Politics of Regulatory Convergence' (1992) 46 *International Organization* 265–87, at 267).

the boundaries between, and indeed the nature and forms, of the state, the market, and the firm. However, to the extent that their role entails the displacement of the focus of contestation from political concepts of 'national interests' to issues expressed and debated within technicist paradigms, they represent a qualitatively new approach to the management of international affairs, as represented by the frequently-used term 'global governance'.

These networks have in many ways facilitated the international diffusion of regulatory practices, and their co-ordination. The changes that have been introduced in national arrangements for the supervision and regulation of financial markets, institutions, and firms have, to a great extent, resulted from international debates and discussion. There have been emulation and transplantation of regulatory models, as well as movements to establish common approaches and standards, and to ensure co-operation. Nevertheless, this has been in a context of competition between financial centres and national economies to maintain or develop the depth of their capital markets. Thus, the form and degree of regulation has itself become a factor in the competition between markets and the agents active in them.

The new global financial system, based on competing centres and a wide variety of institutions, generates multiple layers of regulation, which are nevertheless loosely co-ordinated through horizontal and vertical networks, to form a regulatory web. Although United States policies and practices have been in the forefront, and the dollar has been the dominant currency, the central paradox has been that the United States authorities by themselves could control only its formal and not its substantive validity as money,[26] since the financial markets were increasingly based in London and other 'offshore' centres.[27] In contrast, during the period of sterling's dominance up to 1914, the bulk of the world's money-capital actually flowed through London. Hence, although the Bank of England was an insular institution (its directors rarely travelled abroad and foreign visitors were received out of courtesy) nevertheless:

> The outside world did matter greatly and indeed it was the world outside Britain that seemed to matter most. The tides that operated on the Bank operated on it through

26 G. Ingham, 'States and Markets in the Production of World Money' in *Money, Power and Space*, eds. S. Corbridge, N. Thrift, and R. Martin (1994) 29–49.

27 The eurodollar market was estimated by the BIS at $7bn in 1963, and had grown to about $91bn by the end of 1972. By that stage, net eurocurrency deposits were estimated at 35 per cent of the US narrow money supply, and 17 per cent of its broad money supply (Padoa-Schioppa and Saccomanni, op. cit., n. 20, p. 239). London was attractive since the Bank of England applied its informal but strict monetary controls only to the clearing banks (which were subject to a 28 per cent liquid asset and an 8 per cent cash ratio), but not to the secondary banks or finance houses, which it regarded as outside its supervisory responsibilities. Foreign-owned banks were treated even more lightly and exempt from all credit and interest rate requirements, except in sterling transactions with residents. The Competition and Credit Control reforms of 1971 introduced a common reserve assets ratio for all banks, but only on sterling liabilities.

various parts of the City, but they did in the main come from outside Britain and were recognised as such.[28]

Thus, by managing sterling through control of the Bank Rate, the Bank was also effectively maintaining the Gold Standard, on which global trade and investment relied.[29] The situation with the dollar after 1960 was radically different: the United States Federal Reserve was neither able to manage it as a global currency, nor was it equipped to do so.[30]

In this new context, national officials attempting to perform their 'public' roles of monetary management and financial supervision were pulled into closer interaction with each other by the shifting forces operating through the financial markets. At the same time, these forces altered the balance of power between the different bodies, groups, and sectors structured around and legitimised by national state institutions. Thus, central banks, and later bank supervisors and financial market regulators, acquired a new importance. Within the Keynesian system of macro-economic controls, the central bankers had played the important but secondary role of managing the public debt, while the national finance ministries used macroeconomic tools to control the domestic economy. The new focus on monetary management placed the central bankers closer to centre stage. While they may have appreciated the new weight given to their concerns, they did not relish either the new responsibilities this entailed, or their exposure to the public spotlight. Their assumption and development of new functions have therefore tended to be reactive, and it has generally been only following scandal, controversy, and the politicization of issues, that even a minimal level of formalization and institutionalization has emerged.

An immediate and continuing concern has been the prudential regulation of banking. However, while this task rapidly became one of central importance, it has also been extremely difficult to define, as banking was transformed by the shift to market-based finance and the internationalization of financial markets. These combined factors affected London earliest and most acutely, so it is not surprising that the Bank of England has played a key role in the development of supervisory arrangements for international banking, and financial markets more generally. The 1970s saw a dual process of reform of the United Kingdom framework, and its international co-ordination, especially through the Basle Committee on Banking Supervision (BCBS) set up on the initiative of the Bank of England in 1974. The emergence of new financial intermediaries and the growth of the euromarkets in the 1960s undermined the City's banking oligarchies, leading to liberalization and then (after the secondary banking crisis of 1974) to a more formalized regulatory

---

28 R.S. Sayers, *The Bank of England 1891–1944* (1976) 9.

29 It can also be said that these internal and international aspects were contradictory, and the tensions they created eventually led to the breakdown of the gold standard, once Britain lost its position as the centre of world trade and finance (Ingham, op. cit., n. 26, pp. 165, 187–8).

30 id.

structure.[31] However, although the 1974 crisis revealed the limitations of the insularity and informalism of the Bank of England's approach to regulation, it continued to see its role as one of protecting the British clearing banks and boosting the City, and to prefer to operate through informal networks. Thus, it was a hesitant participant in the shift to formalized regulation, as reflected in its ambivalent roles in the development of the British banking and financial services legislation,[32] as well as its influence in shaping the nature and work of the Basle Committee.[33]

Although the BCBS has been hailed as a central institution in the new framework of global economic governance,[34] it has seen its role as a minimalist one, and has developed only reactively, every initiative being a response to the latest crisis. While it has been clear since the 1960s that the major cause of financial instability has been the existence of a vast pool of finance exploiting the 'offshore' system, and thus beyond the reach of national regulators, the BCBS has shown no inclination to tackle the problem at its root, concentrating instead on trying to curb its effects. It began by attempting to reinforce national systems of supervision, establishing jurisdictional principles based on parental home country responsibility in

31 The informal and extra-legal methods of 'moral suasion' used by the Bank of England to control credit depended essentially on cartels and old-boy networks (more recently described in relation to the Asian crisis as 'crony capitalism'), which broke down under the pressure of competition from new intermediaries and foreign banks. With the shift to a cost-based allocation of credit in the Competition and Credit Control reforms of 1971 the inadequacies of the supervisory arrangements were quickly revealed by the secondary bank crisis of 1974, caused by the fuelling of a property boom by an over-expansion of credit, based on exploitation of innovative wholesale financing devices and the creative avoidance of reserve assets requirements (M. Moran, *The Politics of Banking. The Strange Case of Competition and Credit Control* (1984) 70–1). This episode has some significant similarities to the financial crises in emergent market economies in 1997, not least in the way financial liberalization exposed the inadequacies of the British regulatory arrangements of the time.

32 The Bank responded quickly to the 1974 crisis, by replacing the Discount Office with a new Banking Supervision Division, but the capital and liquidity requirements which it was to apply were agreed with the clearing banks, who were to be subject only to annual 'discussions' (Bank of England, 'The Capital and Liquidity Adequacy of Banks' (1975) 15 *Bank of England Q. Bull.* 240). The Bank reluctantly accepted the need to put its powers on a more comprehensive legal basis in the 1979 Banking Act, at the price of having the Deposit Protection Scheme included in the statute, against the stiff opposition of the clearing banks (Moran, id., pp. 118–24). However, by the early 1980s it was showing greater independence and professionalism, and played a key role in forcing the Stock Exchange to accept the changes leading to the Financial Services Act (Moran, op. cit., n. 12, pp. 73 ff.).

33 This new phase of central bank multilateralism built on the links forged in the late 1920s, when Montagu Norman took the lead in developing co-operation among the leading central bankers, culminating in the setting up of the Bank for International Settlements (BIS) in Basle: Sayers, op. cit., n. 28, ch. 15.

34 Kapstein, op. cit., n. 22.

the Concordat of 1975.[35] Although this was reinforced by the addition of the requirement of consolidated reporting in 1978, a parallel attempt by the United States authorities for multilaterally agreed reserve requirements for offshore banking failed to overcome British objections, and paradoxically led to deregulation in the United States.[36] The failure of the Ambrosiano Bank due to imprudent euromarket operations, and the developing country debt crisis triggered by Mexico's announcement of default, both taking place in 1982, forced the BCBS to consider more directly the substantive standards of capital and liquidity adequacy to be applied to internationally-operating banks.[37] However, the Accord of July 1988 was achieved only following political manoeuvres outside the Committee, involving a direct approach by the United States authorities to the Bank of England, later extended to Japan.[38]

35 This basic principle was urged by the Bank of England and agreed at the regular G10 central bankers' meeting at the BIS in July 1974 (Moran, op. cit., n. 31, p. 135), following the Herstatt bank crisis and the rescue of the Franklin National Bank. However, the failure to agree a commitment to provide lender of last resort support for Euromarket operations resulted in difficulties for some banks in accessing these interbank markets, which was only resolved by the issuing of an ambiguously supportive statement at the September meeting (Kapstein, id., p. 43).

36 The US Treasury and Federal Reserve (the Fed) had been concerned at the need to increase domestic US interest rates in response to the dollar crisis in the autumn of 1978, and opened multilateral discussions on reserve requirements on offshore banking. In order to overcome objections from London and pressurise the United Kingdom, the Fed in 1981 finally yielded to pressures from US transnational banks to allow the creation of an International Banking Facility (IBF) in New York City. The Fed and the Treasury still hoped that they could insulate domestic banking from this new zone of 'onshore Eurobanking', and use it as a means of pressuring 'offshore' centres; but instead of facilitating tighter controls on euro-banking, it accelerated the move towards national deregulation (J.P. Hawley, 'Protecting Capital from Itself: US Attempts to Regulate the Eurocurrency System' (1984) 1 *International Organization* 131–65).

37 The problem illustrated by the Ambrosiano bank débâcle of the use of holding companies located in jurisdictions with inadequate supervisory facilities was partly tackled by revisions to the Concordat issued in 1983, especially by introducing the 'dual key' principle. A host country should 'discourage and, if legally possible, prevent' the entry of banks with a parent institution established in a country where supervisory arrangements are non-existent or inadequate, or where it has been granted exemption: BCBS, 'Authorisation Procedures for Banks' Foreign Establishments', March 1983. (A convenient collection of BCBS documents was issued in 1997: Bank for International Settlements (BCBS) Basle, *Compendium of Documents Produced by the Basle Committee on Banking Supervision; III vols.*) However, groups could still evade effective supervision, as was shown by the BCCI collapse in 1991 (D.E. Alford, 'Basle Committee Minimum Standards: International Regulatory Response to the Failure of BCCI' (1992) 26 *George Washington J. of International Law & Economics* 241–91; T. Bingham, *Inquiry into the Supervision of the Bank of Credit and Commerce International*, HC (1992) 92–3 198) which led to a new set of minimum standards in 1992, stressing the need to identify a clear home-country authority capable of supervising groups on a consolidated basis. This still left open the question of groups engaged in both banking and financial market operations, exemplified by the Barings collapse in 1995.

38 Kapstein, op. cit., n. 25.

In taking on the task of defining substantive supervisory requirements, in the form of capital requirements, the BCBS ventured into a complex area, since the formulation and enforcement of such standards pose jurisdictional problems, both between countries and between different types of supervisors. The early approach of relying on home country supervision has been greatly modified although not abandoned, culminating in the issuing of the core principles for effective banking supervision in April 1997, prepared after involvement of and consultation with banking supervisors from a number of countries outside the G10. These now seek to establish minimum procedural standards of supervision, which are also linked to the substantive capital adequacy standards by the requirement that supervisors must set appropriate minimum capital requirements, which for internationally active banks must not be less than those established in the Basle Capital Accord. Nevertheless, although as a matter of procedure the Basle standards require consolidated supervision, the Basle capital requirements do not explicitly state that they must be applied to all branches and subsidiaries in a group on a consolidated basis.[39] This is not a minor technical point but a crucial one, since the application of capital requirements to all financial groups on a consolidated basis is essential in combating the use of 'offshore' facilities for regulatory avoidance.

These 'horizontal' jurisdictional issues (between the authorities in various countries) are exacerbated by the 'vertical' jurisdictional problems between different kinds of supervisors. These have increasingly come to the fore as the shift to market-based finance has broken down structural barriers, and created competition between different types of financial intermediary (retail and investment banks, brokers, insurance companies, and so on) as well as a process of concentration to form large financial conglomerates. This creates 'turf battles' between different regulators at the national level, which interact with parallel conflicts at the international level. This has been most clearly seen in the disputes over capital requirements, which arose when the BCBS sought to extend its capital standards to cover not only credit (or counterparty) risks, but also market risks. This both created problems among bank supervisors, and took the committee into the territory of the securities market regulators. Its adjustments to capital requirements for market risks, aiming to make them suitable both for banks and securities firms, met with

---

39 Although within Europe, the EC's Capital Adequacy Directive (CAD) does require this, it does not specify how such consolidation should be done, and has been interpreted differently by the Bank of England (BoE) and the Securities and Futures Authority (SFA). The latter took the view that, in relation to investment business, the CAD did not require consolidation of non-EU affiliates, which has been described as 'an open invitation for UK investment firms to escape . . . any or all UK rules that are found to be onerous, simply by routing business offshore' (R. Dale, *Risk and Regulation in Global Securities Markets* (1996) 214). The difference in the practices of the BoE and SFA have not been resolved by the amalgamation of their supervisory functions within the new Financial Services Authority (FSA), which has so far merely continued to administer their different rulebooks (BoE, 'Consolidated Supervision', issued 30 October 1998; SFA Rulebook Release 22 & 24, ss. 10–200).

opposition from some bank supervisors.[40] Yet, the extension to the trading book of its 'building block' approach to capital provisioning failed to gain approval from the International Organisation of Securities Commissions (IOSCO), whose members were themselves divided.[41] Following the Barings collapse, a tripartite group of banking, insurance, and securities regulators was established, which has been reporting to the G7 on its progress in co-ordinating standards, including capital requirements and procedures for effective supervision of international financial conglomerates.[42]

At the same time, the new focus on market rather than counter-party risk led to a shift from attempting to define requirements internationally-agreed by supervisors, towards establishing criteria for the approval of the risk-management systems of firms themselves, or the so-called internal models approach.[43] Reliance on such internal models may help to deal with the problems of rigidity of formal requirements, which are unresponsive to innovation and result in discretion and potential variability of application by supervisors. However, the use of such models runs the danger of creating self-reinforcing practices among firms and practitioners, so their validity greatly depends on systems of backtesting.[44] The establishment of detailed parameters for backtesting has taken international regulators into even more difficult and arcane regions.[45]

Undoubtedly, the difficulty of the task of establishing acceptable and workable substantive standards for financial firms and market transactions has been greatly exacerbated by the need for them to be both agreed and implemented by a wide diversity of nationally-based regulatory authorities. The provisions in the mounting stacks of documents and standards agreed by bodies such as the BCBS and IOSCO must be integrated into the layers of national legislation, rule-books, and codes. Arrangements for their enforcement depend on even more complex networks of co-operation arrangements established between state regulators as well as self-regulatory

---

40 R. Dale, 'International Banking Regulation' in *International Financial Market Regulation*, ed. B. Steil (1994) 167–96.

41 Steil, id., pp. 203–4; E. Dimson and P. Marsh, 'Capital Requirements for Securities Firms' (1995) 50 *J. of Finance* 821–51, at 832.

42 BCBS, op. cit., n. 37, vol. III, pp. 59, 64.

43 These are based on value at risk (VAR) models, which became publicized in October 1994 when J.P. Morgan made available, over the internet, its RiskMetrics system and the data needed to apply it. They are argued by financial economists to be more consonant with portfolio theory (Dimson and Marsh, op. cit., n. 41; K. Dowd, *Beyond Value at Risk* (1998)), although these are the subject of some controversy among theorists as well as practitioners: see, for example, the debate between Nassim Taleb and Philippe Jorion in (1997) 2(4) *Derivatives Strategy*, available at http://www.derivatives.com/archives/1997/0497fea2.html We are grateful to Kevin Dowd for helping us with insights into the arcana of VAR, and other aspects of financial economics.

44 The indeterminacy of valuation models appears to account, for example, for the £100m losses from options trading identified at Natwest Markets in March 1997.

45 BCBS, op. cit., n. 37, vol. II, p. 144.

bodies such as exchanges.[46] It is hard to avoid the conclusion that these ramshackle co-operation arrangements are far from adequate to maintain oversight over financial markets which, even if they remain substantially local in their roots, are globally interlinked by the ability of a substantial number of financial agents to engage in many types of transactions in and across all markets.

CONCLUSIONS

In a prescient comment issued in July 1997, as the Asian crisis began to break, Henry Kaufman, a senior Wall Street figure, described the global financial system as 'an incubator of risk', and dismissed the initiatives for improved co-operation arrangements given impetus by the G7 meetings at that time as 'modest step . . . [not] remotely adequate to the task of assuring a safe and sound global financial system'. Kaufman specifically pointed to the rapid growth and complexity of derivatives, which 'has multiplied the potential for a shock to career through the financial system. It has increased the capacity of market participants to take speculative positions in financial markets, to trade those positions at a moment's notice, and to use considerable amounts of leverage in the process'. He argued that a global Board of Overseers is needed, not only to avoid 'market meltdown', but also as 'essential for achieving competitive equality among market participants'.[47] Although this might be considered a utopian proposal, it could at least be used as a template against which to evaluate both the network of co-operation arrangements sketched out above, as well as the rather

---

46 Notably, in response to the Barings crash, a grouping of regulatory authorities from sixteen countries responsible for the supervision of the world's main futures exchanges has held meetings and issued a series of documents, beginning with the Windsor Declaration in May 1995, agreeing to promote various measures of enhanced disclosure, and to improve co-operation and measures for protecting customer assets. This was followed by a London Communiqué on supervision of commodity futures markets of July 1997, and a Tokyo Communiqué of October of the same year, which included two annexed sets of guidelines, covering standards of best practice for the design of commodity contracts, and guidance for the components of market surveillance and information sharing. In March 1996 representatives of 49 futures and options exchanges worldwide signed a multilateral information-sharing memorandum of understanding (MOU) at Boca Raton, Florida; it was also open for signature by other market authorities, and within a few months a further five had signed. Although it establishes quite detailed administrative arrangements for information sharing between the exchanges and clearing houses, like all MOUs its legal status is ambiguous, and it may be read primarily as a statement of intention rather than a legally binding document. Indeed, many of the signatories may not yet have the power under national law to provide information to foreign authorities: in Germany, for example, the exchanges did not have such powers, while the new federal authority established partly for the specific purpose of international co-operation (the BAWe) was initially given specific powers only in respect of insider dealing.
47 Personal View column in *The Financial Times*, 7 July 1997.

367

modest plans to improve the 'architecture' of the global financial system put forward following the Asian crises.[48]

The central problem is the ambivalence about the justification for and aims of public oversight. As we hope to have shown, the new dominance of international finance has not been created by independent and irresistible economic forces, and it does not constitute a unitary global financial market. The underlying dynamic of changes in the social structure of finance (the social patterns of saving and investment), has generated new competitive pressures mediated through institutional and regulatory forms, which have played a major part in shaping the new financial system. Far from being a lawless new frontier, financial markets are riddled with regulation at every level, of varying degrees of formalization: the unwritten norms of traders, the often elaborate rulebooks of exchanges and standardized contracts of associations, the laws which authorize exchanges and trading systems and provide for the enforcement of contracts of speculation, the provisions on the treatment of margin advances and set-off in bankruptcy, as well as the prudential rules for financial institutions discussed above. Markets do not and cannot exist independently of rules – they are created and shaped by rules, and the more impersonal the exchange relations involved the more formalized the rules will be.

Market participants understand this very well, and are generally at the forefront of demands for better regulation. The question of course is, who should regulate, and to what end. Not surprisingly, the view of market participants generally favours a maximum of 'self'-regulation, and a minimum of 'external intervention'. However, this still begs the question of which 'self' should regulate, and what is the role of the external intervenor (at every level). The emergence of complex global networks of financial intermediation has, as we have sketched out, resulted from the competitive interactions of regulators as much as traders, taking place within an increasingly multi-layered institutional kaleidoscope. The absence of any external reference-point makes it difficult, if not impossible, for regulators to establish what 'public interest' they should be defending. Consequently, they see their dual role as (i) to facilitate the market, and (ii) to prevent systemic collapse. This goes a long way towards explaining the essentially reactive character of regulatory changes, which routinely have resulted from the latest crisis or scandal. However, it is clearly an inadequate perspective on which to base the desirable public framework for this very central activity. We should recall that money is not just any commodity, but the repository and channel for social value as a whole. The time is overdue for a strong reassertion of the crucial importance of a positive public role in regulating financial markets, not simply to prevent economic collapse. but to ensure that they operate in the broader public interest.

48 'Strengthening the Architecture of the Global Financial System', report of the G7 finance ministers to G7 heads of government for their meeting in Birmingham, May 1998; declaration of G7 finance ministers and central bank governors, 30 October 1998. Available on IMF website http://www.imf.org (accessed 3 November 1998).

[6]
Capitalism's Last Chance?

by George Soros

T he world is in the grip of an acute financial and political crisis. This crisis, if left unchecked, will lead to the disintegration of the global capitalist system. It is a crisis that will permanently transform the world's attitude toward capitalism and free markets. It has already overturned some of the world's longest established, and seemingly immovable, political regimes. Its effects on the relationships between advanced and developing nations are likely to be permanent and profound.

This situation came about unexpectedly, almost out of a clear blue sky. Even the people who expected an Asian crisis—and my firm, Soros Fund Management, was the first to anticipate the inevitability of the 1997 devaluation of the Thai baht that started the global chain reaction—had no idea of its extent or its destructive power.

What makes this crisis so politically unsettling and so dangerous for the global capitalist system is that the system itself is its main cause. More precisely, the origin of this crisis is to be found in the mechanism that defines the essence of a globalized capitalist system: the free, competitive capital markets that keep private capital moving unceasingly around the globe in a search for the highest profits and, supposedly, the most efficient allocation of the world's investment and savings.

The Asian crisis was originally attributed to various contingent weaknesses in specific countries and markets. Most economists focused initially

GEORGE SOROS *is chairman of Soros Fund Management and author of* The Crisis of Global Capitalism *(New York: PublicAffairs, 1998).*

on policy misjudgments that resulted in overvalued currencies and excessive reliance on foreign-currency borrowing. As the crisis spread, it became clear that such economic misjudgments were symptomatic of deeper sociopolitical problems. Political commentators have put the blame on the nexus of sociopolitical arrangements now described pejoratively as "crony capitalism" but previously extolled as "Confucian capitalism" or "the Asian model." There is some truth to these claims. Most Asian governments did make serious policy misjudgments, in some cases encouraged by international investors and the International Monetary Fund (IMF). They allowed investment and property booms to go unchecked and kept their currencies tied to the dollar for too long. In general, the Asian model was a highly distorted and immature form of the capitalist regime.

However, as the crisis has continued to develop, it has become apparent that its spread cannot be attributed simply to macroeconomic errors or specifically Asian characteristics. Why, after all, is the contagion now striking Eastern Europe, Latin America, and Russia, and even beginning to affect the advanced economies and efficient financial markets of Europe and the United States?

Financial Pendulum or Wrecking Ball?

The inescapable conclusion is that the crisis is a symptom of pathologies inherent in the global system. International financial markets have served as more than just a passive transmission mechanism for the global contagion; they have themselves been the main cause of the economic epidemic.

If it is true that the operation of free financial markets was in and of itself the fundamental cause of the present crisis, then a radical reconsideration of the dominant role that deregulated financial markets play in the world is inevitable. In the absence of urgent reforms, this rethinking could produce a powerful backlash against the global capitalist system, particularly in the developing countries on its periphery.

The essential point is that the global capitalist system is characterized not just by global free trade but more specifically by the free movement of capital. The system can be envisaged as a gigantic circulatory system, sucking capital into the financial markets and institutions at the center and then pumping it out to the periphery, either directly in the form of credits and portfolio investments or indirectly through multinational corporations.

Until the Thai crisis, the center was vigorously sucking in and pumping out money, financial markets were growing in size and importance, and countries on the periphery were obtaining an ample supply of capital from the center by opening up their capital markets. There was a global boom in which the emerging markets fared especially well. At one point in 1994, more than half the total inflow of capital to U.S. mutual funds went into emerging-market funds. The Asian crisis reversed the direction of the flow. Capital started fleeing emerging markets such as Korea and Russia. At first, the reversal benefited the financial markets at the center. But since the Russian meltdown in August 1998, the banking and financial systems at the center have also been adversely affected. As a result, the entire world economy is now under threat.

Today's crisis cannot be attributed simply to macroeconomic errors or specifically Asian characteristics.

With the growing realization that the underlying cause of this threat is the inherent instability of deregulated financial markets, the ideology of world capitalism faces a historic challenge. The financial markets are playing a role very different from the one assigned to them by economic theory and the prevailing doctrine of free market capitalism. According to the ideology of free market fundamentalism, which has swept the world since it was pioneered in the early 1980s by Ronald Reagan and Margaret Thatcher, competitive markets are always right—or at least they produce results that cannot be improved on through the intervention of nonmarket institutions and politicians. The financial markets, in particular, are supposed to bring prosperity and stability—the more so, if they are completely free from government interference in their operations and unrestricted in their global reach.

The current crisis has shown this market fundamentalist ideology to be irredeemably flawed. Free market ideology asserts that fluctuations in stock markets and credit flows are transient aberrations that can have no permanent impact on economic fundamentals. If left to their own devices, financial markets are supposed to act in the long run like a pendulum, always swinging back toward equilibrium. Yet it can be demonstrated that the very notion of equilibrium is false. Financial markets are inherently unstable and always will be. They are given to excesses, and when a boom/bust sequence progresses beyond a certain point, it inevitably transforms the economic fundamentals, which in turn can never revert to where they began. Instead of acting like a pendulum, financial markets can act like a wrecking ball, swinging from country to country and destroying everything that stands in their way.

The current crisis presents policymakers with what may be a final opportunity to recognize that financial markets are inherently unstable before the wrecking ball takes aim at the foundations of the global capitalist system itself. What, then, needs to be done?

SAVING CAPITALISM FROM ITSELF

Many of the widely discussed solutions to today's crisis are designed to improve the efficiency of financial markets and impose more market discipline through such means as deregulation, privatization, transparency, and so on. But imposing market discipline means imposing instability. Financial markets are discounting a future that is contingent on the bias that prevails in markets, and the reflexive interplay between expectations and outcomes yields unstable results. Market discipline is desirable, but it needs to be supplemented by another kind of discipline: Public-policy measures are needed to stabilize the flows of international finance required by the global capitalist system and to keep the inherent instability of financial markets under control.

Within the main capitalist countries, strong frameworks of state intervention already exist to protect against financial instability. The United States has the Federal Reserve Board and other financial authorities whose mandates are to prevent a breakdown in its domestic financial markets and, if necessary, act as lenders of last resort. They have been quite successful. I am confident that they are capable of fulfilling their responsibilities. Indeed, now, in the second phase of the current crisis, as the problems of the periphery have begun to spill over into the center and threaten serious financial instability in U.S. markets, stabilizing mechanisms have been brought powerfully into play. The Federal Reserve has urgently eased monetary policy and made clear that it will continue to print money if that is what financial stability requires. More controversially, the Fed has pressured the private sector into organizing a lifeboat for Long Term Capital Management, a hedge fund that the Fed itself declared to be too big to fail.

The trouble is that international mechanisms for crisis management

Stop us before we kill again.

are grossly inadequate. Most policymakers in Europe and the United States worry today whether their countries can be protected from the global financial contagion. But the issue at the global level is much broader and more historically important. Even if the Western economies and banking systems do survive the present crisis without too much harm, those on the periphery have been significantly damaged.

The choice confronting the world today is whether to regulate global financial markets internationally to ensure that they carry out their function as a global circulatory system or leave it to each individual state to protect its own interests. The latter course will surely lead to the eventual breakdown of global capitalism. Sovereign states act as valves within the system. They may not resist the inflow of capital, but they will surely resist the outflow, once they consider it permanent. Malaysia has shown the way. A rapid spread of foreign-exchange controls will inevitably be accompanied by the drying up of international investment and a return to inward-looking economic strategies on the periphery. Economic withdrawal from world markets is likely to be accompanied by political disengagement and domestic repression. (Again, Malaysia stands out as an example.) In short, the global capitalist system will disintegrate.

What can be done to stop this process of disintegration? It is necessary to look beyond transparency, regulation, and other mechanisms that simply improve the efficiency of free markets. The flow of capital—and most importantly of private capital— from the center to the periphery must be revived and stabilized.

In seeking solutions to today's crisis, two common fallacies must be avoided. The first is the mistake of shutting the stable door after the horse has bolted. Reforms designed to improve the global financial architecture in the long term may be desirable, but they will do nothing to help the afflicted economies of today. In fact, the opposite may be true: Greater transparency and tougher prudential requirements are likely to discourage capital flows in the short term, just as the austere financial policies imposed by the IMF to restore the long-term soundness of stricken economies tend to make matters worse in the short term. The second fallacy is to embrace the delusion of market fundamentalism: that if markets can be made more transparent, more competitive, and generally more "perfect," their problems will be automatically solved. Today's crisis cannot be solved by market forces alone.

Emergency efforts to stabilize the world economy must focus on two goals: arresting the reverse flow of capital from the periphery of the global capitalist system to the center and ensuring the political allegiance of the peripheral countries to that system.

President Bill Clinton and Treasury Secretary Robert Rubin spoke in September 1998 about the need to establish a fund that would enable peripheral countries following sound economic policies to regain access to international capital markets. Although the two men did not say so publicly, I believe that they had in mind financing it with a new issue of Special Drawing Rights (SDRs), an international reserve asset created by the IMF to supplement members' existing assets.

Although their proposal did not receive much support at the annual meeting of the IMF in October 1998, I believe that it is exactly what is needed. Loans could be made available to countries such as Brazil, Korea, and Thailand that would have an immediate calming effect on international financial markets. Furthermore, such a mechanism would send a powerful signal because it would reward countries doing their utmost to play by the rules of the global capitalist system rather than succumbing, like Malaysia, to the temptation to cut themselves off. The IMF programs in countries such as Korea and Thailand have failed to produce the desired results because they do not include any scheme for reviving the flow of private capital to these countries or reducing their foreign debt. A debt reduction scheme could clear the decks and allow their domestic economies to recover, but it would force international creditors to accept and write off losses. The problem is that creditors would be unwilling and unable to make new loans, making it impossible to finance recovery in these countries without finding an alternate source of international credit. That is where an international credit guarantee scheme would come into play. It would significantly reduce the cost of borrowing and enable the countries concerned to finance a higher level of domestic activity. By doing so, such a mechanism would help revive not

Reforms designed to improve the global financial architecture in the long term will do nothing to help today's affected economies.

only the countries concerned but also the world economy. It would reward countries for playing by the rules of the global capitalist system and discourage defections along Malaysian lines.

At present, the Clinton proposal is not being seriously pursued because European central banks are adamantly opposed to the issue of SDRs. Their opposition stems from doctrinaire considerations: Any kind of money creation is supposed to fuel inflation. But in using SDRs as guarantees, there would be no new money created; the guarantees would kick in only in case of default.

After the German elections, left-of-center governments are now in power in most of Europe. These governments are likely to prove more amenable to a loan guarantee scheme than their central banks, especially when the recovery of important export markets hinges on it. Japan too is likely to support such a scheme as long as it covers Asia as well as Latin America.

NEEDED: INTERNATIONAL CREDIT INSURANCE

Although I strongly endorse the Clinton proposal, I would go even further. Earlier in 1998, I proposed establishing an International Credit Insurance Corporation. My proposal, however, was premature, as the reverse flow of capital had not yet become a firmly established trend. Moreover, the Korean liquidity crisis in late 1997 was followed by a temporary market recovery that lasted until April 1998. My proposal fell flat then, but its time has now come.

A credit insurance mechanism managed by the IMF could provide the cornerstone for the "new architecture" that policymakers and pundits are talking about these days. The new institution, which could become a permanent part of the IMF, would explicitly guarantee, up to defined limits, the loans that private lenders make to countries. If a country defaults, the IMF would pay the international creditors and then work out a repayment process with the debtor country. The borrowing countries would be obliged to provide data on all borrowings, public or private, insured or not. This information would enable the authority to set a ceiling on the amounts it would be willing to insure. Up to those amounts, the countries concerned would be able to access international capital markets at prime rates plus a modest fee. Beyond these limits, the creditors would be at risk. Ceilings would be set taking into account the macroeconomic policies pursued by individual countries, as well as other overall economic conditions in each country and throughout the world. The new institution would function, in effect, as a kind of international central bank. It would seek to avoid excesses in either direction, and it would have a powerful tool in hand.

The thorniest problem raised by this proposal is how the credit guarantees allocated to an individual country would be distributed among that country's borrowers. To allow the state to make this decision would be an invitation for abuse. Guarantees ought to be channeled through authorized banks that would compete with each other. The banks would have to be closely supervised and prohibited from engaging in other lines of business that could give rise to unsound credits and conflicts of interest. In short, international banks would have to be as closely regulated as U.S. banks were after the breakdown of the American banking system in 1933. It would take time to reorganize the global banking system and introduce the appropriate regulations, but the mere announcement of such a scheme would calm financial markets and allow time for a more thorough elaboration of the details.

The credit insurance plan would obviously help the peripheral countries and the Western banking system to weather the immediate crisis. By providing some inducements for lenders scarred by recent and impending losses, it would help restart the flow of funds from the financial markets toward the peripheral countries. But credit insurance would also strengthen the entire global financial architecture

The Big Fix

The global financial crisis has spawned countless proposals on what to do with the International Monetary Fund (IMF). Herewith some examples:

Tear it down: "Let the IMF be abolished," says economics giant **Milton Friedman** in a November 1998 interview with *Forbes*. "Distribute the assets to each country and let the markets take care of the fallout." His fellow Hoover Institution scholar and former secretary of state **George Shultz** agrees. Instead of throwing money at the IMF, remarks Schultz, Congress should boost the global economy by cutting U.S. taxes by 10 percent across the board.

Clip its wings: The IMF can play a constructive role in crisis management if it avoids finger wagging and excessive interference in a nation's fiscal and monetary policies, says Harvard economics professor and former chairman of the President's Council of Economic Advisers **Martin Feldstein**. He urges the fund to focus on coordinating the rescheduling of international obligations for creditors and debtors and to create a collateralized credit facility to lend to governments that are illiquid but able to repay foreign debts through future export surpluses. The Columbia Business School's **Charles Calomiris** says that instead of doling out cash, the IMF should simply offer advice and encouragement and closely monitor government attempts at macroeconomic reform.

Make it bigger and better: Fleshing out proposals made by President Bill Clinton and British prime minister Tony Blair, the **Group of Seven (G-7)** announced in October 1998 a plan for the fund to extend short-term credit lines to any government that implements IMF–approved reforms, drawing from the recently approved $90 billion increase in the IMF's lendable resources. The G-7 ministers also called for increased collaboration between private-sector creditors and national authorities and the adoption by IMF member nations of a code of financial transparency enforced by annual IMF audits.

Create a new institution: Forget the IMF and World Bank, says **Jeffrey Garten**, dean of the Yale School of Management. Instead, create a global central bank that could provide liquidity to ailing nations by purchasing bonds from national central banks; encourage spending and investment by acquiring national debts at discounted prices; and set uniform standards for lending and provide markets with detailed, credible information on the world's banks.

—FP

and improve financial stability in the long term. At present, the IMF does not have much influence in the internal affairs of its member countries except in times of crisis when a member country turns to the IMF for assistance. The fund may send its staff to visit and consult with country leaders, but it has neither the mandate nor the tools to shape economic policy in normal times. Its mission is crisis management, not prevention. By giving the new agency a permanent role in the surveillance of participating countries, the credit insurance scheme would help avoid both feast and famine in international capital flows.

Credit insurance would also help counteract the IMF's perverse role in the unsound expansion of international credit. IMF programs have served to bail out lenders, which encourages them to act irresponsibly, thereby creating a major source of instability in the international financial system. This defect of the current architecture is often described as "moral hazard." Moral hazard is caused by the asymmetry in the way that the IMF treats lenders and borrowers. It imposes conditions on borrowers (countries) but not on lenders (financial institutions); the money it lends enables debtor countries to meet their obligations, indirectly assisting the banks to recover their unsound loans. This asymmetry developed during the international crisis of the 1980s and became blatant in the Mexican crisis of 1995. In that case, foreign lenders to Mexico came out whole, even though the interest rates that the Mexican government paid them before the crisis clearly implied a high degree of risk. When Mexico could not pay, the U.S. Treasury and the IMF stepped in and took investors off the hook. The asymmetry and the moral hazard in IMF operations could be corrected by loan guarantees. Instead of bailing out foreign lenders to Mexico in 1995, the IMF would have guaranteed investors up to insured levels and then allowed uninsured debt to be converted into long-term bonds and written off. Had this happened, lenders and investors (myself included) would have been much more cautious about investing in Russia or Ukraine.

THE WILL TO STABILITY?

Some will wonder whether it would be possible for the IMF, let alone any new institution, to carry out the complex tasks I propose. Would it establish the right limits on sound international borrowing and be able to supervise the global circulatory system? A new institution would be bound to make mistakes, but the markets would provide valuable feedback and the mistakes could be corrected. After all, that is how all central banks operate and on the whole they do a pretty good job. It is much more questionable whether such a scheme is politically feasible. There is already a lot of opposition to the IMF from market fundamentalists who are against any kind of market intervention, especially by an international organization. If the banks and financial-market participants that currently benefit from moral hazard and asymmetry cease to support the IMF, it is unlikely to survive even in its present inadequate form.

Constructive reform will require governments, parliaments, and market participants to recognize that they have a stake in the survival of the system—and that this stake is far more valuable than any short-term gains that they may make from exploiting the flaws in the existing deregulated system. The question is whether this change of mentality will occur before or after the global capitalist system has fallen apart.

WANT TO KNOW MORE?

The flaws of the global financial system have been the focus of much analysis and debate. Karl Polanyi, in *The Great Transformation* (New York: Rinehart & Co., 1944), argues that capitalism is an anomaly since it embodies a system wherein social relations are defined by economic relations. In previous economic systems, he observes, economic interactions followed from social relations. Robert Kuttner's *Everything for Sale: The Virtues and Limits of Markets* (New York: Alfred A. Knopf, 1997) makes a case for the market's insufficiency in many fields and argues for intelligent intervention to produce better outcomes. In *Has Globalization Gone too Far?* (Washington: Institute for International Economics, 1997), Dani Rodrik posits that the world's leaders must ensure that international economic integration does not further domestic social disintegration.

For more analysis of the link between social relations and economic arrangements, see George Soros' "The Capitalist Threat" (*Atlantic Monthly*, February 1997), which argues that the free market undermines efforts to achieve open and democratic societies. Other works by Soros include: "Toward Open Societies" (FOREIGN POLICY, Spring 1995) in which he proposes that the creation of open societies should be a primary foreign-policy objective; "After Black

Monday" (FOREIGN POLICY, Spring 1988), which advocates a reform of the international currency system; and *The Alchemy of Finance* (New York: John Wiley & Sons, 1987), which describes the "theory of reflexivity" that guides his investment strategies.

Other excellent recent articles include **"The Crisis of Global Capitalism"** (*The Economist*, September 12–18, 1998) in which Jeffrey Sachs argues that world leaders should focus on a "development agenda" and suggests a Group of Sixteen summit—the Group of Eight countries plus eight developing nations—to tackle international financial reform, specifically, the international assistance process. Ricardo Hausmann's article, **"Will Volatility Kill Market Democracy?"** (FOREIGN POLICY, Fall 1997) describes alternatives to the common solutions for stabilizing the intense boom-and-bust cycles that characterize today's markets.

Speeches by Treasury Secretary Robert Rubin over the last six months track the evolution of the official U.S. position on reforming the global financial system. Especially useful are his **"Statement at the Special Meeting of Finance Ministers and Central Bank Governors"** on April 16, 1998, the transcript of the **"Post–Group of Seven Press Conference"** on April 15, 1998, the **"Statement at the 58th Annual Development Committee of the World Bank and the International Monetary Fund"** of October 5, 1998, and the **"Statement to the IMF Interim Committee"** on October 4, 1998.

For links to the texts of these speeches and relevant Web sites, as well as a comprehensive index of related FOREIGN POLICY articles, access **www.foreignpolicy.com.**

[7]

THE ARTICLES OF AGREEMENT OF THE IMF
AND THE LIBERALIZATION OF CAPITAL MOVEMENTS

Jacques J. Polak

In its meeting on April 28, 1997, the Interim Committee of the International Monetary Fund (IMF) "agreed that the Fund's Articles [of Agreement] should be amended to make the promotion of capital account liberalization a specific purpose of the Fund and to give the Fund appropriate jurisdiction over capital movements." This essay analyzes the merits of these two proposed changes in the Fund's Articles. It concludes that the first—making capital liberalization one of the Fund's purposes—although not necessary from an operational point of view, is useful as a signal of the radical change that has taken place in members' attitudes toward restrictions on capital movements. It finds that the second, however—giving the Fund jurisdiction over capital movements—is neither necessary nor helpful in promoting the orderly liberalization of capital movements.

1 A Positive Attitude Toward the Liberalization of Capital Movements

The benefits of substantial freedom of capital movements are not a new discovery for the IMF. The Fund's first history, covering the period from 1945 to 1965, noted the resurgence of the view, dominant before the 1930s, that freedom of capital movements was highly desirable in itself (De Vries, 1969, p. 292). In the 1960s, convertibility on current and (partly) on capital account was still predominantly limited to the industrial countries. In the subsequent decades, however, that picture changed radically. Today, one-fourth of the developing-country members of the IMF have no restrictions on capital movements (Quirk et al., 1995, p. 34) and many other developing countries are moving in the same direction. To cite one striking example: India, which did not become convertible on current account until 1994, is moving rapidly toward a high degree of capital-account convertibility.

The Fund's policies reflect this changed attitude of its members. In spite of the bias toward capital controls contained in the Articles of Agreement, the IMF does not hesitate to "express views" on capital-account issues in the context of its surveillance, financing, and technical-assistance activities (Quirk et al., 1995, p. 5). The provisions on foreign participation in domestic corporations in the recent standby arrangement with South Korea provide a striking example of the extent to which capital liberalization has entered into the Fund's conditionality. But the Fund has also warned against "draw[ing] general conclusions about the consequences of 'capital controls' without reference to the nature of such measures and the circumstances under which they were employed" (IMF, 1995, p. 13). Chile's controls on capital inflows have been generally praised, and Stanley Fischer has noted that Korea and Thailand could have benefited from similar measures (Uchitelle, *New York Times*, January 8, 1998) A fair representation of the current consensus on the subject would seem to be that (1) most capital controls, especially those on capital outflows, are both ineffective (except in the short run) and harmful to the country imposing them, (2) some controls on inflows of short-term funds can be helpful in preventing excessive domestic demand, and (3) some other controls (in particular on inflows of direct investment and portfolio investment) have both negative effects, such as a smaller supply of capital and of the managerial and technological innovation that often accompany direct investment inflows, and potential benefits of a prudential or political character.

In the 1940s, when the Fund's Articles of Agreement were drafted, a liberal regime for payments, even on current account, was an endangered species. It is fortunate that the agreement committed member countries to move toward such a regime. At present, current-account convertibility has been almost universally achieved (even though some sixty member countries still remain technically under the protective umbrella of the transitional provisions in Article XIV), and many countries, in all areas of the world, have become convinced by economic arguments or by the force of global markets that capital-account convertibility is, from most points of view, an equally desirable achievement. In acting on this conviction, they can count on the Fund to help them "liberalize in a manner that does not undermine economic and financial stability" (Fischer, 1997, p. 11).

All in all, this outcome appears to be highly satisfactory and is likely to improve further over time under the gentle prodding of the IMF. Why then is the IMF moving toward the adoption of an amendment to its Articles that would extend its jurisdiction to capital movements and thus "enable the Fund to promote the orderly liberalization of capital movements" (Fischer, 1997, p. 12)?

2 Signaling a New Attitude on Capital Movements

One reason cited for the amendment is the existence in the Articles of several awkward gaps, and some equally awkward provisions, on the subject of capital movements. The promotion of the worldwide flow of capital is not listed among the purposes of the Fund in Article I. This omission is to some extent remedied in Article IV as previously amended, which lists, in one breath, "the exchange of goods, services and capital among countries" as the essential purpose of the international monetary system (although not specifically of the Fund).[1] The Fund has the legal power under Article VI to insist that a member introduce capital controls, but it has never, in my memory, used this power. Article VI also prohibits use of the Fund's general resources "to meet a large or sustained outflow of capital," and an IMF Occasional Paper on capital convertibility (Quirk et al., 1995) suggests that consideration should be given to the revision of that Article. This issue was addressed in 1961, however, when the same matter arose in connection with the proposal for the General Arrangements to Borrow, which were clearly designed to enable the Fund to deal with large capital outflows from reserve centers. Fancy legal footwork on that occasion produced the solution that a "large" outflow of capital could be interpreted as one that absorbed an excessively large part of the Fund's resources; this defused the issue into a purely operational one.

The Fund's Articles of Agreement are, of course, outdated in many other respects. Article VII, for example, still permits members to discriminate against a country whose currency has been declared "scarce." When the membership has agreed that the Fund should perform a new task, however, the Fund has usually found a way to do so without recourse to amendment. Thus, in the last decade, economic growth has de facto become a prime Fund objective, on a par with balance-of-payments equilibrium, even though, at Bretton Woods, growth was deliberately kept out of the Fund's purview, in order not to confuse the tasks of the IMF and the World Bank (Polak, 1991, pp. 17–19). When the World Bank wanted to engage in subsidized lending to low-income countries, it created a new and formally separate international organization, the International Development Association. The Fund achieved a similar outcome by taking a set of decisions establishing the Enhanced Structural Adjustment Facility to administer a separate pool

---

[1] The same Article also remedies to some extent one or perhaps two other shortcomings of the original Articles by the introduction of "the objective of fostering orderly economic growth with reasonable price stability" as a guideline for members' policies.

of resources contributed by members. More recently, the Fund has moved into governance and the avoidance of "nonproductive" government expenditure, again without expressing the need for an amendment to support these moves. As noted above, moreover, the Fund has whole-heartedly embraced capital liberalization in its surveillance, financing, and technical-assistance activities without being hindered by a lack of mandate or from the dated provisions of Article VI.

It is thus not necessary to add the liberalization of capital movements to the Fund's purposes. Yet it would seem desirable to do so and, at the same time, to eliminate the stale provisions of Article VI as a sign of official recognition of the substantive benefits that members would derive from greater freedom for capital movements. It does not follow, however, that it would also be a good idea for the Fund to assume jurisdiction over restrictions on capital movements. Indeed, as demonstrated by the discussion below, it would not.

3   Fund Jurisdiction over Restrictions on Capital Movements?

The Fund's *Annual Report for 1997* (p. 39) expresses the view that

> The Fund, given its mandate and its universal membership, should play a central role in promoting capital account liberalization and fostering the smooth operation of international capital markets. The Fund should also be prepared to advise its members in determining how the removal of restrictions should be sequenced with supporting structural and macroeconomic reforms. Likewise, the Fund [is] well placed to assess whether temporary imposition of controls [is] appropriate to address surges in capital inflows and outflows.

These observations are followed by the conclusion that most of the Fund's directors support an amendment of Article VIII that would extend the Fund's jurisdiction to capital movements, but no arguments are presented as to why such an amendment would promote the objectives mentioned. There are four good reasons to doubt that it would:

• The extension of the Fund's jurisdiction to capital movements involves much more than the deletion of the word "current" before "transactions" at various places in Article VIII. It does not simply broaden the Fund's jurisdiction from current transactions to all transactions; it introduces, in addition, two new concepts: (1) The existing Articles consider restrictions from the point of view of the balance of payments and accordingly address only *outpayments* of foreign exchange. By contrast, the current drive aims at liberalizing both *inflows* and *outflows* of capital, and thus at removing restrictions that members may maintain for other than balance-of-payments reasons. (2) Although the existing Articles give the Fund jurisdiction over *payments* and *transfers* for current international transactions, leaving any jurisdiction over the transactions themselves to another international institution, the new jurisdiction sought for the Fund would refer to the capital movements themselves. Under the new proposals, therefore, the Fund would find itself legislating both outside its designated field of business (balance of payments) and across areas of jurisdiction of another international organization, the World Trade Organization, which is also approaching, although from a very different angle, the subject of capital movements among its membership (Ostry, 1997).[2] Such a significant expansion of the jurisdictional scope of the organization should be undertaken only if there is a clear benefit in terms of the objectives to be achieved.

• In that connection, a look at the Fund's experience with the removal of restrictions on current payments may be useful. The Fund's first history, for all its caution and reticence, shows that experience to have been far from happy. In the 1950s, the Fund's executive board engaged in a difficult debate on all aspects (including scope, periodicity, and form) of the consultations that the Articles mandated to be held with "any members retaining any restriction inconsistent with Article VIII, Sections 2, 3, or 4." The history mentions "vexing issues" that could not be settled, "jurisdictional disputes," and "fears of the Fund overstepping the mark" (De Vries, 1969, pp. 232–237). By 1965, more than a decade after the consultations had begun, Article VIII had been accepted by only eleven developing countries (not counting Saudi Arabia and Kuwait), all in Northern Latin America and the Caribbean, and three of these (Guatemala, Mexico, and Panama) had accepted convertibility from the start. By that time, moreover, the Fund had come to acknowledge "that there was no simple solution for the continuing restrictions" of developing countries and, although denying any legal basis for leniency based on countries' low income levels, as had been sought by UNCTAD, the Fund was "nonetheless careful, in implementing its policies, to take into consideration . . . problems related to

[2] The Interim Committee showed its awareness of the risk of potential conflict implied in bringing all capital movements under the Fund's jurisdiction and stated that "in both the preparation of an amendment to its Articles and in its implementation, the members' obligations under other international agreements will be respected. In pursuing this work [sic], the Committee expects the IMF and other institutions to cooperate closely" ("Statement," 1997).

economic development" (De Vries, 1969, p. 294). It moved away from trying to convert countries to the "true faith" of convertibility and toward education and technical assistance. For the next twenty-five years or so, the consultations with developing countries soft-pedaled (perhaps more accurately, ignored) the obligation of those countries to remove themselves from the "transitional arrangements" of Article XIV, and only a few countries took that step. The Fund continued to rely on suasion and never used its power under Article XIV, Section 3, to "make representations to any member that conditions are favorable for the withdrawal of any particular restriction, or for the general abandonment of restrictions." Still, countries did substantially liberalize their payment regimes during that time, making it possible for many of them to move to Article VIII in the 1990s, when the Fund initiated a drive to that effect.

This experience with restrictions on current transactions suggests a similar trade-off between two roles the Fund staff can play with respect to restrictions on capital movements. If given jurisdiction over such restrictions, the staff is likely to become the enforcer of the new legal code, making sure at each step that any policy it recommends or endorses can pass the test of the new Article. If not burdened with this legal task, the staff can be the unbiased adviser of member countries on the benefits and costs of capital liberalization and a reliable source of information about best practices in this field. It is a matter of concern that, even before the revised Articles have been drafted, the expected future code of conduct is casting its shadow ahead to color the staff's attitude toward restrictions on capital movements. One staff publication expresses "a general distaste for [capital] controls as a way of addressing balance of payments difficulties" (Quirk et al., 1995, p. 6). For any capital restriction to receive staff support, it must, it appears, be labeled as "temporary" or "for a transitional period." The notion that some controls on capital inflows may be useful on a permanent or long-term basis for stability or for prudential reasons seems to be beyond the pale.

- Even on matters of considerable importance to the system, jurisdiction is not the only option the Fund has to influence members' policies. The Fund learned that lesson after the collapse of the par value system destroyed its approval jurisdiction on exchange rates. The early discussions on reform in the Committee of Twenty (1972–1974) focused on reestablishing an approval regime in the form of a system of "stable but adjustable par values" with allowance for countries to "adopt floating rates in particular circumstances, subject to Fund authorization, surveillance and review" (IMF, 1974, p. 12). When the time came to codify the results of the reform exercise, however, a provision requiring a country to seek Fund approval to float its currency proved unacceptable. At the same time, countries that wanted to maintain fixed rates were not prepared to accept Fund jurisdiction over the level of their rates, or changes in them, if the currencies of other countries continued to float. Thus, the only acceptable regime, as embodied in the amended Article IV, was one in which countries would be free to adopt the exchange *arrangements* of their choice, but in which their exchange-rate *policies* would be subject to "firm surveillance." Over the next twenty years, this deregulated regime allowed countries to experiment with a variety of exchange-rate arrangements, and it allowed the Fund, although the Fund no longer had the power to approve changes in rates, to influence members' exchange-rate policies by surveillance, conditionality, and technical assistance.

• The need for experimentation, rather than for the adoption of a new dogma, applies as much to the subject of capital liberalization as it did—and does—to the choice between fixed and floating rates. The Asian crisis has shown that there is still much to learn about the costs and benefits of capital decontrol. It is also worth noting that the broad support noted earlier for the liberalization of capital movements relates to the *process* of removing unnecessary, ineffective, and counterproductive restrictions, rather than to an *end result* of complete freedom of capital movements. I doubt that the consensus goes as far as the view that "economic logic advocates the dismantling of capital controls" or that "it is generally agreed that efficiency criteria argue for completely free exchange systems" (Guitián, 1996, p. 186). At that level of abstraction, the benefits to world welfare to be achieved by the unrestricted freedom of capital movements could equally well be claimed for the free movement of people; indeed, the European Union introduced both freedoms at about the same time. Yet it would seem (let us say) premature to argue that the Fund should consider bringing the immigration policies of its members under its jurisdiction.

The four considerations presented above would seem to support the conclusion that, rather than seeking Fund authority over capital restrictions, it would be more efficient to stick with the present deregulated regime, in which the Fund *promotes* the orderly liberalization of capital movements by means of the three instruments already at its disposal, that is, surveillance, conditionality, and technical assistance.

References

De Vries, Margaret G., "Exchange Restrictions," in J. Keith De Vries, ed., *The International Monetary Fund 1945–1965*, Vol. 2, Washington, D.C., International Monetary Fund, 1969, pp. 217–348.

Fischer, Stanley, "Capital Account Liberalization and the Role of the IMF," paper presented at the International Monetary Fund's Seminar on Asia and the IMF, Hong Kong, September 19, 1997.

Guitián, Manuel, "The Issue of Capital Account Convertibility: A Gap between Norms and Reality," in Manuel Guitián and Saleh M. Nsouli, eds., *Currency Convertibility in the Middle East and North Africa*, Washington, D.C., International Monetary Fund, 1996, pp. 169–188.

International Monetary Fund (IMF), *International Monetary Reform—Documents of the Committee of Twenty*, Washington, D.C., International Monetary Fund, 1974.

———, *International Capital Markets*, Washington, D.C., International Monetary Fund, 1995.

———, *Annual Report for 1997*, Washington, D.C., International Monetary Fund, 1997.

Ostry, Sylvia, *A New Regime for Foreign Direct Investment*, Group of Thirty, Washington, D.C., 1997.

Polak, Jacques J., *An International Economic System*, Chicago, University of Chicago Press, 1953.

———, *Financial Policies and Development*, Paris, Development Centre of the Organisation for Economic Co-operation and Development, 1989.

———, *The Changing Nature of IMF Conditionality*, Essays in International Finance No. 184, Princeton, N.J., Princeton University, International Finance Section, September 1991.

Quirk, Peter J., Owen Evans, and staff, *Capital Account Convertibility, Review of Experience and Implications for IMF Policies*, Occasional Paper No. 131, Washington, D.C., International Monetary Fund, 1995.

"Statement of the Interim Committee on the Liberalization of Capital Movements under an Amendment of the Articles," attached to the Communiqué of the Interim Committee of the Board of Governors of the International Monetary Fund, Hong Kong, September 21, 1997.

[8]

THE POLITICAL ECONOMY OF A BILATERAL INVESTMENT TREATY

By Kenneth J. Vandevelde*

One of the more remarkable developments in international law in the mid-1990s is not what it appears to be. The massive and sudden[1] proliferation of bilateral investment treaties (BITs),[2] now constituting a network of more than thirteen hundred agreements involving some 160 states,[3] appears to reflect the triumph of liberal economics in the sphere of international investment. In fact, however, it constitutes only a momentary convergence of nationalist interests.[4] If the BITs are to construct the liberal international investment regime they seem to promise, then they must be modified in important and substantial ways.

I. THE POLITICAL ECONOMY OF INVESTMENT POLICY

In this century, international political economy has been dominated by three theories about the relationship between the state and economic activity: economic liberalism, economic nationalism and Marxist economics.[5] Economic liberalism has been associated with a fundamentally different international investment policy than economic nationalism and Marxist economics. This section briefly describes each of these three theories

---

* Professor of Law and Dean, Thomas Jefferson School of Law. The author wishes to thank Marybeth Herald for her comments on an earlier draft of this article.

[1] Although the first bilateral investment treaty was concluded in 1959, more than two-thirds of the agreements have been signed since 1990. For a listing, see UNITED NATIONS CENTRE ON TRANSNATIONAL CORPORATIONS [UNCTC], BILATERAL INVESTMENT TREATIES IN THE MID 1990s (forthcoming). The International Centre for Settlement of Investment Disputes separately compiled a list of more than 1100 treaties involving 155 countries through the end of 1996. See INTERNATIONAL CENTRE FOR SETTLEMENT OF INVESTMENT DISPUTES [ICSID], BILATERAL INVESTMENT TREATIES 1959–1996 (1997).

[2] On the BITs, see generally RUDOLF DOLZER & MARGRETE STEVENS, BILATERAL INVESTMENT TREATIES (1995); KENNETH J. VANDEVELDE, UNITED STATES INVESTMENT TREATIES: POLICY AND PRACTICE (1992) [hereinafter U.S. INVESTMENT TREATIES]; Kenneth J. Vandevelde, *U.S. Bilateral Investment Treaties: The Second Wave,* 14 MICH. J. INT'L L. 621 (1993); Mohamed I. Khalil, *Treatment of Foreign Investment in Bilateral Investment Treaties,* 8 ICSID REV. 339 (1992); Robert K. Paterson, *Canadian Investment Promotion and Protection Treaties,* 29 CAN. Y.B. INT'L L. 373 (1991); Jeswald Salacuse, *BIT by BIT: The Growth of Bilateral Investment Treaties and Their Impact on Foreign Investment in Developing Countries,* 24 INT'L L. 655 (1990); Kenneth J. Vandevelde, *The Bilateral Investment Treaty Program of the United States,* 21 CORNELL INT'L L.J. 201 (1988); Adeoye Akinsanya, *International Protection of Foreign Direct Investment in the Third World,* 36 INT'L & COMP. L.Q. 58 (1987); Eileen Denza & Shelagh Brooks, *Investment Protection Treaties: United Kingdom Experience,* 36 INT'L & COMP. L.Q. 908 (1987); Palitha T. B. Kohona, *Investment Protection Agreements: An Australian Perspective,* 21 J. WORLD TRADE L. 79 (1987); T. Modibo Ocran, *Bilateral Investment Protection Treaties: A Comparative Study,* 8 N.Y.L. SCH. J. INT'L & COMP. L.Q. 401 (1987); M. Sornarajah, *State Responsibility and Bilateral Investment Treaties,* 20 J. WORLD TRADE L. 79 (1986); Pamela B. Gann, *The U.S. Bilateral Investment Treaty Program,* 21 STAN. J. INT'L L. 373 (1985).

[3] The UN Centre on Transnational Corporations counted 1306 BITs as of the end of 1996. UNCTC, *supra* note 1.

[4] On the circumstances that have given rise to the current flurry of BIT negotiations, see Kenneth J. Vandevelde, *Sustainable Liberalism and the International Investment Regime,* 19 MICH. J. INT'L L. 373 (1998).

[5] *See* GEORGE T. CRANE & ABLA AMAWI, THE THEORETICAL EVOLUTION OF INTERNATIONAL POLITICAL ECONOMY (1997); INTERNATIONAL POLITICAL ECONOMY (C. Roe Goddard, John Passe-Smith & John Conklin eds., 1996) [hereinafter Goddard et al.]; THE INTERNATIONAL POLITICAL ECONOMY: PERSPECTIVES ON GLOBAL POWER AND WEALTH (Jeffrey A. Frieden & David A. Lake eds., 1995) [hereinafter PERSPECTIVES]; INTERNATIONAL RELATIONS THEORY: REALISM, PLURALISM, GLOBALISM (Paul R. Viotti & Mark V. Kauppi eds., 1993); TORBJORN L. KNUTSEN, A HISTORY OF INTERNATIONAL RELATIONS THEORY 237–39 (1992); and ROBERT GILPIN, THE POLITICAL ECONOMY OF INTERNATIONAL RELATIONS (1987).

of political economy and then identifies the essential distinction between liberal and illiberal investment policies.

Economic Nationalism

Economic nationalism, which finds its origins in the seventeenth-century doctrine of mercantilism, appeared contemporaneously with the rise of the nation-state as the dominant form of European political organization.[6] Theorists such as Nicolò Machiavelli and Thomas Hobbes laid the theoretical groundwork for the absolutist state, in which all considerations were subordinate to raison d'état.[7] Economic nationalism holds, accordingly, that a state's economic policy should serve its political policy.[8] Economic nationalists generally seek to enhance or preserve their state's position within the international community by protecting or increasing the economic resources available to the state.[9] Economic nationalists thus are willing to regulate economic activity to the extent necessary to further national political policy.

Postwar national policy in the Third World states of Africa, Asia and Latin America has generally emphasized political independence and economic development. Economic nationalists in these states traditionally prescribed a policy of import substitution industrialization, under which developing states sought to promote enterprises that would manufacture goods to displace imports from developed states.[10]

Similarly, economic nationalist developing states have sought to control inward and outward investment flows. They have employed interventionist measures, such as protective tariffs,[11] tax incentives,[12] investment screening,[13] and performance requirements,[14] to attract those foreign investments that would further their development policy, to prevent establishment of those investments that would not, and to ensure that investment, once established, would continue to operate in accord with national policy.[15] At the

---

[6] *See* CRANE & AMAWI, *supra* note 5, at 5.

[7] *Id.;* GILPIN, *supra* note 5, at 31–32.

[8] *See* CRANE & AMAWI, *supra* note 5, at 5; Jeffrey A. Frieden & David Lake, *International Politics and International Economics, in* Goddard et al., *supra* note 5, at 25, 31–32; GILPIN, *supra* note 5, at 31. Of course, those interests are defined by those who, at any given moment, hold power within the state. *Id.* at 48.

[9] *See* GILPIN, *supra* note 5, at 32.

[10] *See* JOHN RAPLEY, UNDERSTANDING DEVELOPMENT: THEORY AND PRACTICE IN THE THIRD WORLD 27–44 (1996).

[11] Protective tariffs encourage foreign investment because they make it expensive for a foreign producer to export to the protected economy, thus creating an incentive to establish a production facility inside the territory of the target economy and thereby avoid the tariff. *See* RICHARD CAVES, MULTINATIONAL ENTERPRISE AND ECONOMIC ANALYSIS 27, 31–34 (2d ed. 1996); BO SODERSTEN & GEOFFREY REED, INTERNATIONAL ECONOMICS 474 (3d ed. 1994); UNCTC, THE DETERMINANTS OF FOREIGN DIRECT INVESTMENT: A SURVEY OF THE EVIDENCE 33–34, 42, UN Doc. ST/CTC/121, UN Sales No. E.92.II.A.2 (1992).

[12] Out of 103 states surveyed in the early 1990s, only 4 did not offer some kind of tax incentive to foreign investment. *See generally* UNITED NATIONS CONFERENCE ON TRADE AND DEVELOPMENT [UNCTAD], INCENTIVES AND FOREIGN DIRECT INVESTMENT 46, UN Doc. UNCTAD/DTCI/28, UN Sales No. E.96.II.A.6 (1996); UNITED NATIONS CONFERENCE ON TRADE AND DEVELOPMENT, DIVISION ON TRANSNATIONAL CORPORATIONS AND INVESTMENT [UNDTCI], WORLD INVESTMENT REPORT 1995 at 291, UN Doc. UNCTAD/DTCI/26, UN Sales No. E.95.II.A.9 (1995).

[13] Investment screening refers to mechanisms that require prior approval for, or prohibit entirely, the establishment of foreign investment. Such mechanisms typically are embodied in a foreign investment code.

[14] There is no widely accepted definition of a performance requirement, but generally the term is considered to refer to regulations on the use of inputs and outputs by the investment. Performance requirements may stipulate, for example, that the investment use local content, employ local workers, or export a certain percentage of the production. A 1985 study found that half of the foreign investments surveyed were subject to some type of performance requirement involving either export targets or domestic content. *See* CAVES, *supra* note 11, at 222.

[15] *See* Rhys Jenkins, *Theoretical Perspectives and the Transnational Corporation, in* Goddard et al., *supra* note 5, at 439, 445–46.

same time, they have imposed restrictions on outward investment[16] to prevent a loss of capital,[17] although in recent years some developing states have begun to encourage outward investment so as to gain access to foreign markets or needed assets such as natural resources, less expensive labor and technology.[18]

Economic nationalism for developed states has typically called for adopting interventionist measures to promote and protect investments in foreign territory.[19] Promotional measures have included the provision of information, technical assistance, financing and investment insurance,[20] while protective measures have encompassed the use of military force, economic sanctions and diplomacy.[21] Economic nationalism in developed states may also take the form of restrictions on outward investment.[22]

As this overview suggests, economic nationalists do not in all cases favor or oppose foreign investment. Economic nationalists in developed and developing states may perceive international investment flows as beneficial in one case and detrimental in another. The common theme, however, is that international investment should be regulated to ensure that it promotes national political policy.

Economic Liberalism

Economic liberalism emerged as a critique of mercantilism. As a growing merchant class challenged the power of the European monarchs in the eighteenth century, liberal political theorists, notably John Locke, rejected the Hobbesian concept of an absolutist state and argued that the state existed solely to promote individual liberty. Liberal economic theorists, particularly Adam Smith and David Ricardo, sought to demonstrate that free markets, unfettered by state regulation, would result in the greatest prosperity for all.[23]

Liberal economics has thus been concerned more with the production of new wealth than with the distribution of existing wealth.[24] And, in conformity with the classic liberal regard for individual liberty, economic liberals prescribe minimal intervention by the state in the market.[25] In their view, the state's role should be limited to protecting private

[16] *See* WORLD BANK, THE EAST ASIAN MIRACLE: ECONOMIC GROWTH AND PUBLIC POLICY 235–37 (1993). Controls on outward investment are imposed by the great majority of developing states, including those with transitional economies. *See* UNDTCI, *supra* note 12, at 308, 321–31.

[17] Of course, outward foreign investment does not necessarily lead to a loss of capital. In fact, one economic nationalist criticism of inward foreign investment is that it leads to a net loss of foreign exchange through repatriation of the returns on the investment. *See* text *infra* at note 54. Indeed, the establishment of foreign investment may not entail the loss of any capital even initially by the home state because the investment may be financed through funds borrowed in the host state. *See* UNDTCI, *supra* note 12, at 346–49. In other words, in a particular case, the effect of a prohibition on outward investment may simply be to prevent a home state investor from acquiring control over foreign assets.

[18] *See* UNDTCI, *supra* note 12, at 322–23, 331–39.

[19] *See* GILPIN, *supra* note 5, at 241–45.

[20] *See* UNDTCI, *supra* note 12, at 313–21.

[21] *See* Shah M. Tarzi, *Third World Governments and Multinational Corporations: Dynamics of Host's Bargaining Power, in* PERSPECTIVES, *supra* note 5, at 154, 163; Kenneth J. Vandevelde, *Reassessing the Hickenlooper Amendment,* 29 VA. J. INT'L L. 117 (1988).

[22] Such controls, however, have largely disappeared in developed states. For example, as of the end of 1994, only three members of the Organisation for Economic Co-operation and Development retained controls on outward foreign direct investment: Japan, Portugal and Turkey. *See* UNDTCI, *supra* note 12, at 310. Restrictions on outward investment may not necessarily involve restrictions on capital movements. They also may be in the form of limitations on technology transfer, which could have the effect of impeding certain outward investment flows. Loss of technological lead is one potential cost to a home state of outward investment. *See* DOMINICK SALVATORE, INTERNATIONAL ECONOMICS 379 (5th ed. 1995).

[23] CRANE & AMAWI, *supra* note 5, at 6–7, 55–58; Frieden & Lake, *supra* note 8, at 26.

[24] *See* GILPIN, *supra* note 5, at 27, 43–45; RAPLEY, *supra* note 10, at 8.

[25] *See* CRANE & AMAWI, *supra* note 5, at 55; MICHAEL P. TODARO, ECONOMIC DEVELOPMENT 85–86 (5th ed. 1994); Frieden & Lake, *supra* note 8, at 27; Jenkins, *supra* note 15, at 442–43.

624 THE AMERICAN JOURNAL OF INTERNATIONAL LAW [Vol. 92:621

rights of property and contract[26] and correcting market failures.[27] Liberalism seeks to insulate the market from politics[28] and favors an autonomous legal system to protect private property against state interference and to enforce bargained-for exchanges in the market.

Liberal economics as developed by Smith and Ricardo advocated a policy of free trade that permits each state to specialize in the production of goods and services in which it has a comparative advantage, and then trade its products for others that it wants but cannot produce as efficiently.[29] Through economics of specialization and scale, a state maximizes its productivity. As a result, liberalism has been associated with a policy of export-led growth.[30]

Liberalism also has advocated the free movement of capital across borders.[31] Free movement of capital complements free trade in three different ways. First, to the extent that barriers to trade exist, they can be circumvented by capital movements.[32] Second, a state's ability to produce goods for trade depends on its endowment of the factors of production—capital, labor, land and technology.[33] Foreign investment augments the supply of the factors of production and thereby facilitates a state's production of goods for export.[34] Third, foreign subsidiaries can trade with their parent companies at lower transaction costs than with unaffiliated companies, facilitating international trade.[35]

Economic liberals, however, do not in all cases favor foreign investment. State action to promote the establishment of foreign investment in a sector of the economy in which the state does not enjoy a comparative advantage, for example, is antithetical to liberal principles. The liberal doctrine in essence is that the state should permit the market to determine the direction of international investment flows.

Marxist Economics

Marxist economics emerged in the nineteenth century as a critique of liberalism.[36] The Marxist contention was that increasing efficiency would lead to a surplus of capital, causing the return to investors to diminish over time.[37] To maintain profitability, investors would be forced to invest abroad in developing states, where the relative scarcity of capital would permit them to earn a higher return on their investment.[38] The result

---

[26] *See generally* Paul H. Rubin, *Growing a Legal System in the Post-Communist Economies*, 27 CORNELL INT'L L.J. 1 (1994); Tamar Frankel, *The Legal Infrastructure of Markets: The Role of Contract and Property Law*, 73 B.U. L. REV. 389 (1993).

[27] *See* Frieden & Lake, *supra* note 8, at 27–28; GILPIN, *supra* note 5, at 29; RAPLEY, *supra* note 10, at 7.

[28] GILPIN, *supra* note 5, at 29.

[29] A state has a comparative advantage in a good if its opportunity costs to produce the good are lower than those of another state. For a discussion of the theory of comparative advantage, see SODERSTEN & REED, *supra* note 11, at 3–71; PETER B. KENEN, THE INTERNATIONAL ECONOMY 46–85 (3d ed. 1994).

[30] *See* RAPLEY, *supra* note 10, at 59–76.

[31] *See* E. WAYNE NAFZIGER, THE ECONOMICS OF DEVELOPING COUNTRIES 110–13 (3d ed. 1997); TODARO, *supra* note 25, at 531–33.

[32] For example, if a state enacts a protective tariff, a foreign producer can establish a production facility in the protected market and thereby sell in that market while avoiding the tariff. *See* note 11 *supra*.

[33] The traditional view is that productivity at any given level of technology depends on the endowments of land, labor and capital. Because technology was assumed to be a constant, it was not treated as a factor of production. Modern economics, however, treats technology as a variable determining productivity, whether classified as a factor of production or not. *See* KENEN, *supra* note 29, at 46–48.

[34] The most obvious effect of a foreign investment is to increase the capital supply, but it may have other effects on productivity. The investment, for example, may bring in foreign currency, which can be used to purchase scarce resources, thus augmenting the "land" endowment; or it may provide employee training, thus improving the quality of the labor pool; or it may introduce new technology.

[35] *See* SALVATORE, *supra* note 22, at 379; GILPIN, *supra* note 5, at 270.

[36] *See Introduction: International Politics and International Economics*, in PERSPECTIVES, *supra* note 5, at 1, 11.

[37] *See* GILPIN, *supra* note 5, at 36–37.

[38] *See* Frieden & Lake, *supra* note 8, at 29–30; CRANE & AMAWI, *supra* note 5, at 10, 83–85.

would be the industrialization of the developing world, which was a necessary step in the transition from feudalism to capitalism and then ultimately to socialism.[39] The benefits to developed states, however, would be uneven, leading to international conflict over control of markets in developing states.[40]

Marxists in recent years have focused on the potentially detrimental effects of foreign investment on developing states. Twentieth-century neo-Marxists have developed the dependency theory of foreign investment,[41] which regards foreign investment as a form of neocolonialism that subjects the local economy to foreign control and promotes underdevelopment.[42] Dependency theorists have called for reducing the economic ties between developed and developing states,[43] including the screening out of foreign investment from developed states, particularly if it does not demonstrably contribute to the host state's developmental objectives, and in some cases expropriating those foreign investments that are already in existence.[44] Contemporary Marxists are concerned about the distributional consequences of a liberal investment regime[45] and thus favor state intervention in the economy to ensure a more equal distribution of wealth.[46]

The Critique of Liberal Investment Policy

As the foregoing suggests, economic liberals espouse an outward-looking philosophy that regards integration into the global economy as the key to economic development.[47] They favor the removal of barriers to transfrontier investment flows that inhibit global integration and diminish the production of wealth. Further, liberals contend that the negative effects ascribed to foreign investment are often in fact attributable to flawed host state regulatory efforts and thus the proper response is less, rather than more, regulation.[48]

Particularly within developing states, economic nationalists, with their emphasis on nation building and economic development, have found common cause with Marxist economists, who advocate a more equal distribution of wealth within the international community.[49] These theorists share an inward-looking philosophy[50] and are generally suspicious of unregulated foreign investment. They support intervention in the economy when necessary to ensure that foreign investment conforms to their political goals of promoting the national independence and economic development of Third World states.

---

[39] Early Marxist theory thus saw foreign investment as beneficial to developing states.

[40] *See* GILPIN, *supra* note 5, at 38–40, 270–73; Jenkins, *supra* note 15, at 450–52; CRANE & AMAWI, *supra* note 5, at 85.

[41] *See generally* RAPLEY, *supra* note 10, at 18–20; NAFZIGER, *supra* note 31, at 106–08. For a summary of dependency theory, see Theotonio dos Santos, *The Structure of Dependence, in* Goddard et al., *supra* note 5, at 165; Immanuel Wallerstein, *Dependence in an Interdependent World, in id.* at 176.

[42] *See* INTERNATIONAL RELATIONS THEORY, *supra* note 5, at 455–58; SUBRATA GHATAK, INTRODUCTION TO DEVELOPMENT ECONOMICS 65 (3d ed. 1995); M. SORNARAJAH, THE INTERNATIONAL LAW ON FOREIGN INVESTMENT 43–45 (1994); TODARO, *supra* note 25, at 81–82; NAFZIGER, *supra* note 31, at 106–07; Jenkins, *supra* note 15, at 448–50; RAPLEY, *supra* note 10, at 18–20.

[43] *See* NAFZIGER, *supra* note 31, at 107–08; GILPIN, *supra* note 5, at 291–94; RAPLEY, *supra* note 10, at 20; SORNARAJAH, *supra* note 42, at 43–45; CRANE & AMAWI, *supra* note 5, at 15; RICHARD GRABOWSKI & MICHAEL P. SHIELDS, DEVELOPMENT ECONOMICS 10 (1996).

[44] *See* CRANE & AMAWI, *supra* note 5, at 14–15; GRABOWSKI & SHIELDS, *supra* note 43, at 4–10; TODARO, *supra* note 25, at 81–84; GHATAK, *supra* note 42, at 66–67.

[45] *See* GILPIN, *supra* note 5, at 56.

[46] *See* Frieden & Lake, *supra* note 8, at 30.

[47] *See* GILPIN, *supra* note 5, at 265–70; TODARO, *supra* note 25, at 85–86, 484–86.

[48] *See* TODARO, *supra* note 25, at 85–86; Jenkins, *supra* note 15, at 442–43.

[49] *See* CRANE & AMAWI, *supra* note 5, at 21. Gilpin, for example, sees dependency theory as drawing equally on Marxist economics and economic nationalism. GILPIN, *supra* note 5, at 282–88.

[50] The philosophy is inward looking in that it favors greater reliance on domestic resources by using local producers to supply goods and local markets to consume them.

Their concern about a liberal foreign investment regime is twofold.[51] First, foreign investment may not produce the promised increase in efficiency. Dependency theory, for example, asserts that foreign investment fosters underdevelopment rather than economic growth in developing states.[52] The essence of the argument is that the subsidiary in the developing state will be operated for the benefit of the parent company and thus will transfer resources from the developing to the developed state rather than in the other direction.[53] It is alleged, for example, that foreign investment may reduce both foreign currency reserves[54] and employment.[55] Even where they accept the liberal economic analysis as essentially correct in theory, critics of liberalism point to extensive market failures in developing states that they believe will prevent an unregulated market from delivering the promised growth.[56]

The second concern is that, even where the promised productivity materializes, increased productivity and economic development are not the same thing.[57] Economic development theory, particularly since the 1970s, has emphasized that economic development requires both increased productivity and a more equitable distribution of wealth.[58] From this perspective, the real goal is development, not simply increased productivity, and liberalism promises only the latter. The second concern thus focuses on the distributional consequences of foreign investment. These consequences are both internal and external.

Foreign investment redistributes wealth and power internally in that not all members of the society will benefit equally or at all and some may be disadvantaged by it.[59] The benefits may be most likely to accrue to better educated urban populations[60] or to politically dominant ethnic groups,[61] which serves only to reinforce or extend existing gaps between the wealthy and the poor.[62] Alternatively, the creation of new centers of wealth, power and opportunity may weaken the position of traditional elites.[63]

Foreign investment redistributes wealth and power externally by transferring control over local assets to persons who are outside the national political system.[64] This may be

---

[51] TODARO, *supra* note 25, at 533–35.

[52] *See* GILPIN, *supra* note 5, at 247, 285–88; CRANE & AMAWI, *supra* note 5, at 14; RAPLEY, *supra* note 10, at 18–20.

[53] *See* SORNARAJAH, *supra* note 42, at 43–45.

[54] The concern is that the foreign investment may deplete foreign currency reserves through the purchase of imported inputs from the home state or another state, the payment of royalty or management fees to the parent company, and the repatriation of profits. SALVATORE, *supra* note 22, at 178; TODARO, *supra* note 25, at 532.

[55] The foreign investment may substitute capital-intensive means of production for labor intensive, reducing employment while raising productivity. *See* note 126 *infra*.

[56] *See* TODARO, *supra* note 25, at 87, 588–91; GRABOWSKI & SHIELDS, *supra* note 43, at 268–73.

[57] *See* NAFZIGER, *supra* note 31, at 38, 163–64.

[58] *See* GHATAK, *supra* note 42, at 34, 242–43; TODARO, *supra* note 25, at 132.

[59] Thus, foreign direct investment may be opposed by potential local competitors who are unable to compete with much larger transnational enterprises. *See* GHATAK, *supra* note 42, at 169. In Mexico, for example, liberalization of foreign investment regimes favored the export sector, while disfavoring firms that manufactured for the local market. *See* Alex E. Fernandez Jilberto & Barbara Hogenboom, *Mexico's Integration in NAFTA: Neoliberal Restructuring and Changing Political Alliances*, in LIBERALIZATION IN THE DEVELOPING WORLD 138, 150 (Alex E. Fernandez Jilberto & Andre Mommen eds., 1996).

[60] *See* TODARO, *supra* note 25, at 534.

[61] *See* Amy L. Chua, *The Privatization-Nationalization Cycle: The Link Between Markets and Ethnicity in Developing Countries*, 95 COLUM. L. REV. 223 (1995).

[62] *See* TODARO, *supra* note 25, at 533. The fact that foreign investments generally pay relatively high wages has been cited as an indication that foreign investment exacerbates inequality, particularly between urban and rural sectors of the economy. GHATAK, *supra* note 42, at 169.

[63] *See* UNITED NATIONS TRANSNATIONAL CORPORATIONS AND MANAGEMENT DIVISION [UNTCMD], FORMULATION AND IMPLEMENTATION OF FOREIGN INVESTMENT POLICIES 25–26, UN Sales No. E.92.II.A.21 (1992).

[64] *See* EDWARD M. GRAHAM & PAUL R. KRUGMAN, FOREIGN DIRECT INVESTMENT IN THE UNITED STATES 86–93 (1995).

particularly objectionable where the enterprise subject to foreign control is important to the host state's military defense, cultural identity or other vital interests.[65] Indeed, the Marxist critique of foreign investment characterizes it as a recolonialization of the host state.[66] The apprehension about foreign control ranges from fears of intervention in the political process to concerns about cultural imperialism.[67]

The critique of liberalism is not limited to developing states. Economic nationalists in developed states may fear inward foreign investment, particularly that from other developed states, for many of the same reasons that economic nationalists in developing states fear it.[68] Economic nationalists also may fear outward investment because of concerns that it will transfer productive capacity, hence employment, abroad.[69]

II. THE LIBERAL IDEOLOGY OF THE BITs

BITs present themselves as quintessentially liberal documents. The typical BIT cites two goals in its preamble: the creation of favorable conditions for investment by nationals and companies of one party in the territory of the other, and increased prosperity in both states.[70] In short, the avowed purpose of a BIT may be distilled into five words: increased prosperity through foreign investment. The preamble thus affirms the basic liberal doctrine that free movement of capital will yield greater productivity.

Further, the history of the BITs indicates that a principal inducement for states to enter into a BIT has been precisely that it affirms liberalism. Although the first BIT program was inaugurated in 1959 by Germany,[71] BIT negotiations proceeded throughout the 1960s at a largely desultory pace. In the ten years from 1959 through 1968, only seventy-four BITs were concluded, that is, fewer than eight per year worldwide.[72] Of these seventy-four, half were concluded by Germany.

The pace of negotiations did not noticeably change until the mid-1970s, when ideological debates concerning the standard of compensation for expropriation that was required by customary international law emerged as the central issue in discussions of international investment law.[73] Developed states proposed the negotiation of BITs providing for prompt, adequate and effective compensation for expropriation as an antidote to economic nationalist assertions that expropriated investors were entitled to no more than national treatment and Marxist claims that no compensation at all was owed.[74] Thus, the BITs acquired a distinct ideological purpose. Indeed, the United States was unwilling

[65] *See* CAVES, *supra* note 11, at 252.

[66] *See* DEAN HANINK, THE INTERNATIONAL ECONOMY: A GEOGRAPHICAL PERSPECTIVE 234 (1994). The colonialization is not seen as merely economic. There is concern that multinational companies will seek to exercise political control over the state in order to protect investment, *see* TODARO, *supra* note 25, at 534, although direct political intervention by foreign investments seems a "thing of the past." UNTCMD, *supra* note 63, at 26.

[67] *See* TODARO, *supra* note 25, at 534; GILPIN, *supra* note 5, at 247–48.

[68] For a discussion of economic nationalist concerns about foreign direct investment in the United States, see Jose E. Alvarez, *Political Protectionism and United States International Investment Obligations in Conflict: The Hazards of Exon-Florio*, 30 VA. J. INT'L L. 1 (1989); GRAHAM & KRUGMAN, *supra* note 64, at 59–67, 79–90.

[69] Economic nationalists do not inevitably oppose outward investment flows. As noted in text at note 19 *supra*, economic nationalists in developed states often favor the promotion and protection of outward investment. Although economic nationalists agree that investment activity should further national policy, they may disagree over national policy itself and thus about the desirability of capital movements.

[70] BIT preambles sometimes recite other goals as well, such as improved economic relations between the two parties.

[71] The first BIT was that between Germany and Pakistan, which was signed on November 25, 1959, and entered into force on November 28, 1962. The first BIT to enter into force, that between Germany and the Dominican Republic, was signed on December 16, 1959, and entered into force on June 3, 1960.

[72] For chronological listings of the BITs, see UNCTC, *supra* note 1, and ICSID, *supra* note 1.

[73] *See generally* SORNARAJAH, *supra* note 42.

[74] *See* VANDEVELDE, U.S. INVESTMENT TREATIES, *supra* note 2, at 21.

628 THE AMERICAN JOURNAL OF INTERNATIONAL LAW [Vol. 92:621

to negotiate any BIT that did not embrace the prompt, adequate and effective standard, despite the fact that the treaty might have offered real protection in other respects for foreign investors, because any such protection would have been insufficient to justify the ideological consequences of agreeing to a weaker compensation standard.[75]

In direct response to United Nations General Assembly debates on the measure of compensation, the United States launched its BIT program in 1977.[76] Several other developed states also inaugurated their programs in the 1970s.[77] France concluded its first BIT in 1972,[78] the United Kingdom in 1975,[79] Austria in 1976,[80] and Japan in 1977.[81] During the ten years from 1977 to 1986, some 153 BITs were negotiated, meaning that the pace of negotiations in the decade starting in the mid-1970s was about double that of the first decade of the program.

The pace of negotiations quickened a second time in the early 1990s, with the collapse of the Soviet Union and the transformation of the Central and East European economies from socialism to free markets.[82] Conclusion of a BIT represented a relatively easy way for these states to demonstrate their renunciation of Marxist economics and their commitment to a liberal economic regime. For example, some 196 BITs were signed in 1996 alone,[83] an astonishing contrast to the fewer than 8 per year signed in the 1960s.[84]

BITs have therefore been concluded in many cases because they symbolize a commitment to economic liberalism. The sincerity of that commitment, however, can be measured by examining the provisions of the BIT.

III. THE SUBSTANCE OF THE BITs

Liberal economic theory rests on a seeming contradiction. On the one hand, liberalism abhors state intervention in private economic arrangements.[85] On the other hand, liberalism demands a state that is willing and able to protect private contract and property rights and to correct market failures.[86] Liberalism thus favors limited state intervention in private affairs, but intervention nonetheless.[87]

As this might suggest, a liberal international investment regime would rest on three principles: investment neutrality, the principle that the state should not interfere with transfrontier investment flows; investment security, the principle that the state should protect private investment; and market facilitation, the principle that the state should facilitate the operation of the market by correcting market failures.

---

[75] *See id.* at 25–26.

[76] The United States began to prepare for treaty negotiations in 1977, but did not sign its first BIT, that with Egypt, until 1982. *Id.* at 29, 35.

[77] The claim here is not that the affirmation of liberalism is the only or even the dominant purpose of the BITs. Indeed, as will be argued below, BITs are primarily economic nationalist documents. The claim is only that a purpose of BIT negotiations in the 1970s and early 1980s was to counteract illiberal ideological hostility to foreign investment and that the BITs were held out as liberal instruments. In other words, BITs were intended to affirm liberalism, even if they were not primarily liberal documents.

[78] France signed its first BIT, with Tunisia, on June 30, 1972. France and Tunisia also had exchanged notes relating to investment in 1963. UNCTC, *supra* note 1.

[79] The United Kingdom signed its first BIT, with Egypt, on June 11, 1975. *Id.*

[80] Austria signed its first BIT, with Romania, on September 30, 1976. *Id.*

[81] Japan signed its first BIT, with Egypt, on January 28, 1977. *Id.*

[82] *See* Michael Mandelbaum, *Coup de Grace: The End of the Soviet Union*, FOREIGN AFF., Winter 1991–92, at 164; Michael Mandelbaum, *The Bush Foreign Policy*, FOREIGN AFF., Winter 1990–91, at 5; Coit D. Blacker, *The Collapse of Soviet Power in Europe*, *id.* at 88.

[83] *See* UNCTC, *supra* note 1.

[84] *See* text *supra* at note 72.

[85] *See* text *supra* at note 25.

[86] *See* text *supra* at notes 26–27.

[87] *See* UNCTAD & WORLD BANK, LIBERALIZING INTERNATIONAL TRANSACTIONS IN SERVICES: A HANDBOOK 50 (1994).

An economic nationalist investment regime, by contrast, would retain for the state the prerogative to intervene in the economy when necessary to serve distributional or other goals and thus would reject the principle of investment neutrality.[88] Capital-exporting states adhering to an economic nationalist ideology, in accordance with the goal of preserving existing wealth, would favor investment security;[89] while capital-importing states, in accordance with the protectionist stance characteristic of economic nationalism,[90] would wish to preserve their right to exclude or regulate capital and thus would be skeptical of investment security to the extent that the principle undermined that prerogative. Market facilitation is not inherently inconsistent with economic nationalism, but neither is it a core principle of that ideology, since economic nationalists take a regulatory, rather than a facilitative, stance' toward the operation of the market.[91] Economic nationalists, in other words, can favor a properly functioning market, but only if it is consistent with their political goals.

Marxist economics, particularly as practiced in the socialist states of the Second World, essentially rejected all three principles. The state exercised complete control over the economy, which made both investment neutrality and investment security impossible.[92] Further, the planned economies operated by these states abolished the market,[93] rendering market facilitation superfluous.

If the BITs are in fact liberal instruments, they should contain provisions intended to advance all three principles: investment neutrality, investment security and market facilitation. If they are Marxist instruments, they should reject all three principles. If economic nationalist documents, they should be expected to buttress investment security (because they have been drafted by capital-exporting states), while generally avoiding investment neutrality and perhaps showing little interest in market facilitation. This part considers the extent to which the provisions of a typical BIT advance each of these principles.

Investment Neutrality

Investment neutrality provisions should ensure that the host and home states will not discriminate among investments on political grounds. This entails permitting investment to cross borders freely (access) and avoiding action that discriminates among investments on the basis of nationality of ownership (nondiscrimination).

With respect to access, the typical BIT provides that each party shall admit investment by investors of the other party, but subject to the laws of the first party.[94] In effect, local law rather than the BIT determines whether a particular foreign investment may be established.[95] Nor do the BITs require the host state to permit the entry of technical or

---

[88] *See* text *supra* at notes 11–22.
[89] *See* text *supra* at notes 19–21.
[90] *See* text *supra* at notes 11–15.
[91] *See* text *supra* at notes 11–22.
[92] *See* RAPLEY, *supra* note 10, at 44–45.
[93] *Id.* at 44.
[94] Typical is Article 2(1) of the BIT between Germany and Dominica. Treaty concerning the Encouragement and Reciprocal Protection of Investments, Oct. 1, 1984, Dominica-Ger., *reprinted in* 2 ICSID, INVESTMENT PROMOTION AND PROTECTION TREATIES (loose-leaf).
[95] The United States BITs represent an exception. They guarantee to covered investors national and most-favored-nation treatment with respect to the establishment of investment in the host state. Each party, however, is allowed to specify in an annex to the treaty sectors of the economy within which it reserves the right to deny national treatment, MFN treatment or both. See, for example, Article II(1) of the Mongolia–United States BIT. Treaty Concerning the Encouragement and Reciprocal Protection of Investment, Oct. 6, 1994, U.S.-Mong., S. TREATY DOC. NO. 104-10 (1995). Thus, the United States exception is a qualified one.

managerial personnel needed in connection with the operation of the investment.[96] Further, where the host state does permit establishment of an investment, most BITs allow the imposition of performance requirements as a condition of the right of establishment.[97] The typical BIT also imposes no requirement on home states to permit outward investment flows.

BITs typically provide two important guarantees of nondiscriminatory treatment of investment,[98] once established: a guarantee of national treatment and a guarantee of most-favored-nation treatment.[99] Most BITs, however, except from these provisions concessions involving taxes[100] and those made to other states as part of an agreement establishing a regional economic integration organization (REIO), such as a customs union or free trade area.[101]

Given the content of these provisions, the BITs do not fare well as instruments of investment neutrality. They guarantee no right of access for capital or persons to the host state, they leave the home state with unlimited discretion to prohibit or regulate outward investment flows, the obligation of the host state not to discriminate applies only after investment is established, and the postestablishment obligation of nondiscrimination on the part of the host state is subject to important qualifications.

Further, because BIT protections apply only to foreign investment, the BIT investment protection provisions actually serve to undermine the principle of investment neutrality.[102] For example, the nondiscrimination provisions of the BIT do not prohibit the

---

[96] The U.S. BITs are very unusual in that they do have such a provision, but are subject to the host state's immigration laws. The purpose of the provision in the case of the U.S. BITs is to trigger the applicability of a U.S. statute that authorizes issuance of a visa to a person who is entitled to it under the treaty. Thus, the BIT provision entitles covered investors to an entry visa for the United States, but only as long as the U.S. statute so authorizes. *See* VANDEVELDE, U.S. INVESTMENT TREATIES, *supra* note 2, at 95–98; Treaty Concerning the Encouragement and Reciprocal Protection of Investment, Jan. 19, 1993, U.S.-Kyrg., Art. II(3), S. TREATY DOC. NO. 103-13 (1993).

[97] The BITs concluded by the United States again represent an exception. Most U.S. BITs, especially those concluded in recent years, contain a prohibition on performance requirements. The Moldova–United States BIT, for example, states: "Neither Party shall impose performance requirements as a condition of the establishment, expansion or maintenance of investments, which require or enforce commitments to export goods produced, or which specify that goods or services must be purchased locally, or which impose any other similar requirements." Treaty Concerning the Encouragement and Reciprocal Protection of Investment, Apr. 21, 1993, U.S.-Mold., Art. II(6), S. TREATY DOC. NO. 103-14 (1993). This language, which was typical of U.S. BIT practice until the mid-1990s, was replaced by a more detailed provision quoted at note 147 *infra*.

[98] In addition to the guarantees of national treatment and MFN treatment discussed in the text, many BITs separately prohibit the impairment of investment by unreasonable or discriminatory action. *See, e.g.,* Agreement concerning the Promotion and Reciprocal Protection of Investments, Chile-Den., May 28, 1993, Art. 3(1), *reprinted in* 5 ICSID, *supra* note 94. In the U.S. BITs, this provision prohibits impairment by arbitrary and discriminatory action. *See, e.g.,* the U.S.-Moldova BIT, *supra* note 97, Art. II(2)(b).

[99] The BIT between Estonia and the United States, for example, provides that

> [e]ach Party shall . . . treat investment . . . on a basis no less favorable than that accorded in like situations to investment . . . of its own nationals or companies, or of nationals or companies of any third country, whichever is the most favorable, subject to the right of each Party to make or maintain exceptions falling within one of the sectors or matters listed in the Annex to this Treaty.

Treaty for the Encouragement and Reciprocal Protection of Investment, Apr. 19, 1994, Est.-U.S., Art. II(1), S. TREATY DOC. NO. 103-38 (1996).

[100] For example, the Estonia-U.S. BIT, *id.*, Art. X(2), states that "the provisions of this Treaty . . . shall apply to matters of taxation only with respect to the following: (a) expropriation . . . ; (b) transfers . . . ; or (c) the observance and enforcement of terms of an investment agreement or authorization."

[101] See, for example, the Estonia-U.S. BIT, *id.*, Art. II(10).
A customs union is an arrangement among states under which they eliminate barriers to trade among themselves, while maintaining a common trade policy toward nonmember states. The REIO exception usually also applies to free trade areas, which are arrangements under which states eliminate trade barriers among themselves but maintain separate trade policies with respect to nonmember states.

[102] The preference for foreign investors created by BITs will be of practical significance in only very limited circumstances. Host state investors have natural advantages that, all else being equal, will usually give them a competitive advantage that foreign investors must offset through greater efficiency.

host state from offering special concessions to foreign investors and, in the event that the investment climate in the host state deteriorates, only foreign investors will be protected by a BIT.[103]

Investment Security

Most of a typical BIT is directed at protecting the security of the investment after it is established. First, there usually is a broad provision guaranteeing that covered investment will receive fair and equitable treatment, full protection and security and, in some cases, treatment no less favorable than that required by international law.[104] Second, BITs virtually always contain a provision restricting the host state's right of direct or indirect expropriation to situations where the expropriation is for a public purpose, nondiscriminatory, in accordance with due process, and accompanied by compensation,[105] most often, prompt, adequate and effective compensation or some equivalent formulation.[106] Third, most BITs require national and MFN treatment with respect to the payment of compensation for damage to investment caused by war or civil disturbance.[107] Fourth, many BITs have a provision guaranteeing the right of investors to transfer the investment and the returns on the investment into a freely convertible currency.[108] Fifth,

---

The preference, however, is not without significance. In Colombia, for example, successful legal action was taken to invalidate a portion of the Colombia–United Kingdom BIT on the ground that the treaty granted special treatment to foreign investors. *Court rejects treaty clause*, FIN. TIMES, Aug. 16, 1996, at 5 (U.S. ed.).

[103] Developing states, for example, often offer special incentives to foreign investors not available to domestic competitors. *See* WORLD BANK, *supra* note 16, at 228–31.

[104] For example, the Jamaica–United States BIT provides that "[i]nvestments shall at all times be accorded fair and equitable treatment, shall enjoy full protection and security and shall in no case be accorded treatment less than that required by international law." Treaty Concerning the Reciprocal Encouragement and Protection of Investment, Feb. 4, 1994, U.S.-Jam., Art. II(2)(a), S. TREATY DOC. NO. 103-35 (1994).

This provision generally is understood not to require that foreign investment be protected absolutely, but only that the host state take reasonable measures to protect it. *See* VANDEVELDE, U.S. INVESTMENT TREATIES, *supra* note 2, at 77. Note, however, that the provision requires protection against private as well as public actors. *Id.*

[105] See, for example, Article III(1) of the Jamaica-U.S. BIT, *supra* note 104.

[106] *See* DOLZER & STEVENS, *supra* note 2, at 108–17. On the equivalency of some of these other formulations in U.S. BITs, see VANDEVELDE, U.S. INVESTMENT TREATIES, *supra* note 2, at 120–37.

[107] For example, the Latvia–United States BIT provides, in Article III(3):

> Nationals or companies of either Party whose investments suffer losses in the territory of the other Party owing to war or other armed conflict, revolution, state of national emergency, insurrection, civil disturbance or other similar events shall be accorded treatment by such other Party no less favorable than that accorded to its own nationals or companies or to nationals or companies of any third country, whichever is the most favorable treatment, as regards any measures it adopts in relation to such losses.

Treaty for the Encouragement and Reciprocal Protection of Investment, Jan. 13, 1995, U.S.-Lat., S. TREATY DOC. NO. 104-12 (1995).

A number of BITs specifically require payment of prompt, adequate and effective compensation for at least certain war and civil disturbance losses. *See, e.g.*, Treaty Concerning the Reciprocal Encouragement and Protection of Investment, Feb. 26, 1986, U.S.-Cameroon, Art. IV.2-3, S. TREATY DOC. NO. 99-22 (1986). Such provisions are unusual, however, because the compensation they cover for war and civil disturbance losses is often required in any event by the general provision on expropriation. *See* VANDEVELDE, U.S. INVESTMENT TREATIES, *supra* note 2, at 214.

[108] The United States–Uzbekistan BIT, for example, provides, in Article V(1):

> Each Party shall permit all transfers relating to a covered investment to be made freely and without delay into and out of its territory. Such transfers include:
>
> (a) contributions to capital;
> (b) profits, dividends, capital gains, and proceeds from the sale of all or any part of the investment or from the partial or complete liquidation of the investment;
> (c) interest, royalty payments, management fees, and technical assistance and other fees;
> (d) payments made under a contract, including a loan agreement; and
> (e) compensation pursuant to Articles III [relating to expropriation] and IV [relating to losses due to armed conflict], and payments arising out of an investment dispute.

some BITs require the host state to observe any commitments into which it may have entered with respect to investments,[109] which may include, in particular, the investment agreements that host states often sign with investors to induce them to invest. Finally, the BITs provide for binding third-party arbitration of disputes between the investor and the host state[110] or between the home and host states.[111]

The protection provided by the BITs is principally against state interferences with investment, rather than private interferences. BITs, for example, do little to protect intellectual property rights against private infringement or to provide for effective resolution of disputes between the investor and other private parties.

The investment protection provisions of the BIT nevertheless are quite strong. In particular, they provide protection against the most important sources of noneconomic risk facing foreign investment, specifically expropriation, currency exchange controls, and war and civil disturbances, and they establish legal mechanisms to enforce those protections.[112]

Treaty Concerning the Encouragement and Reciprocal Protection of Investment, Dec. 16, 1994, U.S.-Uzb., S. TREATY DOC. NO. 104-25 (1996).

Exchange controls protect the foreign currency reserves of a state against depletion, but also prevent the investor from enjoying the return on its investment. The investor earns profits in the currency of the host state, but if the currency cannot be exchanged for another and if the investor does not want to use the currency for reinvestment or consumption in the host state, then the value of the return is lost.

At the same time, since states need to husband foreign currency to purchase essentials available only from foreign sources, some states have insisted on the right to impose exchange controls in some circumstances. Some BITs, for example, have exceptions permitting exchange controls for a limited time when foreign currency reserves reach very low levels. These exceptions typically require both that the investor be permitted to transfer a certain percentage of the investment each year while the controls are in place and that the controls be imposed on an MFN basis. *See, e.g.,* Treaty Concerning the Reciprocal Encouragement and Protection of Investment, Mar. 12, 1986, U.S.-Bangladesh, Protocol, para. 4, S. TREATY DOC. NO. 99-23 (1986).

In view of these conflicting considerations, the free transfers provision is often controversial in negotiations. *See* VANDEVELDE, U.S. INVESTMENT TREATIES, *supra* note 2, at 143.

[109] See, for example, the Jamaica-U.S. BIT, *supra* note 104, states in Article II(2)(c) that "[e]ach Party shall observe any obligation it may have entered into with regard to investments."

[110] See, for example, the Albania–United States BIT, Article IX. Treaty Concerning the Encouragement and Reciprocal Protection of Investment, Jan. 11, 1995, U.S.-Alb., S. TREATY DOC. NO. 104-19 (1995).

[111] The Ecuador–United States BIT, for example, provides in Article VII:

1. Any dispute between the Parties concerning the interpretation or application of the Treaty which is not resolved through consultations or other diplomatic channels, shall be submitted, upon the request of either Party, to an arbitral tribunal for binding decision in accordance with the applicable rules of international law. In the absence of an agreement by the Parties to the contrary, the arbitration rules of the United Nations Commission on International Trade Law (UNCITRAL), except to the extent modified by the Parties or by the arbitrators, shall govern.

2. Within two months of receipt of a request, each Party shall appoint an arbitrator. The two arbitrators shall select a third arbitrator as Chairman, who is a national of a third State. The UNCITRAL Rules for appointing members of three member panels shall apply *mutatis mutandis* to the appointment of the arbitral panel except that the appointing authority referenced in those rules shall be the Secretary General of the Centre.

3. Unless otherwise agreed, all submissions shall be made and all hearings shall be completed within six months of the date of selection of the third arbitrator, and the Tribunal shall render its decisions within two months of the date of the final submissions or the date of the closing of the hearing, whichever is later.

Treaty Concerning the Encouragement and Reciprocal Protection of Investment, Aug. 27, 1993, U.S.-Ecuador, S. TREATY DOC. NO. 103-15 (1993).

[112] Some measure of the importance of these three types of risk is suggested by the fact that they are the risks typically covered by investment insurance programs, such as those offered by the Overseas Private Investment Corporation and the Multilateral Investment Guarantee Agency. *See* Maura B. Perry, *A Model for Efficient Foreign Aid: The Case for the Political Risk Insurance Activity of the Overseas Private Investment Corporation*, 36 VA. J. INT'L L. 511 (1996); George T. Ellinidu, *Foreign Direct Investment in Developing and Newly Liberalized Nations*, 4 DET. C.L. J. INT'L L. & PRAC. 299 (1995); IBRAHIM I. F. SHIHATA, MIGA AND FOREIGN INVESTMENT: ORIGINS, OPERATIONS, POLICIES AND BASIC DOCUMENTS OF THE MULTILATERAL INVESTMENT GUARANTEE AGENCY (1988).

Market Facilitation

Market facilitation provisions are those directed at curing market failures. A few BITs have transparency provisions that require the host state to make public laws relating to investment, thus addressing in a small way one type of market failure: lack of information.[113] The typical BIT, however, has no provisions aimed at curing market failures.[114]

IV. REASSESSING THE IDEOLOGY OF THE BITs

In their strong promotion of investment security, the BITs clearly reject Marxist economics, with its redistributionist impulse[115] and its disregard of private property rights. Indeed, as noted above,[116] an important impetus for the negotiation of BITs for the past two decades has been to affirm liberal principles while also signaling a rejection of Marxist economics, whether in the form of calls for a sovereign right to engage in uncompensated expropriations or in the form of planned economies.

The alternative to Marxism offered by the BIT, however, is not economic liberalism but economic nationalism. By providing strong protection against uncompensated expropriation, exchange controls and other host state interferences with foreign investment, the BITs promote important economic nationalist goals of capital-exporting states.

The protection of foreign investment, of course, is also fully consistent with liberal economic theory. Liberalism is distinguished from the typical home state's version of economic nationalism by its insistence upon investment neutrality, that is, its separation of the market from politics,[117] and to a lesser extent by its concern for market facilitation.[118] As has been seen, however, the commitment of the BITs to investment neutrality is weak and heavily qualified[119] and they virtually ignore market facilitation.[120] By exalting investment security over investment neutrality and market facilitation, home states make clear that their dominant interest in concluding BITs is in the economic nationalist policy of promoting their investments, rather than in creating a liberal investment regime.

The BITs also leave host states free to pursue a variety of economic nationalist policies. They universally allow investment screening[121] and local participation requirements[122] and most permit performance requirements.[123] The BITs impose no obligation on a host state to reduce tariffs and through their REIO exception facilitate the maintenance

---

[113] *See, e.g.,* the Albania-U.S. BIT, *supra* note 110, Art. II(5). On the general problem of lack of information in developing states, see GRABOWSKI & SHIELDS, *supra* note 43, at 270–71.

[114] Enterprises, particularly those that are vertically integrated, often deal with various market imperfections, such as lack of information, by acquiring foreign subsidiaries and thereby creating an internal market. *See* SODERSTEN & REED, *supra* note 11, at 472; SALVATORE, *supra* note 22, at 379. In this sense, merely facilitating foreign direct investment can reduce the effect of market imperfections. At the same time, foreign direct investment, especially that involving horizontal integration, can reduce competition, thereby creating a market failure. *See* note 182 *infra.*

[115] Of course, all law may be considered redistributive, in the sense that it promotes a different result than would have occurred in its absence and thus redistributes burdens and benefits within a society. To the extent that BITs are redistributive, however, they tend to reinforce the position of wealthy foreign investors at the expense of their economically weaker domestic competitors, making their redistributive consequences inconsistent with Marxist economics.

[116] *See* text *supra* at notes 70–84.

[117] *See* text *supra* at note 28.

[118] *See* text *supra* at notes 26–27.

[119] *See* text *supra* at notes 94–103.

[120] *See* text *supra* at notes 113–14.

[121] *See* text *supra* at notes 94–95.

[122] BITs generally have no specific prohibition on local participation requirements as a condition of the establishment of the investment. The national treatment provision of the U.S. BITs, however, would prohibit treatment of foreign investments that differed from treatment of local investments.

[123] *See* text *supra* at note 97.

634   THE AMERICAN JOURNAL OF INTERNATIONAL LAW   [Vol. 92:621

of trade-diverting economic integration agreements.[124] Host states also enjoy the right to offer tax incentives to investors on a selective basis without violating the nondiscrimination provisions of the BITs.[125]

The interventionist measures permitted by the BITs are antithetical to economic liberalism. For example, in their failure to create a right of establishment for investors, the BITs acquiesce in government screening that may result in inefficient allocations of resources. Consequently, host states may screen out investments that would introduce efficiency-enhancing technology in order to protect a labor-intensive, but inefficient, domestic industry that employs more people.[126] Much the same can be said of the BITs' tolerance of other interventionist tactics, such as local participation requirements,[127] trade-diverting customs unions,[128] protective tariffs[129] and tax incentives.[130] In each case, the BIT permits the host state to choose economically inefficient behavior in furtherance of its political goals.

The subordination of economic considerations to political considerations is a defining feature of economic nationalism.[131] The BITs place a great deal more importance on protecting the interests of home state investors and preserving the political prerogatives of the host state than on promoting economic efficiency.

It is important to note nevertheless that BITs are in fact liberalizing documents. They prohibit much postestablishment discrimination among investors, thus liberalizing the regime in which foreign investment operates. The security they provide for investment is as important to a liberal investment regime as the investment neutrality and market facilitation that they are less successful in fostering. And the investor-to-state arbitration provisions are a critically important step in transferring protection of private investment from the political to the legal realm, a key tenet of liberalism. The conclusion and implementation of a BIT almost certainly results in a more liberal investment regime than would otherwise exist.

In creating a more liberal investment regime, however, the home state appears to be seeking to protect its own investment, rather than enhancing global productivity. Indeed,

---

[124] *See* text *supra* at note 101. Customs unions are referred to as trade diverting when they divert trade from a nonmember state that has a comparative advantage in a good to a member state that does not, with the result that the welfare of member states is diminished. *See* SODERSTEN & REED, *supra* note 11, at 323–43; SALVATORE, *supra* note 22, at 302–05; TODARO, *supra* note 25, at 511. Many economic integration agreements among developing states in particular are trade diverting. *See* SALVATORE, *supra* note 22, at 315.

[125] *See* text *supra* at note 100.

[126] Capital-intensive, high-technology foreign investment may have the effect of reducing employment by displacing local enterprises that are more labor intensive. *See* SALVATORE, *supra* note 22, at 40; HANINK, *supra* note 66, at 84; TODARO, *supra* note 25, at 235–36; CAVES, *supra* note 11, at 228; GHATAK, *supra* note 42, at 169.

[127] Because high-technology companies (for reasons of security or quality control) prefer to operate through subsidiaries that they control rather than through licensees, *see* CAVES, *supra* note 11, at 77, host states requiring local participation are likely to steer investors toward licensing rather than direct investment and thus lose the opportunity to obtain the newest technology, *see id.* at 170. Or they may simply encourage the investor to utilize old technology. *See* SALVATORE, *supra* note 22, at 37.

[128] *See supra* note 124.

[129] Tariffs sometimes have been used to attract foreign direct investment. The problem is that the investment is not competitive once the tariff barriers have been removed because the investment was established in a sector of the economy in which the host state does not enjoy a comparative advantage. *See* UNCTC, *supra* note 11, at 3–4, 64, 67; GRAHAM & KRUGMAN, *supra* note 64, at 50.

[130] Tax incentives often have been found to be ineffective in attracting new investment because of their temporary nature and because they may be matched by other states. *See* CAVES, *supra* note 11, at 205, 220; UNCTAD, *supra* note 12, at 46–51; UNTCMD, *supra* note 63, at 54; UNCTC, *supra* note 11, at 37. Thus, their principal effect may be simply to reduce the amount of tax revenue received by the host state. *See* UNTCMD, *supra* note 63, at 54; UNCTC, *supra* note 11, at 60; CAVES, *supra* note 11, at 203. Indeed, there is evidence that overly generous incentives may discourage investment because they are perceived as a danger sign. UNCTC, *supra* note 11, at 50.

[131] *See* text *supra* at note 8.

it is not clear that home states promote liberalism for its own sake in any aspect of a typical BIT. Rather, the BITs generally are liberal in character only when it is incidental to providing security or preferential treatment for home state investors.[132]

The U.S. BITs are the most successful in establishing a liberal investment regime because they have more extensive investment neutrality provisions than most other BITs. More specifically, they grant to covered investors limited rights to establish investment[133] and they prohibit certain performance requirements.[134] Because these requirements limit only the host state, however, the U.S. BITs actually reflect a greater commitment to liberalism by the capital-importing state than by the capital-exporting state.

V. CONCLUSION

Nationalism Behind the Liberal Facade

In summary, BITs affirm liberal economic theory and are liberalizing to some extent in their impact. The agreements, however, are driven principally by economic nationalism. Both parties proceed for largely nationalist reasons but find in a limited embrace of liberalism a way to advance their greater interest in acquiring or protecting wealth.

For the developing states, a symbolic embrace of liberalism is one way to create the kind of political and economic climate that may lure foreign investment needed for economic growth.[135] Further, there is some empirical evidence that economic growth in developing states is correlated with reductions in inequality,[136] suggesting that liberalization may well be the best path for economic development, even where development is defined in terms of both increased production and a more equal distribution of wealth.

At the same time, behind the facade of liberalization, developing host states have retained in the BITs considerable discretion to employ interventionist tactics associated with nationalist and Marxist economics.[137] The problem for the developing state, however, is that it may not exercise its discretion well. Political pressure, corruption or administrative ineptitude[138] may cause the host state to take illiberal action in the name of economic development that diminishes the welfare of the state as a whole or that only aggravates existing inequalities.[139] Thus, the goal of economic development may be best served if the commitment to liberalism is genuine.

The public embrace of liberalism serves the nationalist interests of the home state as well. The investment security provisions of the BIT are effective ways of protecting the home state's existing (and future) investments. At the same time, the BIT's qualified commitment to investment neutrality permits the home state to dictate the circumstances under which its investors will be permitted to invest abroad, while leaving its investors

---

[132] Almost all of the typical BIT's provisions are intended to provide investment security. *See* text *supra* at notes 104–12. The investment neutrality provisions generally are limited to MFN and national treatment requirements that do no more than protect existing home state investment against discrimination, while there typically are no market facilitation provisions. *See* text *supra* at notes 94–103, 113–14.

[133] *See* note 95 *supra.*

[134] *See* note 97 *supra.*

[135] Generally, a favorable attitude toward foreign investment is highly valued by investors in deciding where to invest abroad. *See* UNCTC, *supra* note 11, at 43.

[136] *See* Kenneth J. Vandevelde, *Investment Liberalization and Economic Development: The Role of Bilateral Investment Treaties*, 36 COLUM. J. TRANSNAT'L L. 501, 516 (1998).

[137] *See* text *supra* at notes 11–22, 46.

[138] Even the most well-intentioned and competent developing state government may operate with such limited information about its economy that economic planning can be extremely difficult. *See* RAPLEY, *supra* note 10, at 61.

[139] *See* GHATAK, *supra* note 42, at 364; RAPLEY, *supra* note 10, at 47, 64–67; TODARO, *supra* note 25, at 584–86; GRABOWSKI & SHIELDS, *supra* note 43, at 273–76.

636   THE AMERICAN JOURNAL OF INTERNATIONAL LAW   [Vol. 92:621

who do invest abroad in a legally preferred position within the host state,[140] the perfect outcome from the perspective of an economic nationalist home state.

The problem for the home state is that its long-term interests may be better served by a genuine liberalism, rather than nationalism in liberal garb. Developing states need foreign investment and they currently are willing to affirm liberalism publicly to get it.[141] The time will come, however, when developing states will not feel the same compulsion to attract foreign investment and may be tempted to renege on their promise of investment security. This will be particularly true if inward foreign investment does not appear to be contributing to economic development, either because it has failed to raise productivity sufficiently[142] or because it is exacerbating existing inequalities.[143] At that point, the capital-exporting states may wish that they had nurtured a more genuine commitment to liberalism among the capital-importing states.

Toward Genuine Liberalism

No state has adopted a purely liberal international investment policy. States have important interests other than maximizing productivity, such as ensuring an acceptable distribution of wealth and protecting national security, that may necessitate deviations from the liberal model.[144] These interests will inevitably lead even an avowedly liberal state to intervene in the market on at least some occasions.[145]

As has been noted, the danger of policies that justify interventions in the market is that they may provide a pretext for illiberal measures undertaken as a result of corruption, clientism or incompetence.[146] Further, one intervention tends to create pressure for others that will extend or even counterbalance the effects of the first.[147] Accordingly, the establishment of a genuine, even though qualified, liberalism can be facilitated by the creation of rules that provide some basis for evaluating and limiting state interventions in the market. BITs can promote liberalism by both requiring states to liberalize their international investment regimes and acknowledging the necessity of, and imposing some controls on, the inevitable departures from liberal principles.

If BITs are to promote a liberal investment regime in this manner, they must be restructured. The following measures would effect such a restructuring.

(1) The BITs would guarantee to investors the right to acquire or establish investment in the host state, including in former state enterprises undergoing privatization. Since every state reserves the right to screen foreign investment to some extent, it almost certainly will be necessary to permit states to designate some sectors of the economy in which they will continue to screen or impose conditions on investment.[148] Nevertheless, there should be a commitment not to expand the number of sectors in which access is denied or limited and to reduce the number of such sectors over time.[149]

---

[140] *See* text *supra* at notes 102–03.

[141] *See* Vandevelde, *supra* note 4.

[142] This may occur, for example, because of market failures in the host state, *see* TODARO, *supra* note 25, at 588–89, or because of the effects of host state regulation of the investment. *See* GILPIN, *supra* note 5, at 26; 69; RAPLEY, *supra* note 10, at 60–63.

[143] *See* TODARO, *supra* note 25, at 533–34.

[144] *See* Vandevelde, *supra* note 136, at 517.

[145] *See* Vandevelde, *supra* note 4, at 393–94.

[146] *See* text *supra* at notes 138–39.

[147] Vandevelde, *supra* note 4, at 394–95.

[148] Even the U.S. BITs, which are unique in guaranteeing MFN and national treatment with respect to the right to establish investment, permit the parties to designate sectors of the economy that will be exempt from the obligation of MFN and national treatment. *See* note 99 *supra*.

[149] The model is the General Agreement on Tariffs and Trade (GATT), which, in Article XXVIII *bis*, provides fo a series of negotiating rounds in which member states negotiate reductions in tariffs. General Agreement on Tariffs and Trade, Oct. 30, 1947, TIAS No. 1700, 55 UNTS 188. Eight such rounds have been conducted since 1947.

(2) The BITs would contain commitments by each party to permit the establishment or acquisition of investment by its nationals or companies in the territory of the other party. That is, the BITs would impose investment neutrality obligations on home as well as host states.

(3) The BITs would restrict the use of performance requirements as a condition of the establishment or operation of the investment.[150] Performance requirements represent a compromise between closing a sector of the economy to foreign investment and permitting foreign investment in that sector unconditionally. Just as a host state may be unwilling to open a sector at all, so may it be willing to open that sector only if it can impose performance requirements. Permitting foreign investment subject to performance requirements in some sectors thus may be the price of opening those sectors to foreign investment. As in the case of prohibitions on establishment, however, permissible performance requirements would be limited to certain sectors of the economy and qualified by a commitment to reducing them over time.

(4) The REIO exception in the BITs would be limited to arrangements that have a net liberalizing effect on trade.[151] In effect, the BITs would limit the exception to arrangements that are consistent with the GATT.[152]

(5) The taxation exception[153] would be eliminated or, at a minimum, restricted to concessions included in double taxation treaties.[154] Double taxation treaties typically allocate between the two parties the right to tax certain income that both states might otherwise tax and do not grant tax incentives for specific investors.[155] Alternatively, the BITs would specify the sectors of the economy in which discriminatory taxation would be permitted, while committing the parties to reducing the number of sectors over time.

---

[150] On the prevalence of performance requirements, see note 14 *supra*. U.S. BITs generally prohibit certain types of performance requirements, but most BITs do not specifically address them. Language illustrative of that currently used in the U.S. BITs may be found in Article VI of the United States–Uzbekistan BIT, which states:

> Neither Party shall mandate or enforce, as a condition for the establishment, acquisition, expansion, management, conduct or operation of a covered investment, any requirement (including any commitment or undertaking in connection with the receipt of a governmental permission or authorization):
>
> (a) to achieve a particular level or percentage of local content, or to purchase, use or otherwise give a preference to products or services of domestic origin or from any domestic source;
> (b) to limit imports by the investment of products or services in relation to a particular volume or value of production, exports or foreign exchange earnings;
> (c) to export a particular type, level or percentage of products or services, either generally or to a specific market region;
> (d) to limit sales by the investment of products or services in the Party's territory in relation to a particular volume or value of production, exports or foreign exchange earnings;
> (e) to transfer technology, a production process or other proprietary knowledge to a national or company in the Party's territory, except pursuant to an order, commitment or undertaking that is enforced by a court, administrative tribunal or competition authority to remedy an alleged or adjudicated violation of competition laws; or
> (f) to carry out a particular type, level or percentage of research and development in the Party's territory.
>
> Such requirements do not include conditions for the receipt or continued receipt of an advantage.

U.S.-Uzbekistan BIT, *supra* note 108, Art. VI.

[151] REIO exceptions are inconsistent with investment neutrality. As a practical matter, however, it may prove difficult to conclude a BIT without such an exception because the party that belongs to a customs union may not wish to extend the concessions it has made to other customs union members to all parties with which it concludes a BIT. The proposal in the text thus represents a compromise.

[152] *See* GATT, *supra* note 149, Art. XXIV.

[153] *See* text *supra* at note 100.

[154] This is as opposed to advantages provided by tax treaties generally or by legislation.

[155] *See* ORGANIZATION FOR ECONOMIC CO-OPERATION AND DEVELOPMENT, MODEL TAX CONVENTION ON INCOME AND ON CAPITAL (1992).

(6) The BITs would grant investors the right to enter the host state in connection with their investment[156] and grant investments the right to employ managerial and technical personnel of their choice, regardless of nationality.[157] Steps would be taken to minimize the subordination of this provision to host state immigration laws, such as by providing that entry visas shall be granted to top managerial personnel of the investor, unless the employee falls into a category of aliens generally excludable on noneconomic grounds.[158]

(7) Investment agreements offering special incentives to investors would be enforceable through the BITs only to the extent that they are consistent with BIT principles. Investment incentives would not be permitted unless they are available on a nondiscriminatory basis to all investors.[159] Alternatively, the BITs would specify the sectors of the economy in which discriminatory incentives would be permitted, with a commitment to reducing the number of sectors over time.

(8) The BITs would have more elaborate provisions on transparency, requiring states to make public not only laws relating to investment, but also information about the business climate and investment opportunities.[160] The obligation would be placed on both home and host states.[161] This is an important way that states can address a key market failure in developing states.[162]

(9) The BITs would require basic levels of protection for intellectual property rights.[163] Because there already is an increasingly complex network of multilateral intellectual property agreements,[164] one approach would be simply to require the BIT parties to

---

[156] For a typical U.S. BIT provision, see note 96 *supra.*

[157] A typical U.S. BIT provision states: "Companies which are legally constituted under the applicable laws or regulations of one Party, and which are investments, shall be permitted to engage top managerial personnel of their choice, regardless of nationality." Ecuador-U.S. BIT, *supra* note 111, Art. II(5).

[158] Thus, an employee could be excluded because of a prior criminal record, if such persons are normally excludable. The employee could not be excluded, however, merely on the basis of nationality.

Some host states will want to retain the discretion to exclude third-country nationals because of hostile relations between the host state and the third state. Accommodation of these kinds of concerns almost certainly is a political necessity.

[159] For example, a state that revises its tax code to provide for accelerated depreciation schedules should apply such schedules to all investors. The experience in east Asia suggests that tax incentives are more effective in raising productivity when the state tries generally to encourage investment, rather than attempting to target the tax incentives. WORLD BANK, *supra* note 16, at 231.

[160] The U.S. BITs, for example, typically provide that "[e]ach Party shall make public all laws, regulations, administrative practices and procedures, and adjudicatory decisions that pertain to or affect investments." Mongolia-U.S. BIT, *supra* note 95, Art. II(7).

[161] Many developed states already provide various types of information and technical assistance to their investors seeking to invest in developing states. *See* UNDTCI, *supra* note 12, at 314–15. Such information, however, appears often to be outdated, *see id.,* and thus there could be real value in requiring the two parties to cooperate in exchanging and disseminating such information.

[162] The development of a mechanism for the exchange of information is crucial to the development of markets. *See* GRABOWSKI & SHIELDS, *supra* note 43, at 270–71. Because information dissemination is directed at curing a market failure, there should be no objection on liberal grounds to state involvement in this activity. Some liberals, however, particularly adherents of the Chicago school of economics, are wary of any state action intended to remedy market failure. They note that governments can fail just as markets do and that state efforts to cure market failures may simply create new problems, whether because of the state's incompetence or because of the political motivations of state actors. *See* Warren J. Samuels, *The Chicago School of Political Economy: A Constructive Critique, in* THE CHICAGO SCHOOL OF POLITICAL ECONOMY 1, 13 (Warren J. Samuels ed., 1993); GRABOWSKI & SHIELDS, *supra* note 43, at 267, 273–76.

[163] In general, strong intellectual property protection is correlated with the attraction of foreign direct investment. CAVES, *supra* note 11, at 50. This is particularly true for investment involving research and development. *See* EDWIN MANSFIELD, INTELLECTUAL PROPERTY PROTECTION, FOREIGN DIRECT INVESTMENT, AND TECHNOLOGY TRANSFER 19 (1994). Failure to protect intellectual property tends to encourage foreign producers to prefer licensing over direct investment and exporting to the host state over either alternative, thereby foreclosing access to the latest technology. *See* CAVES, *supra* note 11, at 170.

[164] For a good overview of the subject and the text of the major agreements, see INTERNATIONAL INTELLECTUAL PROPERTY ANTHOLOGY (Anthony D'Amato & Doris Estelle Long eds., 1996).

adhere to certain existing multilateral agreements for intellectual property protection and leave the task of detailed regulation to the other agreements.

(10) The BITs would require host states to provide investors with effective means of resolving private disputes involving investments in those states.[165] A liberal investment regime requires that the state protect property and contract rights against private as well as public infringement.[166]

(11) The BITs would protect all investment in the host state, regardless of nationality. In principle, of course, there is no reason that a BIT cannot protect domestic as well as foreign investors.[167] This would ensure genuine investment neutrality and create a host state constituency in support of an enduring liberal investment regime. Any investment injured as a result of a violation of a BIT provision, including investments owned by host state nationals, would be authorized to invoke the investor-to-state dispute provisions.

If this last proposal were adopted, conclusion of a single BIT could obviate the need for a host state to conclude additional BITs, since all investment would be covered. Some home states, however, probably would wish to conclude additional BITs with the host state, in part to obtain further protections not included in the first BIT concluded by the host state, in part to provide a common legal framework for all of their investors investing abroad, and in part to give themselves the right to invoke the state-to-state dispute resolution mechanism.

This particular proposal will meet with skepticism from those concerned about the problem of free riding by home states with which the host state has no BIT.[168] Further, the fact that investors of other home states were protected by a host state's first BIT would reduce the incentive of those other states to conclude BITs with the host state, in turn reducing the host state's ability to obtain reciprocal guarantees from those other home states and thereby eliminate free riding. This problem would be ameliorated to some extent, however, by the fact that a state that regarded itself as a victim of free riding would be able at the same time to free ride on other states' BITs to which it was not a party.[169]

One way to address the free rider problem would be to limit protection in the territory of the host state only to investments of investors from the two BIT parties. Such a provision would assure protection for host state investments, without creating a free rider problem. This approach is less desirable from the standpoint of investor neutrality, but the host state will move toward greater neutrality as it concludes more BITs, reducing the number of foreign investors not under BIT protection.

---

[165] Typical language found in the U.S. BITs provides that "[e]ach Party shall provide effective means of asserting claims and enforcing rights with respect to investment, investment agreements, and investment authorizations." Mongolia-U.S. BIT, *supra* note 95, Art. II(6).

[166] *See* text *supra* at note 26.

[167] The protection of local as well as foreign persons is a well-established practice in international human rights treaties. *See, e.g.,* International Covenant on Civil and Political Rights, Dec. 16, 1966, Art. 2(1), 999 UNTS 171 ("Each State Party to the present Covenant undertakes to respect and to ensure to all individuals within its territory and subject to its jurisdiction the rights recognized in the present Covenant . . .").

[168] After concluding its first BIT, a host state would find that it had granted protection to all foreign investors, even though it had concluded a BIT with only one other state and had not obtained any reciprocal rights for its investors in the territory of any states other than the one with which it concluded the first BIT. These other states thus would be able to enjoy a free ride on the one BIT concluded by the host state.

[169] This assumes, of course, that the state was a capital exporter as well as a capital importer and that all BITs adopt this proposal. The first state to include this language in its BITs obviously will have the greatest free rider problem, since it will have granted rights to all foreign investors, without any guarantee that its investors will benefit from any other state's BITs.

Beyond the BITs

Provisions comparable to those found in the BITs already have been included in a number of regional and sectoral agreements.[170] In May 1995, the Organisation for Economic Co-operation and Development (OECD) decided to commence negotiation of a multilateral agreement on investment that would include many of the same provisions that have become typical of the BITs.[171] Negotiations originally were to have been completed by the date of the OECD ministerial meeting scheduled for mid-1997,[172] but as of April 1998 a number of issues remained unresolved.[173] The negotiating group was scheduled to reconvene in October 1998.[174] Some have proposed that similar negotiations be initiated under the auspices of the World Trade Organization (WTO).[175] The discussions within the OECD and potentially the WTO hold out the prospect that the network of thirteen hundred bilateral treaties, with supplementing regional and sectoral instruments,[176] will someday be largely supplanted by a single multilateral instrument.

A multilateral agreement on investment has much to commend it as an instrument of liberalism. Multilateral agreements that command widespread adherence tend to universalize norms and thus give broad scope to the core liberal principles of investment security and investment neutrality.[177] Multilateral agreements are usually of indefinite duration and thereby create the kind of long-term commitment that is essential to the success of a liberal policy.[178] Because they will seem to represent a global consensus, norms adopted in a multilateral negotiation will have greater and more enduring legitimacy than those adopted in a bilateral setting and for that reason will be more productive of long-term investment security and neutrality.[179] In short, all else being equal, a multilateral agreement is likely to be more genuinely liberal than a network of bilateral treaties.

As the OECD negotiations have demonstrated, however, negotiation of a multilateral agreement is a complex undertaking because of the difficulty of balancing the desire for investment neutrality and security against the necessity of accommodating compromises. The more genuine liberalism of a multilateral agreement may be effectively undermined by the extensive qualifications that could be the price of gaining widespread adherence.[180]

Whether structured as a multilateral agreement, a series of regional agreements or a network of BITs, a liberal investment regime can deliver the promise of greater prosperity only if the market is properly functioning. None of the BITs has yet to address pervasive

---

[170] For a compilation of these agreements, see UNCTAD, INTERNATIONAL INVESTMENT INSTRUMENTS: A COMPENDIUM (1996).

[171] See ORGANISATION FOR ECONOMIC CO-OPERATION AND DEVELOPMENT [OECD], TOWARDS MULTILATERAL INVESTMENT RULES 3 (1996).

[172] *Id.* at 9.

[173] The April 1998 working draft of the agreement and an accompanying commentary may be found on the OECD's Web site ⟨http://www.oecd.org⟩.

[174] OECD Meeting at Ministerial Level: Paris, 27–28 April 1998, OECD News Release (Apr. 28, 1998).

[175] OECD, *supra* note 171, at 36–37.

[176] *See, e.g.,* North American Free Trade Agreement, Dec. 8, 11, 14 & 17, 1992, ch. 11, 32 ILM 289, 639 (1993); Energy Charter Treaty, Dec. 17, 1994, pt. II, 34 ILM 360, 385 (1995).

[177] *See* Vandevelde, *supra* note 4, at 396.

[178] *See* Vandevelde, *supra* note 136, at 527.

[179] *See* Vandevelde, *supra* note 4, at 397.

[180] Some of the difficulties of a multilateral agreement could be avoided or deferred by seeking to conclude a series of regional agreements liberalizing investments. There is a lively debate, however, over whether the negotiation of regional agreements accelerates or undermines the process of global liberalization through multilateral agreements. *See* James Michael Lawrence II, *Japan Trade Relations and Ideal Free Trade Partners: Why the United States Should Pursue Its Next Free Trade Agreement with Japan, Not Latin America,* 20 MD. J. INT'L L. & TRADE 61 (1996); Frank J. Garcia, *NAFTA and the Creation of the FTAA: A Critique of Piecemeal Accession,* 35 VA. J. INT'L L. 539 (1995).

problems of market failure that may distort or inhibit the flow of capital to its most efficient use, especially in developing states.[181] For example, the small size of local markets renders developing states particularly susceptible to restrictive business practices,[182] which may be addressed in part through international agreements.[183] The problem of externalities may necessitate agreements on environmental standards.[184] The problem of markets segmented along national boundaries may call for, among other things, agreements to harmonize tax policies to prevent tax-induced market distortions.[185] The problem of the immobility of labor may demand agreements on immigration to facilitate the movement of persons necessary for the operation of an investment.[186] The absence of public goods, such as physical infrastructure and educational facilities, may require substantial financial resources,[187] which could be mobilized through multilateral arrangements. Each of these problems raises its own complexities and difficulties, but each must be addressed on the way to liberalizing international investment flows.

In concluding the vast network of BITs, the nations of the world have affirmed a thousand times over that they seek a liberal investment regime. If they are sincere, and perhaps they are not, there is much work to be done.

[181] *See* TODARO, *supra* note 25, at 589.

[182] *See* UNCTAD & WORLD BANK, *supra* note 87, at 47. Indeed, foreign investment involving horizontal integration often reduces competition because the transnational enterprise proceeds by acquiring its local competition. *See* SODERSTEN & REED, *supra* note 11, at 469.

[183] The danger of leaving regulation of monopolies solely to host state discretion is that it may be used as a facade for economically nationalist activity or the regulatory process may be captured by host state producers. *See* UNCTAD & WORLD BANK, *supra* note 87, at 42–44, 47.

[184] *See* NAFZIGER, *supra* note 31, at 338.

[185] *See* CAVES, *supra* note 11, at 245–46.

[186] *See* UNCTAD & WORLD BANK, *supra* note 87, at 45. The relationship between labor and capital movements thus presents an interesting paradox. The text suggests that international movement of capital is in some cases facilitated by the international movement of labor. At the same time, one of the reasons that capital moves across borders is precisely that labor does not. In other words, the capital seeks out inexpensive labor. Thus, the complete international mobility of labor would eliminate one of the reasons for the international movement of capital. The point in the text is not that immigration barriers should be removed to permit complete mobility of labor, but only that it may be necessary to relax them in particular instances to attract foreign investment. On the relationship between the movement of capital and the movement of labor in the services sector, see *id.*

[187] Vandevelde, *supra* note 4, at 397.

[9]

The Constitutional Strictures of the Multilateral Agreement on Investment

David Schneiderman

One hears that economic globalization has no "explicit political or authority structure" (Cox 1992: 301), and beyond the administrative reach of citizens and states (Albrow 1997: 64). The emergence of a transnational regime of rules for the protection and promotion of foreign investment challenges directly the proposition that global capital has no tangible, institutional fabric. The investment rules regime, itself the product of inter-state bargaining, has as its object the removal of domestic blockages to the free movement of capital across national borders and the establishment of a market presence in all economic spaces. I want to suggest that this regime is constitution-like: that it has as its object placing legal limits on the authority of government, isolating economic from political power, and assigning to investment interests the highest possible protections—the kind of characteristics Karl Polanyi more than 50 years ago associated with constitutionalism (Polanyi 1957: 225).

In the modern era constitutional thought has placed great emphasis on the fact that constitutionalism is not just about limitations on government action. Constitutional rules facilitate, rather than simply inhibit, open democratic government (Elkin 1993). The innovation of Madisonian republicanism, Stephen Holmes reminds us, was to devise precommitment strategies in the form of constitutional rules that could free citizens from having to generate new rules in every successive generation. Constitutionalism, according to this account, releases citizens to dedicate themselves to the pursuit of particular legislative goals (Holmes 1995: 162).

The counter-narrative to the Madisonian version worries about the motivations of constitutional framers. Epitomized by the work of Charles Beard, framers are characterized as exercising domination and control over present and successive generations through constitutional rules (Beard 1935). Constitutionalism, according to this account, disables democratic politics and facilitates the self-interest of the few. Sheldon Wolin reminds us that constitutions are about the

> *The emergence of a transnational regime of rules for the protection and promotion of foreign investment challenges directly the proposition that global capital has no tangible, institutional fabric.*

"highest of all political stakes"—they are about constraining power, about privileging certain forms of politics over others (Wolin 1989: 3–4).

I want to argue that the structuration of a supranational economic order raises similar anxieties. These modern forms of constitutionalism are not merely "constitutive rules" that help frame political discourse (Holmes 1995: 163); rather, they concern limitations on the state's ability to regulate marketplace activities. They are intended to freeze and roll back state measures that impede the flow of foreign direct investment. They take shape through a series of bilateral, regional, and transnational agreements which have proliferated in the 1990s—there are more than 1,500 such bilateral investment agreements in place involving almost 170 countries (UNCTAD 1998: 59)—all of this done under the guise of "globalization."

Constitutionalism, admittedly, is not ordinarily associated with the global diffusion of the forces of production and the compression of the time-space continuum, attributes usually associated with globalization. But I want to argue that this regime of investment rules is an emerging form of supranational constitution which can supersede and overtake domestic constitutional norms. In this short paper, I want to focus on the new regime of investment rules as represented by the draft Multilateral Agreement on Investment (MAI).

The twenty-nine member countries of the OECD began the task in 1995 of completing a binding and enforceable agreement for the protection and promotion of foreign direct investment. It is not that investment flows between these countries is impeded; rather, the objective was to set very high standards for the protection of investment which countries in the so-called 'developing' world would then be pressured to adopt. Negotiations in Paris came to a halt three years later, and were suspended entirely in November 1998, partly because of resistance to the agreement in the U.S. Congress, the withdrawal of France from the negotiating table, and the coordinated action of citizen organizations in Canada, France, New Zealand and elsewhere. These groups revealed the contents of the OECD closed-door negotiations process and publicized the MAI as the ultimate eclipse of democratic rights by corporate rule (Clarke and Barlow 1997). Whatever the future of a multilateral agreement—negotiations may shift to other venues, like the World Trade Organization (WTO 1996)—the rules codified in the draft MAI represent much of what is captured in other investment agreements, like the North American Free Trade Agreement and bilateral investment treaties, and what is likely to be captured in future agreements, like the Free Trade Area of the Americas.

I want to argue that the draft MAI, and the investment rules regime more generally, are a part of what Stephen Gill calls "the new constitutionalism."[1] The new constitutionalist proposals are institutionalized at the macro-political level, such as the OECD, and "imply or mandate the insulation of key aspects of the economy from the influence of politicians or the mass of citizens by imposing, internally and externally, 'binding constraints' on the conduct of fiscal, monetary, trade and investment policies" (Gill 1995: 412). It is a form of precommitment strategy concerned not with decision rules, but with placing substantive and binding constraints on state capacity to regulate the market. An emphasis on the binding constraints inherent in the new constitutionalism makes parallels between the new and the old constitutionalism plausible. Missing from the equation, however, is the idea of popular sovereignty. States admit-

> *... the draft MAI, and the investment rules regime more generally, are a part of ... "the new constitutionalism". ... Missing from the equation, however, is the idea of popular sovereignty.*

tedly are the authors of the very regime which is realigning the bounds of permissible state action. Whatever the authority of governments to commit to these binding constraints, as I argue below the resulting regime is an inadequate mechanism for the exercise of self-government in the face of the mounting pressures of economic globalization.

First, I highlight the features of the new investment rules regime as exemplified by the draft MAI. Those familiar with that regime are encouraged to proceed to the second part, where I discuss how these features replicate those of domestic constitutions. I conclude with some brief thoughts about bringing 'the people' back in to discussions about the new constitutionalism.

I. The Rules of the Game

States are pursuing codification of the rules for foreign investment in a number of arenas. Through bilateral, regional, and multilateral agreements, rules for the protection of FDI have emerged as a priority item for the international legal system. The draft MAI was just one manifestation of this truly transnational phenomenon.

The key provisions of the draft consolidated MAI text of April 1998 replicated many of the provisions of NAFTA's investment chapter and those of most bilateral agreements on investment. These key provisions concerned: (1) the scope of covered investments, (2) the treatment of investments (involving the so-called principle of non-discrimination), (3) investment protection, (4) enforcement, and (5) reservations and exceptions.

Scope

The draft MAI proposed a very wide definition of the term "investment." It was intended to cover most every kind of economic interest. The definition of investment encompassed "all recognised and evolving forms of investment," including investment in any business enterprise; ownership of shares, stocks and bonds; rights under contract; intellectual property rights; and every kind of property right, both tangible and intangible. Moreover, the section was meant to be an illustrative, and not an exhaustive, list of protected investment interests. The MAI was intended to protect both established and prospective investments (although claims arising prior to the MAI entering into force would not have been covered by the agreement).

Treatment

There are two aspects to the so-called principle of non-discrimination: national treatment and most favoured nation status. First, under provisions requiring "national treatment" investors of a contracting party were entitled under the MAI to "treatment no less favourable" than that available to nationals within the host state. States, in other words, were not entitled to prefer local economic concerns over the interests of investors who have their home in another OECD country. Conversely, foreign investors were entitled to be treated as if they already were domicile within (or citizens of) the host state.

Secondly, "most favoured nation" status mandates that foreign investors are entitled to treatment no less favourable than that available to foreign investors of any other (third) country. The European Commission sought a special exemption from this basic tenet, and this caused some concern among the other delegations (Picciotto 1998: 759).

The "non-discrimination" provisions operated both prior to and after an investor had entered the host state. Non-resident foreign investors who wished merely to establish a presence in the host country, then, were entitled to equal treatment with domestic nationals even before they made any investment. There would have been no possibility, then, of screening investments or attaching any conditions to their entry.

Connected to these provisions were express prohibitions on "performance requirements" such as rules requiring the use of local labour or products (except for the promotion of health or the environment) or investment incentives. Entry and exit rights for both corporations and their key personnel also were guaranteed. The prohibition on performance requirements likely would have had the effect of prohibiting a wide range of policy tools including the requirement that investors achieve certain levels of domestic content, purchasing and employment preferences, technology transfers, and insisting that investors be headquartered in the investing state.

Protection

The MAI also established general levels of protection for investments. States were required to provide "fair and equitable treatment and full and constant protection and security"of foreign investments. The standard of treatment must have been no less favourable than that required by international law. Nor could a state have impaired by "unreasonable" or "discriminatory" measures the value of an investment.

It is not surprising also to find, as it is typical in most investment agreements, protection from expropriation and nationalization (the "takings rule"). This section prohibited measures that "directly or indirectly" expropriated or nationalized an investment, and measures that had an effect equivalent to nationalization and expropriation. As drafted, the section could have posed a potentially significant barrier for the ability of states to intervene in the marketplace (a matter to which I will return). Those measures that amounted to expropriation or nationalization were prohibited outright by the MAI unless they were in the public interest, non-discriminatory, and in accordance with the due process of law. Takings were required to be accompanied by prompt, adequate and effective compensation payable at fair market value, without delay, and fully realizable and transferable. This is the standard of compensation known as the "Hull Formula," advocated by former U.S. Secretary of State Cordell Hull and long championed by the U.S. as the standard of compensation "recognized" in international law.

Drawn from the vague language of the 14th amendment to the U.S. Constitution, "due process of law" was defined in the draft agreement. Due process included, in particular, the right to prompt review of a case by an investor, including valuation and payment of compensation, by independent judicial authorities within the expropriating state. This right of investors to prompt review of their case was independent of the investor-state mechanism I turn to next.

Investor standing

North Americans rightly can lay claim to having been party, in NAFTA, to one the first international investment agreements to grant standing to sue not only to contracting state parties (the usual practice in international law) but to investors themselves. The MAI replicated this right of standing to sue for foreign investors. States and investors alike were entitled to trigger mechanisms for the settlement and conciliation of complaints that a state had breached the terms of the MAI, and, in the event of irreconcilable difference, to resolution of a complaint before international trade tribunals whom were entitled to issue declarations, orders for compensatory damages, and restitution. Foreign investors had the additional option of suing in the domestic courts of the offending state. In any event, the decisions of trade tribunals were entitled to be registered and enforceable within those domestic courts.

Exceptions

It was intended that some general exceptions would be available to state parties—exceptions such as those relating to the protection of "essential security interests." These exceptions would not have been available in the case of expropriation or nationalization. Taxation measures were specifically "carved out" of the draft agreement, but the takings rule would continue to apply if a measure went too far. A proposal to except measures to protect cultural industries was tabled by Canada, and supported by a number of similarly concerned countries—a highly objectionable position so far as the U.S. was concerned (U.S. International Trade Commission 1998).

Each party state, in addition, would have been entitled to list specific reservations (or non-conforming measures) to the MAI. No further measures could have been listed after the agreement came into force and these reservations would have been rolled back, "with a view to their eventual elimination" (Witherell 1995: 11).

> *Constitutionalism encompasses those formal institutional arrangements that give binding effect to the basic norms by which a political community is organized. To the extent that the MAI reflects these characteristics, the demands of popular sovereignty and self-government requires that this constitution be rejected. The agreement . . . institutionalizes a legal incapacity to act in a wide variety of economic matters—it is not enabling, but largely disabling.*

The stated objective of the MAI was to both "standstill" and "rollback" non-conforming measures. Save for the general exceptions and country-specific reservations, parties would not have been entitled to deviate from these commitments, and any changes could only have further liberalized, or further protected, foreign investment.

II. The Making of A Constitution

I turn now to the main object of this essay: to interrogate the status of the MAI as a form of constitutionalism. Does the MAI exhibit some of the same features and characteristics as domestic constitutions? The following discussion is not meant to be exhaustive, but illustrative.

Constitutionalism encompasses those formal institutional arrangements that give binding effect to the basic norms by which a political community is organized. To the extent that the MAI reflects these characteristics, the demands of popular sovereignty and self-government requires that this constitution be rejected. The agreement freezes existing distributions of wealth and privileges with what Sunstein calls "status quo neutrality"(Sunstein 1993: 41). It does not merely commit citizens to certain, pre-determined institutional forms through which politics is practised; rather, it institutionalizes a legal incapacity to act in a wide variety of economic matters—it is not enabling, but largely disabling. At bottom, I argue that the MAI represents a form of constitutional pre-commitment binding across generations that unreasonably impairs our capacity for self-government.

The constraining model of constitutionalism resolves the tension between majoritarian democracy and the protection of minority interests in favour of limits on government action. The MAI similarly resolved this tension in favour of foreign investors by legally constraining governments from pursuing a range of legislative strategies. That is, the agreement placed binding limits on what governments could and could not do. This is an understanding of constitutionalism congenial to public-choice accounts. It is a view distrustful and fearful of democratic self-government, seen as captive of particularistic interests. The MAI resolved the problem of rent-seeking by removing from public discussion a range of matters in order to achieve "stability" and "efficiency" in the practice of normal, day-to-day politics (Posner 1987: 4).

I have said that the MAI was binding across generations. This is achieved by setting a high threshold for amendment or repeal. In Canada, for instance, the consent of at least seven out of ten provinces and Parliament is needed in order to achieve any substantive constitutional change. In the case of NAFTA, unanimity is required to amend its terms while six months notice is required for a state to withdraw unilaterally. This, of course, is not easily achieved. The MAI made withdrawal not only practically impossible but legally onerous. According to the draft MAI, no state was permitted to withdraw until five years after the agreement came into force. After the initial five year period, a state could have withdrawn after six months notice but the MAI would have continued to apply to existing investments for a period of fifteen years after a notice of withdrawal. In other words, no state would have been able to withdraw until at least 20 years and six months had passed since the MAI's coming into force. In addition, each of the 29 state parties had a veto over subsequent changes (however, no consent was required for any new state to accede to the terms of the MAI).

Constitutions often have binding enforcement mechanisms, like judicial review, in order to enforce the terms and conditions of these pre-commitments. In the case of the MAI, state parties were entitled to trigger a dispute settlement mechanism which could lead ultimately to binding arbitration before an international trade tribunal composed of "recognized experts" in the field (Sornorajah 1997). These awards would have been registerable in the court system of the rogue state and enforceable as if they were judgements obtained in the domestic court system. These rights of enforcement were meager compared to those available to the foreign investor who claimed abrogation of the MAI. Investors were entitled to launch litigation to enforce the agreement within the domestic court system of the contracting party in addition to being entitled to trigger the dispute settlement mechanism, ordinarily available only to the contracting states. This would have been license to meddle significantly in public policy development within state parties.

Constitutional text ordinarily establishes both an institutional framework for the operation of government and a series of textual limits on what governments can and cannot do. This can take the form of either a structural or a rights-based approach. Canada and the United States have adopted both approaches. According to each of their federal arrangements, the constitution expressly limits government at the national and provincial or state level according to a division of legislative powers (though, oftentimes, little regard have been given to these limits). The U.S. Bill of Rights and the Canadian Charter of Rights and Freedoms limit outright what governments at both levels are entitled to do. These limits are expressed in vague and abstract constitutional guarantees that call for judicial review in order to both give meaning to and enforce these rights. One important distinction between the regimes is that, under the division of powers in Canada, governments together have the power to do anything and that, under the Canadian Charter, there is no reference to property rights (or what are called "pure" economic rights).

The MAI also contained vague and abstract language, such as the principle of "national treatment," standards of reasonableness and arbitrariness, and the requirement of due process. They are deliberately vague concepts, as they were intended to capture or threatened to capture a wide range of state activity that impacted negatively on international capital. In order to make the stronger point about the constitutional nature of the MAI, I want to focus here on the MAI text as it concerns the prohibition on nationalization and expropriation.

If the investment rules regime has attained hegemonic status, it might seem odd to focus on rules prohibiting expropriation and nationalization. These kinds of prohibitions appear to pose no significant problem for state sovereignty. After all, this is a time when there is an apparent convergence across states on the dominant value system, and an apparent absence of alternatives, through which happiness and prosperity can be secured. Yet, I would argue that the removal of this policy option from the stable of instruments for controlling investment is a serious limitation on state sovereignty. And I would argue that the MAI takings rule had the potential of disrupting significantly state regulation of the marketplace. This is not commonly acknowledged by proponents of free trade and investment rules. Indeed, public discussion about expropriation and nationalization usually invites only the worst kind of red-baiting. But the brief six year experience under NAFTA's investment chapter suggests that we should not be sanguine about its effects.

Interested third party investors within United States have invoked NAFTA's takings rule even before any regulatory measure has been adopted. It was used to help subvert implementation in 1993 of Ontario's public auto insurance plan (Campbell 1993: 92–93). The Government of Canada's proposal for the plain packaging of cigarettes triggered an intervention on behalf of three of the biggest U.S. tobacco manufacturers, including Phillip Morris, before a Parliamentary Committee studying the proposal. The tobacco companies argued that legislating the plain packaging of cigarettes amounted to an expropriation of their investment interest

... the MAI, as well as NAFTA and the global web of bilateral agreements, are intended to secure well into the future the ideological politics of the neo-liberal state at the supranational level in the form of a "new constitutionalism."

and threatened to sue for hundreds of millions of dollars should the Government proceed; the initiative was abandoned (Schneiderman 1996). The cancellation of contracts to privatize an airport terminal in Toronto entered into by a previous federal administration also triggered threats of litigation under NAFTA. It was reported that Lockheed Corporation, the U.S. aerosnace conglomerate and a member of the consortium that was awarded the contract to privatize, would challenge the federal action under NAFTA's expropriation provisions (Globe & Mail 1994). This undoubtedly helped shape the government's response in providing compensation for the cancellation. Admittedly, none of these charges led to the filing of formal complaints and the triggering of NAFTA's dispute settlement mechanisms (under which successful foreign investors would be entitled to sue for damages). But, it would be fair to say that these charges have played a significant role in shaping the range of social policy choices available to these governments. In short, NAFTA's takings rule, and its potential restatement in the MAI, has helped to institutionalize a discourse of limited government that will constrain

administrations from pursuing a variety of measures to regulate the marketplace.

Arbitral proceedings, nevertheless, have been launched by foreign investors under NAFTA's investment chapter. The Ethyl Corporation of Virginia sued the Government of Canada for imposing a ban on the import and export of the toxic gasoline additive MMT. The classification of MMT as a "dangerous toxin," Ethyl claimed, amounted to an expropriation under NAFTA. The characterization of the legislative measure as an "expropriation" was important to Ethyl's strategy, as there are no exceptions for the promotion of health or the environment when it comes to expropriations in NAFTA or the draft MAI. The federal government has since settled the Ethyl claim for 13 million US dollars (Schneiderman 1999). Since the settlement with Ethyl, other complaints have been launched against Canada. S.D. Myers Incorporated of Ohio has launched a claim under NAFTA for losses following a temporary ban on the export of PCB-contaminated waste to the United States from 1995 to 1997 (Wagner 1999:491–95).

This expansion of what constitutes an expropriation parallels recent developments in U.S. constitutional law. The Fifth Amendment prohibition on takings of property unless for a "public purpose" and with the provision of "just compensation" appears to have resurfaced as a limitation on government action. The U.S. courts traditionally have distinguished between exercises of the police power jurisdiction, or regulation, and what may be a taking requiring the provision of compensation. The U.S. Supreme Court in a series of recent cases has, in accordion-like fashion, correspondingly been shrinking what falls within "regulation" while expanding the category of what is a "taking." The magnitude of these decisions is in some dispute, but they do indicate "a willingness to impede the liberal economic agenda" (McUsic 1996: 610). These developments also correspond with recent decisions by international trade tribunals and the published views of international trade scholars.

Seen in this light, the broad scope of the MAI expropriations clause is consonant with these developments, but not all of them. The provisions concerning property in the new constitution of the republic of South Africa offers a less stringent standard for the protection of a class of investment interests. The new South African constitution attempts to distinguish more clearly between what is a regulation and what is a taking, and has provided expressly for the redistribution of land and water rights notwithstanding these provisions. Moreover, the standard of compensation in the event of a taking is less strict than that found in the MAI: compensation is required to be "just and equitable" taking into account a number of factors including the history of the property, amount of state investment, and the property's market value (Schneiderman, Forthcoming). In this way, the South African position is more consistent with the position of countries in the southern hemisphere which, prior to the 1990s, adopted the standard of "appropriate compensation" in contrast to the stringent Hull formula of adequate, effective, and prompt compensation.

III. Conclusion

The draft MAI would have posed a significant challenge to democratic politics at a time when state capacity is being challenged at every front. It is reasonably clear that the MAI, as well as NAFTA and the global web of bilateral agreements, are intended to secure well into the future the ideological politics of the neo-liberal state at the supranational level in the form of a "new constitutionalism." As foreign investors increasingly have standing to sue before domestic courts and international arbitration tribunals, unmediated by the foreign policy goals of party states, those states host to foreign investment will be forced to abandon social policy initiatives that impact negatively on investment interests.

All of this makes the new constitutionalism suspect. While surely providing high levels of stability to investment interests, it destabilizes the capacity for self-government represented by constitutional rules that enable democratic processes to work — the rules of parliamentary procedure, as Owen Fiss calls them (Fiss 1996: 118). While the new constitutionalism resembles the old constraining version of constitutionalism, it also departs from the old in a number of important ways. One way is that the 'people' are nowhere in the equation. Here, the transnational movement against the MAI, much of it conducted over the Internet, suggests new possibilities for citizenship practices to countervail the power of transnational capital and neoliberal ideology (Vallely 1999). These new coalitions, by themselves, only are inchoate forms of self-government and not merely a place of last resort. Citizens in OECD countries still have available to them popularly elected assemblies. It is in these places where the forces of "globalization" are making felt their presence and where displacement by democratic forces, though remote, still remains a possibility.

David Schneiderman is associate professor, Faculty of Law, University of Toronto. Many thanks to Mark Graber for comments.

References

Albrow, Martin, *The Global Age*, Stanford: Stanford University Press, 1997.

Beard, Charles A., *An Economic Interpretation of the Constitution of the United States*. New York: MacMillan, 1935.

Clarke, Tony and Maude Barlow, *MAI: The Multilateral Agreement and the Threat to Canadian Sovereignty.* Toronto: Stoddart, 1997.

Cox, Robert, "Global Perestroika," in Robert W. Cox and Timothy J. Sinclair, eds., *Approaches to World Order.* Cambridge: Cambridge University Press, 1996.

Elkin, Stephen L., "Constitutionalism's Successor" in Stephen L. Elkin and Karol Edward Soltan, eds., *A New Constitutionalism: Designing Political Institutions for a Good Society.* Chicago: Chicago University Press, 1993.

Fiss, Owen M., *Liberalism Divided: Freedom of Speech and the Many Uses of State Power.* Boulder: Westview Press, 1996.

Gill, Stephen, "Globalisation, Market Civilisation, and Disciplinary Neoliberalism" *Millenium: Journal of International Studies* 24 (1995): 399–423.

Globe &Mail, "U.S. Firms Considers Pearson Challenge" 20 July 1994.

Holmes, Stephen, *Passions and Constraint: On the Theory of Liberal Democracy.* Chicago: Chicago University Press, 1995.

Jackson, John H., *The World Trading System: Law and Policy of International Economic Relations,* 2nd ed. Cambridge: The MIT Press, 1997.

McUsic, Molly, "The Ghost of *Lochner:* Modern Takings Doctrine." *Boston University Law Review* 76 (1996): 605–67.

Picciotto, Sol, "Linkages in International Investment Regulation: The Antinomies of the Draft Multilateral Agreement on Investment," *University of Pennsylvania Journal of International Economic Law* 19 (1998): 731–768.

Polanyi, Karl. *The Great Transformation* Boston: Beacon Press, 1957.

Posner, Richard. "The Constitution as Economic Document," *George Washington Law Review* 56 (1987):4.

Schneiderman, David, "Investment Rules and the New Constitutionalism," *Law and Social Policy* [forthcoming].

Schneiderman, David, "MMT Promises: How the Ethyl Corporation Beat the Federal Ban," *Encompass Magazine* Vol.3, No. 3 (February 1999) 12–13.

Schneiderman, David, "NAFTA's Takings Rule: American Constitutionalism Comes to Canada," *University of Toronto Law Journal* 46 (1996): 499–537.

Sornorajah M., "Power and Justice in Foreign Investment Arbitration," *Journal of International Arbitration* 14 (1997): 103–140.

Sunstein, Cass R., *The Partial Constitution.* Cambridge: Harvard University Press, 1993.

U.N. Conference on Trade and Development, *World Investment Report 1998: Trends and Determinants.* United Nations: New York and Geneva.

U.S. International Trade Commission, "Cultural Protectionism and the MAI," *International Economic Review* (June/July/August 1998): 1–4.

Vallely, Paul, "How the Web Saved the World" *The Independent on Sunday* (10 January, 1999) Culture:1.

Wagner, J. Martin, "International Investment, Expropriation and Environmental Protection," *Golden Gate University Law Review* 29 (1999): 465–527.

Witherell, William H., "The OECD Multilateral Agreement on Investment," *Transnational Corporations.* 4 (1995): 1–14.

WTO Secreteriat, "Trade and Foreign Direct Investment," *World Trade and Arbitration Materials* 8 (1996): 37–100.

Weiler J.H.H., *The Constitution of Europe: "Do the Clothes Have an Emperor?" and Other Essays on European Integration.* Cambridge: Cambridge University Press, 1999.

Wolin, Sheldon, *The Presence of the Past: Essays on the State and the Constitution.* Baltimore: Johns Hopkins University Press, 1989.

Endnote

1. This should be distinguished from what Stephen Elkin describes as the new constitutionalist thinking: designing institutions which have a deliberative model of lawmaking at their core (Elkin 1993: 134). On the WTO system and European Union as constitutional regimes, see Jackson (1997) and Weiler (1999), respectively.

Part III
The Multilateral Development Banks

[10]

THE WORLD BANK AT THE MILLENNIUM*

Joseph E. Stiglitz

In the aftermath of World War II and in the wake of the Great Depression (surely one of the underlying causes of the war itself),[1] the countries of the world created three international institutions designed to facilitate economic cooperation: the General Agreement on Tariffs and Trade (GATT), the International Monetary Fund (IMF) and the International Bank for Reconstruction and Development (IBRD). GATT (which has since evolved into the World Trade Organisation) was to work on lowering trade barriers among nations and on preventing the beggar-thy-neighbour trade policies that were seen as a contributing factor to the breadth and depth of the Great Depression. The IMF was to provide liquidity and to sustain the international payments system (the gold standard that was reinstituted after the War). And the IBRD, known more generally as the World Bank, was primarily to facilitate the reconstruction of war-damaged Europe, and then to reach beyond that to aid in the development of what later became known as the Third World.[2]

It is now more than fifty years since the creation of these institutions. Over that half-century, they have evolved enormously, especially in response to changing economic circumstances and changing needs. The 1971 abandonment of the gold standard by the United States (and subsequently by the rest of the world) clearly necessitated a change in the functioning and perhaps in the very role of the IMF. The collapse of the Soviet Union posed a new set of challenges to the international institutions – namely facilitating the transition of the former Communist countries to a market economy. The fiftieth anniversary of the Bretton Woods institutions (IMF and World Bank) was marked by criticism from a vocal international group dedicated to the notion that 'Fifty Years Is Enough', reflecting a view among certain groups that these institutions had done as least as much or more harm than good. As the World Bank has

---

* The views presented here are solely those of the author and not those of any institution with which he is or has been affiliated. The author would like to acknowledge the helpful comments and assistance of Halsey Rogers and Maya Tudor.

[1] The link between economic well being and social and political stability had clearly been of concern to Keynes, one of the key founders of the Bretton Woods institutions. Recall his *The Economic Consequences of the Peace* (1920), in which with clairvoyant insight he saw the dangers of the adverse consequences of the reparations payments being imposed on Germany by the Versailles Treaty. We have, unfortunately, been reminded of this link over the past year. One of the most severe economic downturns of the postwar period is the depression that has fallen upon Indonesia, where output in 1998 is projected to be 16% below its 1997 level (which itself was dampened by the crisis which began in October 1997). It is somewhat ironic that the Indonesian depression was in no small measure caused by the social and political upheaval, itself induced in part by contractionary monetary and fiscal policies that had already reinforced the economic downturn that followed the currency and financial sector crises.

[2] The first 'development' loan was given to Belgium, to help the Congo. See Kapur *et al.* (1997), p. 98.

worked over the past few years to redefine itself, that cry is heard much less often today. Similarly, in spite of considerable hesitancy and a lively debate over the IMF's role and competence, the U.S. Congress did increase its funding, perhaps in the recognition that if the IMF did not exist, it would have to be reinvented.

As the world moves into the next century, it is appropriate to re-examine how these institutions are and should be evolving. I shall focus my remarks especially on the World Bank, but I shall look at that institution through the broader perspective of the global economic architecture. And I shall look at these institutions through the lens of modern public finance, macroeconomics, and development theory.

1. Global Public Goods and the Theory of Market Failures

The Bretton Woods organisations are public institutions, designed to facilitate collective action at the global level. At the time the Bretton Woods institutions were founded, there was not as clear a concept of the role of collective action as there is today. Still, Keynes and his compatriots grasped the notion that there were imperfections of capital markets that might impede the flow of capital, say from more to less developed countries. Keynes and his contemporaries were keenly aware that market economies do not always work well—indeed, the Great Depression can be viewed as the most massive market failure that the world had experienced since the beginning of capitalism. He demonstrated how appropriate government intervention could help the economy pull out of an economic downturn. While at the time his ideas were viewed as radical, they were in a sense very conservative, for they maintained a faith in the market economy: beyond maintaining overall macroeconomic stability, government did not have to play any role in resource allocation. Thus, even at the founding of these institutions, there was a curious blend of a recognition of a massive market failure and a faith both in markets and government—or at least in the ability of government to effectively address the key market failures.

Since Keynes, the intellectual foundations of that belief have been subject to extensive scrutiny. Economic fluctuations in general (and the Great Depression in particular) are the tip of an iceberg, the most dramatic manifestations of the market failures that are pervasive in the economy.[3] But while we have come to recognise that markets are not generally even constrained Pareto-efficient,[4]

[3] For an articulation of this view, see Greenwald and Stiglitz (1987). While it was widely recognised that Samuelson's neoclassical synthesis, arguing that once macroeconomic problems were solved, markets provided an efficient resource allocation, lacked foundations, another strand of thought (real business cycle and new classical theory) tried to develop a consistent intellectual framework by arguing that markets worked efficiently all the time. To be sure, there were economic fluctuations, but these were the efficient market responses to external shocks. While employment did vary, it was only because individuals chose to enjoy more leisure at certain times (like recessions), in response to these changing economic circumstances.

[4] The general theorem is articulated in Greenwald and Stiglitz (1986), who show that when information is imperfect and markets incomplete—that is, essentially always—there exist interventions in the market which respect these limitations and which can make some individuals better off without making anyone else worse off.

there has also grown a greater recognition of the limitations of government.[5] Government and markets are seen today more as complements, each providing a check on, and facilitating the functioning of, the other.[6] The recent failures in Russia have brought home forcefully the importance of the institutional infrastructure required to make markets work. This includes having appropriate legal and financial institutions, ensuring competition and contract enforcement, providing for bankruptcy, and enhancing the safety and soundness of banks. At the same time, public institutions have also made more extensive use of market mechanisms.

The modern analysis of collective action thus *begins* with a discussion of market failures, but then moves on to consider whether public interventions can improve matters, and how those interventions can best be designed. It recognises the presence of agency problems in both the public and the private sector.[7]

We are concerned here with collective actions, and therefore with market failures, at the global level. Here, the concept of global public goods is essential. Following Samuelson's definition of the concept of public goods (in 1954), it became clear that the benefits of some public goods extended only within a limited geographic region. There thus developed a theory of *local public goods*.[8] More recently, it has become clear that there are public goods whose benefits extend well beyond national borders to the global level. These are *global public goods*.[9] Five major examples have been discussed in the literature: economic coordination, environment, knowledge, international security, and humanitarian assistance. Various international institutions have been created to facilitate collective action in each of these areas. As these five public goods overlap to some degree, not surprisingly, so do the mandates of the institutions, a theme to which I shall return later in this essay.

In analysing the evolving role of each of the Bretton Woods institutions, it is necessary to identify their core mission and the market and/or public failure that necessitates collective action at the global level. Why, for instance, might non-cooperative action lead to Pareto-inferior outcomes?

Answering the latter question might not be as easy as it seems. Standard neo-classical theory, for instance, argues that it is in the interests of each country to adopt a policy of free trade: what is sometimes referred to as a policy of unilateral disarmament is a Nash equilibrium. But there is considerable evidence that GATT and WTO have played a central role in moving the world towards a freer trade regime (though they have been more successful in reducing tariffs on manufacturing goods, of concern to more industrialised countries, than in removing trade barriers in agriculture, the comparative advantage of parts of the less developed world). To understand that role, one

---

[5] For a general articulation of this view, see Stiglitz (1989).
[6] This view has been put forward, e.g. by Hellman *et al.* (1997), Aoki *et al.* (1997) and World Bank (1997*c*).
[7] See Stiglitz (1991), Krueger (1987), Shleifer and Vishney (1994), Edlin and Stiglitz (1995).
[8] For early discussions, see, for instance, Tiebout (1956) and Stiglitz (1977 and 1983).
[9] See Stiglitz (1995) and the *Economic Report of the President* (1997) and Stiglitz (1999) UNDP paper.

has to move beyond the neoclassical model. But once one does that, a concern for intellectual consistency should make one wary of returning to that same model in analysing trade policies more generally.

Understanding the non-cooperative equilibrium is important in identifying the kinds of interventions that are likely to be desirable at the international level. For instance, McKibbin (1988) concludes his analysis of the role of international macroeconomic coordination in a context in which countries face inflationary pressures by saying:

> A comparison of policies under cooperation and non-cooperation clearly shows that the non-cooperative equilibrium is contractionary relative to the cooperative equilibrium.

If that is correct, then international cooperative action should attempt to induce countries to take more expansionary policies than they would of their own accord.[10]

2. Core Mission

Today, the World Bank's core mission remains the promotion of economic growth and the eradication of poverty in the less developed countries. The instruments used to pursue that objective have changed over the years, to be sure. Over the Bank's history, the balance of its effort has shifted from large-scale, growth-oriented projects toward projects, programmes, and policy advice that more explicitly incorporate the poverty reduction goal. Individual projects remain the core of the Bank's work, and many of these projects have been shown to be quite successful at reducing poverty and its effects, whether by reducing severe malnutrition in Tamil Nadu, India or by helping spur a dramatic increase in girls' education in Bangladesh.[11]

But the Bank has learned over the years that successful projects are not enough: because of fungibility of funds, the net benefit from financing any individual project is in fact the net benefit of the *marginal* government project— whether Bank-supported or not. Recognition of that fact has led the Bank to an increased focus on whether, taken as a whole, the government's actions and the institutional environment support the goal of poverty reduction. Decisions on the *overall* lending portfolios for the poorer countries (those eligible for subsidised IDA loans) are increasingly based on indicators of macroeconomic and sectoral policies and institutions, as well as governance, because these variables are strong predictors of performance on poverty reduction. And poverty assessments now underlie virtually all of the periodic Country Assistance Strategies that guide our lending programme in each country. It is largely the increasing availability of poverty data, a result of

---

[10] Interestingly, this view seemed to predominate in the early days of the Bank, when the Bank's shareholders were reluctant to provide funds for Belgium, partly because of its exclusively *contractionary* monetary policy. See Kapur *et al.* (1997), p. 98.

[11] See World Bank (1999) for a detailed review of Bank efforts and performance on poverty reduction.

household surveys often supported by the Bank, that has helped make that shift pos-sible.[12]

Even as the Bank has pursued and refined its mission of long-term economic development and poverty reduction however, it has increasingly focused on a multitude of other issues. It has become more involved in post-conflict situations, for example, helping countries recover as they emerge from years of civil war. And as the world has turned its attention to global environmental issues, the Bank has not only integrated these concerns into its development agenda (for example, through mandatory environmental assessments of its projects), but has actively promoted work on specific issues. For instance, the World Bank has addressed concerns about greenhouse gases through the Global Environment Facility[13] and through promoting 'carbon trading'.[14] At the same time, the Bank has also been involved in a number of 'bail-out' packages, which have had the effect of providing liquidity support to countries in crisis.

The core mission of IMF continues to be quite distinct: stabilisation, both of the monetary system and of the world economy in general. Like the World Bank, the Fund too has evolved over time, especially in its assistance to the countries in transition and to less developed countries, in its Enhanced Structural Adjustment Facility (ESAF) programme.

2.1. *Governance*

An understanding of the precise roles that these international economic institutions *ought* to play should reflect an understanding of the market failures that need addressing at an international level—a topic to which most of this essay is directed. But as a preface, let me note that to assess the *actual* functioning of these institutions and their ability to fulfill ideal roles, it is necessary to understand the governance of these institutions. As we noted, modern approaches to the economics of the public sector focus not only on market failures, but also on the capacity of political institutions to address those failures. While the Bretton Woods institutions are political institutions, they are not directly but indirectly accountable to the peoples of the world through the representatives of their governments (the executive directors). In fact, the institutions are not even directly accountable to the chief executives of their 'shareholder' countries:[15] the IMF is accountable to ministries of finance and central banks, while the World Bank is accountable to ministries

---

[12] In Africa, for example, virtually every country has by now carried out at least one such survey, and most have done so within the past five years (World Bank, 1999).

[13] Which helps pay for incremental costs associated with environmentally beneficial projects.

[14] It has been exploring the creation of a Prototype Carbon Fund (PCF), which would facilitate carbon trading at the global level under the Clean Development Mechanism and could be expanded to incorporate trading in emission permits.

[15] Voting rights in these international institutions are markedly different from in the United Nations, where, in the General Assembly, each country gets a single vote, regardless of its size. In the IMF and the World Bank, voting rights are proportional to the contributions of the countries that support those institutions, which, in turn, are related to their GDP. Thus, the United States has the largest 'vote'.

of finance and either aid agencies (in the case of donor countries) or economic ministries (in the case of recipient countries). Democratic accountability has been further weakened as central banks have increasingly succeeded in achieving greater independence, often with the encouragement of the IMF itself.[16]

The World Bank's broad mission of promoting development requires it to work actively with a large number of ministries in each developing country— on environment, labour markets, health, education, judicial systems. This in turn necessitates it taking into account a wide range of perspectives. This has become even more true in recent years, as views of development have changed from a more narrow focus on solving certain technical problems, like lowering tariffs, to a broader one of the transformation of society.[17] In response, the World Bank has attempted to engage not only all of these ministries, but also civil society (which in many cases has proven to be an important agent for change).

Differences in governance structures and in borrowing-country counterparts clearly affect the policy prescriptions offered by the two institutions. Different agencies (and the constituencies they represent, or with which they are most closely affiliated) have different priorities, and those priorities will show up most glaringly when it becomes necessary to make hard choices. Central bankers focus predominantly on stabilisation, or even more narrowly on containing inflation, arguing that such policies are a precondition for growth. By contrast, development ministries—not to mention environment and labour ministries—typically focus on the country's longer-term development, broader quality-of-life issues, impacts of policies on workers, and more broadly, issues of equity and sustainability. What is important is ensuring that any major policy shift be preceded by a full discussion that draws on all of these diverse viewpoints.[18]

2.2. *Special Interests vs. National Interests*

When I served as Chairman of the Council of Economic Advisers, it was clear that different agencies in the government serve (and see as their mission

---

[16] My point here is not to discuss whether there might be advantages that result from independence to offset the presumed disadvantage arising from weaker democratic accountability, but only to focus on some of the *consequences*. Note, however, that while there is some argument that independence leads to better performance of economies in terms of certain intermediate variables (like inflation), there is no evidence that in terms of the variables of ultimate concern, output and real incomes, and their growth variability, that performance is superior. See Alesina and Summers (1993). And even in terms of the former, questions have been raised. Stiglitz (1998 f). Some countries, like India, without independence, but a strong anti-inflation consensus, have pursued low inflation policies. On the other hand, independence of the central bank in Russia has enabled it to pursue a more inflationary policy than the government might have desired. Independence in countries without democratic institutions raises further problems: Had the Indonesians been persuaded to have an independent central bank during the Suharto era, the transition to a more democratically accountable regime might have been even more difficult.

[17] For articulations of these views, see Wolfensohn's address to the Annual Meetings of the World Bank and IMF (Wolfensohn, 1998) and my Prebisch lecture at UNCTAD (Stiglitz, 1998 b).

[18] The section below on 'Overlapping Jurisdictions' will elaborate on this point.

serving) different constituencies. Indeed, only at the very top is there typically much focus on the *national interest*. Special interests are so powerful that even near-Pareto-efficient improvements are frequently blocked.[19] Democratic processes within countries resolve these conflicts, attempting to find policies that accommodate different interests and thereby reach broad consensus. Without such consensus, policies will often not be sustainable. They will be undone with the next change of political winds and, even while they are in effect, they will not yield full benefits simply because of the uncertainty that arises from political vicissitudes.

It should not be surprising then that any international economic agency reporting to central banks and finance ministries reflects the views and interests of those agencies and their constituencies more than it does the views and interests of others. Many central banks do not seek to achieve equitable representation on their boards, and while they may claim that they bear in mind the overall economic interests of the country, they may face tradeoffs in which different groups bear the risks and reap the benefits associated with different policies. Labour unions, financial institutions, and business firms may all look at those tradeoffs differently (in American parlance, workers, Main Street, and Wall Street may each have different views). Indeed, even technical matters—probability judgments—that cannot be cleanly separated out as forming Bayesian probabilities requires the specification of a loss function, and each group has a different loss function.[20]

There are thus real risks associated with delegating excessive power to international economic agencies, and a real challenge involved in making these institutions take positions that are more reflective of stances that might have evolved if they were indeed more democratically accountable. Essential to this democratic accountability is increased transparency and increased public discussion of the positions and policies of these institutions. The World Bank is committed to pursuing policies of increased transparency and public dialogue, not only within the developing countries with which it deals, but also in its own operations.

Agency problems arise at several levels. Not only may an institution not serve the *general interest* and weigh the welfare or perspectives of certain groups more than others, but the institution can actually become an interest group itself, concerned with maintaining its position and enhancing its power. This problem becomes particularly alarming when the power and prestige of an international organisation is pitted against the weak position of a developing country that is appealing to the international community in a time of crisis. Like any prudent lender, international institutions have an obligation to see that their funds are not squandered and will be repaid. Usually, repayment is not so much at issue as enforcing international codes of conduct: democracies do not like to see international institutions, which they created and support, being used to prop up corrupt regimes that immiserate their citizens. But in

---

[19] Stiglitz (1997*b*).
[20] Stiglitz (1998 *f, g*).

both cases, there are elements of judgment calls—what reforms are necessary to ensure, or increase the likelihood of recovery? What reforms could be postponed? What reforms should be postponed?[21] Where does one cross the line, with both the reforms themselves and the manner in which they are forced upon the country, undermining democratic processes and ideals?[22]

Asymmetries of information make it difficult to curtail agency problems. When a particular prescription fails, the doctor always has an incentive to suggest that it was the patients' fault for not following the prescription precisely. One sometimes hears the defence of failed policies that 'the policies were correct, but the implementation was faulty'. But modern medicine has taken upon itself recognition of these 'implementation' problems. Doctors are aware of human fallibility, of systematic problems—such as patients' inability to follow a difficult regimen over a long period of time—and have worked out ways that enhance the likelihood of success (for example, by looking for pills that need to be taken less often). To suggest that the policy of financial or capital market liberalisation would have worked, if only the government had had adequate regulatory institutions, misses the point that few developing countries have such institutions and that those weaknesses should have been addressed prior to the deregulation. To put it another way, consider a traffic analogy. When a single car has an accident on the road, one is inclined to blame the driver or his car; when there a dozens of accidents at the same spot however, the presumption changes. It is likely that something is wrong with the design of the road. The fact that there have been, by some reckonings, financial crises in 100 countries in the past quarter-century suggests that there are systematic problems.[23]

My point here is not an exegesis of the most recent set of crises, or even more broadly, of the policies which might have led to them. Rather, my intent is to point out that those who advocated those policies have an incentive to

---

[21] For instance, consider what would have happened if the United States had undertaken a thorough reform of its preferential taxation of real estate and its misguided agricultural policies in the midst of the S&L crisis in 1989. Clearly, these were distortionary policies that not only interfered with the overall efficiency of the economy, but also were directly related to the real estate boom at the root of the crisis. Yet had those policies been reformed during the crisis, the collapse of a small but important segment of the U.S. financial system would have overtaken the entire system. As a result, one effect of that collapse—the recession of 1991–2—would almost undoubtedly been far more severe. Timing of reforms is critical, and the midst of a crisis was clearly the wrong time for those reforms.

[22] Feldstein (1998) argues that many of the conditions imposed on Korea by the IMF in the bailout of December 1997 crossed that line. For instance, whether or the extent to which the Central Bank should be independent, and whether its exclusive mandate should be the maintenance of price stability, are hotly contested propositions even among economists. They are ultimately political decisions. Indeed, in the United States, when Senator Mack proposed changing the charter of the Federal Reserve Board from its current broad mandate, which includes 'maximum employment, stable prices, and moderate long-term interest rates' (Board of Governors, 1994) to an exclusive focus on price stability, I and others in the Clinton Administration had little trouble convincing the President that, should the Senator pursue in advocating this change, the issue should be made a central one in the upcoming election. The threat sufficed to bury the proposal. Korea did not have a history of inflation, such as might warrant inclusion of such a major political reform as a condition for receiving assistance.

[23] Caprio and Klingebiel (1997). For more extensive discussion of these issues, see World Bank (1998*b*) and Furman and Stiglitz (1998).

defend them as appropriate, as well as an incentive to argue that any apparent failures are the fault not of the policies, but of those who implemented them.[24] It is important to recognise these potentially perverse incentives, for they suggest that the policy framework generally, and the policy prescriptions individually, may be maintained longer than the 'evidence' would suggest is reasonable.[25]

2.3. *Transparency*

Public scrutiny serves a useful function in limiting the distortions and abuses that arise from agency problems at every level. Such public scrutiny is especially important for the international financial institutions, for several reasons. First, in the services they provide, these institutions are monopolists or near-monopolists. Market discipline thus cannot provide its usual check. Even if an institution developed a bad reputation and was often thought to misdiagnose problems, it might be turned to in a time of crisis simply because it was the only game in town. Second, the natural asymmetries of information are large: few outside the institutions and the affected governments[26] have the up-to-the minute knowledge required to assess the accuracy of the diagnosis or the likelihood of success of the therapy. Third, the magnitude of the asymmetries of information is endogenous. There is an especial danger: the institutions recognise their 'market power' in the flow of information, and there will therefore be strong pressures on and within the various international agencies to 'collude' to restrict the flow of information, and in particular, information that might be interpreted as critical of one another.[27] (Indeed, as in other arenas, collusion is facilitated by the need for cooperation and by procedures designed to check some of the natural rivalries that might exist between the organisations.) Finally, as we have noted, the governance structure is such that there is not broad-based accountability.

Natural proclivities for secrecy[28] in the public sector generally are only reinforced by the cultures of the governing ministries and the markets from which they draw many of their key personnel. Central banks have had a long tradition of secrecy, which is only now slowly changing. In financial markets,

---

[24] See Stiglitz (1998*d*).

[25] The tendency of managers with failing projects to delay abandoning them has long been noted in the organisational literature, which has referred to the phenomenon as 'escalating commitment'. The phenomenon appeared puzzling to economists, who repeated the maxim that bygones should be treated as bygones: previous investments should be treated as sunk costs. At each moment, the issue should be, what is the best policy going forward. But the economists' naïve reasoning ignored the agency problem: the manager's personal reputation was at stake. See Jensen and Meckling (1976) and Staw (1981).

[26] One other group typically does have considerable knowledge—the lenders who are part of the bail-out—but they have obvious vested interests.

[27] What may be at stake is not so much the reputation of the institution or agency as a whole, but of particular individuals who have been influential in making the decisions. These individuals have, of course, an incentive to make it seem that what is at stake is not their own personal reputation, but that of the institution.

[28] See Stiglitz (1998*a*) for a discussion of some of the incentives for secrecy at play within public agencies, and the conflict between public and private interests.

knowledge may be the key not only to power, but, more importantly, to money—the real currency of the realm. There are those who argue that public discussions will roil the market; yet there have been no studies demonstrating this and no evidence that the policies of more complete disclosure, such as those recently instituted by the Bank of England, have had any adverse effects on market stability. Moreover, even if there were a conflict or tradeoff between openness and democratic accountability on the one hand and a slight increase in market volatility on the other, it is not apparent to me that such a conflict should be automatically resolved in favour of the markets. Recent emphases on the importance of transparency suggest that there is a widespread belief that greater transparency will actually enhance the functioning of the markets.[29] In general, I suspect that markets respond more readily to fundamentals than to the pronouncements of international bureaucrats, and an increased flow of information should reduce the importance of any particular piece of information. Specifically, it is especially hard to believe that analyses of actions taken in the beginning of a crisis would have much impact weeks later. The standards of disclosure should be at least up to those of the Freedom of Information Acts of the countries with the greatest degree of democratic accountability, with confidentiality exceptions spelled out clearly, and with public debate on these exceptions.

2.4. *Organisational Checks*

While the most important check on agency problems is that provided by public scrutiny, well-managed organisations, aware of these difficulties, can and do design complementary internal checks. The World Bank has several. One of the functions of the Development Economics Center (which is also responsible for conducting research) is to comment on the policies and practices being pursued by the Bank's operations. What is their development impact? To what extent are funds fungible? To what extent does the loan change the way resources are being allocated? Can the project be designed in a way that enables us to extract broadly applicable lessons? Will the country be better off after the loan, enough better off to compensate for the greater burden of debt?

Another group, the Operations Evaluation Department, is devoted to evaluating the Bank's projects. This group reports directly to the Board, and in that way obviates some of the agency problems that would arise if it reported to the Bank's management, whose performance it judges.

The Bank also relies heavily on outsiders—for example, through peer review of its research proposals, an Inspection Panel which independently evaluates whether the Bank has abided by its own chartered policies and procedures, and so forth.

---

[29] It is of course, possible that there may be some hypocrisy in these stances. For a more extended discussion of the relationship between transparency and economic performance, and a discussion of the political economy of transparency, see World Bank (1997*c*), Kaufmann *et al.* (1998) and Furman and Stiglitz (1998).

The questions posed by these various groups are often uncomfortable, but the internal scrutiny serves the organisation, and development more broadly, well.

3. Adapting to a Changing World

While the broad mandate of the World Bank has not changed in recent decades, the way in which it works to accomplish that mandate has changed. In this part of the paper, I want to trace out how changes in the global economy, as well as new perspectives on development, have led to changes in both what the Bank does and how it does it.

3.1. *New Views of Development*

Views about development have changed in the Bank, as they have in the development community more broadly. Today, there is a concern about broader objectives, entailing more instruments, than was the case earlier.[30] Development is concerned not only with increasing GDP, but also with raising living standards more broadly. It is concerned with democratic, equitable, and sustainable development.[31] Development is seen as a transformation of society: a dual economy is not a developed economy, and many of the earlier strategies did little to promote this broader transformation of society. It is true that earlier strategies diverged markedly in their views concerning the role of the state: they varied from the planning approaches that characterised development strategies within the Bank while Hollis Chenery served as Chief Economist, to the focus on trade liberalisation and privatisation in the years in which Anne Krueger served in that same capacity, and later to the emphasis on macro-stability as a series of macroeconomists held the position. What all of these approaches had in common was a belief that solving certain technical problems to achieve a more efficient allocation of resources was the key to successful development.[32] But successful development requires not only addressing these technical issues, but a transformation that puts educational and political development at its centre.

Indeed, there has been considerable questioning of earlier strategies even in their more narrow definitions. While the development strategies of the last twenty years have focused on market-based reforms,[33] they have often failed to

---

[30] See Stiglitz (1998 *d*).

[31] This broader agenda often brings the Bank beyond the traditional domains of economic analysis. There has been some concern whether in doing so the Bank is going beyond its charter, which proscribed it from entering into politics. But it has increasingly become recognised that issues like corruption, transparency and democratic processes have profound effects both on development and poverty. See, for instance, Knack and Keefer (1997), Sen (1997) and World Bank (1997 *a*).

[32] For a brief discussion of these different positions, see Stiglitz, (1997 *a*).

[33] It is clear that the prescriptions that came to be called the Washington Consensus are not sufficient for development, since many countries that followed the precepts have still failed to achieve even moderate levels of growth. Beyond this, there is even a question whether they are necessary for successful development. China, which is by all accounts the most successful of the low-income countries

establish the institutional infrastructure required to make markets work. Economic theory emphasised that to make markets work, both the competition and the incentives provided by private property are necessary. The emphasis on one over the other was not based on any body of theory or evidence. The contrast between the experiences of China and Russia has raised questions about the reform strategy emphasising privatisation over competition: China focused on competition, and saw its per capita GDP increase almost eight-fold in two decades; Russia ignored competition policy, and, even after privatisations and other reforms that were supposed to improve efficiency, saw its output decline markedly. Moreover, privatisations in many countries that did not accompany those changes with effective regulatory and competition policies showed that while private monopolies could more efficiently exploit consumers than could the public monopolies they were replacing, privatisation did not necessarily lead to either lower prices or much greater market access. East Asia demonstrated that successful development was possible, but its leading economies adopted economic policies that differed in several key respects from the orthodoxy often advocated by the international financial institutions.[34] And the East Asia crisis has reinforced the message that weak financial institutions can be as disruptive to macroeconomic stability as can high levels of inflation.

Thus, the broadening of objectives and instruments has necessitated both developing new competencies and re-examining old strategies. What separates more developed from less developed countries is not only a scarcity of capital, but a disparity in knowledge. Bridging the knowledge gap has thus become central to the Bank's strategy (World Bank, 1998 a, b). Less developed countries differ from more developed countries in part because their market institutions that work less effectively. Development strategies must be based on an understanding of why markets do not function well. And while they should work to enhance the effectiveness of market institutions, public policy will be badly misguided if it does not take into account the limitations of markets. Government plays a vital role in providing the underlying institutional infrastructure required to make markets work well. Thus, increasing the effectiveness of the state at the same time that one focuses attention on its basic roles is central to development strategies.[35] All of these changes are based on advances in understanding of economics, including the revolutionary changes presented by information economics and the integration of modern finance into the main corpus of economic thought.

---

and which accounted in aggregate for two-thirds of the entire increase in incomes among the low-income countries between 1978 and 1995, did not follow many of the key precepts of the Washington consensus. For further discussion on the Washington Consensus, see Williamson (1990). Throughout this paper, I have in mind a somewhat different conception of the Washington consensus than the one originally outlined by my colleague John Williamson (1990), who coined the term. As Williamson (1997) himself notes, the term has evolved over time to signify a set of 'neoliberal' policy *prescriptions*, rather than the more descriptive usage that he originally intended in discussing reforms undertaken by Latin American economies in the 1980s.

[34] See World Bank (1993) and Stiglitz (1996).

[35] See World Bank (1997*a*, 1998*b*).

3.2. *Changing Markets*

Changes in the world we deal with have also forced changes in what the Bank does and how it does it. In particular, globalisation—the marked expansion in global markets for goods and capital—has had a profound effect on the World Bank and other international institutions associated with global economic policy. We noted that the World Bank was founded partly on the presumption that capital markets are imperfect, and that without the role of government, there would be insufficient flows of capital from the more to the less developed countries. The World Bank borrowed in international capital markets and relent the money to needy member countries. The high credit rating of the World Bank enabled these countries to tap into the global capital markets at more favourable terms than they could on their own. Presumably, either there were market irrationalities that led private lenders to charge excessively high interest rates, or else the World Bank was more effective in enforcing contracts than were private lenders (or both). In either case, the World Bank represented an improvement in the functioning of capital markets.

The huge increase in the flow of private capital to emerging markets – with long-term flows increasing from less than $50 billion in 1990 to almost $250 billion in 1996 and $290 billion in 1997 – raised the spectre that these capital market imperfections might have been overcome. Indeed, by early 1997 many countries had access at terms comparable to those offered by the World Bank. Even then, however, it was clear that there were large gaps: most low-income countries, especially in Africa, did not have access to international capital markets; funds flowed freely only to a few select countries.[36] And funds were not going to all sectors, but went disproportionately to finance infrastructure projects from which cost recovery was possible. Other sectors that were equally important for successful development, such as health and education, received almost no private funds.

Within the World Bank, this changing marketplace led to a redirection of lending, to those sectors and those countries that did not have easy access to the market—that is, wherever the impediments to the flow of capital seemed to remain important. The Bank increasingly asked itself how could it work more effectively to complement the market, for example by offering credit guarantees that would leverage its limited resources. In recent months, it has been involved in several such credit enhancements.[37] The Bank is in effect testing whether the Modigliani-Miller theorem applies to these transactions, by assessing whether its actions have indeed reduced the market imperfections or have simply led to a repackaging of the risk.

The events of 1997 and 1998 raised, however, some profound questions about some of these large private capital flows. The instability of the flows imposed enormous costs on the recipient countries. While foreign direct

---

[36] While South Asia and Sub-Saharan Africa together received only 6% of FDI and 12% of the aggregate net resource flows to all developing countries, the East Asia region received 44% of FDI and 34% of the aggregate net resource flows. See World Bank (1998e).

[37] Examples from 1998 include credit guarantees for a repo facility in Argentina and for a power plant in Thailand.

investment remained relatively stable, the reversals of short-term flows were both sudden and enormous (amounting in East Asia to over 10% of GDP). At a time when countercyclical investment would have been desirable, private finance for infrastructure projects was cancelled. There thus appeared to be a continuing countercyclical role for the Bank even in this area and in those countries where the private sector had been of increasing importance. The experience in this and previous crises showed that in periods not only of crisis, but also of economic slowdown, the net flow of private funds may quickly be withdrawn from developing countries, often exacerbating their economic weaknesses. The international institutions have a clear role to play in offsetting these destabilising forces of private capital markets.

Changes in global capital markets and changes in views of development interacted to lead to a shift in the focus of activities within the bank. While the Bank has continued to be a major source of capital (with outstanding loans totaling $106 billion in 1998, plus an additional $51 billion committed but not yet disbursed),[38] it has increasingly thought of itself as a Knowledge Bank.[39] Knowledge, it will be recalled, is one of the central international public goods. The accumulation, processing, and dissemination of knowledge in development, as well as working more broadly to close the knowledge gap, is the special responsibility of the World Bank.

The two activities of the Bank are complementary. Knowledge, particularly knowledge about the institutions and policies that make market economies work better, leads to higher returns and better allocation of capital. Recent research at the World Bank[40] has shown that in countries pursuing sound economic policies and good economic institutions—more than half of the developing countries, encompassing a much larger share of the population—development assistance is highly effective in promoting growth. Receiving assistance equal to 1% of GDP increases growth by 0.5%, reduces poverty by 1%, and increases private capital flows by 1.9% of GDP.

The World Bank has a role to play in providing such advice that extends beyond the public-good nature of knowledge. It is, and is widely perceived to be, an honest broker.[41] There is always a concern that there may be a conflict of interest in the private provision of such information—that a private consulting firm may recommend, for instance, provisions of a telecom bill that benefit the firm's other consulting clients more than they do the country itself.

---

[38] See World Bank (1998*c*).

[39] See World Bank president James Wolfensohn's 1996 address to the Bank/Fund Annual Meetings in Washington (Wolfensohn, 1996). For a more extended discussion of the concept of knowledge as an international public good, and the role of the World Bank as a Knowledge Bank, see World Bank (1998*b*) and Stiglitz (1998*c*) and the references cited there.

[40] World Bank (1998*a*).

[41] In fulfilling this role, its multinational nature is important. It does not, for instance, represent the interests of the telecommunications company of any particular country.

3.3. *Dealing with the Country*

The changing, broader view of development has necessitated a change in the way in which the Bank interacts with developing-country borrowers. In the past, international agencies typically insisted on a large list of 'conditions' in return for the provision of funds. On the one hand, these conditions could be thought of as part of the loan contract, just as a private lender imposes conditions the use of funds and covenants that restrict more generally the behaviour of the borrower. But the conditionalities imposed often were quite broad. This was especially true of the structural adjustment loans, which provided funds for overall budgetary and balance of payments support rather than for the financing of a particular project. The conditions negotiated with the country often entailed trade liberalisation, privatisation, and macroeconomic stability—all the elements that were central to the Washington consensus reforms. There has been an extensive discussion of this conditionality: whether the mandated reforms were the right reforms, whether they were introduced at the right pace and with the right sequencing, whether reformers paid adequate attention to the more difficult reforms associated with establishing the institutional infrastructure of a market economy, whether the reforms themselves went beyond issues of economics into politics,[42] and whether the imposition of so many conditions,[43] seemingly without prioritisation, tended to weaken country focus.[44] But these questions are not my concern here. There is a more fundamental issue: was imposing conditionality an effective way of changing policies? There is increasing evidence that it was not—good policies cannot be bought, at least in a sustainable way.[45] Equally critically, there is a concern that the way that the changes were effected undermined democratic processes.

As we go forward, the Bank will increasingly work with each borrowing country to develop a broad development strategy. Like a corporate strategy, it would serve as a vision of where the economy is going and what needs to be done to get there. The Bank would then ascertain where within that strategy it has a role. The focus of the Bank will be on capacity-building and consensus-building: helping the country develop the capacity (including think tanks and research institutions) to formulate its own development strategy and democratic institutions to arrive at a national consensus about those strategies.

Our approach has changed along with our understanding. In recent years, the Bank has increasingly recognised that funds are largely fungible, and that the limited funds it has available cannot by themselves make much of a dent on development. As a result, the Bank has focused increasingly on using its funds as 'leverage'. It does this in various ways: financing projects that can be

---

[42] See, for instance, Feldstein (1997).

[43] On this point, see, for instance, Sachs (1996). Overloading the agenda is of especial concern in those countries with limited institutional capacities. Indeed, there have been complaints that the inordinate amount of time that key government officials have had to spend negotiating these conditionalities reduced the amount of time they had available for engaging in constructive development efforts.

[44] See in particular, Stiglitz (1998*e*).

[45] World Bank (1998*a*).

scaled up, so that the learning from successful projects can be transferred both within and between countries; using financing to help create an environment which attracts private capital; and helping to assess the overall expenditure programme and development strategy of the country, rather than just individual projects.

4. Overlapping Jurisdictions

The recent crises have brought to the fore the overlaps in the mandates of various international institutions, and especially of the World Bank and the International Monetary Fund, as illustrated by the call for the Bank to help provide liquidity support. Issues of overlapping jurisdictions have long been a source of concern—and indeed seemed to have been a worry even at the time that the institutions were created, when some suggested that the duties of the Bank and the Fund should be assigned to a single institution.[46]

Before describing the framework within which the two institutions seek to work together, let me say that such overlapping of jurisdictions does not bother me: the two institutions have different mandates, different foci, and different structures of governance. The Bank, as I have noted, focuses on long-run development, the Fund on stabilisation. Given these differences, it is not surprising that occasionally there may be major differences in views concerning economic policy. What may be good for stabilisation today may hinder long-term development. The design of economic policy represents a balancing of concerns, and it is up to the country to make the political decisions about how the various risks are to be balanced. These are not just technical matters to be left to international bureaucrats, as competent as they may be. And it is important that there be more than one source of opinion, of information, of advice. The benefits of a diversity of viewpoints outweigh the costs of the occasional confusion they engender. Resolving—not suppressing—conflicting views is an essential part of democratic processes. These alternative sources of information provide an important check, especially given the lack of direct democratic accountability.

The recent crises in Asia and elsewhere serve as a pointed reminder of the importance of this kind of dialogue. Clearly, the policy responses to those crises had huge distributional consequences. The countries could have adopted other policies that, if not Pareto-dominating, at least would have imposed less risks on some groups (though perhaps more on others) than did the policies that actually were undertaken. Such tradeoffs are again political; economic advisers should simply provide the information about the nature of the tradeoffs and the risks.[47] This is especially true in those arenas where there is not agreement among economists about the consequences of particular policies. There were many economists who warned, for instance, of the dangers of excessively rapid financial market liberalisation in countries that

---

[46] Mason (1973).

[47] This viewpoint was put forward forcefully by John Neville Keynes more than eighty years ago. See Keynes (1917).

lacked the appropriate regulatory structures. In retrospect, there is now a growing consensus that that advice should have been heeded. Should the countries have been confronted with these alternative views, leaving it up to them to make the decision, rather than imposing such reforms as a condition for receiving aid?

An essential part of the transformation that is called development or modernisation is the spread of scientific reasoning—which distinguishes between evidence and ideology and which recognises the limitations of our knowledge and the high degree of uncertainty associated with many of our beliefs. Pretending that there is certainty where there is none is not only dangerous, but may itself set back the development agenda.

The Bank and the Fund have on several occasions worked toward an accord that delineates more clearly their areas of responsibility. Given the Fund's focus on stabilisation, it is natural that it has taken a large responsibility for macroeconomic issues; given the Bank's responsibility for development, it is natural that it should take primary responsibility for structural or microeconomic issues. But the delineation is far from sharp. Issues of macroeconomics and microeconomics are intertwined, as evidenced so clearly in the most recent crisis. It was weak financial institutions and lack of transparency[48]—structural issues lying within the Bank's domain of responsibility—that were assigned much of the blame for the crisis and that underlay the macroeconomic weaknesses.

But it is not only at the onset of the crisis that structural issues have macroeconomic consequences: the pace and design of corporate and financial restructuring has strong aggregate consequences. A policy of forcing countries to meet excessively stringent capital adequacy standards in too short a period of time may lead to a credit crunch that undermines the economic recovery, and—by increasing the incidence of bankruptcy—may actually be self-defeating. At the same time, the conduct of macro policy clearly affects the ability to pursue structural reform: the difficulties of restructuring weak financial institutions in the midst of depression, when firms are going bankrupt by the droves, should be apparent.

Thus, the two institutions, although they differ in their areas of focus and core missions, have important areas of overlapping concern where cooperative action is required. However, the two institutions do not always speak with one voice, which is not surprising given the differences in mandates and governance structure discussed earlier. To some, this is disturbing: there is presumably only one truth, and the international institutions should be leading the less developed countries toward that truth! But to me, open discussion when there is a lack of agreement seems healthy. We should not pretend that there is more certainty about the policies being advocated than the evidence warrants, and disagreements between the institutions reflect both differences in interpretations of the evidence (including differences in models) and differences in objectives.

---

[48] Though there is some controversy even over this diagnosis. See Furman and Stiglitz (1998).

Ultimately, if we believe in democratic processes, the countries must make the decisions for themselves, and the responsibility of economic advisers is only to apprise them of prevailing views concerning those consequences. We do a disservice in pretending that there is more consensus on these matters than there actually is. Moreover, given the weaknesses in the checks on the international institutions, whether through market discipline or direct democratic governance, it is all the more important that different voices be heard. To be sure, the different voices may give rise to a vigorous democratic debate, which may be uncomfortable to those wishing to ensure that their views prevail, but that is one of the 'prices' we pay for democracy.

More recently, the Bank has been called upon to participate in a large number of bailout programmes. While the Bank's charter clearly provides for extending emergency assistance—there is a consensus that such lending poses the danger of diverting the Bank from its core mission.[49] The main reason it has been called upon in these circumstances seems to be that the crisis countries have needed more funding than is available through the IMF. But if the international community believes that liquidity support through bailout packages is effective and desirable, there seems a compelling case that the community should provide sufficient financing to the institution responsible for carrying out this mandate—rather than diverting the funds and focus of other institutions away from their core missions. Still, in supporting the packages in East Asia, the Bank has worked hard to ensure that its support is directed at areas within its central mandate: helping these countries' long-term growth and development strategies and trying to limit the soaring poverty that has accompanied the economic collapses. Thus, while the Fund has tried to encourage short-term borrowing for adjustment and recovery, the Bank has designed its lending programme for a long-term engagement with the country, because it recognises that, for instance, corporate and financial restructuring cannot be done overnight. The Bank has focused on these restructuring issues, as well as issues of corporate and public governance and the development of stronger safety nets. In Thailand, where weaknesses in infrastructure and education were apparent as impediments to its long-term growth even before the crisis, the Bank has continued to support programmes in these areas. While the Bank's programmes in these countries lie well within its core mission, it has responded to the crisis by designing programmes and providing funds far more rapidly than would normally be the case.

5. Concluding Comments

The past fifty years has shown that development is possible, but not inevitable. If development were easy, there would have been more success stories. As the world enters the next millennium, the challenges facing the World Bank, in its core mission of promoting growth and reducing poverty, remain as great as

---

[49] See, for example, James Wolfensohn's address to the 1998 Annual Meetings of the Bank and Fund (Wolfensohn, 1998).

ever. While there has been great progress in reducing poverty, continuing population growth makes the struggle an uphill one: there are now more people living in poverty than there were fifty years ago.[50] East Asia shows both the potential for success and the fragility of that success. While in the 1970s, it is estimated that 6 out of 10 East Asians lived in absolute poverty (defined as income of under US$1 per day), by the mid-1990s, that number had been reduced to 2 out of 10. But as a result of the recent crisis, the World Bank estimates that the number of people living in poverty in the region will double, from 30 million to 60 million.[51]

The Bank will thus have a mission well into the coming millennium. This would be true even if capital market imperfections were eliminated and capital and financial markets behaved far more stably than they have over the course of the previous two centuries. To be sure, what the Bank does and how it does it will undoubtedly evolve with the continuing changes in the global environment and in our understanding of development—that is, both our views of its objectives and our beliefs about how they can most effectively be accomplished. We have, for instance, learned much from the experiences in reform, from both successes and failures. There is a greater recognition of the importance of the institutional infrastructure that is required to make markets work, of the importance of competition, of the key role that governments play, and of the necessity of strengthening the capacity of governments to perform those roles. Deficiencies in the models of the economy which underlay much past advice have become apparent, and new and more appropriate models have been developed; hopefully, the advice proffered will reflect these new perspectives.

That there will be further evolution in the way that the Bank approaches its core mission seems clear, as greater clarity is achieved on the market failures that give rise to a need for public action and on public failures and the ways to mitigate them.

Over the long run, the success of the Bank will depend on its ability to maintain its focus on the broader role of international institutions: addressing the needs for collective action at a global level.

The World Bank

References

Alesina, A. and Summers, L. (1993). 'Central bank independence and macroeconomic performance: some comparative evidence.' *Journal of Money, Credit and Banking* (U.S.), vol. 25(May), pp. 151–62.

Aoki, M., Murdock and Okuno-Fujiwara, M. (1997). 'Beyond the East Asian miracle: introducing the market enhancing view' In (M. Aoki, M. Okuno-Fujiwara, and H. Kim, eds.) *The Role of Government in East Asian Economic Development: Comparative Institutional Analysis.* Oxford: Oxford University Press.

Board of Governors of the Federal Reserve System. (1994). *The Federal Reserve System: Purposes and Functions.* Washington D.C., U.S. Government Printing Office.

[50] While the percentage of the world's population living in absolute poverty (under US$1 per day) has generally declined since the 1970s, the absolute number of poor has risen.

[51] See World Bank (1998*d*).

Caprio, G. and Klingebiel, D. (1997). 'Bank insolvencies: cross-country experience.' In (M. Bruno and
    B. Pleskovic, eds.), *Proceedings of Annual Bank Conference on Development Economics 1996*. Washington,
    DC: World Bank.
Edlin, A. S. and Stiglitz, J. E. (1995). 'Discouraging rivals: managerial rent-seeking and economic
    inefficiencies'. *American Economic Review*, vol. 85 (December), pp. 1300–12.
Economic Report of the President. (1997). Washington, United States Government Printing Office.
Feldstein, M. (1998). 'Refocusing the IMF'. *Foreign Affairs*, vol. 77 (March–April), pp. 20–33.
Furman, J. and Stiglitz, J. E. (1998). 'Economic crises: evidence and insights from east Asia'. *Brookings
    Papers on Economic Activity.* vol 2.
Greenwald, B. C. and Stiglitz, J. E. (1986). 'Externalities in markets with imperfect information and
    incomplete markets'. *Quarterly Journal of Economics*, vol. 101 (May), pp. 229–64.
Greenwald, B. C. and Stiglitz, J. E. (1987). 'Keynesian, new Keynesian and new classical economics',
    Oxford Economic Papers, vol. 39 (March), pp. 119–33.
Hellman, T., Murdock, and Stighlitz, J. E. (1997). 'Liberalization, moral hazard in banking, and
    prudential regulation: are capital requirements enough?' Stanford Graduate School of Business
    Working Paper.
Jensen, M. and Meckling, W. (1976). 'Theory of the firm: managerial behavior, agency costs, and
    ownership structure'. *Journal of Financial Economics*, vol 3. pp. 305–60.
Kapur, ?, Lewis, ? and Webb. ? (1997). *The World Bank: Its First Century*. Washington DC: Brookings
    Institution Press.
Kaufmann, D., Mehrey and Schmukler (1998). 'The East Asian crisis – was it expected?' Unpublished
    paper. The World Bank and Georgetown University (June 22).
Keynes, J. M. (1920). *The Economic Consequences Of The Peace*. New York: Harcourt, Brace and Howe.
Keynes, J. N. (1917). *The Scope And Method Of Political Economy*. New Jersey: Augustus Kelly Publishers.
Knack, S. and Keefer, P. (1997). 'Why don't poor countries catch up? A cross-national test of an
    institutional explanation'. *Economic Inquiry*, vol. 35 (July), pp. 590–602.
Krueger, A. (1987). 'The political economy of the rent-seeking society'. In (J. Bhagwati ed, *International
    Trade*). Cambridge: Cambridge University Press.
Mason, E. (1973). 'How the Bank came into being'. *The World Bank Since Bretton Woods*. Brookings
    Institution Press.
McKibbin, W. J. (1988). 'The economics of international policy coordination'. *Economic Record*, vol. 64
    (December), pp. 241–53.
Sachs. J. (1996). 'Growth in Africa: it can be done'. *The Economist* (June 29), pp. 19–21.
Sen, A. (1997). 'Development strategy at the beginning of the twenty-first century'. London School of
    Economics and Political Science Development Economic Research Programme Working Paper.
    March.
Shleifer, A. and Vishny, R. (1994). 'Politicians and firms'. *Quarterly Journal of Economics*. vol. 109
    (November), pp. 995–1025.
Staw, B. (1981). 'The escalation of commitment to a course of action'. *Academy of Management Review*.
    vol. 6. pp. 577–87.
Stiglitz, J. E. (1977). 'Theory of local public goods', In (M. S. Feldstein and R. P. Inman, eds.). *The
    Economics of Public Services*, MacMillan Publishing Company, pp. 274–333.
Stiglitz, J. E. (1983). 'The theory of local public goods twenty-five years after Tiebout: a perspective', In
    (G. R. Zodrow, ed.). *Local Provision of Public Services: The Tiebout Model After Twenty-Five Years*,
    Academic Press, pp. 17–53.
Stiglitz, J. E. (1987). 'Imperfect information, credit markets and unemployment'. by Mimeo.
Stiglitz, J. E. (1989). 'On the economic role of the state'. In (A. Heertje, ed.) *The Economic Role of the
    State.* Oxford: Basil Blackwell, pp. 9–85.
Stiglitz, J. E. (1991). 'The economic role of the state: efficiency and effectiveness.' In (T. P. Hardiman
    and M. Mulreany, eds.). *Efficiency and Effectiveness*. Dublin: Institute of Public Administration,
    pp. 37–59.
Stiglitz, J. E. (1995). 'The theory of international public goods and the architecture of international
    organizations,' United Nations Background Paper 7, Department for Economic and Social
    Information and Policy Analysis, July.
Stiglitz, J. E. (1996). 'Some lessons from the East Asian miracle,' *World Bank Research Observer*, vol. 11 (2),
    pp. 151–77.
Stiglitz, J. E. (1997*a*). 'An agenda for development in the twenty-first century.' *Proceedings of the Annual
    Bank Conference on Development Economic 1997* (ABCDE). http://www.worldbank.org/html/extdr/
    extme/jssp043097.htm. April 30.
Stiglitz, J. E. (1997*b*). 'Looking out for the national interest: the principles of the council of economic
    advisers,' *American Economic Review*, May, vol. 97.
Stiglitz, J. E. (1998*a*). 'The private uses of public interests: incentives and institutions'. *Journal of
    Economic Perspectives*, vol. 12, no. 2, pp. 3–22.

Stiglitz, J. E. (1998b). 'Towards a new paradigm for development: strategies, policies, and processes'. Given as the 1998 Prebisch Lecture at United Nations Conference on Trade and Development (UNCTAD). Geneva. October 19.

Stiglitz, J. E. (1998d). 'More instruments and broader goals: moving toward the post-Washington consensus.' World Institute for Development Economics Research (WIDER) Annual Lectures 2. The United Nations University, January.

Stiglitz, J. E. (1998e). 'Reflections on the theory and practice of reform.' Paper presented at Stanford University. September 19.

Stiglitz, J. E. (1998f). 'Central banking in a democratic society.' *De Economist* (Netherlands). vol 146, pp. 199–226.

Stiglitz, J. E. (1998g). 'Responding to economic crises: policy alternatives for equitable recovery and development.' Lecture given at North-South Institute, Ottowa. September 29.

Stiglitz, J. E. (1998h). 'Knowledge for development: economic science, economic policy and economic advice.' *Proceedings of the Annual Bank Conference on Development Economics 1998 (ABCDE)*. Washington, D.C., April 20.

Stiglitz, J. E. (1999). Forthcoming. 'Knowledge as a Global Public Good.' In *Global Public Goods*. United Nations Development Programme. New York.

Tiebout, C. M. (1956). 'A pure theory of local expenditures.' *Journal of Political Economy*, vol. 64 (October), pp. 416–24.

Williamson, J. (1990). 'Latin American Adjustment: How much has happened?' Washington, D.C.: Institute for International Economics.

Williamson, J. (1997). 'The Washington consensus revisited.' In (L. Emmerij, ed.) *Economic and Social Development into the XXI Century*. Washington, D.C.: Inter-American Development Bank, pp. 48–61.

Wolfensohn. J. D. (1996). World Bank and International Monetary Fund Annual Meetings Address 1996, http://www.worldbank.org/html/extdr/extme/jssp043097.htm.

Wolfensohn. J. D. (1998). 'The other crisis.' World Bank and International Monetary Fund Annual Meetings Address 1998, http://www.worldbank.org/html/extdr/extme/jdwams98.htm.

World Bank. (1993). *The East Asia Miracle: Economic Growth and Public Policy*. World Bank Policy Research Report. Oxford: Oxford University Press.

World Bank. (1997a). *World Development Report 1997: The State in a Changing World*. Washington, D.C: Oxford University Press for the World Bank.

World Bank. (1997b). 'Helping countries combat corruption: the role of the World Bank.' Poverty Reduction and Economic Management. Washington D.C. September.

World Bank. (1997c). *Proceedings of Annual Bank Conference on Development Economics*. (B. Pleskovic and J. E. Stiglitz, eds.) Washington D.C.

World Bank. (1998a). *Assessing Aid: What Works, What Doesn't and Why*. World Bank Policy Research Report. Oxford: Oxford University Press.

World Bank. (1998b). *The 1998 World Development Report: Knowledge for Development*. Washington D.C.

World Bank. (1998c). *The 1998 World Bank Annual Report*. Website Address: http://www.worldbank.org/html/extpb/annrep98/down.htm#fin.

World Bank. (1998d). *Global Economic Prospects*. Washington, D.C.

World Bank. (1998e). *Global Development Finance 1998*. Washington, D.C.

World Bank. (1999). *Poverty Reduction and the World Bank: Progress in Fiscal 1998*. Washington, D.C.

[11]

THE POLITICAL ECONOMY OF THE WORLD BANK'S LEGAL FRAMEWORK FOR ECONOMIC DEVELOPMENT

LAWRENCE TSHUMA

International Development Law Institute, Rome, Italy

ABSTRACT

Over the last two decades there has been a renewed interest in the role of law in development. The major player in the new law and development movement is the World Bank which provides advice on, and funding for, law reform projects. The Bank's initial foray into law reform issues was through adjustment programmes intended to push back the state from the economy in developing countries in order to liberate markets. Despite the Bank's claim that adjustment programmes are technical and apolitical, they have a negative impact on the livelihoods of many social groups in the countries implementing them. In the 1990s the Bank has expanded lending for law reform programmes as part of its good governance agenda. It promotes a procedural and institutional version of the rule of law as the most appropriate framework for development. This version emphasizes formal equality and is appropriate for neo-liberal capitalist development. It is unsuitable for other strategies of development which emphasize equity and fairness. The Bank's legal framework also emphasizes the importance of legal sector institutional reforms. This is based on new institutional economic explanations of the role of law in influencing individual and social behaviour. The relationship between institutions and human conduct is not direct and is complex. As a result of interactions between formal and informal institutions, the impact of formal reforms is difficult to predict.

INTRODUCTION

SINCE THE end of the 1980s there has been a growth of interest in development circles in the efficacy of law in the process of development. Undoubtedly this upsurge of interest has much to do with the political and economic reforms that have occurred throughout the developing and former communist countries over the last two decades. In the main, these

SOCIAL & LEGAL STUDIES 0964 6639 (199903) 8:1 Copyright © 1999
SAGE Publications, London, Thousand Oaks, CA and New Delhi,
Vol. 8(1), 75–96; 007099

reforms have called for the rolling back of the interventionist state of yester-year from the economy to make way for markets on the one hand, and to restrict its intrusions into the spheres occupied by civil society on the other. Law has been accorded a pre-eminent role in confining the state to its proper place in the new neo-liberal dispensation. It has come to be seen as necessary for creating appropriate conditions for the market to function, as well as for demarcating the spheres for individual and civil society activities.

At the forefront of this renascence has been the World Bank (the Bank) with bilateral donors and regional development banks as major participants. The Bank began addressing law reform issues in the 1980s as part of its adjust-ment programmes. It expanded its lending for law reform in the 1990s when good governance became part of its development agenda (World Bank, 1992; 1995). Regional development banks also provide funding for law reform pro-grammes (Inter-American Development Bank, 1997; Asian Development Bank, 1998). With the collapse of communism in the late 1980s, bilateral aid organisation also took good governance issues on board (ODA, 1993; 1996; SIDA, 1991; OECD, 1993; USAID, 1994). For many people concerned with law and development, the question is whether the new approach departs from previous approaches (Faundez, 1997; McAuslain, 1997). Has a paradigm shift occurred or has the old been repackaged as something new? If a shift has occurred, what are the distinctive features of the new paradigm? If the old has been repackaged to give the appearance of novelty, is there not a danger of repeating the errors of the past?

This article strives to provide some answers to the above questions. It focuses on the work of the World Bank because it has been the bellwether of the renascence and is likely to remain so as long as the programmes are the flavour of the time. Its global reach, the size of its resources and its purported neutrality have given it a competitive edge over regional banks and bilateral aid organisations. Hence its voice carries significant weight in development circles. This article examines the evolution of the Bank's position regarding the role of law in the process of development. It gives an overview of the Bank's legal framework for development. It examines the Bank's claim that the rule of law is a precondition for economic development. It also questions the Bank's claim that its legal framework is economic and apolitical. In addition, the article examines the Bank's concern with institutional reform. It shows that the framework has been influenced by new institutional econ-omic theories of the role of the state and law in economic development. It cautions against some of the claims made by new institutional economists regarding the role of institutions in the development process.

THE EVOLUTION OF THE WORLD BANK'S LEGAL FRAMEWORK FOR DEVELOPMENT

Until the advent of structural adjustment loans in 1980, the Bank provided project loans to member countries as required by Article III of its Articles of

Agreement. As provided in Article III, s. 4(vii), loans made or guaranteed by the Bank should, except in special circumstances, be for the purpose of specific projects of reconstruction or development. Initially, the Bank financed projects in infrastructure, industry and agriculture. During the McNamara presidency in the 1970s, the Bank expanded its lending into new areas such as rural and urban development projects which were targeted at poverty alleviation. These projects were informed by the basic needs approach to development which was initiated by the International Labour Organisation (ILO) and enjoyed popularity in the 1970s.

In 1980 the Bank introduced structural adjustment lending in response to the secular balance of payment and debt crises experienced by many borrowing member countries in the 1970s (Shihata, 1991: 58). Many of the countries turned to the Bank and the International Monetary Fund (IMF) for assistance. The two Bretton Woods institutions diagnosed the causes of the economic crises as largely endogenous. They argued that the state in developing countries had stunted economic growth through excessive and unwise interventions in the economy. The Bank and the Fund have tended to downplay the effects of exogenous factors and structural constraints emanating form the position of developing economies within the global economy. Hence the Bank's structural adjustment programmes and the IMF's stabilisation programmes were designed to address endogenous causes of the crises.

With the advent of structural adjustment loans, Bank lending ventured into the policy domain of borrowing member countries in what may appear, at first blush, to be contrary to the requirement that loans should be for the purpose of specific projects of reconstruction or development. According to Shihata (1991: 60) structural adjustment lending is legally based on the 'special circumstances' exception in Article III, s. 4(vii). The Bank increasingly provided loans for technical assistance and capacity building projects in a number of fields. While the initial focus was on structural adjustment loans addressing the macroeconomic policies of borrowing member countries, a subsequent shift to sectoral adjustment loans took place.

The avowed objective of adjustment programmes was to create a policy environment conducive to growth and development. Since the coming to power of conservative regimes in the United Kingdom and the United States in the late 1970s and early 1980s respectively and their espousal of neo-liberal macroeconomic policies which were adopted by the Bretton Woods institutions, the policy environment conducive to growth and development was conceived as one which permitted the operation of largely self-regulating markets. Hence adjustment programmes sought to roll back the state from the economy in borrowing member countries. This was to be achieved through conditionalities attaching to adjustment loans which required the retrenchment and downsizing of the state. In the main, the reforms adopted by borrowing member countries called for: the abolition of controls on investment, prices and production; the liberalisation of trade in goods and services; the privatization of public enterprises; and labour and market reforms.

The intellectual justification for the downsizing of the state, the centre-piece of adjustment programmes, was found in public choice theory which has exercised a significant influence on the Bank's development policies since the 1980s.[1] Public choice theory posits 'that the state as an institution, the government as a collectivity and politicians, bureaucrats and other individual actors in political processes each act to serve their own interests' (Killick, 1989: 14). It views 'both societal interest groups and elected (non-elected) government officials as purely self-interested, with the latter predominantly concerned to maintain power by attracting and rewarding supporters and favouring certain groups' (Healey and Robinson, 1992: 51). Public choice theory applies the neo-classical economic assumptions of rational individual utility maximization to the analysis of politics and policy formation (Killick, 1989: 15; Mercuro and Madena, 1997: 85).

From the perspective of public choice theory, the Bank viewed statist policies of the 1960s and 1970s as self-serving and rent-seeking attempts by politicians and bureaucrats to maximize surplus. Developing country politicians were said to be in league with urban interest groups (Bates, 1981, World Bank, 1981). Import-substitution policies of the 1960s and 1970s were used as evidence to show the pro-urban and anti-rural bias. Adjustment programmes were intended to roll back the state, to reduce opportunities for rent-seeking, and to create a market-friendly policy environment. They were also intended to reverse the urban bias inherent in import-substitution policies of industrialisation by changing the rural-urban terms of trade (Toye, 1992). Empirical research in a number of African countries did not find evidence of urban coalitions (Skalnes, 1989; Mosley, Harrigan and Toye, 1991).

While lending for law reform projects was not part of the Bank's original project-based lending, it became one of the new areas when the Bank extended its mandate to policy-based lending under structural adjustment programmes (World Bank, 1995). Until the adoption of adjustment lending, the Bank had interpreted its mandate as excluding lending for law reform projects. Its Articles of Agreement require it: to assist in the development of members by facilitating investment of capital for productive purposes; to promote private foreign investment by guarantees and loans; and to promote the balanced growth of international trade and the maintenance of equilibrium in balance of payments by encouraging international investment (Article I). In the pursuit of the above activities, the Bank is required to take into account only economic considerations and is prohibited from engaging in political activities or from being influenced by the political character of its member's decisions (Article IV). Under adjustment lending, loans were conditioned upon the adoption or implementation by borrowing members of laws or regulations reflecting policies agreed upon with the Bank.

GOOD GOVERNANCE AND LAW REFORM

At the beginning of the 1990s lending for law reform projects was given a fillip with the adoption of the Bank's governance agenda. As defined by the

Bank, governance is the manner in which power is exercised in the management of a country's economic resources for development while good governance is synonymous with sound development management (World Bank, 1992: 1). Since the adoption of the governance agenda, there has been a proliferation of law reform projects in the Bank's lending programmes. New lending instruments for law reform have evolved and they include: project or sector investment loans containing funds for legal technical assistance tasks; free-standing technical assistance and institution/capacity building loans to support the institutional dimensions of structural or sectoral programmes, and to facilitate the build-up and strengthening of institutions necessary for a successful implementation of market-oriented reforms and for economic development in general; and grant funding under, among others, the Institutional Development Fund established in 1992 (World Bank, 1995).

In justifying its governance agenda, the Bank argues that its experience showed that programmes and projects it helped finance may have been technically sound but failed to deliver anticipated results for reasons connected to the quality of government (World Bank, 1992: 1). It identifies a number of factors which impede the effectiveness of adjustment and investment operations. These include weak institutions, lack of an adequate legal framework, weak financial accounting and auditing systems, damaging discretionary interventions, uncertain and variable policy frameworks, and closed decision making which increases risks of corruption and waste (World Bank, 1992: 4). Given the apparent shortcomings of the interventionist state in developing countries which adjustment programmes were supposed to address, the institutional incapacity of the state to implement complex reforms should have been foreseen by the Bank. In the 1980s the Bank was, however, more concerned with the downsizing of the state and the creation of conditions for the market than with the capacity of the state to implement the complex reforms imposed by its conditionalities.

Other factors might explain the adoption of the Bank's governance agenda. The collapse of communism created a conducive environment for the emergence of governance as a development issue. The fall of the Berlin Wall and subsequent events in Central and Eastern Europe discredited the only other remaining major developmental vision. Import-substitution programmes which were adopted by many developing countries in the 1960s and 1970s on the basis of dependency and underdevelopment theories of development and nationalist ideologies had already been replaced by adjustment programmes. Capitalist development was therefore seen as the only credible development paradigm. Hence the end of history thesis propounded by Fukuyama (1992). Unlike most developing countries, the countries of Central and Eastern Europe needed something more far-reaching than adjustment programmes. In many of the countries, the basic elements of capitalist development had to be recreated after a hiatus of half a century. In any event, adjustment programmes had not delivered in most of the countries that had implemented them. Good governance programmes emerged as the elixir for the developmental needs of a supposedly post-ideological and more pragmatic world.

Another factor may have been the growing opposition to adjustment programmes in developing countries. Adjustment programmes had an adverse
impact on the livelihoods of large sections of society in developing countries.
This was documented by organizations such as UNICEF which proposed
mitigatory programmes under the slogan of 'structural adjustment with a
human face' (Cornia, Jolly and Stewart, 1987). In the face of growing concern,
the United Nations appointed a Special Rapporteur to look into the impact
of adjustment programmes on economic, cultural and rights. He concluded
that adjustment programmes had a significant impact upon the overall realization of the above rights and the capability of governments to fulfil and
implement them (Turk, 1991). It is therefore hardly surprising that the programmes generated opposition. For while the interventionist state may have
been guilty of most of the charges levelled against it, in some countries it had
provided a protective canopy for some vulnerable social groups. The
response of the Bretton Woods institutions has been twofold. First, they have
relied on counterfactual arguments which posit that the economic circumstances of the affected sections of society would have been worse off without
adjustment programmes. Second, the Bank began to include funding for
social safety nets in its later adjustment programmes. The impact of these programmes has, however, been limited (Turk, 1991; Stewart, 1992)

Opposition to adjustment programmes was not confined to the affected
social groups in developing countries. The term 'governance' made its debut
in Bank literature in 1989 in a report on Sub-Saharan Africa which, among
other things, argued that the sub-continent was facing a crisis of governance
(World Bank, 1989). That the Bank first articulated its concern for governance in its discussion of development problems in Africa may not have been
fortuitous. In the late 1980s the Bank's adjustment programmes in Africa
were strongly challenged by the United Nations Commission for Africa
which suggested, as an alternative, a programme of adjustment with transformation (Adedeji, 1995; Ake, 1996). It may well be that the challenge
nudged the Bank towards the adoption of its governance agenda.

Another factor which might explain the adoption of the Bank's governance
agenda is the success of the developmental state model of the newly industrializing countries of South East Asia (Hamilton, 1986; White, 1987; Wade,
1990). This offered a counterpoint to the Bank's adjustment programmes.
Ripley (1994: 503) summarizes the features of a developmental state as
including: a state in which economic development is top priority, with
welfare of the population being given little importance; a state committed to
private property and markets; state guidance of the market, as engineered by
an elite or technocratic economic bureaucracy; a bureaucracy that enjoys substantial autonomy, with its autonomy guaranteed by powerful political authority, typically though not necessarily an authoritarian regime. The
developmental state plays an interventionist role that goes far beyond the
limits acceptable to neo-classical theory. While it protects infant industries,
its protection differs from import-substitution industrialization in that it discriminates in its support. It promotes social change necessary to development

by redistributing land and repressing labour where necessary. In the face of growing criticism of its adjustment programmes and the apparent success of the developmental state model, the Bank may have been forced to rethink its prescriptions and to counter those aspects of the developmental state model which called its own model into question.

As argued above, the Bank's Articles of Agreement prohibit it from engaging in political activities. This apparent limitation was explained away by the Bank's General Counsel in a memorandum to the Board of Directors which argued that governance may be relevant to the Bank's work if it is addressed in terms of having good order and discipline in the management of a country's resources. He argued that there could well be a need for the Bank to encourage, for example, civil service reform, legal reform, and accountability for public funds and budget discipline (Shihata, 1991: 53–96). His argument was accepted by the Bank's Board and paved the way for the implementation of the governance agenda including law reform.

THE ELEMENTS OF THE BANK'S LEGAL FRAMEWORK FOR ECONOMIC DEVELOPMENT

The Bank has made it clear that it is concerned with law reform only in so far as it relates to economic development. Consequently, revisions of criminal codes, training of police or judges involved in criminal matters, and management of penitentiary institutions fall outside the Bank's remit (World Bank, 1995: 14). Law reform only matters for the Bank if it has implications for good governance. According to the Bank, some of the symptoms of poor governance are the failure to establish a predictable framework of law and government behaviour conducive to development, or arbitrariness in the application of rules and laws. The above symptoms can be cured by a strict adherence to the rule of law conceived as a system comprising abstract rules which are actually applied and institutions which ensure the appropriate application of such rules (Shihata, 1991; World Bank, 1992).

The Bank makes a distinction between the instrumental dimension of the rule of law which focuses on formal elements necessary for a system of law to exist on the one hand, and the substantive dimension which emphasizes the content of law and concepts such as justice on the other. It settles for a limited concept focusing on the processes of formulating and applying rules. For the rule of law to exist under this narrow conceptualization, five rather formalistic elements have to be present. There should be a set of rules known in advance; the rules have to be in force; there should be mechanisms ensuring application of the rules; conflicts should be resolved through binding decisions of an independent judicial body; and there should be procedures for amending the rules when they no longer serve their purpose (World Bank, 1992: 30).[2]

The first element implies the existence of a coherent set of rules; their communication with accuracy, clarity and effectiveness; and the application only of those rules known in advance. This aspect of the rule of law is said to be essential to the creation of a climate of predictability. The second element emphasizes the application and enforcement of law. It addresses the need for effective administration of law, that is the procedures and institutions for implementing rules. The third element deals with the need for the state to exercise power under the authority of the law. It addresses the issue of pre-scribing and proscribing discretionary power.

Conflict resolution is addressed by the fourth element. The Bank argues that the rule of law loses its conflict-resolving and confidence-inspiring func-tion if there is no independent and credible judicial system to assure that private contractual arrangements are respected and that the law is applied uni-formly by the executive. It further argues that confidence in the enforceabil-ity of agreements is required for the proper functioning of an economy and for conducting efficient private economic activities. In addition, it asserts that unreasonable delays, uncertainty, and high costs in enforcing agreements between private parties all tax economic actors inequitably and damage econ-omic efficiency. The fifth aspect addresses procedures for amending the law. The Bank argues that the rule of law is instrumental in creating a climate of predictability and stability. Rules that are constantly or arbitrarily repealed, amended or waived undermine predictability and stability. Publicly known procedures for amending or repealing laws ensure that laws are not arbitrarily repealed, amended or waived (World Bank, 1992: 28–38).

The Bank's World Development Report for 1997 (World Bank, 1997: 41–5) addresses, among other things, the establishment of a foundation of insti-tutions upon which markets rest. These are law and property rights. It dis-cusses the lawlessness syndrome which undermines three foundations for markets. First, markets cannot develop if property rights are not effectively protected from theft, violence and other predatory acts. Second, markets need to be protected from arbitrary government actions such as unpredictable, ad hoc regulations and taxes that disrupt business activity. Third, markets need a fair and predictable judiciary. A well developed judicial system is necessary for monitoring contracts and enforcing disputes (sic). Once the foundations of lawfulness are in place and where the institutional capabilities exist, the next stage is to address other parts of the legal system which strengthen prop-erty rights. Aspects of law contemplated at this latter stage include land titling and the collaterization of movable property, law governing securities markets, the protection of intellectual property and competition law.

The Bank provides a framework for sequencing rule of law reforms which is predicated on the capability of the state. This is defined as the ability to undertake and promote collective actions efficiently (World Bank, 1997: 3). States with weak capabilities are exhorted to concern themselves with minimal functions of providing pure public goods which include law and order and property rights. States with intermediate levels of capabilities are supposed to introduce laws on monopoly regulation and financial regulation. States with strong capabilities should introduce laws addressing problems of missing markets (World Bank, 1997: 27).

TECHNICAL ASSISTANCE, THE RULE OF LAW AND ECONOMIC DEVELOPMENT

The Bank perceives the legal reforms it finances as technocratic and apolitical in character. It emphasises the constraints imposed by its Articles of Agreement on what it should and should not do. In the circumstances, the Bank argues that its concern is with the procedural and institutional aspects of the rule of law since the substantive elements have political connotations that may sometimes lie outside its mandate. It acknowledges that the distinctions between procedural and institutional aspects on the one hand, and substantive aspects on the other, can sometimes be difficult to make in practice (World Bank, 1992: 50–1). The Bank's story-line is that the choice of the direction of law reform is a decision that has to be made by each country taking into account its legal, social, religious, customary, geographic and historical traditions. While outsiders play a useful role in 'informing' the decision-making process, the ultimate decision rests with the authorities of the country (World Bank, 1995: 9). It further argues that in order for technical assistance to bring about the desired results, the recipient governments need to demonstrate a clear commitment to legal reform and to take full ownership of the legal reform process (World Bank, 1995: 19).

For outsiders, the Bank's claim that its role is merely technical is hard to swallow for two reasons. First, given that the Bank conditions its loans on undertakings by governments of the borrowing member countries to implement stipulated macro and sectoral reforms, the argument about each country making its own decisions about the direction of legal reform does not wash. As Faundez (1997: 3) has correctly observed, 'in practice the distinction between the direction of legal reform – a political choice – and the role of external advisers – a technical function – is not always easy to make'. The distinction is more difficult to make if the external advisers not only hold the key to much needed wherewithal but also represent an institution which has its own agenda of what should be done to achieve development.

Second, law reform by its very nature is a political process involving choices about restructuring social relations and the means of achieving them. As conceived by the Bank, law is an instrument of government for achieving economic development. In this respect, it is an instrument of state power and its making and application involve gains and losses for different groups in society. For example, it was well appreciated by some in the Bank that adjustment programmes would hurt the interests of urban groups who, as a result, were likely to resist their implementation. Conventional wisdom of the time was that authoritarian governments were more likely to implement the unpopular reforms than democratic ones. An influential researcher within the Bank, argued that: 'A courageous, ruthless and perhaps undemocratic government is required to ride roughshod over these newly-created special interest groups' (Lal, quoted in Toye, 1992: 88). Despite its claims to the contrary, by advising governments on, and by lending for, law reform programmes, the Bank is involved in a process of social restructuring which involves the use of state power and is therefore political. As some studies have shown, the advice the Bank gives and the reforms it finances have implications for the manner in which power and resources are distributed in a society (Turk, 1991; Stewart, 1992).

The reason why the Bank has chosen the procedural and institutional version of the rule of law is because it is supposed to guarantee stability and predictability which are essential elements of a climate where business risk may be rationally assessed and the cost of transactions lowered (Rigo and Gruss, 1991: 2). A similar argument was advanced by Weber (1978) who argued that the predictability and calculability in the manner in which the legal system operates were important for capitalist development. Weber saw the predictability and calculability of the way the legal system operated as a function of the rationalization and systematization of law. He associated this rationalization and systematization with the rule of law. Yet as Weber had to acknowledge, the development of capitalism in England did not correspond to his theory.

The English experience is not the only known example. The Tiger economies of South East Asia and the Chinese economy have experienced phenomenal rates of economic growth without relying on the procedural rule of law. As indicated, their model of development has come to be known as the developmental state model. The legal framework of a developmental state has a programmatic and instrumental role in the creation and regulation of market relations and property entitlements. The role of law in the developmental state model is to set out developmental goals and programmes and to assign resources and tasks to selected industries and enterprises. Law thus performs allocative functions. In the Bank's model, the allocation of resources is best performed by the market and interventions are only permitted in the event of market failure. From the Bank's perspective, the capacity of the state is essential for facilitating development through the establishment of institutions that underpin and support market relations. For the developmental state model, the capacity of the state is critical for directing development through state interventions in creating markets, redistributing property rights and allocating resources to selected industries and enterprises.

The continuing Asian economic crisis which started in 1997 is seen by the Bank and the Washington consensus as vindicating its development model including its legal framework. The root causes of the crisis are generally believed to lie in the interventionist policies of the developmental state which sought to give administrative guidance rather than free reign to the market. Developmental state policies are said to have created conditions for cronyism, patronage and corruption. It has been argued that the crisis has highlighted the failure of the region's various rule of law reforms to bring transparency and accountability to the dealings of the ingrown circle of privileged bankers, businessmen and politicians (Carothers, 1998: 101). Undoubtedly, most of what has been said about the incestuous relations between politicians, bureaucrats and business people in developing countries and former communist countries is true. What the Asian crisis does is to expose the limitations of policy interventions in the era of globalised markets and highly mobile capital. What it also does is to call into serious question the replicability of the developmental paths followed by the East Asian countries under current global economic conditions. It would, however, be stretching counterfactual reasoning to argue that the Asian countries would have avoided the crisis if they had implemented rule of law reforms.

Despite attempts to present it as universal, the Bank's procedural and institutional version of the rule of law is historically specific for the regulation of social relations in liberal capitalist societies. The precondition for liberal capitalism is the conversion of all the means of production – land, labour and capital – into commodities whose chief value is their exchangeability in the market. Historically, the process of transforming the means of production into commodities involved the use of coercive state power to dispossess large sections of society. The transformation had traumatic consequences for those who were dispossessed of their means of production and who were consequently forced to sell their labour power in order to survive (Polanyi, 1944). Nascent capitalism requires coercive state power unlimited by the rule of law. The ideology of law and order which is part of the Bank's legal framework for development may provide justification for the use of coercive measures by regimes intent on establishing free market relations.

The procedural and institutional version of the rule of law becomes an organizing principle for capitalism once all the means of production have become commoditized and individuals are perceived as owners of commodities which they are free to sell in the market place. As owners of commodities, they are equal and their relations inter se are mediated through the market. Property and contract are the key legal categories under liberal capitalism. The function of legal procedures is to define, demarcate and guarantee social spaces or a framework where property owners are free to maximise their utilities through the exchange of their commodities. Institutions, including the state, function to protect property and bargains entered into voluntarily in the exchange of property. For a society organised around the exchange of commodities, it is necessary to prescribe the manner in which state power is exercised in order to ensure that it does not destabilise private transactions. This is achieved through the formulation and application of abstract and general rules. To ensure that the state does not infringe on the private sphere of civil society, constitutions grant citizens civil and political rights which are enforceable in courts of law manned by independent judges (Habermas, 1991).

Given public choice explanations that the state serves group interests, the procedural version of law is intended to limit, as much as possible, the extent to which politicians and bureaucrats can use the law to tell individuals what to do and how to do it. It should not, however, be assumed from the above argument that the law is not supposed to lay down what individuals can do and how they can do it. On the contrary, the law can lay down what individuals can do and how they can do it as long as the law's commands facilitate competitive market relations. Thus, the litmus test is whether law's commands are market-friendly (Faundez, 1997: 13). Laws which purport to promote substantive values other than through the market are suspect as they are likely to be a smoke-screen for self-serving group interests and will distort the smooth functioning of markets.

The formal equality of liberal capitalism belies the substantive inequality that is experienced by many. For them, the procedural and institutional version of the rule of law as a legitimating ideology for liberal capitalism proves hollow. What they demand is substantive equality. As a result of social struggles for equality, liberal capitalism was transformed into welfare capitalism. Unlike the liberal state, the welfare state goes beyond merely creating a predictable and stable legal framework for commodity owners to exchange their commodities. Its role includes the creation and equitable distribution of wealth. The welfare state has been under sustained attack since the neo-liberal ascendancy in the 1980s. Its ability to create wealth has been undermined by a process that has come to be known as globalization.

Globalisation implies a degree of functional integration between internationally dispersed economic activities (Dicken, 1992: 1). As a result, many economic activities which used to be performed within national boundaries now transcend traditional barriers. A major contributor to the process of globalisation has been the revolution in transport and communication technologies which has facilitated the cross-border movement of goods, services, information and capital. This has diminished the capacity of the state to control the movement of capital and information. Hence governments have been forced to change their traditional regulatory role from one concerned with control to one concerned with facilitating investment and trade. In a globalised world, transnational corporations are relatively free to shop around for jurisdictions which are market-friendly. They thus engage in what has come to be called regulatory arbitrage. In the circumstances, the capacity of the welfare state to create wealth has been undermined. Recent interest in the so-called 'Third Way' shows ongoing concerns for issues of fairness and equity.

The above historical account should be borne in mind in evaluating the Bank's claim that the procedural and institutional version of the rule of law is a precondition for economic development. Such a claim abstracts a particular historical epoch from its specific context and elevates it to a universal desiderata. Other forms of social development which have emphasised the substantive aspects of the rule of law such as fairness and equality on the one hand, and the subjection of markets to social regulation on the other, are discounted. For many, development is understood as going beyond formal equality. Hence the basic needs approach which the Bank subscribed to in the 1970s as well as the current sustainable development approach which the Bank purports to subscribe to. After the initial excitement, Central and Eastern Europeans woke up to the inadequacies of the formal equality offered by liberal capitalism. Hence the deja vu reflected in the election of former communist parties to power in Poland and Hungary a few years back.

To some, the Bretton Woods institutions are engaged in a mission to replicate liberal capitalism throughout the world (Gray, 1998). This may be a futile attempt given that in its spread, capitalism builds on the social relations it finds on the ground. The result is a global capitalist economy characterised by unevenness and various forms of capitalism ranging from bureaucratic to communitarian versions.

LEGAL SECTOR INSTITUTIONAL REFORM AND ECONOMIC DEVELOPMENT

The Bank also emphasizes legal sector institutional reform as an important element for development. Cotterrell (1992: 48–9) has remarked that the prerequisites for establishing the most ambitious modern assumptions about the capabilities of legislation include the accumulation of state power available for enforcement, the professionalization of interpretation and application of legal doctrine, the institutionalization of elaborate adjudicative processes and the development of efficient legislative institutions. The above issues constitute the Bank's legal sector institutional reform programme. In order to understand the Bank's interest in legal sector institutional reform, it is necessary to look at new institutional economic theories of the role of law in economic performance. The new institutional economic paradigm has exercised a significant influence on the Bank's development work in the 1990s, including its legal framework for development.[3]

According to Blaug (1992: 109–10), institutionalism as an economic methodology relies on a mode of explanation called pattern modelling because it seeks to explain events or actions by identifying their place in a pattern of relationships that is said to characterize the economic system as a whole. Institutionalists subscribe to the idea of group behaviour under the influence of custom and habit, preferring to view the economic system more as a biological organism than as a machine. Leys (1996: 36) observes that that new institutional economics is 'supposed to rest on the assumption of rational individuals maximizing their utilities and nothing more, and should (in its most optimistic version, at least) be capable of being integrated with economics and modelled mathematically'. It would appear that new institutional economics attempts to combine the explanatory power and methodological advantages of institutionalism's holistic approach on the one hand with those of neo-classical economics' atomistic approach on the other.

The central claim of new institutional economics is that economic performance hinges on institutions (North, 1990; Picciotto and Wiesner, 1998). This is captured in the new institutionalist mantra that institutions matter. North (1990: 3) defines institutions as 'the rules of the game in a society or, more formally, the humanly devised constraints that shape human interaction'. For Nugent (1998: 9) 'an institution is a set of constraints that governs the behavioural relations among individuals and groups'. In some definitions, institutions include organizations (Nugent, 1998) while in others they exclude them (North, 1990). Examples of institutions include conventions, codes of conduct, norms of behaviour, statute law and common law, property rights and contracts. They may be formal or informal; and they may be created or they may develop over time.

It has been argued that new institutional economics broadens the neo-classical model to deal with situational constraints by recognizing the crucial role of institutions, organizations and political economy restrictions (Wiesner, 1998: xi). Mercuro and Madena (1997: 130–1) identify two fundamental building blocks for new institutional economics. The first is that individuals are assumed to rationally pursue their self-interest subject to constraints which include the definition and existence of property rights and transaction costs, as well as the recognition of the limited computational capacity of the human mind – the so-called bounded rationality postulate. The second building block is the idea of wealth maximization – the search for institutional structures that enhance society's wealth-producing capacity.

The key analytical concepts of new institutional economics are property rights, contracting and transaction costs. Property rights are social institutions that determine the value of an asset by setting the range of its productivity or exchangeability. Contracting is the process through which property rights are established, assigned or modified (Mercuro and Madena, 1997: 131). New institutional economics draws a distinction between the process of physically transferring the asset and the transacting process through which legal rights to the asset are transferred. New institutional economists argue that in many developing and former communist countries, the absence of institutions such as security of property rights and the enforceability of contracts leads people to rely on self-enforcing contracts where the physical transfer of assets occurs at the same time as the transacting process. In these countries, contracts which are not self-enforcing depend on private reputation. They argue that economic development depends on transactions which are not self-enforcing. Transaction costs are the costs associated with the creation, maintenance, or modification of institutions, such as property rights (Mercuro and Madena, 1997: 131). They are the costs associated with negotiating, measuring and protecting property rights, and monitoring and enforcing contracts.

Transaction costs create uncertainty for those engaging in exchange. There is the risk that a party to a contract might engage in opportunistic behaviour and might not perform their side of the agreement. It is therefore necessary to have an institutional framework which minimizes risks and uncertainties associated with exchange. The state provides that institutional framework. It has been argued that: 'Without the state, its institutions, and the supportive framework for property rights, high transaction costs will paralyze complex production systems, and specific investments in long-term exchange relationships will not be forthcoming' (Eggertsson, 1990: 317, quoted in Mercuro and Madena, 1997: 136). Wiesner (1998: xi–xii) argues that the state is the most critical institution because of its comparative advantage to promote collective action at least cost to society. He adds that if the government fails to provide the institutional infrastructure (information, property rights, governance) within which competitive markets can thrive, it becomes extremely difficult to overcome development constraints.

Incentives play an important part in new institutional economic analysis. 'Institutions matter because incentives trigger motivation and action in both public and private sectors' (Wiesner, 1998: xii). Institutional economics purports to show how law structures incentives, influences human behaviour and, consequently, economic activity. Institutions such as law and property rights minimise transaction costs and therefore structure incentives that shape economic behaviour and performance. Equally, institutions such as courts which enforce contracts create stability and reduce transaction costs thus providing incentives to economic actors. Changing the institutional framework results in a change in the incentive structure which in turn triggers motivation and action. Undoubtedly this explains the attractions of new institutional economic theory of the role of law for the Bank. Hence the important role accorded to institutional reform within the Bank's legal framework for development.

INSTITUTIONAL REFORM AND DEVELOPMENT: A FEW PERTINENT QUESTIONS

The Bank's legal sector institutional reform programme focuses on the enforcement of laws, the professionalization of interpretation and application of legal doctrine, the institutionalization of adjudicative processes, and the development of efficient legislative institutions on the basis of the discredited assumptions of the law and development movement of the 1960s as well as the new institutional economic explanations of the role of law in influencing human behaviour. Shihata (1995: 130) argues that the law and development movement has demonstrated that law, though normally a reflection of the prevailing political, social, cultural, economic, financial and other realities of a given society, can also be used as a proactive instrument to further promote development. The truth of the matter is that the old law and development movement went into a crisis because it discovered that the instrumental role of law did not work or produced unintended consequences.[4] New institutional economic explanations of the role of law in shaping human behaviour raise a number of methodological and theoretical questions.

The interrelationship between social constraints and individual human behaviour has a long history in the social sciences. The structure–agency relationship in sociology and the culture–structure relationship in anthropology have dealt with concerns similar to those of new institutional economics. The apparent contribution that new institutional economics makes is the capability of modelling mathematically the interrelationship between institutions and human behaviour. There are, however, a number of methodological and theoretical issues which call for caution. The 'rules of the game' definition so beloved by new institutional economists is very vague. It may be argued that the legal framework for development is based on a limited number of institutions – property rights, contracts, and transaction costs. While this is true, it raises issues about the choice of these institutions. Leys (1996: 39) has noted a tendency 'to argue that, because some aspect of observed reality can be modelled, that aspect is determinative or a key one'.

Nugent (1998: 9–10) has identified a number of methodological difficulties. These relate to the difficulties of identifying the determinants of institutions because of the multidimensional nature of their definition; differences in scale or level of institutions; the variations in sources of institutions; the infrequency of institutional change; and the fact that the determinants of many institutions may have occurred so long ago that the relevant data are difficult or impossible to obtain and relevant questions cannot be defined. Then there is the related problem of identifying the effects of institutions. Another difficulty arises when different institutions are functionally interdependent making it difficult to separate determinants from effects and to identify the direction of causality. Nugent points out that the link between institutions and development is not necessarily a simple and direct one.

Given the above difficulties, new institutional economists have been unable to conduct empirical tests of the influence of institutions on development. This has not, however, deterred them from carrying out proxy tests. One such test which was conducted by economists at the Bank sought to measure the relationship between the quality of institutions and economic development (World Bank, 1997; Chhibber, 1998: 39–41). It involved a survey of over 3600 local forms in 69 countries. The survey sought to get an idea of the private sector's perception of the institutional environment. The two key indicators that the survey relied upon were the predictability of rule making and the perception of political stability. The survey concluded that there was a correlation between the quality of a country's institutions and economic development. Be that as it may, correlation is not synonymous with causality. The relationship between the quality of institutions and economic development could be mutually reinforcing. Economic development might lead to better institutions as much as better institutions might result in better economic growth.

One of the central claims of new institutional economics and the Bank's legal framework is that law structures incentives and therefore influences behaviour and economic performance. While many people would not deny that individuals act in a rational manner, many would question the postulate that individuals only act to maximise utility albeit under constraints imposed by the limited computational capacity of the human mind. Weber (1978: 24–6) identified four ways of orienting social action: instrumentally rational, value-rational, affectual and traditional. As he observed, it would be unusual to find concrete cases of social action which were oriented only in one or another of these ways. The different ways are ideal types. Thus an explanation which gives pride of place to strategic action and excludes other ways of orienting action provides explanations whose validity can only be partial. For Bourdieu (1990: 190), the source of social action lies in the interaction between institutions and the habitus which is a lived environment comprising practices, understandings, inherited expectations and customs. The habitus comprises psychological, sociological, cultural as well as physical elements. In this respect, it is very complex and is unlikely to be amenable to modelling.

The Bank's legal institutional reform focuses on formal law and its institutional framework. Legal pluralism has long highlighted the diversity of normative orders or semi-autonomous fields which interact and overlap with formal law and its institutional framework.[5] These normative orders or semi-autonomous social fields are capable of rule setting and rule enforcement. They thus influence behaviour. Moreover, their interaction with formal law may produce results quite different from those intended by the authorities. The unintended consequences of land titling in Kenya come to mind. Kenya's land reform programme was initiated by the colonial administration in the 1950s and involved attempts to transform indigenous tenure through the consolidation of fragmented peasant holdings and registration. The objective of the reforms was to convert land into a commodity. The reforms were continued after independence. Contrary to expectations, land has continued to be subdivided for inheritance purposes, and most of the subdivisions have gone unrecorded thus making nonsense of the registers. The land reforms floundered against customary usage (Bruce, 1986; Barrows and Roth, 1990).

New institutional economics does acknowledge the role of informal institutions. It would, however, appear that because informal institutions do not lend themselves to modelling, they have not enjoyed as much attention from new institutionalists and the Bank as formal institutions. In the literature, informal institutions have been associated with the concept of social capital (Serageldin and Grootaert, 1998). The concept of social capital was developed by Bourdieu (1977; 1986; 1987). He defined it as consisting of 'resources based on connections and group membership' (1987: 3–4). Putnam (1993: 163–85) sees social capital as inhering in horizontal social relationships rather than in vertical relationships. The examples of social capital he gives are 'norms of reciprocity', 'networks of civic engagement' and 'trust'. In his view, these forms of social capital are found in horizontal social relationships such as tower societies, guilds, mutual aid societies, co-operatives, unions, soccer clubs and literary societies. Putnam argues that social capital undergirds economic and institutional performance. Ellickson (1997) sees social capital as consisting of two components: the stock of previous co-operation among members and the presence of a credible system for enforcing norms through self-help and other non-legal means.

The conclusions of Putnam's empirical study of the reform of political institutions in Italy have important implications for institutional reform. His first conclusion is that: '*Social context and history profoundly conditions the effectiveness of institutions*' (1993: 182, original emphasis). His argument is that institutions perform far better in regions rich in social capital than in those poor in social capital. His second conclusion is that '*changing formal institutions can change political practice'* (1993: 184, original emphasis). The final conclusion is that *'most institutional history moves slowly'*. Where institution building (and not merely constitution writing) is concerned, time is measured in decades' (1993: 184, original emphasis). Ellickson (1997) argues against attempts by the state or an international organisation such as the World Bank to nurture social capital from above. In his view, such efforts are paradoxical because they attempt to use hierarchical planning to improve spontaneous social structures. These are sobering conclusions. They reinforce the argument that informal institutions may interact with formal institutional reforms in ways that produce results different from those contemplated by the architects of the reforms. They cast doubt on explanations which purport to predict responses to institutional and legal reforms. Finally, they bring out the long-term nature of institutional reforms.

Another problematic issue with new institutional economic explanations of law and the Bank's legal framework is their use of the efficiency criterion to evaluate law. While efficiency is a central principle in economic analysis, it is not a legal principle. The question is whether legal reforms should use the efficiency criterion in justifying a particular law over another. Mercuro and Madena (1997: 184–7) identify a number of problematic issues arising out of the application of the efficiency criterion to law. First, they question the ability of economists to render meaningful efficiency judgements on the grounds that since wealth itself is a function of rights, there is no unique wealth-maximising result; any such result is relative to the initial distribution of entitlements. Efficiency analysis therefore takes for granted what is at issue.

Second and more important, they point out that some critics have argued that the wealth-maximisation criterion favours those who already have wealth, with the result that the invocation of the efficiency norm merely serves to reinforce the existing power relations within the economic system and makes the market system the arbiter of rights. A more fundamental issue they raise is whether efficiency should be the principle, or one of the principles, to be used in determining the basic ordering of society. If the answer is in the affirmative, the next question relates to the weight that should be given to efficiency when it conflicts with other ethical and/or political principles. Unlike economics which is concerned with efficiency, law is concerned with principles of equity and justice.

Undoubtedly, it would be unwise for law reformers to ignore efficiency concerns, especially in the area of economic law reform. The point to emphasise, however, is that efficiency should not be used to trump other fundamental concerns such as equity and fairness which provide law with its legitimacy. Efficiency concerns tend to disregard the distributional dimensions of reforms. The experience of adjustment programmes shows that a singular concern with efficiency has harmful consequences for many sections of society. Ultimately, efficiency cannot provide a legitimating ideology for reforms.

Conclusion

In the last decade the World Bank has become increasingly concerned with the role of law in the development process. The first wave of reforms was part and parcel of adjustment programmes and was intended to roll back the state from the economy. Adjustment programmes had a negative impact on the livelihoods of large sections of society in developing countries. Despite the Bank's claim to the contrary, legal reforms associated with adjustment programmes had significant political implications in developing countries. They contributed to the disempowerment of large sections of society. The second phase of reforms has been associated with the Bank's governance agenda. The Bank has designed a legal framework for development which revolves around a procedural and institutional version of the rule of law. This version of the rule of law which emphasizes formal equality in the market place is appropriate for liberal capitalism. The version is suited to the needs of a neo-liberal economic development strategy that hinges on largely self-regulating markets. Other development strategies have appreciated that self-regulating markets are not benign in their operations. Hence the presence of strategies such as the basic needs approach and the sustainable development approach which have emphasised substantive equality and fairness.

The Bank's legal framework for development also emphasises the role of legal institutional reform in structuring incentives and influencing individual and social behaviour. The relationship between institutions and human behaviour is not so clear cut. While there may be a correlation between institutions and economic development, it should be remembered that correlation is not synonymous with causality – the impact of formal reforms cannot be predicted with precision. The interaction between formal and informal institutions may produce unintended consequences. The above methodological and theoretical issues call into question some of the claims made by new institutional economists and the Bank about the role of law in development. When all is said and done, the new programmes on law and development have the hallmarks of the old ones.

Notes

The views expressed in this article are those of the author and do not represent the official views of the International Development Law Institute.

1. See for example the striking similarities between the World Bank's report on Sub-Saharan Africa (World Bank, 1981) and the work of Robert Bates (Bates, 1981) one of the leading public choice theorists. Leys (1996: 80) points out that the Banks World Development Report for 1986 which focused on agricultural policy adopted Bates' analysis without qualification and summarized it virtually word for word.
2. Fuller (1969) made a similar argument. He argued that a number of procedural purposes must exist before a legal system could be said to be in operation. He

argued that legal norms must be general, publicly promulgated, sufficiently prospective, intelligible, free of contradictions, sufficiently constant, congruently administered, and must not require the impossible.

3. This quite evident from reading the World Bank's Development Report for 1997 (World Bank, 1997) and Picciotto and Wiesner (1998).
4. For an excellent summary of the crisis of the law and development movement, see Faundez (1997).
5. For an excellent review of legal pluralism, see Engle-Merry (1988).

REFERENCES

Adedeji, A. (1995) 'Economic Progress: What Africa Needs', pp. 226–42 in K. Mengistaeb and B. I. Logan (eds) *Beyond Economic Liberalization in Africa*. Cape Town: SAPES.

Ake, C. (1996) *Democracy and Development in Africa*. Washington DC: The Brookings Institute.

Asian Development Bank (1998) *Law and Development at the Asian Development Bank, Office of the General Counsel*. Manila: Asian Development Bank.

Barrows, R. and Roth, M. (1990) 'Land Tenure and Investment in African Agriculture: Theory and Evidence', *Journal of Modern African Studies*, 28(2): 265–97.

Bates, R. (1981) *Markets and States in Africa*. Berkeley: University of California Press.

Blaug, M. (1992) *The Methodology of Economics*. Cambridge: Cambridge University Press.

Bourdieu, P. (1977) *Outline of a Theory of Practice*. Cambridge: Cambridge University Press.

Bourdieu, P. (1986). 'Forms of Capital', pp. 241–58 in J. G. Richardson (ed.) *Handbook of Theory and Research for Sociological Education*. New York: Greenwood.

Bourdieu, P. (1987) 'What Makes a Social Class? On the Theoretical and Practical Existence of Groups', *Berkeley Journal of Sociology* 32: 1–18.

Bourdieu, P. (1990) *In Other Words: Essays Toward a Reflexive Sociology*. Cambridge: Polity.

Bruce, J. W. (1986) 'Land Tenure Issues in Project Design and Strategies for Agricultural Development in Sub-Saharan Africa', Land Tenure Center, LTC Paper No. 128, University of Wisconsin-Madison.

Carothers, T. (1998) 'The Rule of Law Revival', *Foreign Affairs* 77, 2(1): 95–106.

Chhibber, A. (1998), 'Institutions, policies, and development outcomes', pp. 34–46 in R. Picciotto and E. Wiesner (eds) *Evaluation and Development: The Institutional Dimension*. New Brunswick (USA) and London: Transaction Publishers.

Cornia, G. A., Jolly, R. and Stewart, F. (1987) *Adjustment with a Human Face: Protecting the vulnerable and promoting growth*. Oxford: Oxford University Press.

Cotterrell, R. B. M. (1992) *Sociology of Law*. London: Butterworth Law.

The Economist (1997) 'Time to Roll Out a New Model', Vol. 347 Number 8062, March 1–7. London: The Economist Newspaper Ltd., pp. 83–4.

Dicken, P. (1992) *Global Shift: The Internationalization of Economic Activity*. New York and London: The Guilford Press.

Ellickson, R. C. (1997) 'Comment on "Contracting, Enforcement, and Efficiency: Economics beyond the Law" by Avner Greif', *Annual World Bank Conference on Development 1996*, 266–70.

Engle-Merry, S. (1988) 'Legal Pluralism', *Law and Society Review* 22: 869–96.
Faundez, J. (1997) 'Legal Technical Assistance', pp. 1–24 in J. Faundez (ed.) *Good Government and Law: Legal and Institutional Reform in Developing Countries*. Basingstoke and London: Macmillan Press.
Fukuyama, F. (1992) *The End of History and the Last Man*. New York: Free Press.
Fuller, L. (1969) *The Morality of Law*. New Haven: Yale University Press.
Gray, J. (1998) *False Dawn: The Delusions of Global Capitalism*. London: Granta Books.
Habermas, J. (1991) *The Structural Transformation of the Public Sphere: An Inquiry into a Category of Bourgeois Society*. Cambridge, Massachusetts: MIT Press.
Hamilton, C. (1986) *Capitalist Industrialisation in Korea*. Boulder: Westview.
Healey, J. and Robinson, M. (1992) *Democracy, Governance and Economic Policy: Sub-Saharan Africa in Comparative Perspective*. London: Overseas Development Institute.
Inter-American Development Bank (1997) *Modernization of the State and Strengthening of Civil Society*. Washington DC: Strategic Planning and Operational Policy Department.
Killick, T. (1989) *A Reaction Too Far: Policy and the Role of the State in Developing Countries*. London: Overseas Development Institute.
Leys, C. (1996) *The Rise and Fall of Development Theory*. Nairobi: EAEP.
McAuslain, P. (1997) 'Law, Governance and the Development of the Market: Practical Problems and Possible Solutions', pp. 25–50 in J. Faundez (ed.) *Good Government and Law: Legal and Institutional Reform in Developing Countries*. Basingstoke and London: Macmillan Press.
Mercuro, N. and Madena, S. G. (1997) *Economics and Law: From Posner to Post-Modernism*. Princeton, New Jersey: Princeton University Press.
Mosley, P., Harrigan, J. and Toye, J. (1991). *Aid Power: The World Bank and Policy-Based Lending in the 1980s* (2 volumes). London: Routledge.
North, D. C. (1990) *Institutions, Institutional Change and Economic Performance*. Cambridge: Cambridge University Press.
Nugent, J. (1998) 'Institutions, markets and development outcomes', pp. 7–23 in R. Picciotto and E. Wiesner (eds) *Evaluation and Development: The Institutional Dimension*. New Brunswick (USA) and London: Transaction Publishers.
Overseas Development Administration (1993) *Taking Account of Good Government*. London: ODA.
Overseas Development Administration (1996) *Law, Good Government and Development: A Guidance Paper*. London: ODA.
OECD (1993) *DAC Orientations on Participatory Development and Good Governance*. Paris: OECD.
Picciotto, R. and Wiesner, E. (eds) (1998) *Evaluation and Development: The Institutional Dimension*. New Brunswick (USA) and London: Transaction Publishers.
Polanyi, K. (1944) *The Great Transformation: The Political and Economic Origins of Our Time*. Boston: Beacon Press.
Putnam, R. D. (1993) *Making Democracy Work: Civic Traditions in Modern Italy*. Princeton, New Jersey: Princeton University Press.
Rigo, A. and Gruss, H. J. (1991) *The Rule of Law*. Washington DC: World Bank Legal Department.
Ripley, J. (1994) 'New Directions in the Political Economy of Development', *Review of African Political Economy* 62: 495–510.
Sarageldin, I. and Grootaert, C. (1998) 'Defining social capital: an integrating view', pp. 203–17 in R. Picciotto and E. Wiesner (eds) *Evaluation and Development: The Institutional Dimension*. New Brunswick (USA) and London: Transaction Publishers.

Shihata, I. F. I. (1991) *The World Bank in a Changing World: Selected Essays Vol. I.* Dordrecht, Boston, London: Martinus Nijhoff Publishers.

Shihata, I. F. I. (1995) *The World Bank in a Changing World: Selected Essays Vol. II.* The Hague, Boston, London: Martinus Nijhoff Publishers.

Shihata, I. F. I. (1997) *Complimentary Reform: Essays on Legal, Judicial and Other Institutional Reforms Supported by the World Bank.* The Hague: Kluwer Law International.

SIDA (1991) *Making Government Work.* Stockholm: SIDA.

Skalnes, T. (1989) 'Group Interests and the State: An Explanation of Zimbabwe's Agricultural Policies', *Journal of Modern African Studies* 27(1): 85–107.

Stewart, F. (1992) 'The Many Faces of Adjustment', pp. 176–231 in P. Mosley (ed.) *Development Finance and Policy Reform: Essays in the Theory and Practice of Conditionality in Less Developed Countries.* New York: St Martin's Press.

Toye, J. (1992) 'Interest Group Politics and the Implementation of Adjustment Policies in Sub-Saharan Africa', pp. 176–231 in P. Mosley (ed.) *Development Finance and Policy Reform: Essays in the Theory and Practice of Conditionality in Less Developed Countries.* New York: St Martin's Press.

Turk, D. (1991) *The Realisation of Economic, Social and Cultural Rights.* United Nations, E/CN.4/sub.2/1991/17.

USAID (1994) *Weighing in on the Scales of Justice: Strategic Approaches to Donor-Supported Rule of Law Programs.* Washington DC: USAID Office of Evaluation.

Wade, R. (1990) *Governing the Market: Economic Theory and the Role of Government in East Asian Industrialisation.* Princeton, New Jersey: Princeton University Press.

Weber, M. (1978) *Economy and Society*, Vols 1 and 2. Berkeley, Los Angeles and London: University of California Press.

White, G. (1987) *Developmental States in East Asia.* New York: St Martin's Press.

Wiesner, E. (1998) 'Introduction', pp. xi–xiv in R. Picciotto and E. Wiesner (eds) *Evaluation and Development: The Institutional Dimension.* New Brunswick (USA) and London: Transaction Publishers.

World Bank (1981) *Accelerated Development in Sub-Saharan Africa: An Agenda for Action.* Washington DC: The World Bank.

World Bank (1989) *Sub-Saharan Africa: From Crisis to Sustainable Growth – A Long Term Perspective.* Washington DC: The World Bank.

World Bank (1992) *Governance and Development.* Washington DC: The World Bank.

World Bank (1995) 'The World Bank and Legal Technical Assistance: Initial Lessons, Policy Research Paper 1414'. Washington DC: The World Bank.

World Bank (1996) *World Development Report 1996: From Plan to Market.* Oxford: Oxford University Press.

World Bank (1997) *World Development Report 1997: The State in a Changing World.* Oxford: Oxford University Press.

[12]

EVOLUTION OF THE GOVERNING LAW FOR LOAN AGREEMENTS OF THE WORLD BANK AND OTHER MULTILATERAL DEVELOPMENT BANKS

By John W. Head*

I. INTRODUCTION

The Issues and Their Importance

What is the governing law for loan agreements entered into by the World Bank[1] and other multilateral development banks (MDBs) in carrying out their public sector lending? That question was first definitively addressed about thirty-five years ago.[2] This article examines the question anew, against the backdrop of recent developments in practice, especially at the newest of the MDBs, the European Bank for Reconstruction and Development (EBRD).

The issue is important because the legal rules that govern the loan agreements of the World Bank and the other main MDBs—the Asian Development Bank (ADB),[3] the Inter-American Development Bank (IDB),[4] the African Development Bank (AFDB)[5] and

* Professor of Law, University of Kansas. The author wishes to thank friends at the European Bank for Reconstruction and Development, especially Mr. Gerard Sanders, and the World Bank for contributing ideas and suggestions for this article. The author also wishes to thank Mr. Aron Broches for his helpful comments on an earlier draft of the article. Some of the observations in the article draw on the author's experience as a consultant to the EBRD at various times in the years 1993–1995. All views expressed here, however, are the author's and not necessarily those of the EBRD or its staff. Research support from the University of Kansas is gratefully acknowledged.

[1] The World Bank consists of two legally separate, but closely related, institutions: the International Bank for Reconstruction and Development (IBRD), established in 1945 following the Bretton Woods conference, and the International Development Association (IDA), established in 1960 to provide more concessional financing for the less economically developed countries, many of which were at that time gaining political independence. A more encompassing term, "World Bank Group," refers to the IBRD and IDA, plus the International Finance Corporation, established in 1956 to engage in private sector financing, the Multilateral Investment Guarantee Agency (MIGA), established in 1988 to provide guarantees against various types of noncommercial risks faced by foreign private investors in developing countries, and the International Centre for Settlement of Investment Disputes (ICSID), established in 1966 to provide conciliation and arbitration facilities for the settlement of disputes related to transnational investments. *See* IBRAHIM F. I. SHIHATA, THE WORLD BANK IN A CHANGING WORLD 7–13 (1991); THE WORLD BANK, 1992 ANNUAL REPORT 4 (1992) [hereinafter WB 1992 REPORT]. For descriptions of the World Bank and the World Bank Group, see generally SHIHATA, *supra. See also* John W. Head, *Supranational Law: How the Move Toward Multilateral Solutions Is Changing the Character of "International" Law,* 42 KAN. L. REV. 605, 629, 642 (1994) [hereinafter *Supranational Law*]; John W. Head, *Environmental Conditionality in the Operations of International Development Finance Institutions,* 1 KAN. J. L. & PUB. POL'Y 15, 16–17 (1991) [hereinafter *Conditionality*].

[2] Aron Broches, *International Legal Aspects of the Operations of the World Bank,* 98 RECUEIL DES COURS 297 (1959 III). *See further* text at and note 17 *infra.*

[3] The ADB, headquartered in Manila, was established in 1965. *See* AGREEMENT ESTABLISHING THE ASIAN DEVELOPMENT BANK, Dec. 4, 1965, 17 UST 1418, 571 UNTS 123 (entered into force Aug. 22, 1966). The ADB started functioning in December 1966. ASIAN DEVELOPMENT BANK, 1994 ANNUAL REPORT (inside front cover) (1995) [hereinafter ADB 1994 REPORT]. For general information about the history and operations of the ADB, see DICK WILSON, A BANK FOR HALF THE WORLD (1987).

[4] The IDB, headquartered in Washington, D.C., was established in 1959. *See* AGREEMENT ESTABLISHING THE INTER-AMERICAN DEVELOPMENT BANK, Apr. 8, 1959, 10 UST 3029, 389 UNTS 69 (entered into force Dec. 30, 1959), *amended* Jan. 28, 1964, 21 UST 1570, *amended* Mar. 31, 1968, 19 UST 7381, *amended* Mar. 23, 1972, TIAS No. 7437. For information about the history and operations of the IDB, see generally INTER-AMERICAN DEVELOPMENT BANK, BASIC FACTS—INTER-AMERICAN DEVELOPMENT BANK (1991); INTER-AMERICAN DEVELOPMENT BANK, 1994 ANNUAL REPORT (1995) [hereinafter IDB 1994 REPORT].

[5] The AFDB, headquartered in Abidjan, Côte d'Ivoire, was established in 1963. *See* AGREEMENT ESTABLISHING THE AFRICAN DEVELOPMENT BANK, Aug. 4, 1963, 510 UNTS 3 (entered into force Sept. 10, 1964). For current information about the operations of the AFDB, see generally AFRICAN DEVELOPMENT BANK, 1993 ANNUAL REPORT (1994) [hereinafter AFDB 1993 REPORT].

214

the EBRD[6]—bear directly on the interpretation and application of those agreements, which in turn bear on the likelihood that the loans made under those agreements will be repaid and, ultimately, on the stature of the institutions themselves and the support they receive from the international community. Most of the MDBs, especially the World Bank, are coming under increasing criticism on many fronts.[7] For example, some political leaders in the United States and other relatively rich industrialized countries with large stakes and heavy influence in the World Bank[8] have urged that financial support for it be sharply reduced;[9] and some leaders in less economically developed countries have advocated that loans from the World Bank not be repaid.[10]

---

[6] The EBRD, headquartered in London, was established in 1990. *See* AGREEMENT ESTABLISHING THE EUROPEAN BANK FOR RECONSTRUCTION AND DEVELOPMENT, May 29, 1990, 29 ILM 1077 (1990) [hereinafter EBRD CHARTER] (entered into force Mar. 28, 1991). For general information about the history and operations of the EBRD, see IBRAHIM F. I. SHIHATA, THE EUROPEAN BANK FOR RECONSTRUCTION AND DEVELOPMENT (1990); Head, *Supranational Law*, *supra* note 1, at 635–49; EUROPEAN BANK FOR RECONSTRUCTION AND DEVELOPMENT, 1994 ANNUAL REPORT (1995) [hereinafter EBRD 1994 REPORT].

[7] *See, e.g.*, Patricia Adams, *The World Bank's Finances: An International S&L Crisis*, POL'Y ANALYSIS NO. 215 (Cato Institute), Oct. 3, 1994, at 1 (claiming that the World Bank "must be shut down" because "its irresponsible lending exposes Western taxpayers to a possible World Bank bailout on a scale comparable to the U.S. savings-and-loan bailout"); Carol Barton, *Structural Adjustment: Deadly "Development,"* GLOBAL ADVOCATES BULL., Oct. 1994, at 1, 2–5, 27, 31, 33–35 (criticizing the World Bank for its structural adjustment lending). For a more comprehensive assessment of the World Bank, see generally BRUCE RICH, MORTGAGING THE EARTH—THE WORLD BANK, ENVIRONMENTAL IMPOVERISHMENT, AND THE CRISIS OF DEVELOPMENT (1994). Rich asserts that World Bank lending has caused "profound human and ecological damage," and expresses the hope that readers will exert political pressure to either "radically reinvent the institution or stop funding it." *Id.* at xii–xiii. Many analyses, of course, run in the other direction. *See, e.g.*, Henry Owen, *The World Bank: Is 50 Years Enough?*, FOREIGN AFF., Sept.–Oct. 1994, at 97, 108 (concluding that criticisms from both right and left are incorrect and that the World Bank has a good record).

[8] Under the weighted voting system that applies in each of the MDBs discussed herein, voting power is concentrated in the Group of Seven (G–7) industrialized states (the United States, Japan, Germany, France, the United Kingdom, Canada, and Italy), closely reflecting the capital subscriptions held by those states. *See* THE WORLD BANK, 1994 ANNUAL REPORT 183–86, 201 (1994) [hereinafter WB 1994 REPORT] (showing aggregated voting powers as 44.4% and 47.4% for G–7 member countries of the IBRD and the IDA, respectively); INTERNATIONAL FINANCE CORPORATION, ANNUAL REPORT 1994, at 114–15 (1994) [hereinafter IFC 1994 REPORT] (showing aggregated G–7 voting power as 53.1% in the IFC); ADB 1994 REPORT, *supra* note 3, at 142–43 (showing aggregated G–7 voting power as 45.4% in the ADB); IDB 1994 REPORT, *supra* note 4, at 128–29 (showing aggregated G–7 voting power as 44.1% in the IDB); AFDB 1993 REPORT, *supra* note 5, at 106–09 (showing aggregated G–7 voting power as 24.6% in the AFDB); EBRD 1994 REPORT, *supra* note 6, at 52 (showing aggregated G–7 voting power as 56.7% in the EBRD).

[9] *See, e.g.*, Jim Lobe, *U.S.-Aid: Clinton's 1996 Budget Holds Line on Foreign Aid*, Inter Press Service, Feb. 6, 1995, *available in* LEXIS/NEXIS, MDEAFR Library, CURNWS File (noting efforts by some Republican leaders of Congress in early 1995 to reduce U.S. financing of IDA); Jim Lobe, *Finance: World Bank Soft-Loan Facility in Limbo*, Inter Press Service, Jan. 5, 1996, *available in* LEXIS/NEXIS, WORLD Library, ALLNWS File (noting the success of those efforts as of late 1995 and the dim prospects for future U.S. funding for IDA); Rose Umoren, *World Bank, NGOs Trade Blame as IDA Slips Away*, Inter Press Service, May 30, 1995, *available in* LEXIS/NEXIS, NEWS Library, INPRES File (quoting a World Bank official as saying that future U.S. support for IDA "will be very minimal" and suggesting that the battle to secure IDA's future has been virtually lost); Patricia Feeney, *Fair Shares for the Rich*, THE GUARDIAN, Mar. 11, 1995, at 24, *available in* LEXIS/NEXIS, MDEAFR Library, CURNWS File (noting similar pressures in Canada and Britain to reduce aid programs); Nicholas Eberstadt & Clifford M. Lewis, *Privatize the World Bank*, WALL ST. J., June 27, 1995, at A12 (proposing partial elimination of the World Bank and privatization of the remainder). For a description of some past efforts in the U.S. Congress to reduce financial support for the World Bank, see Jonathan Earl Sanford, *U.S. Policy Toward the Multilateral Development Banks: The Role of Congress*, 22 GEO. WASH. J. INT'L L. & ECON. 1, 42–45 (1988).

[10] *See, e.g.*, *Bulgarian Refining Board Proposes Plan*, FIN. TIMES E. EUR. ENERGY REP. (London), Sept. 1992, *available in* LEXIS/NEXIS, WORLD Library, ALLNWS File (reporting that Bulgaria's Neftochim refining company proposed suspending payments on a World Bank loan in order to strengthen the company's finances); Raul Ronzoni, *Uruguay: Leftists Struggle to Unite Before 1994 Elections*, Inter Press Service, Nov. 16, 1993, *available in id.*, CURNWS File (noting that one member party in Uruguay's left-wing coalition espoused "non-payment of the foreign debt"). Perhaps the most public high-level threat in this regard came in 1987, when Romania threatened to suspend repayment of its $1.9 billion debt to the World Bank. *See* Jan Krcmar, *Romania Threatens to Suspend World Bank Debt Repayment*, Reuters, Dec. 3, 1987, *available in id.*, ALLNWS File. Several instances of such suspensions have in fact occurred in recent years. *See, e.g.*, *Panama Holding Debt Talks in New York—Banker*, Reuters, Mar. 21, 1995, *available in id.* (noting that "Panama halted all foreign debt payments in 1987, but [later] reached restructuring agreements" with lenders); *Congo Pays Off World Bank Loan Arrears*, Reuters, July 1, 1994, *available in id.* (noting the Congo's arrears of about $100 million to the World Bank); *Zambia: Government Pays 50m Dollars Arrears to World Bank*, British Broadcasting Corp., Feb. 11, 1992, *available in id.*

In a commercial setting, such antagonistic circumstances as these (criticisms from shareholders and threats of default by borrowers) would prompt a lender to ensure that the legal agreements under which it extends loans are expressly made subject to a specified body of law that would prove favorable—or at least not unfavorable—to the lender in case of default or dispute. Indeed, the importance of including a clear and favorable choice-of-law provision in any international contract is a common theme in international commercial and financial practice.[11]

Applied to the World Bank and the other MDBs, this consideration suggests that their loan agreements should include a definitive provision making the agreement subject to a system of law that the lender could count on to protect it in case the borrower defaults on payment or challenges the agreement in a way that makes dispute settlement and enforcement necessary. In particular, an MDB would probably want the governing law provisions in its loan agreements to specify some system of law other than that of the borrower. Otherwise, the lender (the MDB) could face numerous problems.

For example, if World Bank loan agreements could be construed as being subject to local law, some public sector borrowers (states and state-owned enterprises)[12] might try claiming that obligations undertaken in such an agreement—for example, the obligation

---

(discussing Zambia's arrears to the World Bank); *Nicaraguan Officials to Meet with World Bank*, Reuters, July 24, 1991, *available in id.* (noting Nicaragua's arrears to the World Bank); *Peru Craves Big Writedown; Citi to Lend $1 Billion Bridge*, AM. BANKER–BOND BUYER, Nov. 30, 1992, *available in* LEXIS/NEXIS, BANKING Library, ALLNWS File (noting Peru's arrears to the World Bank). For a list of World Bank member countries behind in their loan payments to the World Bank as of mid-1994, see WB 1994 REPORT, *supra* note 8, at 168.

[11] "[A] clause which specifies the applicable law is essential" in drafting an international contract with an eye to resolving any potential disputes between the parties. Jay M. Vogelson, *Dispute Resolution, Enforcement and Termination of Agreements, Governing Law, Choice of Forum, and Jurisdiction, in* NEGOTIATING AND STRUCTURING INTERNATIONAL COMMERCIAL TRANSACTIONS 109, 110 (Shelly P. Battram & David N. Goldsweig eds., 1991). In case the contract specifies arbitration as the means of settling disputes thereunder, "it is important for the arbitration clause itself to designate the law applicable to the arbitration." *Id.* at 117. A choice-of-law clause provides certainty and predictability to the application and construction of the terms of an agreement and to the enforcement of the rights and remedies established thereunder. Raymond M. Auerback, *Governing Law Issues in International Financial Transactions*, 27 INT'L LAW. 303, 308 (1993). Such certainty and predictability are important in the case of loans for the simple reason that, "once the lender has parted with its funds, it will be extremely vulnerable." *Id.* at 316. For other references to the importance of including clear provisions on governing law in international commercial and financial agreements, see Michael Gruson, *Governing-Law Clauses in International and Interstate Loan Agreements—New York's Approach*, 1982 UNIV. ILL. L. REV. 207, 207; MARTIN HUNTER, JAN PAULSSON, NIGEL RAWDING & ALAN REDFERN, THE FRESHFIELDS GUIDE TO ARBITRATION AND ADR 31 (1993) [hereinafter FRESHFIELDS GUIDE].

[12] Both the IBRD and the IDA may make loans to member states, state-owned enterprises or private entities. If a loan is made directly to a state-owned enterprise or a private entity, the IBRD is required (and the IDA is permitted) to have the loan guaranteed by the government of the member state in which the project is being carried out. *See* ARTICLES OF AGREEMENT OF THE INTERNATIONAL BANK FOR RECONSTRUCTION AND DEVELOPMENT, July 22, 1944, Art. III, §4(i), 60 Stat. 1440, 2 UNTS 134, *amended* Dec. 16, 1965, 16 UST 1942, 606 UNTS 294 [hereinafter IBRD CHARTER] (entered into force Dec. 27, 1945), *reprinted as amended Dec. 17, 1965, in* 1 BASIC DOCUMENTS OF INTERNATIONAL ECONOMIC LAW 427 (Stephen Zamora & Ronald A. Brand eds., 1990) [hereinafter BASIC DOCUMENTS]; ARTICLES OF AGREEMENT OF THE INTERNATIONAL DEVELOPMENT ASSOCIATION, Jan. 26, 1960, Art. V, §2(d), 11 UST 2284, 439 UNTS 249 [hereinafter IDA CHARTER] (entered into force Sept. 24, 1960). Because the purpose of the IDA is to alleviate the burden of external financing on poorer countries, IDA loans (technically called "credits") have traditionally been made only to member states, instead of to state-owned enterprises or private entities. Aron Broches, *The World Bank, in* INTERNATIONAL FINANCIAL LAW—LENDING, CAPITAL TRANSFERS AND INSTITUTIONS 251, 262 n.72 (Euromoney Publications, 1980); WB 1992 REPORT, *supra* note 1, at 4; THE WORLD BANK, WORLD BANK OPERATIONAL MANUAL, at OP 7.00 ¶2, ¶3 n.4 (loose-leaf, July 1994) [hereinafter WB OPER. MAN.]. The ADB, the IDB and the AFDB also make all or nearly all of their loans to states and state-owned enterprises. *See* John W. Head, *International Contracting Opportunities Under Projects Financed by the World Bank and Related Institutions*, INT'L CONTRACT ADVISOR, Spring 1995, at 41, 44 [hereinafter *Contracting*]. The EBRD is required by its charter to make 60% of its loans to the private sector (that is, to entities that are neither (1) owned or controlled by the state, nor (2) enjoying the benefit of a guarantee by the state or a state-owned entity), although it has had some difficulty in reaching that target because of changed political circumstances in its countries of operation. *See* Head, *Supranational Law, supra* note 1, at 647–48. *See also* Matthew H. Hurlock, *New Approaches to Economic Development: The World Bank, the EBRD, and the Negative Pledge Clause*, 35 HARV. INT'L L.J. 345, 372 (1994). The IFC lends exclusively to the private sector. *See* IFC 1994 REPORT, *supra* note 8, at 1.

to follow certain procedures for the procurement of goods[13] or to refrain from applying loan proceeds to payment of taxes on goods imported into the country for use in projects financed by the World Bank[14]—are void because of inconsistency with local law. If, on these grounds, the borrower were to stop following the World Bank's procurement guidelines or to use loan proceeds to pay import tariffs on project-related goods, financial support for the World Bank itself could crumble.[15]

Beyond that, if World Bank loan agreements were subject to local law, the validity of the agreements themselves might, in extreme circumstances, be thrown into question. In a borrowing country where the executive and judicial branches of government are engaged in sharp political rivalry, for instance, a citizens' group might persuade a court to declare a loan agreement with the World Bank to be null and void on grounds that it is inconsistent with the state's public policy—for example, the policy of protecting the state's rights of sovereignty and self-determination. Indeed, a legal attack on the validity of a loan agreement might even be made by the executive branch itself, especially in a borrowing member country that has experienced a radical change in leadership, resulting in a refusal to repay the World Bank loan.[16]

A Changing Institutional Landscape

These questions, as they relate to the governing law for World Bank loan agreements, were addressed in 1959 when Aron Broches, then the General Counsel of the World Bank, presented a set of Hague Academy lectures.[17] In presenting what is generally regarded as the traditional World Bank view, Broches posited (1) that loan agreements of the World Bank with member states were governed by international law,[18] and (2) that its loan agreements with state-owned entities were not governed by international law but nonetheless "excluded" the operation of municipal law.[19]

---

[13] World Bank loan agreements typically require that goods and services for a project financed with World Bank funds be purchased in accordance with the bank's procurement guidelines, which generally require that internationally competitive bidding procedures be followed. WB OPER. MAN., *supra* note 12, at OP 7.01, ¶3 (July 1994). For an overview of World Bank procurement guidelines, see THE WORLD BANK, BIDDING FOR CONTRACTS IN WORLD BANK FINANCED PROJECTS 10 (n.d.). *See also* Broches, *supra* note 12, at 256 n.32. Other MDBs typically impose the same requirements. *See* Head, *Contracting, supra* note 12, at 47.

[14] *See* INTERNATIONAL BANK FOR RECONSTRUCTION AND DEVELOPMENT, GENERAL CONDITIONS APPLICABLE TO LOAN AND GUARANTEE AGREEMENTS—DATED JANUARY 1, 1985, §5.08 [hereinafter IBRD 1985 GENERAL CONDITIONS]. The manner in which these General Conditions are incorporated into a particular loan agreement is discussed in text at and notes 27–44 *infra*.

[15] In the relatively rich industrialized states, political support for continued participation in the MDBs turns in part on the fact that contracts under MDB-financed projects can usually be awarded only to persons from member states of that MDB. For a statement of that general criterion, see THE WORLD BANK, GUIDELINES—PROCUREMENT UNDER IBRD LOANS AND IDA CREDITS 7 (1985). The EBRD is an exception in this regard. It does not impose any country-eligibility criteria. *See* EUROPEAN BANK FOR RECONSTRUCTION AND DEVELOPMENT, PROCUREMENT POLICIES AND RULES 3 (1992, rev. Aug. 1994). For an example of how procurement eligibility bears on U.S. political support for MDB participation and funding, see U.S. DEPARTMENT OF THE TREASURY, THE MULTILATERAL DEVELOPMENT BANKS: INCREASING U.S. EXPORTS AND CREATING U.S. JOBS 3 (1994).

[16] The threats to refuse repayment of World Bank loans referred to in note 11 *supra* all seem to have been founded on political and economic grounds, rather than legal grounds. However, as pointed out in text at and notes 102–05 *infra*, unprecedented legal changes are now under way in many former Soviet republics. In that climate of radical legal change and uncertainty, it seems likely that as World Bank and other MDB loans in those countries increasingly come due for repayment, internal pressure for nonpayment might take the form of legal challenges. For a discussion of some other specific disputes that might arise if an MDB loan agreement were expressly or impliedly made subject to local law, see *infra* part V of this article.

[17] Broches, *supra* note 2. These 1959 lectures were recently reprinted in ARON BROCHES, SELECTED ESSAYS—WORLD BANK, ICSID, AND OTHER SUBJECTS OF PUBLIC AND PRIVATE INTERNATIONAL LAW (1995) [hereinafter ESSAYS]. Some of Broches's views also appeared in abbreviated form in a 1956 article that he coauthored with the World Bank's then-current General Counsel and another World Bank attorney. *See* Davidson Sommers, A. Broches & Georges R. Delaume, *Conflict Avoidance in International Loans and Monetary Agreements*, 21 LAW & CONTEMP. PROBS. 463, 476–78 (1956).

[18] Broches's reasoning on this point is discussed in text at notes 55–57, 65–78 *infra*.

[19] Broches's reasoning on this point is discussed in text at notes 58–61, 79–86 *infra*.

Since the time of Broches's lectures, the law and operations of the MDBs have developed greatly. There are now more member states,[20] more loans[21] and more MDBs. Whereas 1959 saw only two such entities in operation—the International Bank for Reconstruction and Development[22] and the International Finance Corporation[23]—there are now no fewer than seven main international development finance institutions,[24] headquartered on four continents and operating in a growing variety of political and economic circumstances.[25]

Of all these institutions, the one that departs most from the World Bank model is the most recently formed, the EBRD. The set of standard legal terms used in public sector loans extended by that institution reflects some important developments since the time of Broches's lectures in 1959. Specifically, one of the EBRD's standard terms relates directly to governing law: EBRD loan agreements, whether with member countries or state-owned enterprises, are explicitly made subject to public international law, which the EBRD standard terms define in a way that incorporates existing rules of international treaty and contract law and encourages the development of new customary rules.[26]

Part II of this article identifies and explains the main provisions of World Bank loan agreements that are relevant to the issue of governing law. Part III summarizes the traditional World Bank view—expressed by Broches and repeated by others—on the effects of those provisions, which remain substantially unchanged since 1959. Part IV explains the corresponding provisions of EBRD loan agreements, noting especially how and why they depart from those of the World Bank. Part V then offers an assessment of the new EBRD approach and concludes that it represents an important step forward in the evolution of MDB loan and guarantee agreements.

II. The Structure and Relevant Provisions of World Bank Loan Agreements

The General Conditions and Project-Specific Loan Agreements

The legal provisions governing a typical World Bank loan appear in at least two main documents: a set of General Conditions[27] and a project-specific Loan Agreement[28]

---

[20] In 1959 the IBRD had 68 member states. Broches, *supra* note 2, at 304. As of June 1994, it had 177 member states. WB 1994 REPORT, *supra* note 8, at 15.

[21] By 1959 the IBRD had made "more than two hundred loans . . . for a total equivalent of $4,500 million" ($4.5 billion). Broches, *supra* note 2, at 301. By June 1994, the IBRD had made 3,660 loans for a total equivalent of about $250 billion, and the IBRD and IDA combined had made 6,105 loans for a total equivalent of about $334 billion. WB 1994 REPORT, *supra* note 8, at 233. *See also infra* note 94.

[22] *See supra* note 1. As explained there, the IBRD is one of the two entities that constitute the "World Bank." The other one, the IDA, did not exist in 1959.

[23] *See supra* note 1. IFC operations do not require government guarantees. *See* ARTICLES OF AGREEMENT OF THE INTERNATIONAL FINANCE CORPORATION, May 25, 1955, Art. I(i), 7 UST 2197, 264 UNTS 117 (entered into force July 20, 1956).

[24] The IBRD, IDA, IFC, ADB, IDB, AFDB and EBRD. These are defined in text at and notes 1, 3–6 *supra*.

[25] For a description of the political and economic "mandates" of the EBRD, see Head, *Supranational Law*, *supra* note 1, at 636–41; SHIHATA, *supra* note 6, at 441–42.

[26] *See* text at notes 119, 131–37 *infra*.

[27] *See* IBRD 1985 GENERAL CONDITIONS, *supra* note 14. In addition to this set of General Conditions, there are others. In 1993, the IBRD issued GENERAL CONDITIONS APPLICABLE TO LOAN AND GUARANTEE AGREEMENTS FOR SINGLE CURRENCY LOANS—DATED FEBRUARY 9, 1993 [hereinafter IBRD 1993 GENERAL CONDITIONS]. The IDA has its own separate set of General Conditions. *See* INTERNATIONAL DEVELOPMENT ASSOCIATION, GENERAL CONDITIONS APPLICABLE TO DEVELOPMENT CREDIT AGREEMENTS—DATED JANUARY 1, 1985 [hereinafter IDA 1985 GENERAL CONDITIONS].

[28] *See* WB OPER. MAN., *supra* note 12, at OP 7.01, ¶¶3–6 (July 1994). Most World Bank loans are project loans rather than balance-of-payments loans. A World Bank project loan is designated for a particular project that is described in detail in the Loan Agreement, reflecting decisions reached through negotiations between World Bank staff and government officials about the specific goods and services to be purchased with the loan proceeds. *See id.* The World Bank also engages in balance-of-payments support, called adjustment lending. This takes the form of loans conditioned on the making of certain economic and financial policy adjustments by the borrowing member country. *See* Head, *Supranational Law*, *supra* note 1, at 629; SHIHATA, *supra* note 1, at 25–27, 58–59.

International Economic Regulation

between the World Bank and the borrower. If the borrower is a member state that will relend some or all of the loan proceeds to a state-owned enterprise, there might also be a Project Agreement between the World Bank and that state-owned enterprise.[29] If the loan is made directly to a state-owned enterprise as borrower, there will also be a Guarantee Agreement between the World Bank and the member state providing the guarantee.[30]

At the center of these agreements are the General Conditions. The General Conditions "set forth certain terms and conditions generally applicable to loans made by the [World] Bank."[31] They apply whenever, and to the extent that, a particular Loan Agreement or Guarantee Agreement incorporates them by reference,[32] which they typically do.[33] If any inconsistency exists between the General Conditions and a Loan Agreement or Guarantee Agreement, the Agreement prevails.[34] The General Conditions include numerous definitions[35] and standard terms on commitment charges,[36] repayment,[37] withdrawal from the loan account,[38] the currencies to be used for various purposes,[39] loan suspension and cancellation,[40] exchange of information,[41] arbitration[42] and effectiveness.[43]

With standard provisions thus established on a bankwide basis in the General Conditions, individual loan agreements can be shorter, focusing on the aspects of the transaction at issue. A typical loan agreement, for example, will specify the loan amount, the interest rate, detailed obligations of the borrower to carry out the project being financed, and any special conditions to be satisfied before loan disbursement can begin.[44]

The Standard Provisions Most Relevant to Governing Law

The standard provision bearing most directly on the issue of governing law for World Bank loan agreements appears in the first sentence of section 10.01 of the General Conditions now in force[45] and is substantively unchanged from the provision appearing in the very first World Bank loan agreements of the late 1940s.[46] The sentence reads as

---

[29] *See* WB OPER. MAN., *supra* note 12, at OP 7.01, ¶¶3–6 (July 1994).

[30] See *supra* note 12 on the need for state guarantees. *See also* WB OPER. MAN., *supra* note 12, at OP 7.01, ¶7 (July 1994).

[31] IBRD 1985 GENERAL CONDITIONS, *supra* note 14, §1.01.

[32] *Id.*

[33] Broches, *supra* note 2, at 305. *See also* WB OPER. MAN., *supra* note 12, at OP 7.01, ¶3 (July 1994); Head, *Conditionality, supra* note 1, at 17.

[34] IBRD 1985 GENERAL CONDITIONS, *supra* note 14, §1.02.

[35] *Id.*, §2.01.

[36] *Id.*, §3.02.

[37] *Id.*, §3.04.

[38] *Id.*, Art. V.

[39] *Id.*, Art. IV.

[40] *Id.*, Art. VI.

[41] *Id.*, §§9.01, 9.02.

[42] *Id.*, §10.04.

[43] *Id.*, §§12.01, 12.02, 12.03, 12.04.

[44] *See* WB OPER. MAN., *supra* note 12, at OP 7.01, ¶¶3–6 (July 1994). For an example of a World Bank loan agreement including these and other details, see the Loan Agreement for the Shanghai Environment Project, between the People's Republic of China and the International Bank for Reconstruction and Development, Loan No. 3711 CHA (June 2, 1994). This and other World Bank loan agreements are available to the public, for a fee, through the World Bank Public Information Center (1818 H Street, N.W., Washington, DC 20433; fax (202) 477-6391).

[45] *See* IBRD 1985 GENERAL CONDITIONS, *supra* note 14, §10.01; IBRD 1993 GENERAL CONDITIONS, *supra* note 27, §10.01; IDA 1985 GENERAL CONDITIONS, *supra* note 27, §10.01. All portions of Article X of each of these sets of General Conditions are identical in all relevant respects, and henceforth this article refers only to the IBRD 1985 General Conditions.

[46] *See* INTERNATIONAL BANK FOR RECONSTRUCTION AND DEVELOPMENT, GENERAL CONDITIONS APPLICABLE TO LOAN AND GUARANTEE AGREEMENTS—DATED MARCH 15, 1974, §10.01 [hereinafter IBRD 1974 GENERAL CONDITIONS]; INTERNATIONAL BANK FOR RECONSTRUCTION AND DEVELOPMENT, LOAN REGULATIONS NO. 3—DATED JUNE 15, 1956, §7.01 (applying to loans made to member states) [hereinafter WB 1956 LOAN REGULATIONS]; INTERNATIONAL BANK FOR RECONSTRUCTION AND DEVELOPMENT, LOAN REGULATIONS NO. 4—DATED JUNE 15, 1956, §7.01 (applying to loans guaranteed by member states). Broches quotes the first

follows: "The rights and obligations of the Bank, the Borrower and the Guarantor under the Loan Agreement and the Guarantee Agreement shall be valid and enforceable in accordance with their terms notwithstanding the law of any State or political subdivision thereof to the contrary."[47]

This provision is as close as the General Conditions come to specifying a governing law. It obviously is not a typical governing law provision,[48] as it does not affirmatively designate any particular legal system (for example, "the laws of New York" or "English law"). Instead, it is narrow and negative in character: domestic law (that is, the law "of any State or political subdivision thereof") will *not* apply—will be, in effect, overridden by the terms of the agreement—in case of a conflict between those terms and that domestic law. The implications of this formulation are discussed below in part III.

A second provision in the World Bank's General Conditions also throws some light on the question of governing law. Section 10.04 is addressed to dispute settlement. It provides that any controversy between the parties to the Loan Agreement or the Guarantee Agreement that has not been settled by agreement of the parties "shall be submitted to arbitration by an Arbitral Tribunal as hereinafter provided."[49] It then sets forth the procedures by which the arbitration will be conducted: within specified time periods triggered by one party's notification of a desire to pursue arbitration, a three-person arbitral tribunal will be constituted to hear the dispute,[50] in accordance with procedures it establishes largely on its own,[51] and to render a decision that will be enforceable in national courts.[52] Despite these detailed provisions—section 10.04 is longer than any other section in the General Conditions—section 10.04 does not include a provision on the governing law to be applied by the arbitral tribunal.

These are the main provisions in the World Bank's General Conditions that relate to the issue of governing law for World Bank loan and guarantee agreements.[53] We now turn to the views expressed by Broches on that subject in 1959.

---

sentence of §7.01 of Loan Regulations No. 3 and then states that "[t]his formula was drafted in 1947, when the Bank was about to undertake its first loan transaction." Broches, *supra* note 2, at 344. *Accord,* Hugh N. Scott, *The Enforceability of Loan Agreements Between the World Bank and Its Member Countries,* 13 AM. U. L. REV. 185, 190 (1964).

[47] IBRD 1985 GENERAL CONDITIONS, *supra* note 14, §10.01. The second sentence of that provision states that none of the parties may claim "that any provision of these General Conditions or of the Loan Agreement or the Guarantee Agreement is invalid or unenforceable because of any provision of the Articles of Agreement of the Bank." For an analysis of the 1956 version of this sentence (which was somewhat broader in coverage because it included "or for any other reason" at the end), see Broches, *supra* note 2, at 362–63, 368–69. For a comparison with the corresponding provision in the EBRD's standard terms, see *infra* text at note 111.

[48] For a sample of a governing law provision, see VED P. NANDA, *Forum Selection and Choice of Law Clauses in Transnational Contracts, in* 1 THE LAW OF TRANSNATIONAL BUSINESS TRANSACTIONS, App. 5A (loose-leaf, July 1995) (reading in pertinent part as follows: "This contract . . . shall be governed by and enforced in accordance with the laws of . . . ."). On governing law provisions and the various purposes to be served by them in international contracts, see FRESHFIELDS GUIDE, *supra* note 11, at 31–40. For such a discussion in the context of international project loan agreements involving private sector lenders, see generally Kimmo Mettälä, *Governing-Law Clauses of Loan Agreements in International Project Financing,* 20 INT'L LAW. 219 (1986).

[49] IBRD 1985 GENERAL CONDITIONS, *supra* note 14, §10.04(a).

[50] The instituting party is to notify the responding party of the claim being made, the relief being sought, and the name of the arbitrator it has appointed. Within 30 days after such notification, the responding party is to name the arbitrator it has appointed. *Id.*, §10.04(d). The parties are then expected to agree on a third arbitrator (the "Umpire"), but if they cannot agree within 60 days after the instituting party's notification, the Umpire will be appointed by the President of the International Court of Justice or, failing that, by the Secretary-General of the United Nations. *Id.*, §10.04(c), (e).

[51] The arbitral tribunal "shall decide all questions relating to its competence and shall, . . . except as the parties shall otherwise agree, determine its procedure," subject to a few other procedural matters covered in §10.04. *Id.*, §10.04(g).

[52] *Id.*, §10.04(k). An exception exists in the case of an arbitral award against a member state: the state's sovereign immunity, to the extent it is claimed, is not waived by operation of §10.04. *Id. See also* Broches, *supra* note 12, at 259.

[53] A third set of provisions in the World Bank's General Conditions bear on the legal status of World Bank loan agreements upon signature—that is, on the legal significance of the act of signing them. Section 12.01 of the General Conditions provides that a Loan Agreement and Guarantee Agreement "shall not become

III. THE LEGAL CHARACTER OF WORLD BANK LOAN AGREEMENTS

The Traditional View in a Nutshell

The traditional view of the legal character of World Bank loan agreements, as articulated by Broches in 1959, may be summarized thus:

(1) *Agreements with members.* Every loan agreement between the World Bank and a member state, and every guarantee agreement (which is by definition with a member state[54]), is an international agreement "governed by international law,"[55] as both parties to such agreements have international legal personality. These agreements are " 'treaties' in the broad sense of the term, as a matter of international law,"[56] and are registered with the United Nations as such.[57]

(2) *Agreements with nonmembers.* A loan agreement between the World Bank and a nonstate borrower (for example, a state-owned enterprise) "is certainly not an international agreement governed by international law,"[58] since the nonstate party does not have international legal personality. Such an agreement does, however, "partake[ ] of the international character"[59] of the dealings between the World Bank and the member state, which justifies "insulating it from the effect of municipal law."[60] Reflecting these attributes, such agreements are not registered separately with the United Nations but are provided instead "as an annex to the related guarantee agreement."[61]

Broches posited these views in 1959, at about the beginning of his tenure as General Counsel of the World Bank.[62] They had apparently not changed in 1980, when he wrote a brief overview of the World Bank after completing two decades in that position.[63] In expressing these views, Broches set forth a number of key propositions about the World Bank, its legal character, and the legal basis for its relations with both members and nonmembers.[64] Several of those warrant attention.

---

effective until evidence satisfactory to the Bank shall have been furnished to the Bank . . . that the execution and delivery of [those Agreements] on behalf of the Borrower and the Guarantor have been duly authorized or ratified by all necessary governmental and corporate action." IBRD 1985 GENERAL CONDITIONS, *supra* note 14, §12.01(a). This provision suggests that the Loan Agreement and Guarantee Agreement are not legally binding and effective immediately upon signature, a suggestion that is bolstered by §12.03. It provides that the Loan Agreement and Guarantee Agreement "shall enter into effect on the date upon which the Bank dispatches to the Borrower and to the Guarantor notice of its acceptance of the evidence required by Section 12.01." *Id.*, §12.03(a). In explaining these provisions, Broches has pointed out that "it is clearly not contemplated that the loan agreement [or the guarantee agreement] will come into force upon signature." Broches, *supra* note 2, at 392. Between the time of signing and the time of effectiveness, the borrower has the "option" to proceed with the loan or not, *id.* at 394, and "is under no obligation to bring the agreement into force." *Id.* at 397.

[54] See *supra* note 12 on the need for state guarantees.

[55] Broches, *supra* note 2, at 353.

[56] *Id.* at 405.

[57] *Id.* at 353.

[58] *Id.* at 351.

[59] *Id.* at 352.

[60] *Id.*

[61] *Id.* at 354. As Broches noted, *id.* at 353, Article 102 of the UN Charter provides for the registration of "every treaty and every international agreement." World Bank loan agreements and guarantee agreements with members are registered with the United Nations pursuant to that provision. *Id.*

[62] For information on Broches's career, see BROCHES, ESSAYS, *supra* note 17, at xiii.

[63] See Broches, *supra* note 12, at 254, 258–59. Moreover, as noted in note 17 *supra*, Broches's 1959 lectures were reprinted in 1995 without any indication that his views on the legal character of World Bank loan agreements had changed over the intervening period.

[64] In expressing views about World Bank loan agreements and these underlying legal issues, Broches was largely reflecting the views of the World Bank Legal Department, based on legal provisions that were developed before he became General Counsel. In particular, his 1959 Hague Academy lectures were intended less as an exposition of his own personal views on these matters than as an explanation of World Bank practice, and its legal moorings, as developed institutionally. Telephone conversation between the author and Aron Broches (June 25, 1995).

Legal Foundations of the Traditional View

First, Broches took the position, supported by extensive argument, that the World Bank is "a subject of international law, that is to say it possesses international personality."[65] Like many other international organizations, he said, the World Bank has the legal capacity to enter into treaties.[66] Not all international agreements between subjects of international law (for example, a state and an international organization) are treaties, since those subjects "may, if they choose, subject their agreements to municipal law,"[67] instead of international law.[68] Loan agreements entered into by the World Bank and its member states, however, are not of a type commonly made subject to municipal law;[69] instead, such agreements contain numerous provisions that "taken as a whole *implicitly* negative any inference that the agreements belong to the sphere of municipal rather than international law."[70]

Broches next turned to the then-current equivalent of section 10.01 of the General Conditions quoted above,[71] in which the rights and obligations created in World Bank loan agreements were made "valid and enforceable in accordance with their terms notwithstanding the law of any state, or political subdivision thereof, to the contrary."[72] He acknowledged that this formulation was not as straightforward as stating that "the rights . . . of the parties shall be governed by international law,"[73] but he explained that this "somewhat unusual and negative formulation"[74] reflected the uncertainty in 1947 (when the language was first drafted)[75] over the legal nature of international organizations and their legal capacity.[76] Nonetheless, Broches asserted, the effect of the provision "is not merely to de-nationalize [World Bank loan] agreements [with member states[77]], but to subject them in all respects to international law."[78]

Broches then turned his attention to loan agreements between the World Bank and entities other than states[79]—for example, state-owned enterprises. Reflecting the view then held that only international persons contracting among themselves were capable of having public international law govern their agreements, Broches reasoned that a loan agreement between the World Bank and an entity other than a state "is certainly not an international agreement governed by international law," as it is "an agreement between a subject of international law and an entity which does not possess that qual-

---

[65] Broches, *supra* note 2, at 328. *See also id.* at 326.

[66] *Id.* at 329, 338.

[67] *Id.* at 339.

[68] This view was expressed later in the 1969 Vienna Convention on the Law of Treaties, which included in its definition of a treaty the criterion that it is to be "governed by international law," suggesting that some international agreements between subjects of international law may nonetheless be governed by municipal law. *See* Vienna Convention on the Law of Treaties, May 23, 1969, Art. 2(1)(a), 1155 UNTS 331, 8 ILM 679 (1969) (entered into force Jan. 27, 1980) [hereinafter 1969 Vienna Convention].

[69] Broches, *supra* note 2, at 343.

[70] *Id.* at 344.

[71] *See supra* text at note 47.

[72] Broches, *supra* note 2, at 344 (quoting WB 1956 LOAN REGULATIONS, *supra* note 46, §7.01).

[73] *Id.*

[74] *Id.* at 345.

[75] *See supra* note 46.

[76] Broches, *supra* note 2, at 344. *See also* Scott, *supra* note 46, at 190.

[77] As noted above, Broches was at this point in his lectures referring to §7.01 of the Loan Regulations applicable to loan agreements with member states. *See supra* notes 46, 72.

[78] Broches, *supra* note 2, at 345. Specifically, as another World Bank attorney has explained, "[t]he interpretation of the agreement will depend on international law, the rights of the parties will be given effect by international law and the remedies available to enforce these rights will be those available under international law." Scott, *supra* note 46, at 190. The applicability of international law is pertinent to the arbitration provisions in the General Conditions. Although those provisions "contain no standards or suggestions to guide the arbitrators in making their decision," it may be assumed that "the arbitrators would, like the International Court of Justice, look to international custom and the general principles of law recognized by civilized nations." *Id.* at 191–92.

[79] Broches, *supra* note 2, at 351.

ity.''[80] Broches acknowledged that it might not be immediately evident how the provisions of such an agreement could be superior to conflicting provisions of municipal law.[81] He explained that the kind of guarantee required by the World Bank when making a loan to a nonmember was unusual, in that the guarantor's obligation was ''as a primary obligor, and not as surety merely.''[82] Therefore, the loan agreement with the nonmember was to be seen in fact as ''only one element . . . in the dealings on the international level between the [World] Bank and its member, and partakes of the international character of these dealings.''[83]

It appears that the World Bank approach, as explained by Broches, leaves the World Bank loan agreement with a nonmember in a legal no-man's-land, since it is not, strictly speaking, governed either by international law[84] or by municipal law.[85] In the latter respect—insulation of such an agreement from municipal law—Broches explained that, ''while the borrower could not contract itself out of the application of municipal law, the [World] Bank and the guaranteeing member may do so in respect not only of their own relationship but also . . . of that between the [World] Bank and the borrower.''[86]

IV. A NEW APPROACH—THE EBRD'S STANDARD TERMS AND CONDITIONS

Practical Concerns in a New Setting

The issue of governing law for World Bank loan agreements apparently has never been formally addressed through arbitration or in attempted litigation.[87] Indeed, since Broches's 1959 lectures the subject has apparently received only slight attention, mainly in the 1960s[88] and early 1980s;[89] in 1982 one commentator reasoned that, although it might be advisable for the World Bank to reformulate section 10.01 to specify interna-

---

[80] *Id.*
[81] *Id.*
[82] *Id.* at 352.
[83] *Id.*
[84] *Id.* at 344.
[85] *Id.* at 352.
[86] *Id.* Broches also pointed out that it made sense for the pertinent provision in Loan Regulations No. 3 and Loan Regulations No. 4, applying to loan agreements with members and nonmembers, respectively, to be drafted identically (rather than differently to reflect the different types of borrowers in the two cases) because in many circumstances where the World Bank made a loan to a nonmember, "the transaction could as well take the form of a loan to the member government," *id.,* and that the World Bank's "legal position should be essentially the same in result, regardless of the technique adopted." *Id.* at 353.
[87] *See* Mark Augenblick & Delissa A. Ridgway, *Dispute Resolution in World Financial Institutions,* 10 J. INT'L ARB. 73, 82 (1993) (noting that "there has never been an actual arbitration between any major multilateral development bank and a borrower"). *See also* Broches, *supra* note 12, at 259 (noting that as of 1980, the World Bank arbitration provisions "ha[d] never been invoked").
[88] At a conference held in 1968 under the auspices of the American Society of International Law, several legal officers from MDBs and similar entities offered views on certain legal aspects of loan agreements entered into by their institutions. FOREIGN DEVELOPMENT LENDING—LEGAL ASPECTS 5, 239–57 (Seymour J. Rubin ed., 1971). In the course of those discussions, Broches reiterated a point he had made in his 1959 lectures: that a World Bank loan agreement typically does not come into force upon signature. *Id.* at 248. As pointed out in note 53 *supra,* provisions on this issue appear in §12.01 of the World Bank's General Conditions. For a related discussion about effectiveness of World Bank loan agreements, see GEORGES R. DELAUME, LEGAL ASPECTS OF INTERNATIONAL LENDING AND ECONOMIC DEVELOPMENT FINANCING 33 (1967) (noting that under the IBRD loan regulations, a loan agreement normally becomes "effective at some time after the date of signature, since conditions of effectiveness" take time to be fulfilled). For other scholarship appearing in the 1960s about legal aspects of World Bank loan agreements, see generally Scott, *supra* note 46; and Cecil J. Olmstead, *Public Economic Development Loan Agreements; Choice of Law and Remedy,* 48 CAL. L. REV. 424 (1960).
[89] *See* Georges R. Delaume, *Issues of Applicable Law in the Context of the World Bank's Operations* [hereinafter *Applicable Law*], *in* 2 THE TRANSNATIONAL LAW OF INTERNATIONAL COMMERCIAL TRANSACTIONS 317 (Norbert Horn & Clive M. Schmitthoff eds., 1982) [hereinafter COMMERCIAL TRANSACTIONS]. Although other references to the traditional World Bank view as expressed by Broches have appeared occasionally, they generally have offered no criticism or analysis of it. *See, e.g.,* 2 PHILIP WOOD, LAW AND PRACTICE OF INTERNATIONAL FINANCE §1.07[2][b] (loose-leaf, Apr. 1983); 1 GEORGES R. DELAUME, TRANSNATIONAL CONTRACTS—APPLICABLE LAW AND SETTLEMENT OF DISPUTES §1.14 (loose-leaf, Dec. 1989) [hereinafter CONTRACTS].

tional law as the governing law, there was no urgency to making such a reformulation because "not a single case has arisen in which recourse to arbitration proved necessary."[90] That being the case, it might seem unnecessary to open the subject now.

However, as noted above, the institutional landscape has changed dramatically since 1959,[91] especially because of the emergence of the regional MDBs—the ADB, the IDB, the AFDB and the EBRD.[92] The first three of these largely adopted the World Bank's General Conditions for purposes of their own lending operations.[93] As a result, the overall volume of lending undertaken by all MDBs under the legal regime established by the World Bank, as described in parts II and III above, is more than a hundred times greater now than it was in 1959.[94] On the basis of this fact alone, it seems appropriate to review the governing law and enforceability of the loan agreements under which these operations are conducted.

Beyond that, however, lies another important development. The newest of the MDBs, the EBRD, departs in several respects from the mold on which its predecessors were patterned.[95] It faces some different challenges that make the issue of governing law important enough to warrant a fresh examination.

For example, the EBRD is the first MDB designed to facilitate directly the privatization of state-owned enterprises. As part of its overall mandate of "fostering the transition of Central and Eastern European countries towards open market-oriented economies,"[96]

---

[90] Delaume, *Applicable Law, supra* note 89, at 323. Delaume's reasoning, in pertinent part, was as follows:

> The practice of many international organisations reveals . . . that contracts between them and domestic law persons are no longer necessarily rooted in municipal law . . . [but can be governed by] international law.

> [Therefore] the question arises whether it might be advisable for the [World] Bank to take a second look at Section 10.01 and to clarify its meaning. Admittedly the negative formulation of that old provision is awkward. Admittedly also, to give, as Mr. Broches did, a dual meaning to a single provision which should govern both the relationship between the Bank and one of its members and that between the Bank and a borrower other than a member is an invitation to criticism. Rather than approaching the basic issue in this timid fashion, the Bank might be better advised to . . . provide, firmly and in a positive way, that its loan/guarantee agreements, whether concluded with a member country or not, are always subject to international law . . . . Such a reformulation of Section 10.01 would be in line with modern trends of legal thinking and would dispel the ambiguities of Section 10.01 in its present form.

Id. Delaume went on to say, however, that redrafting §10.01 was not likely to "entail dramatic practical consequences" because it "has never been put to the test of international adjudication." He therefore saw no "urgency" to redraft the section. *Id.* at 323–24.

[91] *See* text at and notes 20–25 *supra.*

[92] *See supra* notes 3, 4, 5 and 6.

[93] *See, e.g.,* ASIAN DEVELOPMENT BANK, ORDINARY OPERATIONS LOAN REGULATIONS—DATED 1 JULY 1986 [hereinafter ADB 1986 LOAN REGULATIONS]. Although presented in a slightly different order, the ADB's standard terms are virtually identical in substance to the World Bank's standard terms, including in particular those on enforceability and arbitration. *Compare* IBRD 1985 GENERAL CONDITIONS, *supra* note 14, §§10.01, 10.04 *with* ADB 1986 LOAN REGULATIONS, *supra,* §§10.01, 10.04, respectively. The same similarity is found with the standard terms used by the AFDB. *Compare* IBRD 1985 GENERAL CONDITIONS, *supra,* §§10.01, 10.04 *with* AFRICAN DEVELOPMENT BANK, GENERAL CONDITIONS APPLICABLE TO LOAN AGREEMENTS AND GUARANTEE AGREEMENTS §§13.01, 13.04 (Nov. 23, 1989) [hereinafter AFDB 1989 GENERAL CONDITIONS]. The standard terms used by the Inter-American Development Bank are silent on the governing law (they do not even include an exclusion-of-local-law provision like the one in §10.01 of the World Bank's General Conditions), but they do contain arbitration provisions closely similar to those of §10.04 of the World Bank's General Conditions. *See* INTER-AMERICAN DEVELOPMENT BANK, GENERAL CONDITIONS (ORDINARY CAPITAL), §§9.01–9.06 (1994) [hereinafter IDB 1994 GENERAL CONDITIONS].

[94] *See supra* note 21. As noted there, cumulative lending by the World Bank in 1959 totaled about $4.5 billion. By 1994, cumulative public sector lending by all the MDBs except the EBRD (which in fact also largely followed World Bank practice on governing law in its public sector loan agreements until 1994) had exceeded $470 billion. *See* WB 1994 REPORT, *supra* note 8, at 229; ADB 1994 REPORT, *supra* note 3, at 10; IDB 1994 REPORT, *supra* note 4, at 39; AFDB 1993 REPORT, *supra* note 5, at 45.

[95] On why the EBRD can be considered a "third generation international financial institution," see Head, *Supranational Law, supra* note 1, at 641–44.

[96] EBRD CHARTER, *supra* note 6, Art. 2(1). *See also id.,* Art. 1 (same), and Art. 11(3) (requiring that loans to the state sector not exceed 40% of the EBRD's total loans, guarantees, and equity investments). On the EBRD's "economic mandate," see Head, *Supranational Law, supra* note 1, at 640–41 and sources cited there.

the EBRD is expected, according to its charter, to "invest[ ] in the equity capital of any state-owned enterprise to facilitate its transition to private ownership and control."[97] Thus, the distinction between private sector financing of the type conducted by the International Finance Corporation[98] and public sector lending of the type conducted by the World Bank[99] becomes fuzzy in the case of the EBRD. Both types of financing take place, in substantial amounts, in the same lending institution (the EBRD), conceivably with the same borrower over time.[100] Nonetheless, because private sector operations do differ in important respects from public sector operations,[101] issues of governing law and validity for purposes of public sector transactions would best be clearly articulated.

Moreover, the EBRD is working in a political environment that is very different from those faced by other MDBs on their establishment. Most of the EBRD's countries of operations are undergoing wrenching political transformations from subordinate political entities within the Communist world to independent sovereign states experimenting for the first time in decades (or perhaps ever) with democratic institutions.[102] Indeed, one of the purposes of the EBRD is to facilitate that very change, by promoting "the principles of multiparty democracy [and] pluralism."[103] Largely because of these political transformations, the legal foundations in the EBRD's countries of operations are typically shaky, with radical changes in the legal systems and constitutions appearing as the norm rather than the exception.[104] In such a setting, it makes sense both from the perspective of the EBRD and from that of its borrowers to be as clear as possible about the legal nature and enforceability of EBRD loan agreements.[105]

---

[97] EBRD CHARTER, *supra* note 6, Art. 11(1)(ii)(b). Various other types of investments are also authorized. *See generally id.*, Art. 1.

[98] *See supra* notes 1, 23.

[99] *See supra* notes 1, 12.

[100] As further evidence of the EBRD's aim of making its public sector loans subject, as much as possible, to the rigors of private sector terms, the explanatory notes to Article 14 of the EBRD Charter (which provides that the EBRD "may" require a state guarantee in lending to a state-owned enterprise) emphasize the importance of weaning state-owned enterprises away from government dependence. *See Chairman's Report on the Agreement Establishing the European Bank for Reconstruction and Development, reprinted in* SHIHATA, *supra* note 6, at 166, 174 (pointing out "that a state-owned enterprise would be more likely to respond quickly to market forces, and to make the transition to market-oriented economies, if that enterprise could not rely on a government guarantee to discharge its responsibilities under a Bank loan"). *See also* Hurlock, *supra* note 12, at 380.

[101] The differences between private sector and public sector operations in the EBRD appear in various forms. For example, the EBRD's procurement guidelines distinguish clearly between those applicable to public sector operations and those applicable to private sector operations. *See* EUROPEAN BANK FOR RECONSTRUCTION AND DEVELOPMENT, PROCUREMENT POLICIES AND RULES 8, 21 (1993); EUROPEAN BANK FOR RECONSTRUCTION AND DEVELOPMENT, FINANCING WITH THE EBRD 12 (1994). The same distinction appears in the EBRD's disbursement procedures. *See* EUROPEAN BANK FOR RECONSTRUCTION AND DEVELOPMENT, DISBURSEMENT HANDBOOK FOR PUBLIC SECTOR LOANS 4–5 (1994). Indeed, in the EBRD's first couple of years of operations, a sharp organizational division between public sector and private sector operations existed. *See* EUROPEAN BANK FOR RECONSTRUCTION AND DEVELOPMENT, 1992 ANNUAL REPORT 79–80 (1993).

[102] When the EBRD's charter was drafted, there were to be 8 countries of operations (that is, member countries eligible to borrow); by early 1993 (less than two years after it commenced operations), the breakup of the Soviet Union and Yugoslavia had resulted in an increase from those 8 to 25 countries of operation. *See* Head, *Supranational Law, supra* note 1, at 645–46.

[103] EBRD CHARTER, *supra* note 6, Art. 1. For a description of the EBRD's "political mandate" and how it distinguishes that institution from the other MDBs, see Head, *Supranational Law, supra* note 1, at 636–38.

[104] For a partial survey of legal and constitutional changes in the countries of Central and Eastern Europe and central Asia, see A.B.A., CEELI UPDATE, Fall 1995, at 3–32 (reporting on recent work of the ABA's Central and East European Law Initiative in legal and constitutional reform in 20 states in Eastern and Central Europe and central Asia). For assessments of the constitutional changes in some of those countries, see Eric Stein, *International Law in Internal Law: Toward Internationalization of Central–Eastern European Constitutions?*, 88 AJIL 427 (1994) (focusing on the Czech Republic and the Slovak Republic); Gennady M. Danilenko, *The New Russian Constitution and International Law, id.* at 451 (focusing on Russia).

[105] Another legal issue—jurisdiction—also points in favor of carefully setting forth the legal nature of EBRD loan agreements. The EBRD Charter, like the IBRD Charter, provides that legal actions may be brought against the institution, by parties other than member countries, "in a court of competent jurisdiction in the territory of a country in which the [EBRD] has an office." EBRD CHARTER, *supra* note 6, Art. 46; *see also* IBRD CHARTER, *supra* note 12, Art. VII, §3. The EBRD has offices in more than a dozen of its countries of operation. *See* EBRD 1994 REPORT, *supra* note 6, back cover. If, in suing the EBRD in a local court, an individual or

Given these circumstances, it is not surprising that the EBRD has taken a new approach to the formulation of certain standard terms and conditions for its public-sector lending operations. Unlike the other regional MDBs, whose standard loan terms are modeled directly on the World Bank's General Conditions,[106] the EBRD's Standard Terms and Conditions depart from the World Bank's approach in several ways. The following paragraphs discuss the key provisions of those Standard Terms and Conditions that bear on the subject of this article—governing law.

EBRD Standard Provisions on Enforceability and Dispute Resolution

The EBRD first established a set of Standard Terms and Conditions (STCs) for public sector loans in March 1994,[107] after about three years of operations.[108] Minor revisions were made to the STCs in September 1994.[109]

The provisions on enforceability and dispute resolution appear in sections 8.01 and 8.04, respectively, of the STCs. The first of these is closely similar in content to the corresponding provision in the World Bank's General Conditions[110] and reads as follows:

> The rights and obligations of the parties to the Loan Agreement and the Guarantee Agreement shall be valid and enforceable in accordance with their terms notwithstanding any local law to the contrary. No party to either such agreement shall be entitled under any circumstances to assert any claim that any provision of either such agreement is invalid or unenforceable for any reason.[111]

On the subject of dispute resolution, however, the STCs depart rather dramatically from the World Bank model. As explained above, the World Bank's General Conditions attempt to provide in detail for every eventuality in the establishment and operation of an arbitral tribunal if a dispute should arise that cannot be settled by agreement of the parties; but the General Conditions do not specify a governing law to be applied by such a tribunal.[112]

---

group in one of those countries of operations makes reference to an EBRD loan agreement, the court would need to understand the nature of that agreement.

[106] *See supra* note 93.

[107] *See generally* EUROPEAN BANK FOR RECONSTRUCTION AND DEVELOPMENT, STANDARD TERMS AND CONDITIONS (Mar. 1994) [hereinafter EBRD MARCH 1994 STCs]. Section 1.01 of the STCs provides that "[a]ny loan agreement or guarantee agreement of the Bank for an operation made to, or guaranteed by, a member of the Bank may provide that the parties to that agreement accept the provisions of these Standard Terms and Conditions." *Id.* §1.01. As other provisions in the STCs confirm, this opening section makes the STCs generally applicable (subject to modification in particular transactions) to every agreement with a party having a financial obligation to the EBRD under a public sector loan; that is, applicable (1) to the loan agreement where the loan is made to the member state, and (2) to both the loan agreement and the guarantee agreement where the loan is made to an entity other than the member state (for example, a state-owned enterprise) and is guaranteed by the member state. *See, e.g., id.* §§4.01, 6.01(a)(ii), 7.01(a), 7.04, 8.01, 8.04(a), 9.01–9.05, and 10.03 (either imposing obligations simultaneously on both the borrower and the guarantor, as in §8.01, *quoted in* text at note 111 *infra,* or referring to both the loan agreement and the guarantee agreement as being instruments governed by the STCs). In this respect, §1.01 of the EBRD's STCs uses the same general formulation as those in the corresponding sets of standard terms of most of the other MDBs. *Compare id.* §1.01 *with* IBRD 1985 GENERAL CONDITIONS, *supra* note 14, §1.01, ADB 1986 LOAN REGULATIONS, *supra* note 93, §1.02, and AFDB 1989 GENERAL CONDITIONS, *supra* note 93, §1.01.

[108] The EBRD approved its first loan in June 1991. *See* EUROPEAN BANK FOR RECONSTRUCTION AND DEVELOPMENT, 1991 ANNUAL REPORT 20 (1992).

[109] *See generally* EUROPEAN BANK FOR RECONSTRUCTION AND DEVELOPMENT, STANDARD TERMS AND CONDITIONS (Sept. 1994) [hereinafter EBRD SEPTEMBER 1994 STCs]. The changes included, inter alia, a minor revision to the method of calculating the commitment charge. *Compare id. with* EBRD MARCH 1994 STCs, *supra* note 107.

[110] *See* IBRD 1985 GENERAL CONDITIONS, *supra* note 14, §10.01.

[111] EBRD SEPTEMBER 1994 STCs, *supra* note 109, §8.01. The second sentence of the STC provision is somewhat broader in coverage than the second sentence of the corresponding World Bank provision, quoted in note 47 *supra.*

[112] *See supra* text at notes 49–52.

Section 8.04 of the EBRD's STCs differs from those World Bank provisions in three ways. First, section 8.04(a) elaborates on the requirement that the parties initially "endeavour to settle amicably any dispute or controversy between them" before proceeding to arbitration.[113] Second, section 8.04(b) provides that, if arbitration is necessary, it shall be carried out "in accordance with the UNCITRAL Arbitration Rules."[114] Reference to the UNCITRAL Rules naturally was not possible when the World Bank provisions were being formulated, because these rules did not exist until 1976. Third, section 8.04(b) then enumerates certain specific terms pertinent to the application of the UNCITRAL Rules, such as the number of arbitrators (three),[115] the place of arbitration (The Hague),[116] the language to be used in the arbitral proceedings (English),[117] and the law to be applied by the arbitral tribunal.[118]

It is especially on this last point—the law to be applied—that the dispute resolution provision of the STCs departs radically from the corresponding provision in the World Bank's General Conditions. Section 8.04(b)(v) prescribes "public international law" as the law to be applied. That clause reads as follows:

> (v) The law to be applied by the arbitral tribunal shall be public international law, the sources of which shall be taken for these purposes to include:
>
> (A) any relevant treaty obligations that are binding reciprocally on the parties;
> (B) the provisions of any international conventions and treaties (whether or not binding directly as such on the parties) generally recognised as having codified or ripened into binding rules of customary law applicable to states and international financial institutions, as appropriate;
> (C) other forms of international custom, including the practice of states and international financial institutions of such generality, consistency and duration as to create legal obligations; and
> (D) applicable general principles of law.[119]

This enumeration of the sources of public international law for the purposes of arbitration under an EBRD loan agreement roughly parallels the enumeration of "sources" in Article 38(1) of the Statute of the International Court of Justice,[120] which provides that the Court is to apply treaties, custom and general principles in deciding

---

[113] EBRD SEPTEMBER 1994 STCs, *supra* note 109, §8.04(a), which reads as follows:

> The parties to the Loan Agreement and the Guarantee Agreement shall endeavour to settle amicably any dispute or controversy between them arising out of such agreements or in connection therewith. To this end, at the initiative of any party to either such agreement, the other party or parties shall meet promptly with the initiating party to discuss the dispute or controversy and, if requested by the initiating party in writing, shall reply in writing to any written submission made by the initiating party concerning the dispute or controversy.

In contrast, the World Bank provisions make only passing reference to the possibility that a dispute might be "settled by agreement of the parties." *See* IBRD 1985 GENERAL CONDITIONS, *supra* note 14, §10.04(a).

[114] For the UNCITRAL Arbitration Rules, Apr. 28, 1976, see 2 BASIC DOCUMENTS, *supra* note 12, at 1019, and 15 ILM 701 (1976). For an overview of the rules and their status, see 2 BASIC DOCUMENTS, *supra*, at 1015–18.

[115] EBRD SEPTEMBER 1994 STCs, *supra* note 109, §8.04(b)(i).

[116] *Id.*, §8.04(b)(iii). The specification of a place of arbitration is important for (among other things) the enforcement of an arbitral award. For example, the New York Convention requires each contracting state to enforce arbitral awards made in the territory of other contracting states. United Nations Convention on the Recognition and Enforcement of Foreign Arbitral Awards, June 10, 1958, Arts. I, III, 21 UST 2517, 330 UNTS 3 (entered into force June 7, 1959).

[117] EBRD SEPTEMBER 1994 STCs, *supra* note 109, §8.04(b)(iv).

[118] *Id.*, §8.04(b)(v).

[119] *Id.*

[120] INTERNATIONAL COURT OF JUSTICE, STATUTE Art. 38(1) [hereinafter ICJ STATUTE]. The enumeration of "sources" of international law in Article 38 can be traced back to at least about 1919, as the language of that article is virtually identical to the wording of Article 38 of the governing Statute of the ICJ's predecessor, the Permanent Court of International Justice, *reprinted in* ANTONIO S. DE BUSTAMANTE, THE WORLD COURT 353 (Elizabeth F. Read trans., 1925). *See also* IAN BROWNLIE, PRINCIPLES OF PUBLIC INTERNATIONAL LAW 714–16 (4th ed. 1990).

disputes submitted to it.[121] However, the language of section 8.04 of the STCs reflects the fact that one of the parties to arbitration thereunder will be an "international financial institution"[122]—that is, an international organization having personality in international law.[123]

This initiative taken by the EBRD in its dispute resolution provisions—specifying an applicable law rather than remaining silent (or relying on inference) as in the World Bank's General Conditions—represents a significant step forward in the evolution of the governing law for MDB loan agreements.[124] As explained above, the traditional view of World Bank loan agreements was (1) that if between the World Bank and a state, they were governed by international law as treaties, and (2) that if between the World Bank and an entity other than a state, they were not (and could not be) governed by international law but could be insulated from local law (and were so insulated by operation of the General Conditions) on grounds that they "partake[ ] of the international character of [the] dealings" between the World Bank and the relevant member state.[125] In contrast, the EBRD's STCs have swept all such agreements—with states and nonstates alike—into the ambit of public international law.[126] While this innovation would have been difficult to defend in 1959,[127] it seems appropriate today, for two reasons.

First, it is now well accepted that international law can be chosen as the governing law in contracts involving one or more parties that are not subjects of international law, that is, entities that are not states or international organizations.[128] This legal develop-

---

[121] ICJ STATUTE Art. 38(1)(a)–(c). A fourth clause lists judicial decisions and the teachings of publicists, as "subsidiary means for the determination of rules of law."

[122] EBRD SEPTEMBER 1994 STCs, *supra* note 109, §8.04(b)(v)(B), (C).

[123] For the Charter provision establishing the legal personality of the EBRD, see EBRD CHARTER, *supra* note 6, Art. 45. Section 8.04(b)(v) of the STCs also reflects some other developments that have occurred since the time that Article 38 of the ICJ Statute was first drafted. For example, §8.04(b)(v)(B) reflects the fact that international conventions can give rise to rules of customary international law, a proposition confirmed by the ICJ in the North Sea Continental Shelf Cases (FRG v. Den.; FRG v. Neth.), 1969 ICJ REP. 3, 42 (Feb. 20).

[124] Another feature of the EBRD's new dispute resolution provisions that is directly related to the applicable law provision is its adoption of the UNCITRAL Arbitration Rules. *See* text at and note 114 *supra*. Although beyond the scope of this article, several aspects of that topic warrant analysis and evaluation—for example, the merits of selecting the UNCITRAL Arbitration Rules, the significance of specifying The Hague as the place of arbitration, and the relationship between the provisions of §8.04 and pertinent EBRD Charter provisions.

[125] *See* text at and notes 82–83 *supra*.

[126] As noted above, it is clear from various provisions of the EBRD's STCs that they apply to all "public sector" loan and guarantee agreements; that is, to all loan and guarantee agreements relating to loans made to or guaranteed by a member. *See supra* note 107. That the STCs' governing law provisions in particular are applicable to all such agreements, including those made with nonstates, is evident from the wording of §8.04. Section 8.04(a), quoted in full in note 113 *supra*, provides that "[t]he parties to the Loan Agreement and the Guarantee Agreement shall endeavour to settle any dispute or controversy between them arising out of such agreements or in connection therewith." Section 8.04(b) then makes "any such dispute or controversy"— whether arising out of the loan agreement or the guarantee agreement—subject to arbitration and directs the arbitral tribunal to apply public international law as defined therein.

[127] As noted in text at note 80 *supra*, the view most widely held in 1959 was that an agreement with a nonstate entity as a party could not have international law as its governing law. For the same view expressed in 1956, see Sommers, Broches & Delaume, *supra* note 17, at 470 (noting that national and international tribunals had not supported the view that loans involving both a private sector entity and a state should be governed by international law rather than municipal law). Indeed, it was not entirely beyond dispute in the 1950s that *any* agreement involving an international organization such as the World Bank—even an agreement with a state— could be governed by international law. Broches devoted quite a few pages in his 1959 lectures to proving that international organizations, including the World Bank, can (and often are) authorized to enter into agreements governed by international law. *See* Broches, *supra* note 2, at 316–38. For a summary of current views on treaty-making powers of international organizations, see BROWNLIE, *supra* note 120, at 683–84. *See also* DELAUME, CONTRACTS, *supra* note 89, §1.11.

[128] For discussions indicating that international law can be chosen as the governing law in contracts involving at least one party that is not a subject of international law (i.e., at least one party that is not a state or an international organization), see Mettälä, *supra* note 48, at 240–41 (noting that even "a private lender and a private borrower could also choose public international law to govern their loan agreement," although certain obstacles present as of 1986 would probably dictate against widespread use of that option). For many years, certain types of contracts between states and private parties, including oil concession contracts, have often included provisions designating international law as the governing law. *See* Fernando R. Tesón, *State Contracts*

ment reflects in part the growing emphasis on party autonomy in the selection of governing law provisions.[129]

Second, the body of "public international law" is now substantial and extensive enough, at least as it is broadly defined in the EBRD's STCs,[130] to serve as the governing law for an MDB's public sector loan and guarantee agreements. That body of law includes formally promulgated rules on treaty interpretation;[131] the binding character, formation, validity and performance of both treaties[132] and contracts;[133] and commercial and financial terms used in international transactions.[134] It also includes rules deriving from the operations of the MDBs themselves, such as formal guidelines on the procurement of goods and services for MDB-financed projects;[135] written interpretations of their own

---

and *Oil Expropriations: The* Aminoil-Kuwait *Arbitration*, 24 VA. J. INT'L L. 323, 324 (1984). *See also* Delaume, *Applicable Law, supra* note 89, at 322. Delaume points out that the availability of international law as the governing law for an agreement involving one party lacking personality in international law was influenced by Article 42 of the Convention on the Settlement of Investment Disputes between States and Nationals of Other States, Mar. 18, 1965, 17 UST 1270, 575 UNTS 159 (entered into force Oct. 14, 1966). Delaume, *supra*, at 322 (noting that while Article 42 of the ICSID Convention applies only to foreign investments, it illustrates the wider principle that any "international person in its relations with domestic law persons [has] the authority to contract under [international law]").

[129] *See* Mettälä, *supra* note 48, at 228–29 (noting that, although some limitations do exist, "[t]he autonomy of the parties to choose the law governing their agreement is . . . accepted as the basic rule in almost all jurisdictions."). *See also* DELAUME, CONTRACTS, *supra* note 89, §1.01 (noting that in general "the parties to transnational contracts enjoy a large degree of autonomy in selecting the [governing law]"); NANDA, *supra* note 48, §5.03[1], at 5-101, 5-102, §5.03[3][a], at 5-126, 5-127, §5.03[3][b], at 5-131 (noting the acceptance of party autonomy in selecting governing law under U.S. law, under the EC Convention on the Law Applicable to Contractual Obligations, and under the laws of certain other countries). The UNCITRAL Arbitration Rules, *supra* note 114, expressly uphold the principle of party autonomy. Article 33 provides that "[t]he arbitral tribunal shall apply the law designated by the parties as applicable to the substance of the dispute."

[130] For the sources of public international law enumerated in §8.04(b) of the EBRD's STCs, see text at note 119 *supra*.

[131] *See, e.g.*, 1969 Vienna Convention, *supra* note 68, Arts. 31, 32; Vienna Convention on the Law of Treaties between States and International Organizations or between International Organizations, Mar. 21, 1986, Arts. 31, 32, UN Doc. A/CONF.129/15, 25 ILM 543 (1986) (not yet entered into force) [hereinafter 1986 Vienna Convention]. A loan agreement between an MDB and an entity other than a state is not a treaty, if the usual definition of "treaty" is used. *See, e.g., id.*, Art. 2(1)(a) (defining "treaty" as requiring that all parties thereto are either states or international organizations). However, a loan agreement between an MDB and a state *is* a treaty, and therefore is subject to the rules on treaty interpretation appearing in the two Vienna Conventions on treaties, which are generally considered to codify custom in most respects. *See* MICHAEL AKEHURST, A MODERN INTRODUCTION TO INTERNATIONAL LAW 123 (6th ed. 1987) (noting that most provisions in the 1969 Vienna Convention codify customary international law). *Accord*, BROWNLIE, *supra* note 120, at 604. It seems logical to interpret the terms as they appear in an MDB loan agreement with a state the same when they appear in identical form in an MDB loan agreement with an entity other than a state.

[132] *See, e.g.*, 1969 Vienna Convention, *supra* note 68, Arts. 7–18, 26–27, 42–62; 1986 Vienna Convention, *supra* note 131, Arts. 7–18, 26–27, 42–62.

[133] *See, e.g.*, International Institute for the Unification of Private Law, UNIDROIT Principles of International Commercial Contracts, Arts. 1.3, 2.1–2.22, 3.1–3.20, 6.1.1–6.2.3 (1994) [hereinafter UNIDROIT Principles], *reprinted in* MICHAEL JOACHIM BONELL, AN INTERNATIONAL RESTATEMENT OF CONTRACT LAW 157 (1994). As Bonell points out, it is anticipated that the UNIDROIT Principles "may . . . play a role in interpreting and supplementing international instruments." *See id.* at 110. Rules governing international contracts also appear in the United Nations Convention on Contracts for the International Sale of Goods, Apr. 11, 1980, UN Doc. A/CONF.97/18, 19 ILM 668, 671 (1980) (entered into force Jan. 1, 1988) [hereinafter CISG]. The UNIDROIT Principles, *supra*, Arts. 4.1–4.8, include rules on contract interpretation similar to those of treaty interpretation given in the 1969 and 1986 Vienna Conventions. For the less comprehensive, but generally similar, rules of contract interpretation appearing in the CISG, *supra*, see Arts. 8, 9.

[134] *See, e.g.*, INTERNATIONAL CHAMBER OF COMMERCE, PUB. NO. 500, UNIFORM CUSTOMS AND PRACTICE FOR DOCUMENTARY CREDITS (rev. 1994); INTERNATIONAL CHAMBER OF COMMERCE, INCOTERMS 1990 (1990) (a set of internationally consistent commercial terms setting forth allocation of costs, risks and functions to be undertaken by parties to international sales transactions). Some general principles applicable to contracts for civil works projects, a mainstay of MDB lending, appear in the FIDIC conditions of contract. *See* Fédération Internationale des Ingénieurs-Conseils, *Conditions of Contract (International) for Works of Civil Engineering Construction* (3d ed. 1977), *reprinted in* 2 COMMERCIAL TRANSACTIONS, *supra* note 89, at 421.

[135] *See, e.g.*, THE WORLD BANK, GUIDELINES—PROCUREMENT UNDER IBRD LOANS AND IDA CREDITS (1995); ASIAN DEVELOPMENT BANK, GUIDELINES FOR PROCUREMENT UNDER ASIAN DEVELOPMENT BANK LOANS (1981); EUROPEAN BANK FOR RECONSTRUCTION AND DEVELOPMENT, PROCUREMENT POLICIES AND RULES (1992); AFRICAN DEVELOPMENT BANK, RULES OF PROCEDURE FOR PROCUREMENT OF GOODS AND SERVICES (1991). For other

loan, guarantee, and project agreements;[136] and principles drawn from customary MDB practice in applying and enforcing key provisions of those agreements.[137] At a time when MDBs are undertaking dramatic changes in the transparency and public accountability of their operations,[138] the corpus of these MDB-specific rules, both written and customary, can be expected to grow quickly.

In sum, the EBRD's standard provisions on enforceability and dispute resolution constitute both an adoption of and a departure from the traditional World Bank approach. Section 8.01 of the EBRD's STCs insulates the loan agreement and guarantee agreement generally from local law—providing, in essence, that local law is *not* the governing law for those agreements—and section 8.04 goes further to provide that international law shall always serve as the governing law for purposes of arbitrating disputes arising under such agreements, whether or not the other party to that agreement is the state.

V. ASSESSMENT AND CONCLUDING OBSERVATIONS

The new approach currently taken in the EBRD's STCs relating to the governing law for public sector loan and guarantee agreements has much to recommend it. As explained above, the two pertinent provisions clearly support the status of all such agreements as being governed by public international law,[139] whether or not the borrower is a state. This is an advantage over previous MDB practice because it more accurately reflects the current reach of public international law and because it puts all these agreements on the same legal foundation, subject to scrutiny under a single set of rules. Most important, it affords greater certainty with regard to the nature of the governing law and the procedures and standards by which disputes are to be resolved.

Perhaps an example will serve to illustrate how this new approach could make an important difference in the relations between an MDB and its borrowers and member states. Assume the following facts. In 1995 an MDB approves a loan for the expansion of a coal-fired power plant in state A. The borrower is company X, a power corporation that is wholly owned by state A. State A is the guarantor. In 1997 a dramatic change in the government of state A brings to power a regime that is ideologically hostile to foreign investment and development assistance.

The new government decides to challenge several aspects of the loan arrangements. First, the government imposes a special charge on the payment of interest due on the loan, so that the state-owned entity makes a smaller net payment to the MDB than is provided for in the loan agreement. Second, the government prohibits the MDB's staff

---

references to World Bank procurement policies, see *supra* note 13. Other international organizations have also developed formal rules on procurement. *See, e.g.,* United Nations, *Common Principles and Practices Governing Procurement of Goods and Services by the United Nations System of Organizations, reprinted in* UNITED NATIONS DEVELOP-MENT PROGRAMME, GENERAL BUSINESS GUIDE FOR POTENTIAL SUPPLIERS OF GOODS AND SERVICES TO THE UNITED NATIONS SYSTEM 73–86 (11th ed. 1991).

[136] Most MDBs have published extensive sets of rules in the form of operational manuals that explain, among other things, various policies reflected in loan and guarantee agreements. Some of these sets of rules and explanations, including the entire World Bank operational manual, are publicly available. *See, e.g.,* WB OPER. MAN., *supra* note 12, at OP 7.01 (July 1994) (explaining use of covenants in World Bank loan agreements, including covenants on procurement), OP 7.20 (July 1994) (explaining security arrangements, including the use of negative pledge clauses).

[137] For an example of how such customary practice might bear on the interpretation of various provisions of MDB loan agreements, including those governing suspension of loan disbursements in "extraordinary" circumstances, see *infra* part V.

[138] *See, e.g.,* WB 1994 REPORT, *supra* note 8, at 74, 75 (noting the establishment of an independent Inspection Panel to investigate complaints that the World Bank has not followed its own policies and procedures on design or implementation of projects, and noting the establishment of a Public Information Center to provide public access to World Bank documents, including appraisal reports and evaluation reports).

[139] Further support for this view of the status of such agreements might come from registering them with the United Nations. That subject is beyond the scope of this article but does warrant consideration. An obvious starting point for such consideration would be the World Bank practice and Broches's explanation of it. *See* text at and notes 57, 61 *supra*.

members from visiting the power plant concerned, allegedly on grounds that such visits could compromise national security interests. Third, the government orders company X, the borrower, to sell a large portion of its assets and remit the proceeds to the state treasury, leaving company X weak financially and institutionally. Fourth, the government orders company X to relax its environmental protection measures associated with the power plant, so that the operation and expansion activities of the plant meet local environmental standards but not those expected by the MDB. Fifth, the government orders that, in awarding all future supply contracts for the plant's expansion, company X must follow procurement procedures recently adopted by a regional trading bloc of countries that have agreed to give each other preferential treatment in bidding for government contracts.

Each of these actions by the government of state A could have legal ramifications under the loan and guarantee agreements relating to the power plant project. Those agreements probably would incorporate standard provisions (1) disallowing the imposition of "any taxes" on the making of interest payments under the loan;[140] (2) requiring state X to afford "all reasonable opportunity" for the MDB's staff members to visit the project site:[141] (3) permitting the MDB to suspend disbursements under the loan if an "extraordinary situation" arises that makes it improbable that the project will be carried out or that the borrower or the guarantor will be able to perform its obligations under the loan or guarantee agreement;[142] (4) requiring the MDB-financed project to be carried out "in accordance with sound environmental . . . standards;[143] and (5) requiring all goods financed under the MDB loan to be purchased in accordance with the MDB's procurement rules,[144] with the terms of the loan agreement taking priority over "the law of any State or political subdivision thereof to the contrary."[145]

Each of those provisions in the agreements is open to interpretation. Does the term "any taxes" include a "charge" on interest payments? What is a "reasonable opportunity" to visit a project site? When is a situation "extraordinary" enough to warrant suspension of loan disbursements? How stringent must environmental protection measures be to qualify as meeting "sound" standards? Should the term "law of any State or political subdivision thereof" be construed to include rules deriving from a regional agreement between neighboring states?

Without a clear provision on governing law in the MDB's loan and guarantee agreements with borrower X and state A, the answers to these questions of interpretation are fraught with uncertainty. On the other hand, with public international law specified as the governing law, the interpretation of these terms becomes much less uncertain. For instance, it becomes unnecessary to consider the wide array of possible approaches

---

[140] For examples of such standard provisions, see IBRD 1985 GENERAL CONDITIONS, *supra* note 14, §8.01(a); ADB 1986 LOAN REGULATIONS, *supra* note 93, §7.01(a)(i); EBRD SEPTEMBER 1994 STCs, *supra* note 109, §6.01(a)(i); AFDB 1989 GENERAL CONDITIONS, *supra* note 93, §11.02(a).

[141] For examples of such standard provisions, see IBRD 1985 GENERAL CONDITIONS, *supra* note 14, §9.01(c); ADB 1986 LOAN REGULATIONS, *supra* note 93, §6.04; EBRD SEPTEMBER 1994 STCs, *supra* note 109, §5.02(b); AFDB 1989 GENERAL CONDITIONS, *supra* note 93, §12.08(e).

[142] For examples of such standard provisions, see IBRD 1985 GENERAL CONDITIONS, *supra* note 14, §6.02(e); ADB 1986 LOAN REGULATIONS, *supra* note 93, §8.02(f); EBRD SEPTEMBER 1994 STCs, *supra* note 109, §7.01(a)(vi); AFDB 1989 GENERAL CONDITIONS, *supra* note 93, §8.01(d).

[143] *See* EBRD SEPTEMBER 1994 STCs, *supra* note 109, §4.02(a). For a reference to how the increased concern over environmental effects of MDB-financed projects has been reflected in the loan agreements of the World Bank and the ADB, see ASIAN DEVELOPMENT BANK, ENVIRONMENT PAPER NO. 10, ENVIRONMENTAL LOAN COVENANTS: HELPING ENSURE THE ENVIRONMENTAL SOUNDNESS OF PROJECTS SUPPORTED BY THE ASIAN DEVELOPMENT BANK 9–27 (1992).

[144] *See supra* note 13.

[145] For examples of such standard provisions, see text at note 47 *supra* (quoting the pertinent World Bank provision); text at note 111 *supra* (quoting the corresponding but slightly broader EBRD provision); ADB 1986 LOAN REGULATIONS, *supra* note 93, §10.01; AFDB 1989 GENERAL CONDITIONS, *supra* note 93, §13.01(a).

to treaty and contract interpretation, ranging from a strictly textual approach[146] to a policy-oriented one.[147] Instead, the proper method of interpretation is probably the contextual approach generally accepted in public international law via the 1969 Vienna Convention on the Law of Treaties.[148] In addition, guidance on some of the issues, such as what constitutes a set of "sound" environmental standards, could be drawn from customary international law, as reflected in a growing body of treaties and state practice.[149] Moreover, if public international law is defined for these purposes to include rules emerging from the customary practice of international financial institutions,[150] the positions that the MDBs have taken in the past in interpreting the terms at issue—"any taxes," "reasonable opportunity," and so forth—could be persuasive in settling the dispute between state *A* and the MDB in the foregoing example, or in preventing the dispute from arising in the first place.

Indeed, the value of a clear provision on governing law for MDB loan and guarantee agreements stems more from its role in the *prevention* of disputes than from its role in the *adjudication* of disputes. If the agreements relating to the power plant loan in the foregoing example have clearly specified from the outset that they will be governed by the rules of public international law, including customary rules deriving from the practice of international financial institutions, the government of state *A* will be less likely to take action inconsistent with those rules.[151] In short, a clear and effective provision on governing law can prevent disputes by bringing greater certainty to the legal obligations of the parties.[152]

---

[146] *See, e.g.*, EDWARD SLAVKO YAMBRISIC, TREATY INTERPRETATION—THEORY AND REALITY 9–10 (1987) (explaining the "clear sense" approach, under which it is often not permissible to look beyond the word being interpreted in order to examine its context or the intention behind its use).

[147] *See generally* MYRES S. MCDOUGAL, HAROLD D. LASSWELL & JAMES C. MILLER, THE INTERPRETATION OF AGREEMENTS AND WORLD PUBLIC ORDER (1967).

[148] *See* 1969 Vienna Convention, *supra* note 68, Arts. 31, 32. *See also* text at and notes 131, 133 *supra*. For a comparison of these three competing approaches to treaty interpretation, see BURNS H. WESTON, RICHARD A. FALK & ANTHONY D'AMATO, INTERNATIONAL LAW AND WORLD ORDER 59–63 (1990).

[149] For examples of the quickly growing body of international environmental law, see generally UNITED NATIONS ENVIRONMENT PROGRAMME, MULTILATERAL TREATIES IN THE FIELD OF THE ENVIRONMENT (Iwona Rummel-Bulska & Seth Osafo eds., 1991); BASIC DOCUMENTS OF INTERNATIONAL ENVIRONMENTAL LAW (Harald Hohmann ed., 1992).

[150] As noted in text at note 119 *supra*, the EBRD's STCs do that by referring to custom arising from "the practice of . . . international financial institutions."

[151] The preventive role of a provision specifying public international law as the governing law could be important also when a borrower or guarantor is contemplating more hostile action than those posited in the foregoing example. For instance, state *A* might consider declaring that the loan and guarantee agreements are null and void—and that state *A* and company *X* are relieved of all their financial obligations thereunder— on grounds that those agreements were entered into under a predecessor government and hence are no longer binding. Without a clear provision on governing law, there is little to prevent the government (or an arbitral tribunal or court, if the case were to proceed that far) from choosing any one of a range of theories regarding state succession. On the other hand, with a clear prescription of public international law as the governing law, the likelihood of such an outcome is reduced. *See, e.g.*, 2 WOOD, *supra* note 89, §4.10[2] (Feb. 1984) (noting the divergence of opinions among states on succession to debt claims; then pointing out the gradual development of rules of public international law on the subject as a result of the International Law Commission's work on treaties governing state succession).

[152] Another factor—a member state's desire for a continuing flow of MDB loans—serves as a powerful incentive to prevent disputes or to dissolve them informally. For references to this important practical consideration, see W. Paatii Ofosu-Amaah, *The World Bank—Legal Aspects of Its Recent Lending Activities, in* 2 COMMERCIAL TRANSACTIONS, *supra* note 89, at 305, 309 (noting that "[t]he main sanction that the [World] Bank maintains [to prevent the borrower from acting contrary to the bank's expectations under a loan agreement] is the ability not to extend further loans or credits to such a borrower."); ASIAN DEVELOPMENT BANK, *supra* note 143, at 57–58 (explaining in the context of ADB operations the practice of "quasi-conditionality," which is "the practice by which the Bank requires covenants associated with one loan to be honored [to the satisfaction of the ADB] before the processing of another loan can be advanced or completed"). However, the existence of this *practical* consideration, stemming from the usually superior bargaining position of an MDB, does not diminish the importance of establishing *legal* certainty as a means of preventing disputes from arising between the MDB and its borrowers.

Bringing greater certainty to these issues also serves a larger purpose: that of evaluating and improving the MDBs. As noted above, the MDBs face increasing scrutiny and criticism.[153] That is natural, given the growth in their lending volumes[154] and their corresponding influence in the international economic system. Indeed, whether one agrees or disagrees with particular criticisms, it seems beyond doubt that a close and critical evaluation of MDB operations—on economic, political, environmental and social grounds—is a valuable and productive exercise, for it can yield improvements in those operations.

However, there is nothing to gain, and much to lose, when MDBs unnecessarily leave their operations open to challenge on *legal* grounds. This is what the MDBs (with the exception now of the EBRD) do by retaining vague provisions on governing law in their loan and guarantee agreements. That vagueness invites legal challenge and dispute on a wide range of issues, as the foregoing example illustrates.

Such legal challenge and dispute, in turn, can undermine support for the MDBs in the international community, especially in the member states that provide the most financial backing for them.[155] Governments of those states would be unlikely to continue that backing did in fact start challenging or circumventing expectations on such things as environmental standards[156] and procurement procedures.[157]

This outcome would be quite unfortunate, not necessarily because of the result itself (undermining support) but because of the reason for it. The MDBs, like the other major economic and trade institutions that have arisen since World War II—the International Monetary Fund (IMF) and the World Trade Organization (established recently on the foundations of the General Agreement on Tariffs and Trade and its aborted predecessor, the International Trade Organization)[158]—are founded on the principle that overall public benefit is served by facilitating open market-oriented economic decisions and increasing international transactions.[159] We cannot fairly judge the effectiveness of the World Bank and other such institutions in pursuing that principle if their operations are derailed for extraneous reasons.

The risk of derailment is greater in respect of MDB operations in the former Soviet republics than it has been so far anywhere else in the world. Much of the harshest

---

[153] *See* text at notes 7–10 *supra*. For a recent example of scrutiny of the AFDB, see *Development Banking: Double Trouble*, ECONOMIST, May 14, 1994, at 81 (referring to an external report criticizing the AFDB for having a top-heavy bureaucracy riddled with political intrigue, and for haphazard monitoring of loans).

[154] For information on cumulative lending volumes of the MDBs, see text at and note 94 *supra*. Annual lending by the MDBs recently amounted to about $35 billion. *See* Head, *Contracting, supra* note 12, at 43–44.

[155] On the capital subscriptions of G–7 states, as reflected in voting rights, see *supra* note 8.

[156] For an illustration of the importance placed by the U.S. Congress on environmental sustainability of MDB-financed projects, see the International Development and Finance Act of 1989, Pub. L. No. 101-240, tit. V, §521(a) (codified at 22 U.S.C. §262m-7(a) (Supp. V 1993)) (prohibiting U.S. support for MDB loans unless an environmental impact assessment of the project is undertaken first and submitted to the MDB's governing board).

[157] *See supra* note 15. The significance of procurement is illustrated also by the fact that the EBRD's STCs, like the World Bank's General Conditions, expressly authorize the institution to publish information on the contracts awarded under loans it makes, including the nationality of the party to whom the contract was awarded. *See* EBRD SEPTEMBER 1994 STCs, *supra* note 109, §4.04(b); IBRD 1985 GENERAL CONDITIONS, *supra* note 14, §9.07(b). Such information, broken down by nationality of winning contractors, typically appears in the MDBs' annual reports. *See, e.g.,* WB 1994 REPORT, *supra* note 8, at 60–63 (showing, e.g., that as of mid-1994, U.S. suppliers had been awarded a cumulative total of about $23 billion in World Bank contracts).

[158] For an overview of the ideological foundations of the IMF, see RICHARD W. EDWARDS, JR., INTERNATIONAL MONETARY COLLABORATION 4–8 (1985). For an overview of the ideological foundations of the International Trade Organization, the General Agreement on Tariffs and Trade, and the World Trade Organization, see JOHN H. JACKSON, WILLIAM J. DAVEY & ALAN O. SYKES, JR., LEGAL PROBLEMS OF INTERNATIONAL ECONOMIC RELATIONS 293–98 (1995).

[159] This principle appears in the charters of these institutions. *See, e.g.,* ARTICLES OF AGREEMENT OF THE INTERNATIONAL MONETARY FUND, July 22, 1944, Art. I(ii), 60 Stat. 1401, 2 UNTS 39 (entered into force Dec. 27, 1945); AGREEMENT ESTABLISHING THE WORLD TRADE ORGANIZATION, *opened for signature* Apr. 15, 1994, Preamble, 33 ILM 1144 (1994) (entered into force Jan. 1, 1995); IBRD CHARTER, *supra* note 12, Art. I(iii).

criticism of the World Bank's sister institution, the International Monetary Fund—and much of the threatened or actual suspension of payments to that institution by its borrowing members—occurred just after the IMF dramatically increased its lending to debt-ridden countries caught up in the debt crisis of the early 1980s.[160] Now, in the 1990s, the World Bank and the EBRD are lending vast sums of money to public sector borrowers in Central and Eastern Europe and central Asia,[161] where political and legal stability is tentative at best. It should come as no surprise if some of those borrowers are tempted to renege on those loans in a few years when they start coming due for repayment.[162] In anticipation of that, it is important and timely that the governing law for the agreements under which the loans are being provided be as clear as possible, and in particular that those agreements be understood to hold the borrowing countries and their state-owned enterprises to international standards.

---

[160] *See* John W. Head, *Suspension of Debtor Countries' Voting Rights in the IMF: An Assessment of the Third Amendment to the IMF Charter*, 33 VA. J. INT'L L. 591, 598–601 (1993).

[161] *See* WB 1994 REPORT, *supra* note 8, at 230–33 (showing total IBRD and IDA lending as of mid-1994 for the four largest borrowers among the former Soviet republics—Belarus, Kazakhstan, Kyrgyzstan and Russia—as nearly $3.5 billion, with Russia alone accounting for almost $2.9 billion of that total). Although the EBRD's annual report does not distinguish clearly between private sector and public sector loans in reporting on EBRD operations, it can be inferred that the EBRD has made a total of at least ECU 2.19 billion ($2.70 billion) in public sector loans, since total private sector operations (which are often for smaller amounts than public sector loans) account for 62% of all projects and the total of all EBRD financings is ECU 5.77 billion ($7.10 billion). *See* EBRD 1994 REPORT, *supra* note 6, at 14–15.

[162] Typically, public sector loans made by the MDBs have "grace periods" of several years during which no repayment of principal is required, so that repayments under such loans made by those institutions in 1994 are not required until around 1999. *See, e.g.,* WB 1994 REPORT, *supra* note 8, at 234–38. *See also* WB OPER. MAN., *supra* note 12, at OP 3.10, Ann. D (Sept. 1994) (showing 3–5-year grace periods under most IBRD loans and 10-year grace periods under IDA loans).

Part IV
The World Trade Organization

[13]

The Great 1994 Sovereignty Debate: United States Acceptance and Implementation of the Uruguay Round Results

JOHN H. JACKSON*

Sovereignty, strictly, is the locus of ultimate legitimate authority in a political society, once the Prince or "the Crown," later parliament or the people.

* * *

Sovereignty, a conception deriving from the relations between a prince and his/her subjects, is not a necessary or appropriate external attribute for the abstraction we call a state .... For international relations, surely for international law, it is a term largely unnecessary and better avoided.

* * *

For legal purposes at least, we might do well to relegate the term sovereignty to the shelf of history as a relic from an earlier era. To this end, it is necessary to analyze, "decompose," the concept; to identify the elements that have been deemed to be inherent in, or to derive from, "sovereignty;" in a system of states at the turn of the twenty-first century.[1]

I. INTRODUCTION

It is a privilege and an honor to be invited to contribute to this *festschrift* volume for so distinguished an international law scholar and teacher as Louis Henkin. Indeed it is a formidable challenge—what can one say that could rise to even the shadow of the standard that Professor Henkin represents. The way that I have chosen to *try* to reach that shadow, however, is to address one of the many issues on which Professor Henkin has written and that seems to be of great interest to

---

* Hessel E. Yntema Professor of Law, University of Michigan Law School, Ann Arbor, MI 48109. Copyright © John H. Jackson, 1997.

1. LOUIS HENKIN, INTERNATIONAL LAW: POLITICS AND VALUES 9-10 (1995).

158   *COLUMBIA JOURNAL OF TRANSNATIONAL LAW*   [36:157

him.[2] For this reason I have chosen to comment on the concept of "sovereignty," which puzzles many of us toiling in the international legal vineyards. I must confess that I also chose this subject because it intrigues me too, and because recently I have had the experience of participating in some major policy debates which engage this concept, namely the 1994 debate in Congress (and other forums) about whether the United States should ratify the treaty embodying the results of the massive decade-long trade negotiation known as the Uruguay Round. This means, of course, that the reader must be aware that I speak at least partly as a "participant observer,"[3] hopefully in the best sense of that empirical technique. Thus, the reader is entitled to appraise my judgments accordingly. Professor Henkin himself has written from experiences and will understand the approach.

This brief contribution is designed to complement some of Professor Henkin's thoughts on the subject of sovereignty, and to build on them such as is known to me from his writings. The approach I will take here is to examine one particular "case"—the 1994 Uruguay Round debate—to explore how the concept (or, more appropriately, the concepts) of sovereignty played a role in various policy discussions. Through the examination of this specific case, I will illustrate how the concepts of sovereignty were used (differently in different contexts) and point out the more specific and disaggregated policy issues to which they were linked. In some sort of nominal sense, my views may appear to be somewhat contrary to parts of Professor Henkin's views, especially in those instances when he speaks of relegating "the term

---

2. *See id.*

3. *See Results of the Uruguay Round Trade Negotiations: Hearings Before the Senate Finance Comm.*, 103d Cong. 114 (1994) (March 23, 1994, testimony of John H. Jackson, Hessel E. Yntema Professor of Law, University of Michigan) [hereinafter *Jackson March Testimony*]; *The World Trade Organization and U.S. Sovereignty: Hearings Before the Senate Comm. on Foreign Relations*, 103d Cong. (1994) (June 14, 1994, testimony of John H. Jackson, Hessel E. Yntema Professor of Law, University of Michigan), *available in* 1994 WL 14188767 [hereinafter *Jackson June Testimony*]. Uruguay Round Agreements Act, Pub. L. No. 103-465.

In addition to the above, the reader may be interested in some of the articles published about the Uruguay Round legislative debate, including the following: William J. Aceves, *Lost Sovereignty? The Implications of the Uruguay Round Agreements*, 19 FORDHAM INT'L L.J. 427 (1995); Claudio Cocuzza & Andrea Forabosco, *Are States Relinquishing Their Sovereign Rights? The GATT Dispute Settlement Process in a Globalized Economy*, 4 TUL. J. INT'L & COMP. L. 161 (1996); Julie Long, Note, *Ratcheting Up Federalism: A Supremacy Clause Analysis of NAFTA and the Uruguay Round Agreements*, 80 MINN. L. REV. 231 (1995); Samuel C. Straight, Note, *GATT and NAFTA: Marrying Effective Dispute Settlement and the Sovereignty of the Fifty States*, 45 DUKE L.J. 216 (1995).

sovereignty to the shelf of history as a relic from an earlier era"[4] or doing away with the "S word."[5] Yet behind and beyond this "nominal sense," it should be clear that I am using the word "sovereignty" in a different context than Professor Henkin. Indeed, Professor Henkin himself notes that it is necessary to "decompose" the word, and to identify which elements of the concept are "appropriate and desirable for a state in a system of states at the turn of the twenty-first century."[6]

I could, of course, fashion a new word (or perhaps more modernly, a new phrase with a catchy acronym), but the observable fact is that the word "sovereignty" is still being used widely, often in different settings which imply different "sub-meanings." Consequently, I cling to the word and will use it, knowing that most of my readers should understand it. As I use the word it will not always (indeed almost never) signify the more "antiquated" definition (that is also ambiguous and multi-definitional). In broad brush I see the "antiquated" definition of "sovereignty" that should be "relegated" as something like the notion of a nation-state's supreme absolute power and authority over its subjects and territory, unfettered by any higher law or rule (except perhaps ethical or religious standards) unless that nation-state consents in an individual and meaningful way. It could be characterized as the nation-state's power (embodied in the Prince?) to violate virgins, chop off heads, arbitrarily confiscate property, and all sorts of other excessive and inappropriate actions.

No sensible person would agree that such an antiquated version of sovereignty exists at all in today's world. A multitude of treaties and customary international law norms impose international legal constraints (at least) that circumscribe extreme forms of arbitrary actions on even a sovereign's own citizens. Of course some theories can explain these constraints as having been "consented to" by sovereigns, but these explanations cannot always explain the observable phenomena of modern-day international law applications. Furthermore, policy advocates and political representatives make the argument that their government should decline to accept a treaty because it takes away the nation's sovereignty *even when* it consents. Indeed, in this sense *all* treaties "take away sovereignty," and so the argument of some would seem to deny the validity of *any* treaty acceptance. Let us indeed "relegate" or abolish such use of the "S" word.

---

4. HENKIN, *supra* note 1, at 10.

5. Louis Henkin, *The Mythology of Sovereignty*, AM. SOC'Y INT'L L. NEWSL., Mar.-May 1993, at 1.

6. HENKIN, *supra* note 1, at 10.

But then what does "sovereignty," as practically used today, signify? I will suggest a tentative hypothesis: most (but not all) of the time when "sovereignty" is used in current policy debates, it really refers to questions about the allocation of power; this is normally government decision-making power. I would argue that most of the sovereignty objections to joining an international treaty are arguments about the allocation of power among different levels of different human institutions, mostly governmental. That is, when a party argues that the U.S. should not accept a treaty because it takes away U.S. sovereignty to do so, what that party most often really means is that he or she believes a certain set of decisions should, as a matter of good government policy, be made at the nation-state (U.S.) level and not at an international level. Often this is not articulated and the objection to a treaty is stated in generic and opaque terms, sometimes with "religious fervor," so that the argument seems easy to dismiss. When stated so broadly, opaquely, and categorically, the sovereign argument frequently appears unrealistic. It assumes a degree of independent action for a nation state that in a "real" sense hardly exists anyway. When viewed as a question of allocation of power, however, the debate only begins with the "sovereignty" objection; it must continue with an analysis demonstrating why it is better or worse for such a power shift to occur in certain circumstances.[7] As discussed below, this is rarely done, but ought to be done if the argument is to be persuasive.

I suggest that the allocation of power issue, as often embraced by an invocation of the "sovereignty" argument, is part of a very complex and vast landscape of issues relating to allocation of power for all types of government (and non-government) decisions in our world today. First, there is a question of "vertical" allocation of power: at what level should a decision or armed intervention be made? An international body? A national body (federal level)? A sub-federal entity? A local neighborhood? Where should a decision about which pot-holes to fill, which streets to repair, be made? For contrast, where should a decision about standards for products moving in international trade be made? What are the elements for deciding such questions? Second, there are also "horizontal" power allocation questions. Should a certain decision be under the control of the legislature, the executive, the judiciary,

---

7. The concept of "subsidiarity," currently very heavily debated in Europe, is clearly closely related to this discussion. I do not intend here, however, to get into the middle of the European debate on this subject.

another government entity, or even a non-government (such as private business) entity?[8]

When sovereignty objection arguments are "decomposed" and examined for underlying reasons, it becomes clear that there is merit to scrutinize closely what is at stake for a nation in accepting the constraints of an international treaty.[9] Clearly what is at stake will differ with the size, power, population, economic circumstances, etc., of the nation-state. A large and powerful state would more likely be hesitant to accept obligations to an international decision-making procedure that would most probably result in decisions contrary to the national goals of such a powerful state. This might be because of a one-nation one-vote decision-making structure with a large membership of mini-states whose national goals are inconsistent with those of the large states. Consequently, what often becomes important is the actual "constitutional" structure of the international institutions put in place by the treaty.[10]

By way of contrast, small countries might find that membership in certain types of treaty-based international institutions actually "enhance sovereignty" in certain real senses. By such membership, they may feel less threatened by other nations that are much larger and more powerful. For example, a dispute settlement mechanism might, in the view of a small country, redress some of the imbalance of power when it comes to handling disputes or sources of tension about the way either nation has been applying its international economic policies (such as trade barriers).

Part of the challenge for international law and international relations is to analyze the "decomposed" arguments. This may help

---

8. Market economics obviously has much to say about the last in this list. *See generally,* RICHARD G. LIPSEY & PAUL N. COURANT, MICROECONOMICS (8th ed., 1994).

9. *See Jackson June Testimony, supra* note 3, at 3-4.

This does not mean that it is frivolous to carefully study the question, as this hearing is designed to do. It is important to assure ourselves that if there develops the rare situation when an international body or rule system operates in a manner to abuse the rules or abuse the procedures of an organization so as to threaten the vital interests of the United States, that the U.S. will still retain the tools to take appropriate counter measures. In the case of the WTO, I believe that the U.S. and other nations are protected in that respect. Among other protections, the WTO Charter allows for withdrawal with a brief six month notice. It is also the case that this Congress is likely to specify in the implementing legislation that the WTO Charter and the Uruguay Round rules are not "self-executing," so again in the rare case of serious abuse of international procedures the U.S. would maintain its own constitutional freedom to act even if inconsistent with international rules. In such a case, of course, the U.S. could be in breach of its international legal obligations and might face counter-measures.

10. *See id.*

nations with divergent perspectives to consider the broader and longer-term perspectives of both national policy and international policy objectives, and to better understand the risks of developing international institutions as weighed against the advantages of such development.

In looking behind the surface of the Uruguay Round Treaty debate in the United States in 1994, we can readily see many issues stirred together. This is why I believe much of this 1994 activity can be termed the "Great Sovereignty Debate" of this decade. It may not have been much noticed in this context. That is partly because the debate occurred in many different forums. These included several committees of the U.S. Congress, the floor of the House and the Senate, and many forms of the media (*e.g.*, radio, television, newspapers, journals, etc.). Yet if one follows the threads of the debate about the U.S. accepting the Uruguay Trade Round results, one constantly discovers references to "sovereignty" as addressing essentially power allocation issues.[11] These include my own statements responding to the arguments of others.[12]

Consequently, in the three remaining sections of this paper, I will explore the 1994 debate. In Part II I will outline the background context of the debate and some of the specific parts of it. In Part III I will discuss in somewhat greater detail the various ways the "sovereignty argument" was used in the debate over whether the United States should accept the Uruguay Round negotiation results. This will be the core of my analysis, and will suggest a number of different contexts and, therefore, different meanings of the "sovereignty objection." In Part IV I will draw some tentative conclusions or perspectives from the material addressed in Part III.

What are some of the different issues discussed? Even in Part III, I will not attempt in this short space to provide a complete and exhaustive inventory of all the different possible "decomposed" policy questions to which sovereignty arguments were addressed in the 1994 debate. However, to illustrate some of the specific issues, I will discuss sovereignty issues in four broad categories, including elements of the World Trade Organization (WTO) decision-making procedures, the structure of the new WTO dispute settlement process, and some questions about the constitutional and other arguments regarding U.S. internal law and procedures and how they would be affected by U.S. acceptance of the Uruguay Round results. Many particular issues are thus discussed below. These include: the implications and risks of the

---

11. For relevant hearings, see URUGUAY ROUND AGREEMENTS ACT: A LEGISLATIVE HISTORY OF PUBLIC LAW NO. 103-465 (Bernard D. Reams, Jr. & Jon S. Schultz eds., 1995).

12. *See Jackson June Testimony, supra* note 3.

WTO treaty text regarding potential decisions of the WTO affecting national economic regulation; the effect of the WTO dispute processes on domestic environmental standards; and the interrelationship between the U.S. constitutional federal structure and the effects of the WTO institutional procedures.

II. GATT, THE URUGUAY ROUND AND THE WTO: THE BACKGROUND FOR THE 1994 DEBATE

A. *The General Agreement on Tariffs and Trade: A Half-Century Trade Treaty*

Looking back over the 1946-1996 history of the General Agreement on Tariffs and Trade (GATT) allows one to reflect on how surprising it was that this relatively feeble institution with many "birth defects" managed to play such a significant role for almost five decades. It certainly was far more successful than one might have predicted in the late 1940s.

The GATT, often described as the major trade organization and the principal treaty for trade relations, was technically neither. As a treaty, it never itself came into force. It was always applied "provisionally" by the Protocol of Provisional Application (P.P.A.).[13] In addition, technically the GATT was not intended to be an organization. The negotiators in the drafting conferences in 1946 (New York), 1947 (Geneva), and 1948 (Havana) expected the International Trade Organization (I.T.O.), created by their draft treaty-charter, to be the institutional framework to which the GATT (an agreement among "contracting parties" to liberalize trade restrictions) would be attached. When the U.S. Congress refused to approve the I.T.O. Charter, declared dead by 1951, the GATT, which came into (provisional) force in 1948 by the terms of the P.P.A., became the focus of attention as a possible institution where nations could solve some of their trade problems. An attempt in 1955 to create a small mini-organization to solve institutional problems also failed. Yet the GATT, through a series of major trade rounds designed to gradually reduce tariffs and other trade barriers (culminating in the Uruguay Round which was the eighth round) along with an increasingly important set of relatively precise (and complex)

---

13. Protocol of Provisional Application to the General Agreement on Tariffs and Trade, *signed* Oct. 30, 1947, 61 Stat. A2051, 55 U.N.T.S. 308.

rules, was able to achieve an astonishing amount of world trade liberalization.

The relative lack of treaty clauses that could serve as a basis for a trade institution, and the ambiguity of those that were contained in the GATT, became increasingly troublesome as the GATT grew in scope and detail in order to cope with a fascinating set of concrete problems of international economic relations. While most of this story has been told elsewhere[14] and need not occupy us here, several institutional problems in particular relate to the general notion of "sovereignty" and deserve mention.

One of these problems was embedded ambiguously in GATT article 25 regarding decisions of the "Contracting Parties" (C.P.s) acting jointly.[15] The treaty language was extraordinarily broad due to the historical context that expected an I.T.O. charter to oversee and supervise what could be done. Article 25 stated that the contracting parties would meet from time to time "for the purpose of giving effect" to the agreement, and "with a view to facilitating the operation and furthering the objectives of this Agreement." The procedure was mostly one nation one vote, with decisions taken by a majority of votes cast. Despite the generality of the language, however, it is fair to say it was not used to its limit; indeed the contracting parties appeared cautious and arguably never used this authority to impose any new substantive obligation on any nation state. Instead a powerful practice developed of taking major decisions by "consensus," which although not itself defined, generally appeared to require at least the absence of objections from any C.P.[16] When we discuss the "sovereignty" arguments about

---

14. *See, e.g.,* JOHN H. JACKSON, WORLD TRADE AND THE LAW OF GATT: A LEGAL ANALYSIS OF THE GENERAL AGREEMENT ON TARIFFS AND TRADE (1969); John H. Jackson, *The World Trade Organization: Watershed Innovation or Cautious Small Step Forward?*, THE WORLD ECONOMY 11 (1995) [hereinafter Jackson, *The World Trade Organization*]; John H. Jackson, *The Uruguay Round and the Launch of the WTO—Significance and Challenges, in* THE WORLD TRADE ORGANIZATION: THE MULTILATERAL TRADE FRAMEWORK FOR THE 21ST CENTURY AND U.S. IMPLEMENTING LEGISLATION 5 (Terence P. Stewart ed., 1996) [hereinafter Jackson, *The Uruguay Round*]; JOHN H. JACKSON, THE WORLD TRADING SYSTEM (2d ed., forthcoming 1997).

15. Note that the terms "member" or "membership" were not used.

16. The Agreement Establishing the World Trade Organization contains a definition of the "consensus" decision-making procedure: "The body concerned shall be deemed to have decided by consensus on a matter submitted for its consideration, if no member, present at the meeting when the decision is taken, formally objects to the proposed decision." The Agreement Establishing the World Trade Organization, *opened for signature* Apr. 15, 1994, art. IX n.1, 33 I.L.M. 1144, 1148 (1994) [hereinafter WTO Agreement]. *See also* JOHN H. JACKSON, THE WORLD TRADING SYSTEM: LAW AND POLICY OF INTERNATIONAL ECONOMIC RELATIONS 49-50

membership in the new WTO described below, it should be remembered that most of the nations concerned were already previously committed to the broad GATT language.

A second major problem concerned the dispute settlement procedures of the GATT With only the sparse GATT treaty text to look to, an extraordinarily elaborate (and some argue very successful) dispute settlement procedure was developed in reliance on several decades of GATT practice. During its existence, the GATT procedure handled over 233 formal disputes (and was the background for many more that were settled or abandoned).[17] As practice developed, disputes were considered by a panel of experts (usually three but sometimes five individuals) not to be guided by any government. A report of this panel was sent to a "Council" of the GATT C.P.s (again not a treaty body but one constituted by practice and a resolution of the C.P.s). If the Council "adopted" the report, it was considered binding on the parties. But the decision to adopt the report had to be by "consensus." Thus, the C.P. that "lost" the panel proceeding (as indicated in the report) could "block" the adoption, leaving matters in limbo. Increasingly this was recognized as an anomaly for an effective dispute settlement procedure, and during the 1980s the C.P.s, and panels, struggled with ways to overcome this and other similar "birth defects." The Uruguay Round (U.R.) results contain important provisions on this issue, and instigate further "sovereignty" arguments, as we shall see.

B.   *The Uruguay Round Trade Negotiations 1986-1994*

Almost as soon as the seventh trade round, the "Tokyo Round" of 1973-1979, was at an end, some planning began for a next round. The Tokyo Round was the first to address extensively non-tariff barriers, using the treaty technique (to avoid the difficulties of amending the GATT) of proposing a series of about ten stand-alone "side agreements" or "codes" on various subjects. C.P.s could then pick and choose which ones they would accept.

The eighth round was launched formally at Punta del Este, Uruguay, in September 1986 with an incredibly ambitious agenda. The

---

(1997).

17. *See* JACKSON, *supra* note 16, at 99; ROBERT E. HUDEC, ENFORCING INTERNATIONAL TRADE LAW: THE EVOLUTION OF THE MODERN GATT LEGAL SYSTEM 287 (1993) [hereinafter HUDEC, ENFORCING INTERNATIONAL TRADE LAW]; ROBERT E. HUDEC, THE GATT LEGAL SYSTEM AND WORLD TRADE DIPLOMACY (2d ed., 1990).

Uruguay Round agenda called for further work on the "goods" or "product" rules of trade, with attention to revisions of the Tokyo Round codes and some new measures. But even more formidable was the U.R. participants' ambition to bring into the GATT trading system new subjects such as trade in services (potentially embracing 155 or more specific service sectors such as transport, tourism, financial services, professional services (accountants, lawyers, engineers, etc.)), and also to develop rules for "trade related intellectual property" (T.R.I.P.s) questions. It was not surprising that the original goal of completing this round at a Brussels Ministerial meeting in December 1990 was not achieved. After the "Brussels Impasse," negotiations continued. They were largely concluded by December 15, 1993 (after intensive negotiations during the last half of 1993), and formally concluded at the final Ministerial Meeting at Marrakech, Morocco, on April 15, 1994. These dates were primarily controlled by the provisions of the United States "fast track" legislation that specified the procedure by which the U.S. Congress would consider its approval of the U.R. results.

A key element of the U.R. negotiation approach was the "single package" ideal by which every nation would have to accept the whole U.R. results as one entire package, or stay out of the U.R. treaty system. This was in contrast to the "GATT à la carte" approach, as the Tokyo Round results were called. This U.R. approach also established an entirely new treaty for nations to join, thus avoiding the troublesome amendment requirements of the GATT The GATT, after a transition period, was to be formally abandoned (with some nations exercising the formal right under the GATT and P.P.A. language to withdraw from those treaties upon sufficient but brief notice).

In the U.R. package two very important institutional structures are established: 1) the new World Trade Organization as a formal international organization; and 2) a new Twenty-Seven-Article Dispute Settlement Understanding (D.S.U.) of twenty-five pages that specify and control the dispute settlement procedure while correcting some of the "birth defects," especially the "blocking" problem.

The WTO Agreement provides, for the first time, a formal international trade organization charter and structure. The "charter" is quite short—about fifteen pages. But it embraces four annexes which include altogether about 26,000 pages of text, schedule commitments, and other matters. Undoubtedly this treaty is a record for its length. With the breadth of subject matter it is also extraordinarily complex and loaded with potential impacts as well as with ambiguities (inevitable when drafting involves 130 or more participating nations). The WTO charter becomes a sort of "umbrella" for this whole single package, with only a few "optional" texts ("plurilateral agreements" in Annex 4) included as part of the single package.

The D.S.U., which is contained in Annex 2, is strikingly significant—as the history of the first two years of the WTO already demonstrates. Over three times the prior GATT annual rate of dispute process initiations occurred during that time.[18] One of the most interesting features of the D.S.U. is the creation for the first time of an "appellate procedure," plus the virtual "automatic adoption" of panel and appeal reports.[19] No longer will a "sovereign state" be able to block consensus adoption of a dispute report. This obviously gives rise to sovereignty arguments.

When negotiators struggle with the concepts of "sovereignty" as implying ultimate choice for the nation-state, the "realism" of such a choice was certainly difficult for many. The U.R. package is incredibly far-reaching, and certainly, as a matter of treaty law, imposes a number of constraints on nation-state members. Of course, the argument is that the members accepted these constraints. But looking at this history realistically, one can see some qualifications about "acceptance." Major players, such as the United States and the European Union took many months to complete elaborate domestic constitutional procedures, with extensive debates about various aspects. The parliament of a country like Costa Rica, however, took less than one hour! For many small countries, (Costa Rica, one might add, is not atypical), the choices were not very extensive. To stay out of the new trade system could put whole economies in jeopardy, give up "rule based" leverage that the new procedures might afford small nations, and prevent participation in the development of new rules, as well as the elaboration and interpretation of the extensive U.R. texts.[20]

---

18. *See* World Trade Organization, *Overview of the State-of-Play of WTO Disputes*, constantly updated at the following Web site, <http://www.wto.org/wto/dispute/bulletin.htm>. By mid-1997, over 88 disputes were documented. During the 1950s: 53 complaints; 1960s: 7 complaints; 1970s: 32 complaints; and 1980s: 115 complaints. *See* HUDEC, ENFORCING INTERNATIONAL TRADE LAW, *supra* note 17, at 287.

19. *See* Understanding on Rules and Procedures Governing the Settlement of Disputes [hereinafter DSU], Annex 2 of WTO Agreement, *supra* note 16, arts. 16-17, 33 I.L.M. 1226, 1235-37 (1994). *See infra* Part III.C.

20. *See* Implementing the Uruguay Round (John H. Jackson & Alan O. Sykes, eds., forthcoming 1997) (manuscript at 399, on file with authors) (volume of works by 13 authors including analysis of 11 different countries' implementation processes).

C.   *United States Acceptance of the Uruguay Round Results: The Uruguay Round Trade Agreements Act of 1994*

Since the Trade Agreements Act of 1974, the United States Congress has considered approval of all major trade agreements (GATT rounds and Free Trade Agreements such as the N.A.F.T.A.) under a procedure known as the *fast track.* While somewhat intricate and based on a interesting history, the fast track is essentially a "statutory" treaty approval procedure designed for what in U.S. domestic law are called "Executive Congressional Agreements." This contrasts with the constitutional requirement of Senate approval by a two-thirds vote.[21]

Under the fast track process, the U.S. Congress approves a statute (usually proposed by the President after treaty negotiations with foreign states) that authorizes ("delegates power to") the President (sometimes with certain conditions) to accept a proposed treaty. After both houses of the U.S. Congress approve such a statute and the President signs it, this law is the basis for further Presidential action "ratifying" or accepting the proposed treaty. The U.S. Congress usually also includes in the statute the measures that it wishes to enact into domestic law so as to implement the treaty. Whether the treaty itself becomes part of U.S. domestic law is a separate question which depends on the U.S. doctrine of self-executing treaties. However, as to the trade treaties of 1979 and subsequently, statutory phrases and legislative history provide that these treaties are not self-executing, with some possible minor exceptions.[22]

The fast track adds several features to the standard Congressional procedure (as embodied in the rules of the House and the Senate). First, the proposed statute may not be amended once it is introduced. Second,

---

21. It should be noted that the term "executive agreement" used in United States domestic law to contrast with "treaties" for which a separate constitutional procedure exists is confusing. Clearly both of these categories of international agreement are, under international law, "treaties."

22. *See* JOHN H. JACKSON ET AL., LEGAL PROBLEMS OF INTERNATIONAL ECONOMIC RELATIONS 147 (3d ed. 1995) [hereinafter JACKSON ET AL., LEGAL PROBLEMS]; JACKSON, *supra* note 16, at 75; JOHN H. JACKSON ET AL., IMPLEMENTING THE TOKYO ROUND: NATIONAL CONSTITUTIONS AND INTERNATIONAL ECONOMIC RULES 169-70 (1984); STATEMENT OF ADMINISTRATIVE ACTION FOR THE NORTH AMERICAN FREE TRADE AGREEMENT, TITLE I, SECTION 101, H.R. DOC. NO. 103-59, at 10 (1993); STATEMENT OF ADMINISTRATIVE ACTION FOR THE URUGUAY ROUND TRADE AGREEMENTS, TITLE I, SECTION 101, H.R. DOC. NO. 103-316, at 12 (1994). *See also* STATEMENT OF ADMINISTRATIVE ACTION FOR THE NORTH AMERICAN FREE TRADE AGREEMENT, SECTION 102(B), H.R. DOC. NO. 103-59, at 13 (discussing the relationship of the agreement to State Law).

once introduced the bill must be considered and discharged from committees of the U.S. Congress within specified time periods. Finally, the floor debate in both houses on this bill is strictly limited. The whole procedure is designed to take a maximum period of 90 to 120 days (depending on some technicalities), and to ensure that the U.S. Congress will vote ("up or down") on the whole proposed bill to accept the treaty that has been negotiated. Thus, foreign countries should be assured that at least the U.S. Congress will consider the results negotiated, and will not (at this step) "reopen the negotiations" through a variety of amendments to the domestic statute, etc.

Other features of the fast track include various deadlines for submission of the near final negotiation results to the Congress, and for the signing of the agreement (subject to national approval procedures, *i.e.*, a referendum). In addition, the fast track provides for extensive consultation with the Congress throughout a negotiation, and the practice has developed that during the specified Congressional consultation period (recently 120 days) before the treaty is signed, key Congressional committees will work extensively with Administration officials to prepare the draft proposed legislation. The fast track process is eagerly sought by foreign nations who begin a trade negotiation with the U.S. But this procedure has also been criticized by opponents of trade treaty legislation as "undemocratic" or "unconstitutional," or possibly as another track towards "infringement on U.S. sovereignty."[23]

The Uruguay Round results were "signed" on April 15, 1994. During the ensuing months the U.S. Trade Representative's office and its officials worked with the Congress to develop a proposed statute. For various reasons (and some miscalculations) the proposed bill was not sent to the Congress until September 27, 1994. Consequently, the timing restrictions of the fast track procedures did not call for a final vote until after the November 1994 congressional elections—at a "lame duck" special session. In fact, the votes were held in the House of Representatives on November 29, 1994, with approval by a vote of 288 to 146. The Senate vote took place on December 1, 1994, with approval by a vote of 76 to 24. During 1994, many congressional hearings in a large number of different committees were held on the Uruguay Round results and the proposed statute (including some ancillary issues). In a number of these hearings the issue of sovereignty was an important focus in one way or another. Combined with a general public debate in

---

23. *The World Trade Organization and U.S. Sovereignty: Hearings Before the Senate Comm. on Foreign Relations*, 103d Cong. (1994) (testimony of Ralph Nader, Center for Responsive Law), *available in* 1994 WL 14188790.

all the various media, as well as many academic, business and other public forums, 1994 was a year for a truly major and historical U.S. debate about questions of this nation's economic treaty participation and its relation to various concepts of sovereignty.[24]

III.   THE U.R. IMPLEMENTING ACT: DECOMPOSING THE SOVEREIGNTY ARGUMENTS

With the background outlined above in mind, we now look more closely and specifically at some of the various issues discussed in the Great 1994 Sovereignty Debate. There will be no attempt here to present an exhaustive inventory of all the varied arguments relating to sovereignty; this would require a much longer work to accommodate. Rather, we will examine certain sets of related arguments in four parts (A through D, below). The basic question is, what did the opponents of the U.R. mean when they argued that the U.S. should not accept the Uruguay Round results because it "detracts from or takes away U.S. sovereignty?" And what did the proponents mean when they said that such arguments did not lead to the opponents' conclusions?

It should be immediately noted that although the conclusion (to accept or not to accept) is basically bipolar, the arguments are not necessarily so. Specific sovereignty considerations may add up to a conclusion one way or the other, but merely because a small bit of sovereignty is taken away does not mean that no treaty should be accepted. Offsetting policies may make it appropriate to "give up some sovereignty" in order to achieve some important policy results. A classic situation is represented by the "prisoner's dilemma," in which independent actions by a group of players can result in worsening the

---

24. *See generally* URUGUAY ROUND AGREEMENTS ACT: A LEGISLATIVE HISTORY OF PUBLIC LAW NO. 103-465, *supra* note 11.

Four hearings, in particular, are useful in trying to understand the discussion in this article. *See Uruguay Round of Multilateral Trade Negotiations: Hearing Before the Senate Finance Comm.*, 103d Cong. (1994); *Trade Agreements Resulting from the Uruguay Round of Multilateral Trade Negotiations: Hearings Before the Comm. on Ways and Means and its Subcomm. on Trade in the House of Representatives*, 103d Cong. (1994); *The World Trade Organization and U.S. Sovereignty: Hearings Before the Comm. on Foreign Relations*, 103d Cong. (1994); *S.2467, GATT Implementing Legislation: Hearings Before the Comm. on Commerce, Science and Transportation in the Senate*, 103d Cong. (1994).

situation for all but cooperation can prevent such a result.[25] Likewise it should be noted that sovereignty "loss" can have a number of different meanings, which different persons weigh differently in their policy advocacy. For example, loss of sovereignty could mean:

1) any diminution of a nation's right/power to pursue certain domestic policies without:

> for example, interference by notions of international law constraints, regardless of whether these operate effectively or whether they cause domestic law changes which in turn pose practical or "real" constraints (*e.g.*, because of international economic interdependence); interference by international law institutions in a manner that changes domestic law and the constraints it offers; or constraints of international treaty law norms which, although ignorable, can result in retaliation, compensation, or other counter actions by other nations or players;

2) treaty acceptance might cause external influences on domestic policy in certain ways disadvantageous to the opponent of the treaty:

> for example, an opponent may fear that certain domestic special interests (*e.g.*, large corporations) may have greater abilities than most groups to influence the international body; thus, they might be able to achieve results by the remote pressure of international decisions or norms that could not otherwise be achieved at the national government level.[26]

A.   *General Implications of Accepting Substantive Treaty Norms*

Some of the sovereignty arguments of U.R. opponents are aimed at the mere fact of accepting treaty obligations for certain subjects. Other objections may relate to the implications of becoming part of the treaty institutions. This sub-part will explore the former. Later sub-parts will deal with institutional questions.

Focus for the moment on the question of acceptance of a treaty with various substantive norms, but no institutions—for example, no

---

25. This is a classical trade policy argument. *See, e.g.,* JACKSON ET AL., LEGAL PROBLEMS, *supra* note 22, at 33; PETER B. KENEN, THE INTERNATIONAL ECONOMY 125 (2d ed. 1989).

26. For different subjects, this can operate in different directions, so it is not impossible to find a particular domestic interest opposing some treaties and favoring others, even though both "diminish national sovereignty."

joint decision-making powers or dispute settlement procedures—are contained in the treaty. In other words, consider in the abstract only the fact of accepting a series of substantive treaty norms. When an opponent to such acceptance argues that the treaty "takes away sovereignty," what is he or she likely to mean?

Clearly, acceptance of *any* treaty, in some sense reduces the freedom of scope of national government actions. At the very least, certain types of actions inconsistent with the treaty norms would give rise to an international law violation. The amount of constraint might then vary not only with the institutional mechanisms for enforcement, but also with the national domestic government structure or political attitude towards international norms. Some skeptics might dismiss an international norm as ineffective and, thus, not constraining. But if a treaty norm were self-executing or directly applicable in a domestic legal system, it could have a greater constraining effect. Even without those effects, a treaty can have important domestic legal effects, such as influencing how domestic courts interpret domestic legislation.[27] Beyond that, a treaty norm even without domestic legal effect can have weight in some domestic policy debates where some advocates will stress that positions contrary to their views would raise serious international or treaty concerns. Thus, the sovereignty objection can be directed more to the question of where a decision should be made, and what influences on that decision should be permitted.

It can also be observed that the lack of direct effect of a treaty in domestic law is considered a possible protection against sovereignty diminution. This is because without direct effect, a nation normally can decide how to respond to a complaint that its actions have breached international law, and one response possible is to ignore the complaint and live with the breach. This may not be particularly admirable but it can act as sort of a buffering process, or safety valve, against international action that might be deemed overreaching or otherwise inappropriate.[28]

Finally, it should be noted that the legal ability to withdraw within a reasonable period of notice time arguably reduces the concern about infringement on sovereignty. This option seemed to be interesting to some of those worried about the sovereignty arguments. The Uruguay Round treaty provisions allow withdrawal upon six months notice.

---

27. Restatement (Third) of the Foreign Relations Law of the United States § 114 (1990).

28. *See* John H. Jackson, *Status of Treaties in Domestic Legal Systems: A Policy Analysis*, 86 Am. J. Int'l L. 310 (1992).

Whether this is a realistic option for nations today, in the light of their considerable dependence on international trade and the trade system of the GATT/WTO, is a somewhat different question that can also be considered.[29]

Related to the considerations mentioned above, some general objections to a treaty are driven by the substance of particular issues. Many environmental advocates and groups in the 1994 debate were concerned that specific treaty clauses would "trump" U.S. environmental law, or even state laws, such as California's, and would harmonize downward the more stringent U.S. law about which the environmentalists were justifiably proud. Thus, important questions were raised about the legal and practical effect of the WTO and U.R. treaty norms on particular subjects, and sovereignty objections became objections to the substance of the international norms, at least to the extent that those norms appeared not to give enough leeway to domestic U.S. political institutions to adopt more appropriate higher standards.

B.   WTO Decision-Making Procedures: Risk to Sovereignty

Some of the sovereignty objections in the 1994 debate were targeted towards the institution of the WTO. Various opponents to the treaty argued that the WTO posed risks to U.S. sovereignty because decisions could be made in the WTO that would override U.S. law. This objection engages a number of particular clauses of the WTO, as well as the legal effect of potential WTO decisions on U.S. domestic law. As to the latter, testimony pointed out that WTO decisions did not have self-executing or direct legal effect in U.S. law. Consequently, once again there was an element of buffering protection which in realistic terms gave the national government some opportunity to resist inappropriate international decisions.[30]

But more significant, perhaps, is the fact that the decision-making procedures of the WTO have been significantly circumscribed by negotiated treaty text. In fact, by comparison to the loose language of the GATT—which would have remained in effect if the WTO had failed to emerge—the WTO had many more protections for national sovereignty. These protections were significantly enhanced in the treaty

---

29. *See* WTO Agreement, *supra* note 16, art. XV(2), 33 I.L.M. at 1152.

30. *See The World Trade Organization and U.S. Sovereignty: Hearings Before the Senate Comm. on Foreign Relations*, 103d Cong. (1994) (testimony by Rufus Yerxa, Deputy U.S. Trade Representative), *available in* 1994 WL 14188843 [hereinafter *Yerxa Testimony*].

drafting that went on during the fall of 1993, spurred by the U.S. negotiators and other countries who worried about some of the general treaty text of the previous U.R. drafts.

To be more specific, but without going into these matters in depth,[31] an examination of a series of specific decision-making powers for the WTO general bodies shows protections such as super-majorities (often three-fourths requirement of all the members, not just those voting—a very difficult target to achieve) and prohibitions against changing the substantive rights and obligations of the members without more difficult amending or treaty negotiation procedures. In addition, an emphasis on consensus decision-making is manifested in a number of provisions, sometimes with fall-backs to voting only after providing a period of time for an attempt to achieve consensus. Indeed, some of these provisions could be seen to give a "de facto veto" power to a few of the most powerful trading entities. These features can be seen in the texts relating to:

- amending the WTO and subsidiary agreements (article X);
- adopting a formal "interpretation" (article IX:2);
- adopting waivers (article IX:3 & 4);
- adding Pluralateral Agreements (optional agreements) to Annex 4 (article X:9); and
- changing the Dispute Settlement Understanding in Annex 2 (article X:8).

Most sovereignty objections clearly were aimed at power allocation. Members of the Congress were concerned whether the allocation of power regarding WTO decision-making was an inappropriate infringement on U.S. sovereign decision-making. Certainly, this allocation was more protective of national government decision-making than either the GATT or many other international organizations in today's world (although few of those organizations have such an extensive impact on national economies). It was clear in the U.R. negotiation that there was no possibility of achieving any formal weighted voting (such as in the International Monetary Fund or International Bank for Reconstruction and Development), or even a small special body with added power like vetoes or special competence (such as the United Nations Security Council). Thus, the negotiators

---

31. *See* Jackson, *The World Trade Organization, supra* note 14; Jackson, *The Uruguay Round, supra* note 15; *see also Jackson June Testimony, supra* note 3; *Jackson March Testimony, supra* note 3.

greatly restricted the decision-making powers of the WTO bodies, even to the point of concern that the WTO will be hamstrung by inaction derived from its "consensus" culture.

C. *WTO Dispute Settlement Process and the Sovereignty Arguments*

The issue of a nation-state's participation in an international dispute settlement procedure poses sovereignty questions of a different sort. If a nation has consented to a treaty and the norms it contains, why should it object to an external process that could rule on the consistency of that nation's actions with the treaty norms? It might be argued that such objections manifest a lack of intent to follow the norms—sort of accepting the treaty with fingers crossed behind the back. Indeed, there may be some elements of this thinking in this context. It could also be suggested, however, that a nervousness about international dispute settlement procedures reflects a government's desire to have some flexibility to resist future strict conformity to norms in certain special circumstances, particularly circumstances that could pose great danger to essential national objectives. This sort of an "escape clause" idea would allow a nation to accept norms with sincere intent to follow them except in the most severe and egregious cases of danger to the nation or to its political system.[32]

Apart from these escape clause notions, however, there is also an institutional concern that the dispute settlement procedures may not be objective, may be subject to procedural irregularities and overreaching, or may have other important defects that even other nations would recognize but that are not redressed by the treaty or its institutional structure. This danger, either at the outset or developing at some later time, could legitimately constrain a nation's willingness to enter into stringent commitments to a dispute settlement procedure.

Clearly some of these considerations played a part in the U.S. Great 1994 Sovereignty Debate. The objections raised to dispute settlement procedures may, thus, not be objections to the substance of the rules discussed in the previous sub-part, but may be objections to the nature, stringency, or automaticity of the enforcement mechanisms for those rules. Since international institutions are generally less sophisticated or elaborate than most national institutions, various problems can be feared. These might include the difficulty of changing treaties and

---

32. Candidly, though, it may also be noted that danger to the political fortunes of the ruling party in such nation may take on great weight in these considerations.

treaty norms that may become seriously out of date, or the methods of filling in the details of seriously ambiguous texts (a problem often associated with treaties drafted by many countries). The text of the WTO charter may contain some of these problems. An example is the super-majority procedure included in that text for decisions on "formal interpretations." Likewise, the Dispute Settlement Understanding (D.S.U.) contains a number of hedges that reflect concerns about international dispute settlement.

The D.S.U. continues some of the GATT dispute procedures as developed through practice over forty years, but it now includes an elaborate treaty text to govern this practice and adds a number of new features. As in the GATT, a dispute is initiated by a request for consultations by a disputant (or group of complainants), and the consultation period is a prerequisite for further procedures. If no settlement is achieved, then the D.S.U. now makes clear that the complainant is entitled to a panel procedure, and rules spell out the process for forming a panel (usually three impartial individuals). The rules correct some problems seen in GATT by requiring stricter time limits and fall-back procedures when the parties cannot agree to certain aspects such as the panel's composition or its terms of reference. Much more attention is made in the rules to third party participation. Initial experience demonstrates a great desire to use this opportunity to participate. But only "members," (*i.e.*, nation-states or independent customs territories) can bring cases or participate formally. As in GATT, the panel receives oral and written arguments and "testimony," and formulates a report that is sent to the Dispute Settlement Body (D.S.B.), where the parties may comment and urge changes.[33]

The major change in the D.S.U., however, is the elimination of "blocking" when the D.S.B. considers the report. The report is deemed adopted unless there is a consensus against adoption (the "reverse consensus"), and since the winning party could always object and block the consensus, the adoption is considered to be virtually automatic. The *quid pro quo* for this automaticity, however, is a provision that, for the first time, allows for an appeal. If an appeal is taken, then the report is not adopted. Instead, an appellate panel of three individuals, drawn from a permanent roster of seven individuals (with renewable four-year staggered terms),[34] considers the first level report, receives arguments from the parties, and writes its own report. This report also is sent to the

---

33. *See* D.S.U., *supra* note 19, arts. 11-16, 33 I.L.M. at 1233-35. The D.S.B. has the same members as the WTO General Council, except for its Chairman.

34. *See* D.S.U., *supra* note 19, art. 17, 33 I.L.M. at 1236-37.

D.S.B. where the same reverse consensus rule applies to adoption, again making it virtually certain to be adopted. It is this automaticity that worries some diplomats and critics of the WTO system, although in many other international tribunals automaticity, in the sense of no opportunity to block a report, also exists.

The D.S.U. then has a series of detailed rules regarding an enforcement phase if a losing party is unwilling to carry out the recommendations of the panel as adopted by the D.S.B.. These rules provide for "compensation" through trade measures, and for certain other pressures such as continuous monitoring to enhance the implementation of the dispute results.

In the U.S. 1994 debate, some interests testified that the U.S. should include in its implementing legislation certain measures regarding dumping law, even if those would appear to be vulnerable to dispute settlement procedure challenge at some future time.[35] Other witnesses argued against the WTO partly because the dispute settlement procedure was tougher, and no longer permitted a single nation to "block" acceptance of a panel report. There was criticism of the GATT panels ("decisions by three faceless bureaucrats in Geneva"), and, thus, of the likely form of the WTO panels. Criticism was targeted at the secrecy of the procedures, the lack of opportunity of private groups (non-government organizations, etc.) to offer views and evidence, the potential conflicts of interest of the panelists, and the possibility that the WTO secretariat lawyers would be biased and have too much influence on the panels, etc.[36] Indeed, although there have been important efforts to "open up" the WTO procedures (even those relating to decision-making discussed above), many constructive critics of the WTO feel there is much more that must be done.[37]

A very important consideration affecting a nation's willingness to accept the WTO dispute settlement procedures is its view of the way the treaty and its institutions should play a role in that nation's international economic diplomacy. The U.S. and many other nations have often expressed the view that the GATT and now WTO treaty texts are vitally important to improving a rule-oriented international economic system

---

35. *See Results of the Uruguay Round Trade Negotiations: Hearings Before the Senate Finance Comm.*, 103d Cong. 108 (1994) (testimony of Steven R. Appleton, representing the Semiconductor Industry Association).

36. *See Jackson June Testimony, supra* note 3.

37. This author shares many, but not all, the concerns expressed. *See* John H. Jackson, *World Trade Rules and Environmental Policies: Congruence or Conflict?*, 49 WASH. & LEE L. REV. 1227 (1992).

that should enhance the predictability and stability of the circumstances of international commerce. This enhancement, in turn, should allow private entrepreneurs to plan better for longer term investment and other decisions. In short, a basic goal is to reduce the "risk premium" associated with commerce between nations with vastly differing governmental and cultural structures.[38] If a nation wishes to benefit from these policies, then it becomes difficult for it to oppose dispute settlement procedures when they impinge on it. There is a reciprocity element in these conditions, and this must be taken into account in reflecting on the weight to be given sovereignty objections.

The U.S. has explicitly made these considerations part of its diplomacy and has often expressed the view that the rules of the GATT and the WTO are vital for U.S. commerce, particularly U.S. exports.[39] The U.S. was the most frequent initiator of dispute settlement procedures in the GATT and continues in the WTO with the same approach. It learned very early in the WTO history that to appear to "thumb its nose" at the dispute procedures posed very serious diplomatic risks to its status in the WTO and therefore to the potential usefulness of the WTO to the U.S.[40]

How does all this fit with the sovereignty objections? Again, it is abundantly clear that "sovereignty" is not a unitary concept, but is a series of particular considerations that I suggest are centered around the problem of allocation of power. Thus, when an objection is made to the U.S. accepting the WTO because of the WTO dispute settlement procedures, the specific (decomposed) issues of that objection are substantially different from those regarding the problem of treaty norm application or the institutional structure of decision-making. In addition, the sovereignty objection really can be a series of specific objections about the nature or details of the dispute procedure. These in turn must be considered in the aggregate (unless there were options that allowed a nation to accept some details but not others), and that aggregate weighed against the policy advantages of belonging. "Sovereignty" thus is not a magical wand that one waives to ward off any entanglement in the international system. It is a policy-weighing

---

38. *See, generally, e.g.*, DOUGLASS C. NORTH, INSTITUTIONS, INSTITUTIONAL CHANGE AND ECONOMIC PERFORMANCE (1990).

39. *See Yerxa Testimony, supra* note 30. *See also*, USTR *Identification of Trade Expansion Priorities (Super 301) pursuant to Executive Order 12901 (last modified*, October 1, 1996) <http://www.ustr.gov/reports/12901report.html>.

40. *See* John H. Jackson, *U.S. Threat to New World Trade Order*, FINANCIAL TIMES, May 23, 1995, at 13; Ben Wildavsky, *The Big Deal*, NAT'L. J., June 24, 1995, at 1650; Jagdish Bhagwati, *The U.S.-Japan Car Dispute: A Monumental Mistake*, INT'L AFFAIRS, June 1996, at 261.

process. And the policies most often address the question of allocation of power: should this nation accept the obligation to allow certain decisions affecting it (or its view of international economic relations) to be made by an international institution rather than retaining that power in the national government?

As heroic as they may appear, the dispute settlement procedures of the WTO have a number of features that are obviously designed to protect the sovereignty of the WTO members and to prevent too much power from being allocated to the dispute process. Many different illustrations could be described here, but only four subjects will be discussed to keep this text manageable. These four subjects are: 1) the obligation to comply with a panel ruling; 2) the legal precedent effect of a panel report; 3) the standard of review by which the WTO panels examine national government actions; and 4) the broad question of judicial activism or concerns about panels stretching interpretations to achieve certain policy results that they favor. Of course, part of the background of these subjects is the detailed procedures or panel processes and the persons who are on the appellate body roster to be panels. The credibility of these procedures, and, thus, the likely willingness over time of members to accept panel results, is affected by the personnel and the content of the procedures. Of the seven roster members, for example, three are chosen from large trading powers (U.S., E.U., and Japan), while the rest hail from smaller or less powerful members (Philippines, New Zealand, Egypt, and Uruguay). Since policy perceptions about sovereignty might sometimes differ between large and small nations, this majority could create some concerns (at least until practice suggests these are not troublesome) for larger members (who are the most frequent participants in the procedures).

1. Legal Effect and Obligation of a Panel or Appeal Report

One of the interpretive issues that has grown in importance since the WTO came into effect is whether the result of a dispute settlement process obligates the losing respondent to a complaint to change its laws or practices to conform to the panel recommendation. One might think the answer to this should be obvious and affirmative, and certainly most other international tribunal procedures would embrace this result. However, the D.S.U. has much language concerning enforcement and implementation and much of the focus of the language is on compensation. If a nation, particularly a large nation, has the option to perform or compensate, it may have the sense that in many cases brought by small countries, compensation could be relatively painless (small in amount). Thus, such a nation may feel its sovereignty is better protected by the availability of the compensation option.

In fact, U.S. government officials testified to this effect in the Great 1994 Sovereignty Debate, and argued that no international body could require the U.S. (not even in the loose sense of an international law norm) to do anything. In the view of this author, this interpretation is incorrect and not likely to be embraced by future panel reports. The language of the D.S.U. includes a number of clauses that call for an obligation to perform according to panel findings. The D.S.U. makes compensation only a fall-back when performance does not occur, and keeps a matter under surveillance as long as performance has not occurred. Yet it was interesting that as part of the sovereignty debate, U.S. officials thought it would be useful to argue to the public and to the Congress as they did.[41]

2. Precedent or Other Effect of Panel Reports

Some discussion about the precedent effect of GATT panels, and now WTO panels, has occurred. Under GATT it was not always clear what the legal effect of the GATT Council adopting a panel report was.[42] Clearly the general international law rule suggests that there is no strict precedential effect such as *stare decisis*. This author has argued that the real intended effect is only that of "practice," which over time and combined with other practice can have effects on interpretation. But concerns about this have been discussed in GATT councils (leading in some cases to reluctance to adopt a panel report which could be a bad precedent).[43]

The WTO and the D.S.U. seem to attempt to foreclose the use of precedent for panel reports. The WTO text specifies a particular super-majority procedure for formal interpretations.[44] This seems to suggest that the WTO system does not give power to the panels to create any

---

41. *See generally* John H. Jackson, *The WTO Dispute Settlement Understanding: Misunderstandings on the Nature of Legal Obligation*, 91 AM. J. INT'L L. 60 (1997).

42. *See* John H. Jackson, *The Legal Meaning of a GATT Dispute Settlement Report: Some Reflections, in* TOWARDS MORE EFFECTIVE SUPERVISION BY INTERNATIONAL ORGANIZATIONS ESSAYS IN HONOUR OF HENRY G. SCHERMERS 149 (Niels Blokker & Sam Muller eds., 1994).

43. Discussions by author with GATT Secretariat Personnel (1995).

44. "The Ministerial Conference and the General Council shall have the exclusive authority to adopt interpretations of this Agreement and of the Multilateral Trade Agreements . . . . The decision to adopt an interpretation shall be taken by a three-fourths majority of the members." WTO Agreement, *supra* note 16, art. IX(2), 33 I.L.M. at 1148.

formal interpretations, *i.e.*, any formal precedents. Thus, the panel reports are binding only on the parties to the particular proceeding, much like the World Court rule.[45] Of course, the reports will have considerable persuasive effect, at least when well-reasoned. Thus, in at least one WTO case won by multiple complainants against a respondent, the complainants reportedly argued most vigorously among themselves about which of several theories should be expressed in the report as the basis of the decision.

The WTO Charter provisions on interpretations can be combined with the thrust of some of the D.S.U. language to reinforce the view that panel reports are not to act as formal interpretations. During the last months of the U.R. negotiation (fall 1993), U.S. negotiators were reportedly eager to prevent the panels from ruling on the WTO Charter itself, but in the end the D.S.U. clearly provides the contrary view.[46] Here again one sees a sovereignty concern not itself significant enough to change a final decision to accept the treaty affecting a specific treaty detail.

3. Standard of Review

There are two standard of review problems in the WTO dispute settlement procedures: that of the Appellate Body review of first level panel reports, and that of the standard of review of any WTO panel regarding judgments about member government actions that might be inconsistent with the treaty norms. It is the latter that will be taken up here.

---

45. For example and contrast, article 94 of the U.N. Charter states: "Each Member of the United Nations undertakes to comply with the decision of the International Court of Justice in any case to which it is a party." U.N. CHARTER, art. 94. Similarly, the Statute of the International Court of Justice, article 59, implies such obligation, stating: "The decision of the Court has no binding force except between the parties and in respect of that particular case." Statute of the I.C.J., *signed* June 26, 1945, art. 59, 59 Stat. 1055, 3 Bevans 1179.

46. "The rules and procedures of this Understanding shall also apply to consultations and the settlement of disputes between Members concerning their rights and obligations under the provisions of the Agreement Establishing the World Trade Organization." D.S.U., *supra* note 19, art. 1, 33 I.L.M. at 1226. For reports on the negotiations in the U.R. working group on Dispute Settlement see INSIDE U.S. TRADE, Oct. 1, 1993, at 7; Nov. 5, 1993, at 1; Nov. 19, 1993, at 19; Nov. 26, 1993, at 1; Dec. 17, 1993, at 1.

The standard of review, related sometimes to (*inter alia*) the "margin of appreciation" concept,[47] is a critical element of allocating power between an international tribunal and a national government. This issue was very prominent in the "end game negotiations" of the U.R. Some negotiators supported a text that would embody a significant limitation on the degree to which WTO panels would second-guess national governments on decisions regarding trade rules, such as anti-dumping rulings. The U.S. negotiators tried to obtain treaty language that would follow the domestic U.S. administrative law approach known as the *Chevron Doctrine*.[48] Other nations objected, and in the end compromise language with considerable ambiguity was placed in the anti-dumping text but not applied to disputes on other matters (at least until a later study occurred). The D.S.U. does not itself have an explicit text on this type of "standard of review" but there are some clauses that might support a cautious approach by the WTO panels.[49] In the first two appellate body reports, there is panel language that suggest such caution. One states, for example, that "WTO members have a large measure of autonomy to determine their own policies on the environment (including its relationship with trade), their environmental objectives and the environmental legislation they enact and implement."[50]

4.   Judicial Activism or Panel "Overreaching"

Clearly there was some concern about the potential power of WTO panels. This was expressed in hearings during 1994, as well as in negotiations and discussions in various public and confidential forums. The other matters expressed above may sometimes influence panel caution in this regard, but some language in the D.S.U. seems to be

---

47. *See* Ronald St. John Macdonald, *The Margin of Appreciation, in* EUROPEAN SYSTEM FOR THE PROTECTION OF HUMAN RIGHTS 83 (Ronald St. John Macdonald et al. eds., 1993); Steven Croley & John H. Jackson, *WTO Dispute Procedures, Standard of Review, and Deference to National Governments,* 90 AM. J. INT'L L. 193 (1996).

48. Steven P. Croley & John H. Jackson, *WTO Dispute Procedures, Standard of Review, and Deference to National Governments,* 90 AM.J. INT'L L. 193, 202 (1996).

49. *See, e.g.,* D.S.U., *supra* note 19, art. 3(2), 33 I.L.M. at 1227.

50. United States—Standards for Reformulated and Conventional Gasoline, Appellate Body Report and Panel Report, World Trade Organization, WT/DS2/9, 20 May 1996, at 30. *See also* Japan—Taxes on Alcoholic Beverages, Report of the Appellate Body, World Trade Organization, WT/DS8,10,11/AB/R, 4 October 1996, at 22. Both documents are available at World Trade Organization, *Overview of the State-of-Play of WTO Disputes* (last modified Jan. 23, 1997) <http://www.wto.org/wto/dispute/bulletin.htm>.

designed for the same end. In particular, the D.S.U. says "[r]ec-ommendations and rulings of the D.S.B. cannot add to or diminish the rights and obligations provided in the covered agreements."[51] The proposal for a U.S. national review panel to report on the correctness of WTO panel reports affecting the U.S. could be another caution, as described below.

D. The Uruguay Round, U.S. Law, and Implications for Sovereignty Issues

Several significant issues of U.S. constitutional and other law also, sometimes oddly, became embroiled in the sovereignty debate. Only four particular issues will be very briefly described here.

1. The Famous U.S. Section 301

A considerable amount of venom has been expressed by U.S. trading partners towards U.S. *Section 301*.[52] This statute has a special role in the U.S. constitutional division of power between the Congress and the President, delegating to the President the authority to retaliate with trade sanctions against certain "unreasonable or unfair" foreign government actions that damage U.S. commerce. This statute has sometimes been used by the U.S. to apply trade sanctions against other nations in a manner inconsistent with U.S. treaty obligations, and major U.R. participants were determined to rein in U.S. unilateralism. This determination was part of the impetus for improved dispute settlement procedures and for the WTO Charter itself.

The U.S. Congress made it very clear, however, that it would not tolerate changes in *Section 301*, and the Executive negotiating position followed that mandate. Consequently, except for some minor proce-dural amendments, *Section 301* remains intact. Yet, in explaining its position (in ways too complex to recount here), the United States argued that *Section 301* could not be found inconsistent with U.S. WTO obligations (in the absence of some specific action). Indeed, *Section 301* does call for use of the WTO dispute settlement procedures. This statute, however, was perhaps the most important political bellwether

---

51. D.S.U., *supra* note 19, art. 3(2), 33 I.L.M. at 1227.

52. *See* Trade Act of 1974 § 301, 19 U.S.C. § 2411 (1994). *See, e.g., Services of the European Commission, in* REPORT ON U.S. BARRIERS TO TRADE AND INVESTMENT 11-12 (1994).

184   COLUMBIA JOURNAL OF TRANSNATIONAL LAW   [36:157

of the sovereignty considerations in the Congress during the 1994 debate.

2. The Treaty Clause and the Fast Track Statutory Approach

Another intriguing manifestation of sovereignty concerns was the interesting debate about the constitutionality of the fast track procedure for approving the U.R. and the WTO Two levels of sovereignty concerns were raised in this context (demonstrating that the allocation of power concept goes deeper than just the federal level of a nation-state).[53] It was argued that, despite various precedents to the contrary, there were sovereignty concerns when an international agreement required major national commitments and membership in an international organization that might involve yielding U.S. sovereignty to global institutions. It was asserted, moreover, that the constitutional requirement that treaties be approved by a two-thirds vote of the Senate, was the only appropriate procedure. In addition, regarding the second level of "sovereignty" arguments, it was argued that the purpose of the Senate treaty approval requirement was particularly to protect the sovereignty of U.S. sub-federal states. The Senate, it was argued, was a better protector of such states' rights since each state had equal representation there (two senators) and was traditionally, it was claimed, more assiduous in protecting states' rights.

This portion of the 1994 debate also involved various other constitutional arguments, and an interesting Senate Commerce Committee hearing in October with two debating law professors.[54] In the end, the fast track procedure was followed, and the Senate voted 76 to 24 in favor of the statute with its delegation to the President. It can,

---

53. *See S.2467, GATT Implementing Legislation: Hearings Before the U.S. Senate Commerce, Science and Transportation Comm.*, 103d Cong. 290-339 (1994) (Statements and discussion of Laurence H. Tribe and Bruce Ackerman); Bruce Ackerman & David Golove, *Is NAFTA Constitutional?*, 108 HARV. L. REV. 4 (1995); Laurence Tribe, *Taking Text and Structure Seriously: Reflections on Free-Form Method in Constitutional Interpretation*, 108 HARV. L. REV. 6 (1995); "Statutory Procedure for Approval of the Uruguay Round Trade Negotiations and the WTO" Treaty Clause Memorandum sent to various members of Congress and Executive Branch Officials, dated November 11, 1994. Signatories included: Professors Bruce Ackerman, Yale University; Abram Chayes, Harvard University; Kenneth Dam, University of Chicago; Charles Fried, Harvard University; David Golove, Arizona University; Louis Henkin, Columbia University; Robert Hudec, University of Minnesota; John H. Jackson, University of Michigan; Harold Hongju Koh, Yale University; Myres McDougal, Yale University (on file with author).

54. *See* Detlev Vagts, *International Agreements, the Senate and the Consitution*, in this volume, *supra* p. 119.

thus, be argued that this was yet another precedent for following the statutory procedure (at least for trade treaties or other matters related to the Commerce Clause of the U.S. Constitution), and was also an opinion by three-fourths of the U.S. Senate favoring the constitutionality of the statutory approach.

3.   Sub-Federal States in the United States

The question of sub-federal States of the United States received considerable attention in the 1994 Uruguay Round debate. This debate, along with the prior North American Free Trade Agreement (N.A.F.T.A.) debate, were the first times since the origin of the GATT that such attention was given to state interests. A major concern of the states was the potential for a broad scope treaty like the U.R. to invalidate many different state laws governing areas such as economic regulation, environmental affairs, product safety and health standards, etc. (insofar as these were left to the states by Congress or other federal bodies). An organization of state Attorneys General posed "sub-federal sovereignty objections" to the U.S. Office of the Trade Representative, and this office worked with state officials to include language in the 1994 Uruguay Round Agreements Act[55] designed to protect state interests, particularly interests of states in potential dispute settlement proceedings that might be brought at the WTO against certain state laws. State laws had already been subject to such proceedings under the GATT in the Canadian challenge to state alcoholic beverage regulations. A GATT panel concluded that many of these state laws were inconsistent with GATT obligations such as the national treatment requirement that imports be treated no less favorably than domestic products.[56]

The result for the U.R. Implementing Act was several lengthy sections that gave state government officials various procedural rights to participate and provide input into the U.S. handling of WTO disputes affecting them. After this text was negotiated, state officials indicated satisfaction with the approach and removed their objections to U.S. acceptance of the U.R. treaty.[57]

---

55. 108 Stat. 4809 (1994).

56. United States Measures Affecting Alcoholic Malt Beverages, GATT Panel Report, *adopted* June 19, 1991, GATT Doc. No. DS23/R; G.A.T.T ., 39 BASIC INSTRUMENTS AND SELECTED DOCUMENTS 206.

57. *See* JOHN H. JACKSON ET AL., INTERNATIONAL ECONOMIC RELATIONS: CASES, MATERIALS AND TEXTS 1168 (3d ed., 1995); Matt Schaefer & Thomas Singer, *Multilateral Trade Agreements and U.S. States: An Analysis of Potential GATT Uruguay Round*

4.   The Proposed "WTO Dispute Settlement Review Commission"

One of the more explicit manifestations of sovereignty concerns, regarding power allocation in the 1994 debate was a compromise proposal between the U.S. President and the Senate Majority Leader. A Democratic President needed votes in a Republican-dominated Senate to achieve passage of the Uruguay Round Agreements Act, and in late November 1994, a few days before the congressional votes were scheduled, the Majority Leader proposed the idea of a statutory "Commission." This Commission would have been composed of five U.S. federal judges who would review the adopted WTO panel reports adverse to the United States, judging them against a list of four particular criteria. The Commission would then advise the Congress whether it found any panel report to be contrary to any one of these criteria. If the Commission were to make determinations of the contrary nature for three reports, then the Congress would consider a resolution to withdraw from the WTO (giving the requisite six-month notice required by the U.R. agreements). This proposal (as of this writing in August 1997) has not become law, although a series of attempts were made to enact it in 1995 and 1996. Nevertheless, the proposal, its findings, and its criteria, all reveal an explicit concern for various aspects of the sovereignty objections discussed above.

The draft legislation[58] listed the following finding:

[t]he continued support of the Congress for the WTO is dependent upon a WTO dispute settlement system that:

A)   operates in a fair and impartial manner;

B)   does not add to the obligations of or diminish the rights of the United States under the Uruguay Round agreements; and

C)   does not exceed its authority, scope, or established standard of review.

The Bill therefore set forth four specific criteria for evaluating WTO dispute reports, asking whether the panel had: 1) exceeded its authority or terms of reference; 2) added to the obligations of, or

---

Agreements, J. OF WORLD TRADE, Dec. 1992, at 31; Statement of Administrative Action for the Uruguay Round Trade Agreements, Title I, Section 102, H.R. Doc. 103-316, at 15 (1994); Letter from Michael Carpenter (Attorney General of Maine), Heidi Heitkamp (Attorney General of North Dakota), Charles W. Burson (Attorney General of Tennessee) to Michael Kantor (U.S.T.R.) (July 27, 1994) (on file with author).

58. *See A Bill to Establish a Commission to Review the Dispute Settlement Reports of the World Trade Organization and for Other Purposes*, S. 16, 104th Cong. (1995).

diminished the rights of the United States; 3) acted arbitrarily or capriciously or engaged in misconduct, etc.; or 4) deviated from the applicable standard of review including that in article 17.6 of the antidumping text.

Perhaps little needs to be added to the paragraphs quoted above; they clearly show the concerns about some aspects of the WTO dispute settlement system which relate to the broader power allocation concepts of sovereignty. Many observers felt that the final sanction of withdrawal would never be exercised by the Congress or signed into law by the President. And some observers felt that it was very unlikely that the Commission would ever find a WTO dispute report contrary to the criteria stated, although those criteria have significant ambiguities and could be interpreted in different ways depending on the judges who made up the Commission. Nevertheless, there was a perception, particularly among other members of the WTO, that the mere existence of this Commission could subtly influence the work of WTO panels, which might then be hesitant to take positions contrary to U.S. interests, and thereby lose some of their impartiality. Some foreign diplomats suggested that it would be necessary for their governments to adopt a similar procedure to "redress this tilt."

IV. SOME CONCLUDING PERSPECTIVES

Sovereignty, in practical terms, is still an important argument in many government policy debates. It has an emotional appeal and is often used in a blunt and undifferentiated way as a surrogate argument by opponents of some government proposal. Yet when the context of some of the sovereignty arguments is analyzed in detail, it can be demonstrated that there are worthwhile policy issues raised at least in some circumstances, and at least if we abandon some antiquated definitions of the concept of sovereignty. In this article I examined sovereignty arguments and suggested that most often they raised policy issues about allocation of power, particularly as between international institutions or norms and national or even sub-federal levels of government.

When some of the policy debates are approached in this manner, it becomes clear that there are many facets and many details to the policy issue of appropriately allocating power. In the context of treaty acceptance, for example, questions are raised about the domestic law effect of international norms, about the nature of international decision-making processes that can generate secondary norms obligating the nation-state, about details of dispute settlement procedures affecting the credibility and efficiency of those procedures, and about questions of internal domestic allocation of power that are raised by international treaties, other norms, and institutions. When we examine some of these details in a "decomposed" or disaggregated way, we can more easily determine how to weigh some of the disadvantages of those details against advantages of strengthened international norms and institutions. This process, in turn, may assist governments in evaluating the important policy considerations involved in participating in international institutions. This approach to sovereignty arguments may lead to better government decisions by forcing those who use sovereignty objections against policy proposals to make such objections more concrete and explicit so that they can be better compared to contrasting arguments.

[14]

Rethinking liberalization and reforming the WTO

Martin Khor

In his presentation at the World Economic Forum in Davos, Switzerland on 28 January, *Martin Khor*, Director of the Third World Network, argued that trade liberalization does not necessarily lead to economic growth and could even, if pursued in a "big-bang" manner, contribute to a vicious cycle of financial instability, debt and recession. It is in this context that the credibility problems facing the WTO today should be addressed, with a view to making development the overarching aim of the multilateral trading system. We reproduce below the full text of the presentation.

I: The need to rethink liberalization policies

We meet in the aftermath of a global financial crisis as well as the aftermath of the collapse of the Seattle WTO Conference. It is thus urgent and timely to examine and reexamine what is the right approach developing countries should take towards integration in the world economy, and towards liberalization of trade, finance and investment.

On financial liberalization, there are new lessons to learn from the recent events. It is now clear that financial liberalization, especially when done inappropriately, was the main cause of the East Asian economic crisis. Many of the affected countries, which had been in the forefront among countries of the South in global economic integration, are now cautious and reviewing their approach to financial openness.

On trade liberalization, the issue is even more complex. The failure at Seattle provides an opportunity to reexamine the record and to reformulate what is an appropriate approach for trade policy and thus also for the future role of the WTO.

There is a strong paradox or contradiction in the manner developing countries in general and many scholars take towards this issue. On one hand, it is almost invariably repeated that "we are committed to trade liberalization which is positive for and essential to growth and development." On the other hand, many developing countries also notice and are now actively complaining that trade liberalization has net negative results for their economies or has marginalized them.

Why are there so many criticisms that the global free-market or free-trade system has not benefited countries or people equally? That there is a growing gap between rich and poor countries? And that trade liberalization has caused problems to developing countries, especially the poorer ones?

It is often asserted in the mainstream literature that there has been growth for all, that liberalization has benefited "the world" etc. But such generalizations are a fallacy.

It is simply not true that "we are all gainers, there are no losers", as some leading proponents of the Uruguay Round and the WTO would have it. Some have gained more than others; and many (especially the poorest countries) have not gained at all but may well have suffered severe loss to their economic standing.

In fact, only a few countries have enjoyed moderate or high growth in the last two decades whilst an astonishing number have actually suffered declines in living standards (measured in per capita income). The UN Development Programme's *Human Development Report 1999* (p. 31) states: "The top fifth of the world's people in the richest countries enjoy 82% of the expanding export trade and 68% of foreign direct investment – the bottom fifth, barely more than 1%. These trends reinforce economic stagnation and low human development. Only 33 countries managed to sustain 3% annual growth during 1980-96. For 59 countries (mainly in Sub-Saharan Africa and Eastern Europe and the CIS) GNP per capita declined. Economic integration is thus dividing developing and transition economies into those that are benefiting from global opportunities and those that are not."

One of the important things to understand about trade liberalization is that if it is imposed upon countries that are not ready or able to cope, it can contribute to a vicious cycle of financial instability, debt and recession.

A clear explanation of why trade liberalization often leads to negative results is found in the UN Conference on Trade and Development's (UNCTAD) *Trade and Development Report 1999*. It focuses on the behaviour and balance between imports and exports, and finds that rapid trade liberalization has contributed to the widening of the trade deficit in developing countries in general. The report finds that rapid trade liberalization led to a sharp increase in imports but that exports failed to keep pace. For developing countries (excluding China), the average trade deficit in the 1990s is higher than that in the 1970s by 3 percentage points of GDP while the average growth rate is lower by 2 percentage points.

This latest important UNCTAD finding corresponds with several recent studies that show there is no automatic correlation between trade liberalization and growth. Countries that rapidly liberalized their imports did not necessarily grow faster than those that liberalized more gradually.

The problem in trade liberalization is that a country can control how fast to liberalize its imports (and thus increase the inflow of products) but cannot determine by itself how fast its exports grow. Export growth partly depends on the prices of the existing exported products (and developing countries have suffered from serious declines in their terms of trade) and also on having or developing the infrastructure, human and enterprise capacity for new exports (which is a long-term process and not easily achieved).

It also depends on whether there is market access especially in developed countries. Herein lies a major problem beyond the control of the South, for, as is well known, there are many tariff and non-tariff barriers in the North to the potential exports of developing countries. Unless these barriers are removed, the South's export potential will not be realized.

Thus, trade liberalization can (and often does) cause imports to surge without a corresponding surge in exports. This can cause the widening of trade deficits, deterioration in the balance of payments and the continuation or worsening of external debt, all of which constrain growth prospects and often result in persistent stagnation or recession.

This should lead us to conclude that trade liberalization should not be pursued automatically or rapidly and in a "big-bang" manner. Rather, what is important is the quality, timing, sequencing and scope of liberalization (especially import liberalization), and how the process is accompanied by (or preceded by) other factors such as the strengthening of local enterprises and farms, human resource and technological development, as well as the build-up of export capacity and markets. A logical conclusion must be that if conditions for success are not present yet in a country, then to proceed with liberalization can lead to specific negative results or even a general situation of persistent recession. Thus, to pressurize such countries to liberalize would be to help lead them into an economic quagmire.

Developing countries must have the ability, freedom and flexibility to make strategic choices in finance, trade and investment policies, where they can decide on the rate and scope of liberalization and combine this appropriately with the defence of local firms and farms.

And this is why there should be a freeze on further steps to impose more liberalization on developing countries through new issues or a new round in the WTO Seattle meeting. The rich countries must now correct the imbalances and inequities in the world trading system – they should increase their market access to products from developing countries, but they should not press the developing countries to further open up. Developing countries should be allowed to choose their own rate of liberalization.

II: The failure of Seattle

The spectacular failure of the WTO Seattle meeting had its roots in both the system of decision-making and the substance of the negotiations. In the many months of the preparatory phase, developing countries generally were more concerned about their non-benefits from the WTO Agreements and about the need to correct the problems of implementation. Most of them were not in the frame of mind to consider or welcome the new issues being pushed by developed countries.   T h e latter, on the other hand, were aggressively promoting several new issues, such as investment, transparency in government procurement, competition, a new round of industrial tariff cuts, and finally labour and environmental standards. At Seattle, the US push for labour standards led by President Clinton confirmed the worst fears of developing countries that the WTO was sought to be tilted even more against them by the big powers.

The clash of interests over substance was worsened greatly by the utter disrespect for democratic participation of the majority of members and the great lack of transparency in the multitude of talks held in small groups that the majority had no access to. This was compounded by several manipulative tactics, including the non-incorporation of the views expressed by many members in the negotiating drafts. It became clear that an attempt was being made to railroad developing countries into agreeing to proposals and texts they had not agreed to, had opposed or had not even seen at all. In the end, many developing-country delegations made it clear, including through open statements and media conferences, that they would not join in a "consensus" of any Declaration in which they had no or little part in formulating. The talks had to be abandoned without the issuing of any Declaration or even a short statement by Ministers.

The tasks ahead include the need to address both substance and process. The grievances and complaints of developing countries – that they have not benefitted from the Uruguay Round, and that the problems of implementation of these Agreements have to be rectified – must be urgently and seriously tackled. The process of decision-making and negotiations in the WTO has to be democratized and made transparent. "Green Room" meetings should be discontinued. Every member, however small, must have the right to know what

negotiations are taking place and to take part in them. Until the reforms to the system and to the substance of the WTO take place, the organization's credibility will remain low. And for the reforms to take place, there should be a stop to the pressures being exerted by some of the developed countries to inject yet more new issues into the WTO. The following sections touch on these issues.

III: Lack of benefits for developing countries from the Uruguay Round

Officials from many developing countries are complaining that their countries have not benefited from the WTO Agreements of the Uruguay Round. And that as a result the credibility of the WTO trade system could be eroded. What is the basis of the complaints?

Most developing countries have not yet developed to a stage where they are able to meet the challenge to significantly export to the world market. It was believed, however, that the Uruguay Round would improve their chances by increasing the market access of developing countries' exports to the rich countries' markets.

The hopes were especially on textiles and agricultural products where developing countries have some comparative advantage, and also on some other industrial products. But five years after the Uruguay Round came into effect, these expected benefits have not materialized, and as a result there is a major sense of disillusionment or even betrayal that developing countries in general feel about the developed trading countries.

Some examples of this:

● Market access in industry has not improved

A lowering of Northern countries' industrial tariffs is supposed to benefit those Southern countries with a manufacturing export capacity. Even then, the reduction of average industrial tariffs of developed countries has only been from 6.3% to 3.8%, which means that an imported product costing $100 before duty could enter after duty at $104 instead of the previous $106, which is not a significant reduction. In contrast, many developing countries made huge reductions in their tariffs and bound them. According to WTO expert Mr Bhagirath Lal Das, India's average industrial tariff was reduced from 71 to 32%, Brazil's from 41 to 27%, and Venezuela's from 50 to 31%. "Tariff peaks" (or high import duties on certain products) remain in the rich countries for many industrial products that developing countries export. For instance, the US tariff for concentrated orange juice is 31%. This means that some potential exports of developing countries are still blocked.

● No gains yet from the supposed phasing-out of textiles quotas

The Uruguay Round's Agreement on Textiles and Clothing was aimed at phasing out the special treatment of the textiles and clothing sector, in which the developing countries had for the past quarter century agreed to subsidize the North by allowing quotas to be placed on their exports in this sector. The 10-year phase-out was supposed to be the aspect of the Uruguay Round to most immediately benefit the South, or at least the Southern countries that export textiles, clothing and footwear.

However, textile-exporting developing countries have been extremely disappointed and frustrated that five years after the phase-out period began, they have not yet seen any benefits. This is due to the "endloading" of the implementation of developed countries (that is, the liberalization of most of the products they buy from developing countries will take place only in the final year or years), and the benefits will accrue only at the end of the 10-year phase-out period. Although developed countries have legally complied with the agreement by phasing out quotas proportionately, in fact they have chosen to liberalize on products that are listed but which they have not actually restrained in the past. As a result, developing countries have not benefited. They are now pressing proposals that the developed countries improve the quality of their implementation of the Agreement on Textiles and Clothing.

• Increase in non-tariff barriers such as anti-dumping measures

Developing countries are also concerned and bitter that the supposed improvement of market access through tariff reductions is also being offset by an increase in non-tariff barriers in the rich countries. A major problem has been the use (or rather abuse or misuse) of anti-dumping measures, especially by the US and the EU, on products of developing countries, including on textiles.

The use of such measures (anti-dumping and countervailing measures) against developing countries' products has become more frequent after the Uruguay Round. Many countries have proposed that the misuse of these measures be curbed by amendments to the Anti-Dumping Agreement. However, this is stoutly resisted by the US.

• Continued high protection in agriculture

The Agriculture Agreement was supposed to result in import liberalization and reduction of domestic support and export subsidies for agricultural products especially in the rich countries, and this was expected to improve the market access of those Southern countries that export agricultural products. As it turned out, however, the protection and subsidies have been allowed to remain very high. For example, in the initial year of the agreement, there were very high tariffs in the US (sugar 244%, peanuts 174%), the EU (beef 213, wheat 168), Japan (wheat 353), and Canada (butter 360, eggs 236). The rich countries have to reduce such high rates by only 36% on average to the end of 2000. The tariffs have thus still been very high, making it impossible for developing countries' exports to gain access.

Also, the Agreement has allowed the developed countries to maintain most of the high subsidies that existed prior to the conclusion of the Uruguay Round. For example, they are obliged to reduce their very high domestic subsidies by only 20%. In contrast, most developing countries had no or little domestic or export subsidies earlier. They are now barred by the Agriculture Agreement from having them or raising them in future. There is a great injustice in this very odd situation.

• Conclusion

As seen from these examples, from the viewpoint of countries of the South, one of the major categories of "problems of implementation of the Uruguay Round" is the way the Northern countries have not lived up to the spirit of their commitments in implementing (or not implementing) their obligations agreed to in the various Agreements. This has led to the non-realization of the expected benefits to developing countries of their joining the WTO.

IV: "Implementation problems" faced by developing countries from the Uruguay Round

One of the reasons the developing countries were reluctant to endorse new initiatives or new issues in the Seattle WTO meeting is because they are still struggling with serious problems in their having to implement the Uruguay Round agreements.

The Uruguay Round resulted in several new legally-binding agreements that require developing countries to make drastic changes to their domestic economies in such diverse areas as services, agriculture, intellectual property and investment measures. Many developing countries did not have the

capacity to follow the negotiations, let alone participate actively, and did not really understand what they committed themselves to. Some of the agreements have a grace period of five years before implementation. That period was over at the end of 1999. The problems they will encounter from having to implement these agreements are thus only starting and are bound to get worse.

The following are some of their major general problems:

(a) having to liberalize their industrial, services and agriculture sectors will cause dislocation to the local sectors, firms and farms as these are generally small or medium-sized and unable to compete with bigger foreign companies or cheaper imports; and this could threaten jobs and livelihoods of millions;

(b) the Uruguay Round removed or severely curtailed the developing countries' space or ability to provide subsidies for local industries (due to the Subsidies Agreement) and their ability to maintain some investment measures such as requiring that investors use a minimum level of local materials in their production (this is prohibited by the Trade-Related Investment Measures Agreement);

(c) the Trade-Related Aspects of Intellectual Property Rights Agreement prevents local firms from absorbing or internalizing some technologies over which other corporations (mainly foreign firms) have intellectual property rights (IPRs); this would curb the adoption of modern technology in the South. Also, prices of medicines and other essential products are expected to rise significantly when the new IPR regime takes effect in the next few years.

Problems caused by some agreements

• Agriculture Agreement

The Agriculture Agreement could have severe negative effects on many Third World countries. Most of them (excepting the least developed countries) will have to reduce domestic subsidies to farmers and remove non-tariff controls on agricultural products, converting these to tariffs and then progressively reducing these tariffs. This will impose global competition on the domestic farm sector. Farmers unable to compete with cheaper imports may not survive. Hundreds of millions of small Third World farmers could be affected. There is also a category of developing countries which are net food importers; as subsidies for food production are progressively reduced in the developed countries, the prices of their exports may increase; the net food importers may thus face rising food import bills.

A recent UN Food and Agriculture Organization (FAO) study of the experience of 16 developing countries in implementing the Uruguay Round Agriculture Agreement concluded that: "A common reported concern was with a general trend towards the concentration of farms. In the virtual absence of safety nets, the process also marginalized small producers and added to unemployment and poverty. Similarly most studies pointed to continued problems of adjustment. As an example, the rice and sugar sectors in Senegal were facing difficulties in coping with import competition despite the substantive devaluation in 1994." (FAO Paper, "Experience with the implementation of the Uruguay Round agreement on agriculture, synthesis of country case studies", Sept 1999, prepared by FAO's Commodities and Trade Division)

Many developing countries during the preparations for Seattle had proposed to amend the Agriculture Agreement to take into account their problems of implementation. In most developing countries, small farmers form a large part of the population. Their livelihoods and products (especially food) are the main basis of Third World economies. These livelihoods could be threatened by agricultural liberalization under the Agriculture Agreement. Local food production could also be threatened by cheaper imports. Developing countries would then become more dependent on imports for their food supplies, thus eroding national food security.

To deal with these two serious problems, many developing countries (including India, Indonesia, Egypt, Sri Lanka, Uganda, Zimbabwe, El Salvador etc) have proposed that developing countries be given flexibility in implementing their obligations on the grounds of the need for food security, defence of rural livelihoods and poverty alleviation. They proposed that in developing countries, food produced for domestic consumption and the products of small farmers shall be exempted from the Agriculture Agreement's disciplines on import liberalization, domestic support and subsidies.

• TRIMs (Trade-Related Investment Measures) Agreement

In the TRIMs Agreement, "investment measures" such as the "local-content" requirement (obliging foreign firms to use at least a specified minimal amount of local inputs) will be prohibited for most developing countries from January 2000. This would prevent them from maintaining policies they have had to promote the local firms, to enable greater linkages to the domestic economy, and to protect the balance of payments. Developing countries need these policies because of the low level of development of the local sector, which would not be able to withstand free competition at this stage. Thus, by implementing the TRIMs Agreement, developing countries will lose some important policy options to pursue their industrialization.

In the review of the TRIMs Agreement, which was scheduled to begin in 1999, the problems of implementation for developing countries should be highlighted. The prohibition of the local-content requirement will seriously hinder the efforts of developing countries to promote local industry, save on foreign exchange, and upgrade local technological capacity. There is also a prohibition on investment measures that limit the import of inputs by firms to a certain percentage of their exports. Such measures had been introduced to protect the country's balance of payments. The prohibition of these two investment measures will make the attainment of development goals much more difficult.

The TRIMs Agreement should be amended to allow developing countries the right to have local-content policy and to limit the import of inputs to a certain percentage of a firm's exports.

Several developing countries (including Brazil, India, Indonesia, Malaysia, Pakistan, Uganda and Egypt) had been demanding in the pre-Seattle negotiations in the WTO in Geneva that the TRIMs Agreement be amended to provide developing countries the flexibility to continue using such investment measures to meet their development goals.

• TRIPS (Trade-Related Aspects of Intellectual Property Rights) Agreement

The South's collective loss was most acutely felt in the TRIPS Agreement through which countries are obliged to introduce IPR legislation with standards of protection that are similar to those in Northern countries. This will hinder Southern countries' indigenous technological development. It should be noted that the present industrial countries did not have patent or IPR laws, or laws as strict as will now be imposed through the TRIPS Agreement, during their industrializing period, and this enabled them to incorporate technology design originating from abroad in their local systems.

The agreement will also give rise to increasing technical payments such as royalties and licensing fees to TNCs (transnational corporations) owning most of the world's pat-

ents.

The new IPR regime will also have significant impact on the prices of many products. By restricting competition, the IPR rules will enable some companies to jack up prices of their products far beyond costs and thus earn rents in terms of monopoly revenues and profits. This is clearly seen in the case of computer software.

Also, most Third World countries have in the past exempted agriculture, medicines and other essential products and processes from their national patent laws, but with the passage of the TRIPS Agreement, everything is subject to IPRs unless explicitly exempted. The prices of medicines are expected to shoot up in many countries, and foreign drug sales will increase rapidly at the expense of local products.

The TRIPS Agreement also opens the door to the patenting of lifeforms such as microorganisms and modified genetic materials, thus providing the boost in incentives so desired by the biotechnology industry. Many environmentalists are concerned that this will be detrimental to the global environment as the present lack of controls and accountability in biotechnology research and application will likely accelerate biodiversity loss and could threaten natural ecosystems.

For plant varieties, the TRIPS Agreement does permit countries the option to introduce either patents or an alternative "effective" *sui generis* system of intellectual property protection. This has to be implemented by January 2000. Many farmers' groups (especially in India, where huge farmers' demonstrations and rallies have been held against GATT/WTO) and environmentalists are concerned that in the end Third World farmers will be disallowed the traditional practice of saving seed for the next season's planting (if the seed used is under the intellectual protection of a company) but forced to purchase the seeds from companies.

Given these many problems, the TRIPS Agreement should be amended to take into account development, social and environmental concerns. Meanwhile, the grace period before implementation should be extended. Many developing countries have made formal proposals before and at Seattle that a review of the agreement along these lines be made and that there should be an extension of the implementation deadline. So far the US and the EU have turned down these requests, insisting that the laws already created cannot be changed.

Recently there have been calls from some eminent economists and from some NGOs to take the TRIPS Agreement out of the WTO altogether. TRIPS is a protectionist device, and should have no place in an organization that is supposed to be committed to liberalization.   Moreover IPRs is not a trade issue. By locating it in the trade system, the road is open to overload the WTO with more and more non-trade issues.

Conclusion

These are only a few examples of how developing countries are facing immense problems now and especially in future. They are unable to absorb the changes they are required to make to their economic and social policies. Thus, many of the countries are correctly arguing that they need time to digest the Uruguay Round, that some of the rules that are unfair and that generate serious problems should be reviewed, and that until these are satisfactorily resolved there should not be fresh demands on them to liberalize further, especially through new issues such as investment and government procurement.

Given the serious problems faced by developing countries in implementing their Uruguay Round commitments (and in the developed countries' not properly implementing their commitments), there should be a review of the Agreements with a view to amending them. In fact, many of the Agreements themselves mandate that reviews be carried out four or five years after their coming into force.

The next three to five years of the WTO's activities should focus on the review process, so that the opportunity to rectify the defects of the Agreements can be taken. This review process would in itself be a massive task, involving analyses of the weaknesses of the various Agreements, assessments of how they have affected or will affect developing countries, proposals to amend the Agreements, and negotiations on these proposals.

V: Why the WTO should not take on new issues

A major reason for the failure at Seattle was the reluctance and refusal of many developing countries to allow the WTO to be given the mandate to take on more new issues for negotiating new agreements, which had been proposed by some of the developed countries. Saying no to the proposed new issues makes much sense.

If the WTO is to improve its already poor credibility, it should focus in the next few years on reviewing problems of implementing the Agreements and make the necessary changes in the Agreements. These will be enormous tasks. They will not be properly carried out if there is a proliferation of new issues in a new round. The extremely limited human, technical and financial resources of developing countries and their diplomats and policy-makers would be diverted away from the review process to defending their interests in the negotiations on new issues. The limited time of the WTO would also be mainly engaged in the new issues.

There will be little time for examining, reviewing and improving the existing Agreements, and the problems arising from their implementation will increase through time and accumulate, and manifest themselves in social and economic dislocation and political instability in many countries.

If this is not enough, most of the proposed new issues would also have the most serious consequences for the South's future development. Issues such as investment rules, competition policy and government procurement do not belong in the WTO (which is supposed to be a trade organization) in the first place. They are sought to be placed there by the developed countries to take advantage of the enforcement capability (the dispute settlement system) of the WTO, so that disciplines can be effectively put on developing countries to open their economies to the goods, services and companies of the developed countries. Other issues relate to labour, social and environment standards. These too should not enter the WTO as issues to be negotiated into new agreements. If they do so, then these issues are likely to be made use of by developed countries as protectionist devices against the products and services of developing countries.

Should the developed countries continue to push and pressure for these new issues, then the WTO will continue to be split, and moreover other pressing issues such as the problems resulting from the existing Agreements would not be tackled. Developing countries should therefore not accept and developed countries should refrain from injecting these new areas into the WTO.

VI: Conclusions

The multilateral trade system faces a crisis and a crossroads. To resolve the crisis of identity and credibility, the following should be considered:

1. Review the record of liberalization and take a more realistic approach. This requires a slowdown or stop to pressures being put on developing countries for further liberalization. After all, if the developed countries continue after so many years to maintain such high protection in agriculture, textiles and some industrial products (and argue that they

need more time to adjust), they have no basis to insist that developing countries must continuously liberalize in services or industrial products on the supposed ground that such liberalization is automatically good for them.

2. Reassert the objective of the trade system as primarily the development of developing countries, which form the majority of the membership. Liberalization or "free trade" should not be the operational aim. The goal should be development. Therefore there should be a shift of emphasis away from removing what is considered "trade-distorting" to instead removing the obstacles to development, or to review and rectify policies or practices that are "development-distorting." The goal and dimension of development must be primary in WTO rules and assessment of proposals or measures. The "special and differential treatment" principle should be greatly strengthened operationally, far beyond its present weak state.

3. The problems of implementation of the Uruguay Round agreements should be given top priority at the WTO. There is a danger that after the Seattle failure, these problems will again be sidelined as focus is given to the problem of participation and transparency. It must be recognized that the main cause of the Seattle failure was the disillusionment of many developing countries with the inequities of the rules and the negative effects these would have on their economies and societies.

To restore credibility to the trading system in the eyes of developing countries, the following should be done:

(a) Developed countries should take measures to greatly increase market access for developing countries' products, such as in agriculture, textiles and industrial products (where there are now high tariffs); moreover they should stop taking protectionist measures such as anti-dumping measures;

(b) In the many areas where developing countries face problems in implementing their obligations (such as in TRIMs, TRIPS and agriculture), a review and change of the existing rules should be done on an urgent basis. For a start, the sets of proposals put forward by developing countries during the preparations for Seattle (many of which are contained in the draft Ministerial text of 19 October, with more contained in the compilation of proposals) should be treated with urgency by the WTO General Council. A mechanism should be set up to consider these proposals and to rectify the problems (including through amending the agreements) as soon as possible;

(c) In the meanwhile, where the transition period for developing countries has expired (for example, in TRIPS and TRIMs), an extension should be given at least until the review process is completed. There should also be a moratorium on bringing dispute cases against developing countries on issues where the reviews are taking place.

4. Serious consideration should also be given to trimming the WTO so that it can carry out its tasks of regulating trade relations for the benefit especially of developing countries. In areas where it has accumulated a mandate that is inappropriate, steps should be considered to hive off these aspects. For example, it should be seriously discussed whether the TRIPS Agreement should remain within the WTO.

5. There should not be pressures to introduce new issues such as investment, competition, procurement, and labour and environmental standards as these would overload the system further and lead to tremendous systemic stress and great tensions and divisions in the organization.

6. The system and culture of decision-making in the WTO must undergo serious reform. This cannot be done in a rush

(continued on page 10)

(continued from page 15)

but has to be considered carefully, in a process in which all members have full participation rights. The exclusive Green Room meetings (which do not have the mandate of the full membership, and which are not officially announced, nor their results made generally known) should be discontinued. Manipulative methods (such as at Seattle where chairpersons of groups declared there was a consensus view when there was none, or when points made by some members were ignored) should stop. At meetings where issues are discussed and drafts are made and negotiated, there should be transparency and participation, where each member is given the right to be present and to make proposals. Even if some system of group representation is considered, all members should be allowed to be present at meetings and have participation rights. The Secretariat should also be impartial and seen to be impartial. Whatever results from the reform process, if there is one, the system should reflect the fact that the majority of members are now from developing countries, which have as much a stake or more in a truly fair and balanced multilateral system as the developed countries, and therefore the system must be able to provide the developing countries with the means with which to voice their interests and exercise their rights.   □

[15]

Assessing the General Agreement on Trade in Services

Half-Full or Half-Empty?

Pierre SAUVÉ[*]

I. INTRODUCTION

The ink was barely dry on the Final Act of the Uruguay Round before a growth industry—a service one at that—was spawned, one which consists of assessing, for business, the outcome, scope and practical meaning of what was the most ambitious and comprehensive set of multilateral trade negotiations ever undertaken. This article seeks to contribute to the burgeoning literature by focusing on the outcome of seven years of negotiations in one of the so-called "new" areas covered by the Uruguay Round, namely trade in services.

The term "trade in services" applies to international transactions involving such diverse fields as distribution, tourism, banking, insurance, transport, telecommunications, construction or consulting engineering. Services trade relates both to trade in goods (services are, indeed, often embodied in goods) and the international movement of capital, particularly direct investment, and of people, particularly highly skilled individuals.

That the world of multilateral trade diplomacy now contains a body of legally binding disciplines aimed at the liberalization of trade and investment in services hardly seems surprising. Promoting greater efficiency in service industries, including first and foremost a strong services infrastructure, is indeed what the processes of economic growth and development seem to be all, or increasingly, about. Services account, on average, for close to three-quarters of production and employment in most industrialized countries and, in many emerging countries, for shares that are rapidly converging towards the levels of many countries of the Organization for Economic Co-operation and Development (OECD).

The need for the multilateral trading system to catch up with the times appears all the more justified when viewed against the growing importance of services in world trade. In today's global market-place, international trade and investment in the services

---
* Principal Administrator, Trade Directorate, Organization for Economic Co-Operation and Development, Paris, France.

The views expressed in this article are personal and should not be attributed to the OECD or its Member countries. The author is grateful to Bernard Hoekman, Petros C. Mavroidis, Peter Morrison, Janet West, Americo Beviglia Zampetti and Marie-Pierre Faudemay for helpful comments and suggestions.

sector are increasingly prominent features of commerce. Driven by far-reaching innovations in information technology, increasing specialization and product differentiation, as well as by government policies of deregulation, privatization and unilateral liberalization in investment and trade regimes, trade in services has consistently grown faster than merchandise trade throughout the last decade.[1]

Although large in domestic economic terms and increasingly important in trade terms, the services sector remains heavily protected in many countries—developed and developing. Because services are not tangible in a physical sense, trade in them is free from tariff barriers. Rather than operating at the border, protection for services typically surfaces deep inside borders and finds its origin in domestic regulatory regimes.[2] The size, increasing tradability and high degree of protection, characteristic of most countries' services sectors, suggest that the liberalization of international trade and investment in services holds the potential for major gains in economic growth and efficiency. The negotiation of the General Agreement on Trade in Services (GATS) in the context of the Uruguay Round represented an attempt to realize those gains by negotiating mutually acceptable rules for governmental actions affecting international transactions in services and providing a needed institutional setting in which to pursue the progressive dismantling of impediments to trade and investment in services and the movement of people (consumers and suppliers alike).

For all the apparent normalcy of the Uruguay Round's outcome on the services front, the successful negotiation of the GATS represent a milestone in multilateral rule-making. With the successful incorporation within the incipient WTO structure of disciplines on goods (GATT), services (GATS), investment (Trade-Related Investment Measures—TRIMs) and intellectual property (Trade-Related Aspects of Intellectual Property Rights—TRIPs), all of which are now subject to an integrated (and much improved) dispute settlement mechanism,[3] the scope of the multilateral trading system has never been broader, nor its reach more encompassing.

---

[1] The average annual growth rate of trade in services over the last decade was 9.5 percent, as compared to 7.1 percent for merchandise trade. According to the GATT Secretariat, cross-border trade in services stood as just over US$ 1,000 billion at the end of 1993, or 21.1 percent of global trade (goods plus services). As many services are not tradable, producers of such services generally must contest foreign markets through an established presence, i.e. through foreign direct investment (FDI). According to GATT estimates, investment-related trade in services amounted to some US$ 3,000 billion in 1993. By way of comparison, GATT places total merchandise trade in 1993, at US$ 3,600 billion. FDI in services accounts, moreover, for a large share of the total stock of inward FDI in most host-country markets. As of the early 1990s, some 50 percent of the global *stock* of FDI was in service activities. The share of annual flows to many countries has often been much higher in recent years. For more data on trade and investment in services, see *Liberalizing International Transactions in Services: A Handbook*, United Nations Conference on Trade and Development (UNCTAD) and The World Bank, United Nations, New York, 1994.

[2] GATT experience in liberalizing trade in goods suggests that it is far more difficult to deal effectively with the non-tariff barrier-type measures that typically impede service imports than with border measures. This fact creates a major hurdle for the negotiation of any agreement aimed at liberalizing trade and investment in services, a hurdle that has been much in evidence in recent regional attempts at such liberalization (e.g. in North America, Europe or Australia and New Zealand). For a discussion of the scope of regional attempts at the liberalization of trade and investment in services, see Bernard Hoekman and Pierre Sauvé, *Liberalizing Trade in Services*, World Bank Discussion Papers No. 243, The World Bank, Washington, D.C., 1994.

[3] For a short summary of the main improvements contained in the Final Act of the Uruguay Round in the area of dispute settlement, see Pierre Sauvé, *A First Look at Investment in the Final Act of the Uruguay Round*, 28 J.W.T. 5, October 1994, pp. 5–16.

While a significant and welcome achievement, the establishment of the GATS remains only a first (somewhat tentative and imperfect) step in the direction of trade and investment liberalization for services. It is important to keep this in mind when assessing the Agreement. Policies affecting international transactions in services were new issues for most trade negotiators, and the negotiating process was naturally characterized by a large element of "learning-by-doing".[4] It should, therefore, come as no surprise that the GATS does not imply a move to "free trade" in services any time soon. Indeed, as with merchandise trade under the GATT, that is arguably not its core objective. Five decades of recurring trade in goods negotiations conducted under GATT auspices have led to a gradual reduction in average tariff levels and to the use of non-tariff measures being progressively "civilized". With the creation of the GATS, the international community is embarking on a similar journey, one that may be expected to be equally long, winding and occasionally bumpy.

This article's assessment of the GATS proceeds along three paths. It first sketches out the Agreement's structure and key provisions. Second, it briefly assesses the Agreement from a rule-making perspective, focusing in particular on some of the "architectural" changes that may already need to be envisaged to strengthened the Agreement. Third, it attempts a preliminary assessment of some of the practical implications of the GATS for globally active service-supplying firms.

II. THE GATS AT A GLANCE

The architecture of the GATS rests on three pillars:
(i) a framework agreement, which defines the obligations accepted by Members of the Agreement;
(ii) eight annexes, which address horizontal (e.g. movements of natural persons to provide services) and sector-specific (e.g. financial services,[5] telecommunications) matters; and
(iii) schedules of specific commitments that Member countries have chosen to make and which apply to service sectors, subsectors or activities listed therein, subject to sector- or activity-specific qualifications or conditions.

In addition, a number of Ministerial Decisions, dealing with such issues as the establishment of a work programme on trade in professional services or the terms of reference of future negotiations on maritime transport services, are attached to the Final Act of the Uruguay Round and affect the operation of the GATS. The difficulties— conceptual and political—underlying the services negotiations display their effects in the

---

[4] For an excellent depiction of the political economy underpinnings of the GATS negotiations, see Bernard Hoekman, *The General Agreement on Trade in Services*, in *Readings on the New World Trading System*, OECD, Paris, 1994. See also P. David Lee, *Services: The Continuing Agenda*, paper presented to the Ninth Annual Conference of the Centre for Trade Policy and Law on the Future of the Trading System, Ottawa, 31 May 1994.

[5] The difficulties inherent in reaching an acceptable package of trade-liberalizing commitments in the area of financial services (including insurance) are illustrated by the fact that the GATS contains two Annexes, one Understanding and one Ministerial Decision dealing specifically with that sector.

Agreement's complex architecture as well as in the considerable amount of unfinished business, both in terms of substantive rule-making and of liberalization commitments, left for completion after the Uruguay Round (see Table 1).

General obligations are contained in Parts I and II of the framework. As Table 1 indicates, there are fifteen Articles in Parts I and II, the most important of which being Articles I (Scope and Definition) and II (Most-Favoured-Nation Treatment). Under Article I, the GATS applies to measures (i.e. governmental actions) by Members (understood to include subnational governments, e.g. state, provincial and local governments) affecting trade in services, "services" being defined as including "any service in any sector" with the exception of those supplied in the exercise of governmental functions.[6] The definition of "trade in services" was a central issue of the negotiations, the substantive issue being whether the GATS would apply only to cross-border trade in services (as many developing countries initially wished) or would also include transactions requiring the relocation of factors of production (investment or people), that is "commercial presence" or "establishment" and temporary movement of service suppliers. In the end, the Agreement captured all possible modes of supplying services:

(i)   cross-border supply from the territory of one Member into the territory of any other Member (e.g. a long-distance telephone call, international shipping);

(ii) the provision of services involving the movement of consumers to the location of suppliers (e.g. a German tourist atop Mount Kilimanjaro);

(iii) the provision of services through an established presence in a foreign territory (e.g. the U.S. subsidiary of a British bank); and

(iv) the provision of services requiring the temporary cross-border movement of natural persons (e.g. a Canadian consulting engineer operating in Indonesia). It is important to note that the definition covers all modes of supply in principle only; that is, the extent to which specific modes can be used by foreign service suppliers is determined wholly by a country's schedule of commitments.

Article II codifies the unconditional most-favoured-nation treatment (MFN) principle, making it one of the Agreement's core—and arguably the most important—general obligations. Under the MFN rule, Members of the GATS are committed to treating services and service providers from one Member in the same way as services and service providers from any other Member. MFN treatment *per se*, of course, is not a liberalizing condition, as is evidenced by the fact that a country that bans all trade with any non-national supplier would be acting in a manner consistent with the MFN principle. None the less, the adoption of an unconditional MFN rule may be expected to provide export opportunities in many sectors, even if specific commitments on market access and national treatment have not been entered in national schedules, given

---

[6] Examples of such services include activities of central banks and monetary authorities and social security or public retirement systems. The GATS specifies that such services are covered by the Agreement in circumstances where they are provided under competitive conditions.

TABLE 1: THE STRUCTURE OF THE GENERAL AGREEMENT ON TRADE IN SERVICES

Framework

Preamble

Part I   Scope and Definition

Article I   Scope and Definition

Part II   General Obligations and Disciplines

Article II   Most-Favoured-Nation Treatment
Article III   Transparency
Article III *bis*   Disclosure of Confidential Information
Article IV   Increasing Participation of Developing Countries
Article V   Economic Integration
Article V *bis*   Labour Markets Integration Agreements
Article VI   Domestic Regulation
Article VII   Recognition
Article VIII   Monopolies and Exclusive Service Suppliers
Article IX   Business Practices
Article X   Emergency Safeguard Measures
Article XI   Payments and Transfers
Article XII   Restrictions to Safeguard the Balance of Payments
Article XIII   Government Procurement
Article XIV   General Exceptions
Article XIV *bis*   Security Exceptions
Article XV   Subsidies

Part III   Specific Commitments

Article XVI   Market Access
Article XVII   National Treatment
Article XVIII   Additional Commitments

Part IV   Progressive Liberalization

Article XIX   Negotiation of Specific Commitments
Article XX   Schedules of Specific Commitments
Article XXI   Modification of Schedules

Part V   Institutional Provisions

Article XXII   Consultation
Article XXIII   Dispute Settlement and Enforcement
Article XXIV   Council for Trade in Services
Article XXV   Technical Co-operation
Article XXVI   Relationship with Other International Organizations

Part VI   Final Provisions

Article XXVII   Denial of Benefits
Article XXVIII   Definitions
Article XXIX   Annexes

(continued)

TABLE 1: *Continued*

Annexes

Annex on Article II Exemptions
Annex on Movement of Natural Persons Supplying Services under the Agreement
Annex on Financial Services
Second Annex on Financial Services
Annex on Telecommunications
Annex on Air Transport Services
Annex on Negotiations on Basic Telecommunications
Annex on Negotiations on Maritime Transport Services

Ministerial Decisions

Decision on Institutional Arrangements for the General Agreement on Trade in Services
Decision on Certain Dispute Settlement Procedures for the General Agreement on Trade in Services
Decision on Negotiations on Basic Telecommunications
Understanding on Commitments in Financial Services
Decision on Financial Services
Decision on Professional Services
Decision on Negotiations on Movement of Natural Persons
Decision on Trade in Services and the Environment
Decision on Negotiations on Maritime Transport Services

Source: Compiled by the author.

that many Members already maintain relatively open services markets. Many countries, particularly developing ones, had been concerned that a "conditional" MFN rule would have prevented them from benefiting from GATS concessions if they did not accept a certain level of liberalization. Article II, however, allows a Member to maintain a measure inconsistent with MFN treatment provided that the measure is listed and meets the conditions of the Annex on Article II exceptions. The latter Annex specifies that such exemptions, which are not "in principle" to be maintained beyond a period of ten years, are "in any event" subject to periodic review and are to be negotiated away in subsequent liberalizing rounds. The words "in principle" and "in any event" would appear to allow for the possibility of extending exemptions beyond ten years, although the ease with which the Council for Trade in Services would allow this to happen remains to be seen.[7]

Because the level of market openness varies significantly across countries, a binding requirement to apply unconditional MFN treatment was resisted by service industry representatives in a number of industrialized countries. They argued that unconditional MFN would allow countries with restrictive policies to maintain the *status quo* and "free ride" in the markets of more open countries. Whether for reasons of preserving negotiating leverage, protecting culturally sensitive sectors or maintaining the predominantly bilateral nature of international agreements in some sectors, pressure for

---

[7] For a critical assessment of the treatment of MFN-related matters in the GATS, see Brian Hindley, *Two Cheers for the Uruguay Round*, Trade Policy Review 1994, Centre for Policy Studies, London, 1994, pp. 17–20.

MFN derogations were most acute in the areas of telecommunications, financial services, maritime transport, audio-visual services and air transport services.

Other framework provisions of the GATS deal *inter alia* with the following issues:

— transparency, requiring all relevant laws, regulations and administrative guidelines affecting trade in services to be published;

— economic integration, allowing Members to belong to agreements liberalizing trade and investment among or between themselves, e.g. Canada in the North American Free Trade Agreement (NAFTA), provided that certain conditions relating to scope of coverage and the absence of new discriminatory measures *vis-à-vis* third-country Members are met;

— recognition of education, standards, licences or certificates of other Members, allowing for harmonization or mutual recognition arrangements through negotiations or autonomously;

— domestic regulation, acknowledging Members' right to regulate service activities, subject to ensuring that regulatory regimes do not constitute unnecessary barriers to trade or nullify the value of specific commitments entered into national schedules;

— behaviour of public monopolies, aimed at ensuring that these behave consistently with a Member's MFN obligations and do not abuse their dominant position (e.g. by using their monopoly receipts to cross-subsidize services provided in a competitive environment);

— behaviour of private operators, calling on Members to consult with a view to removing private business practices that restrict competition or distort trade[8] and to providing information on business practices deemed to have such effects;

— government procurement, for which the development of multilateral negotiations are envisaged within two years of the Agreement's entry into force;

— emergency safeguards, for which procedures are to be envisaged within three years of the Agreement's entry into force;

— freedom for payments and transfers for current transactions in sectors where specific commitments have been taken, except if taken to safeguard the balance of payments (such safeguards are to be temporary and non-discriminatory in nature, and subject to multilateral surveillance);

— subsidies, for which, in recognition of their potential distortive effect on trade, negotiations aimed at developing multilateral disciplines are envisaged (though no timetable has been agreed);[9] and

— exceptions for reasons of health, safety, consumer protection or national security, analogous to those applicable to merchandise trade under the GATT.

The GATS framework is completed by institutional and final provisions, chief

---

[8] Article IX on business practices reflects a welcome recognition of the fact that private behaviour can restrict trade. The inclusion of business practices in the GATS opens the door to future work in this area, particularly in light of the trade policy community's growing interest in competition policy matters and its recognition of the contribution that competition policy disciplines can make to solving market access problems.

[9] There is, mercifully, no reference to anti-dumping for services in the GATS.

among which are those dealing with the establishment of a Council for Trade in Services to administer the Agreement and with dispute settlement and enforcement matters. The latter provisions need be read in the context of the integrated dispute settlement system adopted in the Understanding on Rules and Procedures Governing the Settlement of Disputes, which provides that suspension of concessions is not limited to the concessions resulting from the GATS, but that cross-sectoral retaliation between goods, services and intellectual property-related matters is permissible under certain conditions.[10]

It is important to understand—and this is arguably one of the architectural weaknesses of the GATS—that many of the obligations described above are triggered only when a Member schedules a specific commitment. These, then, become conditions of such commitments. Two of these—those relating to transparency and monopoly suppliers—contain provisions that are both generally applicable and conditional in nature while others, most notably in the areas of payments and transfers and domestic regulation, are wholly conditional. There would appear to be little *a priori* reason why so many of the GATS general obligations are conditional in nature—traders and investors would stand to gain much, for instance, from the regulatory certainty stemming from the general, rather than selective, application of disciplines on payments and transfers. Similarly, why should the obligation for regulatory regimes affecting trade in services to be administered in a "reasonable, objective, and impartial manner" apply only in scheduled sectors? One can only hope that, in the context of future negotiating rounds, Member countries come to appreciate the policy-signalling benefits to be derived from a more robust framework for underpinning the liberalization of trade and investment in services. Meanwhile, the selective, *à la carte*, approach to rule-making embodied in the GATS must be viewed as weakening the overall Agreement.

Such structural weakness is nowhere more visible than in the GATS' approach to liberalization commitments. This approach is described in Part III of the Agreement. There are three Articles in Part III—Market Access, National Treatment and Additional Commitments (Articles XVI, XVII and XVIII respectively). Market access is not defined under Article XVI. Rather, agreement was reached on six categories of measures which, unless specified in Members' schedules, are prohibited in principle. These six categories define what, in effect, is meant by market access for services and are made up of both non-discriminatory and discriminatory quantitative restrictions.[11] These consist of limitations on:

---

[10] Appended to the Final Act of the Uruguay Round are Ministerial Decisions dealing with Institutional Arrangements and Certain Dispute Settlement Procedures for the GATS. The object of the former Decision is to empower the Council for Trade in Services, the supreme WTO body responsible for administering the GATS, to establish subsidiary bodies as appropriate, including sectoral committees such as that dealing with Trade in Financial Services. The latter Decision provides that panels for disputes in specific sectors should have the necessary expertise, including in regulatory matters, relevant to the specific sector concerned, a concern most vividly expressed in the area of financial services.

[11] Where quantitative restrictions to access apply in a discriminatory fashion, they also violate the Agreement's National Treatment Article (Article XVII). This is the case of the last two categories of measures listed under Article XVI.

(i)   the number of service suppliers allowed;

(ii)   the value of transactions or assets;

(iii)   the total quantity of service output;

(iv)   the number of natural persons that may be employed;

(v)   the type of legal entity through which a service supplier is permitted to supply a service (e.g. branches *versus* subsidiaries for banking); and

(vi)   the participation of foreign capital in terms of a maximum percentage limit of foreign shareholding or the absolute value of foreign investment.

Unlike the GATT, the GATS does not enshrine the right to national treatment. Rather, the obligation to treat foreign services and service providers no less favourably than like domestic services and service suppliers applies selectively to sectors and activities on the terms and conditions inscribed in the Members' schedules of specific commitments. The GATS codifies the recognition that such treatment may not always be identical to that applying to domestic services or suppliers (this is often the case, for instance, of cross-border trade in professional or financial services), so long as it does not worsen the competitive conditions faced by foreign services and suppliers. The Article on Additional Commitments allows for commitments to be undertaken on measures that go beyond the current purview of some of the provisions of the Agreement, for example in areas such as government procurement or professional licensing.

Determining the exact scope of the GATS involves the interplay of a number of parameters. While the Agreement's sectoral coverage is universal in nature (with all services covered except those supplied in the exercise of governmental authority, e.g. social security), specific commitments on market access and national treatment are scheduled by mode of supply and apply only to listed service sectors, subsectors or activities, subject to commitment-specific conditions, qualifications and limitations, either across all modes of supply or for a specific mode. The GATS thus adopts what has been called a "hybrid" approach to scheduling commitments, combining a positive list approach to sectoral coverage with a negative list approach to non-conforming measures (i.e. measures that violate the market access and national treatment provisions) maintained in sectors entered into a Member's schedule.[12] The extent of liberalization is, therefore, reflected in the number of restrictions (which may pertain to each of the four possible modes of supply) that are included in each Member's schedule of commitments in conjunction with the number of service industries that are listed

---

[12] Under a positive list approach, a sector is, for all intents and purposes, excluded from virtually all but the MFN obligation of the GATS if it is not listed in a Member's schedule. Under the obverse, a negative list approach (which was used in the NAFTA), only those services that are specified in Members' lists of non-conforming measures are excluded from the scope of an agreement; that is, services not specified are automatically subject to all obligations. The clearest advantages of a negative list approach lie in its greater transparency (since a failure to list non-conforming measures implies their full and immediate liberalization) as well as the fact that all new services entering the market-place automatically enjoy the benefits of the agreement (i.e. are automatically "bound at free"). An interesting account of the political economy considerations which underpinned the hybrid approach to scheduling adopted in the GATS can be found in Hoekman, *op. cit., supra,* footnote 4, pp. 4–5. As well, see Harry G. Broadman, *GATS: The Uruguay Round Accord on International Trade and Investment in Services,* The World Economy, Vol. 17, No. 3, May 1994, pp. 281–292.

therein. Under this hybrid approach, "free" trade in any particular mode of supply applies to the services sectors inscribed without any qualification in a Member's schedule. Unless noted otherwise, commitments made in schedules are bound; that is, a Member may not impose new measures restricting market access or national treatment for a sector listed in its schedule without compensating affected Members.

While their large number illustrates quite vividly the difficulties encountered by negotiators in coming to terms with their subject-matter (indeed, their very inability to bring the negotiations to a successful conclusion), the eight Annexes and nine Ministerial Decisions that are appended to the GATS and the Final Act of the Uruguay Round form an integral part of the Agreement. These fall into three categories:

(i)   those addressing horizontal issues (exceptions to the MFN treatment principle; movement of natural persons);

(ii) those addressing sectoral specificities (air transport, telecommunications, financial services); and

(iii) those detailing the modalities of ongoing negotiations on both horizontal (movement of natural persons) and sectoral issues (financial services, maritime transport, basic telecommunications and professional services).

The Annex on Article II Exemptions specifies the conditions under which Members may derogate from the GATS' core MFN principle. Apart from those sectoral or horizontal issues for which negotiations are pending, MFN exemptions are to relate to existing measures only; that is, those applied at the time the Uruguay Round was completed in mid-December 1993 (although some of the exemptions scheduled are future measures drafted as existing measures, e.g. future agreements pertaining to the temporary admission of agricultural workers). The Annex specifies that the Council for Trade in Services is to review all exemptions granted for a period of more than five years. In that review, the Council is to determine whether the conditions which created the need for an exemption still prevail and to specify the date of any further review. As mentioned earlier, the Annex provides that MFN exemptions are not to exceed a period of ten years "in principle" and shall "in any event" be subject to negotiation in subsequent trade-liberalizing rounds.[13]

The Annex on Movement of Natural Persons Supplying Services under the Agreement establishes that Members may negotiate specific commitments applying to the temporary entry of all categories of natural persons. This Annex stipulates that the GATS does not apply to measures affecting people seeking access to the employment market of a Member, or to measures regarding citizenship, residence or employment on a permanent basis. It specifies that natural persons who are service suppliers or are employed by a service supplier originating in a Member of the GATS shall be allowed to

---

[13] It is important to note, however, that the Annex on Article II Exemptions does not lay down criteria or conditions for the inclusion of exemptions and most of the exemptions scheduled in Members' MFN exemption lists are for an indefinite period of time. For instance, twenty-six of the twenty-eight exemptions scheduled by the European Union are for an indefinite period, and all MFN exemptions entered by the United States are not time-bound. For a good description of the policy underpinnings of Annex II exemptions, see *Liberalizing International Transactions in Services, supra*, footnote 1, at pp. 172–173.

provide services in accordance with the terms and conditions (e.g. a domestic means test for all incoming labour) of specific commitments relating to the entry and temporary stay of such persons. The development of this Annex was—and remains—of particular interest to developing countries, given the comparative advantage many of them enjoy in labour-intensive services (e.g. construction services, software development, engineering design). Recognition of the fact that most developed countries had not included categories of greatest interest to developing-country exporters led to the adoption of a Ministerial Decision calling for negotiations to continue beyond the conclusion of the Uruguay Round and aimed at achieving higher levels of commitments by GATS Members. Such negotiations are to be completed no later than six months after the entry into force of the WTO (i.e. by the end of June 1995).

The Annex on Financial Services contains language that limits—indeed carves out—liberalization obligations with respect to services supplied in the exercise of governmental functions (e.g. central bank activities) and the application of domestic regulation for prudential reasons.[14] The Annex also lists and defines the range of activities falling under the rubric of "financial services". The Understanding on Commitments in Financial Services that was appended to the Final Act of the Uruguay Round and was spearheaded (but dropped since, for all intents and purposes) by OECD countries, established a specific formula—a first-best scenario of sorts—that signatories could adhere to on a voluntary basis with a view to achieving a higher degree of liberalization.[15] Finally, and perhaps most importantly, a Ministerial Decision on Financial Services stipulates that negotiations in the sector will be extended for six months following the entry into force of the WTO. At the end of this period, Members will be free to improve, modify or withdraw all or part of their commitments in the sector without offering compensation and will be allowed to finalize their positions relating to MFN exemptions in respect of financial services.[16]

The Annex on Telecommunications recognizes the dual role of telecommunications—as a crucially important sector in its own right but also as a means of supplying a host of services (e.g. financial services, engineering designs or intra-corporate and value-added telecommunications services). The Annex aims at ensuring that any service supplier is accorded access to and use of public telecommunications transport networks and services—so-called basic services—on reasonable and non-discriminatory terms and conditions for the supply of a service included in its schedule.

---

[14] The latter remain, however, subject to dispute settlement to the extent that they might be used as a means of avoiding a Member's commitments or obligations under the Agreement.

[15] It is worth noting that U.S. negotiators recently announced that they would no longer pursue the so-called "two-track" approach foreseen in the Understanding. For an excellent survey of the agenda for future GATS-related work in the area of trade in financial services, see *The Outcome of the Uruguay Round: An Initial Assessment*, Supporting Papers to the Trade and Development Report 1994, UNCTAD, United Nations, New York, pp. 177–181.

[16] For a comparison of the treatment of financial services in the NAFTA and the GATS, see Pierre Sauvé and Brenda Gonzalez Hermosillo, *Implications of NAFTA for Canadian Financial Institutions*, The NAFTA Papers, C.D. Howe Commentary, No. 44, C.D. Howe Institute, Toronto, April, 1993.

The Annex, therefore, does not, in itself, result in liberalization in any sector, including telecommunications, without the inclusion of a negotiated commitment.

The Annex on Negotiations on Basic Telecommunications relates to the negotiation of market access and national treatment commitments in this subsector and was largely included to address concerns, particularly those of the United States, relating to the application of the MFN principle in the sector. In accordance with the Ministerial Decision on Negotiations on Basic Telecommunications, GATS Members have agreed to pursue, up to 30 April 1996, negotiations aimed at liberalizing the provision of basic telecommunications services. Members participating in these talks have agreed, up until the implementation date of the results of the negotiations, to apply a standstill; that is, not to apply in the sector any MFN-inconsistent measure that might improve their negotiating leverage.[17]

The Annex or Air Transport Services carves out from the overall GATS coverage all "hard" traffic rights and directly related activities that might affect the negotiation of traffic rights, thereby avoiding the need for all Members to schedule MFN exemptions relating to existing (or future) bilateral air agreements. The Annex, however, specifies that the GATS does apply to aircraft repair and maintenance services, the marketing of air transport services or computer reservation systems, only to the extent that a Member inscribes commitments for these activities. Mindful of the far-reaching economic and regulatory changes that are occurring in the sector, both of which involve a steady move away from the restrictive bilateral approaches of the past, the Annex is to be reviewed within five years of the entry into force of the GATS, with a view to considering the possible further application of the Agreement in the sector.[18]

Paralleling, to some extent, the procedures foreseen for financial services and basic telecommunications, the Annex and the Ministerial Decision on Negotiations on Maritime Transport Services effectively suspend all MFN obligations in the sector until 30 June 1996, allowing more time for the negotiation of a mutually acceptable package of market-opening commitments in the sector. GATS Members will be permitted, during this period, to improve, modify or withdraw their offers without offering compensation, and final commitments as well as MFN exemptions are to be scheduled

---

[17] Until the conclusion of the negotiations on basic telecommunications, MFN exemptions will not be applicable, even if entered into a Member's Annex on Article II Exemptions. The outstanding issues that are being considered by the negotiating group on basic services include those relating to licensing, approval and standards-setting procedures for telecommunications equipment, so as to ensure that measures in these areas do not constitute undue barriers to trade. The development of safeguards against anti-competitive practices on the part of dominant suppliers (e.g. monopoly post, telephone and telegraph (PTT) companies) will also probably need to be addressed, as will measures affecting the ability to own, operate or supply telecommunications facilities (e.g. networks) and services. For a good depiction of the key challenges facing negotiators in the sector, see Harry G. Broadman and Carol Balassa, *Liberalizing International Trade in Telecommunications Services*, Columbia Journal of World Business, Vol. XXVIII, Number IV, Winter, 1993, pp. 30–37.

[18] It was unrealistic for anyone to expect that the network of bilateral agreements under the Chicago Convention would be eliminated in the Uruguay Round. Air transport, indeed, is perhaps the best illustration of what might be called the GATS "assignment" problem, that is, the inability of the Agreement's limited tool-box of liberalizing instruments to really effect any significant rollback of discriminatory and anti-competitive practices in the sector. While it is unlikely that air transport will ever lend itself to an MFN-based regime of multilateral liberalization, any move in this direction within the GATS context would require the development of a complementary set of disciplines in such areas as subsidies, investment and competition policy.

at the end of the negotiations. As in the case of basic telecommunications, Members have agreed to a standstill provision during the course of ongoing negotiations. Among the key issues for discussion are the liberalization of international shipping and auxillary services, non-discriminatory conditions of access to, and use of, port facilities and the degree to which the GATS covers—and thus hence may discipline—commercial (i.e. private) practices applying in the sector which may exert trade-restricting effects.

The Ministerial Decision on Professional Services will lead to the establishment of a Working Party on Professional Services whose mandate will be to make recommendations on least-trade-restrictive approaches to licensing and accreditation matters for professional services, a necessary pre-condition for any meaningful expansion of trade and investment in the sector. Priority emphasis is to be given to the development of multilateral disciplines in the accountancy sector, so as to give operational effect to the specific commitments lodged in that sector by some forty-five Members.

III. THE GATS' BIRTH DEFECTS: ANYTHING CONGENITAL?

The GATS has been described, perhaps appropriately in light of the preceding discussion, as a full employment bill for trade negotiators! There are perhaps two main reasons for coming to this conclusion; first, because of the fair amount of substantive rule-making work that remains outstanding, negotiators having been unable *in seven years* to complete the framework. They will thus need to turn their attention in the coming years to developing provisions on issues ranging from safeguards, subsidies and government procurement to procedures for the mutual recognition of professional licensing regimes. The second reason, of greater immediate importance, is that the search for a critical mass of liberalization commitments continues on such a broad sectoral front. This mass of unfinished business greatly complicates attempts at assessing the real world implications of the Agreement as it currently stands. There can be little doubt, however, that the successful completion of such negotiations, particularly those concerned with sectoral liberalization commitments, will be critical to establishing the credibility of—indeed the very need for—the GATS. This, in turn, will have obvious implications for the credibility of the WTO system as a whole.[19]

Before speculating on the possible implications of the GATS for the business community (as users and suppliers of services), it is important to say a few words on some of the rule-making challenges trade negotiators are likely to meet in trying to enhance the quality of the GATS. This is all the more important as the framework agreement itself is something of a *coquille vide* (an empty shell) in the absence of negotiated commitments. The preceding Section has already alluded to a few of the

---

[19] In the words of Canada's negotiator for services during the Uruguay Round: "In the enthusiasm of negotiating national sectoral positions, it will be important not to lose sight of the long-term integrity of the system. Indeed, it should be emphasized that Members need to temper their participation in these negotiations with the realization that they will be of crucial importance in bringing about the full success of the GATS, or possibly of condemning it to a lengthy period of weakness, or even sterility." See Lee, *op. cit.*, *supra*, footnote 4, at pp. 7–8.

framework's architectural shortcomings: ambiguity as to whether the listed MFN derogations will be repealed at the end of ten-year grace periods; and the fact that so few of the GATS' so-called "general provisions" are of truly general application, starting with the core liberalizing instruments of national treatment and market access—both of which apply in a highly selective manner in scheduled sectors only.

The very design of the scheduling process, which allows Members to restrict the contestability of services markets by sectors *and* by mode of supply, may also be viewed as impeding the proper functioning of the Agreement. For instance, the hybrid approach to scheduling yields a mostly unsatisfactory outcome from a transparency point of view. The GATS, indeed, generates no information on sectors, subsectors and activities in which no liberalization commitments are scheduled—quite often the most sensitive ones in which restrictions and discriminatory practices abound. This is a serious shortcoming when one considers the nature and origin of impediments to trade and investment in the services area: regulatory barriers applying at both the national and subnational levels. The across-the-board adoption of a top-down, "list it or lose it", negative list approach, such as that used for services and investment in the NAFTA, would have both significantly enhanced transparency and been more inherently liberalizing by automatically covering (and binding at "free") all new service activities,

A second problem relates to the implications for the liberalization process of scheduling commitments by mode of supply. Somewhat ironically, given the early resistance of many countries to discussing establishment-related trade in services (i.e. investment), the bulk of commitments lodged under the GATS, first and foremost by developing country Members, relates to the commercial presence mode of supply. While such an outcome is hardly surprising when viewed against the establishment-related nature of much "trade" in services, the decision to schedule commitments by mode of supply clearly resulted in fewer commitments on the cross-border movement of services and service suppliers. This is because it provided Members with what could be called an architectural incentive to impose TRIM-like requirements (even where cross-border trade may be feasible or preferable from a business viewpoint) on foreign services and service suppliers, to establish a commercial presence as a pre-requisite for supplying services in their territories.[20]

While the preceding discussion would appear to suggest that the GATS is structurally flawed, that its birth defects are genetic in nature and, therefore, that the Agreement is probably beyond reconstructive surgery, one need not be unduly dismissive. As already noted, many of these shortcomings can be ascribed to the political economy of learning-by-doing. Negotiating in uncharted waters, particularly among a large and markedly heterogeneous group of countries, across an equally broad spectrum

---

[20] The "revealed preference" seems to reflect the perception that commercial presence provides host countries with greater regulatory oversight and strategic bargaining powers, both of which might allow them to benefit more fully from the externalities deriving from an established presence. The structural bias against cross-border supply remains paradoxical given that Article XVI.2(e) (Market Access) focuses, in part, on the so-called right of non-establishment by prohibiting, in sectors subject to market access commitments, measures which mandate a local presence in order to supply a service.

of sectoral specificities and on behalf of ever-shifting coalitions of industry supporters and opponents, could hardly have been expected to generate perfection *ab initio*. Negotiators may therefore take solace in the fact that many—if not most—of the rule-making inadequacies described above can be redressed. This, of course, will require clear political will—a commodity that is often in short supply—and can only be accomplished progressively over a length of time, particularly in view of the negotiating fatigue found in most capitals following the completion of the Uruguay Round.

As was noted earlier, there is no *a priori* reason for not making a greater number of GATS framework provisions truly general in application, start with those pertaining to domestic regulation (Article VI) and to payments and transfers (Article XI). The same outcome could also be generated with regard to the market access and national treatment provisions, though this would require a NAFTA-like conversion to a negative list approach and involve the preparation—most likely over agreed phase-in periods for countries at differing stages of development—of lists (indeed, telephone books) of non-conforming measures maintained at the national and subnational levels by GATS Members. The gains in transparency and in liberalization dynamics afforded by such a conversion would be significant.[21]

One may also be sanguine as regards the scope for moving away from scheduling commitments by mode of supply. For example, the NAFTA has shown that far-reaching liberalization of trade and investment in services can be achieved without any reference to modes of supply. Moreover, it is important to note that nothing in the GATS itself compels Members to schedule commitments by mode of supply, such a methodology having been adopted at the end of the negotiating process in a largely *ad hoc* manner. By generating commercially useful lists of non-conforming measures (suggesting an over-arching body of general obligations to start with), the adoption of a negative list approach in future negotiating rounds would allow the scheduling process to centre more appropriately on the nature of remaining impediments to trade and investment in services rather than on modes of supply, the latter being rigid and somewhat artificial dividing lines bearing little or no relation to the ways in which service-providing firms conduct their affairs in the real world. Indeed, there is every reason to believe that most service providers would not recognize a mode of supply if they came across one!

There remain, however, two sources of concern from a rule-making perspective which cannot be easily swept aside. One such concern relates to the sectoral nature of ongoing negotiations, which may be expected to complicate attempts at achieving an overall balance of benefits, not only because the negotiations will no longer take place

---

[21] A number of developing countries long resisted—indeed successfully fought against—the adoption of a top-down, general obligation-driven, negative list approach under the GATS, mainly owing to the perception that the obligation to list non-conforming measures and freeze (i.e. bind) the regulatory *status quo* would leave them naked in sectors that were either unregulated or where regulatory regimes were largely undeveloped. The NAFTA, of course, broke this deadlock, marking an important precedent even for Canada and the United States, whose 1989 Free Trade Agreement had seen the adoption of a far more timid positive list approach to coverage. What is interesting is that Mexico's proliferating web of regional agreements with countries in Central and South America all adopt the NAFTA approach. This means that a significant number of important GATS signatories have already effected the needed shift towards a negative list approach to sectoral coverage and liberalization.

against the background of a comprehensive negotiating round involving trade liberalization and rule-making in all areas (e.g. goods, services, intellectual property) but also because of clear differences in the negotiating objectives—both offensive and defensive—between the *demandeurs* (typically OECD countries) and *offreurs* (typically the most dynamic developing countries) in many key outstanding areas. A further complication arises from the bureaucratic rigidities—i.e. turf guarding resistance—that the sectoral negotiating process may be expected to generate.

A second source of concern relates to the difficulty of interpreting the precise scope of the Agreement. This problem arises mainly for three reasons:

(i)   the agreement's reach—which concerns all governmental (including subnational) actions affecting trade in services—is potentially extremely broad and extends deep inside the regulatory domains of Member countries;

(ii) such reach is tightly circumscribed by the contents of individual schedules of commitments;[22]

(iii) many of the schedules are drafted in ways which lack clarity, complicating attempts at determining the nature and reach of Members' bindings.

The interaction of the above factors may well incite Members to "test" the GATS, including through recourse to dispute settlement, in order to determine its scope with greater precision. This could easily clog the WTO's integrated system of dispute resolution at a time when the overriding need will be to establish its credibility. What is more, because the resolution of disputes under the GATS will most likely involve interpreting the nature (and intent) of Members' specific commitments (both by sector and mode of supply), questions arise as to whether the evolving body of GATS jurisprudence will generate sufficiently general ramparts with which to repel future challenges.[23] As one GATS negotiator recently put it: "The mixture of new rules, heavier involvement with domestic regulations and regulators, and binding automatic dispute settlement could pose delicate political problems, especially in the early stages."[24]

IV. GETTING DOWN TO BUSINESS: ASSESSING THE REAL-WORLD IMPLICATIONS OF THE GATS

Assessing the magnitude of trade and investment liberalization that was achieved for services in the Uruguay Round is no easy task. With negotiations on so many key sectoral or horizontal fronts—ranging from basic telecommunications, financial services, accounting, and maritime transport to multilateral discussions on the movement of natural persons and government procurement for services—earmarked to proceed for

---

[22] The greater relative importance of these schedules is one of the main features distinguishing the GATS from the GATT.

[23] As one GATS expert recently noted: "The history of the GATT dispute settlement cases relating to disciplines that were less than clear-cut (e.g. subsidies) suggests that there is potential for controversy." Hoekman, *op. cit., supra*, footnote 4, at p. 7.

[24] See Lee, *op. cit., supra*, footnote 4, at p. 7.

several more months or years, it is simply not possible, at this stage, to pass definitive judgments. This explains why the foregoing analysis spent some time dwelling on the architectural or rule-making challenges GATS negotiators will need to confront.

It is worth noting, however, that even if the GATS negotiations had been fully completed by the time the curtain fell on the Uruguay Round, it would be next to impossible to quantify the commercial benefits flowing from the Agreement. This is so for two reasons. First, the disaggregated and comparable data on trade and investment that would be required to conduct such an investigation are generally unavailable. Such data are notoriously bad at the sectoral level, and next to non-existent (as perhaps it should be) at the level of modes of supply. Second, and most importantly, the very nature of the GATS' liberalization exercise, which consists of extracting binding market access and national treatment commitments (by mode of supply) in regard to regulatory practices, does not lend itself easily to quantitative analysis.[25] That being said, it is possible to suggest some of the positive externalities that businesses—both those that provide services and those that use them—are likely to reap in the wake of the GATS, and to sketch in broad qualitative terms what has been achieved by way of liberalization commitments, i.e. to describe what is already locked in by the Agreement.

Despite the Agreement's noted shortcomings, the GATS may be viewed as embodying two broad types of benefits. First, it provides a body of legally binding multilateral concepts, principles and rules with which to pursue, under conditions of considerably heightened (if still imperfect) transparency, the progressive liberalization of trade and investment in services. Prior to the Uruguay Round, no such body of rules was available to civilize—hence, provide the peaceful means to resolve—policy conflicts among nations in a sector now accounting for more than one-fifth of world commerce. The fact that one of the most vibrant segments of the world economy is now subject to a more predictable, rules-based, environment is a welcome achievement.[26] A second benefit of the GATS lies in its potential to raise the economic efficiency of Members' service industries, a process that can be achieved both through improvements in domestic resource allocation and through improved access to lower-cost/higher-quality service inputs. A higher level of domestic efficiency should, in turn, generate increased export opportunities. In practice, export and import opportunities are strongly interdependent; higher-quality and/or cheaper service inputs are frequently necessary for more efficient and competitive domestic production and thus greater exports of

---

[25] For an excellent discussion of the practical difficulties of quantifying the GATS' outcome, see Bernard Hoekman, *Tentative First Steps: An Assessment of the Uruguay Round Agreement on Services*, paper presented at The Uruguay Round and the Developing Countries: A World Bank Conference, Washington, D.C., January 1995.

[26] In the words of the GATT Secretariat: "It is to be noted that liberalization measures generally, and the liberalization of foreign direct investment in particular, have a much greater value when they are set in a *contractual commitment* and embedded in a *multilateral set of rules*, than when they are merely autonomous. The permanence, predictability and confidence that these elements represent greatly reinforce the effects and the value intended in those measures. This is the value of having the GATS, as such, as the centrepiece of bringing services and the liberalization of services to the multilateral arena." (Emphasis in original). See *An Analysis of the Proposed Uruguay Round Agreement, With Particular Emphasis on Aspects of Interest to Developing Countries*, Trade Negotiations Committee, Group of Negotiations on Goods, MTN.TNC/W/122, MTN.GNG/W/30, GATT Secretariat, Geneva, 29 November 1993.

goods and services. Opportunities for both imports and exports of services will, in part, be a function of the specific liberalization commitments undertaken by GATS Members and inscribed in their schedules.

The value of specific commitments on market access and national treatment lodged by GATS Members will, in turn, be a function of the extent to which:

— service sectors, subsectors or activities appear in individual schedules;
— all modes of supply are bound;
— limitations and qualifications apply to market access and national treatment undertakings; and
— exemptions to the MFN principle are listed.

By the end of the Uruguay Round, ninety-seven countries had submitted schedules of specific commitments. Many of the schedules—sixty-one in all—are accompanied by MFN exemption lists. The coverage of Members' schedules varies widely, whether in terms of industry, mode of supply, degree of openness or liberalization (standstill or rollback). Indeed, of the one hundred and fifty-five sectors appearing in the classification list devised by the GATT Secretariat for scheduling purposes, some (least-developed) countries agreed to bind as few as one or two sectors or subsectors. Other countries, developed and developing, have put forward comprehensive sets of commitments covering most broad categories of sectors and many modes of supply.

Virtually all the commitments scheduled under the GATS—including by OECD countries—represent a binding of the *status quo* rather than a rollback of existing restrictions to trade and investment in services. Such a regulatory freeze, which in many cases involves important qualifications and limitations (suggesting that some Members may, in fact, have offered less than the *status quo*), in effect establishes the liberalization frontier which successive rounds of negotiations will have as a central objective to push back.[27]

While the overall outcome on market access and national treatment commitments typically locks in what was already there, that is, provides generally little by way of new or expanded service export opportunities, this is arguably better than was expected until

---

[27] The U.S. International Trade Commission (ITC) recently completed a comprehensive assessment of the likely impact of the Uruguay Round on U.S. service sectors. The findings of the study, which may be loosely applied to Canada given the two countries' specialization in many similar service-producing activities (with the likely exception of the audio-visual sector), have been summarized as follows: "Generally, the Uruguay Round is expected to increase the U.S. trade surplus in the service sector by a small amount (between 1 and 5 percent). Exceptions are the value-added telecommunications sector, which will likely experience a modest improvement (between 5 and 15 percent) and the audio-visual sector, which is expected to benefit by only a negligible amount (1 percent or less). Revenues in the service sectors are generally expected to increase by a small to modest amount (between 1 and 15 percent) under the Uruguay Round. Employment is expected to increase by negligible to small amounts (5 percent or less). U.S. consumers are expected to benefit from the Uruguay Round by a negligible to small degree, owing mainly to lower prices." An interesting aspect of the ITC study is its emphasis on the indirect gains accruing to the services sector from other parts of the Final Act of the Uruguay Round. This is the case mainly for computer and software services, which will likely derive immediate commercial benefits from the TRIPs Agreement, as well as construction and engineering services, which will benefit from the extension to services (including construction) of the GATT Code on Government Procurement. The latter outcome is of particular interest to Canada's world-class consulting engineering industry: see USITC, *Potential Impacts on the U.S. Economy and Industries of the GATT Uruguay Round Agreements*, Investigation No. 332-353, USITC Publication 2790, Washington, June 1994.

near the end of the Round, and almost certainly better than what had been expected at the outset of the negotiations. Even in the absence of liberalization, guaranteeing the maintenance of existing conditions of access by offering a standstill on current regulatory practices can provide important benefits in terms of security of access for foreign service suppliers. The question, as ever, is whether the glass should be viewed as half-full or half-empty, and the reasonableness of the time-horizon over which one may expect the glass to be progressively filled.

Among OECD and Eastern European countries, the glass appears fuller, with Members' bindings generally at free for business services, enhanced telecommunications services, computer and software services, environmental services, tourism, construction and engineering services (excluding the movement of lower-skilled people), as well as a number of professional services. Many developed and developing countries have made commitments on education, health and cultural services. In those sectors where market-opening negotiations are scheduled to continue—i.e. basic telecommunications, maritime transport, financial services, movement of natural persons and professional services (accounting)—the results were mixed, with some countries making commitments and others preferring to await those negotiations. Given the fact that developing countries tend, on average, to have a weaker services sector, their schedules typically include a more limited number of bindings. While representing a useful first step, the schedules of a number of dynamic emerging economies, especially in South-East Asia, are generally regarded as disappointing. The willingness of this latter group of countries to improve their offers in the areas earmarked for further negotiations (particularly in the areas of financial services and basic telecommunications) would do much to enhance the business opportunities stemming from the Agreement. It should be noted, however, that a number of developed countries eschewed commitments in some important sectors or subsectors; for example, audio-visual services, maritime transport (United States) and financial and business services, as well as with regard to the temporary entry of service suppliers.

In overall terms, preliminary indications are that developing countries' schedules have bound around one-fifth of their services sector, whereas industrialized countries' schedules cover around two-thirds of commercially traded services. It is important to note that the effective coverage of country offers will typically be worth less (in some cases, substantially less) than is suggested by simple sectoral coverage. Any data on GATS commitments must, therefore, be handled with care, as account must be taken of the restrictions on market access and national treatment that may continue to apply, as well as the so-called "horizontal headnotes" found in many schedules that maintain access-limiting restrictions across all or many sectors and modes of supply.[28] For this reason, the

---

[28] A further shortcoming of such coverage ratios is that they give each service sector found in the GATS' classification list equal weight, something that is clearly inappropriate. One way to correct for industry size would be to weigh offers by the share of each industry in the total services output. Unfortunately, the detailed data that would be required to do this are typically not reported by individual Member countries. For more on the empirical problems encountered in measuring the value of GATS commitments, see Hoekman, *op. cit.*, *supra*, footnote 4, at p. 7; and *Liberalizing International Transactions in Services*, *supra*, footnote 1, at pp. 147–148.

GATS may be described as an agreement in which there is invariably less than meets the eye!

As was noted earlier, the mode of supply against which the largest number of commitments were scheduled is that relating to commercial presence, followed by that concerned with the movement of consumers (e.g. tourism). Of some concern from an architectural point of view is the fact that the fewest liberalization undertakings have been lodged against the cross-border mode of supply. More positive, however, is the fact that most Members' schedules contain commitments with regard to the mode of supply involving the movement of natural persons. Developed and developing country Members alike have, indeed, made commitments with respect to intra-company transferees—executives, managers, specialists and business representatives—who are linked to the establishment and/or operation of a commercial presence in scheduled sectors. The movement of service providers in categories other than those listed above is generally unbound, pending the completion of ongoing negotiations.[29]

V.   Concluding Remarks

The General Agreement on Trade in Services represents the first multilateral and legally enforceable agreement to establish a body of rules governing international trade and investment in services. The successful negotiation of the GATS means that policies affecting access to service markets—whether these relate to measures affecting trade, investment, regulatory practices or the movement of people—are now central components of an evolving multilateral architecture of rules aimed at supporting and achieving more open and liberal conditions for doing business globally.

That the international community was able, in the Uruguay Round, to lay the foundations of a modernized multilateral trading system can be ascribed to the far-reaching changes in policy and rule-making approaches which gained currency in a growing number of countries, both developed and developing, during the course of the Round. Chief among these was the greater appreciation world-wide of the key contribution of services to promoting economy-wide efficiency gains and of the central role played by investment (hence by investment regime liberalization) as the principal means of securing market access and enhancing the contestability of markets.

While the GATS must be viewed as a useful start—a down-payment of sorts—the analysis presented in this article suggests that there is no fast and easy answer to the question raised in its title. The jury, indeed, is still out as to whether the GATS' glass should be viewed as half-full or half-empty. Only time will tell whether the instrument devised to liberalize trade and investment in services in a multilateral setting will be up to the task for which it has been established. Some degree of caution over the GATS'

---

[29] For a detailed statistical treatment of GATS schedules of commitments by sector and mode of delivery, see Hoekman *op. cit., supra*, footnote 25; and *The Results of the Uruguay Round of Multilateral Trade Negotiations: Market Access for Goods and Services—Overview of the Results*, GATT Secretariat, Geneva, November 1994.

real-life prospects would, none the less, appear warranted. This is so for three main reasons:

(i) the framework Agreement is unfinished, generally weak and contains too few obligations of a truly general nature;

(ii) the approach that has been used for securing liberalization commitments presents a number of architectural deficiencies—it generates insufficient transparency, is not inherently liberalizing, introduces a bias against cross-border trade and may require undue testing through recourse to dispute settlement; and

(iii) the Agreement, up to this point, promises to yield only modest gains by way of new or expanded business opportunities, potentially depriving itself of the support of sectoral constituencies that will be central to its long-term prosperity.

Much of this prosperity, therefore, will depend on the political will of Member countries both to agree to a credible set of liberalization commitments in all the key sectors earmarked for ongoing negotiations (starting immediately in the high-stakes area of financial services) and to confront the need for introducing what, in some cases, may represent significant structural changes to the Agreement's design. Progress on both fronts will be required if the GATS is to fulfil the promises depicted above. The recent experience of regional trading arrangements shows that such rule-making challenges can be successfully met. In the meantime, services negotiators can look forward to a few more years of guaranteed employment and, governments permitting, to a rich harvest of frequent flyer points.

[16]

GATS and the Millennium Round of Multilateral Negotiations

Selected Issues from the Perspective of the Developing Countries

Neela MUKHERJEE*

I. BACKGROUND

The General Agreement on Trade in Services (GATS), under the General Agreement on Tariffs and Trade (GATT) Uruguay Round, was a major step in an unchartered terrain of liberalising trade in services. Such multilateral liberalisation of trade in services is due for review in the year 2000, when a new round of multilateral trade negotiations will begin at the World Trade Organization (WTO). The GATS covers trade in services related to critical infrastructure such as telecommunications, computer software, banking, insurance, health, tourism, transport and business and is expected to generate phenomenal growth in tradable services. Due to a slow takeoff, the full impact of the GATS on world trade is yet to be felt. However, as a fresh round of negotiations is round the corner, this article makes a general assessment of the GATS "architecture", mainly from the point of view of the developing countries, and also offers some generic suggestions to be considered for the new round. Such generic suggestions have been arrived at based on a study of the original schedules of specific commitments in services of 95 member countries of the WTO under the Uruguay Round.

The value of world export of commercial services was US$ 1,310 billion in 1997, which was 19.3 percent of global export of goods and services. Growing at an annual average rate of 8 percent over 1990–1997, commercial service exports assume significance for both industrialised and developing countries as they contribute 70 percent and 50 percent of respective gross domestic products. However, the arena of tradable services is dominated by the industrialised countries, which have accounted for more than 70 percent of such trade in the 1990s.

The GATS, a product of the Uruguay Round, has been an innovative attempt at constructing a realistic framework for liberalisation of trade in services. It has helped in the creation of global space for multilateral trading rules in services. The GATS, unlike other agreements under the Uruguay Round, enjoys considerable latitude in at least three different ways. One such latitude relates to modes of delivery for trade in services, where four such modes, "crossborder trade", "commercial presence", "consumption abroad" and "movement of natural persons" as described below, have been recognised

* Consultant economist, telefax 91-11-6481824, e-mail: neelamuk@del2.vsnl.net.in. The views expressed in this article are in the personal capacity of the author. Thanks are due to Professor Petros Mavroidis and Dr Ajit Mazumdar for their comments and suggestions on the article. All errors and omissions, however, are the sole responsibility of the author.

under the GATS. Another kind of opportunity is with regard to the opening of service sectors, where a positive list approach adopted under the GATS enables a member country to pick and choose those services, tradable and non-tradable, for providing market access and national treatment to other signatories of the GATS. A third kind of leeway is in terms of measures and restrictions, where, under a negative list approach adopted under the GATS, a member country can specify restrictions/limitations on both market access and national treatment and also deviations from the most-favoured-nation (MFN) clause.

So far so good. However one relevant issue is whether the export interests of the developing countries have been included in the GATS rules and regulations. The answer is a straight "no" and, as will be seen in the following sections, the GATS has not proved to be that effective in churning out proportionate gains for developing countries in service trade. In the recent General Council of special sessions at the WTO, concluded in February 1999, it was stated by India and supported by other developing countries that the latter had paid an enormous price for the Uruguay Round and had undertaken major obligations under the Marrakesh Agreement without having commensurate gains. Also Joseph Stiglitz in the Prebisch lecture at the United Nations Conference on Trade and Development (UNCTAD) in October 1998 stated that in terms of a new development paradigm and the responsibility of the developed countries, the outcome of the Uruguay Round had produced no benefits for Africa but instead a net loss of welfare and little in the way of new market access for products that Africa was in a position to export.

Thus from the developing countries' perspective of the new round, two crucial issues in this context are what limitations does the GATS suffer from and what kind of negotiating agenda should developing countries be looking for in the coming round. This article identifies some of the major limitations of the GATS and makes appropriate suggestions for the coming round.

II.   WHAT IS THE GATS?

The GATS, which governs multilateral trading in services, covers, in principle, all service sectors and all measures affecting such trade by the following four modes of delivery:
- crossborder trade (e.g. exporting software in a floppy disc format, sending business reports and computer-to-computer transfer);
- trade by consumption abroad (the movement of consumers from one country to another to avail of foreign services, e.g. medical services);
- trade through commercial presence (the setting up of an establishment in a foreign country, such as an engineering firm for offering engineering services); and
- trade by means of temporary presence of natural persons (movement of service providers from one country to another, as in the case of lawyers travelling abroad to provide legal services).

Most of the services require physical proximity; some are also long-distance services. The modes of delivery of trade in services which are relatively important for developing countries are movement abroad of skilled and semi-skilled service providers from developing countries to deliver such services and consumption of services abroad by foreign firms and individuals visiting developing countries. Presence of natural persons as a mode of delivery is at a premium as it earns foreign exchange and remittances for the developing countries and helps them to meet their international payments obligations.

The GATS can be divided broadly into three parts:

– the first part is the Framework Agreement, which contains basic obligations applicable to all member countries;

– the second part is that of national treatment and national schedules of commitments on market access; and

– the third part consists of a number of annexes and attachments on special situations of individual service sectors.

Initially 95 countries made offers in services under the GATS. It covers 12 service sectors, which are business services, communication services, construction services, distribution services, educational services, environmental services, financial services, health-related and social services, tourism and trade-related services, recreational, cultural and sporting services, transport services and others.

III. IS THE GATS DIFFERENT FROM OTHER AGREEMENTS UNDER THE GATT-URUGUAY ROUND?

Under the GATS, a gradual process of liberalisation has been initiated in services trade, which is similar to the other agreements under the GATT. With regard to the principle of national treatment, the GATS has a subtle difference as compared to the agreements in agriculture and industrial products under the GATT Uruguay Round (see Table 1). The GATS covers the right to national treatment, unless otherwise indicated in the schedule of commitments. There are no general obligations to offer national treatment and market access to foreign suppliers; these obligations are confined to the sectors and sub-sectors specifically included in the individual schedule of commitments of each member, subject to any limitations with respect to different modes of supply (Mattoo, 1997).

Not all sectors of services were covered by the multilateral negotiations of the Uruguay Round. Negotiations in some of the areas proved to be difficult, such as the areas of financial services, movement of natural persons, maritime services, professional services and the GATS rules regarding emergency safeguards, government procurement and subsidies for services. Negotiations on basic telecom services were concluded in February 1977 and those for financial services in December 1997. Sauvé (1995) remarks that the difficulties, both conceptual and political, underlying the services negotiations are amply displayed in the Agreement's complex architecture as well as the considerable amount of unfinished business, both in terms of substantive rule-making and of liberalisation commitments left for completion after the Uruguay Round.

Again, unlike other agreements in the GATT Uruguay Round, which adopt a

TABLE 1: COMPARATIVE FRAMEWORK OF AGREEMENTS IN THE GATT URUGUAY ROUND

	Agriculture	Industry	Services
Objectives	• Tariffication of non-tariff barriers • Full bindings of new tariffs • Reducing levels of domestic support and export subsidies	• Reduction of average tariff levels by one-third • Reduction of tariff peaks and escalation • Increase in tariff bindings	• Right to national treatment to be provided unless otherwise indicated in the schedule of commitments • Multilateral framework of principles for progressive liberalisation of trade in services
Approach	• Negative list*	• Negative list*	• Unfinished business for rule-making and liberalisation • Hybrid approach in the GATS, includes both positive list and negative list**
Action	• Replacing non-tariff barriers by tariffs and reducing them by 36 percent over six years by industrial countries and 24 percent over ten years by developing countries	• Lowering of tariff rates phased in five equal and annual reductions beginning in 1995 • Phasing of Multi-Fibre Agreement (MFA) and non-MFA restrictions over a ten-year period	• Little scope for tariff barriers • Specification of service sectors for liberalisation • Specification of a framework for investment in services • Specification of limitations on market access and national treatment in services sectors and sub-sectors listed in the Schedules of Commitments

Source: Compiled by the author.
Notes: * Those specified in the Schedules are excluded.
          ** For the GATS, a positive list approach is adopted for the sectors, which means sectors that are not specified are excluded from the GATS coverage; and a negative list approach is adopted for measures, which implies that measures limiting market access and national treatment as specified in the Schedules of Commitments in the GATS are excluded from the scope of the Agreement.

negative list approach, the GATS adopts a "hybrid" approach to undertaking specific commitments. Such specific commitments combine a positive list approach to sectoral coverage and a negative list approach to measures that violate market access and national treatment provisions in the schedule of commitments (see Notes to Table 1). In the GATS, there are two kinds of commitments, the horizontal commitments, which run across the service sectors and the sectoral commitments specific to each sector that a member country chooses to offer for liberalisation.

While for agreements in agriculture and industry, the emphasis is on reducing average tariff levels, binding of tariffs and tariffication of non-tariff barriers, the agreement in services has little scope for tariff barriers. As indicated above, the GATS also recognises four modes of delivery of trade in services. One unique feature of the GATS "architecture" is that it specifies a framework for "commercial presence" or, alternatively, foreign direct investment in trade in services in addition to those on "crossborder" trade, "consumption abroad" and "movement of natural persons". This framework is of considerable interest, covering foreign investment issues in services, where trade in services constitutes around 20 percent of total world trade. The framework is especially important in the context of the controversies raised by issues related to a multilateral framework for investment.

IV. THE ANNEX ON MOVEMENT OF NATURAL PERSONS

There are eight Annexes and nine ministerial decisions appended to the GATS, which are integral to it. One important Annex for developing countries is the Annex on Movement of Natural Persons Supplying Services, which establishes that members may negotiate specific commitments applying to the temporary entry of all categories of natural persons. In this regard, six sets of commitments were produced for the purposes of annexing them to the Third Protocol to the GATS. The Protocol entered into force at the end of January 1996 for those members who accepted it by the date and was open for acceptance by other members until the end of June 1996, which was further extended until 30 November 1996. Australia, Canada, the European Communities, India, Norway and Switzerland improved their commitments on movement of natural persons (only five members had ratified their commitments by 30 June 1996). The commitments guarantee new opportunities for individual service suppliers to work abroad on temporary assignments without the requirement that they be linked to commercial presence in the host country. They have the advantage of being sector specific, which enables developing countries to identify export opportunities in the concerned sectors (ESCAP, 1996).

Right from the inception of the GATT Uruguay Round, there were clear areas of disagreement between the developing and developed countries, which have become all the more pronounced in recent years. One grey area of trade in services is the "right of establishment", which serves the interest of the developed countries, and the "right to movement of labour", which the developing countries perceive to be advantageous. For the latter, the Annex on Movement of Natural Persons has been included in the GATS, although not very effectively, as commitments for entry of mainly higher category of personnel have been undertaken, thus overlooking the natural advantage of developing countries in movement of medium- and low-skilled personnel.

V. THE SIGNIFICANCE OF TRADE IN SERVICES FOR DEVELOPING COUNTRIES

The developing countries as a group exported around US$ 303.9 billion of commercial services in 1997, a share of 23.2 percent of world export of services as shown in Table 2. The new round of negotiations in trade in services is of significance for

TABLE 2: INDUSTRIAL AND DEVELOPING COUNTRIES—PERCENTAGE SHARE IN WORLD TRADE
IN SERVICES

Year	1990	1997	1990	1997
Trade in services	Exports	Exports	Imports	Imports
Industrial countries	79.0	70.9	74.6	66.7
Developing countries	16.5	23.2	18.7	26.3
Other countries	4.5	5.9	6.7	7.0
Total	100.0	100.0	100.0	100.0

Source: Estimated from the WTO (1998): *WTO Annual Report* (Geneva).

developing countries on account of the potential trading opportunities that can be created as a result of such negotiations. Even for the least developed countries, services are becoming increasingly important both as direct exports and as inputs into production processes. Tourism and data-processing appear to have great potential (UNCTAD, 1996 and 1998). The role of such new opportunities can be important, given the constraints and trade barriers that such countries are facing in the sphere of merchandise trade, sluggish world demand, rising foreign debt liability and declining trend in net foreign aid flows, coupled with payment imbalances. Given the human resources that they have, liberalisation of market access in selected categories of skilled and semi-skilled labour can help them in providing services in selected areas of business, communication, travel, recreation, transport and construction services.

VI. ISSUES OF CONCERN IN THE MULTILATERAL TRADING RULES OF THE GATS

Although the GATS has helped in the creation of global space for multilateral trading rules in services, it has failed to deliver much gain to the developing countries. In this context, some major limitations and constraints of the GATS are flagged below.

A.   TRADE IN SERVICES HIGHLY SKEWED

To start with, for any multilateral negotiations, trade in services is an unbalanced situation, where most developing countries are traders at the margin and as a group accounted for 23.2 percent of world exports and 26.3 percent of world imports in 1997 as shown in Table 2. From a global trading position, trade in services is the stronghold of the industrial countries, which constitute an average of 70 percent of such trade in the 1990s. Flow of exports is largely one way: from the rich industrial countries to the developing countries. Effectively, most developing countries export two main services, namely labour and tourism. In the case of tourism, there are really no barriers to be removed by the GATS and, as will be seen later, export of labour is highly restricted under the GATS. Thus, liberalised market access offers imply greater benefit for the industrial countries, which are major traders in services and fewer benefits for the developing countries, which are traders at the margin. One implication of the inequitous trade in services between industrial and developing countries is that the scope of cross-retaliation should be limited as an instrument for enforcing obligation (Mazumdar, personal communication).

Data on trade in services clearly show that the United States is leading global trade for transportation, travel and other commercial services, although the picture changes when the European Community and its member States are considered as one. As shown in Table 3, in the area of export of commercial services, the United States is the leading exporter of communication services, followed by Germany, the United Kingdom, Japan and Canada. In the sphere of exporting insurance services, the United Kingdom is the leading country, followed by Canada, the United States, Italy, Germany and France. In the area of export of financial services, such as those services related to banking, insurance and securities, when considered together, the United Kingdom and the United States are far ahead of others, followed by Italy and Germany, both trailing behind. For computer and information services, the United States is the leading exporter followed by the United Kingdom and Germany. For the export of professional and other business services, the United States is followed by Germany, the United Kingdom, Japan, France, Italy and Canada. In the export of construction services, Japan is followed by Germany, France, the United States and Italy. In the export of other business services, such as consultancy services, the United States is followed by Germany, the United Kingdom, Japan, France, Italy and Canada. In receipt of royalties and license fees, the United States has no competitor, with US\$ 30.3 billion received on that account in 1997.

B.   No Commensurate Benefits to Developing Countries

The specific commitments of member countries as contained in the GATS clearly indicate that it is essentially a trade deal for the multinationals from the industrial countries where most developing countries have undertaken commitments to liberalise trade in services without commensurate benefits. The participation of developing countries is more as importers of services rather than exporters of services. The sustainability issues in the context of importing large quantities of services without appropriate openings in exports are quite important, given the precarious foreign exchange position of most developing countries and the mounting trade and fiscal deficits.

As shown in Table 4, developing countries, with an advantageous position with regard to "mobility of labour" have not gained much from the GATS. "Mobility of labour" as a mode of delivery of tradable services, although formally recognised by the GATS, has been restricted considerably by different trade barriers (see Table 4) as compared to "mobility of capital". Out of 13 industrial countries (considering the European Union and its member countries as one), 12 have allowed exclusive entry of higher level personnel as compared to 43 developing countries offering the same out of 72 developing countries. In the case of mobility of capital, as shown in Table 5, the barriers imposed by member countries of the WTO have more to do with issues related to "ownership" and "control"

TABLE 3: TRADE IN COMMERCIAL SERVICES OF INDUSTRIAL COUNTRIES (BILLION OF DOLLARS)

Services sector/country	Canada		United States		France		Germany		Italy		United Kingdom		Japan	
	X	M	X	M	X	M	X	M	X	M	X	M	X	M
Transportation services	6.0	8.3	49.6	46.7	19.3	19.7	18.9	23.1	16.0	24.8	18.3	21.3	21.8	31.1
Travel services	8.8	11.3	85.2	53.4	27.9	16.5	16.5	46.0	29.7	16.6	20.7	28.2	4.3	33.0
Other commercial services	14.5	16.3	94.8	50.1	33.1	25.9	40.0	51.0	26.0	28.7	46.5	19.1	42.0	58.0
Communication services	1.4	1.3	3.8*	9.1*	0.6	0.7	1.9	2.9	0.7	1.1	1.5	1.8	1.4	1.7
Construction services	0.1	0.1	3.4	0.3	3.9	1.8	4.7	6.1	3.3	1.2	–	–	7.9	5.5
Insurance services	2.7	3.5	2.6	n4.8	1.4	1.2	1.9	2.0	2.0	1.8	5.1	0.9	0.3	2.0
Financial services	0.8	1.2	10.1*	4.1*	1.7	1.6	2.6	1.1	3.8	5.0	7.5**	–	1.8	2.7
Computer and information services	1.2	0.7	6.2*,***	0.8*,***	0.5	0.5	2.1	3.0	0.2	0.6	2.5	1.7	1.4	3.5
Royalties and license fees	0.5	2.0	30.3	7.5	2.0	2.5	3.2	4.7	0.5	1.0	4.8	3.5	7.3	9.6
Other business services	7.7	7.4	35.3***	23.2***	21.4	15.8	23.5	31.2	15.1	16.9	21.3	9.5	21.6	31.9
Personal, cultural and recreational services	0.1	0.1	3.1	0.2	1.4	1.8	0.2	2.6	0.4	1.1	3.9	1.7	0.2	1.1

Source: WTO (1998): *WTO Annual Report* (Geneva).

X = Exports, M = Imports

Notes: * Excludes transactions between affiliates, which are recorded under "other business services".

  ** Indicates that the export of financial services is underestimated because earnings of financial institutions are recorded, net of their foreign expenses.

  *** Includes estimates by the Secretariat of the WTO.

TABLE 4: COUNTRY-LEVEL COMMITMENTS IN THE GATS FOR "MOVEMENT OF LABOUR"

Market access commitments for the "movement of natural persons"	Industrial countries	Developing countries
Exclusive entry of higher level personnel	12	43
Restricted entry of other level personnel	1	9
Not mentioned	–	20
Total number of countries	13 (including member countries of EU as one)	72

Source: Derived from the Schedules of Horizontal Commitments of Member Countries, GATS, WTO, 1994.

TABLE 5: COUNTRY-LEVEL COMMITMENTS IN THE GATS FOR "COMMERCIAL PRESENCE"

Market-access commitments for "commercial presence"	Industrial countries	Developing countries
Limitations on foreign equity participation	8	25
Exceptions to such limitations also included	6	17
No limitations on foreign equity participation	4	12
Limitations not stated explicitly/kept unbound	1	35
Limitations on nationality of board members/directors/shareholders/voting rights/etc.	9	9
Limitations on sectors for foreign investment/application of economic needs test	5	18
Total number of countries	13 (including member countries of EU as one)	72

Source: Derived from the Schedules of Horizontal Commitments of Member Countries, GATS, WTO, 1994.

of capital, whereas, for the mobility of labour, the barriers are generally associated with "keeping out" most categories of labour, diffused "entry conditions" for labour migration and limitations on labour's "duration of stay". Through the GATS, mobility of higher level personnel in transnational corporations has been ensured.

Liberalisation of labour services by the industrial countries would constitute the major benefit for developing countries to be weighed against potential losses from exposing their infant industries in telecom, construction, insurance, banking and other services to competition from the multinationals of the industrial countries (Mazumdar, personal communication). Benefits to host countries from foreign direct investment can be assessed sectorally and additional commitments made for opening of labour services. It is important that non-permanent labour movements (encompassing skilled and non-skilled labour, intra-firm transferees and self-employed service providers) should be included in the negotiations to provide symmetry in the treatment of internationally mobile factors of production (UNCTAD, 1998).

C.   "ELUSIVE" ARTICLE IV OF THE GATS

Some damage control measures, undertaken in the GATS through Article IV, Part II, for creating a "level playing field" for the developing countries, remain elusive. Article IV in Part II of the GATS, which aims at creating space for better participation of developing countries, has been virtually ignored in practice. In this Article, it is stated that the industrial member countries and other member countries of the WTO shall facilitate the access of developing countries' service suppliers to commercial and technical aspects, registration, recognition, obtaining of professional qualification and availability of technology for services. The Article also makes provision for special priority for the least developed countries. The other provisions included in the "elusive" Article IV are liberalisation of market access in sectors and modes of supply of export interest to the developing countries; improved access to distribution and information networks; and the strengthening of the domestic services capacity of developing countries, improving its efficiency and competitiveness.

Some of the above provisions have been arranged by the WTO, while the crucial ones are yet to be translated in actual practice. For instance, the WTO has jointly collaborated with multinational organisations such as the International Trade Commission (ITC) and the UNCTAD for technical assistance to developing countries. It has exercised a variety of instruments such as seminars, workshops, technical missions, briefing sessions and training for capacity building of developing countries' personnel. A total of over 600 technical co-operation activities covering all aspects of the WTO have been organised throughout mid-1998 directed towards human development and institutional capacity building. However, not much has been done with regard to the other provisions in Article IV, relating to greater market access in sectors of export interest to the developing countries, improved access to distribution and information networks, etc.

D.   ABSOLUTE SECTORAL TRADABILITY OVERLOOKED

The basic negotiating stance at the WTO has resulted in absolute sectoral agreements for agriculture, industry and services without any formal linking of the three sectors. Comparatively speaking, the inequality of costs and benefits as between developed and developing countries in extending exclusive reciprocal obligations in trade in services is much greater than that of merchandise trade. Even within the services sector, the sub-sectoral offers in market access are discrete and are not linked up. For example, in the services sector, agreement in the telecom sector is absolute without bearing any relationship with that of computer software services. To that extent, negotiations in the WTO have been limited and partial in character. Sectoral agreements in the WTO, treated as water-tight compartments, tend to overlook the fact that elements of sectoral tradability differ widely and cross-sectoral agreements can lead to better options for the developing countries.

E. MYSTIFIED AGREEMENTS

Like other international trade agreements, the WTO agreements including the GATS are a terse mix of economics, business and law, and it is far beyond the human capacity of many developing countries to assess their long-term implications. Many of the developing countries have signed on the dotted lines of such mystified agreements without understanding much of their implications. The countries are now considerably handicapped in applying the technical agreements to their policy framework, yet, formally, they are parties to such multilateral agreements. Although some international organisations, including the WTO, are helping to build the capacity of the member countries, progress on that front has been quite slow. The sectoral agreements in services trade are complex and technical, while the task of de-mystifying such agreements to the general public as principal stakeholders, still remains in a vacuum.

F. COMPLEX TRADE BARRIERS

Another inherent problem of the GATS is that most of the trade barriers imposed on services are opaque and not amenable to easy measurement (Griffith, 1973). On account of varied modalities of services trade, tariff barriers in the case of services trade are not so effective (Mukherjee, 1995). Thus, most countries protect their services sector by means of non-tariff barriers. Such non-tariff barriers take the form of State monopolies, grant of subsidies, capital and labour market restrictions, market reservations, technical standards, administrative regulations, etc. Progressive liberalisation under the GATS would have implications for such non-tariff barriers. Such trade barriers restrict market access, both directly and indirectly, and lower the overall level of developing countries' exports (Laird and Yeats, 1990).

A major problem with "differential treatment" under the GATS is related to the non-tariff barriers, which are not quantifiable. Thus, no across-the-board solution is available similar to the case of the Generalised System of Preferences for multilateral trade in goods (Mazumdar, personal communication). It is also not easy to expect tariffication of such barriers in the millennium round.

G. HIGHLY LIMITED DATA BASE

Another inherent problem of the GATS is the limited information on trade in services. Unlike data on trade related to agriculture and industry, data on trade in services is not well organised and so cannot provide a back up to the kind of intricate negotiations at the WTO. Although some sectoral estimates related to trade in services are available, much work remains to be done in the area of organising data at the global and bilateral/national levels. Both the breadth and depth of data on trade in services requires considerable improvement. In the absence of solid data, quality of negotiations in services is also adversely affected.

There are 12 service sectors where commitments have been made: business services, communication services, construction services, distribution services, educational services, environmental services, financial services, health-related and social services, tourism and trade-related services, recreational, cultural and sporting services, transport services and other services. Comparable trade data is available for only seven sectors and mostly for the major industrial countries. Most of the negotiations have taken place without any valid data base. It is almost groping in the dark and making offers without any knowledge of the impact of such offers on growth, development and other macro-economic and social variables. The other interesting feature is that there is an acute shortage of data on trade in services by different modes of delivery, although the GATS negotiations under the Uruguay Round were essentially based on different modes of delivery of services. Only recently, some estimates on trade in services by modes of delivery have been made available.

H.   FOCUSING ON A NEW AGENDA

Even before the GATS document could be implemented, a new agenda of the WTO, including the multilateral agreement on investment, competition policy and imposition of labour standards, had arrived on the scene. The new agenda is gaining in significance, thus pushing the initial commitments of the Uruguay Round into the background, and making it difficult for the developing countries to keep pace with such rapid developments.

In the special session of the General Council completed on 25 February 1999, a number of developing countries laid emphasis on both Paragraph 8 of the Geneva Declaration (about implementation of the Uruguay Round Agreements and an evaluation of them at the upcoming Third Ministerial Meet of the WTO in 1999) and Paragraph 10, which requires a consensus decision for any recommendation to the Ministerial Meet. In this context, India's view that the issue of fair implementation of special and differential treatment should be tackled first is broadly supported by a range of developing countries such as Pakistan, Egypt, Tanzania, Uganda, Zimbabwe, Indonesia and Malaysia (Third World Network, 1999).

VII. APPROACHING THE NEGOTIATIONS IN THE MILLENNIUM ROUND

The issue is how to approach the coming round of negotiations in trade in services. The issue is especially relevant for the developing countries for deciding on a suitable stance and course of action for the new round. Some generic suggestions for improving upon the present framework on trade in services, are given below:
    – It is important to make efforts to have greater market access for mobility of labour in selected sectors and sub-sectors of services such as business services, travel

services and construction services, if not across the board. It can be a give and take of labour mobility against capital mobility (which is very much a part of the GATS) in selected sectors and sub-sectors as prioritised by the negotiating countries.

— In the year 2000, one useful stance would be to advocate the break-up of sources of service providers related to trade in services rather than accepting the present form of dividing all service providers into two groups: the higher level personnel or Intra Corporate Transferee (ICT) and the rest of the service providers. With this in mind, one way would be to consider inclusion of the International Labour Organisation's occupational categories to be taken into consideration and divide it further both operationally into professional, technical, managerial, administrative workers, etc. and sectorally into sectors and sub-sectors.

— Two factors that some developing countries can find to their relative advantage and use as tools for negotiations are their domestic market size and/or their internal democratic set up, if any. The opening of markets and size of markets can be linked together. For example, India has a large market to offer. It should be able to extract more concessions. If India is opening markets for insurance, in which the possibility of doing business can be considerable, then it should look for commensurate concessions that can be extracted in other tradable sectors/sub-sectors by appropriate modes of delivery.

— With private capital flows and liberalised market access of financial services into developing countries, the vulnerability of such countries towards their payment imbalances is likely to grow, as shown by the Mexican crisis of 1995, South-east Asian crises, and Russian and Brazilian crises of 1997–1999. Such traumatic past experience calls for adequate precautions such as the need for "waivers" in the GATS and temporary reversals and restraints, perhaps stronger than the balance of payments clause in the GATT (Mazumdar, personal communication). Apart from this, for those service sectors which have financial implications, such as insurance and banking, it is important to build adequate safeguards into the market access offers to foreign companies in terms of protection against economic offence, consumer interests, monopolistic/duopolistic practices, cartelisation, transfer pricing, cultural transgression and similar issues.

— Adequate voting rights, citizenship requirements and compulsory caution deposits can be stated as conditions for granting market access offers to foreign companies, at least in those service sectors that involve public dealings.

— Market access in selected service sectors and sub-sectors such as communication services, for which technological/market configurations have not clearly evolved so far or are likely to evolve in a relatively quick pace of time, can be kept "unbound" or partially "unbound".

— Those sectors and sub-sectors which are considered to be the priority areas need to be flagged and a range of incentives, besides easy market access, need to be provided.

— For those service sectors that have cultural implications, such as communication services, appropriate measures can be built into the market access offers to foreign companies for protecting a country's national identity, security concerns and cultural heritage.

– Conditions such as social obligations for capacity building of the local people and adequate local employment provisions can be included in market access offers relating to those sectors in which large flows of funds are likely to take place. Human resource development for higher skills can be placed as an obligation for multi-national corporations. Many countries have actually included such a condition in their Uruguay Round schedules, although the actual implementation of such a condition needs to be checked. The developing countries can strongly advocate the speedy implementation of Article IV, Part II, of the GATS for increasing participation of developing countries.

– Selected obligations related to best practice and best technology can be considered in granting market access offers for most groups of services.

– Scope needs to be created for maintaining flexibility in the terms of negotiations for trade in services and also for finding ways to adopt damage control measures as and when required.

For the new round of commitments/negotiations, the developing countries need to explore better terms for "mobility of labour" and training obligations of multi-national corporations and transfer of technology within a specified period. The point is that the developing countries have a low proportion of world exports, but such countries put together have a sizeable market for foreign investment. This can be a tool for negotiation in granting any concession or commitment with regard to multilateral negotiations in trade in services. Any deal in the coming round should not be based on disproportionate "give and take". The developing countries can offer concessions/commitments against a proportionate commitment from the other side. This can also be extended to bilateral and regional agreements/negotiations.

The developing countries require more research support and input to back up their future discussions and negotiations at the WTO in terms of contracting comparative research projects on markets, trade and investment barriers, labour movements, environmental linkages, competition policy and labour standards. Multilateral trade negotiations for a new round in services call for considerable preparation, background research, understanding of issues, stakeholders' consultations, market surveys and global and local networking for the countries concerned. Such background work helps to identify potential costs and benefits, identifying a range of options, deriving lobbying tactics, taking positions and building on advocacy and campaigning issues. So far, the track record of developing countries in this regard is far from satisfactory, especially in the area of trade in services. In the absence of such background work, options are limited and there is always the danger of falling in line with agreements that barely serve the interests of the developing countries and consequently add little or no value to their current position as traders in services. The upcoming Ministerial Conference of the WTO towards the end of 1999 will provide a general signal for the issues that will dominate the future course of multilateral negotiations in trade in services. Issues proposed in the Ministerial Conference can then be taken up for the millennium round of negotiations.

References

Cline, William R. (1995): *Evaluating the Uruguay Round*, The World Economy, Vol. 18, No. 1, January.

Dubey, Muchkund (1996): *An Unequal Treaty*, New Era Publishing House, Delhi.

ESCAP (1996): *Asian and Pacific Developing Economies and the First WTO Ministerial Conference, Issues of Concern, Proceedings and papers presented at the ESCAP/UNCTAD/UNDP Meeting of Senior Officials, 4–6 September, 1996, Jakarta*, Studies in Trade and Investment 22, Under UNDP Regional Trade Programme (RAS/92/035) (United Nations, New York).

General Agreement on Trade in Services (1994): Schedule of Specific Commitments, different Member countries, GATS/SC, 15 April.

Griffith, Brian (1973): *Invisible Barriers to Invisible Trade*, Trade Policy Research Centre (The Macmillan Press Limited, London).

Group on Negotiations on Services (1991): "Services Sectorial Classification List", Note by GATT Secretariat, Multilateral Trade Negotiations, The Uruguay Round, MTN.GNS/W/120, 10 July pp. 2–3.

ICRIER (1998): *Project Report on Trade in Services*, for Ministry of Commerce.

Laird, Sam and Alexander Yeats (1990): *Quantitative Methods for Trade Barriers Analysis* (New York University Press, New York).

Mattoo, Aaditya (1997): *National Treatment in the GATS—Corner-Stone or Pandora's Box?*, 31 J.W.T. 1, February, p. 107.

Mazumdar, Dr Ajit, Personal communication, Centre for Policy Research, New Delhi and India International Centre, New Delhi.

Mukherjee, Neela (1995): *GATT Uruguay Round, Developing Countries and Trade in Services* (Vikas Publishing House Pvt. Ltd., Delhi).

Mukherjee, Neela (1996): *Exporting Labour Services and Market Access Commitments under GATS in the World Trade Organization*, 30 J.W.T., 5, October, pp. 21–42.

Mukherjee, Neela (1997): *Export of Business Services and Market Access Commitments under GATS: Some implications for Developing Countries*, Asia-Pacific Development Journal, vol. 4, no. 2, December, ESCAP, United Nations.

Mukherjee, Neela (1998): *Non-Tariff Barriers and Trade in Services—A Comparative Assessment of Capital and Labour, Mobility in the GATS Under the World Trade Organization*, 21 W. Comp. 5, September, pp. 79–91.

Nayyar, Deepak (1994): *Migration, Remittances and Capital Flows*, The Indian Experience, Oxford University Press, Delhi.

Noyelle, Thierry (1990): *Business Services and the Uruguay Round Negotiations on Trade in Services*, in UNCTAD, Trade in Services: Sectoral Issues, United Nations Publication, UNCTAD/ITP/26, Geneva.

Noyelle, Thierry (1995): *Barriers to Trade in Labour Services: Proposals for Strengthening GATS commitments on the Temporary Movement of Natural Persons from the Perspective of Developing Countries*, A Report Prepared for the United Nations Conference on Trade and Development, May.

Sauvé, Pierre (1995): *Assessing the General Agreement on Trade in Services, Half-full or Half-empty?*, 29
  J.W.T. 4, August, pp. 125–145.
Third World Network (1998, 1999): Third World Economics, Trends and Analysis, various issues.
UNCTAD (1996): *Strengthening Participation of Developing Countries in World Trade and the Multilateral
  Trading System (TD/375)*, May (United Nations, Geneva).
UNCTAD (1998): *The Least Developed Countries 1998 Report* (United Nations, New York and
  Geneva).
WTO (1998): *Annual Report*, World Trade Organization, Geneva.

[17]

How the World Trade Organisation is shaping domestic policies in health care

David Price, Allyson M Pollock, Jean Shaoul

High up on the agenda of the World Trade Organisation (WTO) is the privatisation of education, health, welfare, social housing and transport. The WTO's aim is to extend the free market in the provision of traditional public services. Governments in Europe and the US link the expansion of trade in public services to economic success, and with the backing of powerful medico-pharmaceutical, insurance, and service corporations, the race is on to capture the share of gross domestic product that governments currently spend on public services. They will open domestic European services and domestic markets to global competition by government procurement agreements, dispute-settlement procedures, and the investment rules of global financial institutions. The UK has already set up the necessary mechanisms: the introduction of private-sector accounting rules to public services; the funding of public-sector investment via private-public partnerships or the private finance initiative; and the change to capitation funding streams, which allows the substitution of private for public funds and services. We explain the implications of these changes for European public-health-care systems and the threat they pose to universal coverage, solidarity through risk-pooling, equity, comprehensive care, and democratic accountability.

On Nov 29, 1999, trade ministers from 134 member states will meet in Seattle, USA, for the latest round of talks at the World Trade Organisation (WTO), an international body founded in 1995 to expand free trade and the free market. The meeting will trigger the arrival of more than 1100 public-interest groups from 87 countries who intend to put forward "the real critique" of the WTO.[1] Seattle will be the setting for an unprecedented worldwide campaign in which consumer groups, trade unions, environmentalists, and public-health activists will highlight the global economic implications of the WTO trade talks, not the least of which is the dismantling of European socialised welfare provision with its publicly stated goals of universality and solidarity.

Many governments are deregulating and privatising public-service funding and delivery (www.imf.org/external/pubs/ft/fandd/1999/03/thobani.htm, available November, 1999). The transformation is being engineered through policy initiatives such as New Public Management, contracting out of services, compulsory competitive tendering (best value), and public infrastructure privatisation through public-private partnerships known variously as the private finance initiative (PFI), build-own transfer (BOT), or build, own, operate, and transfer (BOOT). These policies are generally presented as technical and, therefore, neutral adjustments. There has been little public debate about the way in which the privatisation of public services at national level is linked to the global trade-expansion policies of international institutions, such as the WTO, the International Monetary Fund, and the World Bank. There

is even less understanding of the huge implications of these policies for European traditions of democracy and community risk-sharing.

WTO's expansion of the free market into public-sector service provision

The Geneva-based WTO was established during the Uruguayan round of the General Agreement on Trade and Tariffs. Its aim is economic growth and stability based on free markets and minimum governmental interference. Although the WTO's membership includes 134 nation states (at February 1999), the transnational corporations that sit on all the important advisory committees decide detailed policy and set the agenda. WTO trade agreements have been described as a bill of rights for corporate business.[2,3]

The WTO talks in Seattle will focus on revision of the General Agreement on Trade in Services (GATS), a system of international law intended to expand private-enterprise involvement in the increasingly important service sector. According to the WTO, 160 service sectors are covered by GATS, including telecoms, transport, distribution, postal, insurance, environment, tourism, entertainment, and leisure services. What few people realise is that health care, social services, education, housing, and other services run by government agencies are also included (www.wto.org/wto/services/services.htm, available November, 1999).[4]

The WTO's focus on the service industry reflects the sector's growing commercial importance. As profitability in manufacturing has declined because of international competition, US and European corporations have turned to services as an alternative source of profit. According to the European Commission "The service sector accounts for two thirds of the [European] Union's economy and jobs, almost a quarter of the EU's total exports and a half of all foreign investment flowing from the Union to other parts of the world".[5] In the USA, more than a third of economic growth over the past 5 years has been because of service exports.[6] The World Bank has calculated that in less-developed countries alone, infrastructure development involving some private backing rose from US$15·6 billion

Lancet 1999; **354**: 1889–92

Health Policy and Health Services Research Unit, University College London, London, UK (D Price BSc); Social Welfare Research Unit, University of Northumbria, Newcastle upon Tyne (D Price); Health Policy and Health Services Research Unit, University College London, London WC1H 9EZ (Prof A M Pollock FFPHM); and School of Accounting and Finance, University of Manchester, Manchester (J Shaoul PhD)

Correspondence to: Prof Allyson M Pollock
(e-mail: allyson.pollock@ucl.ac.ukBackground)

in 1990 to $120·0 billion in 1997. Around 15% was direct foreign investment in public schemes.[7] Governments in Europe and the US link the expansion of trade in public services to economic success, and, with the backing of powerful coalitions of transnational and multinational corporations, the race is on to capture the share of gross domestic product governments currently spend on public services. The European Community has set up the European Services Network of multinational industry representatives, led by Andrew Buxton, chairman of Barclays plc, to "advise European union negotiators on the key barriers and countries on which they should focus . . . " (www.gats-info.eu.int/, available November, 1999).

In the USA, the Coalition of Service Industries is calling for a majority foreign ownership to be allowed for all health facilities. "We believe we can make much progress in the negotiations to allow the opportunity for US businesses to expand into foreign health care markets . . . Historically, health care services in many foreign countries have largely been the responsibility of the public sector. This public ownership of health care has made it difficult for US private-sector health care providers to market in foreign countries . . ." (www.uscsi.org; available November, 1999). The US trade delegation goes even further. "The United States is of the view that commercial opportunities exist along the entire spectrum of health and social care facilities, including hospitals, outpatient facilities, clinics, nursing homes, assisted living arrangements, and services provided in the home."[8]

Waiting in the wings of the WTO talks are the US multinationals, including the pharmaceutical industry, long-term-care sector, and the health-maintenance organisations. Known in the mid-1990s as "the darlings of Wall Street," the multibillion dollar business of health-maintenance organisations depends heavily on a mixture of public funding, private health insurance, and user charges.[8] Much of its impressive profitability was brought about by the acquisition of non-profit hospitals in the USA.[9]

However, by 1997, the stock-market boom in health-maintenance organisations had ended,[10] and earnings by these businesses of $700 million in 1996 turned into $768 million losses by 1998.[8] Profits fell because of market saturation, government and employer strategies to contain health-care costs, and high-profile scandals. To restore profitability, the industry has begun to lower benefits, increase premiums, and withdraw from selected markets. It has also tried to capture new markets abroad by acquiring publicly run facilities. The industry has received influential backing for its foreign-acquisitions policy from the US government, the World Bank, and multilateral financial institutions such as the Inter-American Development Bank. These bodies have supported "managed care initiatives that convert public health care institutions and social insurance funds to private management, private ownership, or both."[11]

Health-maintenance organisations target the public funding behind foreign health-care systems. Multibillion-dollar social-security or tax pools are effectively privatised when public health care is redirected through private-sector organisations.

Intention to open public services to international global markets through GATS

Expansion of the private services sector depends on the opening of markets in the traditional areas of public provision. The WTO and the World Bank have carefully

created policies to ensure that such changes take place. But the WTO has found progress slow in health care.[12] When GATS was introduced in 1995, only 27% of WTO members agreed to open hospital services to foreign suppliers.[12] According to the WTO secretariat, some governments have resisted making the hospital sector commercial because they think of hospitals as part of their country's "national heritage".[12] Consequently, 5 years into GATS, the public-service basis of many health-care systems has not been accessible to transnational corporations.

GATS permits member countries to force the removal of barriers to foreign participation in the service industries of other member countries. The WTO now has three main objectives: to extend coverage of GATS, to toughen procedures for dispute settlements so that member states can more easily be brought into line, and to change government procurement rules to create market access.

Extension of GATS—Articles 1.3, 13, and 19

The previous round of WTO ministerial talks (the Uruguayan round) allowed governments to protect health and social services from GATS treatment by defining them as government services. According to GATS Article 1.3, a government service is one "which is supplied neither on a commercial basis, nor in competition with one or more service suppliers". Article 19 of GATS is, however, intended to end this protection. "Members shall enter into successive rounds of negotiations . . . with a view to achieving a progressively higher level of liberalisation."

The WTO secretariat has argued that for services to be classified under Article 1.3 they should be provided free. Many governments initially protected health services from GATS treatment by defining them in this way. But the WTO has highlighted the inconsistencies in this approach.[12] "The hospital sector in many counties . . . is made up of government-owned and privately-owned entities which both operate on a commercial basis, charging the patient or his insurance for the treatment provided. Supplementary subsidies may be granted for social, regional, and similar policy purposes. It seems unrealistic in such cases to argue for continued application of Article I:3, and/or maintain that no competitive relationship exists between the two groups of suppliers of services." In addition, Article 13 of GATS calls for the end of subsidies that distort trade and requires members to negotiate procedures to combat them.

Therefore, according to the WTO, wherever there is a mixture of public and private funding, such as user charge or private insurance, or there are subsidies for non-public infrastructure, such as public-private partnerships or competitive contracting for services, the service sector should be open to foreign corporations. Health-care systems across Europe are vulnerable on all these counts.

Dispute settlement

The WTO uses dispute settlement to implement market access. These procedures enable states to force changes in the domestic laws of other states and to impose retaliatory trade sanctions in areas unconnected with the disputed practice. Current proposals will enable transnational corporations to take legal action against governments that frustrate their foreign-investment aspirations. Dispute settlement is an important means of US influence and a vital weapon in its trade expansion. According to Ambassador Charlene Barshefsky, leader of the US trade delegation and chairperson of the Seattle round, "the

United States has demonstrated a record as the most aggressive user of the WTO dispute resolution process".[6]

Dispute settlement is a form of attack on government powers. The procedures promote the least trade-restrictive regulation, which is voluntary rather than compulsory, involves consumer information rather than prohibition, and puts individual before public responsibility. The US trade delegation has announced that it will be supporting the introduction of regulation in the service sector that "promotes rather than restrains competition".[6]

Creation of market access: government procurement rules

The WTO proposes to use a reformed government procurement agreement as the primary mechanism for opening public services to the private sector. Government procurement rules supply the legal and regulatory framework within which public bodies contract for goods, services, and investment funds. This procedure opens up domestic services and markets to international competition. The influential Euopean Union reform proposals focus on "[unlocking] new potential markets" by extension of private firms' involvement with public services and by creation of contracting rules to ensure "acceptable returns for investors".[13]

Use of government-procurement-agreement reforms to shape health-care policy in the UK

The World Bank has famously described public services as a barrier to the abolition of world poverty.[14] It maintains that "if market monopolies in public services cannot be avoided then regulated private ownership is preferable to public ownership".[11] The WTO sees one of its roles as coordinating the international transfer of such policies. It asks "How can WTO Members ensure that ongoing reforms in national health systems are mutually supportive and, whenever relevant, market-based?"[12]

The UK provides a fascinating insight into the assimilation of the WTO agenda into domestic policy. The UK was one of the first states among more-developed countries to take up two key recommendations of global financial institutions: the introduction to the public sector of commercial accounting and appraisal of commercial investment. Procurement reforms are being used to breach socialised provision to enable private firms to exploit the public-funding base of traditional public services.

Changes to resource allocation

Money now follows the individual to the point of service. In 1991, the National Health Service internal market replaced resource allocation based on area needs with capitation funding. Payments per person are generally seen simply as a cost-containment strategy because they provide organisations with an incentive to withhold care (necesary and unnecessary). However, per-person payments, which are fixed sums of money that lend themselves to copayments and consumer purchases in the private sector, also facilitate the substitution of private funding for public funding (through private insurance and user charges) and private services for public services. Capitation models are promoted by the World Bank (www.worldbank.org/nor/class/module1/sec7i.hbm 7i).

In the UK, the devolution of capitation payments to family-physician fundholders has enabled the substitution of private health insurance and user charges for some

publicly funded care (eg, pharmaceuticals, elective surgery) as well as the diversion of public funds into the private sector (eg, elective surgery, private outpatient clinics, podiatry, physiotherapy, and capital infrastructure).[15,16] The introduction of primary-care groups and primary-care trusts in April, 1999, will accelerate this process.[17,18] Primary-care groups will have an incentive to expand private health insurance and user charges or copayments when their National Health Service per-person budgets are capped, and they will have more freedom to use the private sector.

A copayment template is about to be tried in the UK by the department of employment and education. Next year the department will give a UK£10 000 "individual learning account" to school-leavers to pay for education after age 18 years, as well as training costs in the public or the private sector.[19] Public funds will be triggered by private contributions.

Service delivery changes in creation of corporations

In the UK, National Health Service entities have been re-established on private-sector lines, or corporatised, by the imposition of commercial accounting practices.[20] For example, the sole statutory duties of National Health Service provider trusts (hospital and community services) are financial and not health-care duties; National Health Service bodies must break even after having made a profit for their owners (the government) equivalent to a 6% return on capital. The same will apply to primary-care trusts, which will also be made to behave commercially as if they have shareholders. This resource accounting, which is shortly to be introduced throughout all UK public services, makes public and private sectors seem interchangeable. Resource accounting is a prerequisite for public-private partnerships.

Public-private partnerships

The UK government is outsourcing labour-intensive services and capital-intensive infrastructure projects through public-private partnerships (or private finance initiative in the National Health Service). These changes give the private sector access to public funds, but are presented as offering the public sector access to private funds. The privatisation of public funds has been achieved by almost eliminating new public funding for capital projects such as hospital refurbishment;[21] through the introduction of direct government subsidies to the private sector;[22] and through creation of revenue that can be diverted to the private sector as rental income.[23]

These policies are occurring to a greater or lesser degree in all UK public services and are being widely copied in other more-developed countries.

Implications for health and health care

These structural changes in the financing and delivery of health-care conflict with the principles of universal coverage and shared risk that tax-funded or social-insurance-funded systems generally uphold. The changes provide insurers and providers with the means and making maximum profit the incentive to engineer favourable risk pools. Experience in the USA and more recently in Latin America is that the viability of public and voluntary hospitals and health services is threatened when they have to compete with commercial providers for per-person public funds, private insurance, and copayments.

Typically, the public sector has been left to bear the risk for more vulnerable populations but with diminished risk pools (or pooled funding) to finance care.[11]

Competition for per-person funds among autonomous providers leads to competition for patients. Evidence from the UK shows that such competition has destabilised the provision of care and diverted planning and service priorities away from the needs of their local populations. For example, private-finance-initiative business cases show that hospitals are currently being planned according to trusts' financial needs and not local clinical need: access to the acute sector is controlled by financial imperatives.[25]

Democracy versus consumerism

In the UK, the substitution of market mechanisms and competition has fractured the traditional mechanisms for local accountability. National Health Service providers are governed by trust boards, with no democratic or legal mechanisms to ensure that they uphold the interests of the local communities from which they draw patients.[24,25] Increasingly, the goals of universality and equity are being replaced by consumer sovereignty. This effect is reflected in the growing governmental emphasis on league tables, performance measures, and quality frameworks, rather than on substantive health-care rights, such as to a universal, comprehensive health-care service.

The cumulative effect of these market-based reforms in the UK[21-23,26] and the US[8,9,27-30] is a decrease in the supply of publicly funded services. An early example of this was the long-term-care sectors. Later, despite government recognition of major shortages in the labour force and physical capacity, the introduction of the private finance initiative to the acute hospital sector in the National Health Service has resulted in a reduction of 30% in capacity at the hospitals concerned and of 20% in clinical budgets and workforce.

Inequalities in health

Income and health inequalities continue to widen in the UK.[31] The restrictions on national sovereignty imposed by the WTO through GATS will make it increasingly difficult to reverse these trends. As the UK trade minister, Richard Caborn, goes to Seattle, the UK Government has yet to adopt the first recommendation of its own Independent Inquiry into Inequalities in Health that "all policies likely to have a direct or indirect effect on health should be evaluated in terms of their impact on health inequalities . . . and formulated . . . to reduce such inequalities".[31] Resource accounting, private finance initiatives, outsourcing, capitation, and corporatisation continue to be imposed under the modernisation programme of the "third way", but the government has yet to sponsor a thorough assessment of their impact on health inequalities.

Conclusion

The WTO is stage-managing a new privatisation bonanza at Seattle. Multinational and transnational corporations, including the pharmaceutical, insurance, and service sectors, are lining up to capture the chunks of gross domestic product that governments currently spend on public services such as education and health. The long tradition of European welfare states based on solidarity through community risk-pooling and publicly accountable services is being dismantled. The US and European Union governments are aggressively backing this project in the

interests of their business corporations. But the assault on our hospitals and schools and public-service infrastructure depends ultimately on a promise from one government to another to expand private markets. Such promises can be kept only if domestic opposition to privatisation is held in check. We need to constantly reassert the principles and values on which European health-care systems are based and resist the WTO agenda.

We thank Meri Koivusalo.

References

1   Surman M. Trade wind hits Sea-Town. *Financial Times* 1999; Sept 20: 10.
2   Balanya B, Doherty A, Hoedeman O, Ma'anit A, Wesselius E. WTO millennium bud: TNC control over global trade politics. *Corp Eur Observer* 1999; 4: 3.
3   Mishra R. Beyond the nation state: social policy in an age of globalization. *Soc Policy Admin* 1999; 32: 481–500.
4   Bertrand A, Kalafatides L. The WTO and public health. *Ecologist* 1999; 29: 365.
5   The European Union and World Trade. *Frontier-free Europe* 1999; August/September: 1–4.
6   Office of the United States Trade Representative, Executive Office of the President. USTR 1998 trade policy agenda and 1997 annual report outlines ambitious global trade agenda ahead. Washington, March 2, 1998.
7   Roger N. Recent trends in private participation in infrastructure: public policy for the private sector, note no 196. Washington: World Bank Group, 1999, 1–4.
8   Kuttner R. The American health care system: Wall Street and health care. *N Engl J Med* 1999; 340: 664–68.
9   Kuttner R. Columbia/HCA and the resurgence of the for-profit hospital business, part 1. *N Engl J Med* 1996; 335: 362–67.
10   Levit K, Cowan C, Braden B, et al. National health expenditures in 1997: more slow growth. *Health Affairs* 1998; 17: 99–111.
11   Stocker K, Waitzkin H, Iriart C. The exportation of managed care to Latin America. *N Engl J Med* 1999; 340: 1131–36.
12   WTO Secretariat. Health and social services: background note by the Secretariat S/C/W50, 18 September, 1998 (98-3558).
13   European Commission. Public procurement in the European Union: exploring the way forward. Green Paper. Brussels: European Commission, 1996.
14   World Bank Group. The World Bank development report 1993: investing in health. Washington DC: World Bank, 1993.
15   Heath I. The creeping privatisation of NHS prescribing. *BMJ* 1994; 309: 623–24.
16   Kerrison SH, Corney R. Private provision of "outreach" clinics to fundholding general practices in England. *J Health Service Policy Res* 1998; 3: 20–22.
17   Pollock AM. Snowed under: managing care. *Nov* 1998; 6–7.
18   Pollock AM. The American way. *Health Serv J* 1998; Apr 9: 28–30.
19   Parliamentary Policy: National Youth Agency—youth policy update. 1999, October: 5–6.
20   Shaoul J. The economic and financial context: the shrinking state? In: Corby S, White G, eds. Employee relations in the public services: themes and issues. London: Routledge, 1999.
21   Gaffney D, Pollock AM, Price D, Shaoul J. NHS capital expenditure and the private finance initiative: expansion or contraction? *BMJ* 1999; 319: 48–51.
22   Gaffney D, Pollock AM, Price D, Shaoul J. PFI in the NHS: is there an economic case? *BMJ* 1999; 319: 116–69.
23   Pollock AM, Dunnigan M, Gaffney D, et al. Planning in the new NHS: downsizing for the 21st century. *BMJ* 1999; 319: 179–84.
24   Pollock AM. Where should health servicecs go? Local authorites versus the NHS. *BMJ* 1999; 310: 1580–84.
25   Harrington C, Pollock AM. Decentralisation and privatisation of long-term care in the UK and the USA. *Lancet* 1998; 351: 1805–08.
26   Gaffney D, Pollock AM, Price D, Shaoul J. The politics of the private finance initiative and the new NHS. *BMJ* 1999; 319: 249–53.
27   Kuttner R. The American health care system: health insurance cover. *N Engl J Med* 1999; 340: 163–68.
28   Kuttner R. Must good HMOs go bad? The search for checks and balances. *N Engl J Med* 1998; 338: 1635–39.
29   Kuttner R. Must good HMOs go bad? The commercialization of prepaid group health care. *N Engl J Med* 1998; 338: 1558–63.
30   Kuttner R. Columbia/HCA and the resurgence of the for-profit hospital business, part 2. *N Engl J Med* 1996; 335: 446–51.
31   The Acheson Report. Independent inquiry into inequalities in health report. London: Stationery office, 1998.

[18]

THE WTO TRIPS AGREEMENT AND GLOBAL ECONOMIC DEVELOPMENT

FREDERICK M. ABBOTT*

The global system for the protection of intellectual property rights has entered a new era. The Agreement on Trade-Related Aspects of Intellectual Property Rights ("TRIPS Agreement") that is part of the new integrated World Trade Organization (WTO) system imposes on all Members of the WTO an obligation to establish high levels of intellectual property rights ("IPRs") protection, and to enforce these high levels of protection.[1] The TRIPS Agreement, when read in conjunction with other components of the new WTO system, is enforceable by WTO Member action through the imposition of trade sanctions.[2]

I. THE TRIPS AGREEMENT ERA

The TRIPS Agreement was concluded after seven years of Uruguay Round negotiations, several years of negotiations leading up to the Uruguay Round mandate, and earlier discussions of an anti-counterfeiting code tracing back to the Tokyo Round negotiations.[3] As one of the principal multilateral trade agreements of the WTO, the TRIPS Agreement plays a new and important role in the international economic system. The Agreement was intended to conclude the era of global intellectual property administration under the auspices of

---

* Professor of Law, Chicago-Kent College of Law.
1. Agreement on Trade-Related Aspects of Intellectual Property Rights, Apr. 15, 1994, Marrakesh Agreement Establishing the World Trade Organization [hereinafter WTO Agreement], Annex 1C, LEGAL INSTRUMENTS—RESULTS OF THE URUGUAY ROUND vol. 31; 33 I.L.M. 81 (1994) [hereinafter TRIPS Agreement]. The TRIPS Agreement entered into force on January 1, 1995. *See id.* Regarding the terms of the Agreement, see generally Adrian Otten. *Improving the Playing Field for Exports: The Agreements on Intellectual Property, Investment Measures and Government Procurement, in* GATT URUGUAY ROUND 67 (Thomas Cottier ed., 1995); J.H. Reichman, *Universal Minimum Standards of Intellectual Property Protection Under the TRIPS Component of the WTO Agreement,* 29 INT'L LAW. 345 (1995).
2. With respect to the application of the TRIPS Agreement in the dispute settlement context, and to the imposition of trade sanctions, see Frederick M. Abbott, *WTO Dispute Settlement and the Agreement on Trade-Related Aspects of Intellectual Property Rights, in* INTERNATIONAL TRADE LAW AND THE GATT-WTO DISPUTE SETTLEMENT SYSTEM (E.-U. Petersmann ed.) (forthcoming 1997).
3. With respect to the negotiating history and objectives of the TRIPS Agreement, see Frederick M. Abbott, *Protecting First World Assets in the Third World: Intellectual Property Negotiations in the GATT Multilateral Framework,* 22 VAND. J. TRANSNAT'L L. 689 (1989).

the World Intellectual Property Organization (WIPO) which the Organisation for Economic Co-operation and Development ("OECD") industrial interests perceived as insufficiently forceful, and to initiate a new era of shared competence. In the new era, the primary rules governing the protection of intellectual property would be promulgated at the WTO. WIPO would step back into a secondary role. It would serve as an IPRs convention administrator, as a provider of technical assistance, and as a forum for considering secondary rules changes. The center of IPRs power, and the police function, would move across Geneva to the WTO.

The IPRs-dependent industries of the OECD countries cannot be faulted for pursuing the TRIPS Agreement. The value of their assets is to a greater and lesser extent defined by the level of protection accorded to IPRs. The importance of IPRs as a component of asset value varies across industrial and service sectors, and within narrow industry segments. Natural resources and access to capital are the principal asset components in many industries, such as the petroleum industry, and the value of IPRs is secondary in these industries. In other industries, such as the entertainment industry, IPRs are principal components of asset value. While the importance of IPRs to each OECD industry in 1996 may vary along a relative scale, there are few industries in which IPRs do not play a significant role. Farmers have become dependent on the planting of IPRs-protected seed strains, and are increasingly interested in the production of genetically-engineered produce.

OECD industries claim entitlement to the fruits of their innovative activity in the form of IPRs protection. Debate over the basis of this entitlement traces to the historical beginnings of IPRs protection, and is not a debate that will be resolved in this forum. To some, IPRs are a right of nature, as the ownership of one's own limbs, or one's home. To others, IPRs are purely the product of government. Whatever the fundamental basis of IPRs ownership, it has long been accepted that the scope of the IPR must be defined by government, under a public welfare analysis that balances the interests of IPRs owners and the public, just as government decides the extent of ownership rights afforded by title to land. It should not be doubted that perspectives on the scope of the rights that governments should afford to IPRs have varied over history, and among societies, just as have perspectives on the ownership of real property.

A. Developing Country Interests in the TRIPS Negotiations

It was certainly recognized during the Uruguay Round TRIPS negotiations that the proposed agreement would have an impact on the interests of developing countries.[4] Many developing countries did not historically provide high levels of IPRs protection within their national legal systems. If, as a consequence of the TRIPS negotiations, those countries agreed to provide such protection, and if the IPRs to be protected were preponderantly held by OECD country enterprises, then the recognition of IP ownership rights would logically lead to a transfer of wealth from the developing to industrialized economies, at least over the short term. There was, and is, substantial agreement concerning this likely short term impact.[5] The developing countries initially resisted negotiation of the TRIPS Agreement because they foresaw this economically undesirable outcome.

In the final analysis, the developing countries accepted the TRIPS Agreement. There were doubtless a variety of reasons for the change in perspective that took place over the course of the Uruguay Round, and different developing countries involved in the negotiations would have had different motivations for accepting the Agreement. Nevertheless, it is clear that the TRIPS Agreement was part of a package bargain.

The bargain included an agreement by the industrialized countries to reduce levels of agricultural export subsidies. This was of particular importance with respect to the European Union which provides massive subsidies for its farmers' exports of important staple crops such as wheat. The EU subsidies allow its farmers to undercut the prices of developing country farmers, and thereby diminish developing country export opportunities. The United States agreed to press the EU for concessions on agricultural subsidies, at least partly in exchange for developing country acceptance of the TRIPS Agreement. In addition to concessions on subsidies, the industrialized countries made substantial concessions with respect to imports of tropical products, and agreed to gradually phase out quotas on textile products.

In the TRIPS Agreement itself there are some important concessions to developing country interests. Most importantly, substantial

---

4. The developing country perspective on the TRIPS Agreement is discussed in Abbott, *supra* note 3, at 713-14.

5. *See, e.g.,* Carlos A. Primo Braga & Carsten Fink, *The Economic Justification for the Grant of Intellectual Property Rights: Patterns of Convergence and Conflict,* 72 CHI.-KENT L. REV. 439 (1996).

transition periods are built into the Agreement, so that most obligations will not apply to developing country Members (and Members in transition from centrally-planned to market economies) until five years after the WTO Agreement has entered into force.[6] In respect to countries that did not maintain patent protection for all areas covered by the TRIPS Agreement, there is an additional five-year period to extend product patent protection to new areas.[7] This additional five-year patent transition period is tempered with respect to pharmaceuticals and agricultural chemicals by a so-called "mailbox" provision.[8] A ten-year transition period generally applies to the least developed WTO Members.[9] Industrialized country Members agree to provide incentives for their enterprises to transfer technology to least-developed Members,[10] and to provide—on mutually agreeable terms—financial and technical assistance to developing and least-developed Members.[11] Rules with respect to the granting of compulsory licenses leave substantial discretion in the hands of national authorities.[12] The United States, at least, would have preferred tighter limits on the granting of compulsory licenses. The compulsory licensing provisions at least in part represent a concession to developing country interests.

Up to and through the Uruguay Round negotiations, the United States pursued an aggressive trade policy toward developing countries which it considered not to be adequately protecting U.S. IPRs interests.[13] One of the motivations of the developing countries in accepting the TRIPS Agreement was to ameliorate this constant pressure from the United States. The WTO Agreement includes a commitment by Members to use the WTO dispute settlement mechanism as the means to settle trade disputes within the scope of the WTO Agreement (including the TRIPS Agreement).[14] Thus, there is

6. *See* TRIPS Agreement art. 65:2. The general obligation of WTO Members to apply provisions of the TRIPS Agreement did not arise until January 1, 1996 (one year after the date of entry into force of the WTO Agreement). *See id.* art. 65:1. Provisions regarding national and most favored nation treatment, and respect for the Paris and Berne Conventions, also apply to developing Members one year after entry into force of the Agreement.

7. *See id.* art. 65:4.

8. The mailbox provision requires developing Members to expeditiously establish a mechanism for receiving patent applications, to eventually grant patents based upon prior art in existence when the application is filed, and to grant exclusive marketing rights for the product following regulatory approval (for a period not to exceed five years). *See id.* art. 70:8-9.

9. *See id.* art. 66:1.

10. *See id.* art. 66:2.

11. *See id.* art. 67.

12. *See id.* art. 31.

13. *See* Frederick M. Abbott, *Public Policy and Global Technological Integration: An Introduction*, 72 Chi.-Kent L. Rev. 345, 346 n.3 (1996).

14. *See* WTO Agreement art. 23 (Dispute Settlement Understanding).

the appearance of a bargain between the United States and the developing countries: if they abide by their TRIPS Agreement commitments, the United States will not unilaterally decide that they are failing to live up to their international obligations and impose trade sanctions.[15]

Finally, it is certainly possible that the Uruguay Round would have failed as a whole if the TRIPS Agreement was not accepted by the developing countries. This would have had an adverse impact on all countries. Nevertheless, the developing countries could have ill afforded the potential result of more restricted access to major industrialized markets. The general advantages that would result from a successful conclusion of the Uruguay Round were thus an inducement to acceptance of the TRIPS Agreement.

---

15. Though not directly TRIPS Agreement-related, a unilateral U.S. action against Japan (regarding its automotive sector) immediately following entry into force of the WTO Agreement raised considerable concern about the nature of the Uruguay Round bargain. The United States ignored prescribed WTO dispute settlement procedures in a highly visible way, and authorized the imposition of trade sanctions against Japan contrary to WTO rules. For background regarding the U.S.-Japan dispute, see *U.S., Japan Strike Deal on Autos; Address Parts, Dealerships, Repairs,* 12 Int'l Tr. Rep. (BNA) 11 (July 5, 1995). The United States appeared to serve notice that it might well ignore a principal concession bargained for by the developing countries in the Uruguay Round negotiations; that is, an assurance that it would not unilaterally decide upon violations of international trade law (or find other trade practices "unreasonable") and thereafter impose trade sanctions. Going into the negotiations, perhaps the sorest spot for the developing countries was the unilateral U.S. pursuit of trade sanctions with respect to IPRs-related practices. In acting unilaterally against Japan, the United States signalled an apparent willingness to continue aggressive unilateral action against other WTO Members, including those which it considered to be inadequately protecting IPRs. Since its action against Japan in respect to the automotive sector, the United States has pursued several complaints regarding TRIPS Agreement matters within the WTO framework. It may be that the negative worldwide reaction to the action against Japan persuaded U.S. trade officials that policy could be more effectively carried out within the framework built during the Uruguay Round negotiations. Nevertheless, the U.S. Congress has legislatively authorized the United States Trade Representative ("USTR") to impose TRIPS Agreement-related trade sanctions on WTO Members which are in compliance with the TRIPS Agreement, in essence codifying an aggressive unilateral approach to assuring protection of IPRs. In connection with implementation of the Uruguay Round agreements, the United States amended its section 301 legislation to provide that "unreasonable" foreign country acts, policies or practices include those which deny "fair and equitable . . . provision of adequate and effective protection of intellectual property rights notwithstanding the fact that the foreign country may be in compliance with the specific obligations of the Agreement on Trade-Related Aspects of Intellectual Property . . . ." 19 U.S.C. § 2411 (1994) (section 301(d)(3)(B)). That the United States may impose trade sanctions on a WTO Member despite its compliance with the TRIPS Agreement is difficult to reconcile with the spirit of the WTO Agreement. Presumably, the United States would intend to apply this rule to matters outside the scope of the TRIPS Agreement.

"Unreasonable" foreign country acts and practices provide the basis for discretionary action by USTR, whereas unlawful or "unjustifiable" practices entail a mandatory response (though subject to significant exceptions).

B. Continuing Uncertainties

Some attention was paid to the interests of developing countries in the TRIPS Agreement negotiating process. There remains, however, little doubt that the driving force behind the negotiations was OECD country industry groups that perceived a significant and growing threat to their valuable commercial assets represented and protected by IPRs. During the Uruguay Round negotiations, these groups devoted their efforts to assembling data intended to demonstrate the extent of this threat. They also promoted the idea that higher levels of IPRs protection would be in the best interests of the developing countries. The arguments are by now quite familiar: (1) OECD countries have high levels of IPRs protection; (2) OECD industries are very innovative; (3) if developing countries adopt high levels of IPRs, their industries will be very innovative; (4) if developing countries do not adopt high levels of IPRs, their scientists and other innovators will leave because they will not be adequately rewarded for their innovation; and (5) if developing countries do not adopt high levels of IPRs, then industrialized country IPRs-holders will not transfer technology to them.[16]

By way of contrast, a recent study under United Nations auspices sought to determine what correlation there had been between developing countries that grant high levels of IPRs protection and the level of foreign investment,[17] the assumption being that increased foreign investment stimulates economic development. This study found an absence of correlation. The developing countries that have received the highest levels of Foreign Direct Investment ("FDI") over the past decade were the same countries that appeared on the USTR's list of the worst IPRs violators — Argentina, Brazil, North Korea, the People's Republic of China ("PRC"), Thailand, etc.[18] Moreover, developing countries without other strong economic attractions, but which

---

16. The Uruguay Round negotiations generated a particular form of economic analysis of the relationship between IPRs and economic development: the "industry-" or "quasi-industry-sponsored" study. These were studies by lawyers and economists working with a consultancy or similar industry interest in the outcome of the work, that set out in advance to demonstrate the benefits to developing countries of enhanced levels of IPRs protection. *See, e.g.,* INTELLECTUAL PROPERTY RIGHTS: GLOBAL CONSENSUS, GLOBAL CONFLICT? (R.M. Gadbaw & T. Richards eds., 1988); Robert Sherwood, The Benefits Developing Countries Gain from Safeguarding Intellectual Property (June 1988) (manuscript cited in Abbott, *supra* note 3, at 693 n.16).

17. *See* U.N. Transnational Corps. & Management Div., Dep't of Econs. & Soc. Dev., *Intellectual Property Rights and Foreign Direct Investment*, ST/CTC/SER.A/24 (1993) [hereinafter *Foreign Direct Investment*]; *accord* Edson Kenji Kondo, Patent Laws and Foreign Direct Investment: An Empirical Investigation, UMI Dissertation Services (May 1994).

18. *Foreign Direct Investment, supra* note 17, at 3-4.

granted high levels of IPRs protection (e.g., Nigeria) have not attracted higher levels of FDI than other similarly situated countries.

The arguments suggesting that higher levels of IPRs protection will benefit the developing countries are logical. They may in small or large part be correct. But the train of logic is not supported by empirical evidence.[19] More importantly, these arguments capture only a small part of how IPRs and their globalization might effect economic development. For example, if a U.S. business refuses to transfer its manufacturing data to a developing country because that country does not recognize its patents, and after the developing country agrees to grant patent protection the U.S. business transfers its technology and begins to manufacture there, the developing country may experience an IPRs-related welfare gain. But there are a number of possible scenarios under which the local welfare gain may be greater, for example if a local group had been able to finance the start-up of its own manufacturing facility and obtain a reasonably-priced license of the technology. It is not just a question of whether technology will be transferred, but under what conditions.

There remains considerable uncertainty concerning the impact of the TRIPS Agreement on global economic development.[20] The past five years have seen an increased attention by economists to the relationship between IPRs and international economic development, and IPRs and trade.[21] While it is clear that substantial progress is being

19. *See, e.g.*, Keith E. Maskus, *Trade-Related Intellectual Property Rights, in* COMMISSION OF THE EUROPEAN COMMUNITIES. EUROPEAN ECONOMY, No. 52, at 172 (1993), stating:

In truth, there is little systematic evidence that natural market mechanisms for appropriating returns on innovation have been eroded and that stronger patents would correct the situation. This is an unfortunate gap in our understanding of the situation and leaves unresolved the important empirical question of whether greater protection of IPRs would call forth substantially more inventive activity. This question lies at the heart of the debate over international protection of IPRs.

20. Up to and through the 1980s. the relationship between IPRs and international economic development was the subject of few studies by economists. This scarcity was noted in, for example, Carlos Alberto Primo Braga, *The Economic of Intellectual Property Rights and the GATT: A View from the South*, 22 VAND. J. TRANSNAT'L L. 243, 254 (1989). One excellent early study was EDITH TILTON PENROSE, THE ECONOMICS OF THE INTERNATIONAL PATENT SYSTEM (1951). Among studies that had been done, the absence of empirical referents was striking. The typical article would read more or less as follows: assume a two-country/two-good world. Assume that the effects of a trademark are X. If a trademark does X, and X is introduced into a developing country economy, and assuming that X is as to a developing economy as it is to an industrialized economy, then mathematical analysis suggests that Y will occur. See, for example, M.L. Burnstein, *Diffusion of Knowledged-Based Products: Application to Developing Economies*, 22 ECON. INQUIRY 612 (1984), with reference to patents. Though these studies may well have had value in suggesting areas where empirical research would be valuable, they did not appear to provide a solid foundation for international IPRs policy planning.

21. Primo Braga and Fink's contribution to this Symposium reviews these studies in detail. See Primo Braga & Fink, *supra* note 5, at 446-53: *see also* Maskus, *supra* note 19, at 157.

made in collecting empirical data and refining tools of analysis, the conclusions that have been reached to date only begin to illuminate the relationship between IPRs and international economic development. The contribution by Primo Braga and Fink to this Symposium reflects the *state of the art* in this field, and its authors use care in offering conclusions. Having reviewed the economics literature concerning the impact of higher levels of IPRs on developing countries, the authors observe:

> This brief review underscores the limitations of normative recommendations concerning changes in the rules for IPRs at world level. The strengthening of IPRs protection will have different welfare implications depending on the characteristics of each country. Generalizations can only be made if strong assumptions are adopted. For example, if one assumes that the supply of innovations in the South (i.e., in the developing world) is rather inelastic and that IPRs regimes are of limited relevance in influencing trade, foreign direct investment, and technology transfer, then it follows that the [TRIPS] Agreement is in essence an exercise in rent transfer. A much more optimistic view of its welfare implications for developing countries, however, can be put together if the opposite assumptions are held.[22]

Yet in the midst of a sea of theoretical and doctrinal controversy concerning the nature of IPRs and their potential impact on public welfare, it may nevertheless be possible to reach consensus at a high level of abstraction on the impact of the TRIPS Agreement on global public welfare. *The TRIPS Agreement in some undetermined measure enhances the economic advantages of holders of IPRs capital.* It is as if to say that all holders of $100 capital now have $101. We do not know what the capital owners will do with their increased assets, or whether an additional $1 can buy additional market share. Perhaps it might merely be said that before the TRIPS Agreement the $100 capital was rather insecure and subject to rapid dissipation, and now it is more secure. This is still an economic advantage. Perhaps it will be easier for more persons to accumulate $100 in the future. Perhaps the formation of capital on a global basis has been facilitated. But in any event, it would seem uncontroversial to suggest that IPRs capital has been made more secure, and that in this sense the value to its holders has been increased. This, after all, was the whole point of the TRIPS negotiations.[23] There is a risk that the higher level of IPRs security

---

22. Primo Braga & Fink, *supra* note 5, at 443 (footnotes omitted).

23. IPRs concentration may be exacerbated by more effective systems for the globalization of IPRs made possible by WIPO-administered conventions like the Patent Cooperation Treaty ("PCT").

will lead to or embed a stratification and concentration of IPRs ownership in OECD country-based enterprises, with public consequences both in the developing and industrialized countries. Public policy makers must now earnestly turn to this other side of the TRIPS equation.

II. The TRIPS Agreement, IPRs Concentration, Technological Integration, and Public Welfare

A. The Sources of Concern

1. Technology "Have" and "Have Nots"

Trademarks are used to generate demand for products in developing and developed markets throughout the world. Patents protect the innovation embodied in the products being marketed. The entertainment media and software industry are increasingly important factors in the international economic arena, and the protection afforded by copyright has taken on a new importance. Ubiquitous trademarks, patented technology, and commercially valuable copyrighted material are preponderantly owned by OECD country-based enterprises.[24] A comparable ownership allocation applies to investment capital.[25] As noted earlier, during the Uruguay Round negotiations, OECD country industry groups promoted the idea that higher levels of IPRs protection would stimulate inventive activity in the developing countries, and would provide a secure environment which would encourage FDI and a higher level of technology transfer from the North to the South. Presumably in consequence, the disparity in ownership of IPRs between developed and developing countries would be self-correcting over time. However, neither the occurrence of this self-correcting effect nor its time frame are certain. If the dis-

---

24. See, *for example*, Primo Braga & Fink, *supra* note 5, at 442 n.8, observing: "By 1982, of the 200,000 patents awarded by developing countries, for example, 175,000 (87.5%) were awarded to foreign patentees. For the major developing countries, the share was around 79%." See also, for example, Maskus, *supra* note 19, at 157; Carlos A. Primo Braga, *Trade-Related Intellectual Property Issues: The Uruguay Round Agreement and its Economic Implications*, in The Uruguay Round and the Developing Economies (1995) (presented at the World Bank Conf., Jan. 26-27, 1995); the annual White Paper of the Japanese Ministry of International Trade and Industry, JETRO, White Paper on International Trade: Japan 1992 (1992) (discussing the importance of technological leadership in Japan vis a vis its Asian work-sharing partners) [hereinafter MITI White Paper]; and Teresa Riordan, *Which Companies Had the Most Patents in 1994? It Depends on Which Set of Statistics You Believe*, N.Y. Times, Apr. 3, 1995, at D2 (indicating high concentration of patent grants to large multinational enterprises).

25. *See* D. Greenaway, *Trade and Foreign Direct Investment*, in European Economy No. 52, at 103, 105 (1993). For example, the "rest of world" outside the OECD in 1988 held 6.3% of the total world stock of FDI.

parity in technological expertise and IPRs ownership will not be self-correcting, or if the time frame for correction is lengthy, is this a concern of the international community?

Assume arguendo that the global economic system is or becomes sharply divided between technology "have" and "have not" countries. At least some public policy planners in the United States and Japan view the maintenance of technological dominance as critical to sustained economic growth in an increasingly competitive international economy.[26]

There are at least two fairly realistic risks that may be associated with a substantial skewing of the international trading system among the technological haves and have nots. The first is that the developing country governments will determine that market opening and the provision of IPRs protection do not constitute effective pro-growth policies, and they will revert to import substitution policies and market closure in order to protect their markets from technologically dominant suppliers. A reversion to import substitution policies would most likely lead to a replay of the period of stagnant developing country economic activity such as what occurred from the late 1960s to the mid-1980s. Market closure and stagnant economic development in the developing countries impacts not only the directly affected states and their nationals, but also has negative consequences for OECD country trade and investment, and for the international financial system. The Mexican Peso Crisis of 1994-95 demonstrated the extent to which global economic markets have become interdependent, and highlighted the risks associated with such interdependence.

The second potential consequence is the emergence of threats to security, i.e., minimum public order. If Japan treats the PRC, the Korean Peninsula, and Southeast Asia as a cheap labor haven, and the United States treats Mexico and other Latin American countries in a similar way, antagonistic political relations may result. The United States is virtually immune from military threat to its territory,[27] but U.S. investments in Latin America (and elsewhere) are not secure

---

26. The emergence of advanced technology as a key component of economic growth in the industrialized countries is a major theme of both LAURA D'ANDREA TYSON, WHO'S BASHING WHOM? (1992) and LESTER THUROW, THE COMING CLASH (1992). The MITI WHITE PAPER, *supra* note 24, at 103, notes that within Japanese international work-sharing arrangements, the higher value-added high technology component of manufacturing processes tends to take place in Japan, while the lower value-added labor intensive components are performed in Southeast Asian countries. The pursuit of policies of technological dominance, and the pursuit of benign technology transfer policies, may not be mutually exclusive, but they are facially inconsistent.

27. Though potential terrorist threats to internal security should not be discounted.

from civil or military capture. Because of its comparatively weaker military forces and its geographical situation,[28] Japan is in a more tenuous position than the United States with respect to both its external investments and its territory.

A pattern of wealth accumulation among the technologically sophisticated (e.g., well-educated), and the existence of a disenfranchised "underclass," is a phenomenon visible in the national sphere.[29] The creation of a schism between rich and poor in the national sphere has manifested itself in domestic security difficulties.[30] The occurrence of a similar phenomenon on the international plane can be envisaged, even if not as a "most likely" scenario. The EU has experienced some significant public order disturbances arising out of immigration from the poorer developing world. The potential for alleviating international minimum public order concerns might justify attempts by the OECD to prevent the continuation or exacerbation of a sharp skewing between standards of living in the developed and developing worlds.

But assume that the international trading system could be divided among the rich and poor, the technology haves and have nots, for an indefinite period without threat to the international economic system as a whole, and without raising minimum public order concerns. There is nevertheless an important place for *humanitarian* concern in the international economic system. From the founding of the General Agreement on Tariffs and Trade ("GATT") forward, the community of international economic specialists has maintained a strong bias in favor of promoting human rights and human dignity through special attention to the interests of developing countries. There is every indication among the present generation of international economic specialists that a strong interest persists in promoting human rights as a core goal of the international economic system.

2. Technology Concentration in the OECD

The concentration of technological expertise and IPRs ownership in large-scale OECD enterprises is not exclusively an industrialized developing country problem (or potential problem). Assuming, arguendo, that extending high levels of IPRs protection on a global basis

---

28. The proximity of Japan to the PRC and North Korea is of more concern from a security standpoint than the proximity of the United States to Mexico and Canada.

29. *See, e.g.*, JOHN KENNETH GALBRAITH, THE CULTURE OF CONTENTMENT (1992).

30. For example, the South Los Angeles riots following the Rodney King verdict and the proliferation of drug-related violence.

solidifies the dominant or quasi-dominant position of existing large-scale enterprises in the global industrial and services sectors, the pattern of concentration will not only exist in the developing countries. There is a risk that the OECD economies will become more highly stratified among those enterprises that can afford to incur large-scale research and development expenses, as well as global advertising expenses, and those that cannot. It seems at least intuitively apparent that enterprises which achieve scale economies on a global basis, and penetrate the global consumer market, have significant advantages over small competitors and potential competitors, at least as far as the large-scale accumulation of capital is concerned. Would policy makers be satisfied by a world of personal computers dominated by seven large multinational producers, if two were Japanese, three were American, one was Korean, and one was Taiwanese? What if all of these computers used an operating system licensed by the same company? What if they all depended on two companies for their microprocessors? What if all of these producers had become so innovative as a consequence of huge research and development expenditures, and so efficient in production as a consequence of international work-sharing arrangements (taking advantage of the lowest production cost in each country), that it became virtually impossible for a new producer to enter the international market? Though at the moment this is a purely speculative exercise, the question is nevertheless not entirely an esoteric one, as at least some trends toward this result are evident in the computer industry. The global market in automobile production is one in which the number of producers has been consistently shrinking through merger activity, and in which capital barriers to entry have become prohibitive. The basic point is this: while concentration of capital in the OECD countries may be of greatest concern to the "have not" developing countries, it is not an entirely moot issue from an OECD public policy perspective.

In the United States and the EU, competition authorities have long sought to assure that IPRs are not abused.[31] Recently, the U.S. Department of Justice in its IPRs Licensing Guidelines[32] has suggested the IPR should be treated as other forms of property—real

---

31. For a survey of OECD country competition law and practice with respect to IPRs, see OECD, COMPETITION POLICY AND INTELLECTUAL PROPERTY RIGHTS (1989).

32. U.S. Dep't of Justice & Fed. Trade Comm'n, 1995 Antitrust Guidelines for the Licensing of Intellectual Property, 34 I.L.M. 1115 (Apr. 6, 1995) [hereinafter DOJ Guidelines]; *see also* OECD, COMPETITION POLICY AND INTELLECTUAL PROPERTY RIGHTS (1989).

property, for example—in competition law analysis.[33] To paraphrase the Department of Justice, IPRs are another component of capital, like money or machinery.[34] Capital may be abused in a variety of different ways for anticompetitive purposes. However, the ownership of capital is not itself abusive, nor is it evidence of abuse. As with other forms of capital, so it is with IPRs. In the acts of the IPRs owner abuse may be found; but the ownership of the IPR itself is neither evidence of market power, nor certainly of abuse. As the Department of Justice was careful to point out, federal courts in the United States have not been of one mind on this philosophical perspective, some concluding that ownership of IPRs should be equated with market power.[35]

The European Union has actively policed against the abuse of IPRs in the inter-Member, or intra-Union, trade context. There is a rich history of decisional law from the European Court of Justice, as well as a history of policy determination by the European Commission, that places significant limitations on market allocation based on IPRs.[36]

In addressing potential IPRs-related concentration problems at the intra-OECD level, the principal focus of public policy planners should be on the development and effective application of competition law rules relating to IPRs. The contributions by Wolfgang Fikentscher and Ernst-Ulrich Petersmann to this Symposium analyze in detail some of the important ongoing efforts to improve the interna-

---

33. See DOJ Guidelines, *supra* note 32, at 1120 ¶ 2.1.

34. The DOJ Guidelines state:

That is not to say that intellectual property is in all respects the same as any other form of property. Intellectual property has important characteristics, such as ease of misappropriation, that distinguish it from many other forms of property. These characteristics can be taken into account by standard antitrust analysis, however, and do not require the application of fundamentally different principles.

Id.

35. See *id.* at 1121 n.10.

36. EU and U.S. policies with respect to importation of goods place on markets with the consent of IPRs holders is described and analyzed in Frederick M. Abbott (Co-Rapporteur), *First Report to the Committee on International Trade Law of the International Law Association on the Subject of Parallel Importation*, presented at ILA Helsinki Biennial Conf. (Aug. 1996). The European Court of Justice, from the virtual inception of the European Economic Community, has grappled with the question whether Member State IPRs laws may be used to restrict the free movement of goods and services between the Member States. As a general proposition, the ECJ has been hostile to prohibitions on parallel importation within the Union, fashioning a broad "intra-Union exhaustion" rule. With respect to intra-Union exhaustion, see Giuliano Marenco and Karen Banks, *Intellectual Property and the Community Rules on Free Movement: Discrimination Unearthed*, 15 EUR. L. REV. 224, 243-44 (1990) (citing, e.g., Deutsche Grammophon v. Metro (copyright), Centrafarm v. Sterling Drug, and Centrafarm v. Winthrop (patent and trademark)).

tional competition law framework.[37] Of course, if OECD policy-makers are right, and developing country enterprises that make heavy use of IPRs become more competitive with similar OECD enterprises, the potential problem of IPRs concentration in the OECD will be reduced.

B. Responding to Development-Related Concerns

Uncertainty concerning the long range impact of the TRIPS Agreement on the developing countries is not an excuse for ignoring its potential effects. There are a number of useful steps that might be taken to promote and assure that a balance between the private advantages accorded to the holders of IPRs and the public interest is achieved. If it turns out that granting high levels of IPRs protection provides great benefits to the developing countries, it is doubtful that measures taken to promote technological development in these countries will have impeded this result.

1. Filling the Information Gap

A central item on the agenda must be to undertake a comprehensive research program concerning the impact of IPRs ownership on economic development, as well as to identify patterns of concentration in the technology and IPRs fields (and the potential effects of such concentration, if any). Progress in this field of analysis is hampered by the lack of collected empirical data. Economists have made some recent progress in this area, and the economics profession has identified this field as one of urgency. Nevertheless, a higher level of funding and coordination for such activities would certainly be desirable.

There is a critical need in the IPRs-trade arena to work toward the creation of a policy-neutral research and analysis source. It may be that academic economists and social scientists are best suited to filling this role. Alternatively, perhaps a commission(s) in which researchers with a variety of policy perspectives share the same task might produce comparatively objective results.

---

37. See Wolfgang Fikentscher, *The Draft International Antitrust Code ("DIAC") in the Context of International Technological Integration*, 72 CHI.-KENT L. REV. 533 (1996), and Ernst-Ulrich Petersmann, *International Competition Rules for Governments and Private Business: A "Trade Law Approach" for Linking Trade and Competition in the WTO*, 72 CHI.-KENT L. REV. 545, 554-58 (1996).

2. Institutional Responses

Financial resources are at the heart of the technology/IPRs disparity problem. Technology that is owned by OECD-based enterprises can often be licensed, but not cost-free. Developing country students can be trained at OECD institutions of higher learning, but at considerable expense. OECD-based enterprises that develop and own IPRs resources are not charitable institutions, and public planners should not expect them to donate their resources. A lack of available capital at the global institutional level must be taken into account as a significant constraint on any program to transfer technological resources to, or to create technological resources in, the developing countries.

Furthermore, the global political situation is not ripe for the creation of an international technology development and transfer-related institution on a large scale, e.g., WIPO transformed into a global technology world bank. With most OECD countries experiencing what national politicians attack as "cheap-developing-country-labor-induced-underemployment," to suggest that these same politicians should undertake to provide funds to make developing country enterprises more competitive with the OECD industrial base would be unrealistic.

In light of the foregoing constraints, at least five potential responses to the disparity between the technology "have" and "have not" countries are likely to occur, or may be recommended. These are: (1) passive resistance to TRIPS Agreement-based changes by developing countries; (2) an international antitrust approach; (3) work by non-governmental organizations ("NGOs"); (4) the use of domestic tax policy to balance IPRs ownership and the public interest; and (5) the development and implementation of international and regional industrial policy programs.

a. Passive resistance

Perhaps the most likely course of the developing countries with respect to the TRIPS Agreement will be a continuation of past practices. They will continue to resist changes to their IPRs laws, and when they do make changes, they will be slow to enforce them in favor of foreign enterprises. To the extent that the TRIPS Agreement may adversely affect the economic interests of developing countries, passive resistance of this type may under present financial circumstances be the most likely countermechanism.

b. *International antitrust/competition law*

Effective polic'ng of the international economic system against IPRs-related competitive abuses through the use of competition laws would be consistent with present governmental approaches to IPRs and the threat of concentration. The TRIPS Agreement permits Member governments to police against the abuse of IPRs within their own national competition law frameworks.[38] Members are politely encouraged to share information,[39] and the Agreement permits the granting by Members of compulsory licenses to remedy anticompetitive abuses of IPRs.[40] On the other hand, the TRIPS Agreement does not obligate its Members to police against IPRs-related competitive abuses.

Developing countries have a particular interest in the potential application of competition rules with respect to IPRs. Developing markets tend to be less competitive than more highly developed markets in the general market economy environment. This situation arises from a combination of factors affecting developing markets, including the relative absence of effective rule-making and enforcement structures, the presence of smaller numbers of major market participants, concentrations of ownership, and more active government participation as market actor.

There obviously remains much work to be done in constructing an effective international system for protecting against abuses in the IPRs domain. As already noted, the range of activities among governments and scholars regarding efforts to coordinate, if not harmonize, competition law at the international level is extensive. Most likely, this work will proceed through the gradual refinement of competition rules in the TRIPS Agreement, and through a combination of more general programs, within the WTO framework and elsewhere. Special attention will need to be directed to the unique problems faced by developing countries in the effective application of competition rules. Assistance by OECD competition offices in the establishment and operation of developing country competition offices may be very desirable, and might be modeled on the assistance programs operated by WIPO and national/regional IP offices in favor of developing countries.

---

38. *See* TRIPS Agreement art. 40:1-2. An illustrative list of practices refers to "exclusive grantback conditions, conditions preventing challenges to validity and coercive package licensing." *Id.* art. 40:3.

39. *See id.*

40. *See id.* art. 31(k)-(l).

c. *Non-governmental organizations*

NGOs have made important contributions in the field of environmental policy and international trade. NGOs have been less active, or at least less visible and successful, with respect to other aspects of international economic policy. With a more substantial presence in the international IPRs field, NGOs could make important contributions in favor of developing countries.

d. *IPRs-related tax policy*

The TRIPS Agreement does not require that patents, trademarks, copyrights, or other forms of IPRs protection be granted or maintained on a tax free basis.[41] Patent holders, for example, could be required to pay annual taxes based on revenues received from sales of patented products or from patent licenses.

The main limitation on an IPRs-based tax is the national treatment principle as set forth in TRIPS Agreement Article 3. This article requires each Member to treat nationals of other Members no less favorably "with regard to the protection of intellectual property" than it treats its own nationals. Footnote 3 to Article 3 makes clear that the imposition of taxes would be subject to the national treatment principle. It provides that "protection shall include matters affecting the availability, acquisition, scope, maintenance and enforcement of intellectual property rights . . . ."[42] Therefore, in applying IPRs-based taxes to OECD-based enterprises, developing countries must also apply IPRs-based taxes to their own enterprises. In theory, this might discourage innovation by domestic enterprises.

There are, however, two reasons why the national treatment principle should not be an insurmountable obstacle to the use of IPRs-based taxes to balance IPRs-based wealth. First, if the preponderance of industry-related IPRs in a developing economy are owned by OECD-based enterprises,[43] tax burdens will fall disproportionately on these enterprises. Second, under express and customary GATT rules with respect to the GATT Article III (national treatment), the re-

---

41. Taxes are an ordinary incidence of property ownership, and are not expressly precluded by the TRIPS Agreement. The GATT 1994 accepts that national governments will impose taxes with respect to the production and sale of goods. *See, e.g.,* General Agreement on Tariffs and Trade, Oct. 30, 1947, 61 Stat. A-11, T.I.A.S. 1700, 55 U.N.T.S. 194, art. III.

42. *See* TRIPS Agreement art. 3. Application of Article 3 by the developing countries is not subject to transition arrangements, and so applies one year following January 1, 1995. *See* TRIPS Agreement art. 65.

43. The nationality of ownership is an empirical issue which, at least in the fields of patents and trademarks, can be answered by a search of local patent and trademark office records.

quirement that governments treat domestic and imported products on an equivalent basis applies to "like products." Although the "like products" language of GATT Article III is not found in TRIPS Agreement Article 3, there is nothing in the TRIPS Agreement language that would preclude a government from imposing different rates of taxation on the maintenance of IPRs with respect to different classes of products. Thus, pharmaceutical product patent maintenance taxes might be different than mechanical engineering patent maintenance taxes.

It is important to stress that taxation mechanisms are subtle instruments. The goal of any IPRs-related tax policy must be to seek a responsible balance between ownership of innovation and general economic welfare. IPRs-related tax policy must not be confiscatory. IPRs-based taxes would transfer wealth from IPRs holders through governments to the public. There is no assurance that governments will pursue thoughtful public planning any more than there is assurance that private enterprises will do so. It cannot therefore be suggested that IPRs-based taxes are a panacea for the imbalance in technology ownership among OECD and developing country enterprises. Taxes may, however, prove at least to be a bargaining lever by which the developing countries can obtain a higher level of cooperation from OECD-based enterprises.[44] IPRs-based taxes appear consistent with Article 7, "Objectives," of the TRIPS Agreement, which provides:

> The protection and enforcement of intellectual property rights should contribute to the promotion of technological innovation and to the transfer and dissemination of technology, to the mutual advantage of producers and users of technological knowledge and in a manner conducive to social and economic welfare, and to a balance of rights and obligations.[45]

It is also worth noting that IPRs-based taxes might be used in the OECD countries to balance the rights of IPRs holders and the public.

e. *International industrial policy*

Industrial policy refers to governmental efforts to direct private resources toward particular social goals. The U.S. government frequently employs industrial policy, for example, to promote the development of military technologies. The Japanese government employs

---

44. Optimally, the developing countries would seek to coordinate their IPRs-related tax policies so as to avoid presenting private enterprises with the opportunity to bargain over conditions of taxation.
45. TRIPS Agreement art. 7.

industrial policy to maintain high levels of stable employment. All other things being equal, the operation of the free market is preferable to industrial policy because recourse to industrial policy may adversely affect individual interests.[46] Nevertheless, there are circumstances under which the operation of the free market may be less than optimal from a social welfare perspective.

The TRIPS Agreement places an obligation on developed country Members to "provide incentives to enterprises and institutions in their territories for the purpose of promoting and encouraging technology transfer to least developed country Members in order to enable them to create a sound and viable technological base."[47]

There are many mechanisms by which the international community could encourage the transfer of technology resources to developing countries. World Bank loans could be made available for the training of developing country engineers in OECD educational institutions. A multilateral investment agreement could obligate or encourage investing enterprises to hire and train local engineers. International financial institutions in cooperation with developing country governments could finance joint research and development efforts designed to maximize local resources. As earlier observed, international industrial policy directed at enhancing developing country technological capability is wishful thinking in the absence of financial resources. Developing countries may therefore want to explore their own pooling of financial resources, just as OECD-based enterprises pool their resources in research and development ("R&D") joint ventures.[48]

f. Regional integration and industrial policy

The EU is following this path in its various plans for the development of the European technological infrastructure. Title XV of the EC Treaty (as amended by the Maastricht Treaty) is wholly devoted to a program of technology-related industrial policy.[49] The developing countries may well seek to accomplish the goal of pursuing a technological balance with the OECD by emulating the EU regional effort in

---

46. See Frederick M. Abbott, *Trade and Democratic Values*, 1 MINN. J. GLOBAL TRADE 9 (1993), for more detail on this theme.
47. TRIPS Agreement art. 66:2.
48. International agencies such as WIPO might assist in such enterprises.
49. Treaty Establishing the European Community, Mar. 25, 1957, arts. 130f-130p, 1992 O.J. (C 224) 1, [1992] 1 C.M.L.R. 573 (1992); *see, e.g.,* THE FINAL REPORT OF THE EUROPEAN COMMISSION ON RESEARCH AND TECHNOLOGICAL DEVELOPMENT IN THE LESS FAVORED REGIONS OF THE COMMUNITY (STRIDE) (1987).

its research and technological development programs. The Mercosur countries, for example, might seek in their cooperation negotiations with the EU to build ties between Mercosur and EU R&D programs. Similarly, the Andean Pact, which experienced difficulties with the relatively confiscatory technology transfer approach of Decisions 84 and 85, might emphasize a redirection to a regional R&D development program.[50]

A regional institutional approach to technological development, coupled with other approaches, may over the next decades begin to bring into balance the state of technological development in the OECD and developing countries.

3. The Information Revolution as a Non-Institutional Development

The changes to patterns of economic development that may be brought about as a consequence of the information revolution are exceedingly difficult to foresee or predict. What may be observed at the present is that a basic telephone connection and a fairly inexpensive computer can be used to link an individual at virtually any point on the globe to a vast collection of data and human resources. The international system for the protection of IPRs is in various measures designed to restrict open access to data that may be useful in producing goods and services, particularly as such production may conflict with the rights of patent holders. Yet the present proliferation of information, scientific and otherwise, is so extensive that its impact on the distribution and use of knowledge-based resources may be great, even in light of existing IPRs restrictions. The potential results cannot readily be extrapolated from experience.

If the Internet or comparable systems of information transfer remain as open as at present, it may be exceedingly difficult for present

---

50. The Andean Pact countries attempted in the mid-1970s to restructure the international IPRs balance by the adoption of Decisions 84 and 85. *See generally* Frederick M. Abbott, *Bargaining Power and Strategy in the Foreign Investment Process: A Current Andean Code Analysis,* 3 SYRACUSE J. INT'L L. & COM. 319, 346-51 (1975). These Decisions were intended to severely restrict the ability of foreign IPRs-owners to establish and transfer income based on IPRs ownership, and included significant restrictions on IPRs ownership. The Andean Pact countries have gradually adopted a more balanced approach to their technology sectors, and have been moving towards compliance with TRIPS Agreement standards. *See* Andean Group: Commission Decision 313-Common Code on Intellectual Property, 32 I.L.M. 180 (1993); *Colombia's Granting of Drug Patents Raises Questions on Andean Pact Rules,* Int'l Bus. & Fin. Daily (BNA) (Aug. 31, 1994); *Intellectual Property in Andean Accord Worries U.S. Industry, USTR Official Says,* 10 Int'l Tr. Rep. (BNA) 427 (Mar. 10, 1993). The Andean Pact historical progression appears to demonstrate the importance of and difficulties in balancing the interests of IPRs owners and the public, and the Andean Pact effort in the technology and IPRs field is worthy of close study.

holders of knowledge-based wealth to exercise control over their knowledge base. Large-scale private investments in research and development may become international public goods. Moreover, even if holders of IPRs continue to exercise control over technological resources, second-best technologies (e.g., those that have fallen outside patent protection) may be very useful in developing country markets. It must be acknowledged that access to technology alone may not suffice in the absence of investment capital. In this regard, international institutions such as the World Bank may continue to play a substantial role, at least in periods of initial capital formation in developing economies. Nevertheless, in the final analysis, the international institutional response to the problem of disparities in the ownership of IPRs-based wealth may be in the process of becoming less important—with one very significant proviso. That proviso, of course, is that international institutions do not respond to the information revolution by attempting to crush it.

4. Synthesis

The optimal approach to creating and maintaining an equitable balance in the international IPRs system will likely involve a combination of approaches. The goal of the international IPRs system should be to promote innovation, while protecting against the continuation and exacerbation of a stark division of the global economic system among the technological haves and have nots. The importance of the relationship between IPRs and economic development is apparent. Long delays in implementing policies in favor of reducing disparities in knowledge-based wealth seem likely—though not certain—to exacerbate long term problems. Developments in technology itself—embodied in the information revolution—may greatly assist in equalizing the distribution of technology. Initial capital formation may nevertheless remain an obstacle to putting technology to use. Disputes will certainly arise as to the proper means of distributing the fruits of the information revolution. Herein lies the role of the public policy planner — promoting a balance between highly useful private capital formation and the general social welfare of humankind.

[19]

Intellectual Property Rights and Indigenous Knowledge of Biodiversity in Asia*

Antonio G.M. La Viña

Undersecretary for Legal and Legislative Affairs and Attached Agencies, Department of Environment and Natural Resources, Manila, Philippines

Abstract

Biodiversity and indigenous peoples have an intimate link in most of Asia. Almost 70 per cent of the estimated 250 million indigenous peoples in the world live in Asia. The region is also one of the richest in the world in terms of biodiversity, with species richness among terrestrial orders generally in the 40–60 per cent range of global diversity. But as the world's indigenous peoples are increasingly threatened by the destruction of the forests many of them call home, their irreplaceable knowledge is threatened as well. By ignoring the rights of indigenous and other long-term forest dwellers and insisting that forest resources are state-owned, national governments have provided economic and political elites with easy legal access to forest resources and short-term profits have been made by the favoured few. But the costs in terms of forest degradation have been staggeringly high. The disappearance of the tribes and their cultures implies one cost that even the most narrowly pecuniary of economic planners should appreciate: the loss of knowledge of how to use the diverse forest species. This article explores these issues by assessing the intellectual property rights of indigenous peoples in Asia and the legal mechanisms which are open to them to protect these rights.

Key Words

Biodiversity, Indigenous Peoples, Intellectual Property, Indigenous Knowledge, Asia.

This article reflects the law up until 1 January 1997.
* This article is a revised version of a paper presented at the Asian Regional Seminar – Workshop on the Conservation and Protection of Indigenous Knowledge in the Context of Intellectual Property Systems, 24–27 February 1995, Sabah, Malaysia and was originally commissioned by the Southeast Asia Regional Initiative for Community Education (SEARICE) with funding provided by the United Nations Development Program. Research assistance was provided by Ms Mylin Sapiera, however the author is solely responsible for all statements and propositions in the paper.

ASIA PACIFIC JOURNAL OF ENVIRONMENTAL LAW, VOL 2, ISSUES 3 & 4 © *Kluwer Law International*, 1997

ASIA PACIFIC JOURNAL OF ENVIRONMENTAL LAW

Introduction

Biodiversity and indigenous peoples have an intimate link in most of Asia. It is no accident that along with the massive loss of biodiversity, indigenous cultures with their largely undocumented knowledge base are being wiped out. Because indigenous peoples live close to the earth and their individual and collective lives revolve around nature, much of this indigenous knowledge relates to biodiversity, habitats, ecological relationships and patterns.

The loss of "vast archives of knowledge and expertise" is "leaving humanity in danger of losing its past and perhaps jeopardising its future as well".[1] The knowledge base of indigenous peoples is "humanity's lifeline" to a time when human beings accepted nature's authority and learned through trial, error and observation. But as the world's indigenous peoples are increasingly threatened by the destruction of the forests many of them call home, their irreplaceable knowledge is threatened as well.

The spectre of cultural extinction hangs over hundreds of thousands of indigenous peoples who live in the forests of Asia. The tragedy is that the people most threatened by biodiversity loss are the very people who possess knowledge about living in harmony with nature that their countrymen competing for space in the forests need to learn.[2] By ignoring the rights of indigenous and other long-term forest dwellers and insisting that forest resources are state-owned, national governments have provided economic and political elites with easy legal access to forest resources and short-term profits have been made by the favoured few. But the costs in terms of forest degradation have been staggeringly high.[3] Moreover, all those people who live entirely in and off the rainforests are, due to the enormous amount of practical knowledge they have gained, the only ones who have mastered the art of exploiting the rainforests on a sustainable basis. Knowledge passed on through tens of generations about food plants, medicinal species, edible insects and their larvae, and the collection of wild honey among others have value almost beyond imagination.[4]

The disappearance of the tribes and their cultures implies one cost that even the most narrowly pecuniary of economic planners should appreciate: the loss of knowledge of how to use the diverse forest species.[5] The medicinal and other

---

1   Eugene Linden "Lost Tribes, Lost Knowledge" *Time* 23 September 1991 at 46.
2   Kenton Miller and Laura Tangley *Trees of Life: Saving Tropical Forests and their Biological Wealth* (Beacon Press, Boston: 1991) 15.
3   Owen J. Lynch "Community Based Tenurial Strategies For Promoting Forest Conservation and Development In South and South East Asia" (Presented at the Second Annual International Association For The Study of Common Property (IASCP) Conference, Winnipeg, Canada, 28 September 1991) 8 .
4   Marius Jacobs *The Tropical Rain Forest: A First Encounter* (Springer-Verlag, Berlin: 1988) 15.
5   In Thailand, for example, the Lua harvest more than 200 wild plant species for food and other purposes. These people are also consummate land-use planners; they designate different categories of forests around their villages and declare some off limits to farmers and wood collectors. In Zaire, the elf pygmies of the Ituri forest gather more than 100 species of forest plants to eat and to make tools, baskets, dyes, and medicines. See Miller and Tangley, note 2 at 16.

properties of the thousands of species present in the forest are prohibitively expensive to assess if done from random samples of vegetation. Much more efficient is a program of ascertaining the uses of species as known to tribal peoples. Little of the knowledge of how to use forest species has been recorded. Recording and using the knowledge that is now the near exclusive domain of indigenous tribes should be done with all due haste because of the unique value of such knowledge and because it supports a strong argument for maintaining intact significant tracts of the forests on which these groups depend for their survival.[6]

There are fears, however, that passing this knowledge on to the dominant society would represent a "last theft" from the tribes. Hence, the tribes' lands and their right to exist must be guaranteed, independent of any economic value that the dominant society may see in preserving their cultures. Once all useful knowledge has been gathered from the tribes, they cannot be destroyed with impunity. In the end therefore, their right to exist is not a question of economic value but one of human rights.[7]

This dilemma is particularly crucial as played out in Asia where most of the world's indigenous peoples live. Almost 70 per cent of the estimated 250 million indigenous peoples in the world live in Asia.[8] This same region is also one of the richest in terms of biodiversity, with species richness among terrestrial orders generally in the 40–60 per cent range of global diversity.[9] The Asia Pacific region includes:

> three of the eight natural realms of the planet including the very extensive Malesian rainforests stretching from Myanmar to New Guinea, the world's richest subtropical and temperate forest systems in China and Indonesia, extensive monsoon and semi-desert habitats in India, Indochina and China and the world's most extensive high altitude deserts on the Tibetan plateau.[10]

The marine biodiversity of the region is just as impressive. The marine areas of the region extend to two oceans – the Indian and the Pacific – which account for more than half the marine organisms of the world.[11]

The major threats to this Biodiversity are the "loss of habitat of living species and unsustainable levels of utilisation of renewable resources".[12] According to Mackinnon:

> These threats can be further categorised as logging, fuel collection, over hunting, land conversion, climate change, desertification, pollution, spread of exotic species, etc. In the most

---

6   See Philip M. Fearnside "Environmental destruction in the Brazilian Amazon" in David Goodman and Anthony Hall (eds) *The Future of Amazonia* (Houndmills, Basingstoke: 1990) 191–192.
7   Ibid.
8   Asian Development Bank *Working Paper On Indigenous Peoples* (Asian Development Bank, Manila: 1994) 1.
9   John Mackinnon "Analytical Status Report of Biodiversity Conservation in the Asia-Pacific Region" (Paper prepared for the Regional Conference on Biodiversity Conservation sponsored by the Asian Development Bank: 6–8 June 1994) 2.
10 Ibid.
11 Ibid.
12 Ibid.

ASIA PACIFIC JOURNAL OF ENVIRONMENTAL LAW

industrialized parts of the region, pollution and acid rain are seriously threatening natural habitats. Wildlife trade is also a growing problem which is very difficult to control.[13]

Indigenous Knowledge in Asia

The range and breadth of indigenous knowledge in Asia is well-recorded and documented. Its utility has also been recognised. Indigenous knowledge in Asia includes information about natural resource management and utilisation systems – particularly on agriculture and the use of forest resources, traditional medicine and pharmaceuticals, and crafts and artistic designs.

In south-east Asia, traditional healers have been documented as using about 6,500 plants.[14] Asian indigenous communities possess what has been called "an enormous reservoir of cultural information that can provide useful guidance as to which pieces of the natural world are worth a closer look".[15] The implications of this information are described by Kloppenburg:

> Tapping this reservoir of knowledge has already proven effective. Three quarters of the plants that provide active ingredients for prescription drugs originally came to the attention of researchers because of their uses in traditional medicine. Accordingly, the NCI (National Cancer Institute of the United States) collection strategy involves close attention to indigenous medical practice and especially to the expertise of traditional healers and curanderos. Similarly, the USDA's (U.S. Department of Agriculture) crop germplasm acquisition policy now gives priority to obtaining samples for which the ethnic source of the cultivar is described.[16]

Indigenous knowledge of medicinal plants has been described as priceless information. According to one author:

> As with genetic diversity, once lost, it cannot be recovered. Without it, we must use random screening, which is like searching for a needle in a haystack. Past experience is the best argument here: 74 per cent of chemical compounds used as drugs today have the same or related use in Western medicine as they do in traditional medical systems. It has been estimated that ethnobotanical information might have increased the yield of active plants by 50 to 100 per cent in the National Cancer Institute (NCI) research program in the search for anticancer and anti-AIDS drugs.[17]

---

13 Ibid.
14 Jack Kloppenburg Jr "No Hunting! Biodiversity, indigenous rights, and scientific poaching" (Summer 1991) *Cultural Survival Quarterly* 15.
15 Ibid.
16 Ibid.
17 Elaine Elisabetsky "Folklore, Tradition, or KnowHow?" (Summer 1991) *Cultural Survival Quarterly* 10.

The Misappropriation of Indigenous Knowledge

The threat to indigenous knowledge comes from three sources. First, the loss of their territorial base – through the destruction of rainforests or through their displacement by government projects or the commercial utilisation of natural resources – makes it impossible for many indigenous communities to sustain their knowledge as well. Second, indigenous knowledge is also threatened by the introduction of so-called "modern" practices of, among others, agriculture and medicine. These new practices frequently replace traditional practices which ironically are often more sustainable or effective than the former.[18] Third, indigenous knowledge is increasingly endangered by misappropriation of this knowledge by outside researchers. The tragedy is that it is the North or the developing countries which often benefit from this misappropriation or intellectual piracy.

The example of misappropriation that has often been cited is that of the neem tree. The neem tree, which is native to Asia, has been used by local people for centuries for manifold uses: as a pesticide, a medicine, an antiseptic, a contraceptive, as building material, fuel wood and for agriculture. Recently however, over a dozen patents have been granted in developed countries on the medicinal and insecticidal properties of this tree. According to Genetic Resources Action International (GRAIN):

> While Asians consider the neem to be part of a collective heritage, companies in the North are now patenting it. Monopoly rights have been assigned for the use of neem bark against cancer, stable and storable forms of the insecticidal component, neembased toothpaste, etc. All of these uses derive from centuries of indigenous knowledge and local innovation, as well as Asian people's efforts to nurture and conserve the valuable tree. Patenting of the neem in the North has struck many as a classic case of intellectual piracy, where scientists have added nothing fundamental to the understanding and use of the indigenous neem and yet are granted an intellectual and commercial monopoly over it.[19]

Another example is the use of the rosy periwinkle. Irving S. Johnson, former vice-president of research at Eli Lilly and Co, states that:

> two different groups were investigating the plant because of folklore suggesting the use of a tea of the leaves for diabetes. These reports were from the Philippine Islands and Jamaica. The plant, however, grows wild or is cultivated in most temperate and semitropical parts of the world. At the time it could be harvested because of its rampant growth in India and Madagascar, and it was grown commercially in Texas.[20]

18 A new study on indigenous resource utilisation and management systems of Mindanao indigenous peoples concludes that traditional practices continue to be sustainable despite the pressures of population and other outside factors. This study conducted by the College of Agriculture of Xavier University looked at the ways and practices of the Subanen, Mamanwa, Mandaya and Higaonon peoples. Interview with Dr Erlinda Burton, Xavier University, 3 January 1995.

19 Genetic Resources Action International (GRAIN) *Intellectual Property Rights for Whom?* (GRAIN Biobriefing No 4, Pt. Two, June 1994) 2.

20 Josephine Axt et al *Biodiversity, Indigenous Peoples, and Intellectual Property Rights: A Report by the Congressional Research Service to Congress* (Congress of the United States, Washington, DC: 1993) 35–36.

ASIA PACIFIC JOURNAL OF ENVIRONMENTAL LAW

Johnson argues that the traditional knowledge as well as the genetic resources leading to the discovery of the vinca alkaloids and their use in the treatment of cancer came from many sources, not just Madagascar. He points out that if one argues that Madagascar's contribution should be compensated, then all the other countries involved should also be paid. Besides, according to Johnson, the traditional use was a remedy for diabetes while the pharmaceutical company ultimately developed a cancer treatment.[21]

The National Cancer Institute of the United States, for example, is actively undertaking plant collection in different parts of the world, including Asia.[22] It can be presumed that many of these collection efforts are premised on existing research which may include documentation of indigenous knowledge.[23]

Customary Norms on Indigenous Knowledge

The accepted view on how indigenous peoples perceive indigenous knowledge is that such knowledge cannot be owned and that it is to be freely shared.[24] Indeed, this cultural refusal to claim ownership, is a major obstacle that bars the use of intellectual property laws by indigenous communities seeking to protect their rights to their traditional knowledge. As Rural Advancement Foundation International (RAFI) observes:

> There are approximately 15,000 culturally distinct ethnic communities in the world today and, while the diversity to be found among these cultures is both marvellous and extraordinary, most indigenous peoples share a sense of communal responsibility for their land and its living resources. It is rare to find a deeply-rooted culture that permits a patentlike monopoly over the products and processes of life. It is largely because of this communal tradition that many indigenous peoples look upon intellectual property – especially related to life forms – as a kind of blasphemy.[25]

However, this view of "communal ownership" should be qualified. While indigenous peoples generally do not claim to "own", in a western sense, their knowledge, this refusal does not mean that there are no rights attached to such knowledge.

There is enough anthropological data to support the conclusion that such rights exist, that, in fact, much of the information and knowledge considered

---

21 Ibid.
22 Gordon M. Cragg et al "Policies for International Collaboration and Compensation in Drug Discovery and Development at the United States National Cancer Institute: The NCI Letter of Collection" in Tom Greaves (ed) *Intellectual Property Rights for Indigenous Peoples: A Sourcebook* (Society for Applied Anthropology, Oklahoma City: 1994) 83 at 87–88.
23 Ibid.
24 See Southeast Asia Regional Institute for Community Education *Intellectual Property Rights and the Indigenous Peoples* (Southeast Asia Regional Institute for Community Education, Quezon City: 1993) 4.
25 Rural Advancement Foundation International (RAFI) *Conserving Indigenous Knowledge: Integrating Two Systems of Innovation* (United Nations Development Programme, New York: 1994) 3.

indigenous and traditional are not really freely shared with just any person within or outside particular communities. Instead, indigenous knowledge is classified into different categories according to the nature, characteristics, utility and even form of the particular information. The rights of the members of the community, as well as those outside of the community, to share particular knowledge is dependent on these categories. Thus, the knowledge of the medicine man or shaman[26] as well as that of religious and political leaders are usually restricted to those called or chosen to this position. On the other hand, information concerning seed varieties and agricultural practices are more freely shared.

The error in concluding that there are no rights over indigenous knowledge because they are communally held is similar to the mistake of those who assert that indigenous peoples "communally own" their lands. The fact is that "communal ownership" does not exclude private rights (the community can exclude others outside) as well as individual rights (some forms of property are exclusively utilised by members of the community who may exclude even other members).

In the same way that "communal ownership" of lands has been misunderstood, the perception that indigenous communities do not recognise private and individual rights over knowledge and information is based on a lack of documented data over such rights. Indeed, in the course of the study of which this article is one product, the author interviewed many anthropologists who unanimously said that the issue of rights over knowledge has rarely been looked at by anthropologists and that this probably explains why very little documentation exists, and in their own experience, they can cite many examples of community as well as individual rights over knowledge and information, which in fact frequently includes the right to exclude others within and outside the community.

Traditional Healers: Monopoly of Information

Ritual and magic are essential elements in traditional healing practices of many indigenous communities. Their presence is probably the nearest thing to intellectual property rights (IPR). Through ritual, the traditional healer controls the use of knowledge "by connecting the use of a particular treatment with rituals and magic" which he or she alone can perform.[27] Thus, another member of the community would believe that a treatment would not be effective unless accompanied by the healer's ritual.[28]

In the Philippines, for example, the Babaylans of the Manobos clearly restrict information and knowledge on healing rituals to themselves. Violating this

---

26 RAFI observes that there is an argument over whether the ritual used by traditional healers is intended to allow the healer exclusive monopoly over the use of medicinal plants and soils or whether such rituals are for the purpose of strengthening the psychological capacity of the patient to surmount illness: ibid at 3.
27 Axt, note 20 at 34.
28 Ibid.

ASIA PACIFIC JOURNAL OF ENVIRONMENTAL LAW

exclusionary norm subjects the infringer to social ostracism as well as a threat that the *Diwatas* (spirits) will punish him or her.[29] Many traditional healers in southern Africa feel the same way: "that this knowledge should certainly not be available to the public; even within their own societies, much of this knowledge is kept private through ritual and taboo."[30]

To become a healer or priest is a calling that not all persons within the indigenous community are called to or are qualified to be. Among the Lisu in Thailand, for example, to become a *mo muang* (priest), a man must pass a selection test conducted in front of the village spirit shrine. Candidates are usually married men with children and have other family responsibilities. Before they become candidates they must already have a good knowledge of ritual. The position cannot be inherited and for as long as a *mo muang* is a resident in the village where he was "chosen" he cannot give up the post. His duties only end when he leaves the community.[31]

Indigenous Knowledge and Intellectual Property Rights

What is incompatible about the concept of IPR with indigenous knowledge is not so much that the latter is freely shared but the very fact that "ownership" is claimed over it by human beings. It is this cultural refusal to claim ownership over knowledge – as well as many natural resources – that makes resort to IPR rules, as a means of protecting rights to indigenous knowledge, objectionable to many Asian indigenous peoples.

On the other hand, even in cases where information and knowledge are usually shared, many indigenous peoples, in Asia and elsewhere, rightly look with suspicion at efforts by outsiders to document such knowledge and information. Their historical experience – of their lands and minerals being taken away from them – justifies this scepticism. As McGowan and Udeinya observe:

> The resources of indigenous peoples have long been a target of state governments and commercial enterprises. Gold, timber, crops, land, oil, minerals, water, fisheries and art have all been sought or taken from native peoples. Now indigenous knowledge of complex healing systems combining plant medicines, local ecology and spiritual care is yet another resource being taken and used by others. For many indigenous peoples, it looks like more of the same. Many indigenous peoples and healers refuse to share their cultural knowledge with outsiders, viewing this use of their cultural knowledge as yet another resource appropriation without permission, payment, recognition or proper respect.[32]

---

29 Interview with Burton, note 18. See also Erlinda Burton *The Impact of Modern Medical Intervention in the Agusan Manobo Medical System of the Philippines* (Xavier University, Cincinnati, Ohio: 1983).

30 A. B. Cunningham "Indigenous Knowledge and Biodiversity" (Summer 1991) *Cultural Survival Quarterly* 4 at 14.

31 Prasert Chaipigusit "Anarchists of the Highlands? A Critical Review of a Stereotype Applied to the Lisu" in John McKinnon and Bernard Vienne (eds) *Hill Tribes Today: problems in change* (White Lotus-Orstom, Bangkok: 1989) 173 at 181–182.

32 Janet McGowan and Iroka Udeinya "Collecting Traditional Medicines in Nigeria: A Proposal for IPR Compensation" in Greaves, note 22 at 57, 60.

This scepticism is reflected, for example, in knowledge about agriculture – particularly folk seed varieties. Like their brothers and sisters all over the world, most Asian indigenous peoples as well as farmers have traditionally shared seeds freely with each other and with their neighbours. However the increasing private control and manipulation of seeds by private companies for commercial gain is beginning to change this. The result is that many Asian indigenous communities are now reluctant to share their folk varieties freely.[33] While this may be a sad development, it is also necessary. Indeed, the starting point for protecting indigenous knowledge is simply to refuse to share information with outsiders.

Indigenous peoples throughout the world are beginning to see that the protection of indigenous knowledge is intimately linked with the concept of IPR. In the Mataatua Declaration on Cultural and Intellectual Property Rights of Indigenous Peoples, the indigenous peoples present declared that:

> cultural and intellectual property are central to the right of determination and that, although the knowledge of indigenous peoples is of benefit to all humanity, the first beneficiaries of indigenous knowledge must be the direct indigenous descendants of such knowledge.[34]

The Declaration recognises that:

> Indigenous Peoples are capable of managing their traditional knowledge themselves, but are willing to offer it to all humanity provided their fundamental rights to define and control this knowledge are protected by the international community.[35]

In sum, as a Maori leader articulated it, the most fundamental intellectual property right of indigenous peoples is the "right to define what their intellectual property is: the right to determine the extent and the meaning of the body of knowledge which shapes, and is in turn shaped, by their cultural heritage".[36]

Asian Intellectual Property Rights Regimes

The IPR regimes that currently dominate in Asia all originate from the western model of intellectual property rights.[37] The only significant difference between the

---

33 This observation is also true of the Zunis of Africa. See Daniela Soleri et al "Gifts from the Creator: Intellectual Property Rights and Folk Crop Varieties" in Greaves, note 22 at 19, 37.
34 Darrell A. Posey "International Agreements and Intellectual Property Right Protection for Indigenous Peoples" in Greaves, note 22 at 223, 237.
35 Ibid.
36 Southeast Asia Regional Institute for Community Information, note 24 at 23.
37 See generally Arthur Wineburg "The Intellectual Property Regimes of East Asia – An Overview" in Arthur Wineburg (ed) *Intellectual Property Protection in Asia* (Butterworths Legal Publishers, Salem, N. H.: 1991).

IPR systems of the North and the regimes which operate in Asia is the treatment of national interest. Asian IPR systems sometimes exclude or restrict the recognition of intellectual property rights where fundamental national interests are involved.[38]

The particular laws that are relevant to the question of indigenous knowledge and the challenges posed by biotechnology are the laws on patents, copyrights, trade secrets and trade marks. The emphasis of many of these laws has always been on individual interest and national interest and not the interest of specific communities in a state. Unfortunately, in many cases in Asia, national interests – often linked to the interests of elite economic classes – is not equivalent to the interests of communities. Indeed, historically, national interests have often collided with the interests of local communities, particularly indigenous peoples.

Asian IPR systems are individualistic because they are designed to recognise and reward individual inventors. Like western IPR systems, a major objective of Asian IPR laws is to ensure that the rights of inventors and those who support them are protected. Asian IPR regimes are also characterised by an emphasis on national and state interests. This characteristic of statism is found in many IPR laws of Asian countries and is founded on the belief that IPR systems must serve the interests of the nation state.

Like many developing countries, most Asian countries maintain generally less extensive systems of intellectual property protection. They insist on the right to design IPR systems to specific national circumstances. This differential treatment has created friction under international trade laws. China, for example, experienced trade sanctions from the United States for refusing to bow down to demands for stricter enforcement of IPR norms. This is also one reason, among others, why the developed countries insisted on the TRIPS agreement under GATT.

In general, developing countries, including most Asian countries, have seen IPRs as a barrier to development, restricting the ability of industry to innovate and imitate.[39] This perception is reflected in compulsory licensing provisions that are found in many Asian IPR systems. "Compulsory licensing" laws usually require that inventors make their invention available to all those prepared to pay. In some cases, compulsory licenses may be awarded by patent tribunals if the inventor fails to make the invention adequately available to society. Under this system, the right of the patent holder to charge royalties for the use of the invention which presumably, allows inventors to seek a fair return on the research investment, is respected.

---

38 See generally Gunda Schumann "Economic development and Intellectual Property Protection in Southeast Asia" in Francis M. Rushing and Carole Ganz Brown (eds) *Intellectual Property Rights in Science, Technology and Economic Performance: international comparisons* (Westview Press, Boulder, Co: 1991) 157.
39 Ibid.

Patent Systems in Asia

Asian patent systems share the same basic definition of a patent as their western and northern counterparts. A patent is considered a form of industrial property right which is designed to legally protect the invention which must generally be new, and commercially useful. The granting of a patent results in the patentee having a monopoly right over the invention. With such a right, the holder of the patent can exclude others from making, using or selling the invention for a period of about ten to twenty years.

Many patent systems in Asia are rooted in the colonial histories of the states in the region.[40] India, Sri Lanka, Malaysia, Hong Kong, and Singapore borrowed from the British legal tradition. Japan, at least outwardly, looked to Germany, and the Philippines was influenced by US law. Notwithstanding the diverse colonial backgrounds of the patent systems of many Asian states, these systems have much in common. By and large, most Asian patent systems have as common elements:
- restrictive rules on what may be patentable;
- the fact that priority is determined by the first inventor to file;
- the requirement that the patent application must be disclosed to the public;
- the opportunity given to the interested public to oppose the application;
- the requirement of public disclosure for commercial gain prior to filing results in a prohibition on its patenting;
- the fact that some one who invents and patents an improvement is generally entitled (for a fee) to work the pioneer or senior patent;
- provisions allowing compulsory licensing in specified cases;
- a cumbersome registration procedure; and
- an undeveloped enforcement mechanism.[41]

For an invention to be patentable, most Asian patent laws require the same elements as in western IPR systems: the invention must be useful and novel (not publicly known or used by others), and must satisfy the standard of inventiveness or "nonobviousness". The subject of a patent may include any useful process, machine, or composition of matter. In this context, mere discoveries are not patentable.

A review of existing Asian IPR regimes reveals the following conclusions:
- On the basis of the texts of the legal provisions alone, life forms are not patentable in Asia except in Thailand which explicitly allows for the patenting of biotechnological inventions; and
- the works which are patentable remain principally industrial in nature.

40 See Wineburg, note 37 at 2–1 to 2–2.
41 Ibid at 2–2 to 2–3.

ASIA
PACIFIC   ASIA PACIFIC JOURNAL OF ENVIRONMENTAL LAW

The widening of the scope of patent protection in the North have implications for developing countries, including those in Asia. First, even if most Asian
countries continue to exclude genetically engineered life forms from the scope of
patent protection, this restriction may be meaningless in the international and
global context. Indeed, an exclusionary rule may work against the interests of those
Asian countries which are investing heavily on biotechnology as a future industry.[42] Second, the internationalisation of IPR standards mandated by TRIPS may
pressure Asian states to recognise patents from the developed countries even when
these patents cover subject matter not patentable in their respective IPR systems.
While countries like India have so far resisted pressure to amend its patent laws to
recognise lifeforms, there is no guarantee that this refusal is sustainable.[43] Third,
the present texts of Asian patent laws are not – as the experience of the United
States and Europe has shown – absolute barriers to the widening of the scope of
patent protection. At present, Japan, South Korea and Thailand have already
widened the scope of patent protection to include most biotechnological products.
There is no legal barrier to do the same in Thailand. It remains to be seen how the
other countries in the region will respond to this challenge. What is certain is that
in the near future, if it is not happening now, patent applications for genetically
modified life forms will be filed.

A survey of the filing and registration procedures required by Asian patent
systems reveals a very complex and cumbersome process. Patent application goes
through the process of filing, acceptance, opposition, grant and maintenance. In
most cases, publication in an official gazette or in a newspaper is essential. Other
extensive preliminary requirements must be followed.

Enforcing the rights to a patent when violated is even more difficult. In most
cases, weaving through the patent system of an Asian country involves engaging
in both administrative and judicial litigation. Enforcement measures could range
from defending an existing patent in the patent office to civil and criminal law suits
involving infringement.

In sum, the filing and registration of a patent as well as enforcing rights when
they are granted will require substantial financial, administrative and legal resources
on the part of the patent applicant or holder.

---

42 The Philippines for example is committed to develop biotechnology as a "leap-frog" strategy. For example
    some policy makers believe that there is no need to go through the industrialisation phase but that the
    national economy should concentrate on developing knowledge industries as the cornerstone of economic
    development. See Proceedings of the Workshop on Strengthening Knowledge Industries/Infrastructures in
    the Philippines (National Security Council, Manila: 1993).
43 Ashish Kothari, *Beyond the Biodiversity Convention: A View from India* (World Resources Institute,
    Washington: 1994) 73.

Copyright Laws in Asia

Copyrights were traditionally designed to protect works of art and literature. Copyrights as a form of intellectual property are unlike patents in that they do not protect ideas but rather their expression.[44] Copyrights can cover artistic and literary work, computer programs, and commercial designs. Copyright law may also indirectly protect rights relating to biodiversity, including rights of indigenous peoples to their traditional knowledge.

The common elements in Asian copyright systems are:
* the originality of the idea expressed as a condition of granting the copyright;
* protection from unauthorised use, reproduction, distribution, sale, and adaptation; and
* a period of time in which the author's rights are protected, usually the life of the author plus 50 years.

Copyright infringement results in liability for the violator who may be ordered to stop the acts of infringement, to pay damages and to deliver, for confiscation and destruction the infringing texts, materials or devices. Criminal remedies may also be resorted to. However, all these remedies, as in enforcing patent rights, are dependent on the availability of substantial financial and legal resources.

Trade Secrets and Trade Marks Laws in Asia

Trade secrets serve as an alternative to patent protection. Trade secrets can be availed of to protect valuable knowledge which does not meet the requirements for patentability. A trade secret can continue perpetually so long as the formula, information, or device remains secret. In plant breeding, for example, the lines used to produce a hybrid may be defended as secrets indefinitely. The owner of a trade secret may license, disclose, or assign the right to use the trade secret, subject to an agreement to hold the information in confidence.[45]

In the Asian context however, the law on trade secrets is largely undeveloped. Like many developing countries, trade secrets are not encouraged in Asia where monopoly of knowledge and information is perceived principally as an obstacle to national development.

Trademarks are labels attached to tradeable goods bearing the name (or some brand name) of their owners. They are resorted to for the purpose of identifying the source of the goods in question. Trademarks, when registered, are protected for a number of years (from ten to 20 years in Asia) with an option for renewal.

---

44 See Michael A. Gollin "An Intellectual Property Rights Framework for Biodiversity Prospecting" in Walter V. Reid et al (ed) *Biodiversity Prospecting* (World Resources Institute, Washington: 1993) 159 at 175.
45 Ibid at 163–165.

ASIA
PACIFIC   ASIA PACIFIC JOURNAL OF ENVIRONMENTAL LAW

Trademark law can be useful in cases where eco-labelling is appropriate. Trademarks can protect the competitive advantage of the company providing the green product, and the revenues can be returned to the source of the product through licensing and other contractual arrangements. Indeed, a product that is perceived to have been derived in a sustainable way can enjoy a competitive advantage among consumers around the world simply because it is perceived as "green". One example where the approach has worked is in Brazil where indigenous peoples raised funds by sustainably producing nuts and materials for cosmetic products.[46]

In sum, a trademark attesting to the authenticity of indigenous peoples' work would be useful if the trademark were widely known among consumers.

Using IPR Laws to Protect Indigenous Knowledge:
Limitations and Possibilities

The foregoing survey of Asian intellectual property rights laws clearly shows that using IPR laws to protect the rights of indigenous peoples to their traditional knowledge will at best be very limited. Indeed, Asian IPR regimes were clearly not conceived to recognise the intellectual contribution of indigenous peoples.

There are three classes of problems that must be confronted in using Asian patent laws to protect the rights of indigenous peoples. First, there is frequently a cultural obstacle to the claiming of ownership over knowledge of genetic and biological resources. Second, the forms and expression of indigenous knowledge are incompatible with the requirements of patentability. And, third, applying for rights under these laws as well as protecting and enforcing rights once granted are frequently impracticable for indigenous peoples.

Ownership by Indigenous Peoples over Life-forms

Most indigenous peoples in Asia reject the proposition that knowledge of life-forms, whether natural or altered, can be owned. They share this belief with others who oppose such claims on ethical, political or economic grounds. The rejection of claims of ownership over knowledge of living matter flows logically from the refusal of many indigenous peoples to claim, at least in the western sense, ownership over natural, genetic and biological resources themselves. As such, even more unacceptable is the concept of ownership over living products and life processes including the regeneration of life.

Unless changes in the cultural worldview of indigenous peoples with respect to what can and what cannot be owned take place, it would be very difficult for

---

46 Ibid at 173–174.

indigenous communities to even make the first step in all IPR mechanisms – the filing of a claim of ownership. To some extent, this change is happening in the area of land claims where many indigenous communities are now pressing claims of ownership as against the state as well as against private persons.[47]

Whether or not indigenous knowledge fulfils the criteria of patentability becomes the next obstacle to recognition of IPR over indigenous knowledge. One view is that since patents and copyrights are available only for new knowledge, these mechanisms cannot be used to protect traditional knowledge which has existed for a long time.[48]

From a legal point of view however, this is not an insurmountable obstacle. Indigenous knowledge fulfils the criteria of patentability in most cases. Besides, the conflict between international trends in IPR and the rights of indigenous peoples emerged precisely because there is still a substantial amount of knowledge and information which remains within the limited confines of indigenous communities – and not shared by others.

A related problem is that patents and copyrights are conferred on individuals or corporations rather than community ownership.[49] Indeed, the traditional concept of IPR is that they grant private rights to individuals to the exclusion of others within a society. Indeed, under IPR laws, the concept of community invention is not recognised.[50] What is usually required is that an inventor is an individual or a group of named individuals.

This bias in favour of individual ownership is also not an insurmountable obstacle to patenting indigenous knowledge. Fundamentally, patents and other IPR laws grant private rights and not necessarily individual rights. As in the case of land, there is nothing in IPR laws which prohibits communities from claiming ownership over ideas.

Communities however must resort to conventional legal means to acquire juridical personality. And assuming that they find an acceptable mode (such as incorporation), they would still have to contend with the issue of how to keep the IPR rights already granted to them. This is especially difficult if the knowledge patented is shared by different communities.

These questions emphasise the practical difficulties of resorting to prevailing IPR laws as modes of protecting rights to indigenous knowledge.

---

47 In some cases, indigenous peoples even see ownership claims over their territory or ancestral domains as taboo. In one case handled by the Legal Rights and Natural Resources Center, a Philippine non-governmental organisation, a ritual of cleansing had to be undertaken by the indigenous community after they made such a claim. Interview with Atty. Augusto Gatmaytan, 15 February 1995, Manila, Philippines.
48 See Tom Greaves "IPR, A Current Survey" in Greaves, note 22 at 1, 8-9.
49 Ibid.
50 See Gurdial Singh Nijar *A Conceptual Framework and essential Elements of A Rights regime for the Protection of Indigenous Rights and Biodiversity* (Biodiversity Convention Briefings, Third World Network: 1994) 2-3.

ASIA PACIFIC JOURNAL OF ENVIRONMENTAL LAW

The Practical Difficulties of Using Patents

The more difficult obstacles to using patent laws to protect rights to indigenous knowledge are the practical problems associated with the procedures of filing and registering the patent claim, and when granted, protecting the rights conferred. The process of filing and registration as well as enforcement is complex cumbersome and expensive.

In sum, engaging in the patent system will demand unreasonably high technical, financial, administrative and legal resources on the part of indigenous peoples. Clearly, by themselves, most indigenous peoples do not have these resources. The only way that they may successfully use the patent system is if they link up and collaborate with individuals or groups with these resources. Indeed, even if they have the necessary resources, it is probably not advisable from a cost-benefit point of view to use these resources for IPR protection.

These difficulties and obstacles also apply to other IPR laws such as copyrights, trade secrets and trade marks. In particular, the cultural barrier of refusal or reluctance to claim ownership over knowledge of living things remains a formidable obstacle.

Theoretically, communities could document their indigenous knowledge in some tangible medium and obtain a copyright under most Asian laws. Ethnobotanists may also write and publish articles or books on traditional knowledge and voluntarily share the copyright with the indigenous people.[51]

In copyright law, as in the case of patents, the same problem of the individual's versus the community's claim of ownership is present. The "author" of traditional knowledge is rarely an individual but a community.[52] Moreover, the period of protection, if indigenous knowledge is truly to be protected, should continue as long as the community survives. This kind of "perpetual" protection would be incompatible with the copyright system. Moreover, the copyright would only protect the specific expression, not the knowledge being expressed. Under copyright laws, others could still use the knowledge they discover or learn from books, articles, and films.[53]

The law on trade secrets may also be resorted to by indigenous peoples. Among others, a traditional healer's knowledge of the medicinal use of a plant or of a method passed down over generations might be protected as a trade secret. However, the utility of trade secrets is limited because of the difficulty in establishing, protecting, and enforcing them.[54] Theoretically, indigenous knowledge could be considered as a trade secret if others within and outside the community are excluded. But once this knowledge is shared or when it is documented and published, by an anthropologist for example, trade secret rights are extinguished.[55]

---

51 Axt, note 20 at 47.
52 See Southeast Asia Regional Institute for Community Education, note 24 at 21–22.
53 Axt, note 20 at 47.
54 Gollin, note 44 at 163.
55 Ibid.

Finally, utilising the law on trademarks is also not a promising mode of protection. First, it does not meet the needs of communities to protect works that have already been widely copied. Second, the law on trademarks does not protect indigenous knowledge related to biological products or processes but protects only non-living works.[56]

Resorting to the IPR laws which currently prevail in Asia is not, on the whole, a promising strategy for indigenous peoples to take. While small windows of opportunity are available in using IPR laws, applying the conventional IPR approaches to indigenous knowledge is likely to do more harm than good.

On the theoretical plane however, there is nothing inherent in IPR laws which prevents its use by indigenous peoples. Working with other sectors, such as public agencies, academic institutions, or non-governmental organisations, indigenous peoples might succeed in using IPR mechanisms to protect indigenous knowledge. However, to successfully weave through the IPR system, indigenous peoples might be compelled to make fundamental changes in their worldview. Moreover, the costs of engaging in the system would probably outweigh the potential economic benefits. In this sense, the decision to pursue IPR could distract attention and energy from more useful initiatives.

Asian Indigenous Peoples and the IPR Challenge: Response Strategies

The IPR challenge to the indigenous peoples of Asia and elsewhere is not a challenge for indigenous peoples to assert ownership over knowledge or living things. Rather it is how, under the shadow of the widening and strengthening of IPR on the international as well as national level, indigenous peoples can best nurture and protect indigenous knowledge.

At its core, the response to the IPR challenge must consist of efforts to affirm responsibility and control over traditional knowledge and to things produced through its application. The ultimate objective of these efforts is "to preserve meaning and due honour for elements of cultural knowledge and to insure that these traditional universes, and their peoples, maintain their vitality".[57] Other objectives are "to manage the degree and process by which parts of that cultural knowledge are shared with outsiders and, in some instances, to be justly compensated for it".[58]

56 Axt, note 20 at 47.
57 See Tom Greaves "Introduction" in Greaves, note 22 at ix.
58 Ibid.

ASIA PACIFIC JOURNAL OF ENVIRONMENTAL LAW

Towards this end, the response framework to the IPR challenge should be one that allows indigenous peoples "to ensure the intellectual integrity of their ongoing innovations rather than to obtain intellectual property".[59] According to RAFI: "Ultimately, a combination of initiatives, that could collectively be termed the 'intellectual integrity framework' may prove most appropriate."[60]

RAFI proposes a spectrum of initiatives to realise this, including:[61]

- Intellectual Protection – the rights of indigenous peoples to their traditional knowledge should be protected through different mechanisms within and outside the IPR system. Indigenous peoples should not be compelled to endorse or support IPR systems in order to have their intellectual integrity protected.
- Intellectual recognition – the utility of indigenous knowledge should be recognised. Indigenous peoples must work with other sectors to ensure that credit, and compensation where appropriate, is given to indigenous communities for their contribution to the conservation and development of biodiversity.
- Intellectual Development – indigenous peoples must be supported so that they can extend their existing systems of information-exchange and cooperation. Linkages between indigenous peoples and with other sectors – such as farmers, scientists and anthropologists – are essential to attain this objective.
- Intellectual exchange – indigenous peoples should actively participate in the social decision process that characterises the IPR debate. They should discuss the issue among themselves and with others, at the community, national, regional and international level.

Territorial Integrity and Intellectual Integrity

Despite differences in historical and political contexts, most indigenous peoples in Asia and elsewhere share similar problems resulting largely from colonisation.[62] To benefit from local resources and to establish effective political power, the colonisers and subsequently the nation states which replaced them "took the land away from the natives".[63]

A common colonial history has left indigenous groups with four basic needs: "namely the need for (a) cultural protection; (b) recognition of land claims; (c) recognition of individual, economic and social (welfare) rights; and (d) political autonomy."[64]

---

59 See RAFI, note 25 at 36.
60 Ibid.
61 Ibid.
62 See Raizda Torres "The Rights of Indigenous Populations: The Emerging International Norm" (1991) 16 *Yale International Law Journal* 127 at 128.
63 Ibid.
64 Ibid.

All these needs and the rights corresponding to them are however intimately interrelated. Demands for cultural protection, which includes the preservation of traditional subsistence patterns as well as the protection of indigenous religions and languages, cannot be separated from the recognition of indigenous land rights.[65] Without a secure territorial base, cultural rights become meaningless.

The primary struggle then of Asian indigenous peoples continues to be their struggle for territorial integrity. Indeed, the IPR challenge must always be seen in this context for it to be meaningful for them. Initiatives to deal with this challenge must support the primary struggle. The fora provided by the IPR debate should therefore be seen as additional and new opportunities for insisting on territorial recognition.

All IPR related initiatives must be premised on the recognition of the integrity of the territory of indigenous peoples. Without a comprehensive and effective recognition of the right of indigenous peoples to control access and utilisation of their ancestral lands and domains, all efforts to realise the intellectual integrity framework is irrelevant and bound to fail. Moreover, if not linked to the struggle to gain territorial integrity, all initiatives to respond to the IPR challenge would ultimately be diversionary.

Territorial integrity includes the following elements:
- the delineation of ancestral lands and domains;
- the recognition that indigenous peoples communally hold and control (not necessarily "own") these lands as against the state and other private persons;
- the acknowledgment that within indigenous territory, the customary law of the indigenous community must generally be followed; and
- in cases, where history justifies it, the recognition of political autonomy.

The ultimate success of an intellectual integrity framework, as a response to the IPR challenge, is dependent on the degree of success that Asian indigenous peoples attain in realising the elements of territorial integrity. At the same time, the IPR challenge provides new venues and fora for their realisation.

A look at specific national and international response strategies reveals how the IPR challenge presents new opportunities for indigenous peoples to assert their claim for territorial integrity. These are discussed below.

National Response Strategies

Response strategies to the IPR challenge, at the national level, may include:
- the enactment and enforcement of regulations to govern bio-prospecting and access to genetic resources;
- using existing IPR laws, limited as they are; and

65 Ibid at 159.

- legislating new IPR norms and mechanisms such as inventor's certificates, a law protecting folklore, and recognising community intellectual property rights.

Access Regulations and Bio-prospecting

One immediate response of Asian indigenous peoples to the IPR challenge is to lobby and work for the immediate formulation, enactment and enforcement of regulations governing access to the genetic resources within their territory. It is politically possible to attain this because it is also in the interests of most Asian states that these resources are protected from both destruction as well as piracy that may result from bio-prospecting.

At present, bio-prospecting – defined as the research, collection and utilisation of biological and genetic resources for purposes of applying the knowledge derived therefrom to scientific and/or commercial purposes – is happening throughout Asia. This prospecting is done by both foreign and local collectors.

Philippine Bio-prospecting Regulation

A major problem in Asia is that there are no statutes which explicitly regulate bio-prospecting – effectively giving collectors free access to genetic resources. In the Philippines, Executive Order 247 was issued to regulate this activity. It contains provisions on prior informed consent of indigenous and other local communities which may have value for other countries. The regulation is far from perfect. Indeed, some have criticised it for even allowing bio-prospecting at all. Unfortunately, the reality is that this activity is happening and that it is being done by Filipinos themselves – usually for and on behalf of a foreign company. A major goal therefore of the regulation is to ensure that all information about bio-prospecting becomes available to the public, that before the activity is undertaken indigenous and local communities have given their prior informed consent, and that both the country and communities benefit from its result. Above all, what Executive Order 247 does is to make the activity of bio-prospecting transparent so that interested parties may make decisions and act on them with the proper information.

The order requires collectors to enter into a contract with an inter-agency governmental body which includes representation from non-governmental organisations and indigenous people's organisations. However, as part of the process of giving consent, indigenous communities can compel the collector to enter into a Materials Transfer Agreement – containing provisions on compensation, capacity building, and technology transfer – with them.

Corporate Practice

It should be noted that there are companies which specialise in using indigenous knowledge to facilitate prospecting. Shaman Pharmaceuticals, for example, explicitly states that it is committed to developing new therapeutic agents by working with indigenous and local people of tropical forests and in the process contributing to the conservation of biocultural diversity.[66] Shaman is also on record as directly acknowledging ethically and financially the intellectual property rights of indigenous people with whom it works. Their strategy is to immediately compensate indigenous peoples for their contribution.[67]

Whether Shaman will live up to its commitments is a question that remains to be seen. Whether the advantages of entering into an agreement with a company such as Shaman outweigh the dangers is a question every indigenous community must confront. The point however is that the national legal system must provide for minimum rules in which these contractual arrangements can be made. Access and bio-prospecting regulations are ways which this can be provided for.

Rules on access to genetic resources and bio-prospecting are not the only answer to the IPR challenge. However, they have immediate utility. They can, if properly formulated and enforced, slow down the process of genetic and intellectual piracy. And they can give indigenous peoples some breathing space to acquire the needed capacity to make the right decisions.

The Case of Human Genetic Material

Collecting genetic materials from indigenous peoples, as is being done under the Human Genome Project,[68] is a different question altogether and should be excluded from rules regulating access to genetic resources. Collecting and patenting human cell lines have both ethical and political underpinnings and cannot be considered as a simple act of bio-prospecting. Indigenous peoples must lobby and work hard for an absolute prohibition on such activity at least until they can make a more informed stand about the activity.

Using IPR Laws

It was pointed out earlier that using Asian IPR laws to protect the rights of indigenous peoples to their traditional knowledge is at best limited. Existing IPR

---

66 See Steven R. King, Thomas J. Carlson and K. Moron "Biological Diversity, Indigenous Knowledge, Drug Discovery and Intellectual Property Rights" in S. Brush and D. Stabinsky (eds) *Valuing Local Knowledge: Indigenous People and Intellectual Property Rights* (Island Press, Washington: 1996) 167–185.

67 Ibid at 2.

68 See *Patents, Indigenous Peoples and Human Genetic Diversity* (RAFI Communique, May 1993) at http://www.rafi.ca/communique/Fltxt/19932.html (22 January 1998).

laws are not only incompatible with the cultural worldview of most indigenous peoples, but engaging in them also requires legal, financial and administrative resources which most indigenous peoples do not have. Moreover, if they do have such resources, it is far better to spend them on the primary struggle of attaining recognition of territorial integrity.

The only way that existing IPR laws can be used by Asian indigenous peoples is if they work together with public or private institutions, such as government agencies and non-governmental agencies, to acquire and defend patents, copyrights, trade secrets or trade marks. In any case, even in this instance, indigenous communities who choose to engage in the IPR system must be willing to conform to the market and commercial premises of the system. This could include setting aside fundamental cultural and ethical biases.

One way however of using existing IPR laws is to lobby Asian governments not to recognise patents over life forms. There is a cogent argument why national governments of the region should delay recognising such patents. Indeed, as the Crucible Group points out:

> No country should be coerced into adopting an IP system for living materials. There are valid ethical and practical reasons why each country should be allowed to reach its own position and either adopt an existing mechanism for protection, create a new mechanism better suited to national interests, or encourage innovation by other means altogether.[69]

Indigenous peoples should also monitor developments in the national and international arenas, making sure that no patents, copyrights or trade marks are granted for knowledge which is based on indigenous innovation.

Another strategy for dealing with the IPR challenge is to lobby and work for new laws on intellectual property rights, laws which provide for norms and mechanisms more compatible with the nature and characteristics of indigenous knowledge. Examples of such laws includes the recognition of Inventors' Certificates, the UNESCO Model Law on Folklore and a law recognising community intellectual property rights.

Inventors' Certificates is an IPR option which, unlike other IPR laws, is not based on an exclusive monopoly. They discard financial compensation altogether in favour of nonmonetary awards and nonexclusive licensing arrangements. According to RAFI:

> Governments can establish Inventors' Certificates through uncomplicated national legislation; they need only notify WIPO and GATT that this legislation exists. Forms of recognition or compensation can be determined either through legislation or through regulation which can vary by category or by case. Governments can adjust the terms of compensation to promote local innovations in domestic or export markets or to attract a foreign invention where access to that invention is deemed to be in the national interest.[70]

---

69 See The Crucible Group *People, Plants, and Patents* (International Development Research Centre, Ottowa: 1994) 54.
70 RAFI, note 25 at 32.

INTELLECTUAL PROPERTY RIGHTS

Inventors' Certificates would permit governments the flexibility to:

- vary the methods of recognition;
- permit or exclude monetary compensation;
- grant exclusive or nonexclusive licenses;
- ensure that the patented technology is applied or manufactured nationally;
- establish other transfers of technology conditions beneficial to the importing country;
- vary the period of protection; and
- attach any other contractual provisions deemed beneficial.[71]

Another option is to work and lobby for the enactment in Asian states of the Model Law on Folklore, adopted in 1985 by both UNESCO and the World Intellectual Property Organisation (WIPO). According to RAFI: "This model law affords indigenous communities three unique elements that are especially appropriate to the protection of biological products and processes."[72] First, "communities" (rather than specific individuals) can be the legally registered innovators; they can either act on their own behalf or be represented by the State. Second, community innovations are not necessarily fixed or finalised, but can be ongoing or evolutionary and still be protected by intellectual property law. Third, communities retain exclusive monopoly control over their folklore innovations as long as the community continues to innovate.

The Model Law however has been interpreted to exclude scientific inventions. Based on the experience of the application of conventional patent laws, this is not an insurmountable objection. RAFI points out that existing IPR laws:

> expressly excludes protection for plants, animals, pharmaceuticals, and chemicals, but many national patent offices have interpreted the law to permit the patenting of such innovations on the assumption that if legislators had known "then" what they know "now", they would not have made these exclusions.[73]

A similar argument could apply to the case of indigenous knowledge.[74]

Still another new initiative that could be pursued is a law recognising an alternative rights regime for indigenous knowledge.[75] In such a case, the claim of indigenous communities would differ from standard IPR claims which are characterised by individualism and commercialisation. It is based on the premise that indigenous communities create collective rights thus the whole community will be deemed the rightful owner of such creativity or innovation. Nijar points out that

---

71 Ibid.
72 Ibid at 32–33.
73 Ibid.
74 Ibid.
75 See generally Nijar, note 50.

ASIA PACIFIC JOURNAL OF ENVIRONMENTAL LAW

this alternative rights regime rejects "the notion of a oneshot concept of innovation which typifies industrial innovations".[76] It recognises that:

> The creation of indigenous communities is often accretional, informal, and over time. The knowledge is continuous as it modifies, adapts and builds upon the existing knowledge. This would pave the way for the recognition of cumulative innovations and knowledge. This will also mean that the innovation cannot be dealt with without regard to the past, present and future owners' and beneficiaries of the knowledge.[77]

A Word of Caution on New Laws

While the three alternative legal approaches discussed above hold promise for the protection of rights to indigenous knowledge, indigenous peoples must seriously weigh the consequences of supporting the adoption of any or all of them. Progressive as they appear, these alternative approaches are still, at its core, IPR mechanisms. As such, they all require registration procedures as well as elaborate administrative arrangements. Moreover, even if rights to indigenous knowledge were granted under these alternative approaches, enforcing and defending these rights would still require substantial resources from communities. The option of course is to rely on the state for protection and enforcement. Given however the political economy of most Asian states, and the extent of the marginalisation of indigenous peoples within these states, it is probably not realistic to rely on such an option.

An additional factor to be considered is the fact that, as the Crucible Group observes, IPR policy and practice is in such a state of flux that: "not only the rules of the game but the game itself may be changing as science and society grapple with the marketing of a new bio-materials."[78] Given this state of IPR, governments as well as indigenous peoples should not enact policies or legislation that cannot be changed rapidly if new circumstances demand it. Indeed:

> If governments are unable or unwilling to rescind or revise legislation, they would be illadvised to lock into new legislation now. If institutes or people's organizations find it difficult to review and revise policy, they should be equally cautious.[79]

International Response Strategies

The national strategies must be accompanied by a coherent international plan of action. A regional response to the IPR challenge would be an essential step to

---

76 Ibid at 2–3.
77 Ibid.
78 The Crucible Group, note 69 at 11.
79 Ibid at 1.

formulate and implement such a plan. RAFI has proposed different initiatives that may be valuable for Asian indigenous peoples to support. Some of these initiatives are relevant only in the international arena. Others may also be applicable at the national level. Another important avenue for protecting rights to indigenous knowledge at the international level is by resorting to the emerging international law of the human rights of indigenous peoples. Indeed, this may prove to be a more effective legal mechanism for protecting indigenous cultural knowledge than the international law of intellectual property rights.[80] By linking the IPR issue to the primary struggle of indigenous peoples for recognition of territorial integrity as well as political autonomy, a more coherent, relevant and effective response to the IPR challenge will be possible.

Conclusion: The Urgent Tasks

Responding to the IPR challenge demands three urgent tasks from the indigenous peoples of Asia:
- unity within communities;
- unity among peoples; and
- unity with other sectors.

A significant consequence of the IPR challenge is that it could be divisive of indigenous communities and peoples. Because access to indigenous knowledge could translate into commercial gain for outsiders, indigenous communities or persons within such communities will be tempted to enter into contractual arrangements with bio-prospectors or gene collectors. So long as there is prior informed consent and so long as the social decision process of the community, in particular its customary law, is followed, there should be no objection to decisions to enter into these arrangements. The problem arises when consent is not informed, when it is given only by a few or not at all or when it is given outside community processes. To deal with the IPR challenge, an indigenous community must be united.

The IPR challenge could also result in divisions among peoples. Indigenous peoples in one country and within a region could be pitted against each other and end up competing with each other over contractual arrangements. Real disputes over who has prior rights over knowledge, once freely shared, could erupt. Again, indigenous peoples, in countries, in Asia and elsewhere, must be united if they are

---

80 Dean B. Suagee "Human Rights and Cultural Heritage, Developments in the United Nations Working Group on Indigenous Populations" in Greaves, note 22 at 204.

ASIA PACIFIC JOURNAL OF ENVIRONMENTAL LAW

to effectively deal with the IPR challenge. Finally, the IPR challenge demands that indigenous peoples examine closely the need to collaborate with other sectors of their respective societies as well as the international community.

The IPR challenge cuts across sectors. In many ways, the predicament and problems it brings to indigenous peoples is similar to what confronts most farmers of the South. There are, in a real sense, "in the same boat". Indeed, in the IPR issue, an alliance with farmers is justified and essential.

Local scientists from developing countries are confronted with analogous, if not similar, dilemmas as indigenous peoples. The need to conserve genetic resources while local capacity is being built and developed is a common concern shared by both scientists and communities. An alliance between both sectors is therefore desirable for an effective response to the IPR challenge.

Indigenous peoples must also be willing to work with lawyers, anthropologists and other social scientists. The nature of the IPR challenge is that it can only be understood and responded to in a multidisciplinary context.

Working with non-governmental organizations, ranging from environmental organisations to groups specialising in genetic resources and intellectual property, will also be useful. Resort to such organizations would particularly be important for monitoring the dizzying pace of change in IPR policy and practice.

Finally, the State. Most nation states of Asia generally emerged as successors of colonial masters. As such, historically, the Asian states and the indigenous peoples within them were usually at odds with each other. It was often seen to be in the national interest, such as national elites, to disregard the rights of indigenous peoples. Depriving indigenous peoples of their territory was seen as necessary so as to expand state power and control. In the IPR issue, however, national interests and the interests of indigenous peoples may coincide. For it is in the national interest, in an economic and political sense, of many Asian states to restrict the scope of patentability and other IPR protection. It is in the national interest for the state to ensure the conservation of genetic resources as well as the protection of indigenous knowledge. Perhaps, finally, in a common response to the IPR challenge, indigenous peoples and Asian states can be allies. In sum, the IPR challenge is not merely a threat to indigenous peoples. It should likewise be seen as an opportunity to use another approach to securing territorial integrity.

Part V
New Issues

The Dilemma of Regulating International Competition under the WTO System

Ignacio De León

Introduction

The increasing interdependence and globalisation of the world economy has decisively influenced the nature of international relations among states. Particularly, the notion of sovereignty that emerged with the rise of the national state during the sixteenth and seventeenth centuries has tended to become blurred as a consequence of the marked economic integration among domestic economies occurring since 1945.

New communication technologies have erased former barriers to economic exchange; as a consequence, governments are increasingly running into difficulties in exercising their formerly uncontested powers of sovereignty.[1] Indeed, the evaluation of conflicts whose causes are ultimately originated abroad has induced some states (most notably, the United States) to exercise their jurisdiction beyond their borders, thus creating a conflict with the conventional principle of territoriality under international law. In sum, economic integration and globalisation of the world economy has led to a redefinition of the boundaries of sovereign powers, as described by Pescatore.[2]

Increasingly, the new reality has brought about the need to revise those regulations simultaneously affecting multiple jurisdictions. Ultimately, the issue

at stake is whether states can co-ordinate their surveillance over international economic transactions, and whether it is convenient to do so.

The need to reconsider international regulation over economic transactions inevitably uncovers significant problems stemming from the particular nature and importance attached by policy makers to these regulations. These ideas entail entrenched principles about state intervention and individual freedom, and are therefore doomed to conflict. Additionally, the very nature of the phenomenon creates further challenges to the task of harmonising these views. The international economic order, like any other economic order, emerges from the consensus of its participants. This is frequently ignored by policy makers, who assume that public policy goals may be set and reached independently from the will of those affected by these rules.

The problems are increased because the international order lacks a supranational authority to which to refer the conflicts that might arise among its participants. At best, there are sets of imperfect rules loosely defining their terms of enforcement as well as the conditions by which economic agents may reasonably expect others to honour their commitments.[3] These gaps and imperfections in the legal setting encourage opportunistic behaviour from its participants, particularly in the form of protectionism; they can only be resolved through complex and tiresome international negotiations.

This article explores these problems in the light of the challenges arising from the proposed international regulation of competition through antitrust rules.[4] In particular, it examines the proposals aimed

Ignacio De León, Attorney, LL.M. (Lon), M. Phil. (Lon).

1 An explanation of the process of globalisation and its consequences over the international legal system is found in A. Avila, J. Castillo-Urrutia and M. Diaz-Mier, *Regulación del Comercio Internacional tras La Ronda Uruguay*, Editorial Tecnos, Madrid, 1994, pp. 170–179, 209. See also E. J. Mestmacker, "Maintaining Competition", in *International Harmonization of Competition Laws*, C.-J. Cheng *et al.* (eds.), Martinus Nijhoff Publishers, London, 1995, pp. 3–9.

2 P. Pescatore, *Le droit de l'intégration: émergence d'un phénomène nouveau dans les relations internationales selon l'expérience des Communautés Européennes*, A. W. Sijthoff, Leiden, 1972.

3 Such imperfection allows Doern, for example, to distinguish between two different sets of rules in the international sphere, which he names as "regimes" and "institutions". He defines the former as the "array of informal co-operative relationships not centered on specific formal organizations and do not involve binding rules and dispute settlement", whereas the latter "refer to the more entrenched system of values more often centred around organizations." (B. Doern, "The Internationalization of Competition Policy", in *Comparative Competition Policy: National Institutions in a Global Market*, G. B. Doern and S. Wilks (eds.), Clarendon Press, Oxford, 1996, pp. 303–305. Yet even the more integrated set of institutions are frequently characterised by a lesser degree of enforceability if compared to domestic jurisdictions. This is precisely the dilemma of regulation in international economic relations.

4 In this work, we use the term "antitrust policy" as it is traditionally referred to by U.S. authorities and following the practice of the majority of OECD countries, as "the body of laws and regulations governing business practices (horizontal or vertical agreements between enterprises, abuses of dominant positions, monopolization, mergers and acquisitions)." (M. Rowat, *Competition Policy in Latin America: Legal and Institutional Issues*, The World Bank, Washington, D.C.,

to replace current anti-dumping legislation by antitrust rules and their likely effects on international commerce. Therefore, it explores the rationality behind these rules, as well as their intellectual origins. The thesis of the article is that the current proposals promoting antitrust rules to regulate international transactions would regulate rivalry among firms, introducing a disincentive to competition. We argue that these rules do not strengthen the international institutional framework but instead undermine it, as they reintroduce, albeit in new ways, sources of discretion and uncontrolled behaviour that could seriously diminish the expectations of the participants in the international economic order.

The first part of this work describes the current approach upon which the proposals for antitrust rely; in the second part, we propose an alternative approach, in the light of the insufficiencies of this policy to promote competition.

The Problem of Competition in International Trade

Market failures and international trade

The conventional theory holds that there is a need to introduce public interest measures to prevent or to correct the monopolistic manipulations of firms enjoying market power aimed either at increasing prices or excluding competitors from the market. The ultimate goal is to prevent them from extracting monopolistic rents from helpless consumers as well as to ensure their access to a wider array of products than otherwise.

This perspective emerged out of a lengthy process of evolution in economic theory, where eventually positive economic theory began to draw normative conclusions about public policy which were immediately accepted by legislators and policy makers alike. In the beginning, there was a widespread acceptance of the benefits of free trade and free markets in promoting social wealth. Generally, the economics profession agrees that the division of

labour and economic exchange arising thereof are the key to economic development. Public policy should not interfere with market functioning, and therefore should be limited to ensuring peace and order. Yet under the influence of the positivistic intellectual climate dominant during the nineteenth century, economic science came to adopt a different view that eventually led them to reconsider their former expectations about market functioning as well as their normative conclusions about public policy to sustain them towards public interest.[5] In particular, this new appraisal (which still dominates the design and implementation of public policy) stressed the structural weakness of markets in producing social wealth, owing to the existence of inherent "failures" that prevent them from achieving a social optimum. Such failures induce markets to depart from a state of "equilibrium" where otherwise they would allocate resources most efficiently throughout society according to their most valuable uses. For this reason, public policy was called on to regulate the conduct of market participants, in order to ensure that none of them introduced distortions into the system. It is easy to see why this regulation was regarded as introduced to protect a "public interest".[6]

As they inevitably departed from the model of "equilibrium" predicated under the new paradigm of thought, the restrictions that market participants introduced to competition became almost immediately regarded contemptuously, as they were assumed to produce a misallocation of social resources for the benefit of unscrupulous rent-seeker monopolists. Consequently, a new concern arose demanding the control of abusive practices addressed to limit and to exclude competitors. In the international arena, these views challenged the former beliefs about the benefits of free trade, already put into question by the old mercantilist views

---

4 *continued*
1995.Internet:http://www.worldbank.org/html/lat/english/papers/trade/cmp_plcy.pdf.) For the purposes of this work we use the term "competition policy" in a wider sense as compared to the sense attributed in some jurisdictions, notably in Europe. Here, competition policy refers to *any* policy aimed at enhancing competition, regardless the form that it adopts. Consequently, deregulation, liberalisation of trade and the elimination of licences, to name a few, are also measures regarded as part of a competition policy since they promote competition in the marketplace.

5 Although the formation of this true "paradigm" (in the Kuhnian sense of the word) was influenced by several intellectual sources, scientific positivism was perhaps the most noticeable trend. According to its premises, positivism relies on empiricism as a tool for the analysis of reality. The influence of the positivist method still dominates "mainstream" economics to a large extent, as argued by De Alessi (L. De Alessi, "Nature and Methodological Foundations of some Recent Extensions of Economic Theory", in *Economic Imperialism: The Economic Approach Outside the field of Economics*, G. Radnizky and P. Bernholz (eds.), Paragon House Publishers, New York, 1987, p. 52). About the influence of positivistic thinking over the public law paradigm of regulation, see, M. Louglin, *Public Law and Political Theory*, Clarendon Press, Oxford, 1992.

6 A summary of the public interest theory of regulation is found in W. Mitchell and R. Simmons, *Beyond Politics: Markets, Welfare and the Failure of Bureaucracy*, Westview Press, Boulder, 1994, pp. 3–37.

towards international trade implemented through protective tariff barriers. Free trade alone was no guarantee that competition would accrue spontaneously.

This view is widely shared by policy makers and scholars alike. For example, at the 1993 Ministerial Meeting of the OECD countries, the Committee on Competition Law and Policy and the Trade Committee submitted a joint progress report on trade and competition policies. They agreed that globalisation should produce more efficient production and marketing, lower prices and improved product quality and variety, but will fail to do so unless market access and competition can be preserved and enhanced.[7]

Similarly, scholars such as Hoekman and Mavroidis argue that "while a free trade stance greatly reduces the scope of the task facing competition authorities, it does not imply that the need for competition rules disappear. Many products are non-tradeable (*e.g.* many services), or, even if tradeable, competition may be limited to local markets for other reasons. Free trade must therefore be complemented by the freedom of entry, including the possibility to contest markets through foreign direct investment. Even then, certain products may be produced by (natural) monopolies, by firms with global market power, or by firms where natural or 'unnatural' (government-made) barriers to entry restrict contestability."[8] Indeed, in their opinion, free trade could be a risky business: "the more open markets are to foreign products, the greater potential vulnerability to anti-competitive practices of foreign monopolists or cartels."[9]

Finally, the "public interest" view of competition policy views the rules regulating competition as a necessary complement to the rivalry introduced by a liberal trade policy. The implicit premise is that markets alone may create obstacles to their functioning. For this reason, antitrust supporters argue that it is necessary to distinguish between "fair" and "unfair" market behaviour, and to minimise the negative effects of the latter.

Origins of the rules for the protection of international competition

In order to translate into positive law the former theoretical premises, governments began to introduce legislation addressed to restrictions to competition and other unfair practices of market exchanges, both domestically and internationally. The connecting thread between both antitrust legislation and unfair trade practices legislation is evident, as both sets of legislation aimed at the ultimate goal of preserving the "purity and transparency" of market transactions. They emerged in the wake of a generalised trade protectionism, being regarded as a "second best solution" for the lack of competition arising from the foreclosure of international markets to foreign competition. In this sense, they both represented official attempts to administer competition according to some "public standard". Antitrust was merely regarded a complement to trade protectionism, to which unfair trade legislation belonged.[10] It is important to grasp the connection between both policies in order to understand why the proposal aiming for the substitution of antitrust rules for anti-dumping rules would not introduce a true reform to the policy of promoting competition but would merely amount to a restatement of the old policy, albeit supported by a more elaborate theoretical framework, and with a somewhat different scope. In turn, this will lead us to the conclusion that a different approach is needed if policy makers sincerely strive to promote competition.

7 OECD Working Papers, Trade and Competition Policies, No. 35, Paris, 1994, p. 2.
8 B. M. Hoekman and P. C. Mavroidis, Linking Competition and Trade Policies in Central and East European Countries, Policy Research Working paper 1346, The World Bank, Washington, D.C., 1994, p. 3.
9 *ibid.* Further, Trebilcock argues that "While some have argued that completely unrestricted international trade largely obviates the need for domestic competition laws, there are reasons for scepticism about this claim. First, even in the traded goods sector, depreciated exchange rates and transportation costs may often attenuate the impact of import competition, and in the non-traded goods sector, especially the service sector which is an increasingly important element in many domestic economies, import competition will not often be an effective competitive threat, and restrictions on foreign investment (an effective market presence rather than effective market access) may be more salient impediments to offshore competition." (M. Trebilcock, "Reconciling Competition Laws and Trade Policies: A New Challenge to International Cooperation, in *Comparative Competition Policy: National Institutions in a Global Market*, G. B. Doern and S. Wilks (eds.), Clarendon Press, Oxford, 1996, pp. 269–270.

10 For example, Trebilcock argues: "Competition laws were enacted in Canada and the USA late in the last century at the same time as their governments were adopting high tariff policies. Thus, for a good past of the ensuing century, competition laws in these two countries were interpreted and applied in a deep 'second-best' world, where domestic competition was promoted in contexts where foreign competition was often severely restrained by self-imposed protectionist trade policies." n. 9 above, p. 269.

Dumping and subsidies as "unfair" trade practices under international commerce

In the realm of international relations, where trade was fragmented and obstructed by government (tariff and non-tariff) barriers the goal of a policy aimed to promote competition was relatively straightforward: this policy should ensure that commercial relations were conducted in such a way as to reflect the "true" competitive advantages of its participants. It was therefore on the grounds of defining the true competitive advantage of nations that policy makers could ultimately isolate those cases regarded as "unfair" under international trade. Only by protecting trade flows from business or government manipulation could trading countries reasonable expect that imports introduced into their respective domestic markets would truly enjoy a fair advantage over their national production and not be the subject of any artificial support from governments or from monopolistic firms interested in excluding domestic competitors by undercutting prices.

However, it was only in 1947 that these unfair practices in international trade became the subject of multilateral regulation for the first time. The GATT introduced specific legislation dealing with "dumping" and "export subsidies".[11] Conventionally, dumping is defined as "exporting at prices below those charged on the domestic market (or, if none, on a third-country market) or at prices insufficient to cover the cost of the goods sold".[12] On the other hand, export subsidies comprise any help "paid to an industry on products that are exported".[13]

Limitations of the unfair trade legislation to deal with the complexity of competition

The GATT rules on dumping and subsidies represent a first attempt at multilateral control over business conducts regarded as "unfair". However, that these endeavours were insufficient to promote fair competition and even counterproductive became evident as soon as the effects of other forms of trade barriers over commerce decreased in significance, particularly tariff barriers. These obstacles, by allowing an unchecked power on authorities to regulate commerce, disguised the potential effects of unfair trade measures as non-tariff barriers. Such dangers became quite obvious as soon as governments realised the advantages of replacing tariff protection (subject to reduction and relatively easy multilateral surveillance) by more subtle means of trade protection.

To avoid this problem, governments aimed to improve the rules governing multilateral trade. Unlike former rounds of negotiations, mostly addressed to achieve tariff reductions through the most-favoured-nation clause, the Uruguay Round was primarily devoted to improving the rules governing the commercial conduct of its participants. Although the aftermath of the process evidenced a clear improvement in the definition of the rules dealing with export subsidies, it did not solve the problems associated to the exercise of government discretion in the field of anti-dumping. Indeed, the round succeeded in notably improving the ex-ante definition of those ("red") subsidies forbidden under the international rules and those permitted ("green"), thus reducing considerably the number of grey cases of subsidies subject to an ex-post determination of injury ("yellow") which formerly enabled a great deal of discretion on behalf of national trade authorities.[14]

However, in the case of dumping, the round did not succeed in eliminating effectively the substantive sources of administrative discretion which remained almost untouched. Instead it was content merely to deal with the procedural shortcomings of the current legislation, in the expectation of reducing administrative discretion to a tolerable level.[15]

---

11 This regulation is developed in the following way: In regard to anti-dumping, Article VI of the GATT comprises a general definition of dumping and regulates the use of anti-dumping measures; the Uruguay Round Code on Anti-dumping specifies the general framework laid down by GATT's Article VI. In connection with export subsidies, the original GATT agreement regulated subsidies on four levels: 1) Article XVI, paragraph 1 set a loose reporting requirement; 2) Article XVI, paragraphs 3 and 4 regulated the restraints on export subsidies; 3) Article XXIII regulated the restraints over new domestic subsidies; and 4) Article VI governed the imposition of countervailing duties. The Uruguay Round Agreement on Subsidies and Countervailing Measures developed these provisions in a systematic way.

12 J. Jackson, W. Davey and Alan Sykes, *Legal Problems of International Economic Relations*, West Publishing Co., St Paul, Minn., 1995, pp. 671–672.

13 *ibid.*, p. 758.

14 *ibid.*, pp. 769–770. See also GATT Focus Newsletter, GATT Secretariat, Dec. 1993, at 10–11.

15 To name some procedural improvements, the Uruguay Round unified the criteria followed for the determination of injury in both anti-dumping and countervailing cases; it also committed countries to follow an "injury determination" formerly set aside unilaterally by some countries (notably, the U.S.) benefiting from their grandparent's rights; further, the

Thus, the round failed to challenge the key issue, namely, the nature of dumping as an "unfair" behaviour. In this regard, Ordover *et al.*, for instance, argue that selling exports at prices below the home market price is not necessarily indicative of "unfairness", and instead may show a healthy strategy of business rivalry.[16]

Indeed, the unavoidable vagueness in the determination of "dumping" invites national trade authorities to exercise their discretion in determining what imports will be regarded as being sold at a dumping price. This vague character emerges from the very determination of the dumping margin, which is used as the basis of calculation of anti-dumping duties. To calculate the margin of dumping it is necessary to determine the "normal value" of the merchandise; to do so, three alternative rules are followed. The normal value will be calculated on the basis of the price of sale of a similar merchandise in the country of origin, deducting transport and other similar expenses. If this price is not ascertainable, the normal value will be determined by reference to the sale price of a similar merchandise in a third market, again making similar deductions. If it is impossible to ascertain these values, the normal value will be constructed on the basis of its estimated production costs, less deductions.[17]

It is easy to see why these rules amount to absolute uncertainty as to the rights of importers and other participants in international trade. Indeed, it is evident that uncontrolled discretion is granted to the administrative agencies by virtue of these rules. This is so because the determination of what

is a normal value in a specific case depends upon the construction of inevitably arbitrary assumptions. For example, what is a "similar product"? Strictly speaking, the production of one firm will inevitably be different from the rest, particularly if one considers the subjective nature of the costs involved. Thus, "similarity" must be by definition arbitrary. For this reason, it is not surprising that in most cases, anti-dumping authorities find no "similar product" available, and thus determine the normal value of the products with reference to the constructed value. Needless to say, this "constructed value" measure is an even more misleading and arbitrary rule, based upon the false assumption that it is possible to determine objectively the costs involved in producing the goods. Again, similar caveats apply to this case.[18] Finally, there are further minor substantive shortcomings in the anti-dumping legislation, such as the determination of expenses incurred to be considered in the respective deduction.[19]

These circumstances left regulatory gaps to be used by anti-dumping agencies to exercise trade protectionism, which in turn has led to mounting criticism over the rules.[20]

Enforcement of antitrust rules over international trade

Owing to the shortcomings mentioned in the preceding section, commentators are increasingly in

---

15 *continued*
new code introduced a special concern over the transparency and publicity of procedures, and also states general criteria to follow in the submission of evidence, setting minimum limits of dumping margin to open procedures, and so forth (A. Avila *et al.*, n. 1 above, p. 154).

16 These authors correctly point out that a firm may exercise monopoly power in its home market, and sell at lower prices to the export market. This lower price could still be above marginal cost (otherwise, it would be predation, and therefore unfair). The fact that such price *above* marginal costs may still be regarded as dumping, and subject to prosecution by anti-dumping agencies, reveals that the regulation is incapable of making a proper distinction between truly unfair and healthy competitive business behaviour. (J. Ordover, A. Sykes and R. Willig, *Unfair International Trade Practices*, PP-19, C.V. Starr Center for Applied Economics, New York University, Department of Economics, Sept. 1982, pp. 6-16).

17 See Agreement on Implementation of Article VI of GATT, Article II paragraph 2.1 (normal value calculated on the basis of sales made in domestic markets) and Article II paragraph 2.2 (normal value calculated on the basis of sales to a third country, and normal value calculated on the basis of costs of production).

18 The lure of objective costs is indeed one of the most entrenched notions in the models from mainstream economics. This notion is inconsistent with the subjective nature of costs. Indeed, costs represent first and foremost the value foregone as a consequence of adopting a certain course of action. This value cannot be ascertained by anyone other than whoever makes such decision. For an explanation about the subjective nature of value, see T. Taylor, *The Fundamentals of Austrian Economics*, Adam Smith Institute, London, 1980, pp. 14-15, 26-34.

19 A. Avila *et al.*, n. 1 above, pp. 138-139.

20 For example, Messerlin regards anti-dumping rules as "undesirable and perverse" (P. Messerlin, "Should Antidumping rules be replaced by National or International Competition Rules?", 18 *World Competition Law and Economics Rev.* [1995], p. 37). On the other hand, Trebilcock argues: "While the trade liberalization that has occurred in the post-war period under GATT and under various regional trading arrangements—such as the E.C., the FTA (Free Trade Agreement), and now NAFTA (North American Free Trade Agreement)—has mitigated these tensions, many trade restrictions still remain. Such restrictions are now less likely to be in the form of tariffs, and instead take the form of quantitative restrictions and the increasing utilization of trade remedy laws, in particular anti-dumping laws, with many countries adopting anti-dumping regimes for the first time during the 1980s, and utilization rates world-wide growing dramatically during the 1990s." (Trebilcock, n. 9 above, p. 269.) A more extended analysis about the protectionist use of anti-dumping remedies is found in M. Leidy, *Antidumping: Unfair Trade or Unfair Remedy?*, Finance & Development, IMF-World Bank, March 1995.

favour of replacing anti-dumping provisions by a more elaborated set of rules enabling a more proper regulation of the problems associated to competition in international trade. A sophisticated framework is increasingly perceived as necessary to deal with the greater complexity of transnational business transactions in the contemporary world. This initiative is far from being new.[21]

Antitrust rules appear an ideal substitute for anti-dumping legislation for several reasons. First, unlike the attention paid by anti-dumping rules to the protection of domestic competitors, antitrust rules proclaim the promotion of competition in the market place as their foremost goal. In the conventional wisdom, this focus somehow directs legal enforcement towards the "right" goal, namely, the protection of economic efficiency and consumer sovereignty, rather than inefficient domestic producers.[22] In other words, antitrust partisans assume that policy goals, once declared, will inexorably lead to enforcement, at least if the "right" people enforce the policy according to the declared goals. Second,

antitrust is attractive to these scholars because it apparently diminishes government discretion associated to the substantive definition of "dumping", vaguely described under the current anti-dumping statutes. In this regard, the concepts of both discriminatory and predatory pricing[23] appear to provide grounds for more elaborate analysis, and therefore less discretion in the hands of enforcement agencies. Finally, antitrust would allow the incorporation of a cluster of behaviours not covered under the current regulations, which nevertheless constitute expressions of "unfairness" in international trade. For example, F. S. Scherer lists the following conduct deserving international antitrust surveillance, not covered by present unfair trade practices legislation: price fixing or other output restrictions among exporting firms; economic concentration through merger and acquisition; voluntary export restraint;[24] as well as others.[25]

Thus, the present inadequacy of unfair trade legislation in dealing with these issues, and the numerous exemptions to antitrust prosecution allowed to "export" cases, lead to the conclusion that it would be beneficial to adopt international antitrust rules.[26]

However, assuming the need for international antitrust rules, the question emerges: which set of rules should apply? In this connection, scholars frequently regard domestic antitrust legislation as insufficient to deal with international restrictions,

21 The introduction of antitrust rules in international trade is not recent, nor are efforts to develop multilateral antitrust rules. The Havana Charter incorporated specific rules to regulate restrictive business practices, such as the prohibition of price agreements among competitors, fixing sale or purchasing quotas, the limitation of production or fixing production quotas. The Havana Charter would have obliged the members of the proposed International Trade Organization to take appropriate measures to prevent private commercial enterprises that had "effective control of trade" from "restrain[ing] competition, limit[ing] access to markets, or foster[ing] monopolistic control in international trade." (Art. 46, Ch. 5, Havana Charter for an International Trade Organization, U.N. Doc. E/Conf. 2/78 (1948), reprinted in U.N. Doc. ICITO/1/4 (1948).) Later, during the 1970s, much attention on international antitrust was related to the control of multinational enterprises. The aftermath of this focus was the adoption, in 1980, by the U.N. Assembly, of the Set of Equitable Principles Multilaterally Agreed for the Control of Restrictive Business Practices. More recently, the attention on international antitrust has been aroused again, this time associated to the extension of trade disciplines to new areas of regulation, in the Uruguay Round. The history of international antitrust is well explained in N. Yacheistrova, "The International Competition Regulation", 18 *World Competition Law and Economics Rev.* [1994]. See also E. Fox, "Competition Law and the Agenda for the W.T.O.", in *Antitrust: A New International Trade Remedy?*, J. Haley & H. Iyori (eds.), Pacific Rim Law & Policy Association, Seattle, 1995, pp. 2–7.

22 In this regard, Trebilcock argues: "Tensions between the objectives and application of domestic competition laws, and international trade policy have a long genesis." (Trebilcock, n. 9 above, p. 269.) Further, Hoekman and Mavroidis state the following: "Trade policy is consequently often inconsistent with the objectives underlying competition policy. The way this inconsistency is frequently put is that competition law aims at protecting competition (and thus economic efficiency) while trade policy aims at protecting competitors (or factors of production)." (n. 8 above, p. 2.)

23 According to Ordover and Willig, there is evidence of predatory objectives whenever the exclusion of competitors increases the monopoly power of incumbent firms in the market. To be predatory, such increase in monopoly power must be the ultimate cause of the rival's exit from the market (Ordover and Willig, "An Economic Definition of Predation", 91 Yale L.J. 8 [1981]).

24 The proposed inclusion of these agreements under the scope of antitrust is somewhat puzzling, as they are concluded between governments and not firms. Further, they refer not only to dumping situations, but also imports enjoying subsidies, or simply a competitive advantage. About the nature and effects of these agreements in international commerce, see generally *Competition and Trade Policies: their Interaction*, O.E.C.D., Paris, 1984, pp. 16–17.

25 F. M. Scherer, *Competition Policies for an Integrated World Economy*, The Brookings Institution, Washington, D.C., 1994, pp. 43–88.

26 See *Los Nuevos Temas del Comercio*, SP/CL/XXI.O DT No. 13, XXI Reunión Ordinaria del Consejo Latinoamericano, Sistema Económico Latinoamericano. Traditionally, it is assumed that antitrust discretion would work in such way to favour their unenforceability to domestic producers in "export cases". This is the reasoning which leads to the adoption of international antitrust rules. (See, e.g. A. Haagsma, "An International Competition Policy as a Means to Create an Open Global Market Place", in *International Harmonization of Competition Laws*, C.-J. Cheng et al. (eds.), Martinus Nijhoff Publishers, London, 1995, pp. 409–426.)

owing to the numerous exceptions granted to export cartels, as well as other loopholes enabling infringing firms to avoid prosecution in their domestic jurisdictions. Also, and no less important, there are several problems associated with the extraterritorial enforcement of domestic antitrust provisions in various cases. For example, the United States has attempted to exercise its antitrust provisions to prosecute domestic subsidiaries of foreign corporations allegedly involved in manipulations to restrain competition.[27] Despite the rise of a more flexible trend in court decisions which regard the principle of extraterritorial effects in the light of international principles of comity, it is unlikely that such problems will disappear.[28]

For this reason, there is an increasing tendency for commentators to advocate the development of international standards to regulate competition internationally. There is a variety of alternative solutions.

First, the negotiation has been proposed of an international set of ad hoc rules which would be imposed "from the top" into the legislation of states. This solution has already been attempted (albeit unsuccessfully) by a group of trade and competition experts from the Max Planck Institut in Munich;

it adopted the form of a Multilateral Antitrust Code, to be celebrated within the framework of GATT.[29] According to this proposal, there would be a set of five basic principles of consensus which would be incorporated into the domestic legislation of each member country:

1) national enforcement of antitrust laws;
2) observance of a principle of equality as between foreign and domestic competition;
3) enforcement of minimum standards in the regulation of domestic antitrust against restrictive conduct of international dimension;
4) the use of GATT sanctions to ensure the non-discriminatory use of international rules of competition;
5) the Code would apply to transnational cases exclusively.[30]

---

27 The U.S. courts have been particularly active in extending the jurisdiction of the Sherman Act over cartels formed abroad. The principle of extraterritoriality had already been established in the *ALCOA* case (*United States v. Aluminium Co. of Am.*, 148 F.2d 416, 443 2d Cir. 1945). However, it was the Uranium case (*Westinghouse Elec. Corp. v. Rio Algom Ltd. in re Uranium Antitrust Litigation*, 617 F.2d 1248 7th Cir. 1980) which evidenced the difficulties of enforcing the principle, as shown by the diplomatic protest of several states who consequently enacted blocking statutes, such as the Canadian Uranium Information Security Regulations of 1976, or the Australian Foreign Proceedings Act. Furthermore, the claw-back provision of the U.K. Protection of Trading Interests Act of 1980 provides for the recovery of the non-compensatory portion of treble damage awards made by U.S. courts.
28 Decisions such as *Timberlane Lumber Co. v. Bank of America* (574 F. Supp. 1453, 1466 N.D.Cal. 1983) or *Manington Mills Inc. v. Congoleum Corp.* (595 F.2d 1287, 1297 3d Cir. 1979), established a rule of reason based on the principle of "international comity", which lessened the stringency of the extraterritorial principle. As a result of this trend, according to Trebilcock, the U.S. Department of Justice adopted its "DOJ International Antitrust Guidelines" comprising the principles and conditions that the agency would consider before ascertaining its jurisdiction over an extraterritorial case. (Trebilcock, n. 9 above, p. 275; also U. Immenga, "Export Cartels and Voluntary Export Restraints between Trade and Competition Policy", in *Antitrust: A New International Trade Remedy?*", J. Haley & H. Iyori (eds.), Pacific Rim Law & Policy Association, Seattle, 1995, pp. 112–113.)
However, the matter is far from being settled and the objection to allowing a rule of reason in this field still persists, as evidenced in *National Bank of Canada v. Interbank Card Association* (666 F.2d 6, 8 2d Cir. 1981), *Laker Airways Ltd v. Sabena* (731 F.2d D.C.Cir. 1984).

29 BNA Antitrust & Trade Reg. Rep., vol. 64, no. 1628 (Aug. 19, 1993) More recently supporting the idea of an international antitrust code, see Y-P. Chu, "Towards the Establishment of an Order of Competition for the International Economy: With References to the Draft International Antitrust Code, the Parallel Imports Problem, and the Experience of Taiwan, ROC," in *International Harmonization of Competition Laws*, C.-J. Cheng, L. S. Liu and C.-K. Wang (eds.), Martinus Nijhoff Publishers, London, 1995. An alternative view is presented by W. Fikentscher, "On the Proposed International Antitrust Code", in *Antitrust: A New International Trade Remedy?*, J. Haley & H. Iyori (eds.), Pacific Rim Law & Policy Association, Seattle, 1995, pp. 345–357.
30 Scherer also proposes some guidelines that could be incorporated into such an international antitrust code. His proposals are as follows: 1) Following ratification of an international compact, an International Competition Policy Office (ICPO) will be created within the ambit of the new WTO. It will have both investigative and enforcement responsibilities; 2) A year after the new Competition Policy agreement is ratified, all substantial single-nation export and import cartels and all cartels operating across boundaries must be registered, and the mechanisms of their operation must be documented with the ICPO. "Substantial" comprises cartels exceeding $100 million in sales a year. Also, all enterprises originating 40% or more of world exports must register with the ICPO, providing details of their annual sales and the locations of their principal operations; 3) Following a petition of a signatory nation that trade has been restricted or distorted by a monopolistic practice, the ICPO will study the alleged practices, publishing the results of its investigation and recommendations for correction; 4) Within three years after the creation of the ICPO, representatives of the signatory nations will agree upon a common format for reporting information on the supply and international trading activities of substantial enterprises that propose to merge. A previous notification must be filed. The ICPO will distribute the information of the competition agencies of all affected nations; 5) Within five years after the creation of the ICPO, all signatories will enact legislation prohibiting export cartels; 6) Within six years after the creation of the ICPO, all signatories will enact legislation prohibiting import cartels; 7) After seven years, the ICPO will accept complaints about the alleged abuse of monopoly powers by cartels or by any substantial enterprise (40% world's output). 8) After seven years, the ICPO will accept complaints about notified substantial mergers with probable

Secondly, there are proponents of the harmonisation of domestic antitrust standards with international standards; this process would develop international legislation "from the bottom", by means of bilateral or multilateral co-operation agreements negotiated to solve specific problems. This solution has already been followed in agreements entered into by the United States with Canada,[31] Australia,[32] Germany[33] and more recently the European Union.[34]

Third, some scholars assume that endorsing multilateral competition standards is an impractical or difficult goal, and therefore concentrate, perhaps more pragmatically, on the use of the current instruments of control. Under these proposals, they either assign domestic antitrust authorities the task of reviewing the effects of anti-dumping standards when examining a case,[35] or propose an extended interpretation of certain key GATT provisions and principles, which would eventually allow for coverage of restrictive conduct not encompassed by express provisions.[36]

Finally, Fox proposes a more "constitutional" approach which would identify those strengths and limitations of competition as applied to international commerce in order to identify an international agenda of action. This proposal, in her opinion, would overcome the limitations of all the former proposals, either too ambitious or unrealistic (*i.e.* negotiating an international antitrust code) or too narrowly focused (*i.e.* harmonising domestic antitrust criteria) or no solution at all (*i.e.* the use of current GATT provisions).[37]

Shortcomings of Antitrust Policy in Promoting Competition

The different proposals outlined above of antitrust enforcement in international trade are unable to solve the fundamental flaws implicit in the basic assumption of its supporters, namely, that antitrust laws do in fact promote competition, and therefore that they should be enforced in order to promote international trade relations.

Indeed, these proposals present deficiencies on three different levels. First, the model of *perfect* competition and *static* markets underlying antitrust policy bears little resemblance to competition as it

---

30 *continued*
effects (concentrations of more than 40% of world trade). 9) Should a substantial firm continue to control 40% of world trade for a period longer than twenty years on the basis of validly issued patents or copyrights, any signatory nation may require the compulsory licensing of the firm's patents or copyrights within its jurisdiction at reasonable royalties. 10) After seven years, the ICPO will receive complaints concerning monopolistic practices which distort international trade that are not expressly covered above. 11) None of this prevents any signatory nation from implementing more stringent rules within its own national market. (F. M. Scherer, n. 25 above, pp. 91–97.)

31 23 I.L.M., 275.

32 20 I.L.M., 702.

33 Agreement between the Government of the United States of America and the Government of the Federal Republic of Germany relative to Mutual Co-operation on Restrictive Business Practices (1976).

34 Agreement between the Commission of the European Communities and the Government of the United States of America relative to the Enforcement of their Competition Laws, Washington, Sept. 23, 1991.

35 B. Hoekman and P. Mavroidis, Antitrust-based Remedies and Dumping in International Trade, Policy Research Working Paper No. 1347, The World Bank, Washington, D.C., 1994. The goal sought under this proposal is to ensure that domestic markets remain contestable notwithstanding the enforcement of anti-dumping.

36 B. Hoekman and P. Mavroidis, Competition, Competition Policy and the GATT, Policy Research Working Paper No. 1228, The World Bank, Washington, D.C., 1993. Under this proposal, the authors suggest that current GATT rules and case law provide ample scope for disputes to be brought before the GATT that relate to the application and the non-application of existing domestic competition laws of GATT Contracting Parties. In particular, they propose to overcome the limitation that by definition GATT mechanisms apply to private entities by treating anti-competitive measures as resulting from government

36 *continued*
behaviour, either in the form of official approval (*e.g.* an antitrust exemption) or other support (*e.g.* trade barriers). The point is that if a Contracting Party supports business practices leading to a *de facto* if not *de jure* discrimination against foreign products GATT dispute settlement procedures may be invoked. Thus, measures inconsistent with Article III (National Treatment) or with complementary rules on state-trading enterprises and quantitative restrictions (Articles XVII and XI), may give rise to a "violation" complaint under Article XXIII:1 (a). Measures that are not inconsistent with the General Agreement, but nullify or impair an existing concession, may give rise to a so-called "non-violation" complaint under Article XXIII:1 (b).

On the other hand, Trachtman holds that theoretically GATT could apply to those restrictions of competition not enforced or exempted from domestic legislation. These cases could be regarded as domestic subsidies, under GATT's provisions; consequently, they could promote commercial compensation. However, there is little control of the use of domestic subsidies; indeed, GATT provisions deal foremost with the effects of "export subsidies", against which it allows the use of countervailing measures. (J. Trachtman, "International Regulatory Competition, Externalization and Jurisdiction", 34 *Harvard International L.J.*, pp. 47–104.).

In such a framework, antitrust complaints would be presented as government disputes. In other words, they would be brought only if they are supported by a Contracting Party. The conduct must also violate some GATT obligation. Hence, for example, a cartel agreement exemption would not be immediately void, unless the government supports the operation of the cartel through other policies.

37 E. Fox, "Competition Law and the Agenda for the WTO", in *Antitrust: A New International Trade Remedy?*, J. Haley and H. Iyori (eds.), Pacific Rim Law & Policy Association, Seattle, 1995, pp. 1–36.

is in the real world; hence the pretension of antitrust supporters to use this model as a normative landmark is completely unfounded and misleading for public policy purposes. Secondly, antitrust partisans overlook the actual negative effect of antitrust policies, in the light of the incentives that political actors face when designing and enforcing this policy. Thirdly, antitrust policy introduces an *absolute* uncertainty upon the transactions of economic agents, as the discretionary powers of enforcing agencies cannot be submitted to judicial review effectively, owing to the nature of economic evidence as well as to the arbitrary implications of positive economic models upon which antitrust theories are constructed.

Inability of the perfect competition model to deliver adequate normative conclusions

As Petermann aptly observes, the conglomerate of economic activities from different actors in the international sphere comprises an "international economic order".[38] The nature of this order is essentially "dynamic" in the sense that it results from the interaction of its participants. As put by Taylor, "The process of interaction and co-operation is the essence of the market; the market is not something physical but a process."[39] Owing to its nature as process, market events take place in "real" time; they are in constant "disequilibrium". Further, individuals interact in the market in order to unfold hidden information about consumer tastes, to develop cheaper means of production, more effective techniques of distribution, more capable technologies, and in general to overcome their "ignorance" about opportunities of profit. They do so by collaborating and competing one against another.[40]

By contrast, the model of perfect competition underlying antitrust theory depicts efficient markets in exactly the opposite way: complete information (present and future) about consumer preferences, tastes, available resources and technologies; comprising multiple sellers and buyers; and characterised by the presence of a constant "equilibrium" or static relationships among its elements. These conditions ensure that markets allocate resources most efficiently, allocating resources to their best valuable use among members of society.

Under this view real markets are represented as "imperfect" structures chronically departing from the stringent conditions set up by the model, or, to put it differently, subject to "failures" that lessen the level of efficiency which otherwise would accrue. Consequently, there is no wonder that the model possess a normative inclination to hold government intervention necessary to correct these failures. Antitrust policy appears in this context as a single case of justified intervention to put things in order.[41]

While it is true that this positive model is useful to express the mathematical relationships among the variables of the model in order to understand how market forces work, it seems incapable of delivering an accurate picture of competition in the real world. In fact, by assuming a perfect knowledge among market participants, the model eliminates the need of competition to obtain such information.[42]

---

38 E.-U. Petermann, *Constitutional Functions and Constitutional Problems of International Economic Law*, PUPIL 3, University Press Fribourg, Switzerland, 1991.
39 He also adds: "The tendency to ascribe to the market economy the characteristics of being something other than the events caused by the choices and actions of individuals is incorrect." (Taylor, n. 18 above, p. 35.).
40 On the dynamic nature of competition, see F. A. Hayek, "The Meaning of Competition", in *Individualism and Economic Order*, The University of Chicago Press, Routledge, London, 1948, pp. 92–106. Similarly, J. M. Clark, "Toward a Concept of Workable Competition", *The American Economic Review*, Vol. XXX, June 1940; F. Machlup, "Competition, Pliopoly and Profit", *Economica*, Vol. IX (1942), No. 33. More recently, the Austrian School of Economics has developed these seminal ideas and consequently has attempted an alternative explanation of markets and competition as processes performed in the course of time. (See C. Taylor, *The Fundamentals of Austrian Economics*, Adam Smith Institute, London, 1980; also, R. Langlois, "Economics as a Process", Introductory Paper for a Liberty Fund symposium, October 13–15, 1982, pp. 29–44; an

40 *continued*
extensive discussion about the fundamentals of the Austrian view over markets is found in I. Kirzner, *The Meaning of Market Process: Essays in the Development of Modern Austrian Economics*, Routledge, London, 1992. The dynamic view of competition is explained in I. Kirzner, *Competition and Entrepreneurship*, University of Chicago Press, Chicago, 1973.
41 As Langlois argues: "[The conclusions of the perfect competition model] consist in comparing real-world states of affairs with the hypothetical states of affairs that, in the general-equilibrium model, can be shown to be Pareto optimal. It is in this practice—and it is a widespread one—that Demsetz [H. Demsetz, "Information and Efficiency: Another Viewpoint", 12 *Journal of Law and Economics*, [1969], p. 1] branded the 'nirvana' approach, the comparison of actual situations with an impossible ideal. And, to the extent that the failure of competition to live up to this hypothetical standard is taken as justification for government intervention, the welfare comparison necessarily implies a hidden value judgement that such government intervention is the more efficient institutional arrangement." (Langlois, n. 40 above, p. 41).
42 See also generally I. Kirzner, n. 41 above, and G. O'Driscoll, "Monopoly in Theory and Practice", in *Method, Process and Austrian Economics*, I. Kirzner (ed.), Lexington Books, Toronto, 1982, pp. 189–214. The insufficiency of the perfect competition model is thoroughly explained in G. B. Richardson, *Information and Investment: A Study in the Working of the Competitive Economy*, Oxford University Press, London, 1960. A recent work by Machovec explains the origins of the change in the paradigm dominating the study of

Further, the use of this model as a normative yardstick to judge real markets is excessive. This is particularly noticeable in the lack of attention that the model gives to the behaviour of the firm, which is regarded as a "black box". Antitrust policy draws normative conclusions about the behaviour of entrepreneurs, yet its underlying theory completely neglects the analysis of their behaviour in the real world. Obviously, this theoretical limitation seriously undermines the consistency of the policy of developing normative conclusions about business behaviour.[43]

From another viewpoint, these conclusions lead to a new normative appraisal over traditionally suspected restrictive practices. From such a new perspective, such conduct, which currently appears "negative" and restrictive of "perfect competition" (in the sense of departing from the model) would be regarded as positive initiatives displayed by businessmen to facilitate the process of discovery of scattered information and to improve the imperfect assignment of rights granted by the state.[44]

Government failures in the exercise of antitrust policy

A second misconception by supporters of antitrust policy arises from their unfounded assumption that the policy in question is developed and enforced following a "public interest" objective, in principle, the promotion of competition.[45] Empirical evidence presented increasingly shows that such an assumption of benevolence on behalf of governments is proving to be unwarranted, as political agents (bureaucracy, legislators, policy makers, etc.) have clear incentives to diverge from such public welfare, and instead to promote their own welfare.[46] In particular, the empirical studies in the field of antitrust policy are increasingly leading to the following conclusions.

First, that the emergence of the policy is closely related to the protection of local interests in the agricultural sector and some specific industries (*e.g.* railways) which cannot compete with new entrants as the result of the introduction of new technologies reducing production costs.[47]

---

42 *continued*
economics as a result of the introduction of the perfect competition model: F. Machovec, *Perfect Competition and the Transformation of Economics*, Routledge, London, 1995.
43 Critics of the perfect competition model's ability to deliver normative conclusions are numerous. See, for example, F. A. Hayek, *Law, Legislation and Liberty, Vol. 3: The Political Order of a Free People*, University of Chicago Press, Chicago, 1973, chapter 2; also, R. Cordato, *Welfare Economics and Externalities in an Open Ended Universe: A Modern Austrian Perspective*, Kluwer Academic Publishers, Boston, 1992; also, G. B. Richardson, *Information and Investment*, n. 42 above.
44 This occurs, for example, when private parties negotiate dealings to prevent "free riding" from unauthorised parties who would unjustly benefit from the investments made by the contracting parties, with no effort. There are numerous forms of opportunistic behaviour arising from a poor assignment of rights that market participants seek to correct through contractual dealings regarded by antitrust legislation as "restrictive". See H. Lepage, *La nouvelle économie industrielle*, Pluriel (Inédit), Hachette-Librairie Française, Paris, 1989, Chapter "La Théorie Économique des Contrats"; also, B. Klein and K. Leffler, "The Role of Market Forces in Assuring Contractual Performance", *Journal of Law and Economics*, [1979] pp. 297–326; and B. Klein, R. Crawford and A. Alchian, "Vertical Integration, Appropriable Rents, and the Competition Contracting Process", 89 *Journal of Political Economics* [1981], pp. 615–641.

45 The discussion about the goals of antitrust policy involves one of the most debated issues concerning this policy among scholars and policy makers. In this connection, there are two clear trends of thought. On the one hand, there are those that regard antitrust as pursuing economic efficiency, consumer welfare and the promotion of competition. In their view, antitrust should limit itself to ensuring the protection of competition and avoiding any measures that could impair efficient market functioning. On the other, there are those who regard antitrust as a policy guided by socio-political goals, besides the proper functioning of markets. Under this view, the policy should be enforced to protect small and medium enterprises, product diversity and equity in the market place. The concerns under this view are related to the size of modern industrial corporations. The crucial issue here is that there has been no reconciliation between these two conflicting views, and therefore it cannot be stated that antitrust, as it is under positive law, can provide any guidance as to the goals of the policy in international economic relations.
46 A thorough explanation of Public Choice theory is found in W. Mitchell and R. Simmons, n. 6 above, pp. 41–84. The most salient feature of regulation according to this theory is the "capture" of the regulator by regulated industries. (G. Stigler, "The Theory of Economic Regulation", 2 *Bell Journal of Economics and Management Science* [1971], pp. 3–21.) This theory is generally applied to the case of "natural monopolies". In the field of antitrust, the capture occurs too, albeit in more subtle ways. Perhaps the best explanation is found in further refinements of the Capture Theory, arguing that rents are spread among several competing groups and do not benefit only one constituency group, such as the producer: S. Peltzman, "Toward a More General Theory of Regulation", 19 *Journal of Law and Economics* [1976], pp. 211–240. This might explain that antitrust is likely to be shaped by the combined *private* interest of less efficient competitors, government attorneys seeking fame and experience in the field, economists expecting high income from their professional advice as court experts, bureaucracy, litigants, and the like. Several studies dealing with each of these interests have been presented in F. McChesney and W. Shughart (eds.), *The Causes and Consequences of Antitrust: The Public-Choice Perspective*, The University of Chicago Press, Chicago, 1995.
47 T. Di Lorenzo, "The Origins of Antitrust: An Interest-Group Perspective", 5 *International Review of Law and Economics* [1985], pp. 73–90. Also, D. Bourdreaux, T. DiLorenzo and S. Parker, "Antitrust before the Sherman Act", in *The Causes and Consequences of Antitrust: The Public-Choice Perspective*, n. 46 above, pp. 255–270.

Secondly, that the policy is enforced in a way that has little to do with the promotion of competition, and is more related to the protection of particular interests, such as the creation of more bureaucracy and the welfare of law firms and litigants.[48]

Thirdly, that the policy is frequently used by less efficient competitors as a deterrent to competition in order to keep more efficient firms in line or force their exit from the market.[49] In sum, antitrust policy generates costs of enforcement associated to the promotion of grossly inefficient activities and rent-seeking behaviour that are probably more expensive to society than the benefits allegedly brought about by antitrust in terms of enhanced social efficiency.

Discretion of antitrust enforcement and the lack of effective judicial review

Perhaps the most severe limitation of antitrust policy in promoting trade and economic transactions stems from the uncertainty that arises from the discretion exercised by enforcing antitrust agencies. Such discretion is inherent to the nature of antitrust policy,[50] and further it is not possible to exercise judicial control to limit its scope and intensity beyond proper limits. In other words, by its very nature, discretion associated to antitrust enforcement must always be excessive and arbitrary. The lack of control emerges from the impossibility of exercising thoroughly a judicial review of decisions imposing fines or penalties on allegedly misbehaving firms.

Antitrust laws cannot thoroughly define *ex ante* conduct forbidden by legislation; at best they can only describe certain formal features that obscure, rather than clarify, the truth about the restrictive nature of the conducts involved. For example, when listing an exclusive dealing as suspected restrictive behaviour (since it excludes potential competitors

otherwise "enjoying" the possibility of, say, distributing products of a given manufacturer), antitrust statutes cannot determine in advance which of those dealings represents monopolistic behaviour and which is the exercise of a normal business dealing aimed at enhancing efficiency by eliminating the opportunistic behaviour of potential "free-riders" in the market.[51] Antitrust supporters must always resort to *ex post* economic analysis in order to determine, case by case, whether such practices are truly monopolistic and should be eliminated, or whether they are efficient and should be upheld.

The fact that antitrust legislation cannot identify properly what practices are subject to prohibition should already send a signal of warning about its possible negative effects.[52] Nevertheless it is the analysis of the economic evidence that shows the arbitrary character of the antitrust process as a whole. Indeed, the question here is, how do positive economic analysis and evidence enable us to distinguish proper from improper competitive behaviour in the marketplace? In this regard, it must be noticed that the premises upon which antitrust theory builds its normative assumptions about the true nature of restrictive behaviour have been increasingly subject to reappraisal and criticism. In particular, both the doctrine of concentration and the doctrine of barriers to entry, which formerly upheld the economic determinism of the structure-conduct-performance paradigm,[53] have been challenged by new empirical evidence. This new evidence shows that concentration does not determine the fate of competition in markets, and that barriers to entry may be evidence of efficiencies developed by entrepreneurs in highly competitive environments.[54] The models of market behaviour traditionally employed by antitrust supporters cannot serve as normative yardsticks for

---

48 S. Weaver, *The Decision to Prosecute: Organization and Public Policy in the Antitrust Division*, M.I.T. Press, Cambridge, Mass., 1977.

49 A. Rodriguez and M. Coate, "Antitrust Policy for Reforming Economies", 18 *Houston Journal of International Law* [1996], pp. 337; also, W. Baumol and J. Ordover, "Use of Antitrust to Subvert Competition", 28 *Journal of Law & Economics* [1985], pp. 247–266. This is similar to what Bork refers to as "predation through governmental processes" (R. Bork, *The Antitrust Paradox: A Policy at War with Itself*, Basic Books Publisher, New York, 1978, pp. 347–349.)

50 In this regard, I am not alone. See Sir G. Borrie, Q.C., "The Need for Discretion in the Application of Competition Law", in *International Harmonization of Competition Laws*, C.-J. Cheng *et al.* (eds.), Martinus Nijhoff Publishers, London, 1995, pp. 255–267.

51 On the problem of free riding and its contractual solutions, see for example B. Klein and K. Leffler, "The Role of Market Forces in Assuring Contractual Performance", *Journal of Law and Economics*, [1979] pp. 297–326; also, B. Klein, R. Crawford and A. Alchian, "Vertical Integration, Appropriable Rents, and the Competitive Contracting Process", 89 *Journal of Political Economics* [1981], pp. 615–641.

52 F. A. Hayek, *Constitution of Liberty*, Routledge & Kegan Paul Ltd., London, 1960, pp. 205–220. See also S. Selinger, "The Case Against Ex-Post Facto Laws", 15 *Cato Journal* [1995–1996], pp. 191–213. On the consequences of the retroactive laws on individual rights and the Rule of Law, see J. Jowell, "The Rule of Law Today", in *The Changing Constitution*, J. Jowell and D. Oliver (eds.), Clarendon Press, Oxford, 1994, pp. 57–78.

53 J. S. Bain, *Barriers to New Competition*, Harvard University Press, Cambridge, Mass., 1956.

54 See, for example, D. T. Armentano, *Antitrust and Monopoly: Anatomy of a Policy Failure*, The Independent Institute, San Francisco, 1990, p. 1.

policy purposes because economic theory is not really sure about their truthfulness and accuracy.[55]

Further, these shortcomings show the relative value of economic evidence in confirming the existence of restrictive monopolistic behaviour. Economic data can merely state that past actions occurred in a definite way; it cannot predict how economic agents will behave in the future. In this regard, positive economics, upon which antitrust policy relies, cannot attach to a given case under review the consequences predicted by the models of positive economics.[56]

Finally, the very limitations of positive economics in determining with certainty the monopolistic content of a given restrictive practice arise from the impossibility of ascertaining in a particular case whether the conduct subject to analysis is efficient or inefficient. In this regard, the Pareto standard is above all a test measuring interpersonal values, or to be more precise, "assuming" interpersonal values. In other words, it is a test designed to measure "social" efficiency, not individual. For this reason, its operative form entails an assumption that is not possible under antitrust analysis, namely, that the gains and costs of one restrictive agreement can be contrasted with the gains and costs of all other agreements of the same kind. By definition, the standard demands that these *individual* costs and benefits be contrasted with the individual costs and benefits of other similar arrangements in fact entered into by other firms in order to have a *social* account of their convenience.

Such condition is unrealistic in terms of evaluating the personal liability arising from a specific undertaking. Antitrust cannot determine that the efficiencies (and costs) of agreement A are better or worse than those found under agreements B and C. All behaviour (restrictive or not) does bring new improvements over former stages; otherwise the parties would not undertake it.

The question involved in the Pareto standard of whether such individual arrangements bring about efficiencies to third parties (creating positive externalities compensating the negative ones brought by the restriction), to consumers or to society as a whole cannot be solved by balancing the efficiencies and restrictions of the agreement itself. Even within one class of undertakings (say, exclusive distribution agreements) the parties may be motivated to enter into such agreements for various reasons, changing in space and time: the changing preferences of customers may determine that these agreements are more "cost saving" in certain cases as compared to other cases; also, particular products may be likely to be distributed more efficiently by imposing extended periods of time.

The number of examples in this connection is infinite; not to mention those possible examples that could arise if we compare the efficiencies delivered by different kinds of agreements. For example, how can we argue that a franchise is "better" or "worse" (more efficient or less efficient) than another arrangement, say an exclusive supply agreement? That will obviously depend upon the subjective costs involved in the operation to the parties concerned; not on interpersonal ones.

As Rothbard puts it, there is no way that an outside observer can distinguish between purely restrictive behaviour and an efficiency-increasing operation. Efficiency can be increased not only as a result of the advantages resulting from an enhanced plant capacity. The size of the factory is not the only factor the efficiency of which can increase; marketing, advertising, distribution, etc. could also improve. In sum, their difference does not arise from their impact over competition in the marketplace. The difference between these various forms of corporate organisation relies primarily on their permanent or transitory corporate form and not on their profitability. This is why it becomes so difficult

---

[55] In fact, as stated by Langlois, if these models were taken seriously, they would lead to disastrous results. (Langlois, n. 40 above, p. 40).

[56] This observation was made by Mises, who correctly pointed out that this premise is a consequence of the false belief according to which economic behaviour can be assimilated to that of natural phenomena. Physical and natural events are dominated by "laws", since they behave according to patterns of behaviour or regularities easy to predict using empirical evidence. Therefore, past events could somehow "predict" future ones. Yet in the case of economics, this is not possible, as individuals behave purposely, that is, pursuing individual goals that cannot possibly be predicted. (L. Mises, *The Ultimate Foundation of Economic Science: An Essay on Method*, Van Nostrand Company, Inc., Princeton, New Jersey, 1962.) Of course, the positive method has been extremely useful in detecting relationships among its elements, particularly to the idealistic perfect competition model, whose logic, as we have seen, is based upon mathematical *impersonal* relationships. Nevertheless, it is necessary to acknowledge the limitations of the positive model beyond these boundaries, and to apply it cautiously in public policy matters, as Friedman himself agreed. (M. Friedman, "The Methodology of Positive Economics", *Essays in Positive Economics*, M. Friedman (ed.), University of Chicago Press, Chicago, 1953.)

[57] M. Rothbard, *Monopoly and Competition* in "Man, Economy and State: A Treatise on Economic Principles", Vol. II, D. Van Nostrand Company, Inc., Princeton, New Jersey, 1962.

for antitrust rules to distinguish between acceptable and non-acceptable forms of organisation.[57] As Bork emphatically states: "efficiency cannot be studied directly and quantified."[58]

For these reasons, Calabresi finds "pointless" a social welfare test for normative purposes extending to any *ex ante* premise guiding policy attempts: "the set of Pareto superior changes which would make no one worse off and at least one person better off must *ex ante* be a void set. For if strict or fanatical Pareto is the criterion, why wouldn't any change that belonged in the set have already been made? Since, by definition, no one would in any way be hurt by the change, why would anyone object?" He concludes: "the Pareto criterion is of no general use as a normative guide."[59]

For these reasons, it is unreasonable to expect that judicial review can deliver sufficient control over antitrust activity by government officials. For this reason, depending on the level of review allowed under each legislation, judges either state their lack of jurisdiction over the merits of the decision, limiting themselves to a mere formal

revision of its procedural aspects,[60] or end up making statements of social policy, to which they are not

60 This is frequently the case with European laws, where the judicial review of government acts has been traditionally limited to a mere revision of legal formalities due to the continental understanding of the principle of separation of powers which prohibited any interference on the functioning of the executive power. As a result, the understanding of legal rights became severely constrained by the limits provided under positive law, in the absence of an effective judicial protection over government intervention on individual rights. (On the development and consequences of this process, see E. Garcia de Enterria, *La Lengua de los Derechos: La formacion del Derecho Publico europeo tras la Revolucion Francesa*, Alianza Universidad, Madrid, 1994.) It was only after the Second World War that a new constitutionalism emerged, particularly in Germany and those countries which suffered most the positivism of the law as applied by totalitarian regimes. (See Lon. L. Fuller, "Positivism and Fidelity to Law—A Reply to Professor Hart", 71 *Harvard Law Review* [1958], pp. 630–672; also U. Everlin, "El Tribunal de Justicia de las Comunidades Europeas como Tribunal Administrativo", in *La Justicia Administrativa en el Derecho Comparado*, Edit. Civitas, Madrid, 1993, pp. 647 *et seq.*) Yet the pace of judicial control even in these countries is still slow and dominated by formalism. This is the case, for example, of the French judicial review over administrative acts within a special jurisdiction. As argued by Everlin, "In France the Public Administration enjoys a considerable margin of appraisal . . . the courts seem to let themselves become influenced by the allegations of the Public Administration, presuming that it has appraised properly the relevant facts. And of course, they do not review those facts which require a technical or economic analysis." (Everlin, *ibid.*, p. 648.) Furthermore, European scholars highlight the diversity of national jurisdictions in regard to judicial control; as an ex-judge from the European Court of Justice argues: "it is in this area particularly that national interests show their differences". (Lord Mackenzie Stuart, *The European Communities and the Rule of Law*, The Hamlyn Lectures, Stevens and Sons, London, 1977, p. 64.) As contrasted with the French experience, Germany has attempted to develop a more ambitious judicial review. In this country, the emergence of the theory of "essential core of rights" has attempted to provide some protection for individual rights. They have also developed the theory of "unspecified legal concepts" whereby certain concepts contained in statutes lacking a proper legal sense (*e.g.* "competition", "relevant market", "dominance", "market power"), must be interpreted in accordance with social conventions, not according to the whim of the judge. Yet these theories still deny the possibility of questioning the way in which economic theories permeate "social conventions" to influence the judge's appraisal in a given case. Indeed, as we have seen, the "public interest" view of antitrust entails a true paradigm in the Kuhnian sense of the word. These limitations are noticeable in the rulings on European competition policy, notwithstanding certain cases where the European courts have cautiously examined the merits of the cases presented before them, albeit from the models of perfect competition and the "public interest" paradigm of competition policy. (Decision of 17 November 1987, concerning Case 142 and 156/84, *BAT/Phillip Morris*, Rep., 1987, 4487; Decision July 3, 1991, Case C–62/86, *AKZO*. For a different view, see Lord Mackenzie Stuart, *ibid.*, pp. 64–68.)

61 Indeed, it is the legislative power, where the interests of groups within society are balanced and levelled, and not the judicial power which is the proper forum for the discussion of such matters, as rightly observed by Bork (Bork, n. 49 above, pp. 79–80). This is the case in countries where judicial review has few limits (*e.g.* the U.S.).

58 Bork, n. 49 above, p. 192.

59 G. Calabresi, "The Pointlessness of Pareto: Carrying Coase Further", 100 *The Yale Law Journal*, p. 1216. In fact, the attempt to use the Pareto standard in antitrust "efficiency" analysis reveals a misconception about the original use of the standard. The Pareto test is above all an *ordinal* concept of efficiency, and therefore does not reveal any intensity of preference, interpersonal comparability of utilities or conmensurability of different inputs or outputs for its definition. In other words, not even Pareto himself would have agreed to use his test for normative purposes, to make interpersonal comparisons of value: Pareto himself was a convinced ordinalist, who believed that the utilitarian concept of introspective utility was unscientific. Indeed, individuals perceive value differently, as their hierarchy of personal preferences obviously differ. (V. Pareto, *Manual of Political Economy*, Macmillan, London, 1971, p. 113.) In fact, determining an ideal state of affairs following social welfare measures represents an impossible task. Further, while it provides a ranking of allocations of economic goods between individuals, the Pareto test does not permit a ranking of all such allocations. That is to say, there are many different allocations that are Pareto-optimal and which differ with respect to the distribution of real income (*i.e.* utility) among the individuals in society. Therefore, it becomes impossible for the would-be interventionist (antitrust) agency to determine the most adequate allocation considering the distribution of income. (B. Lockwood, *The New Palgrave in Economics: A Dictionary of Economics*, Vol. 3, J. Eatwell, M. Milgate and P. Newman (eds.), Macmillan Press Ltd., 1987, p. 811.) For an extended critique on the use of efficiency as normative yardstick, see M. Rizzo, "The Mirage of Efficiency", 8 *Hofstra Law Review* [1980], pp. 641–658; and M. Rizzo, "Law Amid Flux: The Economics of Negligence and Strict Liability in Tort", 9 *Journal of Legal Studies* [1980], pp. 291–318. In these articles, the author clearly shows the theoretical contradictions of those who pretend to use economic efficiency as a normative yardstick to measure the functioning of the law.

allowed under the constitutional principle of separation of powers.[61]

From another perspective, it is easy to see that the impossibility of identifying what conducts should be regarded as "unfair" or "restrictive of competition" poses an insurmountable problem to any endeavours of harmonising domestic antitrust substantive criteria and/or to develop an international set of antitrust rules. At best, harmonisation is possible in those procedural aspects surrounding the implementation of these rules, as they involve areas of law where consensus has already been built, such as the right not to be condemned without being heard, or the right to submit evidence, and so on. Unlike the *ex post* nature of substantive antitrust issues, such as the definition of a restrictive or inefficient exclusive dealing, these principles involve rules which it is possible to define in advance and can be known by all participants. It is not surprising that the international efforts made so far have been mostly oriented in this direction.

As a consequence of these reasons, it must be concluded that if applied to economic transactions and international trade, antitrust policy bears a high risk of obstructing such transactions. Under such conditions, it is very likely that if implemented to regulate international trade, antitrust will simply reproduce the protectionism of present anti-dumping rules, constituting a new non-tariff barrier. This is not surprising, considering the enormous and uncontrolled degree of discretion vested upon enforcing agencies. It is to be expected that such agencies would be inclined to find anti-competitive the aggressive conduct of foreign firms undermining the position of local firms as a result of what would otherwise be understood as healthy competitive behaviour.[62]

Indeed, the transparency of international trade is endangered by the proposals calling for antitrust intervention. The danger lies in introducing, as part of the institutional framework governing international trade relations, rules and principles that could increase the opportunities for countries to develop opportunistic behaviour and disguised trade protectionism. Indeed, given the considerable (to say the least) amount of discretion entertained by antitrust provisions, there is the risk that by incorporating these provisions into the set of institutions governing trade, the latter will be severely hampered,

rather than being fostered. These terms are easily confused, as shown, for example, by the opinion of Hoekman and Mavroidis in this regard: "We argue that efforts might more productively center on ensuring that current GATT (or post-Uruguay Round) rules and principles enhancing competition are actually applied by contracting parties, and on further attempts to eliminate the 'loopholes' in the GATT allowing contracting parties to impose trade restrictions."[63] In the light of these considerations and the discretion entertained, it is naive to believe that antitrust principles would eliminate "loopholes" of the institutional rules governing trade. Instead a new, large, and unchecked source of discretion would be created.

In the light of the above, it is easy to see that the promotion of competition requires above all a reliable and predictable set of rules enabling participants in international trade to anticipate their strategies in order to obtain information most efficiently. Institutional predictability is the most important ally of any policy truly committed to fostering competition. To this we now focus our attention.

Alternative Proposal for the Promotion of Competition in International Trade Relations: Strengthening Institutions

Regulating competition does not necessarily guarantee its promotion, as antitrust supporters assume. Yet this evidence should not lead us to conclude pessimistically that public intervention is irreconcilable with the promotion of competition and market transactions. Markets can only function within a defined framework of rights, and this is a responsibility of governments, not particular. Hence, advocating against antitrust policy does not belittle government's involvement in promoting competition. On the contrary, it is unthinkable to imagine economic transactions occurring in an institution-free setting. Yet, it should be immediately realised that such intervention bears a different sign and purpose.

The question, then, is what sort of competition policy is compatible with market functioning? This section aims to define an alternative proposal of competition policy.

An alternative competition policy as applied to international transactions acknowledges the para-

---

62 This is, of course, far from embracing antitrust policy as the Magna Carta of economic freedom, as proclaimed naively by the U.S. Supreme Court in cases such as *Northern Pacific Railways v. United States* 356 U.S. 1, 6, 8–9, 10 N.8 (1958) or *U.S. v. Topco Associates Inc.* 405 U.S. 596, 610 (1972).

63 Hoekman and Mavroidis, Competition, Competition Policy, and the GATT, n. 36 above, pp. 2–3.

mount significance of controlling government discretion over trade and economic transactions. Administrative discretion potentially harbours new forms of trade protectionism. In turn, discretion develops in the presence of regulatory gaps; these "loopholes" are used opportunistically by governments to apply non-tariff barriers to trade.

Why does the absence of multilateral rules governing trade generate such restrictions? As it is argued elsewhere,[64] governments tend to behave strategically in their international trade relations. Such strategies are currently based in the mercantilist assumption that exports are praiseworthy, whereas imports should be discouraged.

Based on the "prisoner's dilemma" situation developed under the models of game theory,[65] it is possible to predict that governments will be inclined to favour "own" national firms against their foreign counterparts. Yet the existence of multilateral commitments prevents them from making such distinctions and from discriminating against foreign firms. They will do so only in the presence of regulatory loopholes enabling them to decide according to discretion. Therefore, government discretion should be kept to a minimum and any institution developed to promote trade transactions and business competition should be designed with this goal in mind.

From the perspective of individuals, there are two further conditions that must be met: first, a proper delimitation in the sphere of individual rights, which would encompass not only clarity in the initial assignment of rights over things, but also clear rules on the transmission of such rights. Secondly, it calls for an expedite and efficient dispute settlement mechanism allowing to eliminate any source of interference and uncertainty in the initial allocation or transfer of rights. An efficient dispute settlement system would allow to solve *ex post* conflicts over the use of resources due to a poor *ex ante* identification and assignment of rights.

By no means such initiatives would call for a government retreat of its commitments. There are particular several instances where the formulation of policies addressed to make rights and legal relations more transparent demands particular active government involvement. Consider the case of the

legislation dealing with intellectual property. This legislation aims to identify and protect certain sorts of (intellectual) entitlements over things, whose intangible nature makes them difficult to grasp, let alone to enjoy legal protection. In these cases, governments must entertain into the difficult task of detecting the infringement of these rights, whose legal qualification makes them particularly subtle. For example, how to determine that a product has been reproduced up to the point of creating a confusion in the consumers' perceptions as to the identity of the rightful producer? How to establish that a negative opinion spread about a competitor's product constitutes the denigration of his reputation and therefore a legal wrong? The delimitation of individual rights is frequently difficult and therefore requires particular care and commitment from the government in its enforcement.

The question is therefore, that there are two ways in which government intervention is necessary for market functioning and competition: First, in the *ex ante* definition of entitlements and individual spheres of action, and secondly in the *ex post* intervention aimed to clarify, albeit in an imperfect way, the content of such spheres of action in cases where initial entitlement proves difficult. The ultimate goal of defining rights and entitlements lies on the public interest to prevent unauthorised subjects ("free riders") from obtaining undeserved benefits out of the investments made by legitimate owners. This is a task that governments can perform themselves, or allow individuals to perform: another reason to repeal antitrust policies.[66]

These elements provide the blueprint for the formulation of an adequate competition policy: to ensure economic freedom to market participants in international trade, in order to provide them effective market access which is frequently denied to satisfy the interests of particular groups seeking protection from international trade. This sort of intervention would warrant positive results for the promotion of competition, in a more effective way than chasing elusive monopolistic practices.

In sum, the goal of an alternative competition policy in international trade is to enhance the predictability of market participants through the

64 I. De León and M. Morales, "From Aid to Trade: A new appraisal in the economic relations between the European Union and Latin America", *European Foreign Affairs Review* (forthcoming). Also, Ordover *et al.*, n. 16 above, pp. 10–16.
65 See A. Dixit and B. J. Nabeluff, *Thinking Strategically*, W. W. Norton & Company, New York, 1991.

66 Indeed, antitrust generally subjects contractual arrangements to exclude "free riders" (*e.g.* exclusive dealings) to a rule of reason analysis, in order to determine their restrictive effects. It is overlooked that by their very nature, these agreements are aimed to exclude ("free riding") competitors from the market. Once more, antitrust analysis reveals itself as lacking touch with reality.

reduction of uncertainty on their individual rights. This is possible if, as Petermann suggests,[67] there is an economic constitution in the international economic order, fundamentally integrated by GATT principles to which international trade participants could refer for the protection of their economic rights, in case they are harmed or lessened by trade protectionism.

Indeed, such protection would do more for individual rights and trade than any well-intentioned set of international antitrust rules.

Conclusions

Understanding the problems put forward by the promotion of competition in the contemporary world extends beyond the substitution of a well-intentioned yet inefficient policy by another based on similar premises. Nor the essence of the problem involved here is to "level the playground", and harmonise domestic legislation into a single set of multilateral antitrust principles. The question is, alas, more complex and rejects such easy answers.

The essence of this problem has to do with the nature of the restrictions to commerce and the most expedient way to avoid them. As it is shown, there are conflicting views in this sense, but some views are more realistic than others. It is clear that the role of institutions cannot be ignored, as it has been from the conventional neo-classical analysis nourishing antitrust predictions and theories. A constructive and more profound perspective must not attempt to isolate social reality and market functioning from those sets of rules that enable them to function. Constructing public policies on the basis of ideal worlds cannot lead but to contradictions and institutional failures. The theoretical shortcomings and the enforcement experience of antitrust policy show the possible consequences of these rules as applied to international trade relations. In fact, more than anything, the concerns about restrictive trade and business practices in international trade relations show, in the words of Godek, "an unhealthy anxiety about the imagined ills of capitalism".[68]

So one must be particularly wary about the claims of scholars, particularly (but not exclusively, it is fair to say) in the legal field, who take these policies at their face value without regarding the economic theory and the implications behind resulting from their implementation. It is not possible, but to agree wholeheartedly with Ackerman, when he sarcastically put the matter in these terms: "When they speak so resonantly of 'public policy', do lawyers have the slightest idea what they're talking about?"[69]

---

67 E.-U. Petersmann, n. 38 above.

68 P. Godek, "One U.S. Export Eastern Europe doesn't need", *International Merger Law*, September 1991, p. 3. Also, Regulation, Winter, 1992.

69 B. Ackerman, *Reconstructing American Law*, Harvard University Press, Cambridge, 1984, p. 22.

[21]

Putting Worker and Trade Union Rights in the WTO?

Gerard Greenfield

Some trade unionists and human rights groups argue that the WTO can be reformed by including core labour standards in the WTO agreements. By doing so this will protect basic worker and trade union rights and balance free trade with social guarantees. This notion of including special clauses on social protection in the WTO agreements was originally called the social clause proposal.

Basically, there are three reasons why supporters of the social clause believe it should be included in the WTO.

The first reason is that the ILO is too weak and has failed to prevent the violation of ILO Conventions.

The second reason is that the WTO is considered to have more teeth than the ILO because the WTO can place trade sanctions on those countries where core ILO Conventions are violated.

Third, this will limit the negative social effects of free trade under the WTO and force the WTO to be more socially responsible.

What are core labour standards?

Labour standards refer to the standards set by the International Labour Organisation (ILO). The ILO is an organisation of the United Nations created in 1919. The members of the ILO are governments. Trade unions and employers are not members of the ILO, but participate in ILO meetings at the invitation of their own governments.

The governments which are members of the ILO express their commitment to protecting labour standards by signing the ILO's International Labour Conventions. There are nearly 200 different Conventions signed by ILO members, including the protection of women workers' health, chemical safety in the workplace, the right of workers to organise trade unions, etc. As such these Conventions refer to worker and trade union rights as universal principles common to all countries. However, we should be clear that even if a government is a member of the ILO, it does not have to agree to all of the ILO's Conventions.

In theory once a government signs an ILO Convention it must make sure that the worker or trade union rights protected in that Convention are not violated. This means that the government cannot have laws or policies which violate this right, and the government must make sure that employers do not violate this right. Instead, national laws and policies should follow ILO Conventions by protecting these rights. Of course, there is a very big gap between these principles and reality. There is not a single member of the ILO today which is not violating one or more of its Conventions.

Core labour standards refer to only five ILO Conventions which are considered to be basic trade union and worker rights. These include freedom of association, the right to organise and bargain collectively, freedom from forced labour, equal pay for equal work, and no child labour. (See the BOX for more details).

The next question is how this social clause supposed to work?

How is it supposed to work?

The social clause proposal is based on the idea that if a member of the WTO violates one or more of the core labour conventions then a complaint can be made to the WTO by another member. This complaint is made like any other trade dispute under the WTO. (See Globalisation

Monitor, Issue 2, pp.6-8). A member of the WTO complains that part of a WTO agreement is being violated by another member, and the WTO then forms a panel to judge the case. If the WTO decides that the complaint is true, then it will order that member which is breaking the rules to make changes or face trade sanctions.

Here is an example of how the social clause in the WTO might work:

In the Free Trade Zones in Sri Lanka trade unions are banned. Nearly all of the products made in these Free Trade Zones are exported to other countries. This includes garments exported to the US and the EU. Since trade unions are banned in these Zones, this clearly violates two of the core labour standards - workers' right to organise and freedom of association. This means that a country which imports these garments, such as the US, can make a complaint to the WTO. The WTO would then set up a panel to consider the case. This WTO panel would be supported by the ILO which then investigates whether labour standards are being violated. If the WTO decides that the ban on trade unions in Sri Lanka's Free Trade Zones violates core labour standards, then the Sri Lankan government is ordered to lift the ban on trade unions in the Zones. If it does not, then the WTO will permit the US government to place trade sanctions on Sri Lanka, preventing these goods from being exported to the US. The idea is that these trade sanctions would force the Sri Lankan government to lift the trade union ban.

Although it sounds as though it might be an effective strategy for supporting Sri Lankan garment workers' rights, let us consider the following points about how it would really work in practice.

How will it really work?

1.   Only governments can make complaints to the WTO. Trade unions, NGOs or other social movement organisations cannot. So it is up to the government to decide whether or not it makes a complaint to the WTO about another member's violation of core labour standards. For example, when the AFL-CIO asks the US government to make a complaint to the WTO about the ban on trade unions in Sri Lanka, the US government will make the final decision. It will make this decision with many other political, economic, military and foreign policy considerations in mind. So the decision to use the social clause in the WTO will be a foreign policy decision - not a decision on social justice or workers' rights. So trade unions supporting the social clause proposal are actually encouraging powerful governments to make the final decision on the meaning of workers' rights by letting them use workers' rights as a bargaining tool over other foreign policy and trade issues.

2.   The WTO would treat the violation of core labour standards like any other trade   dispute. This means that the WTO will make its decision based on whether a violation of core labour standards leads to unfair trade. So the ban on trade unions in Free Trade Zones in Sri Lanka is not judged in terms of the violation of worker and trade union rights. It is only judged in terms of whether, as a result of this trade union ban, Sri Lankan garment exports are cheaper and therefore competing unfairly with other garment exports. Again, the real meaning of universal workers' rights will be lost. Everything will be judged in terms of the ideology of free trade.

3.   The trade sanctions which follow a WTO decision are not limited to the product under dispute. We have already seen this when the US won the case in the WTO against the EU over bananas. The US government put trade sanctions on many other imports from the EU, including cheese and telecommunications, not just bananas. So if the US government won a complaint against garment exports from Sri Lanka, then it could place trade sanctions on coffee and tea or any other export. Again, it's up to the government to decide which products it will ban or restrict.

2

4.   When the WTO decides on a trade dispute, it places blame on the governments of member-countries. It does not take into consideration the TNCs operating in those countries.

Let us look again at the example of Free Trade Zones in Sri Lanka. The fact is nearly all of the production in these Free Trade Zones is by foreign companies or subcontractors of foreign companies. So it is clear that these foreign companies benefit from the ban on trade unions, which keeps wages low and allows employers to repress workers. In fact, there are many Hong Kong companies operating garment factories in the Free Trade Zones in Sri Lanka. These garments are exported to the US and EU. Under the social clause proposal, the WTO would rule against the Sri Lankan government and trade sanctions would be placed on the country. It would not target the Hong Kong companies directly involved in this exploitation or any other foreign companies. While the WTO is investigating the case - which could take between two to seven years - the Hong Kong companies could easily avoid the trade sanctions by moving to Cambodia and doing the same thing there. But Sri Lanka would be stuck with trade sanctions on its garments and other exports.

Another example would be sports shoes made in Indonesia. If the US government won a complaint in the WTO against the Indonesian government for violations of workers' rights in the sports shoe industry, then the US could place trade sanctions on any imports from Indonesia. The fact that it is Nike that is using subcontractors which violate worker and trade union rights is ignored. So we have a US TNC making huge profits from the repression of workers' rights in Indonesia, but the ruling of the WTO is only against the country, not the TNC.

In this sense, the proposal for a social clause in the WTO fails to take into the reality of globalisation. TNCs, TNC subcontracting, and relocation of production from country to country are all part of the globalisation strategy. But the proposed social clause strategy only targets countries and their governments.

BOX

The five core labour standards are based on the following ILO Conventions:

Freedom of Association (Convention No 87): This means workers are free to form workers' organisations (such as trade unions) of their own choosing and that these organisations should be free from interference or repression by governments and employers. The idea here is to protect the independence of workers' self-organised unions and to make sure they are free from government or employer control.

Right to Organise and to Collective Bargaining (Convention No 98): This means that workers have the right to organise themselves into trade unions and cannot be stopped by the government or employers. These unions have the right to negotiate with employers on a collective basis. This gives workers the right to bargain with employers collectively instead of individually.

Forced Labour Convention (Convention No 29): This protects workers from being forced to work by political means, and includes protection from slavery and prison-labour. (Note: I use the term 'political', because under capitalism all workers are forced by economic and social means to sell their labour!)

Equal Remuneration Convention (Convention No 100): This gives all workers the right to equal pay for equal work. That means there cannot be wage discrimination based on sex, race or ethnicity. For example, women workers doing the same work as men workers must be paid the same wages as men workers.

Minimum Age Convention (Convention No 111): This means that there must be a minimum age for workers. The idea here is to prevent child labour.

3

[22]

The Fair Trade-Free Trade Debate: Trade, Labor, and the Environment

ROBERT HOWSE and MICHAEL J. TREBILCOCK

University of Toronto

I. Introduction

Many trade scholars—both lawyers and economists—view the increasing preoccupation with "fair trade" as the most fundamental challenge or threat to the liberal trading order that has arisen in recent decades.[1] The fair trade claims that currently generate the most heated debates in the trade community are those related to environmental and labor standards. The *Economist* magazine recently noted that ". . . . labour standards and environmental issues are playing an increasing role in international trade disputes" and are likely to be the central area of conflict between developed and developing countries in the next decade.[2]

Most free traders see recent demands that trade be linked to compliance with environmental and labor standards as motivated by the desire to protect jobs at home against increased competition from the Third World and view many fair traders as charlatans (protectionists masquerading as moralists). Where the demands of fair traders cannot so easily be reduced to protectionist pretexts, free traders are inclined to portray the advocates of linkage as irrational moral fanatics, prepared to sacrifice global economic welfare and the pressing needs of the developing countries for trivial, elusive, or purely sentimental goals.

The attitude of the free traders is reflected in two recent General Agreement on Tariffs and Trade (GATT) dispute panel rulings,[3] both concerning the legality under GATT of U.S. embargoes of tuna imports. The embargoes were targeted, either directly

We are grateful for research assistance by Ari Blicker and Peter Miller and for helpful comments from Lucian Bebchuck, Jagdish Bhagwati, Richard Craswell, Alan Deardorff, Steven Elliot, David Friedman, Douglas Ginsberg, Robert Hudec, Brian Langille, Helen Maroudas, Richard Posner, Alan Sykes, and Darlene Varaleau.

[1] See, for example, J. Bhagwati, "*The World Trading System at Risk, Aggressive Unilateralism,*" and "Fair Trade, Reciprocity and Harmonization", in *Analytical and Negotiating Issues in the Global Trading System* eds. A. Deardorff and R. Stern (Ann Arbor: University of Michigan Press, 1993); R. Hudec, "Mirror, Mirror on the Wall: The Concept of Fairness in the United States Foreign Trade Policy" *Proceedings of the Canadian Council on International Law* 88 (1990).

[2] "War of the Worlds," *The Economist,* October 1, 1994, p. 32.

[3] *United States—Restrictions on Imports of Tuna,* 30 I.L.M. 1594 (1991) (hereinafter, *Tuna/Dolphin I*); *United States—Restrictions on Imports of Tuna,* DS29/R, June 1994 (hereinafter, *Tuna/Dolphin II*). Tuna/Dolphin I is discussed at length in M.J. Trebilcock and R. Howse, *The Regulation of International Trade* (London and New York, Routledge, 1995) pp. 344–350.

or indirectly,[4] at tuna-fishing practices in the Eastern Pacific, particularly those of Mexico, which resulted in the deaths of large numbers of dolphins. Despite some differences in interpretive approach, both panels held that the environmental exemptions in Article XX of the GATT (which refer to protection of animal life and health and to conservation of natural resources) do not extend to trade sanctions targeted at other countries' policies. While neither panel ruling has been formally adopted by the GATT Council, and while there is currently no exemption in Article XX of the GATT that applies to labor rights-based measures (except with respect to restrictions on imports of products of prison labor); the principle that trade sanctions should never be a legally permissible response to the environmental and labor policies of other countries has become an article of faith among most free traders, or at least the beginning point[5] for any discussion of the relationship between GATT rules and global environmental and labour rights concerns.

The notion that there is, or should be, no room whatever within the GATT World Trade Organization (WTO) legal framework for trade measures in response to labor and environmental policies of other countries, has arguably heightened the intuitive discomfort many citizens feel about transferring domestic sovereignty to an international institution like the WTO. It is significant that of all the GATT panel rulings in recent years, only *Tuna/Dolphin I* has attracted widespread attention and scrutiny beyond the trade law and policy community, particularly in the United States. If international trade law simply rules out of court any trade response to the policies of other countries, however abhorrent, then there will be an understandable, and dangerous, temptation to declare that international trade law is an ass. The lesson of the recent heroic exercise to gain congressional approval of the Uruguay Round Agreement, including the provisions establishing the WTO, is that any rules-based approach to international trade is unlikely to be durable unless, in the end, it is able to command significant public legitimacy.

This article suggests the idea of a blanket prohibition of trade sanctions to affect other countries' policies and advocates a more subtle legal and institutional approach to the relationship between trade, environment, and labor rights. We propose a normative framework for disaggregating and evaluating "fair trade" claims relating to labor and environmental standards. In particular, we draw a critical distinction between claims that trade measures should be used to attain a specific non-trade goal or vindicate a specific non-trade value, and arguments for a "level" competitive playing field, evening the odds, or establishing "fair" rules of the game that are internal to the trading system.

Sanctions as a Means of Inducing Other States to Alter their Environmental or Labor Practices

Environmentalists and labor rights activists may advocate trade sanctions as a means of inducing recalcitrant governments and/or firms to meet a given set of labor or envi-

---

[4]*Tuna/Dolphin II* concerned a secondary embargo of tuna from the European Union World Trade Organization (EU), aimed at pressuring the EU to itself impose a primary embargo on tuna from the Eastern Pacific caught in a dolphin-unfriendly way (i.e., with purse-seine nets).

[5]Free traders may often eventually concede some exceptional cases where sanctions ought to be permissible—for instance where both the sanctioning state and the targeted state are signatories to an international environmental agreement that contemplates sanctions.

ronmental standards.[6] This may involve trade restrictions being imposed in the case of a country violating international environmental or labor agreements that it has already signed, or to induce a country to adopt a standard or norm that it has not yet accepted as binding, even in principle. Where the conduct of another state is repugnant to the values and sensibilities of its citizens, a government has a range of responses available to it, escalating from the minimalist response of doing nothing or making diplomatic protests to a maximalist response of declaring and waging war. Economic sanctions, including trade sanctions, can be viewed as falling somewhere in the middle of this spectrum, and have characterized in recent years the main response of a wide variety of states to such practices as apartheid in South Africa and genocide in the former Yugoslavia. The embargo of Iraq is a further recent example of the use of economic sanctions in support of non-trade policy goals. To what extent does the use of trade sanctions to punish, protest, or influence behavior of other states in the name of values external to the trading system itself constitute a challenge or threat to the normative theory of the gains from trade?

The non-trade-related rationales for environment and labor sanctions. An initial issue is whether the ultimate goals of such sanctions can be justified. Here it is useful to identify the main reasons why concerns about environmental and labor laws and practices may legitimately extend beyond national borders.

EXTERNALITIES. In certain circumstances, a country may be able to externalize some of the environmental costs of economic activity within its borders to the nationals of other countries. The classic example is pollution which flows from country A into the territory of country B through common air or water bodies. These spillovers can be of major significance—for example, a significant portion of the acid rain that affects Canada can be attributed to emissions in the United States.

THE GLOBAL ENVIRONMENTAL COMMONS. The commons may be defined as "physical or biological systems that lie wholly or largely outside the jurisdiction of any of the individual members of society but that are valued resources for many members of society. International commons of current interest include Antarctica, the high seas, deep seabed minerals, the electromagnetic spectrum, the geostationary orbit, the stratospheric ozone layer, the global climate system, and outer space.[7] Protection of endangered species might be added to this list. Where unconstrained and uncoordinated, exploitation of these physical and biological systems by nationals of each individual jurisdiction may produce what is widely referred to as the "tragedy of the commons."[8]

SHARED NATURAL RESOURCES. "Shared natural resources are physical or biological systems that extend into or across the jurisdictions of two or more members of international society. They may involve nonrenewable resources (for example, pools of oil that

---

[6]See H.F. Chang, "An Economic Analysis of Trade Measures to Protect the Global Environment", *Georgetown Law Journal* 83 (1995): 4.

[7]O. Young, *International Governance: Protecting the Environment in a Stateless Society* (Ithaca, NY: Cornell University Press, 1994), p.20.

[8]G. Hardin, "The Tragedy of the Commons", in *Managing the Commons* eds. G. Hardin and J. Baden (San Francisco: W.H. Freeman, 1977).

underlie areas subject to the jurisdiction of adjacent or opposite states), renewable resources (for example, straddling stocks of fish or migratory stocks of wild animals), or complex ecosystems that transcend the boundries of national jurisdiction."[9] Property rights to these shared resources cannot easily be assigned on a purely territorial basis, and therefore each sharing state has an interest in the practices and policies of each other sharing state with respect to these resources.

HUMAN RIGHTS. Human rights are frequently and increasingly regarded as inalienable rights that belong to individuals regardless of their national affiliation, simply by virtue of being human. Such an understanding of rights is implicit in the Kantian understanding of human autonomy that has profoundly influenced contemporary liberal theory. Certain labor rights or standards have come to be widely regarded as basic human rights with a universal character. These include: the right to collective bargaining and freedom of association; the right not to be enslaved; the abolition of child labor; and equality of opportunity in employment for men and women.[10] These rights are reflected in the Conventions of the International Labor Organization (ILO). Some of the Conventions have been ratified by a large number of countries; others by far fewer countries.

Although labor rights are conceived of as universal in the ILO Conventions, they are not viewed as absolute. Thus, for example, in the case of the prohibition on child labor, the minimum age of 15 years applies in most circumstances, but in many developing country contexts, the applicable age may be 12 years; as well, child labor in agricultural contexts is generally permitted.[11] Respect for the universal normative content of international labor rights need not entail *identical* labor policies or standards.

INTERNATIONAL POLITICAL AND ECONOMIC SPILLOVERS. Some human rights abuses and some labor practices, particularly violent suppression of workers' rights to organize or associate, may lead to the kind of acute social conflict that gives rise to general political and economic instability. Such instability may spill over national boundaries and affect global security. Increasingly (as the cases of the former Yugoslavia, Rwanda, and Somalia illustrate), "internal" conflicts are capable of raising regional or global security, economic, or social (e.g., immigration and refugee) issues.

ALTRUISTIC OR PATERNALISTIC CONCERNS. Even if they are not directly affected in any of the ways described above, citizens of one country may find the purely domestic environmental practices or policies of another country to be misguided or morally wrong. Similarly, citizens of one country may believe that workers in another country would be better off if protected by higher labor standards. Such a belief may or may not be warranted. For instance, higher minimum wages or other improvements in standards that raise labor costs, may in some circumstances do more harm than good, if the result is a significant increase in unemployment. Proponents of external intervention make the strong assumption that citizens in one country are better able to make these welfare judgments than governments in another country, which seems unlikely to be systematically true, even where the government in the latter country is not democratically

---

[9]Young, *op. cit.*, p. 21.

[10]See, generally, B. Hepple, "Equality: A Global Labour Standard" in *International Labour Standards and Economic Interdependence*, eds. W. Sengenberger and D. Campbell (Geneva: International Institute for Labour Studies, 1994).

[11]*ILO Convention No. 138* (Minimum Age Convention) (1973).

elected or accountable. However, the provision of foreign aid, often with major conditions attached as to recipients' domestic policies, by international agencies such as the World Bank and the International Monetary Fund (IMF) suggests that a welfare presumption against paternalism is not irrebuttable.

The nature of the above concerns differs in important respects. In the case of externalities, the global environmental commons, and shared natural resources, the main normative basis may sound in an argument about economic welfare, primarily the welfare of citizens in the state seeking to invoke trade sanctions but perhaps indirectly also global welfare. In other cases, the most obvious and compelling normative basis for insisting on compliance with minimum standards may have little relation to economic welfare; this is particularly true in the case of universal human rights, including labor rights, where the case for universal recognition of such rights is often premised on a deontological conception of human freedom and equality. Alternatively, in welfare terms, one can conceptualize such rights as involving interdependent utility functions between citizens of different states (unlike externalities and related claims). However, it is important to stress the universal character of such rights in order to distinguish these claims from more *ad hoc* claims of paternalism or altruism, which although also ostensibly grounded in the interdependence of utility functions cannot as readily be justified on a purely deontological basis, rendering these claims contestable in both welfare (or utilitarian) terms and in deonotological terms.

In the following discussion we attempt to identify the kinds of potential welfare effects, both positive and negative, that would need to be considered in any analysis of environmental or labor rights-based trade sanctions.

Scenario 1: trade sanctions or the threat of sanctions succeed in inducing higher environmental or labor standards.
The first scenario is that the country or countries targeted by sanctions, or at least some firms within those countries, change their domestic practices and adhere to or accept the minimum standards.

WELFARE EFFECTS IN TARGETED COUNTRY. With respect to the *domestic welfare of the country or countries that change policies,* if the status quo prior to the alteration of the policies is welfare maximizing (either in the Pareto or Kaldor-Hicks sense), then conforming to higher standards will reduce domestic welfare. Alternatively, the policy change may be welfare enhancing. For instance, in the case of environmental standards, it may lead to a more complete internalization of environmental costs and therefore a more efficient allocation of resources within the domestic economy. Critics of "fair trade" claims from an economic perspective often assume that low environmental or labor standards do in fact reflect a welfare-maximizing outcome for poor countries, but there is no empirical work that appears to provide unambiguous support for such a conclusion. Therefore, the *assumption* that domestic polices' *ex ante* trade sanctions were welfare maximizing has to be based on the view that, absent foreign influence, the domestic political and regulatory processes within these states would maximize welfare based on revealed preferences.

With respect to labor rights abuses, some of the practices that have been singled out as justifying trade sanctions—slave labor camps in China, for instance—would be difficult to characterize as the product of political or regulatory processes likely to maximize welfare based on the revealed preferences of individuals. Since the countries concerned are not genuine democracies, the domestic political process is simply not designed to take into account the preferences of all citizens. Indeed, in a Marxist totalitarian state like China, individual preferences—except for those of the ruling elites—may well count for very little. With respect to low environmental standards, it is true that some countries singled out for attack are liberal democracies where the assumption that domestic political and regulatory processes maximize individual preferences is more plausible (e.g., the call for trade sanctions against the British Colombia forest products industry). However, in these instances it may sometimes be possible to attribute lax environmental standards to the disproportionate influence of powerful industrial interests on the political and regulatory process, or to misguided efforts to protect jobs in a particular firm, sector or region.[12] In the end, knowing whether higher environmental or labor standards is likely to result in an improvement in domestic welfare, defined either in Pareto or Kaldor-Hicks terms, would entail judgments and analysis that go far beyond the disciplinary expertise of trade economists and trade policy experts.[13]

In general, the domestic welfare gains from improved labor standards are most likely to exist where, in the first place, there is a strong case for regulation to correct specific instances of market failure[14] (e.g., information asymmetries in the case of occupational health and safety[15], or where markets fail more radically due, for instance, to the presence of coercion (slave labor, child labor, the use of violence to intimidate workers, etc).

GLOBAL WELFARE EFFECTS. Improvements in environmental standards may increase global welfare where these improvements reduce or eliminate transboundary spillovers and externalities or address the problem of the "tragedy of the commons" or correct other market failures. In the case of the environment, examples of transboundary externalities abound, whether these are conceived of in the traditional sense as spillovers or whether they concern effects on the global environmental commons.

In the environmental area, where they are effective in inducing countries to remove or reduce externalities, and therefore in more fully internalizing the costs of economic activity, trade sanctions may actually lead to an increase in global allocative efficiency.[16] With respect to labor rights or standards, international minimum standards may address in some measure a fundamental distortion in the global labor market, i.e., restrictive

---

[12]For an explanation along these lines of some Canadian environmental policies, see Michael E. Porter and The Monitor Company, *Canada at the Crossroads: The Reality of a New Competitive Environment* (Ottawa: Business Council on National Issues, Supply and Services Canada, 1991), pp. 92–94.

[13]See G. Hansson, *Social Clauses and International Trade: An Economic Analysis of Labour Standards in Trade Policy* (New York: St. Martin's Press, 1983), pp. 168–171.

[14]Some economists have a generally skeptical view of the possibility that minimum standards, for instance in the case of occupational health and safety, can adequately correct for market failure. However, once this skepticism is put to the test through economic modeling, the results are ambiguous. Under some assumptions, minimum standards may be effective in correcting for market failure; under others (e.g., considerable heterogeneity in workers' risk preferences) minimum standards may actually result in greater market distortion. See D.K. Brown, A.V. Deardorff, and R.M. Stern, "International Labour Standards and Trade: A Theoretical Analysis", Fairness-Harmonization Project, University of Michigan, July 1994.

[15]See, generally, C. Sunstein, *After the Rights Revolution: Reconceiving the Regulatory State* (Cambridge, MA: Harvard University Press, 1990).

[16]It is this perspective, reflected in the "polluter pays" principle, that has informed most of the work of the OECD on international environmental standards (although the OECD does not endorse trade sanctions *per se* as a means of achieving internalization of environmental costs). See OECD, *Guiding Principles Concerning International Economic Aspects of Environmental Policies* (26 May 1972) 11 I.L.M. 1172 (1972); OECD, *Council Recommendation on the Implementation of the Polluter Pays Principle* (14 Nov. 14 1974) 14 I.L.M. 234 (1975). See also, G. Feketekuty, "The Link Between Trade and Environmental Policy" Minnesota Journal of Global Trade 2 (1993): 171–178.

immigration policies that prevent people from moving to locations where their labor is more highly valued. Without the threat of exit and often without effective voice in their home countries, they may be vulnerable to oppressive domestic labor policies or practices.[17] There may be possible longer-term impacts of the reduction in oppressive labor practices that would have positive impacts on global welfare—such as accelerated political liberalization as workers become less intimidated, better organized, and generally more capable of asserting their rights.[18] Increasing liberalization of domestic political regimes was linked early on by the philosopher Immanuel Kant[19] and much more recently in empirical work by Michael Doyle,[20] to a reduced threat of global conflict, including a reduced likelihood of war. Resort to practices such as forced labor, child labor (which often amounts to the same thing since, generally, children in these regimes have little say in whether they work or not), and violent suppression of independent trade unions (e.g., the Solidarity movement in Poland) provides a means of resistance to pressures for political and economic reforms—reforms which, it has been suggested, may well in the medium or longer run produce regimes that are significantly less likely to threaten international peace and security.[21]

WELFARE EFFECTS IN SANCTION-IMPOSING COUNTRY. Depending on elasticities of supply and demand, where foreign producers are faced with higher costs due to higher environmental or labor standards, they may be able to pass on some of these costs to consumers in the country that imposed the trade sanctions. However, it may be the case that compliance with minimum environmental or labor standards will not result in significantly higher prices to consumers, where *some* producers in the targeted country are *already* meeting minimum standards. In the case of the environment, for example, producers who have more modern plants or use new technologies that are relatively speaking more environmentally friendly, may not need to incur significant additional costs in order to comply with minimum standards. Similarly, in the case of labor standards, some producers may be meeting minimum standards within existing cost structures. Where, for instance, a producer is located in a part of the country where political and social conditions have allowed trade unions to survive, it may already have had to measure up to basic levels of protection with respect to occupational health and safety. Such a producer may have been able to remain competitive with other producers who have not been meeting minimum standards, through increasing the productivity of

---

[17]See Albert Hirschman, *Exit, Voice and Loyalty: Responses to Decline in Firms, Organizations, and States* (Cambridge, MA: Harvard University Press, 1970).

[18]In the case of Poland, for instance, the beginnings of liberal revolution are found in the gradual recognition of an independent trade union movement, which was able to mobilize broader social forces against the Soviet-bloc regime. See A. Pravaj, "The Workers," in *Poland: Genesis of a Revolution*, ed. A. Brumberg (New York: Vintage, 1983), pp. 68–91.

[19]I. Kant, "Perpetual Peace," in *Kant's Political Writings*, ed. Hans Reiss, trans. H.B. Nisbet (London: Cambridge University Press, 1970).

[20]See Michael W. Doyle, "Kant, Liberal Legacies and Foreign Affairs" *Philosophy and Public Affairs* 12 (1983): 205; and "Liberalism and World Politics" *American Political Science Review* 80 (1986): 1151.

[21]In recent work, Bhagwati has suggested that labor rights-related trade measures might be understood as most justifiable where the labor standards in question can be most clearly assimilated to classical human rights—for instance, prohibition of forced labor, or suppression of collective bargaining, sanctioning of violence to intimidate workers from making demands for a better workplace, etc. From a global welfare perspective, it is these kinds of labor rights that we suggest may lead to welfare gains from the resultant liberalization that occurs where a regime can no longer resist popular demands for a better life through coercive measures (or sanctioning private sector use of coercion).

labor, better employment of technology, etc.[22] However, it must be acknowledged that, making the conventional economic assumption that supply curves, are never infinitely elastic, some adverse price effects on consumers in the sanction-imposing country seem likely, although in many cases these seem likely to be small.

In some circumstances the additional costs that compliance with labor or environmental standards impose on firms in the targeted country may create gains for the domestic producers of like products in the country that imposed or threatened sanctions. This would occur where producers in the sanction-imposing country have the lowest costs of *any* country whose producers comply with the labour or environmental standards in question. In this instance, producers in the sanctions-imposing country will gain both domestic and foreign market share. Consumers, however, will pay more. Nevertheless, in very many instances, the next-lowest-cost producer complying with minimum standards is likely not to be a domestic firm, but a firm in another country. For this reason, compliance with minimum labor or environmental standards will often not confer substantial benefits on producer interests in the country that has imposed sanctions, although there are always likely to be some protective price effects (depending on elasticities of supply).

Scenario 2: the case where trade sanctions fail to induce higher standards.
WELFARE EFFECTS IN THE TARGETED COUNTRY. Here, the welfare effects will depend on how widely or narrowly cast the sanctions are. Perhaps the sanctions with the least negative welfare effects would be those that target the products of only those *firms* that do not meet minimum labor or environmental standards.[23] These sanctions, first of all, may be effective in actually securing some environmental or labor rights benefits even in the absence of a change in *government* policy, if they induce changes in firm behavior. Second, if there exist some producers who are already meeting the standards (e.g., due to deployment of more recent technologies, etc.) or who could meet them without variable costs significantly exceeding those of the most efficient firm not meeting the standards, then the sanctions may have only a small negative welfare effect, mostly shifting export market share to the more efficient producers.

Monitoring and enforcement of firm-specific sanctions may, however, entail much higher administrative costs than an outright ban of a given product from a particular country or countries. An attractive variant on firm-specific sanctions may therefore be a general ban subject to specific exemptions for firms able to satisfy the authorities of the sanctioning state that they are, in fact, in compliance with the environmental or labor standards at issue.

GLOBAL WELFARE EFFECTS. Even where sanctions fail to induce any policy change in the

---

[22]In the case of Mexico, for example, it is often suggested that gross violations of basic international labor rights norms are concentrated in the *maquiladora* region, whereas basic labor rights are respected throughout much of the country, particularly in unionized workplaces. See P. Morici, "Implications of a Social Charter for the North American Free Trade Agreement, in *Ties Beyond Trade: Labour and Environmental Issues under the NAFTA* eds. J. Lemco and W.B.P. Robson (Toronto and Washington D.C.: C.D. Howe Institute and National Planning Association, 1993), pp. 137–138. Morici notes that, even within the *maquiladoras,* "many employers . . . provide workers with a wide range of benefits and a safe working environment, and they adhere closely to strict environmental standards." (p. 138). See also USITC, "Review of Trade and Investment Measures by Mexico," *USITC Report No. 2326* (October 1990).

[23]In practice, however, such targeting will not always be easy. For instance, it is rumored that China falsifies the factories of origin for exported products that are manufactured with forced labor, so that these cannot be traced to the labor camps.

targeted country, there may be some positive effect on global welfare where sanctions result in a decline in the global sales of products that are manufactured in a fashion that creates significant externalities or entail labor rights abuses. If the country imposing the sanctions, or the group of countries imposing them, constitute a major market for the products in question, then global demand will now be met through production that complies with the standards in question. But for this to happen, sanctions must be imposed *consistently*—i.e., against all producers or countries worldwide that do not comply with the standards in question. Otherwise, production may simply be shifted from one firm that is responsible for the negative externalities or abuses in question to another.

Just as with domestic welfare, trade sanctions that are not carefully targeted against only those industries, sectors, or (ideally) firms that actually do not meet higher environmental or labor standards could, in theory, result in significant global welfare losses, shifting production away from least-cost producers in the targeted country to higher-cost producers elsewhere. However, many product areas are characterized by the existence of a variety of rival producers in different countries, often with closely comparable cost structures. In such a case, and assuming that some of these companies will be in compliance with the environmental and labor standards in question, global welfare losses may not in the end be significant. Rivals in compliance with international minimum standards will simply expand their market share. However, there are likely to be some price increases, assuming supply is not infinitely elastic.

With respect to the welfare effects of sanctions that fail to change government policy on those with pro-environmental or pro-labor rights preferences, these will still likely be positive for three reasons. Two of the reasons will be evident from the above analysis. First, if the sanctions are properly targeted at *firms* they may induce higher levels of labor and environmental protection even in the absence of a change in government policy. Second, sanctions, because they reduce world demand for products made in ways that harm the environment or abuse workers' rights, will reduce the levels of these harmful activities. Third, sanctions will provide the moral satisfaction of resisting government policies or practices that violate environmental or human rights norms, even if the government does not change its policies. However, even those with pro-environmental and pro-labor rights preferences may have some of these utility gains offset from utility losses due to the knowledge that sanctions may well cause harm to "innocent" victims of the government's intransigence in the face of sanctions, i.e., workers who lose their jobs, persons who suffer from a country's reduced ability to purchase essential supplies given a reduction in its convertible currency earnings, etc.

WELFARE EFFECTS IN THE SANCTIONS-IMPOSING COUNTRY. Welfare effects on consumers and producers in the sanctions-imposing country are likely to be similar to those in Scenario 1.

SUMMARY. The above analysis has taken into account only the static effects of sanctions. A dynamic perspective could alter the analysis significantly. For instance, higher environmental standards may induce investment in environmentally friendly processes or technologies, ultimately leading to a reduction in environmental compliance costs, or even production costs generally (inasmuch as the new technology is simply more efficient). Similarly, restrictions on the use of child labor may, as with the *Factory Acts* enacted in Britain in the first half of the nineteenth century, lead to political demands for enhanced access to public education.

The very general analysis, above, of the welfare effects of environmentally or labor rights-based trade sanctions outlined above suggests that little can be said, in the abstract, about the likely effects of such sanctions on aggregate domestic welfare in either the targeting or sanction-imposing country, or on global welfare. This clearly distinguishes trade measures of this kind from conventional protectionist trade restrictions, where formal analysis suggests overall net welfare losses, both domestic and global, when one considers the welfare effects of trade restrictions on consumers as well as workers and firms.[24]

PREDICTING THE EFFECTIVENESS OF SANCTIONS. Clearly, as the above analysis suggests, the welfare effects of sanctions will differ considerably depending on whether or not sanctions are actually able to change policies or practices in the targeted country. This underscores the importance of examining whether and when sanctions are likely to be effective in achieving such policy changes.

While there is not much evidence on the effectiveness of environmental or labor rights trade sanctions in particular, significant empirical work has been undertaken with a view to measuring the impact of economic sanctions more generally on state behavior. To our knowledge, the most comprehensive work on this question remains the study by Hufbauer, Schott, and Elliott,[25] which examines 115 instances of the use of economic sanctions over a period of about 40 years. The authors conclude that these sanctions had an overall success rate of about 34% in achieving an alteration of the conduct of the targeting country in the desired direction.[26] Not surprisingly, they found sanctions were more likely to succeed in changing behavior where the policy changes in question were relatively modest, and where the sanctions-imposing country was larger and more powerful than the targeted country.[27] Another important observation in this study is that sanctions are least likely to succeed against intransigent, hostile regimes as opposed to countries that are relatively friendly to the sanctions-imposing state.

Relative to many of the sanctions studied by Hufbauer, Schott, and Elliott, most environmental or labor rights trade sanctions would certainly count as aimed at only modest policy changes,[28] in comparison with sanctions that seek to topple an entire regime, or the removal of a pervasive form of social ordering (e.g., apartheid in South Africa). Moreover, Hufbauer, Schott, and Elliott's general observations on the importance of the relative size of the sanction-imposing and the targeted country, and about friends and enemies, seems consonant with recent evidence about the effectiveness of some environmental and labor rights sanctions. The threat of trade sanctions by the United States has, for instance, been credited with altering fishing practices that harmed endangered species in countries such as Japan, South Korea, Chile, Taiwan, and Peru—all of which could be described as relatively "friendly" states from the U.S.

---

[24]Trebilcock, Chandler, and Howse, *op. cit.* p. 45. See also R.E. Baldwin, "The Ineffectiveness of Trade Policy in Promoting Social Goals," *The World Economy* 8: 109.

[25]G.C. Hufbauer, Schott, and Elliott, *Economic Sanctions Reconsidered: History and Current Policy*, 2d ed. (Washington D.C.: Institute for International Economics, 1990). See also M. Miyagawa, *Do Economic Sanctions Work?* (New York: St. Martin's Press, 1992), and D. Baldwin, *Economic Statecraft* (Ithaca, NY: Cornell, University Press, 1985).

[26]*Ibid.* p. 93.

[27]This is consistent with more recent work by Nossal, which found that sanctions by "middle powers" such as Canada and Australia have been largely ineffective. See K.R. Nossal, *Rain Dancing: Sanctions in Canadian and Australian Foreign Policy* (Toronto: University of Toronto Press, 1994).

[28]In some cases such sanctions might, however, be aimed at goals that imply very significant regime change, for instance, in the case of China, sanctions aimed at inducing respect for the right of labor to organize and bargain freely.

point of view, and all (with the possible exception of Japan) significantly smaller and less powerful than the United States.[29] By contrast, U.S. threats to deny most favored nation (MFN) status to China, a totalitarian quasi-superpower with a hostile ideological system, has made little impact in terms of human rights, including labor rights compliance.

Overall, the evidence suggests that trade sanctions are of limited but real effectiveness, and in this respect they are no different from other, more extreme forms of coercive action such as military force where the record of effectiveness is also extremely mixed (e.g., Lebanon, Bosnia, Somalia, Rwanda, Haiti, and Vietnam). On the other hand, a systematic strategy of isolationism, appeasement, or acquiescence would largely resign us to accept grotesque human rights abuses or indeed attempted genocide without external opposition.

An issue closely related to the effectiveness of economic sanctions is the relative desirability of sanctions as opposed to other instruments for influencing the behavior of other countries and their producers. For instance, the GATT Secretariat has advocated the use of financial inducements as an alternative means to sanctions for influencing countries to adopt higher environmental standards.[30] This proposal has the virtue of attaching a price to the invocation of such sanctions and thus providing some assurance that these higher standards are truly valued for their own sake in the country desiring the changes, especially in cases of ostensible *ad hoc* paternalism or altruism, whereas trade sanctions, lacking such an explicit price (beyond price effects on consumers), may be easily subverted by protectionists. Chang argues, however, that subsidies, as opposed to sanctions, create a perverse incentive for foreign countries to engage in, or intensify, the offensive behavior (or make credible threats to this effect) in order to maximize the payments being offered.[31]

A recent study of the effects of both carrots and sticks on political change in South Africa supports Chang's skepticism about carrots; it concludes that ". . . political strategies that rely on inducements rather than commands are limited in what they can accomplish."[32] Moreover, in cases of transboundary externalities, the global environmental commons, shared natural resources, or universal human rights abuses (in contrast to exchanges of tariff concessions), a principle that victims (or their supporters) should always pay ("bribe") violators to achieve compliance would seem impossible to defend either ethically or politically. However, in some cases financial assistance to enable poor Third World countries to meet higher environmental or labor standards may be warranted or distributive justice grounds.

Another alternative[33] to trade restrictions is environmental and labor rights labeling,

---

[29]S. Charnovitz, "Encouraging Environmental Cooperation Through Trade Measures Through The Pelly Amendment and the GATT", *Journal of Environment and Development* 3 (1994): 3, 2202–2203.

[30]GATT Secretariat, *Trade and the Environment*, GATT Doc. 1529 (Feb. 3, 1992).

[31]Chang, *op. cit.*, pp. 2154–2156.

[32]K.A. Rodman, "Public and Private Sanctions against South Africa," *Political Science Quarterly* 109 (1994): 313,334.

[33]There may also be a further alternative, akin to labeling, through which individual consumers by their investment choices can attempt to discipline socially irresponsible corporate behavior. The phenomenon of socially responsible investing (SRI) refers to the "making of investment choices according to both financial and ethical criteria." For instance, individuals can choose to put their investments in firms that act in a manner consistent with their ethical values or they may choose to refrain from investing in those firms believed to be behaving in a socially unacceptable fashion. The two primary claims advanced by SRI adherents, which distinguish it from other strategies of investment, are: (i) that social screening does not entail a financial sacrifice (i.e., that advancing one's social agenda can be as profitable as investment for purely financial gain) and (ii) that SRI can alter corporate behavior insofar as it seeks to

which allows individuals as consumers to express their moral preferences for environ-mental or labor rights protection.[34] Products that are produced in a manner that meets a given set of labor or environmental standards would be entitled to bear a distinctive logo or statement that informs consumers of this fact. Although labeling may enable individual consumers to avoid the moral "taint" of consuming the product in question themselves, if most consumers have a preference for terminating production altogether (rather than merely reducing consumption and production) by changing a foreign country's domestic policies, then a collective action problem arises as in any approach to influencing behavior that depends upon coordinating action among large numbers of agents. Unless she can be sure that most other consumers will do likewise, the individual consumer may well not consider it rational to avoid buying the product in question.[35]

In sum, neither financial inducements nor labeling programs are self-evidently supe-rior policy instruments to sanctions for influencing other countries' environmental and labor practices. Each has its own drawbacks. However, it must be admitted that little concrete empirical evidence exists that would allow a rigorous comparison of these alternative instruments with sanctions. In addition, the greatest effectiveness might actually be achieved by a combination of more than one of these instruments. Again, in the absence of empirical work, it is difficult to make out a clear-cut case for excluding the use of trade sanctions as an instrument for influencing the behavior of other countries' governments or firms.

The "Systemic" Threat to a Liberal Trading Order

Even in the presence of indeterminate welfare effects many free traders may still reject environmental or labor rights-based trade measures on the basis that such measures, if widely permitted or entertained, would significantly erode the coherence and sustain-ability of rule-based liberal trade. We ourselves, in earlier work, have argued that com-petitiveness-based or level playing field "fair trade" measures, such as countervailing and antidumping duties, already pose such a threat. This is based on the notion that the legal order of international trade is best understood as a set of rules and norms aimed at sustaining a long-term cooperative equilibrium, in the face of ongoing pressures to cheat on this equilibrium, given that the short-term political payoffs from cheating may be quite high (depending, of course, on the character and influence of protectionist interests within a particular country, the availability of alternative policies to deal with

---

channel funds away from firms acting in a socially unacceptable way. While this phenomenon has become quite popular, there is good reason to be skeptical about its ability to deliver on its claims. Specifically, Knoll has suggested that, at best, only one of the claims can be true because each implies the negation of the other. As he explains, "[i]f markets are efficient, the first might be true but the second is false. If markets are inefficient, the second might be true but the first is false." With respect to the second claim, Knoll found that "regardless of the efficiency or inefficiency of the market, the impact of an investor's decision not to invest in a company will have little or no impact on the firm's ability to raise capital and therefore on its activities." For a more thorough discussion, see Michael S. Knoll, "Socially Responsible Investment and Modern Financial Markets" (March 18, 1994, unpublished manuscript).

[34]On environmental labeling, see R. Howse, "Reform, Retrenchment or Revolution? The Shift to Incentives and the Future of the Regulatory State", *Alberta Law Review* 31 (1993): 486–487; D. Cohen, "Procedural Fairness and Incentive Programs: Reflections on the Environmental Choice Program", *Alberta Law Review* 31 (1993): 554–574.

[35]J. Bhagwati and T.N. Srinivasan suggest that environmental values, if sound, "will spread because of their intrinsic appeal." "Trade and the Environment: Does Environmental Diversity Detract From the Case for Free Trade?," unpublished manuscript, July 1994. The fact that moral principles such as those prohibiting murder and theft are inherently sound does not, however, obviate the need to sanction non-compliance with them.

adjustment costs etc.).[36] In the presence of a lack of fundamental normative consensus as to what constitutes "cheating" on the one hand, and the punishment of others' cheating on the other, confidence in the rules themselves could be fundamentally undermined, and the system destabilized.

In considering the systemic threat from environmental and labor rights-related trade measures, it is important to distinguish between purely unilateral measures and those that have a multilateral dimension. The former measures are based upon an environmental or labor rights concern or norm that is specific to the sanctioning country or countries. Here, there is a real risk of dissolving a clear distinction between protectionist "cheating" and genuine sanctions to further non-trade values—the sanctioning country may well be able to define or redefine its environmental or labor rights causes so as to serve protectionist interests. Measures with a multilateral dimension, by contrast, will be based upon the targeted country's violation of some multilateral or internationally recognized norm, principle, or agreement—for instance, a provision in an accord to protect endangered species or one of the ILO Labor Conventions. These norms, principles, or agreements are typically not the product of protectionist forces in particular countries, nor are they easily captured by such forces (although the example of the Multi-Fibre Arrangement suggests that this is not invariably the case).

In *Tuna/Dolphin I*, the judgment that the strictures of Article XX of the GATT would not be adequate to "screen" global as opposed to domestic environmental measures and thereby prevent abuse, is undermined by the fact that the Panel itself had little difficulty in applying (*arguendo*) a least restrictive means test (as developed in the *Thai Cigarette*[37] case) to the facts of *Tuna/Dolphin*. Thus, the Panel noted that even if Article XX were to include measures with non-domestic policy goals, the U.S. ban on dolphin-unfriendly tuna imports could not be considered "necessary" to achieve these goals, since the United States had not exhausted the avenues for a negotiated co-operative solution that would have avoided trade disruption.

It should be possible to build into Article XX of the GATT a series of limits or criteria that are likely to minimize the protectionist abuse of environmental or labor rights[38] trade sanctions, and the corresponding risk of a loss of coherence and integrity in the GATT legal framework. In developing such criteria, we believe it is important to distinguish four different contexts in which environmental or labor rights trade sanctions may be employed: (1) where trade measures are explicitly contemplated in an interna-

---

[36] *Trade and Transitions, op. cit.*, pp. 211–215. This view of the legal order of liberal trade has been greatly influenced by the liberal internationalist perspective of Robert Axelrod and Robert Keohane. According to Axelrod and Keohane, "The principles and rules of international regimes make governments concerned about precedents, increasing the likelihood that they will attempt to punish defectors. In this way international regimes help to link the future with the present. This is as true of arms control agreements, in which willingness to make future agreements depends on others' compliance with previous arrangements, as it is in the GATT, which embodies norms and rules against which the behavior of members can be judged. By sanctioning retaliation for those who violate rules, regimes create expectations that a given violation will be treated not as an isolated case but as one in a series of interrelated actions." R. Axelrod and R.O. Keohane, "Achieving Cooperation Under Anarchy: Strategies and Institutions", in *Neorealism and Neoliberalism* ed. D.A. Baldwin (New York: Columbia University Press, 1993), p. 94.

[37] *Thailand: Restrictions on Importation of and Internal Taxes of Cigarettes* (Report of the Panel) BISD, 37th. Supp. (1989–1990) 200. In this case, the Panel ruled that an import ban could only be found "necessary" within the meaning of Article XX (b), where alternative measures, less restrictive of trade, were not available to achieve the objectives in question.

[38] In the case of labor rights, amending the actual text of Article XX would seem to be necessary, because (apart from products manufactured with prison labor) Article XX does not contain any explicit labor rights justifications for trade restrictions.

tional treaty that establishes labor or environmental standards; (2) where trade measures are not contemplated in the treaty or agreement, but where an independent body, such as a supra-national dispute settlement panel, commission, or monitoring authority, has found the targeted country in violation of international labor or environmental standards; (3) where the sanctions-imposing country or countries themselves have determined that the targeted country is in violation of an international norm or standard, in the absence of an independent ruling by a neutral third party (e.g., international institution); and (4) where the sanctions-imposing country merely asserts a norm or standard of environmental or labor protection as appropriate, in the absence of an internationally recognized norm or standard. Trade sanctions involved to promote environmental or labor protection should be easier to justify in categories (1) and (2) than categories (3) and (4).

Competitiveness-based Arguments for Environmental or Labor-Rights-Based Trade Measures

Unlike the arguments for trade restrictions on environmental and labor rights grounds that we have been discussing up to this point, which have a normative reference point external to the trading system itself, competitiveness-based "fair-trade" claims focus largely on the effects on domestic producers and workers of other countries' environmental and labor policies, and not *per se* on the effects of those policies on the environment and on workers elsewhere. Competitiveness claims are, in principle, indifferent to the improvement of environmental or labor practices in other countries. Hence, in the case of competitiveness claims, trade measures that protect the domestic market or "equalize" comparative advantage related to environmental or labor standards are a completely acceptable *substitute* for other countries raising their standards.

Competitiveness claims usually refer to one of two kinds of supposed unfairness (and, it is often argued as well, welfare losses) that stem from trade competition with countries that have lower environmental or labor standards:

1. It is unfair (and/or inefficient) that our own firms and workers should bear the "costs" of higher environmental or labor standards through loss of market share to foreign producers who have lower costs due to laxer environmental or labor standards in their own country.

2. It is unfair that downward pressure should be placed on our environmental or labor standards by virtue of the impact of trade competition with countries with lower standards.

Competitive Fairness Claim 1

The first kind of claim is, in our view, largely incoherent and in fact in tension with the basic theory of comparative advantage in trade. Assuming there is nothing wrongful with another country's environmental or labor policies along the lines discussed in the first part of this paper, then why should a cost advantage attributable to these divergent policies not be treated like any other cost advantage, i.e., as part and parcel of comparative advantage? In fact, even if all countries had the same level of environmental consciousness, or even the same general environmental standards, approaches to instrument choice as well as the choice of risks on which to concentrate would still differ widely, due to differing climatic and other geographical or demographic conditions. For these reasons, even in a world where all citizens shared the same environmental preferences, environmental laws and regulations would still be likely to differ substantially between countries, and even where they were the same, the costs to industry of complying with those laws and regulations would still likely differ substantially from country to country.

Precisely because the implicit benchmark of fairness is so illusory—i.e., a world where governmentally imposed labor and environmental protection costs are completely equalized among producers of like products in all countries—trade measures based upon this kind of fairness claim are likely to be highly manipulable by protectionist interests. Since, of course, protectionists are really interested in obtaining trade protection, not in promoting environmental standards or labor rights, the fact that the competitive fairness claim in question does not generate a viable and principled benchmark for alteration of other countries' policies is a strength not a weakness—for it virtually guarantees that justifications for protection will always be available, even if the targeted country improves its environmental or labor standards.

Welfare Effects of Trade Restrictions Aimed at Equalizing Comparative Advantage

Trade restrictions will lead to reduced exports, with consequent welfare losses to firms and workers in the targeted country. Since *every* foreign producer whose environmental or labor rights compliance costs are less than those of domestic producers will be vulnerable to trade action, trade restrictions based on equalization of comparative advantage are likely to affect imports, potentially quite dramatically, from a wide range of countries. Firms and workers engaged in the manufacture of like products to those imports targeted by trade restrictions will benefit where the restrictions in question make imports relatively more expensive than domestic substitutes, thereby shifting demand from imports to domestic production. Consumers will pay more, probably substantially more, as domestic producers will price up to the duty imposed by the trade restriction. Here, the welfare effects essentially resemble those from the imposition of a tariff or countervailing duty. Inasmuch as production is shifted from lower to higher cost producers, there is also some loss of global allocative efficiency.

Clearly, overall, these welfare effects entail a shift in wealth to firms and workers in the trade-restricting country from firms and workers in the targeted country as well as from consumers in the trade-restricting country. In our view, it is difficult to construct a theory of distributive justice to support the fairness of these transfers.

Perhaps the transfer between workers and consumers in the trade-restricting countries might be a *prima facie* defense on the grounds that it is just that many people suffer a little to avoid a few (i.e., workers who risk dislocation) from suffering a lot. But, then, why burden consumers? Why not subsidize from general taxation revenue environmental or labor rights compliance costs for industries that, but for such subsidies, could not compete on international markets? If anything, the most coherent distributive justice argument in support of the fairness claim here points to getting rid of countervailing duty law, so that such subsidies can be provided without risk of trade retaliation (but fair traders are not known for their outspokenness in this cause!).

What seems completely unsustainable on grounds of distributive justice is the shift of the costs of higher environmental or labor standards in the trade restricting country from workers and firms in that country to workers and firms in other countries. If, as fair traders vociferously argue, it is unfair to make workers and firms in one's own country pay for the competitive consequences of higher environmental and labor standards in that country, how could it possibly be fair to make workers and firms in another country pay this price? Indeed, shifting the competitiveness costs of one's own environmental or labor standards to workers in other countries seems distributively *perverse*. No matter how high an intrinsic or instrumentalist value we may wish to put on high environmental or labor standards in our own country, there is simply an unsupportable leap of logic in the conclusion that someone else should be paying the price for them. First of all, workers in other countries do not even usually directly benefit from these higher standards, whereas workers in one's own country do. Second, most competitiveness-based fair trade claims are targeted against countries that are poorer than the trade-restricting country, often with lower *per capita* incomes, higher levels of unemployment, and weaker social welfare nets (in some instances, the revenue from trading products may be essential to obtaining foreign exchange to buy essential goods such as medicines and foods).

Competitive Fairness Claim 2

This fairness claim does appear to be based in some concern for environmental and labour rights *per se*, albeit not at the international level but within one's own country. Whereas competitiveness claim 1 presumes that governments will not respond to the competitive implications of higher labor and environmental standards, and simply let firms and workers lose out, the second competitive fairness claim assumes just the opposite—that governments will respond by lowering domestic standards below the optimal level.

We do not believe that, generally speaking, lowering environmental or labor standards is an appropriate response to competitive pressures. There is, in fact, a wide range of alternatives—such as better regulation which reduces compliance costs without lowering standards,[39] investment in training, etc. to increase the productivity of labor[40] and the investment in technologies that are likely to reduce the costs of compliance with environmental standards.

Of course, it is arguable (although there is not much hard empirical evidence on the matter) that governments and/or firms are in fact responding by lowering standards, rather than through these arguably superior activity alternatives. However, these sub-optimal policy responses surely represent a political and social problem within countries that are lowering standards in response to competitive pressures. Again, it seems hardly fair that workers (or firms for that matter) in other countries should bear the burden of avoiding choices in another country that are ultimately attributable to a flawed policy process in that country.

A variation of the claim about the effect of competitiveness pressures on domestic environmental and labor standards suggests the possibility of a form of beggar-thy-neighbor behavior that may, admittedly leave all countries worse off. This is the "race to the bottom," whereby countries competitively lower their environmental or labor standards, in an effort to capture a relatively greater share of a fixed volume of trade or investment.[41] Much like the beggar-thy-neighbor subsidies wars that characterized ag-

---

[39]See R. Stewart, "Environmental Regulation and International Competitiveness" *Yale Law Journal* 102 (1993): 2039.

[40]See W. Sengenberger, "Protection-Participation-Promotion: The Systemic Nature and Effects of Labour Standards," in W. Sengenberger and D. Campbell, eds., *supra* note 10.

[41]"Fair Trade is Free Trade's Destiny," forthcoming in Bhagwatti & Hudec (eds.), *Harmonization and Fair Trade: Prerequisites for Fair Trade?* (MIT, 1996).

ricultural trade among Canada, the United States, and the European Union and other countries during the 1980s, it is not difficult, using the model of a Prisoner's Dilemma game, to show that competitive reduction in environmental or labor standards will typically result in a negative sum outcome,[42] as long as one assumes that before entering the race each country's environmental or labor standards represent an optimal domestic policy outcome for that country.

The "race to the bottom" claim has a different normative basis from the other competitiveness-based claims discussed above. Those claims relate to the proper distribution of the competitiveness costs of maintaining higher environmental and labor standards than one's trading partners. The normative basis for concern over the race to the bottom, by contrast, sounds in the language of Pareto efficiency: the race ends, literally, at the bottom, with each country adopting suboptimal domestic policies, but no country in the end capturing a larger share of the gains from trade.

Frequently, beggar-thy-neighbor regulatory competition is able to flourish much more easily where it is possible to reduce on a selective basis labor or environmental standards to attract a particular investment or support a particular industry or firm. It is more difficult and more costly to engage in these activities where the formal statutory framework of labor or environmental regulation must be altered across the board. Here, some of the provisions in the NAFTA Environmental and Labor Side Agreements may create disincentives to beggar-thy-neighbor competition in as much as these agreements oblige the signatories to enforce effectively those environmental and labor rights laws that are formally on the books. At the same time, it must be acknowledged that effectively monitoring whether a country is fully enforcing its own laws is not an easy task, especially for outsiders.

Finally, it is possible simply to ban by international agreement beggar-thy-neighbor competition. This is, for instance, what Article 1114 of the NAFTA attempts to do, albeit in rather weak legal language, with respect to environmental measures, *inter alia*. Article 1114 (2) states, in part that "The Parties recognize that it is inappropriate to encourage investment by relaxing domestic health, safety, and or environmental measures. Accordingly, a Party should not waive or otherwise derogate from or offer to waive or otherwise derogate from, such measures as an encouragement for the establishment, acquisition, expansion, or retention in its territory of an investor."

Accepting, however, that cooperation is the ultimate solution to the "race to the bottom," a further difficult question remains as to the appropriateness of trade restrictions as a sanction to induce a cooperative outcome. Here, there is important further work to be done in applying the insights of game theory to beggar-thy-neighbor trade conflicts such as, for instance, the agricultural subsidies wars: Did trade retaliation facilitate or frustrate a cooperative solution, i.e., the Uruguay Round Agreement on Agriculture? Just as was suggested in the first part of this paper, the role of unilateral sanctions in inducing rules-based, cooperative solutions to conflict is a complex one. Sophisticated advocates of unilateralism or aggressive reciprocity, such as Laura Tyson[43] and Carolyn Rhodes,[44] argue for trade measures as a means of inducing a rules-based cooperative equilibrium, not as a long-term strategy of non-cooperative behavior. The

---

[42]"Competing Conceptions of Regulatory Competition in Debates on Trade Liberalization and Labour Standards," forthcoming in Bratton, McCahery, & Picciotto (eds.), *International Regulatory Competition and Co-ordination—Perspectives on Economic Regulation in Europe and the United States* (Oxford University Press, 1996).

[43]Laura Tyson, *Who's Bashing Whom?*, (Washington, D.C.: Institute for International Economics, 1992).

[44]C. Rhodes, *Reciprocity, U.S. Trade Policy and the GATT Regime* (Ithaca, NY: Cornell University Press, 1993).

problem, as has been articulated by Bhagwati and others, is that these trade restrictions usually constitute deviations from *existing cooperative outcomes (preexisting GATT rules)*. Therefore, depending on one's standpoint such restrictions may resemble cheating on an existing cooperative equilibrium, rather than inducement to create a new one. One response of the unilateralists and reciprocitarians might be that the "race to the bottom" or "beggar-thy-neighbor" conduct of one's trading partners has, in fact, already put in danger the preexisting cooperative equilibrium, and that no return to a rules-based approach is possible unless new rules are adopted to deal with the "race to the bottom." However, free traders might well respond that an approach to inducing a new equilibrium based upon the use of technically illegal trade measures as a sanction to bring about negotiation of new rules is likely to undermine countries' overall confidence in the rule of law, and therefore actually may complicate the future prospects for rules-based solutions to trade conflict.

In the GATT WTO, there is arguably already a kind of implicit response to this dilemma, to be found in the concept of non-violation nullification and impairment in Article XXIII. In some circumstances, a GATT Panel may find that a Contracting Party's practices, even if not in technical violation of the General Agreement, nevertheless undermine reasonable expectations of another Party as to the benefit that it would receive from GATT concessions. In this situation, trade sanctions may ultimately be authorized, even if the targeted country did not engage in a technical violation of the GATT rules. Where a Contracting Party views the "beggar-thy-neighbor" but technically GATT-legal conduct of another Party as undermining the existing cooperative equilibrium of GATT rules and concessions, it may seek GATT approval of ultimate recourse to unilateral trade measures through making a case that non-violation nullification or impairment has occurred. This procedure prevents each Party being judge in its own cause, and thereby obviates the consequent potentially negative implications for overall confidence in the rule of law. Through this means, trade sanctions or the threat of sanctions, may be used as a legitimate instrument for inducing one's trading partners to bargain towards new or reformed rules to end a "race to the bottom." Thus, even where it could be shown that trade restrictions are appropriate as a means of inducing a cooperative solution, we do not see a justification for taking such measures outside the existing jurisprudential framework of the GATT WTO, or for making the framework more amenable to unilateral actions in which Contracting Parties are judges in their own cause as to whether the existing cooperative equilibrium has been undermined by purported "beggar-thy-neighbor" conduct of other Contracting Parties.

Conclusion

Once carefully disaggregated and scrutinized, "fair trade" claims related to environmental and labor standards are not necessarily groundless, nor self-serving of protectionist interests, nor as threatening to the liberal world trading order as free traders often make out. A concern to protect the rules-based liberal trading order from a loss of coherence and integrity, and a corresponding risk of a new protectionist spiral, has led free-trade oriented economists, policy experts, and lawyers to criticize and often reject wholesale trade measures related to labor and environmental standards, even where there is little persuasive evidence that such measures are welfare reducing or are motivated only by protectionist interests. However, a potentially serious threat to a liberal international trading order is posed by competitiveness-based or level playing field forms of fair trade claims, which we almost entirely dismiss as normatively incoherent and as mostly thinly disguised forms of protectionism. The institutional challenge thus posed is designing trade law regimes (both international and domestic) with the capacity to distinguish credibly between these two classes of claims. We have argued in this paper that this enterprise will entail minimizing to the greatest extent possible the scope for unilateral assertions of fair trade claims and maximizing to the greatest extent possible the role of international treaties, agreements, and norms as the basis of such claims. Free traders, by indiscriminately dismissing all fair trade claims and eliding these two classes of claims, run the risk of being discredited as moral phillistines and thus being marginalized in political debates that do indeed carry serious risks for a liberal international trading order.

Part VI
Legitimacy and Sovereignty

[23]

The Domain of WTO Dispute Resolution

Joel P. Trachtman*

{J}udicial law-making is a permanent feature of administration of justice in every society . . . .[1]

Recommendations and rulings of the D{ispute} S{ettlement} B{ody} cannot add to or diminish the rights and obligations provided in the covered agreements.[2]

I. INTRODUCTION

Many trade diplomats, environmentalists and scholars have expressed concern regarding the magnitude of decision-making power allocated to World Trade Organization (WTO) dispute resolution panels and the WTO Appellate Body. While trade diplomats and scholars have expressed pride at the Uruguay Round achievement of more binding and more "law-oriented" dispute resolution, the same group and a variety of non-governmental organizations (NGOs) and other commentators question the jurisdictional scope of dispute resolution. After all, should these small tribunals, lacking direct democratic legitimacy, determine profound issues such as the relationship between

* Professor of International Law, The Fletcher School of Law and Diplomacy, Tufts University. This paper was presented at a conference on WTO dispute resolution organized by the Harvard International Law Journal and held at Harvard Law School in September 1998. I would like to thank the organizers of that conference, and I am most appreciative of comments and suggestions from participants. I would also like to thank Jeffery Atik, Sung-joon Cho, Jeffrey Dunoff, Peter Gerhart, Robert Howse, Robert Hudec, and Phil Moremen for their comments and suggestions with respect to earlier drafts. I also wish to thank Meg Donovan for her thoughtful and tireless research assistance.

1. HERSCH LAUTERPACHT, THE DEVELOPMENT OF INTERNATIONAL LAW BY THE INTERNATIONAL COURT 155 (1982). *See generally* THE GLOBAL EXPANSION OF JUDICIAL POWER (C. Neal Tate & Torbjörn Vallinder eds., 1995).

2. Understanding on Rules and Procedures Governing the Settlement of Disputes, Apr. 15, 1994, art. 3(2), Marrakesh Agreement Establishing the World Trade Organization, Annex 2, THE RESULTS OF THE URUGUAY ROUND OF MULTILATERAL TRADE NEGOTIATIONS: THE LEGAL TEXTS 404, 405 (1994), 33 I.L.M. 1144, 1227 (1994) [hereinafter DSU]. *See also* Advisory Opinion on the Legality of the Threat or Use of Nuclear Weapons, 1996 I.C.J. 35 (July 8).

trade and environmental values or trade and labor values? Many voices, including this author's, have called for greater international legislation[3] in these important fields.

This Article is intended to outline a more realistic and nuanced view, based on law and economics analytical techniques. It is intended to suggest the reasons why dispute resolution could be the appropriate place to determine these issues. Conversely, it is intended to suggest a way to predict when these issues might better be determined through more specific legislative action. This Article seeks to begin to delineate the role of dispute resolution in the international trade law system.

In order to do so, the Article first analyzes the function and vocation of WTO dispute resolution. Second, it examines two related analytical techniques of law and economics to attempt to suggest the reasons for the assignment of competences to WTO dispute resolution, as opposed to WTO legislation. These two techniques are (i) incomplete contracts,[4] and (ii) rules and standards.[5] The incomplete contracts literature considers the reasons for, and implications of, the fact that all contracts (like all treaties) are necessarily incomplete in their capacity to specify the norms that will be applied to particular conduct. In the rules versus standards literature, a law is a "rule" *to the extent that* it is specified in advance of the conduct to which it is applied. A "standard," on the other hand, establishes general guidance to both the person governed and the person charged with applying the law but does not, in advance, specify in precise detail the conduct required or proscribed. The relativity of these definitions is critical. Furthermore, each law is comprised of a combination of rules and standards. However, it will be useful to speak here generally of rules as distinct from standards.

Finally, the Article applies these techniques to two important examples in the WTO legal system: (a) the kind of trade and environment

---

3. When used in connection with the international legal context, the term *legislate* and all variations thereof refer to the processes and parties involved in specific treaty-making and treaty amendment.

4. *See* Gillian K. Hadfield, *Weighing the Value of Vagueness: An Economic Perspective on Precision in the Law*, 82 CAL. L. REV. 541, 547 (1994). *See also* Ian Ayres & Robert Gertner, *Strategic Contractual Inefficiency and the Optimal Choice of Legal Rules*, 101 YALE L.J. 729 (1992).

5. For an introduction to the rules versus standards discussion in law and economics, see Louis Kaplow, *General Characteristics of Rules*, *in* ENCYCLOPEDIA OF LAW AND ECONOMICS (Boudewijn Bouckaert & Gerrit De Geest eds., 1998); Louis Kaplow, *Rules Versus Standards: An Economic Analysis*, 42 DUKE L.J. 557 (1992). *See also* Cass R. Sunstein, *Problems with Rules*, 83 CAL. L. REV. 953 (1995). The "rules" spoken of in the rules and standards literature are narrower than the category referenced in John Jackson's dichotomy of "rule-oriented" versus "power-oriented" dispute resolution. In Jackson's terminology, "rules" encompass both rules and standards. JOHN H. JACKSON, THE WORLD TRADING SYSTEM 109–11 (2d ed. 1997). Finally, in international trade law, "standards" has a specific meaning, referring to product standards. This meaning is separate from the sense in which "standards" is used here.

conflict exemplified by the recent *Shrimp/Turtle*[6] decision of the Appellate Body, and (b) the problem of non-violation nullification or impairment, addressed in the recent *Film*[7] panel.

This Article addresses neither of the major debates in international trade law: (i) that between power-oriented and law-oriented dispute resolution, defined by Professor John Jackson,[8] and (ii) that of subsidiarity, the question of whether particular competences should be allocated to member states of the WTO or to the WTO.[9] Rather, this Article addresses an interstitial institutional question: once one has decided on the application of law, and once one has decided to empower the WTO, where in the WTO institutional structure should power be exercised?

This interstitial question, however, affects the choice between power orientation and law orientation, as well as the choice between allocation of competences to the state and allocation to the WTO: the design of the institution affects the decision to allocate power to the institution.[10] Thus, within the "rule-oriented" approach, there are both rules and standards, as well as possibly lacunae. In brief, where decision-making authority is allocated to a dispute resolution body, less specific standards are consistent with a transfer of power to an international organization—the dispute resolution body itself—while more specific rules are more consistent with the reservation of continuing power by member states.[11] From a more critical standpoint, it might be argued that allocation of authority to a transnational dispute resolution body by virtue of standards can be used as a method to integrate *sub rosa*, and outside the visibility of democratic controls.[12]

---

6. WTO Appellate Body Report: United States—Import Prohibition of Certain Shrimp and Shrimp Products, AB-1998-4, WT/DS58/AB/R (98-3899) (Oct. 12, 1998) [hereinafter Shrimp/Turtle Appellate Body Report].

7. WTO Panel Report: Japan—Measures Affecting Consumer Photographic Film and Paper, WT/DS44/R (98-0886) (Mar. 31, 1998) [hereinafter Film Panel Report].

8. JACKSON, *supra* note 5. *But see* OLIVIER LONG, LAW AND ITS LIMITATIONS IN THE GATT MULTILATERAL SYSTEM (1985).

9. *See, e.g.*, Joel P. Trachtman, *International Regulatory Competition, Externalization, and Jurisdiction*, 34 HARV. INT'L L.J. 47 (1993); George A. Bermann, *Taking Subsidiarity Seriously: Federalism in the European Community and the United States*, 94 COLUM. L. REV. 331 (1994).

10. *See* Joel P. Trachtman, *The Theory of the Firm and the Theory of the International Economic Organization: Toward Comparative Institutional Analysis*, 17 Nw. J. INT'L L. & BUS. 470, 535–38 (1996-97).

11. On the other hand, where definitive decision-making authority is withheld from the dispute resolution body, standards seem more consistent with retention of state power, facilitating auto-interpretation, while rules seem more consistent with transfers of state power. Furthermore, the nature of the dispute resolution body as a transnational entity versus an inter-national entity affects the analysis of the transfer of state power.

12. *See* Paul B. Stephan, *Accountability and International Lawmaking: Rules, Rents and Legitimacy*, 17 Nw. J. Int'l L. & Bus. 681 (1996-97).

II. THEORETICAL FRAMEWORK DEFINING THE ROLE OF WTO DISPUTE RESOLUTION

It will be recalled that article 3(2) of the DSU provides that the vocation of dispute settlement is to preserve and to clarify rights and obligations under the covered agreements "in accordance with customary rules of public international law."[13] This phrase has been interpreted by the Appellate Body to refer to the interpretative rules of the Vienna Convention.[14]

This section examines the vocation and function of WTO dispute resolution in order to begin to articulate the distinction and relationship between WTO dispute resolution and WTO treaty-making. To understand the role of dispute resolution, one must recognize that dispute resolution is not simply a mechanism for neutral application of legislated rules but is itself a mechanism of legislation and of governance.[15] We must also recognize that today dispute resolution often works in tandem with legislation in that dispute resolution tribunals function in part as agents of legislatures. Moreover, legislatures, intentionally or unintentionally but often efficiently, delegate wide authority to dispute resolution.

A. *The Vocation and Function of WTO Dispute Resolution*

The WTO dispute resolution process begins with a requirement of consultations. If consultations are unsuccessful, the complaining state may request the establishment of a three-person panel to consider the matter. The panel issues a report which may be appealed to the Appellate Body. The panel report, as it may be modified by the Appellate Body, is subject to adoption by the Dispute Settlement Body (DSB) of the WTO. Adoption is automatic unless there is a consensus not to adopt the report.[16]

What is the vocation of WTO dispute resolution? There are several answers. Panels determine the facts. They determine those facts that are relevant under the applicable law, so that they must determine the applicable law and relevant facts concurrently and interactively. Inter-

---

13. DSU, *supra* note 2, art. 3(2).

14. Vienna Convention on the Law of Treaties, May 23, 1969, 1155 U.N.T.S. 331 [hereinafter Vienna Convention]. *See, e.g.*, WTO Appellate Body Report: Japan—Taxes on Alcoholic Beverages, AB-1996-2, WT/DS8,10,11/AB/R (95-0000) (Oct. 4, 1996), at 10, *citing* WTO Appellate Body Report: United States—Standards for Reformulated and Conventional Gasoline, AB-1996-1, WT/DS2/AB/R (95-1597) (Apr. 29, 1996), at 17 [hereinafter Gasoline Report].

15. *See generally* DUNCAN KENNEDY, A CRITIQUE OF ADJUDICATION (FIN DE SIÈCLE) (1998).

16. For a more detailed description of the dispute resolution system of the WTO, see, e.g., Ernst-Ulrich Petersmann, *The Dispute Settlement System of the World Trade Organization and the Evolution of the GATT Dispute Settlement System Since 1948*, 31 COMM. MKT. L. REV. 1157, 1195 (1994); PIERRE PESCATORE, WILLIAM J. DAVEY & ANDREAS F. LOWENFELD, HANDBOOK OF WTO/GATT DISPUTE SETTLEMENT (1991).

estingly, because of a design flaw in the DSU, the Appellate Body has no right of remand.[17] Therefore, the Appellate Body is constrained where it determines to apply law for which the panel has made no findings of fact.

Within the determination of the applicable law are several subfunctions. First, panels (and here the Appellate Body acts as well) determine which law is applicable, by virtue of factors including, but not limited to, the activity, the location, the persons, and the timing. Second, where there is a dispute regarding the meaning of the law, the panel must definitively interpret the law. Third, where the law does not apply by its specific terms but was intended to address the issue, the panel may construe the law. Fourth, the law may have a lacuna and therefore not provide a response.[18] Fifth, where two legal rules overlap, the panel must determine whether both were meant to apply or whether one takes precedence. Sixth, where two legal rules conflict, the panel must determine whether the laws are of unequal or equal stature. If they are of equal stature, the panel must determine how to accommodate both. As shall be discussed in more detail below, one persistent problem of the WTO legal system is the recognition and application of legal rules from outside the system. Penultimately, after the complete determination of the applicable law, the tribunal applies the law to the facts. Finally, the tribunal may fashion a remedy: it may recommend a resolution to be adopted by the DSB.

Dispute resolution is of course a socially immanent governance mechanism to be used to establish a particular type of governance in a particular social setting. Where the applicable legal provision has the characteristics of a rule—clear, self-executing, fully specified in advance and not in need of interpretation or construction—once the facts are determined, the dispute resolution process has little more to do.[19] This is the economist's, and often the political scientist's, erroneously idealized view of dispute resolution: the economist and political scientist often assume that there is a definite applicable law and a discrete set of facts to which the law applies unequivocally. Given this assumption, they expect and conclude that the only question left for analysis is whether the dispute resolution tribunal's decision will meet with compliance.

Where, alternatively, the legal provision has the characteristics of a standard, with need of interpretation or even construction, then the

---

17. *See* David Palmeter, *The WTO Appellate Body Needs Remand Authority*, 32 J. WORLD TRADE 41 (1998).

18. Of course, not to respond is to confer victory on the defendant. *See, e.g.*, Anthony D'Amato, *Legal Uncertainty*, 71 CAL. L. REV. 1 (1983).

19. For an intellectual history of this idea and a substantial critique, see Kennedy, *supra* note 15.

determination of the law and the application of the law to the facts become much more complex.

However, there is yet a third possibility, which is something of a chimera. The third possibility is that there is no applicable law. In one recent decision, the Appellate Body, agreeing with the panel that no WTO law applied, *ratione temporis*,[20] declined to provide a remedy.[21] This decision recognizes that the WTO legal system is a limited one, which does not provide a remedy for every claim.[22]

There is, however, perhaps, another kind of lacuna: one in which there is some applicable WTO law. In these cases, there may be a gap in the international system for applying non-WTO international law that may conflict with WTO provisions. The WTO dispute resolution system is clearly not a court of general jurisdiction, competent to apply all applicable international law.[23]

WTO law does not represent a complete legal answer in multidimensional disputes in the sense that it does not include other law that may articulate policies beyond trade policies. This is the character of some of the recent environmental decisions of WTO dispute resolution bodies.[24] It is not so much a substantive lacuna as a procedural one. There is no mechanism for integrating diverse legal rules, that is, for determining which law takes precedence when diverse laws conflict. The procedural lacuna has substantive effects.

B. *The Relationship between Treaty-Writing and Dispute Resolution*

It is clear that dispute resolution arrangements—and more generally *ex post* enforceability—affect the willingness of states to enter into agreements *ex ante*.[25] After all, what would be the purpose of entering into an unenforceable agreement?[26] Dispute resolution arrangements

---

20. *Ratione temporis* means by reason of time. For example, a law might not apply to conduct that occurred prior to its enactment, depending on whether the law is intended to apply retrospectively.

21. *See* WTO Appellate Body Report: Brazil—Measures Affecting Desiccated Coconut, AB-1996-4, WT/DS22/AB/R (97-0695) (Feb. 21, 1997).

22. A claim for which the law does not provide a remedy is referred to as *non liquet*. *See* Prosper Weil, *"The Court Cannot Conclude Definitively . . ." Non Liquet Revisited*, 36 COLUM. J. TRANSNAT'L L. 109 (1997).

23. *See infra* notes 41–47 and accompanying text.

24. *See* Stefan Ohlhoff & Hannes L. Schloemann, *Rational Allocation of Disputes and "Constitutionalization": Forum Choice as an Issue of Competence*, *in* DISPUTE RESOLUTION IN THE WORLD TRADE ORGANIZATION (James Cameron & Karen Campbell eds., 1998).

25. *See* Trachtman, *supra* note 10. *See also* James D. Fearon, *Bargaining, Enforcement, and International Cooperation*, 52 INT'L. ORG. 269 (1998); Alan O. Sykes, *Protectionism as a "Safeguard": A Positive Analysis of the GATT "Escape Clause" with Normative Speculations*, 58 U. CHI. L. REV. 255 (1991).

26. By "enforceable," I mean not just enforceability in a court of law but also enforceability through reputation or other informal sanctions. Of course, one can find many examples of unenforceable agreements that nonetheless serve a useful purpose. If they are neither formally nor informally enforceable though, they have no direct effect on the parties and may rather be de-

are intended to provide some degree of formal enforceability. Before undertaking further analysis, it is useful to review the complementary role that dispute resolution plays in relation to legislation.

It may appear odd that dispute resolution is at the center of world trade governance. Indeed, it is worthwhile to wonder why the focus is on adjudication, rather than legislation, as the mainstay of legalism in world trade. Of course, dispute resolution plays two roles. First, as noted above, dispute resolution is necessary to the application of legislation. In this regard, dispute resolution is not important for its own sake but as the place where legislation becomes binding and effective.[27] Legislation without adjudication at least raises greater concerns regarding the application and effectiveness of the legislation.[28] It is only in this sense that dispute resolution may properly be considered the cornerstone of international trade law. Second, dispute resolution, as indicated in the quote from Lauterpacht with which this Article began, inevitably interprets and expands upon legislation. In a common law system, indeed, dispute resolution amounts unabashedly to a type of legislation. Even in a civil law system,[29] or one such as the WTO that rejects *stare decisis*, dispute resolution may be a source of persuasive or helpful precedent, that is, of less binding legislation.

C. Interpretation and Construction

In Anglo-American parlance, interpretation refers to the determination of the meaning of words contained in a contract, statute or treaty while construction refers to the determination of the intent of the parties in connection with a matter not specifically addressed in the text of the document. While the distinction may be a matter of degree, construction raises greater questions of legitimacy, of fidelity to the intent of the parties and—in statutory or treaty contexts—of democracy.

The WTO dispute resolution process often involves interpretation: the parties disagree about the meaning of the promises made in the relevant treaty. Virtually every decision involves some dispute regarding the meaning of a treaty obligation[30]—few turn solely on the facts.

---

signed for political theater, that is, to impress domestic constituencies or other onlookers.

27. For a thoughtful game theoretic analysis of the role of dispute resolution in enforcing trade treaties, see Frieder Roessler, Warren F. Schwartz, & Alan O. Sykes, The Economic Structure of Renegotiation and Dispute Resolution in the WTO/GATT System, Feb. 5, 1998 (unpublished manuscript on file with the author).

28. Note the importance ascribed to the recent Rome Agreement to create an international criminal court. *Rome Statute of the International Criminal Court*, United Nations Conference on the Establishment of an International Criminal Court, U.N. Doc. A/CONF.183/9 (1998), *reprinted in* 37 I.L.M. 1002 (1998).

29. *See, e.g.,* MARTIN SHAPIRO, COURTS 28–32 (1981); Michael Wells, *French and American Judicial Opinions*, 19 YALE J. INT'L L. 81, 92 (1994).

30. There are, however, limitations on interpretation. *See* Gasoline Report, *supra* note 14, and

This might be expected given the large amount of new treaty obligations that came into formal existence in 1995 as a result of the Uruguay Round. Some dispute resolution proceedings involve construction. Indeed, one group of decisions that might be categorized as construction decisions are those involving non-violation nullification or impairment. In these cases, by definition, no specific provision of a treaty is violated. The question is whether the treaty should be construed to provide a remedy for acts that nullify or impair concessions despite the lack of specific treaty language. In other types of cases, recent WTO jurisprudence has seemingly rejected construction:

> The legitimate expectations of the parties to a treaty are reflected in the language of the treaty itself. The duty of the treaty interpreter is to examine the words of the treaty to determine the intentions of the parties. This should be done in accordance with the principles of treaty interpretation set out in Article 31 of the Vienna Convention. But these principles of interpretation neither require nor condone the imputation into a treaty of words that are not there or the importation into a treaty of concepts that were not intended . . . .[31]

However, construction occurs where concepts that *are* intended are implicit in the text though they are not expressly articulated. Construction under non-violation nullification or impairment involves only the most generally intended concepts.[32]

D. *Lacunae*

There is only a subtle difference between a context in which construction is called for and a lacuna.[33] Construction is called for where the intent of the parties is determinable, while a lacuna is a case where the intent of the parties is not known. Of course, a tribunal must determine which circumstance is involved in particular cases, and the distinction turns on an interpretation of the intent of the parties. The existence of a lacuna, or *non liquet*, "is an expression of the principles of

---

text accompanying note 59 *infra* ("[A]n interpreter is not free to adopt a reading that would result in reducing whole clauses or paragraphs of a treaty to redundancy or inutility").

31. WTO Appellate Body Report: India—Patent Protection for Pharmaceutical and Agricultural Chemical Products, AB-1997-5, WT/DS50/AB/R (98-3091) (Aug. 24, 1998), para. 45.

32. *See, e.g.*, WTO Panel Report: European Economic Community—Payments and Subsidies Paid to Processors and Producers of Oilseeds and Related Animal-Feed Proteins, Jan. 25, 1990, GATT B.I.S.D. (37th Supp.) at 86 (1991) [hereinafter EEC—Oilseeds Report].

33. *See* PETERSMANN, *supra* note 16, at 1195; Jacques H.J. Bourgeois, *WTO Dispute Settlement in the Field of Anti-Dumping Law*, 1 J. INT'L ECON. L. 259, 271–72 (1998); Pierre Pescatore, *Drafting and Analysing Decisions on Dispute Settlement*, *in* HANDBOOK OF WTO/GATT DISPUTE SETTLEMENT, *supra* note 16; 15 Developed Countries: Uruguayan Recourse to Article XXIII, B.I.S.D. 11S/95 (1963).

self-interpretation and polynormativity that are characteristic of the international legal system."[34] However, "[t]he view prevailing among writers is that there is no room for *non liquet* in international adjudication because there are no lacunae in international law."[35] General principles of law and rules of equity provide rules of decision where custom and convention fail to do so.[36] This perspective is important in light of the *Lotus* doctrine that the principle of sovereignty requires that what is not positively prohibited to states is permitted to them.[37]

International trade law approaches lacunae in a different way. As explained below, the law applicable in WTO dispute resolution is a limited body.[38] There are two main types of cases where this limitation is relevant. First, there are cases where the question, in a violation-type case, is whether there is an applicable provision of WTO law that restricts the conduct in question. Second, there are cases where WTO law does restrict the conduct in question, but that conduct is required under non-WTO law, including either domestic or international law. Alternatively, within this second category, the WTO law may permit conduct that is forbidden under domestic or other international law. This second group of cases may be described as presenting a choice of law or conflict of laws issue. With regard to domestic law, it is clear that applicable WTO law trumps conflicting domestic law, at least as a matter of WTO law.[39] While this outcome is clear in formal legal terms, it raises substantial policy concerns. These policy concerns arise from the fact that the exceptional provisions in article XX of the General Agreement on Tariffs and Trade (GATT) have not been interpreted broadly to except certain types of trade restrictions that arise from the application of non-trade policy.[40] The most notorious examples are in the areas of trade and environment and trade and labor. With respect to conflicts between WTO law and other international law, the outcome is less clear. In the environmental field, there has not been a di-

---

34. Weil, *supra* note 22, at 119. For an example of an international law *non liquet*, see Advisory Opinion on the Legality of the Threat or Use of Nuclear Weapons, *supra* note 2, at 105.

35. Weil, *supra* note 22, at 110.

36. *See, e.g.*, North Sea Continental Shelf (F.R.G. v. Den.; F.R.G. v. Neth.) 1969 I.C.J. 3, 46 (Feb. 20).

37. S.S. Lotus (Fr. v. Turk.), 1927 P.C.I.J., (ser. A) No. 10, at 18-19 (Sept. 7). *See also* Military and Paramilitary Activities in and against Nicaragua (Nicar. v. U.S.), 1986 I.C.J. 14, 135.

38. *See infra* notes 41–47 and accompanying text.

39. *See* Marrakesh Agreement Establishing the World Trade Organization, Apr. 15, 1994, art. XVI(4), THE RESULTS OF THE URUGUAY ROUND OF MULTILATERAL TRADE NEGOTIATIONS: THE LEGAL TEXTS 6, 17 (1994), 33 I.L.M. 1144, 1152 (1994) [hereinafter WTO Agreement]; Vienna Convention, *supra* note 14, art. 27. *See also* John H. Jackson, *The Status of Treaties in Domestic Legal Systems: A Policy Analysis*, 86 AM. J. INT'L L. 310 (1992).

40. General Agreement on Tariffs and Trade, Oct. 30, 1947, art. XX, 55 U.N.T.S. 194, 262, *as amended in* THE RESULTS OF THE URUGUAY ROUND OF MULTILATERAL TRADE NEGOTIATIONS: THE LEGAL TEXTS 519 (1994).

rect conflict between WTO law and other applicable mandatory international law.

E. *References to Non-Substantive versus Substantive Non-WTO International Law in WTO Dispute Settlement*

The mandate to WTO dispute resolution panels, to the Appellate Body, and to the Dispute Settlement Body is clear: apply (directly) only WTO law.[41] Several provisions of the DSU provide this limitation. Article 3(2) provides that the dispute settlement system "serves to preserve the rights and obligations of Members under the covered agreements, and to clarify the existing provisions of those agreements in accordance with customary rules of interpretation of public international law."[42] Article 3(2) further provides that "[r]ecommendations and rulings of the DSB cannot add to or diminish the rights and obligations provided in the covered agreements."[43] This language would be absurd if rights and obligations arising from other international law could be applied by the DSB. The standard panel terms of reference provided under article 7 provides for reference only to law arising from the WTO agreements.[44] Finally, article 11 of the DSU specifies the function of panels to assess the applicability of and conformity with the covered agreements.[45] With so much specific reference to the covered agreements as the law applicable in WTO dispute resolution, it would be odd if the members intended non-WTO law to be applicable.

This limited role of WTO dispute resolution has been confirmed in the recent Appellate Body Report relating to *European Communities–Measures Affecting the Importation of Certain Poultry Products*, holding that

---

41. *But see* David Palmeter & Petros C. Mavroidis, *The WTO Legal System: Sources of Law*, 92 AM. J. INT'L L. 398, 399 (1998) (arguing that the texts of the WTO agreements "do not exhaust the sources of potentially relevant law"). Palmeter and Mavroidis refer to articles 3(2) and 7 of the DSU as the ostensible basis for incorporation of non-WTO international law. However, these provisions refer only to *interpretation* of relevant provisions of WTO agreements "in accordance with customary rules of *interpretation* of public international law." *Id.* (emphasis added). They cannot be taken as making the WTO dispute resolution system a court of general international law jurisdiction. *See also* Thomas J. Schoenbaum, *WTO Dispute Settlement: Praise and Suggestions for Reform*, 47 INT'L & COMP. L.Q. 647, 653 (1998). Schoenbaum argues that article 11 of the DSU, by authorizing panels and the Appellate Body to make "such other findings as will assist the DSB in making the recommendation or in giving the rulings provided for in the covered agreements," provides a kind of "implied powers" allowing the panels and Appellate Body to decide all international legal issues involved in a dispute properly before them. *Id.* While Schoenbaum adduces reasons why this *should* be so, this instruction to make "such other findings" is too general to overcome the more specific language of the DSU limiting panels and the Appellate Body to the "covered agreements." *See also* Gasoline Report, *supra* note 14, at 11. ("[T]he General Agreement is not to be read in clinical isolation from public international law.")

42. DSU, *supra* note 2, art. 3(2).

43. *Id.*

44. *Id.* art. 7.

45. *Id.* art. 11.

a tariff agreement settling a matter between two WTO members does not constitute WTO law applicable by a panel. [46] It is also supported by the recent Appellate Body Report regarding *Argentina—Measures Affecting Imports of Footwear, Textiles, Apparel and Other Items*, suggesting that a purported agreement between Argentina and the IMF would not modify WTO obligations.[47]

While panels and the Appellate Body are only permitted to apply WTO law, they refer to non-WTO international law in two types of cases. First, as specifically authorized by article 3.2 of the DSU, they refer to customary rules of interpretation of international law. This reference does not appear to include substantive non-WTO international law. While article 31(3)(c) of the Vienna Convention, which is taken as reflective of customary rules of interpretation, refers to applicable international law, it does so only to indicate what materials should be taken into account in interpreting treaty texts. Thus, other international law is not directly applicable but is taken into account in a manner similar to the U.S. *Charming Betsy* rule: interpret so as to avoid conflict where possible.[48]

Second, substantive non-WTO international law may be incorporated by reference in WTO law, either by treaty language such as the references in TRIPS to intellectual property treaties[49] or by a waiver such as the Lomé waiver in the recent *Bananas III* decision.[50] More subtly, substantive non-WTO law may indirectly be incorporated by reference in provisions such as article XX(b) of GATT.[51]

---

46. While the Appellate Body allowed that the Oilseeds Agreement might serve as a supplementary means of interpretation of WTO law, it did not apply the Oilseeds Agreement itself as law. WTO Appellate Body Report: European Communities—Measures Affecting the Importation of Certain Poultry Products, AB-1998-3, WT/DS69/AB/R (98-2688), para. 81 (July 23, 1998).

47. WTO Appellate Body Report: Argentina—Measures Affecting Imports of Footwear, Textiles, Apparel and Other Items, AB-1998-1, WT/DS56/AB/R (98-0000), (Apr. 22, 1998), para. 72.

48. Murray v. The Schooner Charming Betsy, 6 U.S. (2 Cranch) 64, 118 (1804). *See generally* Curtis A. Bradley, *The* Charming Betsy *Canon and Separation of Powers: Rethinking the Interpretive Role of International Law*, 86 GEO. L.J. 479 (1998); Ralph G. Steinhardt, *The Role of International Law as a Canon of Domestic Statutory Construction*, 43 VAND. L. REV. 1103 (1990).

49. Agreement on Trade-Related Aspects of Intellectual Property Rights, Apr. 15, 1994, arts. 2, 3, 9, 10, 16, 19, Marrakesh Agreement Establishing the World Trade Organization, Annex 1C, THE RESULTS OF THE URUGUAY ROUND OF MULTILATERAL TRADE NEGOTIATIONS: THE LEGAL TEXTS 365, 368, 370, 373–74 (1994); 33 I.L.M. 1144, 1199, 1203–04 (1994) [hereinafter TRIPS].

50. WTO Appellate Body Report: European Communities— Regime for the Importation, Sale and Distribution of Bananas, AB-1997-3, WT/DS27/AB/R (97-0000), (Sept. 25, 1997), para. 164 [hereinafter Bananas Appellate Body Report].

51. Article XX(b) (as well as paragraphs (a) and (d)) contains a requirement that measures excepted thereunder be "necessary." This requirement has been read on several occasions to require multilateral or bilateral efforts to address the domestic regulatory need. *See, e.g.*, WTO Panel Report: Thailand—Restrictions on Importation of and Internal Taxes on Cigarettes, Nov. 7, 1990, GATT B.I.S.D. (37th Supp.) at 200 (1991).

F. The Choice between Treaty Specification and Delegation to Dispute Resolution

When trade negotiators select the language of a particular provision, they determine the extent to which subsequent specification is delegated to dispute resolution or other processes, as well as the substantive treatment of an issue. In connection with the Anti-Dumping Agreement, for example, the participants in the Uruguay Round agreed on a scope of review of national measures, intending to leave a defined scope for auto-interpretation by WTO members and to provide for reduced scrutiny by a dispute resolution panel of factual matters established by WTO members.[52]

The decision regarding the post-legislative role of dispute resolution is not different in abstract theoretical terms from the decision by a legislature[53] to delegate rule-making or interpretative functions to an administrative agency. Recognizing that dispute resolution tribunals engage in interpretation and construction and are stymied by lacunae, it is important to question how and why particular provisions operate to authorize interpretation and construction.

Not only do treaty writers delegate authority to dispute resolution tribunals, they also maintain complex relationships with both the formal and the informal dispute resolution processes. First is the possibility of legislative reversal: if the authors of the treaty become discontented with the manner of its application, they may change the treaty. Second, and relatively unusual in general international law, is a formal "political filter" device. Although it still exists in attenuated form, this political filter was much more important prior to the 1994 changes to WTO dispute resolution.

As is now well-understood and the subject of much commentary, the Uruguay Round brought about a dramatic shift in the structure of dispute resolution in international trade.[54] Prior to the establishment of the WTO, GATT dispute settlement suffered from many arguable weaknesses. Chief among the perceived weaknesses was the requirement that consensus among the members of the GATT Council (the full membership) be attained in order for the report of a dispute reso-

---

52. Agreement on Implementation of Article VI of the General Agreement on Tariffs and Trade 1994, Apr. 15, 1994, art. 17.6, Marrakesh Agreement Establishing the World Trade Organization, Annex 1A, THE RESULTS OF THE URUGUAY ROUND OF MULTILATERAL TRADE NEGOTIATIONS: THE LEGAL TEXTS 168, 193 (1994).

53. The term is used here in the traditional sense.

54. *See, e.g.*, Andreas F. Lowenfeld, *Remedies along with Rights: Institutional Reform in the New GATT*, 88 AM. J. INT'L L. 477 (1994); G. Richard Shell, *Trade Legalism and International Relations Theory: An Analysis of the World Trade Organization*, 44 DUKE L.J. 829 (1995); Michael K. Young, *Dispute Resolution in the Uruguay Round: Lawyers Triumph over Diplomats*, 29 INT'L LAW. 389 (1995); Miguel Montana i Mora, *A GATT with Teeth: Law Wins over Politics in the Resolution of International Trade Disputes*, 31 COLUM. J. TRANSNAT'L L. 103 (1993).

lution panel to acquire legal effect.[55] Thus, the loser had the ability to block adoption of the panel report. This was a political filter that did not allow politically objectionable decisions to have legal effect. The change made in the DSU reversed the consensus rule: panel decisions are to be adopted automatically unless *rejected* by consensus.[56]

Of course, the representatives of member states continue to have substantial power over the dispute resolution process. One avenue of influence is the ability to establish new treaties or treaty provisions[57] and thereby "legislatively" to reverse the outcome of a dispute resolution determination. A second avenue of influence is through the *exclusive* authority to adopt interpretations of WTO agreements.[58] A third is to specify the "standard of review," as mentioned above.

Thus, perhaps like other tribunals, WTO dispute resolution may be seen as a hybrid, or a confluence of these two types of authority. Of course, positive political theory would analyze the interaction of adjudicative and legislative authority in game theoretic and perhaps other terms, examining how the structure of the relationship between these two bodies affects outcomes.[59]

G. *The Assignment of Competences to WTO Dispute Resolution*

This section examines the mechanisms by which competences to address important issues are assigned to WTO dispute resolution. Many of these issues are largely trade issues, such as the determination of applicable tariffs.[60] Others exist at the margins of WTO law, implicating "trade and . . ." type problems.[61] Any of these issues have the capacity to be "big cases": the *Bananas*[62] decision and the *Computers*[63]

---

55. In the Omnibus Trade and Competitiveness Act of 1988, the United States expressed as its first trade negotiating objective "to provide for more effective and expeditious dispute settlement." Omnibus Trade and Competitiveness Act of 1988, Pub. L. No. 100-418, § 1101(b)(1)(a), 102 Stat. 1107 (codified at 19 U.S.C. § 2901(b)(1) (1988)). *But see* Ernst-Ulrich Petersmann, *Uruguay Round Negotiations 1986–1991, in* THE NEW GATT ROUND OF MULTILATERAL TRADE NEGOTIATIONS: LEGAL AND ECONOMIC PROBLEMS 501, 555 (ERNST-ULRICH PETERSMANN & MEINHARD HILF, ed., 2d ed. 1991) (arguing that this was not a significant problem).

56. DSU, *supra* note 2, art. 16(4). Automatic adoption can be blocked by consensus, or can be forestalled by an appeal.

57. *See* WTO Agreement, *supra* note 39, art. X.

58. *Id.* art. 9(2). *See also* DSU, *supra* note 2, art. 3(9) providing that the provisions of the "Understanding are without prejudice to the rights of Members to seek authoritative interpretation of provisions of a covered agreement through decision-making under the WTO Agreement . . . ."

59. *See, e.g.,* Robert Cooter & Josef Drexl, *The Logic of Power in the Emerging European Constitution: Game Theory and the Division of Powers,* 14 INT'L REV. L. & ECON. 307 (1994).

60. *See, e.g.,* WTO Appellate Body Report: European Communities—Customs Classification of Certain Computer Equipment, WT/DS62, 67, 68/AB/R, (June 22, 1998) [hereinafter Computers Report].

61. *See* Joël P. Trachtman, *Trade and . . . Problems, Cost-Benefit Analysis and Subsidiarity,* 9 EUR. J. INT'L L. 32 (1998) [hereinafter Trachtman, *Trade and . . . Problems*].

62. Bananas Appellate Body Report, *supra* note 50.

63. Computers Report, *supra* note 60.

decision are both "big cases" involving relatively "pure" trade law issues. On the other hand, there are some types of "big cases" that involve non-trade issues, such as the recent *Shrimp/Turtle* decision or the *Film* decision. Of course, the careful reader will respond that the domain of "trade" issues is not so clearly delimited as this paragraph pretends.

The *Shrimp/Turtle* decision is a typical "trade and . . ." circumstance, with national environmental regulation criticized as unduly restrictive of international trade and a breach of WTO obligations. These cases are at the margin of WTO law. In these types of cases, there are two foci. First, is this domestic measure subject to article III of GATT? If it is, is it exclusively subject to article III of GATT and removed from the strict scrutiny of article XI of GATT? Second, if it is not (which is generally the case) and the measure would otherwise be found to violate article XI, is there an exception available under article XX of GATT? Each step in this analysis has involved a good deal of creativity on the part of dispute resolution panels and now the Appellate Body: in none of these cases is the language of the treaty viewed as determinate.

The *Film* case demonstrates the limited distance a panel would be willing to travel to find non-violation nullification or impairment. Again, the treaty language is indeterminate.

We may view the indeterminacy (or incompleteness) or standard-like nature of these treaty provisions as delegation to dispute resolution. In other words, as time goes by, one can increasingly view the decision to draft these provisions as they are, or to leave them as they are, as legislative decisions and as delegations. Two related analytical methods that seek to explain these decisions are reviewed below.

III. WTO DISPUTE RESOLUTION AND THE INCOMPLETE CONTRACTS PERSPECTIVE

This and the following section develop two linked analytical techniques for application to WTO dispute resolution. The first, the incomplete contracts analysis, is largely consistent with the second, the rules versus standards approach.

Professor Hadfield applies an incomplete contracts analysis to statutes which in turn can be applied to treaties.[64] Treaties may be optimally incomplete in that they contain appropriate instructions for decision-makers to complete the "contract" in particular cases. The parameters to consider include (i) the costs of advance specification, (ii) the degree to which the future is unpredictable or stochastic, (iii) the ability to customize to particular facts in specific cases and

---

64. Hadfield, *supra* note 4.

(iv) the potential value of diversity of compliance techniques. This literature, however, tends to treat the legislature as a unitary actor. It will be exceedingly important to recognize that the legislature in this case (as in Hadfield's) is a group of actors that is subject to strategic and social choice limitations on its ability to act.

Oliver Williamson seeks to link the study of the institutional environment, that is, the general legal context external to particular organizations, to the study of the institutions of governance.[65] From a lawyer's perspective, perhaps the most salient difference between the international legal context and the domestic legal context with which Williamson is concerned is the relative thickness of the domestic legal context. This thick domestic legal context is highly articulated and supplies a reliable and predictable mechanism to complete contracts.

This body of law may specify the terms of a relationship where the parties have not done so; it may complete contracts. Take the example of a commercial contract governed by New York or English law. In the event of a dispute, the parties would have an extremely detailed body of statutory and common law that has responded to an enormous history of commercial disputes. This body of law performs the function of a set of terms automatically incorporated by reference in the contract. *Non-liquet* is not permissible in common law courts. The likelihood that the dispute is not governed by statute or precedent is small, and consequently, the likelihood of proceeding to full litigation is also small.

More saliently, even in the absence of precedent, a common law court will create law to apply. The domestic institutional setting is thick with experience and legislation; it reflects the choices of a complex and relatively comprehensive society. The international institutional setting is thin by comparison. And again, more saliently, the international institutional setting may permit *non-liquet*: where positive law does not exist, the complainant may simply lose by default.

The role of general law in completing contracts reminds us that no institution is an island: each exists in a broader institutional setting. This setting penetrates the institutions at various points, to complete contracts and to supply broader institutional rules where appropriate. Thus, each particular institutional setting is really a complex of interacting institutional settings. However, the WTO generally isolates itself from much of the broader institutional setting of public international law.[66] WTO dispute resolution panels and the Appellate Body are limited to the application of substantive WTO law and are not

---

65. Oliver Williamson, *Comparative Economic Organization: the Analysis of Discrete Structural Alternatives*, 36 ADMIN. SCI. Q. 219 (1994).

66. *See* P.J. Kuyper, *The Law of GATT as a Special Field of International Law: Ignorance, Further Refinement or Self-Contained Regime of International Law*, 24 NETH. Y.B. INT'L L. 227 (1994).

authorized to apply general substantive international law or other conventional international law.[67] On the other hand, as noted above, the rules of interpretation of customary international law have been received into WTO law.

Incomplete contracts give rise to strategic action to capture surplus after the contract is entered into: opportunism. Furthermore, "the prospect of *ex post* bargaining invites *ex ante* pre-positioning of a most inefficient kind."[68] Potential opportunism gives rise to transaction costs in order to forestall opportunistic action; one type of transaction cost is the cost of establishing binding dispute resolution mechanisms. Greater duration and complexity make incompleteness more likely; greater asset specificity accentuates the risks of incompleteness and the concomitant transaction costs. The response will be either to complete the contract by greater anticipation, negotiation and specific advance resolution or to create legislative or judicial institutions to resolve future questions.

Williamson adds a critical dimension to this model, which is change. Change in the environment accentuates uncertainty and the incompleteness of contracts. Williamson distinguishes price-based adaptability in the market from coordination-based adaptability in the firm. He links adaptability to asset specificity and finds that in circumstances where there is both (i) frequent need for modification of relationships, especially where prices are not expected to serve as sufficient coordinating statistics and (ii) high levels of asset specificity, hierarchy (firm) may be more responsive than market (contract) forms of relationship.[69] In the context considered in this article, allocation to WTO dispute resolution may be considered more like the firm while allocation to future legislation, with its requirements of log-rolling and deal-making, may be analogized to the market.

By comparison to the domestic context, the international legal context is thin, consisting of two main types of international law: treaty and customary international law. For the purposes of this Article, the first, treaty, corresponds to contract in domestic law: one does not think of it as law emanating from a vertical government in domestic law but instead as "private" promises that the law will enforce. In this context, the second, customary international law, including the law of treaty, is quite limited in scope.

Due to this "thinness," international treaties are often subject to the problem of incompleteness in a way that domestic contracts are not.

---

67. For an explication of some of the concerns regarding reference to non-WTO law, *see* notes 41–47, *supra*, and accompanying text.

68. .Williamson, *supra* note 65, at 279, *citing* Sanford J. Grossman & Oliver D. Hart, *The Costs and Benefits of Ownership: A Theory of Vertical and Lateral Integration*, 94 J. POLIT. ECON. 691 (1986).

69. Williamson, *supra* note 65, at 277–80.

Domestic contract disputes always have an answer: the common law abhors a vacuum. Courts interpret, construct or leave the loss where it falls. In international treaties, especially those without compromissory clauses,[70] the loss more often stays where it falls and auto-interpretation would be expected to intensify this effect. Even if international treaty gaps are potentially filled by valid international law, there may be gaps in the dispute resolution structure that leave the international law unenforceable although valid.

There is another more serious incompleteness of the WTO legal system. It does not countenance the possibility of directly applicable[71] norms from outside the WTO system. Thus, in addition to *substantive* incompleteness, the WTO suffers from *procedural* or *jurisdictional* incompleteness.

In a domestic legal system, dispute resolution processes can be relied upon to complete contracts, to the extent that the parties find that either litigation or arbitration is a cost-effective means to establish the rights they think are theirs. In the international legal system, similar reliability can be constructed but is generally not available. This is not simply another way of referring to the fact that the international legal system is more horizontal than vertical. Rather, it emphasizes the limited array of institutions available in the international legal system.

Milgrom, North and Weingast point out that the medieval law merchant enforcement system "succeeds even though there is no state with police power and authority over a wide geographic realm to enforce contracts. Instead, the system works by making the reputation system of enforcement work better."[72] The system uses formal institutions to supplement an informal mechanism. Reputation is not simply a non-economic value; rather, it is an important source of transaction cost economizing *ex ante*, where formal institutions are not cheaply available to enforce contracts *ex post*. Appeals to reputation may also assist in enforcement *ex post*. The importance of reputation may be magnified in a context where there are multiple transactions entered into by any one person, as in a village community or an increasingly interdependent international society.

In the international legal system, public international law serves the function that a constitution serves in the domestic legal system: it is a

---

70. John E. Noyes, *The Functions of Compromissory Clauses in U.S. Treaties*, 34 VA. J. INT'L L. 831 (1994).

71. By "directly applicable" I mean norms that apply by their own terms, rather than by virtue of their incorporation by reference in the WTO legal system.

72. Paul R. Milgrom, Douglass C. North, & Barry R. Weingast, *The Role of Institutions in the Revival of Trade: The Law Merchant, Private Judges, and the Champagne Fairs*, 2 ECON. & POL. 1, 19 (1990). The synergistic model that establishes institutions necessary to facilitate private sanctions "appears to have been structured to support trade in a way that minimizes transaction costs, or at least incurs costs only in categories that are indispensable to any system that relies on boycotts and [private] sanctions." *Id.*

fundamental component governing the production of the remainder and of the institutional environment for international organizations and for states. It provides a limited set of rules regarding the formation of law and its interpretation, application and enforcement. Thus, it serves as a set of background norms for treaties[73] and other less "constitutional" varieties of customary international law.

In international law, there are fewer institutional and legal structures to complete contracts. First, in international law, there is not a very complete body of customary or other general law that can be applied to supply missing terms to incomplete treaties. However, article 38 of the Statute of the International Court of Justice authorizes that tribunal to refer to applicable customary international law and general principles of law.[74] Second, in general international law, as opposed to the WTO system, there is usually no dispute resolution tribunal with mandatory jurisdiction. Thus, it is often difficult to rely on the ability to complete contracts through dispute resolution mechanisms.

IV. RULES VERSUS STANDARDS

A related literature examines the economics of rules and standards. Instead of dealing with incomplete contracts, this literature deals more directly with different types of law, accepting in advance that there is no *non liquet* in common law. This literature addresses the fact that laws are sometimes established more specifically in advance as rules, or less specifically in advance as standards.

A. Defining Rules and Standards

In the rules versus standards literature, a law is a "rule" to the extent that it is specified in advance of the conduct to which it is applied. Thus, a law against littering is a rule to the extent that "littering" is well-defined. Must there be an intent not to pick up the discarded item? Are organic or readily biodegradable substances covered? Is littering on private property covered? Is the distribution of leaflets by air covered? Any lawyer knows that there are always questions to ask so that every law is incompletely specified in advance and therefore incompletely a rule.

On the other hand, a standard is a law that is, in relative terms, farther toward the other end of the spectrum. It establishes general guid-

---

73. For a new institutional economics perspective on treaty law, see Georg Ress, *Ex Ante Safeguards Against Ex Post Opportunism in International Treaties: Theory and Practice of International Public Law*, 150 J. INST. & THEO. ECON. 279 (1994). *See also* John K. Setear, *An Iterative Perspective on Treaties: A Synthesis of International Relations Theory and International Law*, 37 HARV. INT'L L.J. 139 (1996).

74. *Statute of the International Court of Justice*, June 26, 1945, art. 38, 59 Stat. 1055, T.I.A.S. No. 993.

ance to both the person governed and the person charged with applying the law but does not, in advance, specify in detail the conduct required or proscribed.

The relativity of these definitions is critical. A standard is more apparently and intentionally specified in advance in an incomplete manner. Familiar constitutional standards in the U.S. legal system include requirements like "due process," prohibitions on uncompensated "takings" or prohibitions on barriers to interstate commerce. A well-known statutory standard is "restraint of trade" under the Sherman Act.[75] It is worth noting that the distinction between a rule and a standard is not necessarily grammatical or determined by the number of words used to express the norm; the distinction relates to how much work remains to be done to determine the applicability of the norm to a particular circumstance. Furthermore, this distinction assumes, in line with H.L.A. Hart and contrary to certain tenets of critical legal theory, that language may be formulated to have core meanings, penumbral influence and limits of application.[76] If all language were equally indeterminate, there would be no distinction between a rule and a standard.

Incompleteness of specification may not simply be a result of conservation of resources. It may be a more explicitly political decision either (i) to agree to disagree for the moment in order to avoid the political price that may arise from immediate hard decisions or (ii) to cloak the hard decisions in the false inevitability of judicial interpretation. It is important also to recognize that the incompleteness of specification may represent a failure to decide how the policy expressed relates to other policies. This is critical in the trade area, where the incompleteness of a trade rule often relates to its failure to address, or incorporate, non-trade policies.

Each law is comprised of a combination of rules and standards. However, it will be useful to speak here generally of rules as being separate from standards.

B. The Costs and Benefits of Rules and Standards

Rules are more expensive to develop *ex ante* than standards because rules entail specification costs, including drafting costs, negotiation costs, and strategic costs involved in *ex ante* specification. In order to reach agreement on specification and to legislate specifically, there may be greater costs in public choice terms.[77] This is particularly interest-

---

75. The Sherman Anti-Trust Act, 15 U.S.C.A. §§ 1–7, § 1 (1990).

76. H.L.A. HART, THE CONCEPT OF LAW, chap. VII (2d ed. 1994). *See also* FREDERICK SCHAUER, PLAYING BY THE RULES (1991).

77. *See* Hadfield, *supra* note 4, at 550, *citing* Linda R. Cohen & Roger G. Noll, *How to Vote, Whether to Vote: Strategies for Voting and Abstaining on Congressional Role Calls*, 13 POL. BEHAV. 97

ing in the trade context where treaty-making would be subjected to intense domestic scrutiny while application of a standard by a dispute resolution process would be subjected to reduced scrutiny. On the other hand, in this connection, NGOs have sought to enhance transparency in dispute resolution. In short, while rules require clear decision, standards may serve as an agreement to disagree or they may help to mask or mystify a decision made.[78] Under standards, both sides in the legislative process, at least initially, may claim victory.

Rules are generally thought to provide greater predictability. There are two moments at which to consider predictability. The first moment refers to the ability of persons subject to the law to be able to plan and conform their conduct *ex ante*. This is sometimes known as "primary predictability."[79] The second moment in which predictability is important is *ex post*, after the relevant conduct has taken place. This type of predictability is "secondary predictability."[80] Both types of predictability can reduce costs. For example, where the parties can predict the outcome of dispute resolution, that is, the tribunal's determination of their respective rights and duties, they will spend less money on litigation.

While rules appear to provide primary and secondary predictability, tribunals may construct exceptions in order to do what is, by their lights, substantial justice, and thereby reduce predictability.[81] It may be difficult to constrain the ability of tribunals to do this. Furthermore, as noted below, game theory predicts that some degree of uncertainty—of unpredictability—may enhance the ability of the parties to bargain to a lower cost solution. Thus, simple predictability is not the only measure of a legal norm; one must also be concerned with the ability of the legal norm to provide satisfactory outcomes. In economic terms, one must be concerned with the allocative efficiency of the outcome. This Article considers allocative efficiency below as it examines the institutional dimension of rules and standards.

In order to evaluate the relative allocational efficiency of potential outcomes, one must recognize that there is a temporal distinction between rules and standards. Standards may be used earlier in the development of a field of law, before sufficient experience to form a basis for more complete specification is acquired. In many areas of law, courts

---

(1991).

78. *See* Kenneth W. Abbott & Duncan Snidal, *Why States Act Through Formal International Organizations*, 42 J. CONFLICT RESOL. 3 (1998).

79. For this use of the terms "primary predictability" and "secondary predictability," see William F. Baxter, *Choice of Law and the Federal System*, 16 STAN. L. REV. 1, 3 (1963).

80. *Id.*

81. *See* Duncan Kennedy, *Form and Substance in Private Law Adjudication*, 89 HARV. L. REV. 1685 (1976) (for the idea that tribunals construct exceptions); *see also id.* (giving examples of constructed exceptions in the context of primary and secondary predictability).

develop a jurisprudence that forms the basis for codification, or even rejection, by legislatures. With this in mind, legislatures or adjudicators may set standards at an early point in time, and determine to establish rules at a later point in time.[82] It is clear that a rule of *stare decisis* is not necessary to the development of a body of jurisprudence by a court or dispute resolution tribunal.[83] It is also worth noting that in a common law setting, or any setting where tribunals refer to precedents, the tribunal may announce a standard in a particular case, and then elaborate that standard in subsequent cases until it has built a rule for its own application.

Kaplow points out that where instances of the relevant behavior are more frequent, economies of scale will indicate that rules become relatively more efficient.[84] For circumstances that arise only infrequently, it is more difficult to justify promulgation of specific rules. In addition, rules provide compliance benefits: they are cheaper to obey, because the cost of determining the required behavior is lower. Rules are also cheaper to apply by a court: the court must only determine the facts and compare them to the rule.

C. The Institutional Dimension of Rules and Standards

Another distinction between rules and standards, often deemphasized in this literature, is the institutional distinction: with rules, the legislature often "makes" the decision; with standards, the adjudicator determines the application of the standard, thereby "making" the decision. Again, it is obvious that these terms are used in a relative sense (this caveat will not be repeated). Economists and even lawyer-economists seem to assume that the tribunal simply "finds" the law, and does not make it. Of course, courts can make rules pursuant to statutory or constitutional authority. The hallmark of a rule is that it is specified *ex ante*, not that it is specified by a legislature. At least in the international trade system, however, rules are largely made by treaty and standards are largely applied by tribunals.[85]

But the difference between legislators and courts is an important one; it may affect the outcome.[86] The choice of legislators or courts to make particular decisions should be made using cost-benefit analysis.

---

82. *See* Kaplow, *The General Characteristics of Rules, supra* note 5, at 10.

83. Palmeter & Mavroidis, *supra* note 41, at 400–01.

84. Kaplow, *supra* note 5, at 13–14.

85. This may be partially a function of the absence of binding precedent in the international trade system. The system also lacks depth and frequency to make tribunals make rules. This is not to say, however, that tribunals may not take an announced standard and then elaborate it into a rule. "Necessity" serves as a good example of this ongoing process. A parallel lies in the infrequency of international law adjudication. The International Court of Justice, for example, rarely speaks.

86. *See* NEIL KOMESAR, IMPERFECT ALTERNATIVES (1994).

Such a cost-benefit analysis would include, as a critical factor, the degree of representativeness: which institution will most accurately reflect citizens' desires? There are good reasons why such cost-benefit analysis does not always select legislatures. First, there is a public choice critique of legislatures. Second, even under a public interest analysis, legislatures may not be efficient at specifying *ex ante* all of the details of treatment of particular cases. Third, the rate of change of circumstances over time may favor the ability of courts to adjust. Finally, the strategic relationship between legislators and courts must be analyzed. Thus, in order fully to understand the relationship between rules and standards, the tools of public choice or positive political theory[87] should be brought to bear to analyze the relationship between legislative and judicial decision-making.[88]

D. The Strategic Dimension of Rules and Standards

It is not possible to consider the costs and benefits of rules and standards separately from the strategic considerations that would cause states to prefer a rule as opposed to a standard. Johnston analyzes rules and standards from a strategic perspective. He finds that, under a standard, bargaining may yield immediate efficient agreement, whereas under a rule this condition may not obtain.[89] Johnston considers a rule a "definite, ex ante entitlement" and a standard a "contingent, ex post entitlement."[90] Like Kaplow, he does not here consider the source of the rule, whether it is the legislature or tribunal.

Johnston notes the "standard supposition in the law and economics literature . . . that private bargaining between [two parties] over the allocation of [a] legal entitlement is most likely to be efficient if the entitlement is clearly defined and assigned *ex ante* according to a rule, rather than made contingent upon a judge's *ex post* balancing of relative value and harm."[91] Johnston suggests this supposition may be incorrect:[92] "[w]hen the parties bargain over the entitlement when there is private information about value and harm, bargaining may be more efficient under a blurry balancing test than under a certain rule."[93] This is because under a certain rule, the holder of the entitle-

---

87. *See, e.g.*, John Ferejohn & Barry Weingast, *A Positive Theory of Statutory Interpretation*, 12 INT'L REV. L. & ECON. 263 (1992). *See also* Sunstein, *supra* note 5, at 973.

88. *See* Cooter & Drexl, *supra* note 59.

89. Jason Scott Johnston, *Bargaining Under Rules Versus Standards*, 11 J.L. ECON. & ORG. 256 (1995).

90. *Id.* at 256.

91. *Id.* at 257 (citations omitted).

92. *See also* Carol M. Rose, *Crystals and Mud in Property Law*, 40 STAN. L. REV. 577 (1988); Joel P. Trachtman, *Externalities and Extraterritoriality*, *in* ECONOMIC DIMENSIONS OF INTERNATIONAL LAW, 642, 675 (Jagdeep S. Bhandari & Alan O. Sykes eds., 1997).

93. Johnston, *supra* note 89, at 257.

ment will have incentives to "hold out" and decline to provide information about the value to him of the entitlement. Under a standard, where presumably it cannot be known with certainty *ex ante* who owns the entitlement, the person not possessing the entitlement may credibly threaten to take it, providing incentives for the other person to bargain. Johnston points out that this result obtains only when the *ex post* balancing test is imperfect because if the balancing were perfect, the threat would not be credible. This provides a counter-intuitive argument for inaccuracy of application of standards.[94]

Interestingly, further research as to the magnitude of strategic costs under rules and under standards might suggest that over time, rules provide some of the strategic benefits of standards. This might be so if tribunals develop exceptions to rules in a way that introduces uncertainty to their application. This increased benefit would, of course, be countervailed to some extent by the reduction of predictability that the development of exceptions would entail.

V. APPLYING INCOMPLETE CONTRACTS AND RULES/STANDARDS ANALYSIS TO INTERNATIONAL TRADE LAW

In the following two sections, the *Shrimp/Turtle* case and the *Film* case are explored as examples of the relationship between rules and standards. This Article compares the case-based decision-making by the WTO dispute settlement system under these provisions with the possibility of decision-making by the more political processes of the Committee on Trade and Environment,[95] for example, or more immediate decision-making or treaty-making by the WTO.

The following table summarizes the factors to be considered as derived from the analysis set forth above and their general application to rules and standards, respectively.

---

94. *Id.* at 272.

95. *See infra* note 149 and surrounding text for a discussion of the work of the Committee on Trade and Environment.

Table 1: Costs and Benefits of Rules and Standards		
	Rules	Standards
Administrative cost of formulation	Higher cost	Lower cost
Public choice costs of specification, including costs of transparency	Higher cost	Lower cost
Perceived legitimacy; democracy deficit	Lower cost	Higher cost
Primary predictability—predictability for actors *ex ante*	Lower cost	Higher cost
Secondary predictability—ease of application by dispute resolution tribunal	Lower cost	Higher cost
Opportunity to gain experience prior to specification	Reduced benefit	Increased benefit
Economies of scale with greater frequency	Increased benefit	Decreased benefit
Minimization strategic costs—promotion of bargaining toward efficient agreement	Decreased benefit	Increased benefit

A. Shrimp/Turtle: *Trade and Environment*

Tariff bindings under article II of GATT have more the character of rules,[96] while norms such as the definition of "like products" under article I or III, the necessity test of article XX(b) and XX(d), the "primarily related" test of article XX(g) or the *chapeau* of article XX of GATT[97] seem more like standards. These "standards" involve complex judicial balancing. One could adduce many additional examples.

Thus far, the GATT and WTO Committees on Trade and the Environment have produced no rules. With the exception of the relevant provisions of the Agreement on Technical Barriers to Trade (the "Standards Agreement")[98] and the Agreement on Sanitary and Phytosanitary Measures (the "S&P Agreement"),[99] there has been no additional legislation in the GATT/WTO system addressing the problem of the relationship between trade and the environment.

---

96. *But see* Computers Report, *supra* note 60.

97. *See* Trachtman, *Trade and . . . Problems, supra* note 61.

98. Agreement on Technical Barriers to Trade, Apr. 15, 1994, Marrakesh Agreement Establishing the World Trade Organization, Annex 1A, THE RESULTS OF THE URUGUAY ROUND OF MULTILATERAL TRADE NEGOTIATIONS: THE LEGAL TEXTS 138 (1994) [hereinafter TBT Agreement].

99. Agreement on the Application of Sanitary and Phytosanitary Measures, Apr. 15, 1994, Marrakesh Agreement Establishing the World Trade Organization, Annex 1A, THE RESULTS OF THE URUGUAY ROUND OF MULTILATERAL TRADE NEGOTIATIONS: THE LEGAL TEXTS 69 (1994) [hereinafter S&P Agreement].

1. *Shrimp/Turtle* Panel Decision

It is worthwhile to describe the facts of this case and the panel report[100] before describing the Appellate Body decision[101] and comparing resolution of this type of issue through dispute resolution with resolution through legislation: resolution through standards versus resolution through rules.

The panel convened to examine a prohibition imposed by the United States on the importation of certain shrimp and shrimp products under section 609 of Public Law 101-162 (hereinafter "section 609")[102] and associated regulations and judicial decisions. Section 609 prohibited importation into the United States of shrimp harvested with commercial shrimp-fishing technology that may adversely affect sea turtles. It also provided an exception for shrimp imported from states certified thereunder. The relevant portion of this exception, applicable where sea turtles are otherwise threatened, permits certification if the exporting state adopts a regulatory program governing the incidental taking of sea turtles comparable to that of the United States and with an average incidental taking rate comparable to U.S. vessels. This regulatory program would require "turtle excluder devices" to be used by commercial shrimp trawling vessels operating in areas where turtles are likely to be found.

This case presented an occasion for the Appellate Body to review the contentious trade and environment issues first addressed in 1991 and 1994 in the *Tuna-Dolphin* cases.[103] In both *Tuna-Dolphin* panel decisions (each unadopted) the panels found the U.S. embargoes on foreign tuna to violate, *inter alia*, article XI of GATT,[104] and were not to be exempted under article XX of GATT.[105] Both the 1991 and the 1994 panels found that the U.S. measure, as a regulation of a process rather than a product, was not exclusively covered by article III of GATT, and so was subject to the prohibition of embargoes under article XI. The 1991 panel found that the U.S. measures did not qualify for an exemption under article XX because that provision did not permit the pro-

---

100. WTO Panel Report: United States—Import Prohibition of Certain Shrimp and Shrimp Products, AB-1998-4, WT/DS58/AB/R (98-1710) (May 15, 1998) [hereinafter Shrimp/Turtle Panel Report].

101. Shrimp/Turtle Appellate Body Report, *supra* note 6.

102. 16 U.S.C.A. 1537, § 609(a). Departments of Commerce, Justice, and State, the Judiciary, and Related Agencies Appropriations Act of 1990, Pub. L. No. 101-162, 103 Stat 988 (1989).

103. WTO Panel Report: United States—Restrictions on Imports of Tuna, GATT B.I.S.D. (39th Supp.) at 155, 204, para. 6.3 (1993), *reprinted in* 30 I.L.M. 1594 (1991) [hereinafter First Tuna Report]; WTO Panel Report: United States—Restrictions on Imports of Tuna, DS29/R (1994), *reprinted in* 33 I.L.M. 839 (1994) [hereinafter Second Tuna Report].

104. First Tuna Report, *supra* note 103, para. 5.18; Second Tuna Report, *supra* note 103, para. 5.10.

105. First Tuna Report, *supra* note 103, paras. 5.29, 5.34; Second Tuna Report, *supra* note 103, paras. 5.27, 5.39.

tection of animals outside the territory of the state adopting the relevant measure.[106] Furthermore, it found that the U.S. measures were not "necessary" within the meaning of article XX(b) insofar as the goal sought to be protected by the United States might have been addressed through multilateral negotiations.[107] The 1994 panel left open the possibility that article XX could permit the protection of animals extraterritorially. It did find, however, that the U.S. measures did not qualify for article XX because they were designed, not to directly achieve environmental goals, but to coerce other governments into adopting specific environmental policies.[108]

The *Shrimp/Turtle* panel took a novel, and ultimately unacceptable, approach to interpreting and applying the exemptive provisions of article XX of GATT.[109] Analyzing the *chapeau*, the panel first found that the countries that were certified and those that were not were "countries where the same conditions prevail" and that therefore the U.S. measure was discriminatory.[110] The panel did not even evaluate the U.S. position that different conditions prevail in these two types of countries. Thus, the panel implicitly disrespected the regulatory categories established by section 609.

The panel next turned to the question of whether this discrimination was arbitrary or unjustifiable. Specifically, the panel focused on the word "unjustifiable," arguing that it must be interpreted in light of the purpose of the WTO Agreement[111] as a whole. The panel found that the purpose of the *chapeau* is to prohibit abuse of article XX, and, unfortunately, equated "abuse" with frustration of the broadest purposes of the WTO Agreement.[112] This approach might be acceptable if the purposes of the WTO Agreement were read to include subtleties like maintaining a degree of local regulatory autonomy. This is not the way that the panel read the purposes of the WTO Agreement. By selecting a limited, unidimensional "object and purpose," the Panel pre-

---

106. First Tuna Report, *supra* note 103, para. 5.27.
107. *Id.* para. 5.28.
108. Second Tuna Report, *supra* note 103, para. 5.37.
109. The *"chapeau"* of article XX of the GATT and the relevant exceptions are as follows:
    Subject to the requirement that such measures are not applied in a manner which would constitute a means of arbitrary or unjustifiable discrimination between countries where the same conditions prevail, or a disguised restriction on international trade, nothing in this Agreement shall be construed to prevent the adoption or enforcement by any Member of measures:
    (b) necessary to protect human, animal or plant life or health;
    (g) relating to the conservation of exhaustible natural resources if such measures are made effective in conjunction with restrictions on domestic production or consumption . . . .
    GATT, *supra* note 40, art. XX.
110. Shrimp/Turtle Panel Report, *supra* note 100, para. 7.33.
111. *Id.* para. 7.34, citing the WTO Agreement, *supra* note 39.
112. Shrimp/Turtle Panel Report, *supra* note 100, para. 7.40.

determined that measures having an environmental object and purpose could not be justified under article XX. The Panel stated that

> While the WTO Preamble confirms that environmental considerations are important for the interpretation of the WTO Agreement, the central focus of that agreement remains the promotion of economic development through trade; and the provisions of GATT are essentially turned toward liberalization of access to markets on a nondiscriminatory basis.[113]

The Panel concluded that derogations from other provisions of GATT are permissible under article XX only so long as they "do not undermine the WTO multilateral trading system."[114] As the United States argued in connection with its appeal, this uncompromising allegiance to the international trading system—this unidimensional teleological method of interpretation—contradicts the clear intent of article XX. The panel went further, however, to hold that its examination of whether a measure undermines the multilateral trading system may look not only at the particular measure before the panel but at the possibility of a proliferation of measures that in the aggregate might undermine the system.[115] Again this seems to exceed the clear meaning of article XX.

The panel carefully distinguished this case dealing with unilateral measures by the importing state from possible cases where the importing state acts pursuant to a multilateral environmental agreement.[116] Although the panel's distinction between these circumstances under WTO law is not clear, the panel effectively reserved judgment on this issue. It stated that the "negotiation of a multilateral agreement or action under multilaterally defined criteria is clearly a possible way to avoid threatening the multilateral trading system."[117] Given that multilateral environmental agreements might well be inconsistent with trade goals, one wonders why this is so clear. The panel did not say whether compliance with a multilateral environmental agreement may support the availability of an exception under article XX.

2. *Shrimp/Turtle* Appellate Body Decision

In its arguments to the Appellate Body, the United States argued that the panel had misinterpreted the *chapeau* of article XX, thereby effectively "eras[ing]" article XX from the GATT in any case in which

---

113. *Id.* para. 7.42.
114. *Id.* para. 7.44.
115. *Id.*
116. *Id.* para. 7.50.
117. *Id.* para. 7.55.

there is a "threat to the multilateral trading system."[118] Indeed, the Appellate Body criticized the panel for departing from the text of the GATT and for not examining the ordinary meaning of the text.

In pursuit of this approach, the Appellate Body recalled that in the *Gasoline* case[119] it had focused on the use of the reference to the manner in which the measure is applied, clarifying that the *chapeau* is not concerned with the nature of the measure itself.[120] The design of the measure itself is addressed in the subparagraphs of article XX. The panel, on the other hand, evaluated whether section 609 itself satisfied the criteria of the *chapeau*.[121]

Furthermore, the Appellate Body stated that a teleological interpretation should consider the provision itself being interpreted, not the whole of the WTO Agreement:

> Maintaining, rather than undermining, the multilateral trading system is necessarily a fundamental and pervasive premise underlying the *WTO Agreement*; but it is not a right or an obligation, nor is it an interpretative rule which can be employed in the appraisal of a given measure under the chapeau of Article XX.[122]

The Appellate Body recalled that in the *Gasoline* case, it had examined the object and purpose of the *chapeau*, finding that it is intended to prevent abuse of the exceptions listed in article XX.[123] The panel did not examine the question of whether section 609 was applied in a manner that was arbitrary or unjustifiable discrimination or a disguised restriction within the meaning of the *chapeau*.[124] The Appellate Body further criticized the panel for examining compliance with the *chapeau* prior to determining compliance with any of the following exceptions.[125] It is not possible to determine whether an exception is being abused without first determining whether the exception is otherwise available.[126]

In fact, the Appellate Body completely rejected the panel's line of reasoning: "conditioning access to a Member's domestic market on whether exporting Members comply with, or adopt, a policy or policies unilaterally prescribed by the importing Member may, to some degree, be a common aspect of measures falling within the scope of one

---

118. Shrimp/Turtle Appellate Body Report, *supra* note 6, para. 15.
119. Gasoline Report, *supra* note 14.
120. Shrimp/Turtle Appellate Body Report, *supra* note 6, para. 38.
121. Shrimp/Turtle Panel Report, *supra* note 100, para. 7.29.
122. Shrimp/Turtle Appellate Body Report, *supra* note 6, para. 117.
123. *Id.*
124. *Id.*
125. *Id.* para. 118.
126. *Id.* para. 121.

or another of the exceptions (a) to (j) of Article XX."[127] In an ideal setting, such a wholesale rejection of the panel's reasoning and conclusion would be a basis for remand to the panel for further findings; in fact, lacking the power of remand, the Appellate Body bravely made its own findings.[128]

In a ringing defense of living resources, the Appellate Body found that article XX(g), referring to "exhaustible natural resources," includes living resources such as sea turtles.[129] Referring to the drafting history of article XX(g), which involved discussions of mineral resources, the Appellate Body endorsed an organic approach to interpretation: the words "exhaustible natural resources" "must be read by a treaty interpreter in the light of contemporary concerns of the community of nations about the protection and conservation of the environment."[130] Interestingly, the Appellate Body looked to the inclusion of sea turtles on Appendix 1 (species listed are threatened with extinction) of the Convention on International Trade in Endangered Species of Wild Fauna and Flora (CITES) for evidence of the endangered position of these animals.[131]

Continuing its analysis of the availability of an exception under article XX(g), the Appellate Body examined whether section 609 "relates to" the conservation of exhaustible natural resources.[132] This "relates to" requirement has been construed to require that the measure be "primarily aimed at" this goal. The Appellate Body applied a means-ends analysis, finding that the U.S. measure satisfies this test (despite the fact that it might be construed as aimed at changing exporting state policy, rather than at directly protecting turtles). The Appellate Body also found that the U.S. measure satisfies the third prong of article XX(g): that it is made effective in conjunction with restrictions on domestic harvesting of shrimp.[133]

---

127. *Id.* para. 122.
128. "Having reversed the Panel's legal conclusion . . . we believe that it is our duty and our responsibility to complete the legal analysis . . . ." *Id.* para. 123. This is a substantial departure from the approach taken by the Appellate Body in the *Computers* report, in which the Appellate Body rejected the panel's reasoning, but then failed to continue to provide its own legal analysis. Computers Report, *supra* note 60.
129. Shrimp/Turtle Appellate Body Report, *supra* note 6, § VI(B)(1).
130. *Id.* para. 130.
131. *Id.* para. 132, *citing* Convention on International Trade in Endangered Species of Wild Fauna and Flora, app. 1, Mar. 3, 1973, 27 U.S.T. 1087, 993 U.N.T.S. 243 (1973) [hereinafter CITES]. Importantly, the Appellate Body specifically declined to rule on whether there is a territorial or jurisdictional limitation in article XX(g)—whether the "extraterritorial" nature of the U.S. measure removed it from eligibility for an exception under that provision. It was able to do so because the sea turtles at issue are migratory, migrating to and from U.S. waters. *Id.* para. 133.
132. Shrimp/Turtle Appellate Body Report, *supra* note 6, § VI(B)(2).
133. *Id.* § VI(B)(3).

The Appellate Body then turned to the *chapeau*.[134] Here, the Appellate Body relied heavily on its analysis in the *Gasoline* case to the effect that "the measures falling within the particular exceptions must be applied reasonably, with due regard both to the legal duties of the party claiming the exception and the legal rights of the other parties concerned."[135] This formulation, and its use here, sets up a kind of balancing test for availability of exceptions under article XX. The Appellate Body's application of this balancing test is colored by the language regarding "sustainable development" contained in the first paragraph of the preamble to the WTO Agreement.[136]

The adoption of this balancing test constitutes a recognition that these types of issues are not addressed by a *rule* of WTO law, but that the parties to the WTO Agreement intended the dispute resolution process, and effectively the Appellate Body, to address these issues. As discussed below, the parties to the WTO Agreement have had opportunities, through the Committee on Trade and Environment and elsewhere, especially since the two *Tuna* decisions,[137] to address these issues with rules. Its failure to do so reinforces at least the legitimacy of the dispute resolution process doing so.

By way of engaging in this balancing test, the Appellate Body first engaged in a means-ends analysis, finding the U.S. measure to be too broad and unnecessarily stringent, insofar as it requires foreign governments to adopt essentially the same policies as those applied by the United States.[138] The Appellate Body also noted that the U.S. approach failed to consider the different conditions that pertain in other members' territories.[139] Furthermore, the Appellate Body questioned whether domestic measures alone can be effective and suggested that unilateral measures are not an effective means to the desired end.[140]

During the balancing process, the Appellate Body also found the approach of the U.S. measure, section 609, to be a kind of discrimination in that it does not permit the import of shrimp caught using turtle excluder devices but originating in a state that is not certified.[141] The failure of the United States to engage in international negotiations

---

134. *Id.* § VI(C).

135. *Id.* para. 151, *quoting* Gasoline Report, *supra* note 14, at 22. *See also* Shrimp/Turtle Appellate Body Report, *supra* note 6, paras. 156, 159.

136. The relevant language is as follows:

while allowing for the optimal use of the world's natural resources in accordance with the objective of *sustainable development*, seeking both to protect and preserve the environment and to enhance the means for doing so in a manner consistent with their respective needs and concerns at different levels of economic development . . . .

WTO Agreement, *supra* note 39, pmbl., para. 1 (italics added).

137. First Tuna Report, *supra* note 103; Second Tuna Report, *supra* note 103.

138. Shrimp/Turtle Appellate Body Report, *supra* note 6, paras. 162–64.

139. *Id.* para. 165.

140. *Id.* paras. 167–69.

141. *Id.* para. 165.

further weighed against the U.S. measure. The Appellate Body then pointed out that while the United States signed the as yet unratified Inter-American Convention for the Protection and Conservation of Sea Turtles, that convention contains a requirement to respect article XI of GATT.[142]

At least in part then, the Appellate Body used the balancing test to examine whether the measure at issue was the least trade restrictive device available. In this case, it held that the existence of the Inter-American Convention demonstrated that a less restrictive device was available (at least in terms of its consensual origins, if not in terms of its potential to restrict trade). The Appellate Body also referred to the fact that consensual negotiations in the Inter-American Convention context "marked out the equilibrium line . . . ."[143] Perhaps the Appellate Body felt the need to support its standard-based balancing test determination with this reference to a treaty rule-based determination.

Finally, the Appellate Body found real discrimination in the way that the United States (i) negotiated multilateral agreements and (ii) applied phase-in periods to different countries. It considered this discrimination "unjustifiable" within the meaning of the *chapeau*.[144] The rigidity of section 609, including its failure to distinguish among countries in which different conditions prevail, as well as the lack of transparency of the certification process, led to the further finding that this discrimination was "arbitrary" under the *chapeau*.[145] The Appellate Body went on to impose a requirement of due process in connection with the application of exceptions under article XX of GATT.[146]

Upon review, the Appellate Body's decision in *Shrimp/Turtle* proves itself to be careful and conservative, in addition to politically sensitive. The Appellate Body, very importantly, held open the possibility that unilateral measures may be crafted in such a way, and developed in particular contexts, in which they might satisfy the requirements of article XX.[147] While the Appellate Body declined to reach a number of important issues, and did not explicitly accept that a multilateral environmental agreement would be a sound basis for an exception under article XX, it welcomed environmental measures, and recommended those that are not unilateral.[148]

---

142. *Id.* para. 170, *citing* Inter-American Convention for the Protection and Conservation of Sea Turtles, with Annexes, Caracas, Dec. 1, 1996, signed by the United States, Dec. 13, 1996 [hereinafter Inter-American Convention].

143. Shrimp/Turtle Appellate Body Report, *supra* note 6, paras. 171–72, *discussing* the Inter-American Convention, *supra* note 142.

144. Shrimp/Turtle Appellate Body Report, *supra* note 6, para. 177.

145. *Id.*

146. *Id.* paras. 182, 183, *citing* art. X of GATT.

147. Shrimp/Turtle Appellate Body Report, *supra* note 6, para. 186.

148. *Id.* paras. 185–86.

This decision shows a measured, analytical approach to teleological interpretation, helping to develop the jurisprudential tools of international law. The Appellate Body recognized that the unidimensional teleology of the panel was too blunt an instrument for accurate adjudication. The Appellate Body also refined its interpretative tools by rejecting a strict "original intent" interpretation of article XX(g) in favor of a more dynamic interpretation to fit modern circumstances. In doing so, it aggregated substantial power to itself, both to engage in balancing and to "modernize" the interpretation of article XX.

As the WTO addresses the problem of the intersection between international environmental law and international trade law, it will be interesting to observe the extent to which the Appellate Body will determine the nature of this intersection. For now, the Appellate Body has retained jurisdiction to address these relationships and has articulated a standard, a balancing test, that gives the Appellate Body itself wide flexibility in responding to these problems. In addition, it will be worth observing the extent to which the Appellate Body must transform itself from a "trade court" to a general international court in order to deal with intersections between trade values and other vital considerations such as environment.

3. The Work of the Committee on Trade and Environment

In 1994, the trade ministers who approved the results of the Uruguay Round also approved a Decision on Trade and Environment.[149] This decision called for the formation of the WTO Committee on Trade and the Environment (CTE) with a mandate to make recommendations regarding the modifications of the multilateral trading system needed to "enhance positive interaction between trade and environmental measures." The CTE issued a report at the Singapore Ministerial in 1996.[150] This report did not constitute legislation, and its "approval" at the Singapore Ministerial[151] was not a legislative or treaty-making act. In fact, as set forth in more detail below, the CTE has remained a "talking shop," with no direct legislative impact thus far. However, the lack of direct legislative impact does not mean that the CTE has had no impact on the context of WTO dispute resolution.

---

149. Decision on Trade and Environment, Apr. 14, 1994, World Trade Organization, Report (1996) of the Committee on Trade and Environment, [hereinafter 1996 CTE Report], Annex 1C, WTO Doc. WT/CTE/W/40 (Nov. 7, 1996) [hereinafter Decision on Trade and Environment].

150. CTE Report. *See* Steve Charnovitz, *A Critical Guide to The WTO's Report on Trade And Environment*, 14 ARIZ. J. INT'L & COMP. L. 341 (1997).

151. World Trade Organization: Singapore Ministerial Declaration, adopted Dec. 13, 1996, 36 I.L.M. 218, 224, para. 16 (1997).

a. Cooperation with Dispute Resolution

In its December 9, 1998, report, the CTE noted that in October 1998, Australia, Canada, the European Community and New Zealand expressed satisfaction with the Appellate Body's *Shrimp/Turtle* decision.[152] Moreover, Canada stated that the report would be useful in the formulation of a statement on the interaction between multilateral environmental agreements and WTO rules. This is an example of dispute resolution decisions leading the way for a more political legislative process. In effect, the CTE sees itself in a cooperative project with the dispute settlement process to elaborate the application of article XX of GATT to environmental measures. Thus, the CTE requested the Secretariat to prepare a note on the "GATT/WTO Dispute Settlement Practice Relating to Article XX, Paragraphs (b), (d) and (g) of GATT."[153] This report might be viewed as a kind of "restatement of the law" such as those used in common law systems to organize, codify and perhaps develop common law rules.

The Secretariat also states that in the event of a dispute arising due to the application of a trade measure in a multilateral environmental agreement (MEA), "WTO Members are confident that the WTO dispute settlement provisions would be able to tackle any problems which arise in this area, including in cases when resort to environmental expertise is needed."[154] This expression seems to suggest that further "legislative" or treaty action is not required to address these types of trade and environment problems.[155] Canada also expressed concern that an attempt to legislate more specifically "ran the risk of a result more restrictive than the status quo, which provided, as expressed in the 1996 Report of the CTE, considerable flexibility and would continue to evolve through WTO panels."[156]

> Norway said that the main task . . . was to clarify how two sets of legal commitments (WTO rules and MEAs) were complementary so that conflicts were prevented. There were basically two options:

---

152. Shrimp/Turtle Appellate Body Report, *supra* note 6.

153. GATT Secretariat, *GATT/WTO Dispute Settlement Practice Relating to Article XX, Paras. (b), (d) and (g) of GATT*, WT/CTE/W/53/Rev.1 (Oct. 26, 1998).

154. *Trade and Environment in the WTO* (visited Dec. 29, 1998) <http://www.wto.org/wto/environ/environ1.htm>.

155. *See also* WTO Committee on Trade and the Environment Invites MEA Secretariats to Information Session, and Discusses Items Related to the Linkages between the Multilateral Environment and Trade Agendas, WTO Press Release Press/TE/025 (Aug. 13, 1998) [hereinafter WTO Information Session] ("One point which was noted by Members who spoke on this item was that WTO rules already provide considerable scope for accommodating the use of trade measures necessary for environmental purposes.").

156. *Id.*

(i) rely on evolving jurisprudence (the status quo); or (ii) devise solutions to accommodate MEA trade measures in the WTO.[157]

Thus, the choice between adjudication and legislation—between standards and rules—is explicit.

The CTE has also addressed the problem of jurisdictional lacunae covered earlier in this Article. In its background note on Trade and Environment in the WTO, the WTO Secretariat states as follows:

> A related item concerns the appropriate forum for the settlement of potential disputes that may arise over the use of trade measures pursuant to MEAs; is it the WTO, or is it the dispute settlement mechanisms that exists in the MEAs themselves? There is general agreement that in the event a dispute arises between WTO Members who are each Parties to an MEA over the use of trade measures they are applying among themselves pursuant to the MEA, they should consider in the first instance trying to resolve it through the dispute settlement mechanisms available under the MEA. Were a dispute to arise with a non-party to an MEA, however, the WTO would provide the only possible forum for the settlement of the dispute.[158]

This statement is notable for two reasons. First, the Secretariat seems willing to cede "adjudicative" jurisdiction where both parties to a "trade and environment" dispute are party also to the relevant MEA despite the clear and strong language of article 23 of the Dispute Settlement Understanding establishing that the WTO dispute resolution mechanism is the exclusive forum for determining violations of WTO agreements. Second, the secretariat leaves unanswered the question, in the context of a dispute with a non-party to an MEA, whether—and in what manner—the WTO dispute settlement forum is authorized to "apply" the MEA.

Another cross-jurisdictional question relates to the effect in the WTO system of MEA rules. For example, in the results of the 1992 U.N. Conference on Environment and Development, many WTO members endorsed Principle 12 of the Rio Declaration that "Unilateral actions to deal with environmental challenges outside the jurisdiction of the importing country should be avoided. Environmental measures addressing transboundary or global environmental problems should, as far as possible, be based on an international consensus."[159] It is important to note that Principle 12 is not binding law. On the other hand,

---

157. *Id.*

158. *See* Trade and Environment in the WTO, *supra* note 154. *See also* 1996 CTE Report, *supra* note 150.

159. Rio Declaration on Environment and Development, princ. 12, U.N. doc. A/CONF.151/5/Rev.1 (1992), 31 I.L.M. 874, 878 (1992).

the CTE has spoken of the need legislatively to clarify the legality of "discriminatory trade restrictions applied by MEA Parties against non-parties that involve extra-jurisdictional action."[160] As noted above, the Appellate Body in its *Shrimp/Turtle* decision explicitly refused to do so.

b. Coordination with MEA Secretariats

In addition to coordinating within the WTO, the CTE has also co-ordinated with the secretariats of various MEAs.[161] This coordination role can assist in formulating MEAs that raise fewer trade issues. In theory, it could also assist in formulating modifications to the WTO legal system to reduce potential conflict.

In addition, a number of WTO dispute resolution panels and the Appellate Body, including most importantly the *Tuna* decisions,[162] the *Gasoline* decision[163] and the *Shrimp/Turtle* decision,[164] have considered whether multilateral measures had been attempted in order to determine the compliance of unilateral measures with article XX. These decisions do not directly apply multilateral rules, but use them indirectly to make determinations under the standards of article XX. The *Shrimp/Turtle* Appellate Body report suggests that the balancing test it uses to apply the *chapeau* of article XX may be short-circuited by examination of the "equilibrium line" negotiated in MEAs.[165]

Indeed, in its 1996 Report, the CTE "endorses and supports multilateral solutions based on international cooperation and consensus as the best and most effective way for governments to tackle environmental problems of a transboundary or global nature."[166] Thus, there is a delicate interactive process, not strictly dictated by law, by which WTO dispute resolution, WTO legislation and MEA action are, to a degree, coordinated.

4. Explaining the Relative Dominance of Dispute Resolution

What plausible explanations can be posited for the dominance thus far of WTO dispute resolution in addressing the relationship between trade concerns and environmental concerns?

Some WTO members have provided an explanation that is consistent with a rules/standards analysis:

---

160. 1996 CTE Report, *supra* note 150, at 14.
161. *See, e.g.*, WTO Information Session, *supra* note 155.
162. First Tuna Report, *supra* note 103; Second Tuna Report, *supra* note 103.
163. Gasoline Report, *supra* note 14.
164. Shrimp/Turtle Appellate Body Report, *supra* note 6.
165. *See* Shrimp/Turtle Appellate Body Report, *supra* note 6, para. 170.
166. *See* 1996 CTE Report, *supra* note 150.

> When account is taken of the limited number of MEAs that con-
> tain trade provisions, and the fact that no trade dispute has arisen
> over the use of those measures to date, some feel that there is no
> evidence of a real conflict between the WTO and MEAs; existing
> WTO rules already provide sufficient scope to allow trade meas-
> ures to be applied pursuant to MEAs, and it is neither necessary
> nor desirable to exceed that scope. According to this view, the
> proper course of action to resolve any underlying conflict which
> may be felt to exist in this area is for WTO Members to avoid
> using trade measures in MEAs which are inconsistent with their
> WTO obligations. Any clarification in that respect can be pro-
> vided, as necessary, ex post through the WTO dispute settlement
> mechanism.[167]

This excerpt refers to the relative infrequency, indeed the speculative
nature, of possible conflict between MEA obligations and WTO law.
Of course, there has been substantially more frequent conflict between
unilateral environmental measures and WTO law. As additional disputes occur, the Appellate Body will have opportunities to articulate a
jurisprudence that will be influenced by the scope of MEAs, as well as
by decisions of the CTE and the WTO generally. In turn, the Appellate Body's jurisprudence may stimulate a codification or a negative
codification—a legislative reversal.

If the table of costs and benefits was filled in the trade and environment context, the following might be the result. This filled-in table is
speculative: greater certainty would require more empirical and analytical work. Additionally, it is difficult to quantify and commensurate
among the various costs and benefits. This kind of analysis is merely
meant as a guide to political discourse which would presumably evaluate each of the categories of costs and benefits.

---

167. *Id.* at 14.

Table 2: Costs and Benefits in Trade/Environment Context		
	Rules	Standards
Administrative cost of formulation	Higher cost	Lower cost—status quo
Public choice costs of specification, including costs of transparency	Very high cost given extreme diversity of perspective	Lower cost—status quo
Perceived legitimacy; democracy deficit	Lower cost	Higher cost
Primary predictability—predictability for actors *ex ante*	Lower cost, but depends on avoiding development of substantial exceptions through dispute resolution	Higher cost, but the *Shrimp/Turtle* decision has enhanced predictability
Secondary predictability—ease of application by dispute resolution tribunal	Lower cost, but depends on avoiding development of substantial exceptions through dispute resolution	Higher cost, but the *Shrimp/Turtle* decision has enhanced predictability
Opportunity to gain experience prior to specification	Reduced benefit, although the magnitude of reduction declines as experience is already gained	Increased benefit, especially as dispute resolution decisions raise opportunities for dialog
Economies of scale with greater frequency	Increased benefit, and likely to grow as more intersections between trade and environment arise	Decreased benefit, but may serve as casuist legislature over time, reaping similar economies of scale
Minimization strategic costs—promotion of bargaining toward efficient agreement	Reduced benefit, although the magnitude of reduction may decline as uncertainty of result of rules rises with development of exceptions	Increased benefit given uncertainty of outcome

The above table suggests that as more experience is gained, and as more trade/environment conflicts arise (perhaps due to the increase of trade law, the increase of environmental law, or both), one might expect a shift from standards to rules. While the present analysis is insufficient to suggest that it is time for the legislation of rules in the trade and environment area, it serves first to rebut arguments that it is definitely time for such legislation and second to provide a more discrete matrix of considerations in determining whether rules are appropriate.

B. Film: *Non-Violation Nullification or Impairment*

In contrast to standards that are designed to import non-trade values to the trade system, this Article next examines a "standard" that is designed to address barriers to trade not specifically addressed in the GATT: the concept of non-violation nullification or impairment

(NVNI).[168] This concept may be used to import non-trade values to the trade system, but its use is more limited, as demonstrated by the *Film* decision discussed below. It is a super-standard in the sense that it authorizes substantial construction of norms by dispute resolution. Interestingly, it has been used with remarkable restraint, and in the area of competition policy, has not yet been applied to bind states' actions.

In connection with the recent Kodak-Fuji/United States-Japan dispute regarding access of U.S. photographic materials to the Japanese market, a number of interesting issues were raised as to the coverage of WTO law. The WTO lacks any substantial coverage of competition law,[169] nor does it otherwise specifically address issues of domestic business structure or non-discriminatory general domestic regulation, other than regulation of technical standards and sanitary and phytosanitary standards.

As noted above, the concept of NVNI serves as an invitation to construction, or a catch-all, to limit defection by WTO members through the use of avenues of defection with respect to which they have accepted no positive commitment.[170] In this sense, NVNI might be considered a "super-standard," as it invites the WTO dispute resolution system to evaluate the legitimacy of expectations (derived from the text of agreements) and on that basis to provide a remedy where there is no discrete breach.[171] As Professor Abbott has pointed out, the "nullification or impairment" touchstone in GATT/WTO dispute resolution is consistent with a "private interests" legal system.[172] That is, the question under NVNI is whether one of the parties was deprived of the benefit of its bargain, not whether the general rule of law or broader social interests are demeaned.

Of course, the problem with all of this is in determining what is NVNI, as opposed to a simple exercise of retained sovereignty. This question is not unlike that evaluated above in connection with the *Shrimp/Turtle* case: what is unjustifiable discrimination as opposed to a

---

168. *See* Sung-joon Cho, *GATT Non-Violation Issues in the WTO Framework: Are They the Achilles' Heel of the Dispute Settlement Process?*, 39 HARV. INT'L L.J. 311 (1998).

169. Compare the originally planned International Trade Organization, which included rudimentary coverage of competition law issues. *See, e.g.*, CLAIR WILCOX, A CHARTER FOR WORLD TRADE (1949); WILLIAM DIEBOLD, THE END OF THE I.T.O. (1952). It is also worth noting the 1960 Arrangement by the GATT Contracting Parties for Consultations on Restrictive Business Practices, Nov. 18, 1960, B.I.S.D. (9th Supp.) at 28 (1961). The 1960 Arrangement provides no substantive rules, but calls for consultations in connection with restrictive business practices.

170. *See* Film Panel Report, *supra* note 7, para. 10.35, *quoting* EEC-Oilseeds Report, *supra* note 32, paras. 144, 148.

171. In this regard, it is not dissimilar from a general commercial rule requiring "good faith" or indeed the requirement in article 26 of the Vienna Convention that treaties be performed in good faith.

172. Kenneth W. Abbott, *GATT as a Public Institution: The Uruguay Round and Beyond*, 18 BROOK. J. INT'L L. 31 (1992).

simple exercise of *explicitly* retained sovereignty? Both kinds of decision are, thus far, delegated to the dispute resolution process.

1. Construction under Non-Violation Nullification or Impairment

The availability of recourse under article XXIII(1)(b) of GATT and coordinate provisions for NVNI of tariff concessions is a legislative invitation to extraordinary construction.[173] The original purpose of this provision appears to have been to allow the construction of rights to recourse where specific treaty provisions provide none.[174] There have only been nine cases brought under this concept, but it stands available. Furthermore, the nullification or impairment concept has been construed narrowly because of the dire consequences for sovereignty of broad construction.[175] Furthermore, in the most recent, and most celebrated, non-violation case, *Film,* the U. S. claims were firmly rejected. In that decision, the panel carefully examined whether the United States had legitimate expectations as to the non-existence of certain Japanese government measures.[176]

2. The Film Panel's Approach to Non-Violation Nullification or Impairment

In the *Film* case, the United States complained about various alleged Japanese governmental and quasi-governmental measures that individually or cumulatively had the effect of excluding U.S. film producers (*viz.* Kodak) from the Japanese film market. The United States raised complaints based on both violation of GATT and NVNI. The three types of alleged NVNI measures that the United States attacked were (i) measures that encourage and facilitate the establishment of a market structure that restricts access to traditional distribution channels, (ii) the Japanese Large Scale Retail Stores Law of 1 March 1974, as amended 14 May 1979, which the United States claimed restricted the growth of an alternative means of distribution, and (iii) various Japanese legal rules restricting promotional discounts and premia of

---

173. Article 26(1) of the WTO Dispute Settlement Understanding applies special rules to actions under article XXIII(1)(b) of GATT 1994. *See also* Annex to the Understanding Regarding Notification, Consultation, Dispute Settlement and Surveillance, Nov. 28, 1979, B.I.S.D. (26th Supp.) at 210, 216 (1980).

174. *See* Kuyper, *supra* note 66, at 246–47 (1994). *See also* EEC-Oilseeds Report, *supra* note 32, para. 144.

175. *See* Film Panel Report, *supra* note 7, para. 10.36.

176. Film Panel Report, *supra* note 7. The panel found generally that the United States was sufficiently aware of the measures at issue, or of their possible promulgation at the time that relevant tariff concessions were negotiated, and that the United States therefore failed to show the frustration of legitimate expectations. This decision sets a high standard for future nullification and impairment cases, refusing to engage in broad criticism of at least long-standing domestic measures that may have the effect of reducing the value of tariff concessions.

various types, which the United States claimed had a disproportionate adverse effect on new market entrants.[177] In the background of the U.S. claims was a general perception and argument that Japan had used its Anti-Monopoly Law, and exceptions therefrom, to insulate domestic firms from foreign competition.[178]

The *Film* panel viewed NVNI as an "exceptional remedy for which the complaining party bears the burden of providing a detailed justification . . . ."[179] The panel noted that there have only been eight instances in which NVNI has been considered,[180] and that most of these have involved subsidies. The panel reviewed whether there was a Japanese governmental measure, whether there was a benefit accruing to the United States and whether the Japanese governmental measure nullified or impaired that benefit. We need not review the question of whether there was a Japanese governmental measure here, but note that the panel reviewed this in a fact-specific, case-by-case procedure.[181]

The panel considered benefits that might be nullified or impaired to consist of enhanced market access arising from the change in competitive relationship brought about by tariff concessions, but it found that the United States bore the burden of proof as to its "legitimate expectations" of benefits after successive tariff negotiation rounds.[182] In order for the United States to meet this burden, it was required to show that the Japanese measures at issue were not reasonably anticipated at the time the concessions were granted.[183] Where the measure at issue was adopted after the relevant tariff concession, the panel established a

---

177. Film Panel Report, *supra* note 7, para. 2.7. It is worth noting the parallel between the latter issue and the concerns of the recent European Union case of Criminal Proceedings Against Bernard Keck and Daniel Mithouard, Joined Cases C-267/91 and C-268/91, 1993 E.C.R. I-6097 1 C.M.L.R. 101 (1993). The European Court of Justice, perhaps for similar reasons, found that it should not evaluate non-discriminatory national regulation of selling conditions under its jurisprudence pursuant to article 30 of the Treaty of Rome. Treaty of Rome, Oct. 2, 1997, E.U., 37 I.L.M. 56.

178. Film Panel Report, *supra* note 7, paras. 5.380–.430.

179. Film Panel Report, *supra* note 7, para. 10.30.

180. *See* Film Panel Report, *supra* note 7, para. 10.36, *citing* Report of the Working Party on Australian Subsidy on Ammonium Sulphate, Apr. 3, 1950, GATT B.I.S.D. (Vol. 2) at 188 (1952); WTO Panel Report: Treatment by Germany of Imports of Sardines, Oct. 31, 1952, GATT B.I.S.D. (1st Supp.) at 53 (1953); Uruguayan Recourse, Nov. 16, 1962, GATT B.I.S.D. (11th Supp.) at 95 (1963); WTO Panel Report: EC-Tariff Treatment on Imports of Citrus Products from Certain Countries in the Mediterranean Region, Feb. 7, 1985 (unadopted), GATT Doc. L/5576; WTO Panel Report: EEC-Production Aids Granted on Canned Peaches, Canned Pears, Canned Fruit Cocktail and Dried Grapes, Feb. 20, 1985 (unadopted), GATT Doc. L/5778; WTO Panel Report: Japan-Trade in Semi-Conductors, May 4, 1988, GATT B.I.S.D. (35th Supp.) at 116 (1989); EEC-Oilseeds Report, *supra* note 32, at 86 (1991); WTO Panel Report: United States Restrictions on the Importation of Sugar and Sugar-Containing Products Applied Under the 1955 Waiver and Under the Headnote to the Schedule of Tariff Concessions, Nov. 7, 1990, GATT B.I.S.D. (37th Supp.) at 228 (1991).

181. *See* Norio Komuro, *Kodak-Fuji Film Dispute and the WTO Panel Ruling*, 32 J. WORLD TRADE 161, 188–91 (1998).

182. Film Panel Report, *supra* note 7, para. 10.65.

183. Film Panel Report, *supra* note 7, para. 10.61.

presumption, rebuttable by Japan, that the United States could not have reasonably anticipated the measure.

As part of the test for whether the benefits at issue were nullified or impaired by the measures at issue, the panel considered the Japanese argument that the measures at issue were neutral as to origin and not discriminatory against imports. The panel accepted that non-discriminatory measures could not impair benefits, insofar as they had no disproportionate impact on imports. Here, the panel referred to jurisprudence under article III(4) of GATT.[184] The critical question, however, is the *de facto* impact of the measure, regardless of intent. Thus, for example, in connection with the Japanese Large-Scale Retail Stores law, the panel found that the measures were neutral, considering lack of intent to hinder imports as only one indicator of neutrality.

By imposing the burdens of proof as to the legitimacy of expectations and anticipation of the subject measures, the panel substantially constrains the scope of NVNI. It is not enough for a benefit to be reduced due to some domestic circumstance. First, the circumstance must be a governmental measure: it must arise from governmental action. This constraint assumes a positive role of government. Government action, not government inaction, is subject to criticism. This is a critical distinction in the competition law context. Second, the complaining party must show that the governmental measures were not reasonably anticipated. Thus, longstanding practices or circumstances are protected. This means that the domestic circumstances, as they are, form a background for all concession. As a matter of negotiations, members of the WTO must recognize this and bear the burden of negotiating an end to existing measures that reduce benefits for which they negotiate.

3. Non-Violation Nullification or Impairment and Competition Policy

As noted above, today there is no substantial WTO law relating to domestic competition policy. The Working Group on the Interaction Between Trade and Competition Policy was formed in 1996 pursuant to a decision taken at the WTO Singapore Ministerial Conference.[185] It has engaged in extensive study but has so far made no substantive recommendations.[186]

---

184. Film Panel Report, *supra* note 7, para. 10.86.

185. World Trade Organization, Singapore Ministerial Declaration, Conf. Doc. WT/MIN(96)/DEC/W, para. 20 (Dec. 13, 1996). The declaration cautions that the working group's activities will "not prejudge whether negotiations will be initiated in the future." *Id.*

186. *See* Report (1998) of the Working Group on the Interaction Between Trade and Competition Policy to the General Council, WT/WGTCP/2 (98-4914) (Dec. 8, 1998) [hereinafter Competition Report].

Nor are there any substantial multilateral agreements regarding domestic or international competition policy. It is fair to say that there is even less international competition law than there is international environmental law, and perhaps it is also fair to say that there is less global consensus on international competition law.[187] Using the words of the *Shrimp/Turtle* decision, no legislative "equilibrium line" has been drawn.[188] Furthermore, there is no direct invocation of domestic competition law issues anywhere in GATT, comparable to the references to environmental issues in article XX, or the implicit permission for non-discriminatory domestic regulation in article III.

The *Film* panel followed earlier GATT jurisprudence in applying the concept of NVNI conservatively. It sought disproportionate trade impact in order to determine whether a national measure caused nullification and impairment. It sought evidence of what one might call in domestic law "actual reliance" to find "legitimate expectations." The panel was not asked to mold from NVNI international competition law rules, as perhaps the Appellate Body has been asked to mold from article XX international trade and environment rules.[189] Therefore, one cannot expect a "trade and competition" jurisprudence to develop from the *Film* case. There is insufficient textual authorization.

If the table of costs and benefits of rules and standards was filled in the trade and competition policy context, the following might be the result.

---

187. There are, however, Organization for Economic Cooperation and Development (OECD) statements, as well as bilateral agreements and regional law, for example, with respect to the European Union. Another example is the Australia-New Zealand: Closer Economic Relations-Trade Agreement, Mar. 28, 1983, Austl.-N.Z., 22 I.L.M. 945.

188. Shrimp/Turtle Appellate Body Report, *supra* note 6, para. 171.

189. And yet, this is a case of intersection between trade commitments and other areas of domestic policy: by definition, a "measure" must be a governmental action.

Table 3: Costs and Benefits in NVNI/Competition Context		
	Rules	Standards
Administrative cost of formulation	Higher cost	Lower cost—status quo
Public choice costs of specification, including costs of transparency	Slightly higher cost, but perhaps less diversity of perspective and less NGO interest than in trade and environment	Slightly lower cost; at present, broadest standards or lacuna in international trade law; standard would require agreement on principle
Perceived legitimacy; democracy deficit	Lower cost	Higher cost
Primary predictability—predictability for actors *ex ante*	Lower cost, but depends on avoiding development of substantial exceptions through dispute resolution	Higher cost, with no substantial experience to date
Secondary predictability—ease of application by dispute resolution tribunal	Lower cost, but depends on avoiding development of substantial exceptions through dispute resolution	Higher cost
Opportunity to gain experience prior to specification	Reduced benefit, although the magnitude of reduction declines as experience is already gained	Increased benefit, especially as dispute resolution decisions raise opportunities for dialog
Economies of scale with greater frequency	Increased benefit, and likely to grow as more intersections between trade and environment arise	Decreased benefit, but may serve as casuist legislature over time, reaping similar economies of scale
Minimization strategic costs—promotion of bargaining toward efficient agreement	Reduced benefit, although the magnitude of reduction may decline as uncertainty of result of rules rises with development of exceptions	Increased benefit given uncertainty of outcome

The competition law context differs from the environmental law context insofar as the competition law context is not subject to any relevant WTO law but may, under certain circumstances, be a basis for invocation of the very broadest standard in WTO law, NVNI. The competition law context probably involves lower political costs for agreement of rules than the environmental context because it lacks the NGO attention that environmental policy attracts. Finally, if anything, there has been less experience with competition policy than with environmental policy in the international trade context. Due to the varying effects of these differences, and their incommensurability, it is difficult to say with any certainty that these major differences would indicate that rules would be more likely in the competition policy context than in the environmental context.

VI. CONCLUSIONS: RULES, STANDARDS, AND LACUNAE IN INTERNATIONAL TRADE LAW

This Article begins by exploring the discontinuity between the domain of WTO dispute resolution and the body of general international law. The disparity between the positive law dispute resolution system of the WTO and the more political, natural law style of dispute resolution available in connection with most other forms of international law raises jurisprudential and practical concern. How can a WTO dispute resolution decision ignore other international law? On the other hand, how can the WTO dispute resolution process purport to interpret and apply non-WTO international law? While present WTO law seems clearly to exclude direct application of non-WTO international law, this position seems unsustainable as increasing conflicts between trade values and non-trade values arise. These conflicts may be addressed through standards such as the exceptional provisions of article XX, or by legislated rules regarding the more specific interaction between trade values and non-trade values.

This Article posits that more specific international law is not always a good thing and seeks to provide a taxonomy of factors for consideration in determining the optimal specificity of international law. Lacunae are circumstances where there is no law and no constraint. This is quite different from a standard, where there is law applicable by a dispute resolution tribunal but less explicit guidance to the tribunal as to how to decide. Rules, on the other hand, by definition, leave less discretion to tribunals. Thus, the decision between rules and standards is not a decision between more international law and less international law. While rules may be developed by tribunals, the decision is often an institutional choice between adjudicators and legislators. This observation depends on the perception that tribunals applying standards legislate, even when they purport not to do so. When one chooses between adjudicators and legislators, there is more to consider than simply institutional expertise or competence.

Some of the critical factors in choosing between rules and standards that may change over time include the relative frequency of disputes and the strategic costs of bargaining to an efficient solution under standards versus rules. Interestingly, the public choice costs of specification of rules are increasingly countervailed by the costs in terms of legitimacy of decision pursuant to a standard by a dispute resolution tribunal. The relative costs may vary in different circumstances, and the variation may well depend on NGO interest. There may come a tipping point, at which continued decision by a tribunal pursuant to a standard becomes so illegitimate as to make it more attractive to specify rules. In any event, it is impossible to determine without specific analysis the utility of a rule versus a standard in particular cases.

[24]

Is the WTO Open and Transparent?

A Discussion of the Relationship of the WTO with Non-governmental Organisations and Civil Society's Claims for more Transparency and Public Participation

Gabrielle MARCEAU and Peter N. PEDERSEN*

I. INTRODUCTION

In the last few years the World Trade Organization (WTO) has been under pressure to increase the transparency of its work and public participation in its functions. This is a new phenomenon.

Initially, the work pursued by the governments in the General Agreement on Tariffs and Trade (GATT) of 1947, the WTO's predecessor, was rarely criticised as exclusive and secretive. No one really cared about the GATT. In fact, very few people knew about the GATT (compared, for instance, with the International Monetary Fund or the World Bank). Conceived as a provisional agreement between countries, the administration of which was facilitated by a very modest secretariat, the GATT was concerned primarily with technical matters of international commerce and trade. However, the GATT was not legally an "international organisation"; it handled its scope of work in a pragmatic, efficient, discreet and, arguably, non-transparent manner.

Yet, as the sole multilateral agreement containing trade disciplines, the GATT evolved into a *de facto* forum for countries to undertake negotiations, survey the implementation of such negotiated obligations and develop a system of dispute settlement. For various reasons, including a desire to maintain effective and efficient control of these activities, the GATT countries always insisted that the only actors in the forum be the countries' representatives themselves and that their activities be handled in a pragmatic manner. The secretariat has always been very small, with defined and limited functions. Countries' representatives have always had the exclusive authority to initiate discussions and negotiations, and representation and participation has always been limited to governments' representatives in all forums of the GATT. Non-governmental interest groups have never been formally present in the negotiating room or even in the corridors of the GATT

* Gabrielle Marceau is from the Legal Affairs Division and Peter N. Pedersen is from the External Relations Division, WTO Secretariat. The opinions expressed are strictly personal and cannot bind the WTO Secretariat. Any mistakes are the authors' alone. The authors are most grateful to Nadir Alikhan, Jesse Krier, Rachel Pedersen, Valeska Populoh and Matthew Stilwell for their useful comments on previous drafts.

building. Although the GATT lacked formal and legal existence, the body was a successful institution for 50 years, setting up a system of trade disciplines which have now infiltrated multifarious dimensions of commerce, trade and trade-related areas. From this standpoint, the GATT functioned well.

The GATT 1947 (now called the GATT 1994, but hereafter referred to as the GATT) became one part of the Marrakesh Agreement Establishing the World Trade Organization (WTO Agreement) which entered into force on 1 January 1995. The formal legal personality of the WTO, as an international organisation, is now recognised in Articles I and VIII of the WTO Agreement.[1] Generally, the WTO continues to function as the GATT did. The main actors in the WTO forum remain the Member governments. In all areas of activities, Members must initiate, conduct and terminate actions. The WTO now has a formal Secretariat, the powers of which are still rather limited compared to other international bodies, such as the Commission of the European Communities or the Secretariat of the Organisation of Economic Co-operation and Development (OECD). Throughout the various WTO agreements, and with the limited circumstances of the Trade Policy Review Mechanism, the responsibilities of the WTO Secretariat do not include any investigation or assessment power. Only Members can initiate negotiations in which they are the sole participants. In the area of dispute settlement, initiation of the process, request for the adoption of panel or Appellate Body reports, and surveillance of the adequacy of implementation of the conclusions of dispute settlement reports are limited to Members. Thus, the main focus and *raison d'être* of the WTO are the interests of governments.

The increasing ramifications of international trade, as well as those of the WTO and its far-reaching agreements, such as the Agreement on Trade-Related Aspects of Intellectual Property (TRIPS Agreement) and the General Agreement on Trade and Services (GATS) and dispute settlement mechanism, are changing the dynamics of the old GATT. In recent years many non-governmental organisations (NGOs) have claimed that the rights of citizens and civil society have been infringed by GATT/WTO rules, and that certain interest groups have been able to exercise a disproportionate influence. Consequently, groups have been demanding increased access to and participation in WTO functions to ensure the representation of all interests. To this extent, the WTO should allow for a larger and more diverse number of civil society groups to express their views, independent of the positions of the governments and countries in which they are located.

Many proponents of greater public participation in WTO processes emphasise the wealth of knowledge, resources and analytical capacity in the NGOs' respective areas of expertise. Therefore, NGOs can act as "intellectual competitors"[2] to governments in the quest for optimal policies. One central argument supporting NGO participation in WTO

---

[1] Art. I reads as follows: "The World Trade Organization (hereinafter referred to as 'the WTO') is hereby established". Art. VIII:1 states: "The WTO shall have legal personality, and shall be accorded by each of its Members such legal capacity as may be necessary for the exercise of its function".

[2] Daniel C. Esty, *Non-Governmental Organizations at the World Trade Organization: Co-operation, Competition, or Exclusion*, Journal of International Economic Law, Vol. 1, No. 1, 1998, p. 123.

IS THE WTO OPEN AND TRANSPARENT? 7

matters and greater access to WTO work is the role that NGOs can play in disseminating information at the national level. This could ensure broader public support and understanding for trade liberalisation in general and the functioning of the WTO in particular.

There is evidence,[3] both within as well as outside the WTO, that governments recognise the capacity of NGOs to provide quality input, particularly in the areas of environment and development, drawing on valuable on-the-ground experience. Already, NGO representatives are invited to participate as members of their national delegation in Ministerial Conferences, as well as other WTO meetings. In adopting the guidelines for relations with NGOs, Members recognised the role of NGOs in increasing public awareness. More recently, this has been reflected in a large number of the speeches delivered by Heads of State and Ministers at the Geneva Ministerial Conference as well as in the final declaration of the meeting.[4]

This also confirms that the issue of whether the WTO is open and transparent is not limited to NGO and public participation in the dispute settlement mechanism. The issue of transparency is also about increased access to documents, the decision-making process of governments on trade matters (domestically and in the WTO forum), and greater public participation in WTO meetings, all of which would lead to a better understanding of the activities surrounding the multilateral trading system.

Yet, the purpose of this article is not to assess the legitimacy of NGO claims for greater transparency and further public participation in the WTO. Instead, it discusses the actions that the WTO Members and the WTO Secretariat have taken to increase transparency, to delineate the legal parameters of WTO agreements in this area and, consequently, to highlight the existing limitations that need to be pushed forward should Members decide to change the situation as it stands today.

GATT practice has demonstrated that constructive and open debates are essential for effective negotiations. The evolution of the NGO issue in the context of the multilateral trading system confirms this point. Therefore, the authors hope that this modest contribution on the "state of affairs" of NGO and civil society claims for greater transparency and increased participation in WTO work, as well as the response of the institution, will enrich the on-going discussions.

Section II outlines the history of NGO relations with the WTO, traces the evolution of this relationship through the adoption of guidelines on NGO participation and the

---

[3] For example, the discussion by Charles Dileva, *International Environmental Law and Development*, Georgetown International Environmental Law Review, Winter 1998, p. 525.

[4] These are the claims of the so-called civil society, a concept not easily defined which would include all the individual and collective interests lying outside the more defined and structured interests and powers of governments. Although environmental NGOs (Green NGOs) are generally the most vocal, the very idea of NGOs includes any non-governmental interest group, which is organised enough to be able to express a position on any issue. It would appear that the concept of civil society is perhaps wider than that of NGOs and would also reach the non-organised interest of individuals in society, such as individual consumers. For the purpose of this article, the authors use the practical working definition of NGOs as applied in the day-to-day work in the WTO Secretariat, i.e. that mentioned in Art. v:2 of the WTO Agreement: "non-governmental organisations [non-profit] concerned with matters related to those of the WTO". Whenever the term "interest group" is used, it is intended to cover a wider range of entities including profit, private as well as public and non-profit NGOs.

8 JOURNAL OF WORLD TRADE

Singapore Ministerial Conference, and discusses the recent proposal of the Director-General in this context. Section III examines transparency, publication and notification requirements in the WTO Agreement, and provides a context to understand the scope of NGO claims for greater transparency. Section IV discusses the participation and influence of NGOs and other non-governmental interest groups in the dispute settlement mechanism of the WTO. Section V focuses on the participation of non-governmental interest groups in the policy-making leading to WTO provisions and in the work of the WTO generally. Finally, in section VI, there is a conclusion.

II. THE RELATIONSHIP BETWEEN THE GATT/WTO AND THE NGOS

A. THE HISTORICAL BACKGROUND

Early Considerations on Relations with NGOs

Although the debate about the role of civil society within the multilateral trading system has intensified over the last few years, the issue did receive significant attention during the early, but unsuccessful, attempts to create the International Trade Organisation (ITO). In fact, for the second session of the Executive Committee of the Interim Commission for the International Trade Organisation (ICITO)[5] item 5 on the provisional agenda specifically refers to Paragraph 2 of Article 87 of the Havana Charter, which provides that "the Organisation may make suitable arrangements for consultation and co-operation with non-governmental organisations concerned with matters within the scope of this Charter".[6]

The note prepared by the Secretariat of the ICITO on relations with NGOs provided the Executive Committee with a brief *tour d'horizon* of the arrangements made by the Economic and Social Council (ECOSOC) of the United Nations (UN),[7] as well as the specialised agencies for consultation with NGOs. In addition, the Secretariat's note presented a set of conclusions and recommendations on how the procedures regarding NGOs could be adapted to suit the ITO.

These recommendations never materialised into a concrete set of procedures for dealing with NGOs within the context of the multilateral trading system (particularly as the ITO was never established). They do, nevertheless, merit a few comments, particularly because they have served as the basis of the current WTO guidelines for relations with NGOs[8] and raise a number of issues which remain at the forefront of the WTO-NGO debate today.

The conclusions and recommendations of the Secretariat's note emphasised that as the Havana Charter required the ITO to deal with such an immense number of commercial and technical matters, "it is clearly desirable that the ITO should be able to take full

---

[5] ICITO/EC.2/11, 15 July 1948 (Note by the Secretariat).
[6] Havana Charter, Art. 87, para. 2.
[7] The Constitutional Provision for arrangements with NGOs is found in Art. 71 of the UN Charter.
[8] WT/L/162.

advantage of the knowledge and expertise of the non-governmental organisations in these various fields".[9] However, when it came to defining specific procedures regarding NGOs, the model adopted by the ECOSOC with its provisions for different categories of consultative status was seen as being too rigid and potentially counter-productive. First, rigid categories where certain NGOs had to be consulted as a matter of principle would have eliminated the flexibility of *ad hoc* consultations with specialised NGOs. Second, imposing a system of categories could have generated questions of prestige and rank, and could have been misinterpreted as endorsing certain NGOs as more important than others. Therefore, to circumvent potential conflict, no formal procedure was developed and a flexible case-by-case scenario of consultations was allowed to continue. As will be seen below, this principle of flexibility is a prominent feature of the guidelines for arrangements on relations with NGOs which Members adopted in July 1996.[10]

The Secretariat's recommendations resulted from an evaluation of existing approaches for dealing with NGOs in other inter-governmental fora. Finding them inadequate for the ITO, the Secretariat's note recommended a number of measures which would have institutionalised the role of civil society within the ITO. Based on the Secretariat's note, the Executive Secretary of the Interim Commission for the ITO, Mr Eric Wyndham White, made a number of practical suggestions to the Executive Committee.[11]

Among these suggestions was the idea of adopting a list of "consultants" chosen from the ECOSOC list of NGOs with consultative status, on the recommendation of the Director-General and with the approval of the Executive Board. These NGOs were to be invited to send observers to the Annual Conference of the ITO and receive the Conference documentation. In addition, they would be allowed to propose items for the Conference agenda. The Executive Committee would consider these proposals and would hear the views of the NGOs which had suggested an item for the agenda. For meetings other than the Annual Conference, the Director-General would be entrusted to ensure that consultations with relevant NGOs took place. If a committee and/or a commission deemed it valuable, NGOs would be invited to address the specific meeting directly.

On more general matters, the Director-General would have the authority to set up, if considered appropriate, an advisory committee of representatives of the NGOs. The Director-General would also be given a relatively free hand in deciding whether to distribute NGO documentation to the Annual Conference and would ensure that a comprehensive list of all NGO material received by the Secretariat from listed NGOs be circulated to Members. Such documents were to be circulated in full at the request of any Member government.

Finally, in the event of a difference of opinion between the Director-General and any listed NGOs regarding the implementation of these arrangements, the matter would

---

[9] IcITO/EC.2/11, 15 July 1948.
[10] WT/L/162.
[11] IcITO/EC.2/SC.3/5, 2 September 1948.

be referred to the Executive Board. The arrangements would be subject to review from "time to time",[12] in which the input of the NGOs would be given full consideration.

Interestingly, these very first documents concerning the relationship between the multilateral trading system and civil society reflect the genuine belief that the ITO needed the expertise and experience of specific NGOs to advance and implement the trading agenda. Although these recommendations never materialised into a tangible and formal role for NGOs in the ITO (and subsequently the GATT), they certainly demonstrate that from the very beginning the importance of NGOs as providers of knowledge and experience was recognised. With this is mind, it is hardly surprising that the provisional list of NGOs which might be consulted, found in Annex A of ICITO/EC.2/11, includes a large number of specific business and industry associations. Adding to this impression is the letter from the International Chamber of Commerce (ICC) included in Annex B which, point by point, argues how the deeper involvement of the ICC in the activities of the ITO would support the promotion of an international trade regime.

Despite these early attempts to institutionalise the involvement of NGOs, civil society was not accorded a formal role within the international trade system along the lines of the ECOSOC of the UN. NGOs pursued informal and *ad hoc* contacts with both GATT Contracting Parties and the Secretariat, but were denied accreditation and access to specific meetings and annual conferences. At the Ministerial Meeting in Marrakesh in April 1994, establishing the WTO, no provisions existed for inviting NGOs. Those NGOs that actually attended the Marrakesh Ministerial Meeting had to acquire press credentials and register as members of the press.

Nevertheless, the signing of the Final Act of the Uruguay Round and the Marrakesh Agreement, with or without the presence of civil society, signalled the beginning of an irreversible process of recognising the role that NGOs can play *vis-à-vis* the multilateral trading system.

B.   THE WTO AND NGOs

The purpose of this section is to examine the legal basis of current WTO-NGO relations, and to examine the evolution of this relationship from a practical and procedural perspective.

1.   *Article V:2 of the Marrakesh Agreement*

Article V:2 of The Marrakesh Agreement reads:

> "*The General Council may make appropriate arrangements for consultation and co-operation with non-governmental organisations concerned with matters related to those of the WTO.*"[13]

Although the significance of finally including a reference to NGOs within the framework of the multilateral trading system cannot be overstated, Article V:2 initially

---

[12] WT/L/162.

[13] *The Results of the Uruguay Round of Multilateral Trade Negotiations, The Legal Texts*, p. 9.

provided little guidance as to how civil society could play a more active part in the multilateral trading system. Such clarification and guidance came at a meeting of the General Council in July 1996.

2. The 1996 Guidelines for Relations with NGOs[14]

On 18 July 1996, the General Council adopted a set of guidelines clarifying the framework within which NGOs could work with the WTO. The guidelines acknowledge the importance of NGOs in the public debate and address key issues such as transparency, the derestriction of documents,[15] the role of the WTO Secretariat and WTO Chairpersons, and the restrictions on NGO participation in WTO meetings. Adoption of the guidelines appears to have been propelled by two factors: the need for the clarification of Article v:2 and the Ministerial Conference in Singapore in December 1996.

The last paragraph of the Marrakesh Decision on Trade and Environment of 14 April 1994 is significant, inviting the Sub-Committee of the Preparatory Committee, and the Committee on Trade and Environment, once established, to "provide input to the relevant bodies in respect of appropriate arrangements for relations with inter-governmental and non-governmental organisations referred to in Article v of the WTO".[16] Subsequently, the WTO Secretariat utilised outside funding to organise a Trade and Environment Symposium in June 1994, thereby initiating a process of informal consultations between the Secretariat and civil society—a relatively daring endeavour for the Secretariat at the time. The explicit mention of *symposia* in the 1996 guidelines is largely due to the success of this first symposium and the fact that Members found it to be a useful, if arms-length, exercise in NGO-WTO relations, with the Secretariat serving as a "buffer" between Members and NGOs.

In regards to transparency, the guidelines establish a commitment to ensure that de-restricted documents be made available to the public more systematically and promptly than in the past. The specific issue of derestriction of documents is discussed in more detail below. The launch of the WTO Web Site in September 1995 marks a significant step towards transparency. Visitors to the site have access to comprehensive information about the WTO and the ability to directly submit questions, request information and download de-restricted documents. Currently, the Web Site is visited by an average of 36,000 individual users every month, who download approximately 18 gigabytes or around 15 million pages of documents.[17] The most recent initiative by the WTO Secretariat for greater transparency has resulted in the addition of a special section for NGOs to the WTO Homepage in September 1998.

The guidelines allow the Secretariat manoeuvring room in pursuing dialogues with

---

[14] See Annex A (WT/L/162), below.

[15] At the same General Council meeting on 18 July 1996 Members also adopted the Decision on Derestriction of documents (WT/L/160.REV1). See further discussion, below.

[16] *The Results of the Uruguay Round of Multilateral Trade Negotiations, The Legal Texts*, pp. 469–471.

[17] This makes the WTO Web Site one of the most popular Web Sites among international inter-governmental organisations.

civil society,[18] yet are more restrictive of the WTO Chairpersons' interactions with NGOs. Chairpersons can meet with NGOs in their personal capacity only if the council or committee does not decide otherwise. The guidelines also address the inevitable question of a more direct role for NGOs in the WTO. This matter did receive considerable attention during informal meetings of the General Council, but there was no consensus on giving NGOs a more direct or formal role to play. Members generally held that the character of the WTO, as a legally binding inter-governmental treaty among its Members and a forum for negotiations, bars direct NGO involvement in its affairs. In addition, the General Council has noted that the primary responsibility for consulting with civil society lies in processes at the national level and that, therefore, NGOs should focus their attention on domestic trade policy discussions.

There will be a return to the guidelines below to demonstrate how this framework for interaction with civil society is constantly being reinterpreted. Suffice to say at this point that the adoption of fairly broad guidelines left the Secretariat with a relatively free hand in defining its relationship with NGOs and allowed it to become increasingly pro-active in its undertakings with civil society, as highlighted by the first Ministerial Conference of the WTO in Singapore.

3.   *Discussions on NGO Attendance at the Ministerial Conference in Singapore*

The guidelines only provided the Secretariat with a broad framework for NGO presence at the Ministerial Conference. Considerable work remained in order to achieve an effective and workable model for NGO involvement in Singapore that would also be acceptable to Members. The practical difficulties of hosting a multitude of NGOs were compounded by Members of the consensus-driven WTO remaining sharply divided over NGO attendance and their role in the context of the meeting.

It became increasingly apparent that a growing number of Members were facing domestic pressure to ensure that NGOs would be allowed to play a role at the Singapore Ministerial Conference. In most of the informal meetings of the General Council preparing for the Ministerial Conference, the issue of NGO attendance figured high on the agenda, sparking debate on the merits of inviting civil society to attend the conference, on the modalities for NGO attendance and the procedures for defining which NGOs would be invited.

Members mandated the Secretariat to draw up a proposal for how representatives of civil society would be accommodated at the conference, which, for practical purposes, included close collaboration with the Singapore Mission to the WTO. Essentially, this proposal focused on ensuring that NGOs could attend the Plenary sessions of the Ministerial Conference and would have at their disposal an NGO Centre with adequate facilities for organising their own meetings and workshops. The Secretariat's proposal for inviting

---

[18] The wording of Art. v:2 is repeated in the first paragraph of the guidelines. Particularly important is the reference to organisations "concerned with matters related to those of the WTO", which avoids any specific definition of which NGOs may be consulted.

NGOs to attend the conference in Singapore was specifically designed to ensure that only NGOs whose activities were "concerned with those of the WTO" would be considered.[19] The proposal envisioned a procedure requiring NGOs to submit a written request for registration materials delineating their scope of work within the definition of Article v:2. Following expiration of the deadline, the resulting list of NGOs would be circulated among Members for review and comment. After a period of two weeks, barring objections, registration forms would be forwarded to the NGOs.

Members did not have to approve the NGOs to be invited and, in fact, the Chairman of the General Council specifically stated that there was no reason to take a formal decision on the matter.[20] Instead, Members were encouraged to consult informally with the Secretariat on specific matters relating to the list of 159 NGOs that had submitted registration requests. Consultations did take place shortly after the list of the NGOs was circulated, but instead of resulting in requests for NGOs to be taken off the list, the discussions focused on ensuring that all NGOs had submitted the required description of their activities. Although a number of the NGOs detailed activities in contentious areas surrounding preparations for the Ministerial Conference, all 159 NGOs received registration forms.[21]

Two other issues relating to the NGO presence at the conference were brought up during the informal consultations among Members: defining the status of NGOs at the Ministerial Conference and the danger of creating a precedent for NGO involvement in WTO meetings.

NGO presence at the Ministerial Conference originally appeared on the General Council meeting agenda as a sub-item of a proposal to grant international inter-governmental organisations (IGOs) observer status in Singapore.[22] Some Members expressed concern that granting NGOs observer status would create the impression that these organisations could both participate and intervene at the meetings in Singapore. This discussion of semantics resulted in a concerted effort to replace the word "*observe*" with the more neutral "*attend*" (emphasis added).

Members also voiced concern that approving NGO presence in Singapore would set a precedent for future meetings of the WTO. Members referred to provisions in the newly adopted guidelines for interaction with NGOs to be pursued on an *ad hoc* basis rather than through a formal or institutionalised process. Therefore, it was decided that the issue of NGO attendance at the 1996 Ministerial Conference would not set a precedent for

---

[19] Admittedly, the majority of NGOs can claim that their activities are in some way related to trade liberalisation itself and/or the effects of it.

[20] For further discussion on the position of Members on this issue, see the minutes of the meeting WT/GC/M/13.

[21] The deadline for submission of NGO requests for registration forms was 1 October 1996. The announcement of this deadline and the requirements for applying was made in the 11th issue of the WTO Newsletter, FOCUS, on 27 August 1996, in the Trade and Environment Press Release of 26 August 1996 and on the WTO Web Site. At the close of business on 1 October, 118 requests had been received. Following the circulation of the list of NGOs that had requested a registration form, Members decided to extend the deadline to 15 October to accommodate late requests. In total, 159 requests were received.

[22] Virtually every council or committee in the WTO has a roster of IGOs which have been granted observer status and as a consequence are invited to the formal meetings where they may be invited to make statements.

future conferences and that, for the Geneva event, Members would re-visit the issue "based on the experience from Singapore".

The informal discussions among Members on how to accommodate civil society at the Singapore Ministerial Conference did not address the issue of how to handle the actual accreditation of NGOs in any detail. Hence, the rather awkward task of differentiating between those organisations which could be accredited and those which could not was left to the Secretariat.

The approach taken to this task was a cautious one, particularly because determining which NGO is truly representative and legitimate and which one is not remains controversial. In addition, engaging an investigation of who certain organisations represent was (and is) beyond the resources of the Secretariat. Instead, it was decided that any "non-profit" organisation which could point to "activities related to those of the WTO" would be considered. The Secretariat received a large number of requests for application forms for the Ministerial Conference from private companies and law firms. These companies and firms were informed that in order to qualify for accreditation they would have to register through their respective industry association or professional grouping. This practice of accrediting only "non-profit" organisations was also used for the Geneva Ministerial Conference. However, private entities have been invited to participate in some meetings, e.g. environment and trade facilitation symposia. Although the accreditation process has been done so far on a case-by-case basis, there is little doubt that in the long run a more systematic approach will have to be developed.

The above account demonstrates the importance of the guidelines in developing NGO-WTO relations and in guiding the process towards securing NGO attendance at the Singapore Ministerial Conference. More importantly, however, the account highlights the sensitive and controversial character of NGO presence at the time, and the caution WTO Members exercised in allowing representatives of civil society to play a role at the first Ministerial Conference. It must be emphasised that these sorts of discussions never occurred in the GATT, and that the entire concept of NGOs was still uncharted territory for many delegations and the Secretariat. Thus, it was almost inevitable that the initial steps were so timid and the process so slow.

In retrospect, the period from July to December 1996 was a milestone in WTO-NGO relations because the process of engaging with NGOs was moved forward significantly. Similarly, the significance of the process of confidence-building between the Secretariat and Member countries with respect to interpreting the guidelines and dealing with NGOs cannot be overstated.

4. *The Singapore Ministerial Conference*

Of the 159 NGOs that submitted requests to attend the Ministerial Conference, 108 actually came to Singapore.[23] Each accredited NGO was allowed a maximum of four

---

[23] The difference between the NGOs that received registration forms and those that actually came to Singapore can, to a large degree, be explained by the considerable cost of sending a representative to Singapore for one week.

representatives and the total number of individuals reached 235.[24] The facilities provided for NGOs by the government of Singapore were of a quality that will be difficult to match in the future. The NGO Centre was located in the Westin Hotel, one block away from the Suntec Conference Centre where the week-long Ministerial Conference took place.

Upon arrival at the NGO Centre, registered NGOs were provided with a special green badge allowing them access to the Plenary Sessions of the Ministerial Conference, the press area and the floor level of the Suntec Centre. The NGO Centre consisted of one large conference room and five smaller meeting rooms available for NGO meetings. The main conference room, with a seating capacity of approximately 250 persons, contained a computer facilities area (each NGO was given a separate e-mail account), a document distribution area and TV screens transmitting live from the plenary sessions. In the Suntec Centre itself, two rooms were reserved for NGOs wishing to meet with delegations and an area outside the room where the informal meetings were held was reserved for NGO materials.[25] NGOs were invited to participate in all of the social events taking place during the Conference.

Although some NGOs considered the arrangements insufficient, the prevailing sentiment among NGOs was that the Singapore Conference marked a significant step towards acknowledging civil society. A special feature of the Conference contributed to this sentiment. A taskforce was created to deal with specific problems and requests concerning NGO arrangements. The group, which met early each morning, consisted of representatives from the different segments of civil society and a member of the WTO Secretariat. Apart from serving a practical purpose, these meetings also came to symbolise the confidence-building process between NGOs and the WTO. The co-operative spirit of the NGOs aided the success of these meetings and the process of interaction eliminated some of the misunderstandings which had frustrated communications between NGOs and the WTO Secretariat.

5. *Symposia and the Geneva Ministerial Conference*

Since Singapore, the WTO has continued to pursue interaction with NGOs. The WTO Secretariat has continued to organise NGO activities and launch initiatives to develop a closer dialogue with civil society. The following discussion provides an overview of these activities and delineates the new set of initiatives announced by the Director-General on 15 July 1998.

---

[24] This number is somewhat misleading, insofar as a significant number of additional NGO representatives turned up at the NGO Centre requesting accreditation. These NGOs again had to demonstrate that their activities were trade-related and were subsequently accommodated with a white pass which secured access to the NGO Centre, but not to the Suntec Conference Centre. For an overview of the statistics on NGO attendance at the Singapore Ministerial Conferences, the reader may want to consult Annex B.

[25] NGOs did not have direct access to this area, but Secretariat staff ensured that such material was placed on the two tables outside the meeting rooms.

(a)   *Symposia*

The Trade and Environment Division pioneered the concept of issue-specific NGO symposia as early as June 1994. These symposia were designed to broaden and improve the dialogue between the WTO (in 1994 the GATT) and NGOs on the relationship between international trade, environmental policies and sustainable development. Although the symposia in 1994 and 1997 were both successful insofar as they specifically sought input from NGOs, interest among Members was only moderate. NGOs argued that although the exercise of exchanging views with the WTO Secretariat had been useful, the discussions would only be fruitful if Member governments were present and participated in the dialogue.

In late September 1997, a two-day joint WTO-United Nations Conference on Trade and Development (UNCTAD) NGO Symposium on Trade-Related Issues Affecting Least-Developed Countries was held in Geneva. The timing of this symposium was of particular importance because the High-Level Meeting (HLM) for Least-developed Countries was planned to take place two weeks later. In defining the framework for the Symposium, the first priority was to ensure the participation of NGOs from as many least-developed countries (LDCs) as possible. To achieve this goal, a specific portion of the HLM budget was allotted to finance the attendance of LDC NGOs. The Symposium was attended by approximately 34 NGOs, the majority from LDCs, and a consistent presence of several Member countries.

To maximise NGO-WTO Member interaction, the NGO Symposium was designed to mirror the agenda of the Thematic Roundtables of the HLM, i.e. capacity-building and encouraging investment in LDCs. The conclusions and recommendations of the NGO proceedings were then forwarded to the HLM as an official WTO document. In the end, the two Chairpersons of the NGO Symposium were invited back to Geneva for the HLM to present these conclusions directly. The official submission of the NGO recommendations to the HLM, as well as the direct NGO intervention at the meeting, signified a new level of NGO involvement in the multilateral trading system.

The Trade and Environment Symposium in March 1998 marks another significant improvement in NGO-WTO relations. First, the list of invitees for the Symposium included over 150 individuals from environment and development NGOs, private corporations and academia—reflecting the widening scope of the trade and environment debate. Second, more than 60 individuals from Member countries participated in the two days of panel discussions. Third, the presence of the heads of the WTO, UNCTAD and UNEP on the opening day of the Symposium highlighted that the trade and environment debate crosses not only national, but also institutional boundaries.[26]

In March 1998, the WTO Secretariat also hosted a Symposium on Trade Facilitation, including a large number of NGOs and representatives from large corporations. The

---

[26] A full report on the Symposium was done by the International Institute for Sustainable Development (IISD) and is available from their Web page on the Internet (http://www.iisd.ca).

objective of this Symposium was to help identify the areas where traders face obstacles when moving goods across borders. To this extent, the event provided a direct interface between the practical level (traders) and the trade policy level (officials in capitals and Geneva).

These examples illustrate the evolving relationship between civil society and the WTO, highlighting the increased presence of NGOs at WTO meetings. NGO symposia have become more frequent within the WTO and future activities are being organised by the WTO Secretariat.

(b) *The Geneva Ministerial Conference*

The evolving relationship between the WTO and NGOs, as well as the growing interest of civil society in the work of the WTO, is also highlighted by an account of the May 1998 Geneva Ministerial Conference and 50th Year Celebration of the multilateral trading system.

As in Singapore, the NGOs represented a broad cross-section of environmental, development, business, consumer, labour and farm interests.[27] The same application procedures used for Singapore were applied for the Geneva event, yet this time not a single Member of the WTO approached the Secretariat for consultation on the list of NGOs requesting registration materials.

Of the 152 NGOs that registered to attend the Plenary Sessions in Geneva,[28] 128 NGOs, comprised of 362 representatives, actually attended the Conference at the Palais des Nations. The facilities provided for NGOs, including an NGO Centre, meeting rooms and computer facilities, were similar to those in Singapore, yet a number of arrangements for NGOs marked a significant improvement over the last conference. Most importantly, NGO facilities were housed in the same building as the Ministerial Conference itself, providing representatives of civil society with improved access to delegates.[29] In addition, NGOs were allocated tables near the official document distribution desk to make printed materials available to interested parties. Finally, for the Plenary Sessions of the Ministerial Conference and the 50th Year Celebration a special NGO Gallery with 50 seats was reserved in the General Assembly Hall. These seats were allocated on a first-come, first-served basis and those NGOs that did not receive a seat in the gallery had access to a live transmission of the proceedings broadcast on three TV monitors.

As in Singapore, the Director-General addressed NGOs on the opening day of the Conference. Throughout the three-day event, NGOs were briefed regularly by the WTO

---

[27] For a comparative overview of the statistics on NGO attendance at the two Ministerial Conferences, see Annex B.

[28] Each NGO was allowed to register a maximum of four representatives. In the context of a Ministerial Conference it is also worth noting that for the Geneva event the number of NGO representatives outnumbered members of the media by a very large margin.

[29] Despite these improvements over Singapore, the logistics of the Palais des Nations unfortunately made it impossible to cluster all the NGO meeting rooms in one place.

Secretariat on the progress of the informal working sessions[30]—an improvement on Singapore. NGOs welcomed the briefings as a genuine sign of commitment to ensure transparency and as acknowledgement of the importance of civil society.

Despite overall praise for the Secretariat's efforts to accommodate civil society, some groups criticised NGO exclusion from informal working sessions, the logistical difficulties of finding the various meeting rooms in the Palais des Nations and the very tight security at the Conference. Outside the official event itself, a number of demonstrations against the WTO and globalisation took place. These demonstrations, organised by a relatively large, but loose coalition of international NGOs and local squatters, succeeded in capturing some headlines due to the violence and extensive property damage which ensued. However, the overall impression left by the Geneva Ministerial Conference and the attendance of NGOs was positive and confirmed that this relationship continues to mature.

(c)   *Lessons from the past*

In an effort to maintain and further develop a constructive dialogue with civil society, the WTO Secretariat expends great energy in continuously assessing the value of the various initiatives for all involved parties. The authors' evaluation has relied extensively on the constructive input of NGOs. A number of useful conclusions can be drawn from this review and it is possible to offer recommendations as a result.

First, large symposia often produce equally large frustrations, as NGOs with different agendas compete for "air time". This jockeying for position among NGOs results in poorly focused discussions, general conclusions and the unfortunate impression that the NGO approach to the debate sometimes lacks innovation.

Second, and perhaps the logical extension of the above, issue-specific symposia with limited agendas as well as fewer participants are more likely to produce constructive results. The NGO Symposium prior to the HLM is the best example. The attempt to place NGO symposia back-to-back with meetings of the Committee on Trade and Environment is a timid, albeit fairly controversial, step.[31]

Third, the participation of Member governments in NGO symposia remains crucial for such events to be useful. The idea of an arms-length NGO symposium as a purely political exercise will not achieve optimum results and holds the potential for backfiring.

Solving the above conundrum is complicated by the WTO Secretariat's small size and limited resources. The Secretariat does not have a separate budget for organising NGO symposia, relying entirely on donations from Member countries. In addition, the prospect of an increasing number of issue-specific NGO events is a daunting challenge for a small Secretariat.

---

[30] These working sessions on implementation of existing WTO agreements and the future work of the multilateral trading system took place at the WTO headquarters located near the United Nations.
[31] In September 1998 the Trade and Environment Division held a regional symposium for Latin American government officials in Santiago, Chile. Back-to-back with this meeting, and using the same facilities, an NGO seminar was organised, bringing together the government representatives and a large number of environmental NGOs. Another such WTO symposium followed by an NGO seminar will take place in Harare in February 1999.

The solution probably lies somewhere in the middle, i.e. large NGO events with short introductory plenary sessions followed by "break-offs" into smaller fora. Finding a more appropriate and perhaps creative formula for productive NGO events is one of the issues currently discussed in the WTO Secretariat, and this is certainly an area where input from NGOs would be welcomed. In any event, defining what is to be achieved by hosting an NGO event remains the key issue when deciding on the format.

The experiences from two Ministerial Conferences with NGO attendance should also serve as the basis for reflections on how to better accommodate civil society at the third Ministerial Conference of the WTO to be held in the United States in late 1999.

C. NEW INITIATIVES

Since 1996 the External Relations Division of the WTO Secretariat has served as the overall focal point for NGOs and has been in charge of developing what could be labelled as a systemic approach to the interaction with civil society.[32] Although the process of developing a coherent and active approach to improving the dialogue with NGOs has been slow, the increased attention given to this issue is perhaps best illustrated by a number of new initiatives announced by the Director-General during the General Council meeting on 15 July 1998.

The announcement of these initiatives to enhance the dialogue with civil society should, to a certain extent, be seen in the context of the calls for greater transparency made by a number of Ministers and Heads of State at the Geneva Ministerial Conference and 50th Year Celebration. There is little doubt that these public statements provided the Secretariat with the necessary backing for moving ahead with the interpretation of the guidelines on relations with NGOs.[33]

Immediately following the Geneva event, the Director-General created a taskforce to deal with the issue of how to improve the dialogue with civil society. This taskforce, chaired by the Director-General himself, met twice during the month of June to discuss and propose a number of Secretariat initiatives which, although still within the guidelines, would respond to the calls for greater transparency.

The first of the initiatives announced the beginning of regular briefings by the WTO Secretariat for NGOs on specific meetings. The decision to commence briefings for NGOs was based on a genuine wish to increase transparency and to counter the frequently voiced criticism of excessive secrecy, but a number of other considerations also played a role.

First, previously, briefings were only given to the media and NGOs without press credentials were unable to attend such briefings. Therefore, NGOs were most often left to

---

[32] Of course, other divisions in the WTO Secretariat work directly with NGOs and maintain their own day-to-day contact with representatives of civil society.

[33] Another significant example of political backing for enhancing the dialogue with civil society can be found in the Chair's Statement from the Quadrilateral Trade Ministers' Meeting in Toronto from 30 April to 2 May 1997, which calls for the Director-General to "consult with Members regarding appropriate means for encouraging informal dialogue between WTO working groups and committees and business, non-governmental organisations and other interested parties ...".

use their individual contacts to Member delegations, WTO Secretariat and/or read the papers. Second, as press briefings made the information public anyway, there was little logic in delaying it for others. Third, from a pure efficiency point of view, briefing a room full of NGOs at the same time, as opposed to answering individual phone calls, makes sense for a small Secretariat like that of the WTO. Fourth, although the conventional wisdom has been that NGOs generally do not face the deadlines of the media and, therefore, do not need the information as rapidly, there appears to be a growing convergence in this area. Many NGOs produce weekly newsletters which are distributed electronically to constituencies and members worldwide and, thus, timely information is becoming increasingly important to them.

The inaugural briefing by the WTO Secretariat for NGOs was held on 28 September 1998 with more than 20 Geneva-based NGOs present.[34]

Another of the initiatives announced by the Director-General concerns the compilation and circulation to WTO Members of a monthly list of NGO position papers received by the Secretariat. If Members wish to consult the material in more detail, they may contact the Secretariat to obtain a copy. As the Secretariat receives a substantial number of NGO publications, brochures, newsletters, etc. every week, only position papers which relate to the activities of the WTO will be included on the list.

Since late October 1998, a special NGO section on the WTO Web Site has been in place. This section holds specific information for civil society, e.g. records and statistics from past NGO events organised by the WTO Secretariat in announcements of registration deadlines for ministerial meetings, etc. In addition, the monthly list of NGO position papers received by the Secretariat and circulated to Members will be featured on the NGO Web Site.

Finally, the Director-General announced the first of a series of meetings with representatives of civil society to discuss how to further enhance the dialogue and improve relations. In the past, Director-General Ruggiero has met with individual NGOs on a regular basis and he remains committed to continue this practice. However, the new initiative addresses the more fundamental problem of how to develop the most constructive and efficient mechanism for dealing with NGOs.

In this endeavour, the Secretariat needs the input and ideas from the broadest possible group of NGOs and to this effect the Director-General met with representatives of the environment, development, consumer, business and labour groups on 17 July and again on 5 November 1998. The Director-General has expressed a strong wish to meet with more NGOs in the near future.

It is still too early to say what this process will lead to, but one significant objective of such informal meetings, apart from the confidence-building, is to establish an overall framework within which WTO-NGO relations can continue to evolve. There is little doubt that the new initiatives have opened a window of opportunity to further explore ways in which consultation can take place, but much will also depend on the ability of NGOs to come up with a common position on how to proceed.

---

[34] The NGO briefings are open to all NGOs "concerned with matters related to those of the WTO" and take place in rooms provided by the International Centre for Trade and Sustainable Development (ICTSD).

III.   CLAIMS FOR MORE TRANSPARENCY AND ACCESS TO INFORMATION AND
       DOCUMENTS

Although the WTO has been criticised for lacking transparency and operating in
"secrecy", the WTO Agreement contains multiple notification, publication and transparency
requirements. Most documents are issued as unrestricted under the Decision on
Derestriction, discussed below. These provisions ensure a moderate level of transparency
of WTO and Member country decisions and measures.

As the GATT was, and the WTO is, a contract between countries, these obligations
are addressed to Member countries and all Members are given the right to request
compliance with these obligations. Private citizens cannot challenge the validity of any
publication or notification, or the lack thereof. Because of the reach of the various WTO
obligations and their impacts on non-governmental entities, some agreements do address
requests by "any interested party" and obligate information to be provided upon request.

The following section identifies the existing transparency provisions of the WTO
agreements operating at the domestic publication and WTO notifications levels.

A.   DOMESTIC PUBLICATION

The basic provision of the GATT on transparency is Article X. The first paragraph
obligates Members to publish promptly any measures (laws, regulations, judicial decisions,
etc.) relating to GATT matters, as well as any international agreement affecting international
trade policy, to allow government and trading entities to become familiar with them.

"Publication and Administration of Trade Regulations

1.   Laws, regulations, judicial decisions and administrative rulings of general application, made
effective by any contracting party, pertaining to the classification or the valuation of products for
customs purposes, or to rates of duty, taxes or other charges, or to requirements, restrictions or
prohibitions on imports or exports or on the transfer of payments therefor, or affecting their sale,
distribution, transportation, insurance, warehousing inspection, exhibition, processing, mixing or
other use, *shall be published promptly in such a manner as to enable governments and traders to become
acquainted with them.* Agreements affecting international trade policy which are in force between
the government or a governmental agency of any contracting party and the government or
governmental agency of any other contracting party shall also be published. The provisions of this
paragraph shall not require any contracting party to disclose *confidential information* which would
impede law enforcement or otherwise be contrary to the public interest or would prejudice the
legitimate commercial interests of particular enterprises, public or private."

This paragraph in Article X of the GATT has been interpreted by a few GATT panels,
and the WTO panel, and Appellate Body to mean the following.

 – Such measures *do not have to be published before their entry into force,* as no time-limit or
   delay between publication and entry into force of the measure is specified therein.[35]

---

[35] *EEC—Restrictions on Imports of Dessert Apples, Complaint by Chile,* BISD 36S/33, para. 12.29; *EEC—Restrictions
on Imports of Apples, Complaints by the United States,* BISD 36S/135, para. 5.20–5.23; and *Canada—Import, Distribution
and Sale of Certain Alcoholic Drinks by Provincial Marketing Agencies,* BISD 39S, para. 5.34.

However, the use of a "back-dated" measure is prohibited by such a provision.[36]

- As Article X:1 deals with measures of general application, neither specific quotas allocated nor licenses issued to a specific company or applied to a specific shipment have to be published.[37] However, administrative rulings in individual cases establishing or revising principles or criteria applicable in future cases ought to be published.[38] In any case, Article X does not relate to the substantive content of the measure, but only to its publication.[39]

By exception, Paragraph 2 of Article X prohibits the entry into force of certain limited regulations before publication:

"2.   No measure of general application taken by any contracting party effecting an advance in a rate of duty or other charge on imports under an established and uniform practice, or imposing a new or more burdensome requirement, restriction or prohibition on imports, or on the transfer of payments therefor, shall be enforced before such measure has been officially published."

Some of the WTO multilateral trade agreements cross-reference provisions of Article X of GATT, such as Article 6 of the Agreement on Trade-Related Investment Measures (TRIMS):

"*Transparency*

1.   Members reaffirm, with respect to TRIMS, their commitment to obligations on transparency and notification in Article X of GATT 1994 ... .

3.   Each Member shall accord sympathetic consideration to requests for information, and afford adequate opportunity for consultation, on any matter arising from this Agreement raised by another Member ... ."

Article 12 of the Agreement on the Interpretation of Article VII of the GATT 1994 ("Customs Valuation Agreement") provides:

"Laws, regulations, judicial decisions and administrative rulings of general application giving effect to this Agreement shall be published in conformity with Article X of GATT 1994 by the country of importation concerned."

The Import Licensing Agreement uses the same wording as Article X and refers to the rights of traders to be acquainted with the supplied information.[40] However, the

---

[36] *EEC—Restrictions on Imports of Apples, Complaints by the United States*, as note 35, above.

[37] *EC—Measures Affecting the Importation of Certain Poultry Products*, WT/DS69/AB/R, paras 113–114.

[38] *Japan—Measures Affecting Consumer Photographic Film and Paper*, WT/DS44/R, para. 10.388.

[39] *EC—Measures Affecting the Importation of Certain Poultry Products*, WT/DS69/AB/R, para. 115, referring to *EC—Regime for the Importation, Sale and Distribution of Bananas*, WT/DS27/AB/R, para. 200.

[40] Art. 1.4 reads as follows:

"(a) The rules and all information concerning procedures for the submission of applications, including the eligibility of persons, firms and institutions to make such applications, the administrative body(ies) to be approached, and the lists of products subject to the licensing requirement shall be published, in the sources notified to the Committee on Import Licensing provided for in Article 4 (referred to in this Agreement as 'the Committee'), in such a manner as to enable governments and traders to become acquainted with them. Such publication shall take place, whenever practicable, 21 days prior to the effective date of the requirement but in all events not later than such effective date. Any exception, derogations or changes in or from the rules concerning licensing procedures or the list of products subject to import licensing shall also be published in the same manner and within the same time periods as specified above."

agreement limits the right to obtain further information on the administration of quotas to Members.[41]

Article III of the GATS imposes domestic notification obligations of all laws, regulations and international agreements that may affect the operation of the GATS:

> "1.   Each Member shall publish promptly and, except in emergency situations, at the latest by the time of their entry into force, all relevant measures of general application which pertain to or affect the operation of this Agreement. International agreements pertaining to or affecting trade in services to which a Member is a signatory shall also be published.
>
> 2.   Where publication as referred to in paragraph 1 is not practicable, such information shall be made otherwise publicly available."

Some WTO agreements recognise the legitimate rights of persons outside the government to request and obtain information on these publications. These individuals are defined as "interested parties". The Agreement on Technical Barriers to Trade (TBT Agreement) provides for such a notification requirement in order to ensure that any "interested party" be adequately informed:

> "2.9   Whenever a relevant international standard does not exist or the technical content of a proposed technical regulation is not in accordance with the technical content of relevant international standards, and if the technical regulation may have a significant effect on trade of other Members, Members shall:
>
> 2.9.1 publish a notice in a publication at an early appropriate stage, in such a manner as to enable *interested parties in other Members* to become acquainted with it, that they propose to introduce a particular technical regulation; ... ."

It is interesting to note that Annex B of the Agreement on Sanitary and Phytosanitary Measures (SPS Agreement) contains a similar notification obligation, but refers only to the interests of Members in being well-informed. It also imposes a reasonable period of time between publication and the entry into force of any SPS measure.

> "*Publication of regulations*
>
> 1.   Members shall ensure that all sanitary and phytosanitary regulations which have been adopted are published promptly in such a manner as to enable interested Members to become acquainted with them.
>
> 2.   Except in urgent circumstances, Members shall allow a reasonable interval between the publication of a sanitary or phytosanitary regulation and its entry into force in order to allow time for producers in exporting Members, and particularly in developing country Members, to adapt their products and methods of production to the requirements of the importing Member."

Article 63 of the TRIPS Agreement imposes a publication obligation wider than that envisaged in Article X of the GATT for ensuring that rights-holders are adequately informed:

---

[41] Art. 3.5 reads as follows:

> "(a) Members shall provide, upon the request of any Member having an interest in the trade in the product concerned, all relevant information concerning: (i) the administration of the restrictions; (ii) the import licences granted over a recent period; (iii) the distribution of such licences among supplying countries; (iv) where practicable, import statistics (i.e. value and/or volume) with respect to the products subject to import licensing. Developing country Members would not be expected to take additional administrative or financial burdens on this account; ... ."

"1.   Laws and regulations, and final judicial decisions and administrative rulings of general application, made effective by a Member pertaining to the subject-matter of this Agreement (the availability, scope, acquisition, enforcement and prevention of the abuse of intellectual property rights) shall be published, or where such publication is not practicable made publicly available, in a national language, in such a manner as to enable governments *and right-holders* to become acquainted with them. Agreements concerning the subject-matter of this Agreement which are in force between the government or a governmental agency of a Member and the government or a governmental agency of another Member shall also be published ... .

4.   Nothing in paragraphs 1, 2 and 3 shall require Members to disclose confidential information which would impede law enforcement or otherwise be contrary to the public interest or would prejudice the legitimate commercial interests of particular enterprises, public or private."

The Agreement on Safeguards in Article 3, the Agreement on Subsidies and Countervailing Measures (SCM Agreement) in Article 22 and the Agreement on the Application of Article VI (Dumping Agreement) in Article 12 all provide for domestic notification of any measure through which an investigation is initiated and which may result in an import remedy measure. For instance, Article 12 of the Dumping Agreement provides:

"When the authorities are satisfied that there is sufficient evidence to justify the initiation of an anti-dumping investigation pursuant to Article 5, the Member or Members the products of which are subject to such investigation and other interested parties known to the investigating authorities to have an interest therein shall be notified and a public notice shall be given."

Article 12 of the Dumping Agreement imposes fairly detailed requirements on the contents and the explanation to be provided in these public notifications. Article 22 of the SCM Agreement contains similar obligations. Article 3 of the Safeguards Agreement, although requiring less detailed information, goes further in imposing a "public interest" investigation. This type of participation of interest groups in the domestic process is further discussed in section IV, 2 below.

The Agreement on Preshipment Inspection (PSI Agreement) also provides for notification and transparency requirements. The purpose of the PSI is to establish a system of disciplines for private inspection companies hired by importing countries to examine whether imported goods respect their domestic standards and other regulatory requirements. The PSI Agreement requires Members using preshipment companies to maintain transparent activities.

"*Transparency*

5.   User Members shall ensure that preshipment inspection activities are conducted in a transparent manner.

6.   User Members shall ensure that, when initially contacted by exporters, preshipment inspection entities provide to the exporters a list of all the information which is necessary for the exporters to comply with inspection requirements ... .

8. User Members shall publish promptly all applicable laws and regulations relating to preshipment inspection activities in such a manner as to enable other governments and traders to become acquainted with them."[42]

The Agreement on Trade Policy Review Mechanism (TPRM), which introduced trade policy review to the international trade system, contains an explicit transparency policy statement in Section B:

"*Domestic transparency*

Members recognise the inherent value of domestic transparency of government decision-making on trade policy matters for both Members' economies and the multilateral trading system, and agree to encourage and promote greater transparency within their own systems, acknowledging that the implementation of domestic transparency must be on a voluntary basis and take account of each Member's legal and political systems."

Therefore, the various WTO agreements contain provisions obligating Members to have domestic systems of access to information on laws, regulations and other measures relating to WTO matters. When there is reference to "any interested party", any citizen submitting a request for information on WTO-related laws or regulations should be granted information pertinent to the request. The limited rights of NGOs to challenge compliance with these domestic publication obligations, both domestically and in the WTO forum, is discussed in further detail below.

B. NOTIFICATIONS TO THE WTO

1. *Obligation to Notify the WTO of Laws, Regulations and other Measures*

Generally, Members are required to notify other Members through the WTO Secretariat of all laws and regulations of *general application*[43] concerned with WTO matters. This includes all actions and measures covered by the WTO provisions, especially those actions affecting the rights of other Members, and obligates Members to provide due consideration to requests by other Members for information on such regulations. This obligation, which binds only Member governments, ensures transparency at two levels: first, domestically, individuals and other members of civil society may have access to their own government documents and papers notified to WTO if the domestic system allows for such procedure;[44] second, at the WTO level, most documents notified to the WTO are circulated to all Members, are accessible to anyone who request a copy and, since the adoption of the Decision on Derestriction discussed below, are posted on the WTO Web Site.

The GATT 1947 contained many notification requirements for measures of general

---

[42] Under the PSI Agreement exporting Members are also subject to the same publication requirements. Art. 3.2 of the PSI Agreement states: "Exporter Members shall publish promptly all applicable laws and regulations relating to preshipment inspection activities in such a manner as to enable other governments and traders to become acquainted with them."

[43] Members are also obliged to notify any *specific measure* that affect matters covered by WTO provisions.

[44] For instance, in the United Sates, the government is obliged to make available to the public most of its position papers and other submissions to WTO bodies.

application, such as those mentioned in Articles II:6(b) for modification of schedules, XII:4 and XVIII:12 for balance of payment problems, XV:8 for exchange restrictions reports, XVI:1 for subsidies, and XXIV:7 for regional arrangements.[45] Additional notification requirements, such as those for the export of domestically prohibited goods or for any protective measures affecting imports from less developed countries, existed in the provisions of legal instruments under the GATT 1947.[46] The notifications to the GATT and now to the WTO of laws and measures of general application are parallel to the domestic publication obligation contained in Article X of the GATT.

The general obligation to notify *specific measures* affecting the operation of the GATT has its genesis in the Tokyo Round Decision of the Contracting Parties, whereby any measure affecting the rights of another country had to be notified prior to its entry into force. The Understanding Regarding Notification, Consultation, Dispute Settlement and Surveillance states:

"1.   The CONTRACTING PARTIES reaffirm their adherence to the basic GATT mechanism for the management of disputes based on Articles XXII and XXIII.1 With a view to improving and refining the GATT mechanism, the CONTRACTING PARTIES agree as follows:

Notification

2.   Contracting parties reaffirm their commitment to existing obligations under the General Agreement regarding publication and notification.

3.   Contracting parties moreover undertake, to the maximum extent possible, to notify the CONTRACTING PARTIES of their *adoption of trade measures affecting the operation of the General Agreement*, it being understood that such notification would of itself be without prejudice to views on the consistency of measures with or their relevance to rights and obligations under the General Agreement. Contracting parties should endeavour to notify such measures *in advance of implementation*. In other cases, where prior notification has not been possible, such measures should be notified promptly *ex post facto*. Contracting parties which have reason to believe that such trade measures have been adopted by another contracting party *may seek information on such measures bilaterally*, from the contracting party concerned."[47]

The notification requirement is inscribed into the "GATT mechanism" following a stated reaffirmation of the importance of the GATT dispute settlement mechanism. The two components are inextricably linked. This principle is contained in the Marrakesh Decision on Notification Procedures in a more elaborated form:

"...

Members,

Desiring to improve the operation of notification procedures under the Agreement Establishing the World Trade Organization (hereinafter referred to as the 'WTO Agreement'), and thereby to contribute to the transparency of Members' trade policies and to the effectiveness of surveillance arrangements established to that end;

---

[45] For an exhaustible list of the notification requirements under the GATT 1947, consult the Secretariat Document G/NOP/W/2/Rev.1.

[46] As note 45, above.

[47] Decision of the CONTRACTING PARTIES adopted on 28 November 1979 (L/4907).

...

Agree as follows:

I. *General obligation to notify*

Members affirm their commitment to obligations under the Multilateral Trade Agreements and, where applicable, the Plurilateral Trade Agreements, *regarding publication and notification.*

Members recall their undertakings set out in the Understanding Regarding Notification, Consultation, Dispute Settlement and Surveillance adopted on 28 November 1979 (BISD 26S/210). With regard to their undertaking therein to notify, to the maximum extent possible, their adoption of trade measures affecting the operation of GATT 1994, such notification itself being without prejudice to views on the consistency of measures with or their relevance to rights and obligations under the Multilateral Trade Agreements and, where applicable, the Plurilateral Trade Agreements, Members agree to be guided, as appropriate, by the annexed list of measures. Members therefore agree *that the introduction or modification of such measures* is subject to the notification requirements of the 1979 Understanding.

II. *Central registry of notifications*

A central registry of notifications shall be established under the responsibility of the Secretariat. ...

Information in the central registry regarding individual notifications shall be made available on request to any Member entitled to receive the notification concerned ... .'

This decision led to the creation of a central registry of all notifications and the creation of a working group to improve the system of notification requirements imposed on Members. This system has been criticised, as only representatives of Member countries can consult the registry. The notification requirements developed by the working group have also been criticised as extremely burdensome, especially for developing countries.[48]

It should be noted, however, that often most measures are notified *after* they have been enacted, which reduces the latitude of other Members, and certainly that of non-governmental interest groups, to influence the decision-making process relating to these measures. However, as detailed below, some WTO agreements[49] explicitly obligate Members to notify certain actions and measures first domestically, and to the WTO Secretariat, before their implementation. Some of these WTO provisions also oblige Members to consult with interested parties.

2. *Notification Requirements Contained in the WTO Multilateral Trade Agreements*

The various WTO agreements refer to three types of notifications requirements: annual, regular and one-time-only. Under the Annex 1A agreements (on trade in goods) alone, there are 175 notification requirements. Some agreements require a one-time notification of regulations or laws in place at the entry into force of the WTO, to be

---

[48] This working group issued its report on 7 October 1996. It can be consulted as Secretariat document G/L/112.

[49] Such as the TBT Agreement and some of the trade remedy agreements, i.e. the SCM Agreement, the Dumping Agreement and the Safeguard Agreement.

followed on an *ad hoc* basis by notification of changes in these regulations and laws. There are also 106 *ad hoc* notification requirements, obligating Members to submit notification only if a specific action is taken. There are also 43 "one-time-only" notification require-ments, most of which relate to the implementation of the agreements and were due in 1995 or on a Member's accession. There are also 26 regular, periodic notification require-ments which consist of 17 annual notifications, three semi-annual, three biennial and three triennial notification requirements.

For example the Agreement on Agriculture envisages seven annual notification requirements that relate to:

- tariff and other quota commitments;
- special safeguard provisions;
- total aggregate measurement of support;
- export subsidy, budgetary outlay and quantity reduction commitments;
- total exports in the context of export subsidy commitments;
- total food aid in the context of export subsidy commitments; and
- actions taken under the Decision on Measures Concerning the Possible Negative Effects of the Reform Programme on Least-Developed and Net-food Importing Developing Countries.

The SCM Agreement contains various notification requirements, including the obligation to notify, in advance of its implementation, non-actionable subsidies (Article 8.3 of the SCM Agreement).[50] Another set of examples concerns the requirements under the TBT Agreement:

> "At least once every six months, the standardising body shall publish a work programme containing its name and address, the standards it is currently preparing and the standards which it has adopted in the preceding period ... no later than at the time of publication of its work programme, the standardising body shall notify the existence thereof to the ISO/IEC Information Centre in Geneva."[51]

The TRIPS Agreement and the GATS also contain extensive notification require-ments which, together with the application of the Decision on Derestriction, ensure transparency *vis-à-vis* other Members and *vis-à-vis* the public in general.

(a)   *The possibility of cross-notification*

Another feature of the WTO notification requirements under the various WTO multilateral trade agreements is the opportunity for cross-notification, whereby a Member notifies the WTO of a measure not notified by its originating Member. This process ensures further transparency and forces the originating Member to justify its position regarding such a cross-notified measure. For instance under Article III:5 of the GATS:

---

[50] It is interesting to note that the SCM Committee adopted a decision on 22 February 1995 (before the General Council's Decision on Derestriction adopted on 18 July 1996), that all notifications of national SCM legislation would be made public, i.e. would be circulated as derestricted. See Minutes of the SCM Committee, G/SCM/M/1, paras 40–59. Similar decisions were taken by the ADP Committee for Antidumping Legislation, G/ADP/M/1, paras 37–39 and by the SG Committee for the Safeguard Legislation, G/SG/M/1, paras 37–38.

[51] Annex 3, para. (j) of the TBT Agreement. For an exhaustive list of notification requirements under the Annex 1A Agreement, see Secretariat Documents G/NOP/W/5 and G/NOP/W/14.

"5. Any Member may notify to the Council for Trade in Services any measure, taken by any other Member, which it considers affects the operation of this Agreement."

Similar cross-notifications rights exist under the Agreement for Textiles and Clothing,[52] the SCM Agreement,[53] and the Import Licensing Agreement.[54]

(b) *Request for information and "enquiry points"*

The right to request information flows from the obligation of domestic publication. Some agreements, such as the TBT Agreement and the GATS, also contain obligations on Members to maintain "enquiry points" where any Member, and in some cases any "interested party", can request information on any law, regulation or measure in place domestically. For instance, Article 10 of the TBT Agreement requires Members to maintain enquiry points where *any interested* party may request information:

"10.1 Each Member shall ensure that an enquiry point exists which is able to answer all reasonable enquiries from other Members and *interested parties in other Members* as well as to provide the relevant documents ... ."

Article 6 of the TRIMS Agreement contains a similar obligation, limited only to Members, as does Article III:4 of the GATS:

"Each Member shall respond promptly to all requests by any other Member for specific information on any of its measures of general application or international agreements within the meaning of paragraph 1. Each Member *shall also establish one or more enquiry points to provide specific information to other Members, upon request,* on all such matters as well as those subject to the notification requirement in paragraph 3. Such enquiry points shall be established within two years from the date of entry into force of the Agreement Establishing the WTO (referred to in this Agreement as the "WTO Agreement"). Appropriate flexibility with respect to the time-limit within which such enquiry points are to be established may be agreed upon for individual developing country Members. Enquiry points need not be depositories of laws and regulations."

These enquiry points usually provide information to anyone requesting it.

In the context of dispute settlement procedures, which are generally confidential (including submissions by the parties to the panel), Article 18 of the Understanding on Rules and Procedures on Dispute Settlement (DSU) obliges a party to the dispute to provide a non-confidential summary of its submission at the request of any Member. Unfortunately, the DSU does not provide for any deadline for such obligation. Again, this does not provide any rights to non-governmental interest groups, but leaves them the opportunity to pressure their own governments to require a non-confidential summary of submissions.

---

[52] Art. 7.3 of the ATC Agreement.
[53] Art. 25.10 of the SCM Agreement.
[54] Art. 5.5 of the Import Licensing Agreement.

The system of notifications under the GATT and the WTO is fairly sophisticated and conducive to transparency. Although these obligations are imposed only upon Members, the Decision on Derestriction extends the information to anyone.[55]

3. *Decision on Derestriction*[56]

The full transparency potential of the above-mentioned notification requirements lies with the Decision on Derestriction (WT/L/160/Rev.1) adopted by the WTO General Council on 18 July 1996. Since the adoption of this decision, the WTO principle has been one of *unrestricted circulation of all WTO documents* with few exceptions. Notwithstanding the exceptions mentioned below:

 – any document required to be published under the WTO agreements or containing only publicly available information cannot be restricted; and
 – any Member may circulate any document as unrestricted.

The following list of exceptions refers to the present rules on derestriction:[57]

 – Working documents are derestricted at the time of their adoption or six months after their circulation (as in the case of Secretariat background papers), whichever is earlier.[58]
 – SECRET documents (such as tariff negotiations) are derestricted upon completion of the process. It is difficult to envisage derestriction of these documents, which contain essentially confidential information, before the or a negotiation process is completed.
 – Minutes of meetings are derestricted six months after their circulation. Circulation of minutes normally occurs more than a month after the meeting.
 – Trade Policy Review reports are derestricted at the expiration of the press embargo.
 – Documents relating to working parties on accession are derestricted upon the adoption of the working party report or at the end of the year following the year in which they were circulated.
 – Balance-of-payment documents are considered for derestriction at the end of each six-month period.
 – Documents submitted by a Member requesting restricted circulation are considered for derestriction at the end of each six-month period.
 – Panel reports are circulated as unrestricted unless a Member requests an additional period of restriction, not to exceed ten days. (No Member has ever made use of this ten-day postponement option.)

---

[55] However, as further discussed below, non-Members do not have the right to request enforcement of such notification or any related information.

[56] See Annex C.

[57] During consultations on these procedures, many Members expressed wariness at "automatic" derestriction, which would prevent them from having the final say. Most derestriction provisions, therefore, call for documents to be "considered" for derestriction by Members upon the expiry of the stipulated time periods for restriction.

[58] Working documents of some WTO Committees (Market Access, Balance of Payment (BOP), Committee on Trade and Development (CTD), Trade Policy Review Body (TPRB) are to be considered for derestriction at the end of each six-month period (i.e. January–June, July–December). This was the old GATT practice, and was retained to prevent the new procedure (six months after circulation) being more restrictive than the earlier GATT procedures for the documents of these committees.

Reducing the scope of the exceptions listed in the Appendix of the Decision on Derestriction would improve WTO transparency. Providing for earlier derestriction, barring requests for continued restricted status, would promote this process. The Decision on Derestriction is under review at the present time. Four Members, the United States,[59] the European Communities[60] and Canada[61] have submitted proposals favouring greater transparency and a reduction of the period during which documents remain restricted. Mexico[62] has submitted a proposal which insists, among other elements, on the fact that documents should be derestricted only when they are available in the three official languages of the WTO. A set of other countries have expressed contentment with the status quo and have raised their concern that further opening of the WTO process, including an enlarged distribution of documents as unrestricted, will enable private interest groups to frustrate the negotiation powers of governments in the WTO forum. In this regard, some Members stress the contractual nature of the WTO Agreement and emphasise that the WTO is an inter-governmental forum which should not become prey to interest groups. At publication of this article, the negotiations were still continuing.

As is apparent from the above publication and notification requirements, reinforced with their general circulation pursuant to the WTO Decision on Derestriction, the WTO is committed to principles of transparency and access to information of the formal actions of States in WTO-related matters. However, there are limitations to this transparency principle.

First, WTO notifications (and sometimes even domestic publications) often take place after the actions or measures have been implemented. The domestic arena and internal relations between NGOs and their governments still largely determines the ability of non-governmental entities to access information before the final measures are adopted, published and notified. Accordingly, the possibility for NGOs to influence government decision-making may be limited.

Second, non-governmental entities have no right of action whatsoever in the WTO. Therefore, any interested party can challenge the absence of publication by another WTO Member, but only if their own government takes on their complaint. NGOs cannot challenge the absence of notification by their own government, unless there are domestic mechanisms in place to facilitate this action. On the other hand, a Member (following a request by its own domestic entities for instance) can challenge the absence of WTO notification or domestic publication by another Member. This situation has led to criticism of domestic openness provisions of the WTO Agreement based on the "sovereignty principle", as creating a "paradoxical situation for domestic citizens in relation to foreign governments", as there is "no assurance that those similar rights will be maintained for

---

[59] WT/GC/W/88.
[60] WT/GC/W/92.
[61] WT/GC/W/98. Canada and the United States also put forward together (WT/GC/W106) a revised proposal taking into account some of the claims of Members with regard to their respective first proposal.
[62] WT/GC/W113.

domestic citizens".[63] If the WTO Agreement had a "direct effect" on the domestic laws of a Member, then private citizens and NGOs would be able to challenge their own governments and other entities for failing to comply with WTO publication requirements.

However, few countries "receive" international law obligations directly into their domestic system. Most countries require domestic implementation legislation for international agreements, such as the WTO Agreement, to enter into force domestically. Usually, such implementing legislation either explicitly or implicitly provides that provisions of the WTO Agreement do not have direct effect on the country, consequently depriving private citizens and non-governmental entities of the right to take action against their own government for failure to comply with WTO obligations.[64] Therefore, procedural rights of NGOs to challenge the inadequacy or absence of notification (or other WTO obligations) by their own government or of other governments are limited and most often depend on the domestic law of such country.[65]

Civil society is concerned and affected by policy and events at the international level, yet enormous disparity exists between access to information at the domestic level, where measures are to be published before they are adopted, and at the international level, where citizens and NGOs face a six-month delay in being informed of an action. Correcting this asymmetry propels NGO efforts to increase transparency and the dissemination of documents, consequently strengthening their ability to exert influence in a more timely fashion on the WTO decision-making process.

Finally, it also should be noted that the claims of NGOs for further transparency are not only of a procedural nature, such as access to information. NGOs want to be able to challenge the norms-setting that takes place within the WTO. For instance, NGOs have challenged the TBT and SPS agreements' reliance on the harmonisation efforts of Codex Alimentarius and the International Standards Organisation, international bodies which they argue also lack transparency.[66] Whether such an NGO challenge will be constructive or detrimental for the WTO and international trade depends on the actions Members take in response to the criticism.

IV. PARTICIPATION IN THE DISPUTE SETTLEMENT MECHANISM

A. THE DSU PROCESS

Dispute settlement mechanisms ensure respect for negotiated rules. The new binding set of WTO rules on dispute settlement, the semi-automatic character of the process, and

---

[63] Alice Enders, *WTO Openness*, Washington, IISD's Knowledge Networks Project.
[64] For a discussion on the different constitutions of WTO Members and whether they receive international law directly as monist countries, or indirectly as dualist countries, see Ian Brownlie, *Principles of Public International Law*, 4th Ed. (Oxford, 1990), pp. 32 *et seq.*
[65] See, for instance, the US implementation legislation of the Uruguay Round, which provides that any information submitted or any report made pursuant to Art. 8.3 or 8.4 of the SCM Agreement regarding notified subsidy be published domestically, HR 5110, 27 September 1994, p. 311.
[66] Enders, as note 62, above, p. 18.

the threat of economic sanctions facing a Member not fulfilling its obligations, have led some authors to label the dispute settlement rules of the WTO as the "jewel" of the WTO crown or the "teeth" of the system. Although panels and the Appellate Body are expressly prohibited from adding rights and obligations when adjudicating on disputes,[67] interpretation of WTO agreement provisions is a necessary component of the dispute settlement process. The line between interpretation and providing clearer parameters of the rights and obligations of Members under these agreements is often very fine. Therefore, it is not surprising that many NGOs request the right to provide evidence, interpretations and their positions on the matters at issue in a dispute settlement procedure.

The rules of the dispute settlement mechanism are initiated by WTO Members, and the DSU is administered by the Dispute Settlement Body (DSB), serving as the parliament of Members for deliberations on disputes. A dispute settlement procedure is initiated with a request for consultation by a Member, or group thereof, claiming that benefits under any of the covered WTO agreements are being nullified or impaired by the failure of another Member, or group thereof, to carry out obligations under the agreement(s). If the complaining country pushes the process further, the DSU provides for a set of steps in the dispute settlement that occur almost automatically. Actions by the DSB are necessary for some of these steps to occur. However, the DSU is drafted so that the Members of the DSB must approve or authorise any action requested by one Member unless, by consensus, all Members decide not to. All Members present, including, most importantly, the Member which has interest in pursuing the process, must agree to stop the process. Therefore, the process is in the hands of the complaining party or parties. Even surveillance and compliance with the panel and Appellate Body reports are in the hands of the Members themselves. There is no independent policing authority and retaliation is possible only between Members involved in the dispute.

The formal participation[68] of non-Members in the dispute settlement process is consequently limited. The Appellate Body reiterated that only Members can initiate dispute settlement procedures.[69] However, panels are authorised to obtain information from any source, as is highlighted by Article 13 of the DSU:

> "1. Each panel shall have the right to seek information and technical advice from any individual or body which it deems appropriate. However, before a panel seeks such information or advice from any individual or body within the jurisdiction of a Member it shall inform the authorities of that Member. A Member should respond promptly and fully to any request by a panel for such

---

[67] Art. 3.2 and 3.4 of the DSU.

[68] Jeffrey L. Dunoff has argued that firms and other private interest groups have *de facto* been very active and influential in policy-making and dispute settlement procedures, see in *The Misguided Debate Over NGO Participation at the WTO*, Oxford Journal of International Economic Law, Vol. 1 No. 3, 1998, forthcoming.

[69] See in *Shrimp/Turtles* the Appellate Body in para. 101:

> "It may be well to stress at the outset that access to the dispute settlement process of the WTO is limited to Members of the WTO. This access is not available, under the *WTO Agreement* and the covered agreements as they currently exist, to individuals or international organisations, whether governmental or non-governmental. Only Members may become parties to a dispute of which a panel may be seized, and only Members 'having a substantial interest in a matter before a panel' may become third parties in the proceedings before that panel."

information as the panel considers necessary and appropriate. Confidential information which is provided shall not be revealed without formal authorisation from the individual, body or authorities of the Member providing the information.

2.   Panels may seek information from any relevant source and may consult experts to obtain their opinion on certain aspects of the matter. With respect to a factual issue concerning a scientific or other technical matter raised by a party to a dispute, a panel may request an advisory report in writing from an expert review group. Rules for the establishment of such a group and its procedures are set forth in Appendix 4."

This article offers two points in regards to interpretation of Article 13. First, Article 13 is broad and appears to give full discretion to panels to decide whether and what type of information or technical advice it considers it needs or desires from any source. Second, this provision is addressed only to panels and not to the Appellate Body. Consequently, some legal experts argue that this right to obtain outside information is limited to evidence, as opposed to legal arguments.[70] If Article 13 was intended to cover something other than evidence, which is under the exclusive administration of panels, the provision would also be addressed to the Appellate Body. On the other hand, the second paragraph of Article 13 is broad, referring to "information from any relevant source".

In the recent environmental dispute *United States—Import Prohibition of Certain Shrimp and Shrimp Products*,[71] the panel received two *amicus briefs* submitted by NGOs. The panel acknowledged receipt of the two *amicus briefs*. The NGOs concerned also sent copies of these documents directly to the parties in the dispute. The complaining parties requested the panel not to consider the content of the *amicus briefs* in its examination of the matter under dispute. The defendant, the United States, stressed that the panel could seek information from any relevant source under Article 13 of the DSU and urged the panel to avail itself of any relevant information in the two *amicus briefs*, as well as in any other similar communications.

Taking the position that it had not requested such information under Article 13 of the DSU, the panel informed the parties to the dispute that it did not intend to take these documents into consideration. The panel observed, however, that if any of the parties to the dispute wanted to put forward these documents, or part of them, as part of their own submission to the panel, they were free to do so; the other parties would then have two weeks to respond to the additional material. The United States availed itself of this opportunity by designating Section III ("Statements of Facts") of the *amicus brief* from one of these NGOs, as exhibit to its second submission to the Panel. The complaining parties noted that the *amicus briefs* comprised not only technical advice, but also legal and political arguments, and therefore did not fall within the purview of Article 13. The complainant countries also argued that Article 13 of the DSU did not permit anyone to make unsolicited submissions.

---

[70] Having said this does not eliminate all questions because evidence, as including expertise and technical advice still has to be defined. It should also be noted that as far as the participation of NGOs in dispute settlement proceedings is concerned, this provision is more restrictive than the situation before other courts, such as the European Court of Justice or the International court of Justice, the procedures of which explicitly envisage the possibility for the courts to invite *amicus briefs* from NGOs.
[71] WT/DS58/R.

In its final report the panel ruled:

"7.1 We had not requested such information as was contained in the above-mentioned documents. We note that, pursuant to Article 13 of the DSU, the initiative to seek information and to select the source of information rests with the Panel. In any other situations, only parties and third parties are allowed to submit information directly to the Panel. *Accepting non-requested information from non-governmental sources would be, in our opinion, incompatible with the provisions of the DSU as currently applied... . We noted that the United States availed themselves of this opportunity by designating Section III of the document submitted by the Centre for Marine Conservation and the Centre for International Environmental Law as an annex to its second submission to the Panel.*"

This case was brought before the WTO Appellate Body on 13 July 1998. The appellees, or complainants before the panel, objected to the United States' annexation of NGO submissions, on the grounds that the NGO documents contained more than factual evidence (indeed, they contained extensive legal arguments). In a preliminary ruling dated 11 August, the Appellate Body decided to accept the filing of submissions by NGOs attached to the US submission. The Appellate Body also decided to accept a revised brief notified separately, and arguably independently of the US submission, by one of the NGOs. The Appellate Body ruled:

"83. ... We have decided to accept for consideration, insofar as they may be pertinent, the legal arguments made by the various non-governmental organisations in the three briefs attached as exhibits to the appellant's submission of the United States, as well as the revised version of the brief by the Centre for International Environmental Law *et al.*, which was submitted to us on 3 August 1998. The reasons for our ruling will be given in the Appellate Body Report."[72]

The interesting point is that the legal arguments put forward by some of these NGOs were different from those of the United States. Following a specific question of the Appellate Body on this issue, the United States added that it agreed with the legal arguments in the submissions of the NGOs "to the extent those arguments concur with the US arguments set out in [its] main submission". This was challenged by the appellees as being against the rules of the DSU and the rules of procedure of the Appellate Body. The Appellate Body then ruled:

"91. We admit, therefore, the briefs attached to the appellant's submission of the United States as part of that appellant's submission. At the same time, considering that the United States has itself accepted the briefs in a tentative and qualified manner only, we focus in the succeeding sections below on the legal arguments in the main US appellant's submission States."

In its final report, the Appellate Body reversed the first part of the panel's findings on Article 13 of the DSU with a ground-breaking conclusion that as panels are masters of the panel process, a panel may decide to accept information even if that panel did not initially request such information. The Appellate Body made a distinction between what a panel is "obliged" to do and what it is "authorised" to do with submissions: panels are obliged to take into consideration submissions by parties and are authorised to accept

---

[72] *Shrimp/Turtles*, Appellate Body Report.

submissions by NGOs,[73] whether the panel initially requested these submissions or not:

"104. ... We consider that a panel also has the authority to *accept or reject* any information or advice which it may have sought and received, or to *make some other appropriate disposition* thereof. It is particularly within the province and the authority of a panel to determine *the need for information and advice* in a specific case, to ascertain the *acceptability* and *relevancy* of information or advice received, and to decide *what weight to ascribe to that information or advice* or to conclude that no weight at all should be given to what has been received."

"108. ... In the present context, authority to seek information is not properly equated with a *prohibition* on accepting information which has been submitted without having been requested by a panel. A panel has the discretionary authority either to accept and consider or to reject information and advice submitted to it, *whether requested by a panel or not*. The fact that a panel may *motu proprio* have initiated the request for information does not, by itself, bind the panel to accept and consider the information which is actually submitted. The amplitude of the authority vested in panels to shape the processes of fact-finding and legal interpretation makes clear that a panel will *not* be deluged, as it were, with non-requested material, *unless that panel allows itself to be so deluged*."

"109. ... Moreover, acceptance and rejection of the information and advice of the kind here submitted to the Panel need not exhaust the universe of possible appropriate dispositions thereof ... ."[74]

This decision has been criticised as a departure from the clear wording of Article 13 of the Dsu, which arguably provides the panel with the exclusive authority to "seek" information from any source. However, as this Appellate Body report was adopted by the Dsb on 6 November 1998, NGOs are now expected to forward submissions to panels in disputes addressing issues of concern to them.

Therefore, panels will have to develop working procedures to address:

– initial receipt of NGO submissions;

– *prima facie* examination of the submissions to assess their relevance to the dispute and whether they will be taken into account in the panel adjudication process; and

– procedures for confirming the formal acceptance and distribution of the submissions to all parties to the dispute.

---

[73] "It may be well to stress at the outset that access to the dispute settlement process of the WTO is limited to Members of the WTO. This access is not available, under the *WTO Agreement* and the covered agreements as they currently exist, to individuals or international organisations, whether governmental or non-governmental. Only Members may become parties to a dispute of which a panel may be seized, and only Members 'having a substantial interest in a matter before a panel' may become third parties in the proceedings before that panel. Thus, under the Dsu, only Members who are parties to a dispute, or who have notified their interest in becoming third parties in such a dispute to the Dsb, have a *legal right* to make submissions to, and have a *legal right* to have those submissions considered by, a panel. Correlatively, a panel is *obliged* in law to accept and give due consideration only to submissions made by the parties and the third parties in a panel proceeding. These are basic legal propositions; they do not, however, dispose of the issue here presented by the appellant's first claim of error. We believe this interpretative issue is most appropriately addressed by examining what a panel is *authorised* to do under the Dsu."

[74] "Against this context of broad authority vested in panels by the Dsu, and given the object and purpose of the Panel's mandate as revealed in Article 11, we do not believe that the word 'seek' must necessarily be read, as apparently the Panel read it, in too literal a manner. That the Panel's reading of the word 'seek' is unnecessarily formal and technical in nature becomes clear should an 'individual or body' first ask a panel for permission to file a statement or a brief. In such an event, a panel may decline to grant the leave requested. If, in the exercise of its sound discretion in a particular case, a panel concludes *inter alia* that it could do so without 'unduly delaying the panel process', it could grant permission to file a statement or a brief, subject to such conditions as it deems appropriate. The exercise of the Panel's discretion could, of course, and perhaps should, include consultation with the parties to the dispute. In this kind of situation, for all practical and pertinent purposes, the distinction between 'requested' and 'non-requested' information vanishes."

In this context, the Appellate Body points out that Article 12.1 of the DSU authorises panels to depart from, or to add to, the working procedures set forth in Appendix 3 of the DSU, and in effect to develop their own working procedures, after consultation with the parties to the dispute. Article 12.2 goes on to direct that panel procedures should provide sufficient flexibility so as to ensure "high-quality panel reports", while not unduly delaying the panel process.

A preliminary selection process of NGO briefs will remain under the panels' full discretionary authority. Yet, this selection process will always remain subject to "review" by the Appellate Body, as panels are required, pursuant to Article 11 of the DSU, to act in an "objective" manner as.[75]

The Appellate Body conclusion in the *Shrimp/Turtle* dispute is ground-breaking insofar as it allows NGOs to access the dispute settlement process from now on by submitting their own argument before panels and the Appellate Body. Even if the panel ultimately decides not to accept the submission by a non-party, the latter has still been given the fundamental opportunity to put forward arguments that may be taken by the panel.[76]

NGOs also have other opportunities to influence and participate in the dispute settlement process. Various agreements, such as the Antidumping, the SCM, the Safeguard and the TRIPS Agreements, provide for rights in favour of individuals and non-governmental bodies affected by measures adopted pursuant to these agreements, as did the GATT in some cases. Such agreements oblige WTO Members to have dispute settlement and other forms of mechanisms in place domestically to assess the legal value of the rights of such "interested party or parties".

B. THE RIGHTS OF "INTERESTED PARTIES" IN DOMESTIC DISPUTE SETTLEMENT PROCEEDINGS WHICH MAY LEAD TO WTO PANELS

An important feature of the GATT has always been to ensure that contracting parties maintain an independent domestic system to review decisions by customs authorities regarding customs matters. Article X:3(b) of the GATT provides that:

> "(b) Each contracting party shall maintain, or institute as soon as practicable, judicial, arbitral or administrative tribunals or procedures for the purpose, *inter alia*, of the prompt review and correction of administrative action relating to customs matters. Such tribunals or procedures shall be independent of the agencies entrusted with administrative enforcement and their decisions shall

---

[75] See case law on standard or review and the interpretation of "objective assessment", for instance in the Appellate Body Report in *EC—Measures Concerning Meat and Meat Products (Hormones)*, WT/DS26 and DS 48/AB/R, paras 110–119 and 131–134.

[76] It also remains to be seen whether representatives of NGOs will be attending the meeting of the panel and Appellate Body as jurisprudence now recognises that it is for each Member to decide who attends the meeting as their representatives (Appellate Body report in *Bananas III*, WT/DS27/AB/R and panel report in *National Car*, WT/DS54, 55, 59 and 64/R). If an individual from an NGO were present in the room of the panel or Appellate Body meeting, he or she would be there only as a representative of the Member which invited him or her. It is also conceivable that a party of the panel or the Appellate Body may call such a representative of an NGO to testify or provide evidence in the context of the dispute settlement procedures.

be implemented by, and shall govern the practice of, such agencies unless an appeal is lodged with a court or tribunal of superior jurisdiction within the time prescribed for appeals to be lodged by importers; *provided* that the central administration of such agency may take steps to obtain a review of the matter in another proceeding if there is good cause to believe that the decision is inconsistent with established principles of law or the actual facts."

Under the WTO, this obligation has evolved to take into account the rights of interested parties other than those of Member governments. For instance, Article 12 of the SCM Agreement[77] provides:

"12.1   Interested Members and *all interested parties* in a countervailing duty investigation shall be given notice of the information which the authorities require and ample opportunity to present in writing all evidence which they consider relevant in respect of the investigation in question.

12.1.2   Subject to the requirement to protect confidential information, evidence presented in writing by one interested Member or *interested party* shall be made available promptly to other interested Members or interested parties participating in the investigation.

12.1.3   As soon as an investigation has been initiated, the authorities shall provide the full text of the written application received under paragraph 1 of Article 11 to the known exporters[78] and to the authorities of the exporting Member and shall make it available, upon request, to other *interested parties* involved. Due regard shall be paid to the protection of confidential information, as provided for in paragraph 4."

"12.2   Interested Members and *interested parties* also shall have the right, upon justification, to present information orally. Where such information is provided orally, the interested Members *and interested parties* subsequently shall be required to reduce such submissions to writing. Any decision of the investigating authorities can only be based on such information and arguments as were on the written record of this authority and which were available to interested Members and *interested parties* participating in the investigation, due account having been given to the need to protect confidential information ... ."

"12.9   For the purposes of this Agreement, 'interested parties' shall *include*:

(i)   an exporter or foreign producer or the importer of a product subject to investigation, or a trade or business association a majority of the members of which are producers, exporters or importers of such product; and

(ii)   a producer of the like product in the importing Member or a trade and business association a majority of the members of which produce the like product in the territory of the importing Member."

Although this list is non-exhaustive, as it employs the word "including", it refers essentially to two groups concerned with the imported products under dispute: the importers and exporters, and the domestic producers. However, the last paragraph of Article 12.9 provides that "[t]his list shall not preclude Members from allowing domestic or foreign parties other than those mentioned above to be included as interested parties".

---

[77] The SCM Agreement authorises an importing Member to impose at its border a surtax on imported goods that have been the object of subsidies that are causing injury in the domestic market of that importing country, obliges such an importing country to hold a thorough investigation and to hear the views of private interest groups.
[78] It being understood that where the number of exporters involved is particularly high, the full text of the application should instead be provided only to the authorities of the exporting Member or to the relevant trade association who then should forward copies to the exporters concerned.

More importantly, Article 12.10 obligates the importing country to take into account the views and interests of other non-governmental organisations:

"12.10 The authorities shall provide opportunities for industrial users of the product under investigation, and for *representative consumer organisations* in cases where the product is commonly sold at the retail level, to provide information which is relevant to the investigation regarding subsidisation, injury and causality."

The Dumping Agreement provides in Article 6.12, for a similar mechanism in favour of consumer groups:

"6.12 The authorities shall provide opportunities for industrial users of the product under investigation, and *for representative consumer organisations* in cases where the product is commonly sold at the retail level, to provide information which is relevant to the investigation regarding dumping, injury and causality."

The SCM and Dumping Agreements are often qualified as "producers" agreements, as their main objective is the protection of producers, rather than consumer interests. Although the provisions favouring consumer groups are indeed weaker than those protecting business and trade associations, NGOs could nevertheless make use of these provisions as an opportunity to provide the domestic investigation process with appropriate and relevant information. This NGO input could, therefore, become part of the evidence (and arguments) to be assessed by WTO adjudicating bodies, if such domestic determination is eventually challenged by another Member.

From the perspective of public participation, the Safeguard Agreement is bolder, obligating importing countries to perform a "public interest" investigation to take into account the interest of various stakeholders in the country.

"3.1 A Member may apply a safeguard measure only following an investigation by the competent authorities of that Member pursuant to procedures previously established and made public in consonance with Article X of GATT 1994. This investigation shall include reasonable public *notice to all interested parties* and public hearings or other appropriate means in which importers, exporters and *other interested parties could present evidence and their views*, including the opportunity to respond to the presentations of other parties and to submit their views, *inter alia*, as to whether or not the application of a safeguard measure would be in the *public interest*. The competent authorities shall publish a report setting forth their findings and reasoned conclusions reached on all pertinent issues of fact and law."

"Interested parties" are not defined in the Safeguard Agreement and, thus, could include any interest group. If NGOs get involved in the domestic assessment of the "public interest", their input will become part of the file that will be taken to the WTO dispute settlement procedure, should another Member challenge such domestic determination of public interest (which under the Safeguard Agreement is mandatory).

Article 42 of the TRIPS Agreement, dealing with intellectual property rights held by non-governmental entities, contains provisions in favour of private parties:

"Members shall make available to right holders[79] civil judicial procedures concerning the enforcement of any intellectual property right covered by this Agreement. Defendants shall have the right to written notice which is timely and contains sufficient detail, including the basis of the claims. Parties shall be allowed to be represented by independent legal counsel, and procedures shall not impose overly burdensome requirements concerning mandatory personal appearances ... ."

Article VI of the GATS on "Domestic Regulations" contains provisions similar to those of Article X of the GATT and provides rights for private parties to be informed of decisions that could affect their rights:

"2.   (a)   Each Member shall maintain or institute as soon as practicable judicial, arbitral or administrative tribunals or procedures which provide, *at the request of an affected service supplier,* for the prompt review of, and where justified, appropriate remedies for, administrative decisions affecting trade in services. Where such procedures are not independent of the agency entrusted with the administrative decision concerned, the Member shall ensure that the procedures in fact provide for an objective and impartial review ... ."

"3.   Where authorisation is required for the supply of a service on which a specific commitment has been made, the competent authorities of a Member shall, within a reasonable period of time after the submission of an application considered complete under domestic laws and regulations, inform the applicant of the decision concerning the application. At the request of the applicant, the competent authorities of the Member shall provide, without undue delay, information concerning the status of the application."

This right of consumer groups and other private interested parties is limited, however. If a Member violates an obligation, and no *domestic* avenues exist to pursue a challenge, the individual or NGO has no enforcement tools at its disposal to pressure its government to attend to their complaint. If such individuals or NGOs are not to be heard by their own government (let alone the government of another Member), where can they take their complaint? With the new ruling of the Appellate Body in the *Shrimp/Turtles* dispute, if the matter is taken to the WTO dispute settlement process, anyone could forward its submission directly to an ongoing panel process. Yet in the absence of such WTO dispute settlement process, NGOs (and individuals) do not have any enforcement rights of any WTO obligation.[80]

C.   THE PARTICIPATION OF NGOS IN THE DISPUTE SETTLEMENT MECHANISM UNDER THE PSI, THE SPS AND THE TBT AGREEMENTS

The hybrid nature of the dispute settlement provisions of the PSI Agreement, and arguably the TBT and SPS Agreements, deserve mention. Pursuant to Article 4 of the PSI

---

[79] For the purpose of this section, the term "right holder" includes federations and associations having legal standing to assert such rights.
[80] Art. 11 of the Customs Valuation Agreement also provides for an individual right of appeal in favour of the importer against any determination by such national authority. Art. 11.2 adds: "An initial right of appeal without penalty may be to an authority within the customs administration or to an independent body, but the legislation of each Member shall provide for the right of appeal without penalty to a judicial authority." Art. 16 of the Customs Valuation Agreement has introduced new rights of information in favour of any importer affected by any such decision of the customs authority: "Upon written request, the importer shall have the right to an explanation in writing from the customs administration of the country of importation as to how the customs value of the importer's good was determined."

Agreement, an independent body exists to adjudicate on the dispute between exporters and preshipment inspection bodies that are used by Members for assessing the compatibility of imports and exports with national regulatory requirements. This Independent entity became operational on 1 May 1996. It is constituted of the WTO, the ICC and the International Federation of Inspection Agencies, and is administered by the WTO. The procedural functions of the independent entity resemble those of DSU panels, but the independent entity is inherently different, as it deals with disputes between private individuals. Notably, there are no explicit provisions for non-governmental bodies.

The TBT Agreement contains provisions explicitly addressing actions by non-governmental bodies and standards established by NGOs. It encourages NGOs to follow the provisions of a Code of Good Practice, containing obligations similar to those provided for technical regulations and standards when administered by governments. Thus, the TBT Agreement is a hybrid, providing for obligations on non-governmental bodies, but reserving rights to Members. The TBT Agreement imputes on Members the full liability for actions taken by such NGOs on their territory. Members are obligated to take reasonable measures to ensure NGO compliance with the provisions of Article 2 on non-discrimination and restrictiveness of technical regulations. The same is said of the assessment of conformity by non-governmental bodies and for the preparation, adoption and application of standards by non-governmental bodies which Members shall ensure that NGOs accept and comply with the Code of Good Practice. In addition, Members are prohibited from taking measures which have the effect of directly or indirectly requiring or encouraging such bodies to act in a manner inconsistent with the provisions of Articles 5 and 6.

Notably, Article 14.4 of the TBT Agreement provides that:

> "The dispute settlement provisions set out above can be invoked in cases where a Member considers that another Member has not achieved satisfactory results under Articles 3, 4, 7, 8 and 9 and its trade interests are significantly affected. In this respect, such results shall be equivalent to those as if the body in question were a Member. (Articles 3, 4 and 8 of the TBT Agreement are concerned with obligations imposed on non-governmental bodies.)"

The SPS Agreement also contains provisions dealing explicitly with non-governmental bodies, ascribing Members obligations *vis-à-vis* these NGOs and imputing full liability for their actions or absence thereof. Article 13 of the SPS Agreement provides that:

> "Members shall take such reasonable measures as may be available to them *to ensure that non-governmental entities within their territories ... comply with the relevant provisions of this Agreement.* In addition, Members shall not take measures which have the effect of, directly or indirectly, requiring or *encouraging such ... non-governmental entities to act in a manner inconsistent with the provisions of this Agreement.* Members shall ensure that they rely on the services of non-governmental entities for implementing sanitary or phytosanitary measures only if these entities comply with the provisions of this Agreement."

This type of provision may have a direct impact on the manner in which governments deal with the non-governmental bodies within their own territory. Traditionally, in public international law, countries are responsible for the actions of citizens in their territory. However, it is arguably unbalanced that some of the WTO agreements impose specific responsibilities and obligations on these NGOs generally (such as not to do anything that would contravene the agreement), and subject the activities of NGOs to scrutiny by other Members, without providing equivalent rights of defence or rights to complain against to the same entities.

V.   PARTICIPATION OF PRIVATE CITIZENS AND NON-GOVERNMENTAL ENTITIES IN POLICY-MAKING AND IN MEETINGS OF THE WTO

The WTO is a forum for governments. Thus, non-governmental interest groups do not participate directly in the negotiation process. However, non-governmental groups do exercise influence on WTO procedures and policies through their lobbying efforts and activities at the domestic level. Charnovitz[81] and Esty[82] have compiled a long list of international bodies that pursue consultations with non-governmental entities at the international level. As mentioned above, countries considered such a possibility in the context of the negotiations of the ITO. No such process exists at the moment in the WTO forum and under any of the WTO agreements. Therefore, in order to permit the formal participation of non-Members at the international level of the WTO, or permit them to attend any of its meetings, consensus on this matter would have to be reached.

In light of the Appellate Body report in the *Shrimp/Turtle* dispute, which could elicit a flow of NGO submissions on future disputes, governments may want to consider consulting with relevant NGOs prior to the adoption of any such treaty provisions and throughout their negotiations, because such provisions may eventually lead to a WTO dispute settlement. Yet, the obstacle of national sovereignty complicates consultations between governments and NGOs located within the borders of another Member. To circumvent this problem, negotiation procedures at the WTO may need to be reformulated to incorporate NGOs into the norm-establishment process.

Involving non-governmental bodies in the law-making process is addressed by the TBT Agreement. The TBT Code of Good Practice imposes on Members an obligation to include a representative of a non-governmental body on its delegation, whenever possible.

"G.   With a view to harmonising standards on as wide a basis as possible, the standardising body shall, in an appropriate way, play a full part, within the limits of its resources, in the preparation by relevant international standardising bodies of international standards regarding subject-matter for which it either has adopted, or expects to adopt, standards. For standardising bodies within the territory of a Member, participation in a particular international standardisation activity shall, whenever possible, take place through one delegation representing all standardising bodies in the territory that have adopted, or expect to adopt, standards for the subject-matter to which the international standardisation activity relates."

---

[81] Steve Charnovitz, *Two Centuries of Participation: NGOs and International Governance*, 18 Michigan Journal of International Law, p. 183.

[82] Daniel C. Esty, *Why The World Trade Organization needs NGOs*, 1 Public Participation in the International Trading, 1996, p. 11.

The Code also imposes on such non-governmental bodies the obligation to consult all interested parties before the establishment of any standard:

"H.   The standardising body within the territory of a Member ... shall also make every effort to achieve a national consensus on the standards they develop ... ."

"L.   Before adopting a standard, the standardising body shall allow a period of at least 60 days for the submission of comments on the draft standard by *interested parties* within the territory of a Member of the WTO. This period may, however, be shortened in cases where urgent problems of safety, health or environment arise or threaten to arise ... ."

"M.   On the request of any interested party within the territory of a Member of the WTO, the standardising body shall promptly provide, or arrange to provide, a copy of a draft standard which it has submitted for comments. Any fees charged for this service shall, apart from the real cost of delivery, be the same for foreign and domestic parties."

"N.   The standardising body shall take into account, in the further processing of the standard, the comments received during the period for commenting ... ."

"Q.   The standardising body shall afford sympathetic consideration to, and adequate opportunity for, consultation regarding representations with respect to the operation of this Code presented by standardising bodies that have accepted this Code of Good Practice. It shall make an objective effort to solve any complaints ... ."

Yet, formal participation of NGOs and other non-governmental interest groups in WTO negotiations is non-existent. Business interests and other interest groups, which arguably are well organised and powerful, may exercise influence on a Member's negotiating position. As was emphasised above, this process continues to be played out in the domestic arena of Member countries, and the formal participation of NGOs in the WTO cannot be changed without an amendment of the text of the WTO agreements and its practices.

VI.   Conclusion

The arguments for greater public participation in WTO processes have pointed to the specific expertise, resources and the analytical capacity of NGOs, their role as intellectual competitors to governments and their information activities on the domestic level. Arguably some of these claims are well founded, but resistance within the WTO to greater NGO involvement persists.

To the specific argument that participation of an increased number of NGOs in the WTO would reduce the risk of narrow special-interest driven policies, it remains unclear whether this would effectively deal with special interest problems at the national level. This argument would appear to promote the idea that developing domestic trade policy positions would have to wait for the international discussion to take place. At a time when an increasing number of people are concerned that they are losing control of domestic policies, it would seem highly controversial to shift the policy-making further away from national constituencies. Yet arguably some interests should be addressed at the international level, independently or parallel to any domestic consideration. However, some would argue that interest groups should not have "two bites at the same apple"—one domestically and one internationally.

Furthermore, NGOs argue that States and governments are imperfect representatives of public opinion[83] and that allowing NGO involvement in WTO discussions would permit the organisation to hear important voices on issues which are inherently international and can help to compensate for deficient representation at the national level. Although the concerns of NGOs may be authentic and genuine, their legitimacy and capacity to represent the public interest in this particular context is equally questionable. Questions remain about the actual constituencies, financial backing and transparency of some NGOs. This issue remains highly controversial and further thought should be given as to which NGOs are truly representative and legitimate.

At the same time, developing countries have argued that granting NGOs a more prominent role in the multilateral trading system would exacerbate the current imbalance against developing country interests as the large majority of the powerful NGOs represent Western constituencies. An increasing number of participants may slow down the traditional efficiency of the GATT/WTO and inevitably lead to more informal meetings.

As has been discussed in this article, the ongoing debate over the role of NGOs within the multilateral trading system is rather complex, but the mere fact that the issue is receiving so much attention is a positive sign. There is little doubt that the WTO as an institution has much to learn about and from NGOs, and in this context the experiences of other international IGOs in dealing with civil society are instructive. Expecting rapid changes in attitudes of WTO Members with very different cultural and sociological heritages is unrealistic, taking into account the need to find a common consensus-based approach to defining the appropriate relationship with NGOs.

Such differences among countries are found in numerous other international fora, however, there are three important differences between the WTO and other international organisations. First, the nature and objective of the GATT/WTO has traditionally been limited to trade issues, and the attempt to include wider policy issues in the WTO context is new and controversial. Second, contrary to most international organisations, the GATT/WTO has developed a practice for consensus which inherently complicates the decision-making process. This is both the strength and the weakness of the WTO. Third, the new binding and powerful dispute settlement mechanism further complicates the problem. A WTO Member can now be forced to change its domestic policies and become the object of economic sanctions, if the WTO adjudicating bodies uphold the request of another Member. For Members to allow NGOs direct access to this process can be viewed as providing an outsider with tools that some governments do not even give domestically.

Nevertheless, despite the considerable differences on the scope and modalities of NGO participation in the WTO, much has been achieved, both under the existing guidelines and in application of the provisions of the WTO and its instruments, including the Decision on Derestriction. The recent ruling of the Appellate Body in *Shrimp/Turtles* is another example of the evolutionary interpretation of existing provisions of the WTO agreements which have favoured further public participation in the work of the WTO, including

---

[83] As note 80, above, p. 131.

its dispute settlement mechanism. However, addressing the wide range of NGO demands implies amending "the rules of the game" by the consensus of Members.

The most important point at this juncture of the evolving relationship between the WTO and civil society is that the debate no longer seems to focus on *whether* NGOs should be involved, but on *how* they can be given an appropriate role within the WTO.

ANNEX A: GUIDELINES FOR ARRANGEMENTS ON RELATIONS WITH NGOS

Decision adopted by the General Council on 18 July 1996

1. Under Article V:2 of the Marrakesh Agreement establishing the WTO "the General Council may make appropriate arrangements for consultation and co-operation with non-governmental organisations concerned with matters related to those of the WTO".

2. In deciding on these guidelines for arrangements on relations with non-governmental organisations, Members recognise the rôle NGOs can play to increase the awareness of the public in respect of WTO activities and agree in this regard to improve transparency and develop communication with NGOs.

3. To contribute to achieve greater transparency Members will ensure more information about WTO activities in particular by making available documents which would be derestricted more promptly than in the past. To enhance this process the Secretariat will make available on on-line computer network the material which is accessible to the public, including derestricted documents.

4. The Secretariat should play a more active rôle in its direct contacts with NGOs who, as a valuable resource, can contribute to the accuracy and richness of the public debate. This interaction with NGOs should be developed through various means such as *inter alia* the organisation on an *ad hoc* basis of symposia on specific WTO-related issues, informal arrangements to receive the information NGOs may wish to make available for consultation by interested delegations and the continuation of past practice of responding to requests for general information and briefings about the WTO.

5. If chairpersons of WTO councils and committees participate in discussions or meetings with NGOs it shall be in their personal capacity unless that particular council or committee decides otherwise.

6. Members have pointed to the special character of the WTO, which is both a legally binding inter-governmental treaty of rights and obligations among its Members and a forum for negotiations. As a result of extensive discussions, there is currently a broadly held view that it would not be possible for NGOs to be directly involved in the work of the WTO or its meetings. Closer consultation and co-operation with NGOs can also be met constructively through appropriate processes at the national level where lies primary responsibility for taking into account the different elements of public interest which are brought to bear on trade policy-making.

ANNEX B: NGO PARTICIPATION AT WTO MINISTERIAL CONFERENCES

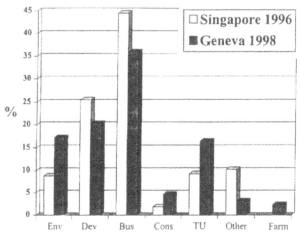

Type of Organisation

	Total No. Orgs	Environment	Development	Business	Consumers	Trade Unions	Other	Farm
Singapore	108	10	27	48	2	10	11	–
Geneva	128	22	26	46	6	21	4	3

ANNEX C: PROCEDURES FOR THE CIRCULATION AND DERESTRICTION OF WTO DOCUMENTS[1]

Decision adopted by the General Council on 18 July 1996[2]

Revision

The General Council *decides* to adopt the following procedures with respect to the circulation[3] and derestriction of documents:

---

[1] A copy of this decision shall be transmitted to the bodies established under the Plurilateral Trade Agreements for their consideration and appropriate action. Furthermore, the decision does not cover documents outside of a formal document series, such as a submission to a dispute settlement panel, or an interim report of a dispute settlement panel submitted to the parties thereto.

[2] In adopting these procedures, the General Council took note that Members attached particular importance to the restricted nature of documents so designated, and that individual governments should proceed accordingly in their handling of such documents.

[3] The words "circulation" and "circulated" when used in this decision shall be understood to refer to the distribution by the Secretariat of documents to all WTO Members.

1.   Documents circulated after the date of entry into force of the Marrakesh Agreement Establishing the World Trade Organization (hereinafter referred to as "WTO Agreement") in any WTO document series shall be circulated as unrestricted with the exception of documents specified in the attached Appendix, which shall be circulated as restricted and subject to derestriction, or consideration thereof, as provided. Notwithstanding the exceptions specified in the Appendix, any document that contains only information that is publicly available or information that is required to be published under any agreement in Annex 1, 2 or 3 of the WTO Agreement shall be circulated on an unrestricted basis.

2.   Notwithstanding the exceptions to paragraph 1 set forth in the Appendix,
   (a)   any Member may, at the time it submits any document for circulation, indicate to the Secretariat that the document be issued as unrestricted; and
   (b)   any restricted document circulated after the date of entry into force of the WTO Agreement may be considered for derestriction at any time by the Ministerial Conference, the General Council, or the body under the auspices of which the document was circulated, or may be considered for derestriction at the request of any Member.

3.   Requests for consideration for derestriction shall be made in writing and shall be directed to the Chairman of the Ministerial Conference, the General Council or the relevant WTO body. Such requests shall be circulated to all Members and placed on the agenda of a forthcoming meeting of the body concerned for consideration. However, in order to preserve the efficiency of work of the body concerned, the Member concerned may indicate to the Secretariat that it circulate to Members a notice advising them of the documents proposed for derestriction and the date proposed for derestriction, which shall normally be sixty days after the date the notice is circulated. These documents shall be derestricted on the date set forth in the notice unless, prior to that date, a Member notifies the Secretariat in writing of its objection to the derestriction of a document, or any portion of a document.

4.   The Secretariat shall prepare and circulate a list of all documents eligible for consideration for derestriction, indicating the proposed date of derestriction, which shall normally be sixty days after the circulation of the list. These documents shall be derestricted on the date set forth in the notice unless, prior to that date, a Member notifies the Secretariat in writing of its objection to the derestriction of a document, or any portion of a document.

5.   If a document[4] considered for derestriction is not derestricted because of an objection by any Member, and remains restricted at the end of the first year following the year in which an objection was raised, the document shall be considered for derestriction at that time.

---

[4] These procedures shall apply *mutatis mutandis* to the consideration for derestriction of a portion of a document that remains restricted as a result of an objection made pursuant to para. 4.

6.   The Secretariat will circulate periodically (e.g. every six months) a list of newly derestricted documents, as well as a list of all documents remaining restricted.

7.   In the light of the experience gained from the operation of these procedures and changes in any other relevant procedures under the WTO, the General Council will review, and if necessary modify, the procedures two years after their adoption.

APPENDIX

(a) Working documents in all series (i.e. draft documents such as agendas, decisions and proposals, as well as other working papers, issued as "-/W/-" documents in a particular series), including documents in the Spec/- series.
Such documents shall be derestricted upon the adoption of the report[5] or of the decision pertaining to their subject-matter, or considered for derestriction six months after the date of their circulation,[6] whichever is earlier. However, working documents relating to balance-of-payments consultations, the Committee on Market Access, the Committee on Trade and Development and the Trade Policy Review Mechanism, shall be considered for derestriction at the end of each six-month period.[7,8] All background notes by the Secretariat, however, shall be considered for derestriction six months after the date of their circulation.

(b) Documents in the SECRET/- series (i.e. those documents relating to modification or withdrawal of concessions pursuant to Article XXVII of the GATT 1994).
Such documents shall be derestricted upon completion of the Article XXVIII process (including such process initiated pursuant to Article XXIV:6) through certification of the changes in the schedule in accordance with the Decision by the CONTRACTING PARTIES to GATT 1947 of 26 March 1980 (BISD 27S/25).

(c) Minutes of meetings of all WTO bodies (other than minutes of the Trade Policy Review Body, which shall be circulated as unrestricted), including Summary Records of Sessions of the Ministerial Conference.
Such documents shall be considered for derestriction six months after the date of their circulation.

(d) Reports by the Secretariat and by the government concerned, relating to the

---

[5] Reference to "adoption" of a report in this decision is intended to mean its adoption by the Ministerial Conference, General Council or other relevant WTO body.

[6] The "date of circulation" means the date printed on the front page of a document, indicating when it has been made available to Members' delegations.

[7] Documents circulated during the period January–June would be considered for derestriction directly after the end of that period. Documents circulated during the period July–December would be considered for derestriction directly after the end of that period.

[8] Notwithstanding these provisions, budget working documents in the Spec/- series shall not be derestricted.

Trade Policy Review Mechanism, including the annual report by the Director-General on the overview of developments in the international trading environment.

Such documents shall be derestricted upon the expiry of the press embargo thereon.

(e) Documents relating to working parties on accession.

Such documents shall be derestricted upon the adoption of the report of the working party. Prior to the adoption of the report, any such documents shall be considered for derestriction at the end of the first year following the year in which they were circulated.

(f) Documents (other than working documents covered by (a) above) relating to balance-of-payments consultations, including the reports thereon.

Such documents shall be considered for derestriction at the end of each six-month period.[9]

(g) Documents submitted to the Secretariat by a Member for circulation if, at the time the Member submits the document, the Member indicates to the Secretariat that the document should be issued as restricted.

Such documents shall be considered for derestriction at the end of each six-month period.

(h) Reports of panels which are circulated in accordance with the provisions of the Understanding on Rules and Procedures Governing the Settlement of Disputes.[10] Such reports shall be circulated to all Members as restricted documents and derestricted no later than the tenth day thereafter if, prior to the date of circulation a party to the dispute that forms the basis of a report submits to the Chairman of the Dispute Settlement Body a written request for delayed derestriction. A report circulated as a restricted document shall indicate the date upon which it will be derestricted.[11]

---

[9] Documents circulated during the period January–June would be considered for derestriction directly after the end of that period. Documents circulated during the period July–December would be considered for derestriction directly after the end of that period.

[10] This provision will be subject to review at the time of review of the DSU, and will be discontinued if there is no consensus on the matter.

[11] The following standard cover note will be placed on panel reports:

"The report of the Panel on [name of dispute] is being circulated to all Members, pursuant to the DSU. The report is being circulated as an unrestricted document from [date] pursuant to the procedures for the Circulation and Derestriction of WTO Documents [document number]. Members are reminded that in accordance with the DSU only parties to the dispute may appeal a panel report, an appeal shall be limited to issues of law covered in the panel report and legal interpretations developed by the panel, and that there shall be no *ex parte* communications with the panel or Appellate Body concerning matters under consideration by the panel or Appellate Body."

[25]

Global Civil Society: Perspectives, Initiatives, Movements

RICHARD FALK

ABSTRACT This article focuses on the efforts of voluntary associations, rooted in a global consciousness, to address the negative impacts of globalization. In part, this encounter reflects the extent to which globalization has been unfolding in recent years in an ideological climate of neo-liberalism. As a result, there has been steady downward pressure on the social agenda of governments and international institutions. Globalization-from-below represents an overall effort to moderate market logic by reference to the following values embodied in "normative democracy", a view of democracy that takes account of the emergence of global village realities: consent of affected peoples; rule of law in all arenas of decision; human rights; effective modes of participation; accountability; support for public goods to address basic needs; transparency; and non-violence as a principle of public order.

1. Note on Terminology

The emphasis of this article is upon social forces that respond to the patterns of behavior associated with the phenomena of economic globalization. As a consequence, it seems preferable on balance to frame such activity by reference to "global civil society" rather than to "transnational civil society". Even so the word "society" is definitely problematic at this stage of global social and political evolution, due to absence of boundaries and weakness of social bonds transcending nation, race and gender. Such a difficulty exists whether the reference is to "transnational civil society" or to "global civil society". But the transnational referent tends to root the identity of the actors in the subsoil of national consciousness to an extent that neglects the degree to which the orientation is not one of crossing borders, but of inhabiting and constructing a polity appropriate for the global village. Such a nascent global polity is already partly extant, yet remains mostly emergent. (For helpful conceptual discussion of these issues of conceptual framing, see Wapner, 1996.)

A similar issue arises with respect to the terminology useful in aggregating the actors. It seems convenient to retain the term non-governmental organizations (NGOs) to designate those actors associated with global civil society because it is accurate and convenient, being so widely used and thus easily recognizable. But it is also somewhat misleading in relation to the fundamental hypothesis of a diminishing ordering capability by the sovereign state and states system. To contrast the actors and action of global civil society with the governments of states, as is done by calling them NGOs, is

Richard Falk, Centre for International Studies, Bendheim Hall, Princeton University, Princeton, NJ 08544, USA.

100   *R. Falk*

to confer a derivative status and to imply the persistence of a superordinate Westphalian world of sovereign states as the only effective constituents of contemporary world order. Until recently this hierarchical dualism was justifiable because the preeminence of the state was an empirical reality, reinforced by the absence of any other significant international actors capable of autonomous action.

To overcome this difficulty of relying upon this somewhat anachronistic statist rhetoric, James Rosenau has proposed an alternative terminology to that of NGOs by calling such entities "sovereignty free actors" (Rosenau, 1990). Besides being obscure, such a substitute terminology is still operating in a Westphalian shadowland in which actor identities are exclusively derived from sovereign actors, namely, states. A comparable problem exists if the reference is to "transnational social forces", although the sense of "transnational" is more flexible and autonomous than "sovereignty free". Another possibility was proposed some years ago by Marc Nerfin (1986), in the form of a framework that recognized the social reality of "the third system" (the first sector being that of states, the second of market forces), from which issued forth civil initiatives of motivated citizens supportive of the global public good.

There is by now a wide and growing literature on "global civil society", especially as related to environmental politics on a global level. (For concise overview see Wapner, 1996; Lipschutz, 1996). For the purposes of this article global civil society refers to the field of action and thought occupied by individual and collective citizen initiatives of a voluntary, non-profit character both within states and transnationally. These initiatives proceed from a global orientation and are responses, in part at least, to certain globalizing tendencies that are perceived to be partially or totally adverse. At present, most of the global provocation is associated directly or indirectly with market forces and the discipline of regional and global capital. As will be made clear, such a critical stance toward economic globalization does not entail an overall repudiation of these developments, but it does seek to regulate adverse effects and correct social injustices.

To focus inquiry further, I also propose to rely upon a distinction that I have used previously: drawing a basic dividing-line between global market forces identified as "globalization-from-above" and a set of oppositional responses in the third system of social activism that is identified as "globalization-from-below" (Falk, 1993, 1995). This distinction may seem unduly polarizing and hierarchical, apparently constructing a dualistic world of good and evil. My intention is neither hierarchical nor moralistic, and there is no illusion that the social forces emanating from the third system are inherently benevolent, while those from the first and second systems are necessarily malevolent. Far from it. One of the arguments of the article is that there are dangerous chauvinistic and extremist societal energies being released by one series of responses to globalization-from-above that are threatening the achievements of the modern secular world that had been based on the normative side of the evolution of an anarchic society of states in the cumulative direction of humane governance. (This normative potential of statism has been most influentially articulated by Hedley Bull, 1977.) To situate the argument, it is important to acknowledge that there are strong positive effects and potentialities arising from the various aspects of globalization-from-above. At the same time, the historic role of globalization-from-below is to challenge and transform the negative features of globalization-from-above, both by providing alternative ideological and political space to that currently occupied by market-oriented and statist outlooks and by offering resistances to the excesses and distortions that can be properly attributed to globalization in its current phase. That is, globalization-from-below is not dogmatically opposed to globalization-from-above, but addresses itself to the avoidance of adverse effects and to providing an overall counterweight to the essentially unchecked influence currently exerted by business and finance on the process of decision at the level of the state and beyond.

2. Deforming Historical Circumstances

The distinctive challenges posed by globalization-from-above have been accentuated by certain defining historical circumstances. Above all, the ending of the Cold War generated an ideological atmosphere in the North supportive of an abandonment of Keynesian approaches to economic policy, and its replacement by a strong version of neo-liberal reliance on private sector autonomy and an economistic approach to social policy, that is, eroding the social compromises between labor and business by way of achieving fiscal austerity, efficient allocation of resources, privatization and international competitiveness. There were other pressures to move in these directions, including a pendulum swing in societal attitudes against "the welfare state" in many states, a generalized distrust of government and public sector approaches to problem-solving, the steadily declining political leverage of organized labor, the waning of industrialism and the waxing of electronics and informatics, an overall disenchantment with ameliorative rhetoric and proposals, and, above all, pressures to neutralize the alleged competitive advantages of countries in the South, especially those in the Asia/Pacific region.

These alleged competitive advantages are associated with the political and economic unevenness of states, and refer especially to cheap skilled labor, minimal regulation and high profit margins that have been supposedly draining jobs and capital away from the North. These differentials have ethically ambiguous consequences, reinforcing neo-liberal rationalizations for harsher economic policy and contributing to chauvinistic backlash politics in the North, while liberating many of the most populous countries in the South from centuries of acute poverty and massive human suffering.

In effect, the material and technological foundation of globalization, based on the possibilities for profitable expansion of business operations without regard to state boundaries, did not necessarily have to be linked to an ideological abandonment of the social agenda and downsizing pressures on public goods, including a disturbing decline in support for mechanisms to protect the global commons and the global public good. Neo-liberal approaches and ideological justifications have been latent in market economies ever since the birth of capitalism during the industrial revolution, but somewhat surprisingly the nastiest features of early capitalism were moderated to varying degrees in the 19th and 20th Centuries in response to the rise of "the dangerous classes", the labor movement, the ordeal of business cycles culminating in The Great Depression, and the adjustments promoted by different versions of "social democracy", and what came to be known in the USA as "liberalism".

Indeed, the recent change in ideological atmosphere can be rapidly understood by the delegitimation of liberalism in the USA since the 1980s, making even those political perspectives of the most socially sensitive leaders in the Democratic Party unwilling any longer to use or accept the liberalism as a label of what came to be derisively called "the L word". What has emerged in this first stage of globalization after the end of the Cold War is a neo-liberal consensus among political élites in the world, powerfully disseminated by a business-oriented and consumerist global media, a power shift that helps explain the economistic orientation of most governments. (For a more historically grounded view of globalization, see Clark, 1997.) In the North, this consensus tends to be justified by reference to the discipline of global capital, or simply by reference to "competitiveness", the struggle for market shares and the virtues of free trade. Such an

102   *R. Falk*

ideological setting is often merged with globalization to make the one indistinguishable from the other.

The evolving perspective of those social forces associated with globalization-from-below is that it remains possible and essential to promote the social agenda while retaining most of the benefits of globalization-from-above (Hirst & Thompson, 1996, 1–17, 170–194). In effect, globalization can be enacted in a variety of governance and fiscal scenarios, including some that are more people-oriented and supportive of global public goods and the goals of the social agenda. The ideological infrastructure of globalization is rather structural, and its reformulation is at the core of the convergent perspectives implied by the emergence of global civil society as the bearer of alternative visions of a more sustainable and compassionate future world order (Falk, 1995). Often this normative convergence is concealed beneath the more particularized banners of human rights, environmental protection, feminism and social justice that have been unfurled within global civil society by issue-oriented social movements that have been transnationally active during the last several decades.

It is also important to acknowledge the limited undertaking of globalization-from-below. It is not able to challenge globalization as such, only to alter the guiding ideas that are shaping enactment. Globalization is too widely accepted and embedded to be reversible in its essential integrative impact. Recent global trends establish the unchallengeable dominance of markets and their integration. In Jeffrey Sachs' words, "...capitalism has now spread to nearly 90% of the world's population, since nearly all parts of the world are now linked through open trade, convertible currencies, flows of foreign investment, and political commitments to private ownership as the engine of economic growth" (Sachs, 1997, p. 11). Sachs points out that only 20 years earlier such conditions pertained to only 20% of the world's population, the rest of humanity being subjected either to command socialist economies or to clumsy Third World efforts to combine capitalism and socialism. Such a shift in so short a time, of course, inevitably produces a fundamental reshaping of the ideas and practices constitutive of world order.

It is this process of economic restructuring according to the logic of markets that establishes the context for globalization-from-below. The strategic question is how can these forces effectively challenge the uneven adverse effects of globalization-from-above as it is currently evolving. These adverse consequences include insufficient attention to environmental protection and resource conservation, failures to offset severe vulnerabilities of social segments, countries and regions that are not currently able to gain sufficient access to the market, and a generalized lack of support for the social agenda and global public goods, including the United Nations (UN), especially in its efforts to coordinate and promote moves to overcome world poverty and to close the gaps that separate rich from poor.

3. Responding to Economic Globalization

There have been varied failed responses to economic globalization, conceived of as the capitalist portion of the world economy. Without entering into an assessment of these failures, it is worth noticing that both Soviet-style socialism and Maoism, especially during the period of the Cultural Revolution, were dramatic efforts to oppose economic globalization that ended in disaster. By contrast, despite the difficulties, the subsequent embrace of the market by China under the rubric of "modernization" and even by Russia (and the former members of the Soviet empire) in the form of the capitalist path have been spectacularly successful. The same is true for many Third World countries that had forged a middle path between socialism and capitalism that made the state a major player in the economy, particularly with respect to public utilities and energy; for most of these countries, as well, the change from a defensive hostility toward the world market to a position of unconditional receptivity has been generally treated as a blessing.

The learning experience at the level of the state has been one of submission to the discipline of global capital as it pertains to the specific conditions of each country. Fashionable ideas of "delinking" and "self-reliance" are in a shambles, perhaps most easily appreciated by the inability of North Korea to feed its population, while its capitalist sibling in South Korea is scaling the peaks of affluence. In effect, the geopolitical managers of the world economy use such policies as a punishment for supposedly deviant states, seeking to legitimize the exclusion under the rubric of "sanctions", a policy often widely criticized in this period because of its cruel effects on the civilian population of the target society. Even Castro's Cuba, for so long an impressive holdout, is relying on standard capitalist approaches to attract foreign investment and open its economy to market forces. Fukuyama's notorious theme about the end of history is partially correct, at least for now, if understood as limited in its application to economic aspects of policy, and not extended to political life (Fukuyama, 1992).

Another direction of response to economic globalization has been negative in the form of backlash politics that looks either at some pre-modern traditional framework as viable and virtuous (as with religious extremists of varying identity, or of indigenous peoples) or ultra-territorialists that seek to keep capital at home and exclude foreigners to the extent possible. These responses, aside from those of indigenous peoples, have a rightist flavor because of their emphasis on the sacred religious or nationalist community of the saved that is at war with an evil "other", being either secularist or outsider. To the extent that such movements have gained control of the state, as in Iran since the Islamic Revolution, or even threatened to do so, as in Algeria since 1992, the results have been dismal: economic deterioration, political repression, and widespread civil strife. Specific causes of these backlash phenomena are related to the failures of globalization and its related secularist outlook, but the correctives proposed have yet to exhibit a capacity to generate an alternative that is capable of either successful economic performance or able to win genuine democratic consent from relevant political communities.

Related to this predominance of market forces is a series of attempts by civil society to avoid the adverse effects of economic globalization. The most effective of these responses have been issue-oriented, often involving local campaigns against a specific project. One notable attempt to enter the domain of transformative politics more generally was made by the green parties in Europe during the 1980s. This green movement often exhibited tactical brilliance in its moves to expose the deficiencies of globalizing trends, especially their dangers to the environment. Its political success was less its ability to mobilize large numbers in support of its causes and programmes, but the extent to which its challenge influenced the whole center of the political spectrum to put the environmental challenge high on its policy agenda. But the green movement's attempt to generalize its identity to provide an alternative leadership for the entire society across the full range of governance or to transnationalize its activities to promote global reform met with frustration and internal controversy that fractured green unity, most vividly in Germany, but elsewhere as well. Those who argued for a new radicalism beyond established political parties within a green framework were dismissed as Utopian dreamers while those who opted for influence within the existing

104   *R. Falk*

framework were often scorned as victims of co-optation or derided as opportunists. The green movement and its political parties have persisted in the 1990s, but as a voice on the margins with neither a credible alternative world view to that provided by globalization nor a sufficiently loyal constituency to pose a threat to the mainstream.

Localism has been another type of response directed at the siting of a nuclear power reactor or dam, mobilizing residents of the area facing displacement and loss of traditional livelihood, and sometimes involving others from the society and beyond, who identify with the poor or nature. These struggles have had some notable successes (Shiva, 1987; Rich, 1994). But these are reactions to symptomatic disorders associated with globalization, and do little more than influence entrepreneurial forces to be more prudent or to make more public relations efforts.

More relevant have been attempts by elements of global civil society to protect the global commons against the more predatory dimensions of globalization. Here Greenpeace has a distinguished record of activist successes, exhibiting an imaginative and courageous willingness to challenge entrenched military and commercial forces by direct action that has had an impact: helping to discourage whaling, protesting against the effort of Shell Oil to dispose of the oil rig Brent Spar in the North Sea, supporting a 50 year moratorium on mineral development in Antarctica and, most memorably, resisting for many years nuclear testing in the Pacific. Rachel Carson's lyrical environmentalism and Jacques Cousteau's extraordinarily intense dedication to saving the oceans suggest the extent to which even single, gifted individuals can exert powerful counter-tendencies to the most destructive sides of an insufficiently regulated market. But these efforts, although plugging some of the holes in the dikes, are not based on either a coherent critique or alternative ideology, and thus operate only at the level of the symptom, while neglecting the disorders embedded in the dynamics of globalization.

Some other efforts to awaken responses have arisen from global civil society on the basis of a more generalized assessment. One of the earliest such initiatives was that promoted by the Club of Rome, a transnational association of individuals prominent in business, science and society that led to the famous study *The Limits to Growth* (Meadows *et al.*, 1972). The argument, tied closely to a sophisticated computer program that was measuring trends in population growth, pollution, resource scarcity and food supply concluded that industrialism as being practised was not sustainable, but was tending toward imminent catastrophe. Around the same time a group of distinguished scientists from various countries working with the British journal, *The Ecologist,* issued their own warning call under the title *Blueprint for Survival* (Goldsmith, 1972). These alarms provoked a debate and led to some adjustments, but the resilience of the world capitalist system was such that no fundamental changes occurred, and the warnings issued as signals soon faded into the cultural noise. Neither a sense of alternative nor a movement of protest and opposition took hold.

The World Order Models Project (WOMP) is illustrative of a somewhat more remote effort to challenge the existing order and find alternatives, through the medium of diagnosis and prescription by a transnational group of independent academicians. The efforts of this group have been confined to the margins of academic reflection on world conditions. Also, until recently, the policy focus and animating preoccupation was centered on war, and then broadened somewhat later to include environmental danger. Although WOMP did produce overall assessments, its background and participants made it less sensitive to the distinctive challenges and contributions of economic globalization (Falk, 1995, 1996, 1997a). As such, its emphasis on war and the war-making sovereign state did not come to terms with either the durability of the state or the need to avoid its *instrumentalization* by global market forces. That is, the principal world order danger is no longer the absolute security claims of the sovereign state, but rather the inability of the state to protect its own citizenry, especially those who are most vulnerable, in relation to the workings of the world economy.

A better connected effort to address overall global issues was attempted by the Commission on Global Governance, as expressed in its main report, *Our Global Neighborhood* (Commission, 1995). This initiative, claiming authority and credibility on the basis of the eminence of its membership drawn from the leading ranks of society, and stressing past or present government service at leadership or ministerial levels, seemed too farsighted for existing power structures and too timid to engage the imagination of the more activist and militant actors in civil society. The Commission report failed to arouse any widespread or sustained interest despite the comprehensiveness and thoughtfulness of its proposals. As an intellectual tool it is also disappointing, failing to clarify the challenge of globalization and the troublesome character of Bretton Woods approaches to world economic policy. As a result, its efforts to anchor an argument for global reform around an argument for "global governance" seemed more likely to consolidate globalization-from-above than to promote a creative equilibrium relying on the balancing contribution of globalization-from-below. In part, this Commission report was unlucky, beginning its efforts in the aftermath of the Gulf War when attention and hopes were centered on the future of the UN and finishing its work at a time when the world organization was widely, if somewhat unfairly, discredited as a result of the outcomes in Somalia, Bosnia and Rwanda. But this was not the fundamental problem, which was more a failure of nerve to address the adverse consequence of globalization, a focus that would have put such a commission on a collision course with adherents of the neo-liberal economistic world picture. Given the claims of "eminence" and "independent funding" that characterize such a commission, it is not to be expected that it would be willing or able to address the structural and ideological deficiencies attributable to the prevailing world order framework. This means that its best efforts confirm pessimism about finding an alternative world picture to that provided by the neo-liberal prism on globalization.

What is being argued, then, is that the challenges posed by economic globalization have not as yet engendered a sufficient response in two connected respects: first, the absence of an ideological posture that is comparably coherent to that being provided by various renditions of neo-liberalism, and that could provide the social forces associated with globalization-from-below with a common theoretical framework, political language and programme; secondly, a clear expression of a critique of globalization-from-above that cuts deeply enough to address the most basic normative challenges associated with poverty, social marginalization and environmental decay, while accepting the emancipatory contributions being made, as well as the unchallengeable persistence of state and market; the political goals of globalization-from-below are thus at once both drastic and reformist.

It is central to realize that the world order outcomes arising from the impact of economic globalization are far from settled, and in no sense pre-determined. The forces of globalization-from-above have taken control of globalization and are pushing it in an economistic direction that considerably instrumentalizes the state on behalf of a set of attitudes and policies: privatization, free trade, fiscal austerity and competitiveness. But there are other options: "sustainable development", "global welfare", "cybernetic libertarianism". The eventual shape of globalization will reflect the play of these diverse perspectives and priorities. The perspectives and priorities of globalization-from-above are being challenged in various ways, but mainly piecemeal. The effort of the final

106   R. Falk

section is to encourage a mobilization of the now disparate forces of globalization-from-below in the direction of greater solidity and political weight. It is my conviction that such mobilization is most likely to occur beneath the banner of democracy, but democracy reformulated in relation to the basic aspirations of peoples everywhere to participate in the processes that are shaping their lives.

The purpose of the next section is mainly to clarify what is meant by "democracy" in relation to the analysis of globalization.

4. Toward Coherence: The Theory and Practice of Normative Democracy

To introduce the idea of "normative democracy" is to offer a proposal for a unifying ideology capable of mobilizing and unifying the disparate social forces that constitute global civil society, and provide the political energy that is associated with globalization-from-below. The specification of normative democracy is influenced strongly by David Held's work on democratic theory and practice, particularly his formulations of "cosmopolitan democracy", but it offers a slightly different terminology so as to emphasize the agency role of global civil society with its range of engagements that go from the local and grassroots to the most encompassing arenas of decision (Archibugi *et al.*, 1995; Held, 1995). Normative democracy also draws upon Walden Bello's call for "substantive democracy", set forth as a more progressive movement alternative to the more limited embrace of constitutional democracy (Bello, 1997). I prefer normative to substantive democracy because of its highlighting of ethical and legal norms, thereby reconnecting politics with moral purpose and values, which calls attention to the moral emptiness of neo-liberalism, consumerism and most forms of secularism. There is also a practical reason: to weaken the political appeal of resurgent organized religion while at the same time acknowledging the relevance of moral purpose and spiritual concerns to the renewal of progressive politics.

Contrary to widespread claims in the West, there is no empirical basis for the argument that economic performance is necessarily tied to constitutional democracy and human rights. Several countries in the Asia/Pacific region, most significantly China, have combined an outstanding macroeconomic record with harsh authoritarian rule. Globalization-from-above is not an assured vehicle for the achievement of Western style constitutional democracy, including the protection of individual and group rights. But democracy, as such, is of the essence of a meaningful form of political action on the part of global civil society, especially to the extent that such action even when revolutionary refrains from and repudiates violent means. In this regard, there is an emergent, as yet implicit, convergence of ends and means on the part of several distinct tendencies in civil society issue-oriented movements; non-violent democracy movements; governments that minimize their links to geopolitical structures. This convergence presents several intriguing opportunities for coalition-building, and greater ideological coherence in the outlook associated with globalization-from-below. Against this background, normative democracy seems like an attractive umbrella for theorizing, not dogmatically, but to exhibit affinities.

Normative democracy adopts comprehensive views of fundamental ideas associated with the secular modern state: security is conceived as extending to environmental protection and to the defense of economic viability (e.g. Mahathir complains about George Soros' financial speculations as jeopardizing Malaysian development successes; *Turkish Daily News*, 1997); human rights are conceived as extending to social and economic rights, as well as to such collective rights as the right to development, the right to peace, the right of self-determination; democracy is conceived as extending beyond constitutional and free, periodic elections to include an array of other assurances that governance is oriented toward human wellbeing and ecological sustainability, and that citizens have access to arenas of decision.

The elements of normative democracy can be enumerated, but their content and behavioral applications will require much amplification in varied specific settings. This enumeration reflects the dominant orientations and outlook of the political actors that make up the constructivist category of "globalization-from-below". It is thus not an enumeration that is a wishlist, but intends to be descriptive and explanatory of an embedded consensus. The elements of this consensus are as follows:

(1) Consent of citizenry: some periodic indication that the permanent population of the relevant community is represented by the institutions of governance, and confers legitimacy through the expression of consent. Elections are the established modalities for territorial communities to confer legitimacy on government, but referenda and rights of petition and recall may be more appropriate for other types of political community, especially those of regional or global scope, while direct democracy may be most meaningful for local political activity; the idea is to be flexible and adaptive.

(2) Rule of law: all modes of governance subject to the discipline of law as a way of imposing effective limits on authority and of assuring some form of checks and balances as between legislative, executive, judicial and administrative processes; also, sensitivity to the normative claims of civil initiatives associated with codes of conduct, conference declarations, societal institutions (for instance, Permanent Peoples Tribunal in Rome).

(3) Human rights: taking account of differing cultural, economic and political settings and priorities, the establishment of mechanisms for the impartial and effective implementation of human rights deriving from global, regional, state and transnational civil sources of authority; human rights are comprehensively conceived as encompassing economic, social and cultural rights, as well as civil and political rights, with a concern for both individual and collective conceptions of rights, emphasizing tolerance toward difference and fundamental community sentiments.

(4) Participation: effective and meaningful modes of participation in the political life of the society, centered upon the processes of government, but extending to all forms of social governance, including workplace and home; participation may be direct or indirect, that is, representational, but it enables the expression of views and influence upon the processes of decision on the basis of an ideal of equality of access; creativity is needed to find methods other than elections by which to ensure progress toward full participation.

(5) Accountability: suitable mechanisms for challenging the exercise of authority by those occupying official positions at the level of the state, but also with respect to the functioning of the market and of international institutions; the ideal of an international criminal court is one mechanism for assuring accountability by those in powerful positions that have been traditionally treated as exempt from the Rule of Law.

(6) Public goods: a restored social agenda that corrects the growing imbalance, varying in seriousness from country to country, between private and public goods in relation to the persistence of poverty amid affluence, pertaining to health, education, housing and basic human needs, but also in relation to support for environmental protection, regulation of economic globalization, innovative cultural activity, infrastructural development for governance at the regional and global

108   *R. Falk*

levels. In these regards, a gradual depoliticalization of funding either by reliance on a use or transaction tax imposed on financial flows, global air travel, or some form of reliable and equitable means to fund public goods of local, national, regional, and global scope.

(7) Transparency: an openness with respect to knowledge and information that builds trust between institutions of governance and the citizenry at various levels of social interaction. in effect, establishing the right to know as an aspect of constitutionalism, including a strong bias against public sector secrecy and covert operations, and criminalizes government lies of the sort recently revealed where for years to protect air force spy missions the CIA lied about alleged "UFO sightings"; internationally, transparency is particularly important in relation to military expenditures and arms transfers.

(8) Non-violence: underpinning globalization-from-below and the promotion of substantive democracy is a conditional commitment to non-violent politics and conflict resolution. Such a commitment does not nullify rights of self-defense as protected in international law, strictly and narrowly construed, nor does it necessarily invalidate limited recourse to violence by oppressed peoples; such an ethos of non-violence clearly imposes on governments an obligation to renounce weaponry of mass destruction and the negotiation of phased disarmament arrangements, but also maximum commitments to demilitarizing approaches to peace and security at all levels of social interaction, including peace and security at the level of city and neighborhood; such commitments suggest the rejection of capital punishment as an option of government.

5. Globalization-from-below and the State: A Decisive Battle

Without entering into detailed discussion, it seems that different versions of neo-liberal ideology have exerted a defining influence upon the orientation of political élites governing sovereign states. Of course, there are many variations reflecting conditions and personalities in each particular state and region, but the generalization holds without important exception (Sakamoto, 1994; Falk, 1997b). Even China, despite adherence to the ideology of state socialism, has implemented by state decree, with impressive results, a market-oriented approach to economic policy. The state can remain authoritarian in relation to its citizenry without necessarily jeopardizing its economic performance so long as it adheres, more or less, to the discipline of global capital, thereby achieving competitiveness by reference to costs of production, savings and attraction of capital. In these respects, neo-liberalism as a *global* ideology is purely economistic in character, and does not imply a commitment to democratic governance in even the minimal sense of periodic fair elections.

Globalization-from-below, in addition to a multitude of local struggles, is also a vehicle for the transnational promotion of substantive democracy as a counterweight to neo-liberalism. It provides an alternative, or series of convergent alternatives, that has not yet been posited as a coherent body of theory and practice, but remains the inarticulate common ground of emergent global civil society. Substantive democracy, unlike backlash politics that closes off borders and identities, seeks a politics of reconciliation that maintains much of the openness and dynamism associated with globalization-from-above, while countering its pressures to privatize and marketize the production of public goods. In effect, the quest of substantive democracy is to establish a social equilibrium that takes full account of the realities of globalization in its various aspects. Such a process cannot succeed on a country-by-country basis as the rollback of welfare in Scandinavia suggests, but must proceed within regional and global settings. The state remains the instrument of policy and decision most affecting the lives of peoples, and the primary link to regional and global institutions. The state has been instrumentalized to a considerable degree by the ideology and influences associated with globalization-from-above, resulting in declining support for public goods in an atmosphere of strong sustained economic growth and in polarization of results with incredible wealth for the winners and acute suffering for the losers. An immediate goal of those disparate social forces that constitute globalization-from-below is to reinstrumentalize the state to the extent that it redefines its role as mediating between the logic of capital and the priorities of its peoples, including their short-term and longer term goals.

Evidence of this instrumentalization of the state is present in relation to global conferences on broad policy issues that had been organized under UN auspices, and were making an impact on public consciousness and behavioral standards in the 1990s. These UN conferences increasingly attracted an array of social forces associated with global civil society, and gave rise to a variety of coalitions and oppositions between state, market and militant citizens organized to promote substantive goals (e.g. human rights, environmental protection, economic equity and development). These UN conferences became arenas of political participation that were operating outside the confines of state control, and were regarded as threatening by the established order based on a core coalition between market forces and geopolitical leaders. One effect is to withdraw support for such UN activities, pushing the organization to the sidelines on global policy issues as part of a process of recovering control over its agenda and orientation. Such a reaction represents a setback for globalization-from-below, but it also shows that the social forces that are associated with the promotion of normative democracy can be formidable adversaries.

Such a process of reinstrumentalization could also influence the future role and identity of regional and global mechanisms of governance, especially to the extent of increasing the regulatory mandate directed toward market forces and the normative mandate with respect to the protection of the global commons, the promotion of demilitarization and the overall support for public good.

6. Conclusion

In this paper it is argued that the positive prospects for global civil society depend very much on two interrelated developments: achieving consensus on "normative democracy" as the foundation of coherent theory and practice, and waging a struggle for the outlook and orientation of institutions of governance with respect to the framing of globalization. The state remains the critical focus of this latter struggle, although it is not, even now, a matter of intrinsic opposition between the state as instrument of globalization-from-above and social movements as instrument of globalization-from-below. In many specific settings, coalitions between states and social movements are emergent, as is evident in relation to many questions of environment, development and human rights. It may even come to pass that transnational corporations and banks adopt a longer term view of their own interests, and move to alter the policy content of globalization-from-above to soften the contrast with the preferences of globalization-from-below. It is helpful to remember that such an unanticipated convergence of previously opposed social forces led to the sort of consensus that produced "social democracy" and "the welfare state" over the course of the 19th and 20th centuries. There is evident reason to preclude such convergencies on regional and global levels as

110   R. Falk

a way of resolving some of the tensions being caused by the manner in which globalization is *currently* being enacted.

References

Archibugi, D., Held, D. (Eds) (1995) *Cosmopolitan Democracy: An Agenda for a New World Order* (Cambridge, Polity).

Bello, W. (1977) Talk at Bangkok Conference on Alternative Security Systems in the Asia-Pacific, *Focus Asia*, March, pp. 27–30.

Bull, H. (1977) *The Anarchical Society: A Study of Order in World Politics* (New York, Columbia University Press).

Clark, I. (1997) *Globalization and Fragmentation: International Relations in the Twentieth Century* (Oxford, Oxford University Press).

Commission on Global Governance (1995) *Our Global Neighbourhood* (Oxford, Oxford University Press).

Falk, R. (1993) The making of global citizenship, in: J. Brecher, J.B. Childs & J. Cutler (Eds) *Global Visions: Beyond the New World Order* (Boston, MA, South End Press).

Falk, R. (1995) *On Humane Governance: Toward a New Global Politics* (Cambridge, Polity).

Falk, R. (1996) An inquiry into the political economy of world order', *New Political Economy*, 1, pp. 13–26.

Falk, R. (1997) Resisting "Globalization-from-above" through "Globalisation-from-below", *New Political Economy*, 2, pp. 17–24.

Falk, R. (1997b) State of siege: will globalization win out?, *International Affairs*, 73, pp. 123–136.

Fukuyama, F. (1992) *The End of History and the Last Man* (New York, Free Press).

Goldsmith, E., Allen, R., Allaby, M., Davoll, J. & Laurence, S. (1972) *Blueprint for Survival* (Boston, MA, Houghton Mifflin).

Held, D. (1995) *Democracy and the Global Order: From the Modern State to Cosmopolitan Governance* (Cambridge, Polity).

Hirst, P. & Thompson, G. (1996) *Globalization in Question* (Cambridge, Polity).

Lipschutz, R.D. (1996) *Global Civil Society and Global Environmental Governance* (Albany, NY, State University of New York Press).

Turkish Daily News (1997) Malaysia PM Mulls Action Against Speculators, 29 July.

Meadows, D.H., Meadows, D.L. & Randers, J. (1972) *The Limits to Growth* (New York, Universe Books).

Nerfin, M. (1986) Neither prince nor merchant: citizen—an introduction to the third system, *IFDA Dossier 56*, Nov./Dec., pp. 3–29.

Rich, B. (1994) *Mortgaging the Earth: The World Bank Environmental Impoverishment and the Crisis of Development* (Boston, Beacon Press).

Rosenau, J.N. (1990) *Turbulence in World Politics: A Theory of Change and Continuity* (Princeton, NJ, Princeton University Press).

Sachs, J. (1997) New members please apply, *TIME*, 7 July, pp. 11–12.

Sakamoto, Y. (Ed.) (1994) *Global Transformation: Challenges to the State System* (Tokyo, United Nations University Press).

Shiva, V. (1987) People's ecology: the Chipko movement', in: R.B.J. Walker & S.H. Mendlovitz (Eds) *Towards a Just World Peace: Perspectives from Social Movements* (London, Butterworths).

Wapner, P. (1996) The social construction of global governance, *American Political Science Association Annual Meeting*, 28–31 August.

[26]

Global Economic Policy-Making: A New Constitutionalism?

Jane Kelsey[*]

It has become fashionable in the burgeoning literature on globalisation to proclaim 'the end of history',[1] that we live in a 'borderless world',[2] the nation-state is a 'historical anomaly'[3] and that corporations will 'rule the world'.[4] Recent visitor to Aotearoa New Zealand, Robert Reich, has predicted a new century where there are 'no national products or technologies, no national corporations, no national industries. There will be no national economies, at least as we have come to understand that concept. All that will remain within national borders are the people who comprise a nation . . .'.[5] State-centred economics, law and government have, it seems, been transcended by a 'new global order' which is irrepressible, irreversible and inevitable. Fans want to move the process faster. Critics seek ways to mitigate its effects. There are no alternatives. Resistance to globalisation is futile.

This paper challenges such representations as simplistic, misleading and disempowering. Rather than focusing on the erosion of state authority it offers a positive assessment of what states can still do—not from any desire to defend the state, but because it is necessary to clarify where the power to make policy and law is located before we can identify how those decisions can be opened to contest.

This in no way denies that very significant inter-connected changes are affecting economic, political and social relations around the world, with important flow-on effects for policy and law. The degree of economic integration and inter-dependency is far greater now than during the Keynesian era. While statistically the levels of international trade, foreign investment and immigration are similar to those in the early twentieth century,[6] this is more than a cyclical reversion. There are qualitative differences in the form and intensity of global economic integration between then and now. Flows of finance capital are more technologically integrated and deterritorialised, and often operate through financial products whose value is unrelated to actual currencies. Transnational production is more horizontally and vertically integrated, with enterprises

---

[*] Professor Jane Kelsey, Faculty of Law, University of Auckland.

[1] Francis Fukuyama, *The End of History and the Last Man*, Avon Books, New York, 1992

[2] K. Ohmae, *The End of the Nation State. The Rise of Regional Economies*, The Free Press, New York, 1995; see also *The Borderless World: Power and Strategy in the Interlinked Economy*, Harper, New York, 1991.

[3] R. Mansbach, 'The Realists Ride Again: Counter Revolution in International Relations' in J.N. Rosenau and H. Tromp (eds), *Interdependence and Conflict in World Politics*, Gower Publishing, Aldershot, 1986 p.224.

[4] D. Korten, *When Corporations Rule the World*, Kumarian Press, West Hartford, 1995

[5] R. Reich, *The Work of Nations: Preparing Ourselves for 21st-Century Capitalism*, Simon and Schuster, London, 1991, p.3.

[6] See N. Woods, 'Editorial Introduction. Globalization: Definitions, Debates and Implications', *Oxford Development Studies*, vol.26, no.1, 1998, pp.5-6.

536 *Otago Law Review* (1999) Vol 9 No 3

adopting a wider range of organisational and legal forms. Patterns of trade and the relative importance of goods and services have changed significantly. There are new forms of consumption and new modes of generating, transmitting and controlling knowledge. There are also new ecological and socio-economic 'externalities'.

All these developments constrain how effectively and autonomously states (defined here to include the executive, legislature and judiciary) can make policy, pass and enforce laws and regulate. Most governments now seek to nudge, rather than steer, the economic developments which affect them. But that does not mean states are powerless or that globalisation is an orderly, coherent, linear process.

The tensions between globalisation and state-centred policy and law have typically drawn two contrasting responses. The first, traditionalist, line comes mainly from governments and international lawyers. This treats globalisation as an unproblematic extension of international law whereby states voluntarily concede the reduction of their autonomy, but claim their sovereignty remains inviolate. A second, less orthodox approach heralds globalisation as a catalyst for the emergence of a pluralist and non-state-centred system of global governance (in the case of James Rosenau) or global law (Gunther Teubner).

These polarised positions treat the state as either omnipotent or moribund. This paper will argue that the state's role is more contingent in the way it facilitates the globalisation of capital through the transformation of policy and law at the national level and the coordination of policy and law internationally. This bifurcation of sites has begun to produce some serious tensions between the domestic and international jurisdictions. The way these tensions are being resolved suggests that states still have some control over the outcome and that domestic political pressures and judicial responses still play an important role.

'External' Sovereignty

The standard government line on globalisation rests on the Westphalian notion of an international community of sovereign states. Its constitutive principles include mutual respect for each other's sovereignty, non-intervention in each other's internal affairs, consent as the basis of obligation to comply with international law and diplomatic immunity.[7] Fully autonomous and self-determining, these states have the sovereign authority to confer on other actors or agencies the right to exercise some of their powers. Equally, the self-determining state can renege on international commitments, refuse to accept international rulings and withdraw from any agreement at any time on its own terms. It cannot be forced to comply. So long as globalisation is conducted through language and protocols consistent with these principles, governments can reject arguments that their sovereignty is diminished.

---

[7] For a discussion of the contemporary relevance of this notion see M. Zacher, 'The decaying pillars of the Westphalian temple: implications for international order and governance', in J.N. Rosenau and E-O Czempiel (eds), *Governance without Government: Order and Change in World Politics*, Cambridge University Press, Cambridge, 1992, p.58.

This position is exemplified in a speech by Minister of Foreign Affairs Don McKinnon to the Otago Foreign Policy School in 1996.[8] Globalisation is accepted as a *fait accompli*, with the consequence that:

> states are less able to act independently and that real economic growth depends on a high level of international interaction. No state is an island any more, nor capable of truly autonomous action. But as with any small space, you need rules of behaviour. On the positive side of the ledger there is a growing realisation and recognition of the concept of a global community. New Zealand is playing an active role in this.... [O]verall it is a changed world. The degree of interdependence we see now is unlikely to be reversed.... But let us be optimistic. There is much to look forward to. Increasing interdependence does not mean a loss of freedom and individuality. It does not mean we cease to have choices about our future.[9]

New Zealand's participation in this global community is mediated through the exercise of the state's external sovereignty. McKinnon contrasts internal sovereignty, which is about 'operating with the consent of the people' including public debate and consultation, with external sovereignty which 'is all about the Government, on behalf of New Zealanders, determining and protecting New Zealand's interests abroad.... We work externally to protect interests and values important to us (and to many other countries).' The disjuncture effectively divorces the government's international actions from their impact on domestic policy and law, and quarantines the exercise of external sovereignty within the 'global community' from domestic participation and scrutiny.

Such a distinction is increasingly difficult to sustain. The exercise of external sovereignty, whether seen as an act of state or as Crown prerogative,[10] may have been defensible when international treaties were primarily concerned with military and strategic matters that had little direct impact on domestic policy and law. But international policy and treaty-making has now penetrated deeply into areas that were previously the domain of domestic law. The potential for direct conflict is very real. Reliance on external sovereignty to avoid addressing this potential invites challenges to both the executive's actions and the legitimacy of the relevant international fora.

These concerns are commonly expressed in terms of a 'democratic deficit'. The simplistic solution is to integrate internal and external sovereignty by rendering the executive accountable to domestic political processes. Demands for greater democratic scrutiny of external treaty-making have gained force in New Zealand in recent years, initially led by Sir Kenneth Keith and the Law Commission[11] and supported by interventions from Clerk of the House David

---

[8] D.McKinnon, 'New Zealand Sovereignty in an Interdependent World', in G.A. Wood and L.S. Leland, *State and Sovereignty. Is the state in retreat?*, Otago University Press, Dunedin, 1997, p.7. The orthodox position was also argued by the Director of the Ministry of Foreign Affairs and Trade legal division in D.MacKay, 'Treaties - A Greater Role for Parliament?', (1997) *Public Sector* vol.20, no.1, p.6

[9] McKinnon, p.12.

[10] For a discussion of the basis for these see M. Gobbi and M. Barsi, 'New Zealand's Treaty-Making Process: Understanding the Pressures and Proposals for Reform', Ministry of Justice, Draft paper 3, June 1997, pp.7-8

[11] New Zealand Law Commission, 'The Making, Acceptance and Implementation

538 *Otago Law Review* (1999) Vol 9 No 3

McGee.[12] They gained further momentum during the recent controversy over the proposed OECD Multilateral Agreement on Investment (MAI), with all opposition parties expressing support during 1997 for some greater parliamentary participation in the treaty-making process.[13]

The government's response has been minimalist. On May 1998, following a report from the select committee on foreign affairs,[14] the then Deputy Prime Minister tabled a notice of motion that requires all treaties subject to ratification, accession, acceptance or approval to be presented to Parliament beforehand. They will be accompanied by a National Interest Analysis (NIA) prepared by the government; however the government rejected the committee proposal that this should address the advantages and disadvantages, and any economic, social, cultural and environmental effects of entering or not entering the treaty. Both the treaty and the NIA will be referred to the Foreign Affairs, Defence and Trade Select Committee which can examine them itself or the chair can refer them to another relevant committee. Government cannot sign the treaty until the select committee has reported back or 35 calendar days have expired.[15]

However, these changes were introduced only as sessional orders for a trial period. They are limited to those international treaties where Cabinet's decision to ratify was taken after 17 December 1997. Reference solely to treaties excludes non-treaty commitments like APEC which are clearly intended to constrain future economic policy decisions and play a critical role within the international circuitry of economic policy-making where binding constraints are imposed. The select committee retains full discretion whether to hold an inquiry and, if so, whether to call for submissions which might contest the NIA. Parliament has no right to vote on the treaty and can therefore impose no constraints on the executive. Parliament will not get to discuss a treaty until negotiations are complete and its content finalised. There is no requirement for a parliamentary mandate to negotiate nor for public discussion at any stage. The Official Information Act still gives the government conclusive grounds to withhold information provided in confidence by another government or international organisation,[16] and information considered likely to cause serious economic damage to the New Zealand economy by premature disclosure of decisions relating to entering

---

of Treaties: Three Issues for consideration', draft paper, July 1995; *A New Zealand Guide to International Law and its Sources*, NZLCR 34, 1996, p.3. See also K.J. Keith, 'New Zealand Treaty Practice: The Executive and the Legislature' (1964) 1 *NZULR* p.272.

[12] See *NZ Herald*, 1 Nov. 1996 and 'Treaties and the House of Representatives', Annex D to *Report of the Standing Orders Committee on its Review of the Operation of the Standing Orders*, 1996, I.18B; See also Ministry of Justice, (Briefing Paper for the Minister of Justice), Oct. 1996, p.51.

[13] Matt Robson MP (Alliance) and Ken Shirley MP (Act) both placed private member's bills in the ballot which would subject treaties to formal parliamentary process. Hon. Mike Moore (Labour) presented a paper to the foreign affairs select committee proposing new rules to increase Parliamentary and select committee scrutiny.

[14] *Inquiry into Parliament's Role in the International Treaty Process. Report of the Foreign Affairs, Defence and Trade Committee*, 1997.

[15] Notices of Motion, 28 May 1998.

[16] Official Information Act 1982, sec.6(b)(ii).

overseas trade agreements.[17] There is no attempt to address the authority under Treaty of Waitangi of the colonial government making unilateral commitments on behalf of its Treaty partner.

The proposed process falls far short of the scrutiny demanded for domestic legislation, regulations or even policy. As a result ministers, who hold office in the short-term, retain the power to lock future governments into pursuing, or refraining from, a particular set of policies, activities or goals. There is clear potential for conflict between commitments by the executive in the international arena and domestic policy and law. Even if there were effective parliamentary and public scrutiny, the potential for conflict between these commitments and future government policies and laws would remain. The fall-back argument is that state sovereignty allows governments to not sign, withdraw from, renege on or alter any international commitments. The examples examined later in this paper put these claims to the test.

Global governance and global law

The sovereignty argument adopts a state-centred perspective on globalisation. It assumes that global economic policy and law are the exclusive sphere of inter-national agencies and inter-governmental agreements. At the other extreme, an increasing number of international relations and some legal theorists argue that non-state systems of law are emerging through globalisation and render the already-dubious traditional concepts of law and government obsolete.

James Rosenau contrasts the unitary image of state-centred *government* with a pluralist concept of *global governance*. This spans formal and informal, international and domestic, state and non-state sources of power, policy-making and regulation.[18] It brings together diverse sites that transcend the territorial boundaries of the state. These develop at different paces and operate through varying forms. Shared commitment to consistent principles, norms, rules and procedures means that all actors, agencies and agreements act in a regular and patterned way. This provides coherence and the sense of an organic whole.[19]

A variant on this is Gunther Teubner's concept of 'global law without a state'. Teubner argues that diverse sectors of civil society (such as multi-national enterprises (MNEs), professions or international employers and employees), faced with globalisation, organise their own 'global law' in relative insulation from the state, official international politics and international public law.[20] This law is produced by 'highly technical, highly specialized, often formally organized and rather narrowly defined, global networks of an economic, cultural, academic or technological nature'.[21] It constitutes a legal order in its own right that depends on neither political nor institutional support. It addresses conflicts that are inter-systemic rather than inter-national. Its approach is flexible and pluralist,

---

17   Official Information Act 1982, sec.6(e)(vi).
18   J. Rosenau, 'Governance, Order and Change in World Politics', in Rosenau and Czempiel (eds.), p.1 at p.4.
19   Rosenau, p.8.
20   G. Teubner, '"Global Bukowina": Legal Pluralism in the World Society', in G. Teubner (ed.) *Global Law Without a State*, Dartmouth, Aldershot, 1997, p.4.
21   Teubner, p.7.

operating through values and principles instead of the structured and rules-based system of state law. The lack of global enforceability is compensated for by the flexibility to adapt to rapidly changing circumstances. Because global law is neither the creation of, nor dependent on, the official legal order it becomes extremely difficult for national politics and international institutions to intervene in global economic transactions or multinational organisations.

Teubner describes *lex mercatoria* or 'the transnational law of economic transactions, as the most successful example of global law without a state'.[22] Contractual arrangements, such as international business transactions, standardised contracts and model contracts create an institutional triangle of contracting, legislation and adjudication. The legislators are the economic and professional associations, and network of international organisations, that contribute to and participate in these processes. The judiciary is the various arbitration and dispute settlement tribunals. The 'system' is pluralist, fragmented and lacks institutional linkages; but this leaves it fluid enough to grow and change with the exigencies of the global economy.

There is considerable evidence of the multi-layered polity on which Rosenau bases his claims of global governance. Transnational enterprises (TNEs) by definition exist supra-nationally. Their inherent flexibility, gross turnover and superior access to finance, technology, skills and economies of scale make them larger and more powerful than many of the national economies in which they operate. Razeen Sally suggests the TNE is 'not only the key economic and commercial actor in structures of international production, but it is also implanted in the institutional arrangements of nation-states, as well as subnational and supranational regions'.[23]

Finance capital flows through what some have termed a nonterritorial 'region' that is nevertheless integrated, operates in real time and exists alongside the territorially-defined spaces called national economies.[24] International financial institutions like the International Monetary Fund and World Bank set conditions that severely constrain the policy options for deeply indebted countries. Regional economic integration agreements also set the parameters for their members and can assume an existence independent of the sum of their parts.[25] There are even transborder administrative and legal jurisdictions that integrate parts of different countries for economic and regulatory purposes.[26] Overlaying these are binding multilateral instruments like the General Agreement on Tariffs and Trade (GATT)

---

[22]   Teubner, p.3.

[23]   R. Sally, 'Multinational enterprises, political economic and institutional theory: domestic embeddedness in the context of internationalization', *Review of International Political Economy*, vol.1, no.1, 1994, pp.161, 162.

[24]   J.G. Ruggie, 'Territoriality and Beyond: problematizing modernity in international relations', *International Organization*, vol.47, no.1, 1993, pp.139, 143.

[25]   These range from federations of states, such as the European Union, to binding regional agreements like the North American Free Trade Agreement (NAFTA) and inter-governmental commitments like the Asia Pacific Economic Cooperation forum (APEC).

[26]   For example, the Transmanche Euroregion links Kent, Calais and three parts of Belgium, the Singapore-Johor-Riau Triangle integrates parts of Singapore, Malaysia and Indonesia.

and related agreements that now operate under the umbrella of the World Trade Organisation (WTO) with their own enforcement mechanisms.

More subtle contributions to global governance come from economic organisations like the OECD, rich countries' clubs (primarily the Group of 7), the credit rating firms (especially Moody's and Standard and Poor's), globally-linked neo-liberal think-tanks (like the World Economic Forum and Mont Pelerin Society), and transnational accounting and consultancy firms (such as Price Waterhouse, CS First Boston, Ernst Young). These are complemented by networks of academics, consultants, advisers and officials who cross-fertilise ideas and implement their common agenda across the globe.

These diverse entities, instruments and actors play a major role in the development of international economic policy and law. They create a climate conducive to, and expectant of, certain commitments and outcomes. They can be influential, and even definitive, in securing change. Sometimes they even exercise autonomous policy and regulatory powers. But they cannot ultimately deliver without the cooperation, or at least the acquiescence, of states.

The evidence for Teubner's 'global law without a state' is less convincing. Peter Muchlinski assessed Teubner's claims that a 'proto-legal' phenomenon is emerging within the organisation of MNEs, on the assumption that global law would at least require consistency and generality of practice, transnational application, and a sense of binding duty among both those to whom it applies and those not directly affected.[27] Teubner identifies contracts governing the interaction between staff, and between different elements of an enterprise, as possible examples of intra-corporate 'global proto-law'. Muchlinski suggests these might equally be described as management practices. Similarly, company codes of conduct which appear like quasi-law may be just another public relations exercise. Muchlinski agrees that codes of conduct across industries or firms could have more claim to proto-legal status. But even this usually rests on recognition by official law through implied terms of consumer contracts, as evidence of standard industry practice when assessing a duty of care in tort, or as the basis for official codes.

Muchlinski finds more substantial evidence of the leverage exercised by MNEs over the development of substantive laws that govern commercial practice. Contractual standardisation is frequently modelled on the practices of major firms, as are the standard terms developed by the international trade associations and agencies like the International Chamber of Commerce (ICC) in which MNEs play a dominant role. Early MNEs effectively created the applicable international investment regimes through contracts between themselves and the local rulers, insisting on protection of property rights against confiscation and external arbitration to resolve disputes.

There is also abundant evidence of their role as a powerful and concerted lobby in the development of national and multilateral regulatory regimes. The degree of influence differs between sectors and industries, and on whether MNEs speak with a single voice on an issue. Some have secured institutionalised roles

---

27   P. Muchlinski, '"Global Bukowina" Examined: Viewing the Multinational Enterprise as a Transnational Law-making Community', in Teubner, (ed.) p.79.

in the decision-making process of their home states, notably in the US,[28] Japan and the European Union. Collectively, MNEs have a formal presence in international fora where global economic policy and law is made, such as the APEC Business Advisory Council (ABAC) and the Business and Industry Advisory Committee (BIAC) at the OECD. In all these examples, however, it is not the MNEs that formally create policy and law. That is still the role of states, either through customary practice or formal instruments.

Rosenau and Teubner fall into the trap of many international relations theorists of trying to construct a coherent global order. In doing so they over-state the stability of the 'system', the unanimity of the participants and the extent to which economic policy and law have converged. My empirical work on diverse sites of global policy and law suggests the situation is more complex and fragile. The so-called 'global economy' is multi-faceted. Each element—such as foreign investment, trade, finance capital, transnational enterprise, information technology flows, financial institutions, regional agreements or international consultancies and think tanks—has its own dynamics.[29] Each exhibits different degrees of autonomy from state intervention nationally and internationally. Each provokes a different response from states, institutions and economic actors, and forms of resistance from those it adversely affects. Each therefore has different implications for the policy, regulatory and legal framework of the state and raises different possibilities for contest.

Their counterparts who advocate critical engagement with globalisation seek an equally ordered and systematic mode of response. International lawyer Richard Falk, for instance, argues that globalisation as a process is inevitable,

---

[28]   As a *quid pro quo* for approving the fast-track process for trade negotiations, the US Trade Act 1974 established a system of trade advisory committees which provide 'public' input into the US negotiating position. This 'public' has been confined to the business community who gain privileged access to information, documents and key officials. A key player is the United States Council for International Business [USCIB] comprising 300 MNCs, service companies, law firms and business associations. It is allied to the International Chamber of Commerce and International Organization of Employers and officially represents US business positions in the main intergovernmental bodies. Its mission is to 'advance the global interests of American business both at home and abroad'.

[29]   The leverage exercised by the International Monetary Fund, the World Bank and the Asian Development Bank, for example, poses quite different issues and arguments from concerns over the power and liability of transnational enterprise. These differ, in turn, from the impact of unregulated capital flows and questions about the appropriateness and effectiveness of re-regulation. The think tanks, consultancies and networks that seek to construct an ideological consensus are different again. The diverse participants in these processes have specific objectives which they pursue with varying degrees of power. Corporate strategies and operational practices vary enormously. States frequently engage in forum shopping depending on which institution's decision-making processes, agenda and status best serves their interests. Some take apparently contradictory positions on the same issues in different fora. The objectives of some players coincide, reflecting different styles of capitalist expansion, different cultures of law, language and human relations, different strategic objectives and ideological or religious beliefs. International agencies themselves have organisational agenda and legitimacy requirements which create turf battles over issues and strategies.

but its form is not. In place of globalisation-from-above he argues for a process of globalisation-from-below that challenges both state-centred and market-oriented paradigms. This would require an 'ideological posture that is comparably coherent to that being provided by various renditions of neo-liberalism, and that could provide the social forces associated with globalisation-from-below with a common theoretical framework, political language and programme.'[30] Falk's quest for coordination and coherence begs the question of who would determine that framework, language and programme. Recent experience suggests that global movements, notably on environmental and development issues, are dominated by Western NGOs. The old and recent history of resistance, and my own empirical work, suggests that challenges to globalisation historically in its imperial and colonial form and today are still largely localised, with some loose coordination internationally. Locking this into the straight-jacket of a global civil society working to a unified counter-ideology seems more likely to neutralise rather than enhance the prospects of an effective contest.

A new constitutionalism

How, then, do we position the state in the making of global economic policy and law? Numerous, sympathetic empirical studies of structural adjustment over the past decade insist that the state has far from withered away.[31] Instead, it is responding to the needs of capital in a different way. Less sympathetic accounts reach a similar conclusion. Gramscian scholar Robert Cox, for instance, argues that welfare interventionism, which was overseen by the state, performed an important role in legitimating and supporting capitalism when it operated mainly at the national level. The state has played a similar role in overseeing the domestic transition to neo-liberalism and facilitating the reorganisation of capitalism internationally.[32]

At the domestic level, this transformation or 'structural adjustment' has broadly coalesced around the policy agenda known as the 'Washington consensus'. Internationally, this agenda has been reflected in the rapidly expanding menu of state-sponsored economic agreements, organisations and arrangements. In the past decade the ideological hegemony of post-Cold War neo-liberalism has become quite explicit. For example, the *Declaration on the Contribution of the [WTO] to Achieving Greater Coherence in Global Economic Policymaking* in 1994 noted that achieving harmony between 'the structural, macroeconomic, trade, financial and development aspects of economic policymaking . . . falls primarily on governments at the national level' but argued that international coherence was important to increasing these policies' effectiveness. '[T]he interlinkages between the different aspects of economic policy require that the international institutions

---

30   R. Falk, 'Global Civil Society: Perspectives, Initiatives, Movements', *Oxford Development Studies*, vol.26, no.1, 1998, pp.99, 105.

31   R. Bates and A. Krueger, *Political and Economic Interactions in Economic Policy Reform*, Blackwell, Oxford, 1993, pp.462-3; and generally, S. Haggard and R. Kaufman, (eds.), *The Politics of Economic Adjustment*, Princeton University Press, New Jersey, 1992.

32   R. Cox, *Approaches to World Order*, Cambridge University Press, Cambridge, 1996.

544   *Otago Law Review*   (1999) Vol 9 No 3

with responsibilities in each of these areas follow consistent and mutually supportive policies'. WTO ministers mandated the Director-General of the WTO to review the responsibilities and mechanisms for cooperation among the Bretton Woods institutions of the World Bank and IMF 'with a view to creating greater coherence in global economic policymaking'.[33] Ironically, just as this hegemony is reaching its height the 'Washington consensus' is being challenged as inappropriate and damaging by leading players within the global economic arena—illustrating, once more, that nothing is forever.[34]

In a world supposedly committed to competitive deregulated markets and reduced state power, the desire for order, coherence, coordination and even convergence seems paradoxical. It is explained as a rational strategy that maximises the benefits from global capitalism and minimises the undesired externalities. These arise partly from market forces and the difficulties facing states in regulating global economic activity. But there is also potential for distortions as self-interested actors seek to intervene. Hence, the need to facilitate and protect deregulated global markets through agreed global rules, with mechanisms for resolving disputes and where necessary enforcing rights. There is a corresponding need to manage non-economic externalities in ways that do not disrupt the equilibrium of market forces. These may achieved through various configurations of parties using a range of modalities and fora. But they are underpinned/constrained by the global economic policy framework.

For example, the plethora of bilateral, regional, plurilateral, multilateral investment agreements follow a common set of core principles and a standard formula, with some variations in the detail.[35] *National treatment* requires signatory governments to treat the investors of other parties to the agreement at least as favourably as their own, and therefore possibly better. *Most favoured nation (MFN) status* prevents a signatory from discriminating between investors of other parties and requires them to give to all the best treatment it gives to any one. This can be limited to non-discrimination between countries which are party to the agreement, or be unconditional and apply to any other agreement under which the signatory has MFN obligations. *Transparency* requires full disclosure to other parties of the rules, policies, practices, procedures and decisions which relate to the subject of the agreement.

'Investment' is broadly defined. Investors' rights are protected from expropriation and nationalisation. Most agreements allow governments to reserve certain activities, sectors, policies or laws from coverage, although they cannot opt out of their commitments on expropriation and nationalisation. These reservations are usually subject to 'standstill', meaning they cannot be added to, and to the expectation of 'rollback' or their reduction and elimination over time. The objective is not to change the country's laws, but to codify them so they

---

33   Final Act Embodying the Results of the Uruguay Round of Multilateral Trade
        Negotiations, MTN/FA III-2, p.1.
34   See R. Stiglitz, chief economist of the World Bank, speech in Helsinki, Finland, 7
        January 1998, www.worldbank.org.
35   During the 1980s and 1990s there was a particularly rapid growth in the number
        and coverage of bilateral investment treaties [BITs]. According to UNCTAD by
        June 1996 nearly 1160 had been completed, two-thirds of these in the 1990s.

cannot subsequently be made more restrictive. Provision is usually made for exit, after due notice is served.

Many agreements also make provision for dispute resolution. Rather than working through their parent state, investors are increasingly given standing to enforce agreements themselves. Settlement or adjudication of disputes generally involves international arbitration.[36] The preferred fora is the International Centre for the Settlement of Investment Disputes (ICSID), established by the World Bank specifically to deal with disputes between states and private foreign investors.[37] ICSID awards must be enforceable under the participating state's domestic law.[38]

Canadian critic of NAFTA and the proposed MAI Tony Clarke has described such agreements as Bills of Rights for TNEs. Investors achieve a status equivalent—arguably superior—to not only citizens, but to nation-states. States and this privileged private category known as 'investors' are treated equally. Private property rights are guaranteed against direct or indirect expropriation, sometimes even when public order breaks down.[39] Senior personnel of an investor are granted quasi-diplomatic status that is immune from many normal immigration rules. Investors are empowered to call a foreign government before a supra-national forum for breaching the agreement and to demand enforcement of any consequent award in that state's domestic courts. In the case of the draft MAI this quasi-Bill of Rights would be entrenched—governments promise not to withdraw for an initial five years, and if they do subsequently withdraw, to continue applying the rules to existing investors for a further fifteen years, irrespective of the policies and laws a new government may wish to pursue.

David Schneiderman of the University of Alberta describes this as a new constitutionalism which in form and substance mirrors many features of the old.[40] Almost all these agreements contain a pre-commitment strategy that binds future generations of citizens to certain pre-determined institutional forms and policies. They are difficult to amend. They often include binding enforcement mechanisms. But they serve a different constituency, conferring privileged rights of citizenship on corporate capital, while constraining the power of the nation state and the democratic rights of its citizens. These agreements variously defer to national laws, supplement them and replace them, in a continuous dialectical relationship. In the process, tensions and conflicts arise between the old constitutionalism and the new.

---

[36] Sometimes an agreement will specify the use of the UN Commission on International Law's model arbitration rules [UNCITRAL]; see Convention for the Recognition and Enforcement of Foreign Arbitral Awards, (UN) (binding) 1958.

[37] Washington Convention on the Settlement of Investment Disputes between States and Nationals of Other States, 1965. The International Chamber of Commerce's Court of Arbitration is also sometimes used, but that deals mainly with private international disputes.

[38] In New Zealand see the Arbitration (International Investment Disputes) Act 1979.

[39] This issue remained unresolved when the MAI negotiations broke down in October 1998.

[40] D. Schneiderman, 'Investment Rules and the New Constitutionalism: Interlinkages and Disciplinary Effects', paper to the Consortium on Globalisation, Law and Social Sciences, New York, April 1997.

Conflicting constitutionalisms

This approach offers a mid-point between the state-centred Westphalian model and non-state global governance and law by recognising the active role of the state in facilitating the links between the global and national. There is still a risk of over-stating the coherence of the process and viewing current developments as linear and determinist. But that is mitigated by recognising the potential for discord as the old constitutionalism is confronted by the new.

One key to understanding the implications of globalisation for domestic policy and law is how states have responded when these conflicts arise. The following examples suggest a combination of factors affects the outcome: the geo-political and economic power of the particular state, the extent of dependence on international capital, the policy inclination of the incumbent government, the willingness of the judiciary and parliament to diverge from the executive and the potency of domestic oppositional forces.

The first example involves a conflict between the investor protection and dispute resolution provisions of NAFTA and the Mexican constitution.[41] As with many Latin American countries, Mexico's 1917 constitution embraced the 'Calvo doctrine'.[42] This entitled foreign investors to national treatment (non-discrimination), but not to better treatment than local investors. The 'Calvo clause' made Mexican national law the only applicable law and the domestic courts the only forum for settling investment disputes. This was intended to ensure that foreign creditors did not secure greater rights than local creditors in claims against the state. NAFTA's investment chapter directly contradicted this by giving foreign investors stronger rights to compensation for expropriation enforceable in international trade tribunals.

The conflict was resolved by formally and informally amending the domestic Constitution. Mexico's President Salinas guaranteed that NAFTA would not be subject to constitutional attack and enacted a Law Regarding the Making of Treaties which empowered the state to negotiate international treaties with enforceable dispute settlement mechanisms.[43] Provision for redistribution of rural lands for collective use under Article 27 of the Mexican Constitution was also radically altered in 1992 to permit individual property holding, relax limits on the number of acres that could be held and extend legal capacity to enter joint-ventures. Opposition to these new land laws was widespread in rural Mexico, most notably in the civil war waged by indigenous peoples and peasants in Chiapas through the Zapatista Liberation Army.

---

41   *Ibid.*

42   See M. Sornarajah, *The International Law on Foreign Investment*, Cambridge University Press, Cambridge, 1994, pp.11, 89, 123.

43   Schneiderman, *op cit.* fn. 40, A. Cânavos, 'Introductory Note', *International Legal Materials*, vol.31, 1990 p.391 and J. Daly, 'Has Mexico Crossed the Border on State Responsibility for Economic Injury to Aliens? Foreign Investment and the Calvo Clause in Mexico after NAFTA', *St Mary's Law Journal*, vol.25, 1994, pp.1147-1193.

The Mexican government's capitulation could be attributed to its relatively weak economic bargaining position, demands from the US government and international financial institutions as conditions for debt refinancing, and the need to maintain the confidence of foreign investors on whom Mexico's open economy now depends. But previous Mexican governments have taken different policy positions; they even seriously threatened a moratorium on the repayment of foreign debt in 1982. This suggests that domestic factors were also important. By the 1990s a new administration committed to neo-liberalism was in control and was determined, with US support, to lock in that regime.[44] Their ability to rewrite the Constitution was assisted by a corrupt political system. While the Constitution has been changed, however, many Mexican people remain committed to the old Constitution—some to the extent of supporting armed resistance. Coupled with the failure of the economic policies to deliver the promised wellbeing, the long-term survival of the new constitutionalism is far from guaranteed.

In the second example similar contradictions have been left unresolved. A bilateral investment treaty (BIT) between Canada and South Africa was signed on 27 November 1995. This contains provisions on property rights, takings and compensation[45] which conflict with the painstakingly negotiated, and deliberately open-textured, provisions for restoration of lands in the South African Constitution.[46] The property rights rule in the Constitution cannot impede measures for affirmative action to redress past discrimination. Compensation provisions are relatively lenient, distinguishing between non-compensable regulation of property and compensable expropriation for purposes including land reform. However, the BIT makes no such distinctions and no reservations against takings are listed in the agreement. The agreement also contains a more onerous expropriation and nationalisation clause than the Constitution. This means that Canadian foreign investors would be treated better than local investors; standards of compensation would also differ. The South African Constitutional Court has final authority to interpret the property rights clause under the BIT.

Judicial interpretation of the constitutional provisions on land will be a sensitive domestic issue that would require political and ethical judgements from the Constitutional Court. If a dispute arises under the BIT before the domestic interpretation of the Constitution is settled the Court will have to weigh additional considerations of South Africa's international obligations and the message it wants to send foreign investors and governments. The Court might resist interpretations that modify the spirit of the Constitution. Equally, it might succumb to pressures to conform with emergent international standards and to harmonise the property rule with the investment rule, so far as that can be done. Any judicial rewriting of the Constitution could damage the legitimacy of the

---

[44]   See P. Krugman, *Pop Internationalism*, MIT Press, Cambridge Massachusetts, 1996, p.165.

[45]   These are common to almost all Canadian BITs, as well as to NAFTA and the draft MAI.

[46]   Schneiderman, *op cit.* fn. 40. At the time of writing in April 1997 Schneiderman noted the BIT had not yet been proclaimed in force.

548 *Otago Law Review* (1999) Vol 9 No 3

Court and provoke a volatile response that impedes the extension of neo-liberal policy and law in the medium term.

The Philippine Supreme Court faced a similar dilemma in 1994 and essentially reinterpreted domestic constitutional provisions to comply with the government's new international commitments.[47] Like many countries emerging from colonial and foreign economic domination, the post-Marcos Constitution of the Philippines had positively embraced economic nationalism. Section 19 of the Declaration of Principles and State Policies in the Philippine Constitution says 'The State shall develop a self-reliant and independent national economy effectively controlled by Filipinos'. Further principles say the Congress shall 'enact measures that will encourage the formation and operation of enterprises whose capital is wholly owned by Filipinos'. In granting rights, privileges and concessions covering the national economy and patrimony, the State 'shall give preference to qualified Filipinos' (section 10). Section 12 says the State 'shall promote the preferential use of Filipino labor, domestic materials and locally produced goods, and adopt measures that help make them competitive'.

In late 1994 the Supreme Court of the Philippines was asked to strike down a Senate motion to ratify the accession to the WTO on the grounds that it was unconstitutional. The Court found in favour of the government almost three years later. The case centred on two main issues. The first was whether the parity provisions and national treatment requirements of the WTO agreements contravened the Constitution. The Court accepted the defence contention that these principles were merely aids to interpretation. Those parts of the Constitution which espoused economic nationalism had to be read in relation to other parts, which the court selectively identified and creatively interpreted.[48]

The second issue was whether the provisions of the Agreement and Annexes would limit, restrict or impair the exercise of legislative power by the Congress or the judicial authority of the Supreme Court. The Court observed that the Constitution contained explicit commitments to 'generally accepted principles of international law'. Invoking orthodox external sovereignty arguments, it noted the self-limiting nature of state sovereignty enabled the executive to sign, and Congress to ratify, such agreements and that the WTO recognised all members' sovereign equality.

The Court insisted its sole concern was whether the Senate had 'gravely abused its discretion amounting to a lack of jurisdiction'. It was not there to review the wisdom of the President and Senate in joining the WTO, nor to pass upon the merits of trade liberalization as a policy. Yet that is patently what happened. The judgement began:

---

[47]   *Tanada and others v. Angara and others*, Republic of the Philippines Supreme Court, Manila, 2 May 1997, per Panganiban J.

[48]   For example, when quoting one of the original Constitutional Commissioners, Bernardo Villegas, that 'economic self-reliance does not mean autarky or economic seclusion', the Court conveniently ignored the remainder of the quote: 'Independence refers to the freedom from undue foreign control of the national economy, especially in such strategic industries as in the development of natural resources and public utilities'; *Tanada v Angara*, p.44.

Liberalization, globalization, deregulation and privatization, the third-millennium buzz words, are ushering in a new borderless world of business by sweeping away as mere historical relics the heretofore traditional modes of promoting and protecting national economies like tariffs, export subsidies, import quotas, quantitative restrictions, tax exemptions and currency controls. Finding market niches and becoming the best in specific industries in a market-driven and export-oriented global scenario are replacing the age-old "beggar-thy-neighbor" policies that unilaterally protect weak and inefficient domestic producers of goods and services. In the words of Peter Drucker, the well-known management guru, "Increased participation in the world economy has become the key to domestic economic growth and prosperity."

and concluded in the 'Epilogue':

Notwithstanding objections against possible limitations on national sovereignty, the WTO remains as the only viable structure for multilateral trading and the veritable forum for the development of international trade law. The alternative to WTO is isolation, stagnation, if not economic self-destruction. Duly enriched with original membership, keenly aware of the advantages and disadvantages of globalization with its on-line experience, and endowed with a vision of the future, the Philippines now straddles the crossroads of an international strategy for economic prosperity and stability in the new millennium.[49]

Opting to endorse this line could be seen as pragmatic realism on the part of the Court. The WTO had been operating for two years, with the Philippines government as an active participant. Parallel commitments had been made in other fora such as APEC, which the government had hosted with great fanfare just six months before. Even before the East Asian collapse, the Philippines was effectively beholden to the World Bank, Asian Development Bank and IMF and, like Mexico, a captive of the need to maintain investor confidence. Also like Mexico, the government was dominated by a political and economic elite who had converted to neo-liberalism.

In effect, the Supreme Court opted to repeal the nationalist economic principles of the Philippines' Constitution. The newly-elected government has announced a review of the constitution in 1999, intended to remove those provisions. But they were drafted in a period of fervent hostility to dominance by foreign powers and TNCs and retain strong domestic support. They will not be easily given away. Indeed, the government and the Supreme Court have faced ongoing pressure. Against a backdrop of widespread civil disruption, the Court subsequently struck down, on technical grounds, a decision to deregulate domestic oil prices agreed to with the IMF.[50] The government was forced to withdraw the price rise. Like Indonesia and Russia, domestic pressures succeeded in forcing the reconsideration of what are often portrayed as watertight IMF demands. This suggests that popular politics, the need for courts and governments to retain some domestic legitimacy, and the potentially disastrous local consequences of imposing these policies and laws are all potential fetters on global policy and law.

---

49   *Tanada v Angara*, p.4 then p.72.
50   *Tatad v Secretary of the Department of Energy*, Republic of the Philippines Supreme Court, Manila, 5 November 1997.

What would happen if domestic courts or Parliament stood firm in asserting state sovereignty and refused to concede to the new constitutionalism? That dilemma currently faces the government of India. Several states have filed an original jurisdictions suit against the Union of India on its accession to WTO on the principal ground that this violates the basic structure of the Indian Constitution, in particular federalism, fundamental rights and the sovereignty and unity of India. Although the suit was filed soon after ratification, it has yet to come up for hearing. The reticence of the previously activist Indian judiciary may reflect a nervousness about the separation of powers and external sovereignty; but it is also politically consistent with their prevarication in the litigation against Union Carbide over Bhopal.[51]

The Indian courts may have been reticent, but the Parliament and the people have not been. The Trade-Related Intellectual Property Rights Agreement (TRIPS) negotiated during the GATT Uruguay Round, and in particular the patenting of seeds and agricultural chemicals to agribusiness like Cargill, have been extremely controversial in India and provoked massive protests. The TRIPS agreement gave developing countries until 2000 to comply, except for national treatment and MFN obligations. They were also exempted until 2005 from providing product patents in areas which were not currently patentable under domestic law. This particularly upset pharmaceutical and agribusiness TNEs who, in return, secured a special provision to protect their interests: Article 70 required such governments, from 1 January 1995, to provide a 'means' for receiving applications for pharmaceutical and agricultural chemical patents, and a mechanism for granting exclusive marketing rights for five years to those applicants where patent applications had been accepted in another WTO country.

The Indian government was initially willing to deliver what other WTO members demanded in complying with Article 70. In March 1995 it issued a Presidential Ordinance that would provide a means to receive such applications and grant exclusive marketing rights, and introduced a bill into Parliament to enact the ordinance into law. This Bill lapsed when Parliament was dissolved in May 1995. The government then administratively directed the Patent Office to continue receiving applications and keep the old applications without disposing of them. This was conveyed to the Parliament in response to a parliamentary question, one of the mechanisms available for formal notification. Between 1 January 1995 and 15 February 1997 some 1339 applications were received and stored.[52]

The US, later joined by the EU, said this was not enough. In July 1996 they asked the WTO to establish a disputes panel to determine whether India was in breach of its obligations under Article 70.[53] (A similar dispute with Pakistan was settled bilaterally.) Upholding the complaint the WTO panel found that Article 70.8(a) required India to establish a 'mailbox' for applications and allocate filing

---

51   See J. Cassels, 'The Uncertain Promise of Law: Lessons from Bhopal', *Osgoode Hall Law Journal*, vol.29, no.1, 1991, p.1; Permanent People's Tribunal on Industrial Hazards and Human Rights, 'Beyond Bhopal', Pesticide Trust, London, 1994.

52   C. Raghavan, 'WTO panel rules against India on TRIPS', *Third World Economics*, no.169, 16-30 September 1997, p.4.

53   Complaint by the US on Patent Protection for Pharmaceutical and Agricultural Chemical Products: violation of TRIPS articles 27, 65, 70, WT/DS50, July 1996

and priority dates to them through legislation. The panel also said it was a legitimate expectation that patents would be granted over matters which, at the time the application was lodged, were not patentable and that those applications would be given priority. India appealed. The WTO Appellate Body upheld the panel's finding that India had failed to preserve the novelty of an invention and filing and priority dates because the mailbox lacked a 'sound legal basis'. It was left to the Indian government to decide how to give it that effect. The Appellate Body disagreed that the 'means' had to eliminate all reasonable doubt about whether the application might be rejected or invalidated in the future. It also rejected the application to TRIPS of the 'legitimate expectations' argument, saying this had been developed in the quite different context of non-violation disputes relating to trade in goods. The WTO required the Indian government to comply with its ruling within eighteen months or face severe retaliatory action.

This dispute highlights the tensions between quasi-judicial supranational fora and the domestic courts. The Appellate Body in this case explicitly considered Indian law and concluded there was no guarantee that the administrative instructions would survive a legal challenge.[54] Its findings were therefore intended to ensure enforcement of an agreement which might well be struck down in the Indian domestic courts. These WTO disputes processes are widely seen to lack legitimacy. Strong criticism of them as non-transparent, undemocratic and run by the majors in the interests of their TNEs has led to calls at the WTO ministerial meeting in Geneva in May 1998 from US President Clinton, supported by the WTO Director-General Ruggiero, for a more transparent process.[55] The three member dispute panel in this case was chaired by the former TRIPS negotiator for Switzerland, a country with a strong chemical and pharmaceutical industry.[56]

In April 1998 the Indian government announced an agreement with the US to comply within 15 months. But what if the Parliament refuses to pass the legislation or popular opposition makes it politically suicidal for government to push the issue? What if the Indian Courts again became activist and declared accession to the WTO unconstitutional? Economic sanctions would probably ensue. But the Indian government, and according to media reports the Indian people, have accepted wide-ranging economic sanctions as the price for demonstrating their nuclear capacity. In such conditions the assertion of national sovereignty is more than academic.

All these examples involve countries which are generally portrayed as powerless victims of the globalisation juggernaut. The record is mixed, and reflects different configurations of domestic and international, economic and political circumstances. How the dominant actor in global economic policy and law, the United States, mediates the tension between the old constitutionalism and the new provides an interesting contrast.

---

with a dispute settlement panel established in November 1996; Complaint by the EC on Patent Protection for Pharmaceutical and Agricultural Chemical Products: violation of TRIPS article 70, para 8 &9, WT/DS 79/1, April 1997.

[54] C. Raghavan, *Third World Economics*, no.176, 1-15 January 1998, p.13.

[55] These speeches are reported on the WTO website at www.wto.org.

[56] C. Raghavan, 'WTO panel rules against India on TRIPS', *Third World Economics*, no.169, 16-30 September 1997, p.4.

552   *Otago Law Review*   (1999) Vol 9 No 3

Article II of the US Constitution empowers the President 'by and with the Advice and Consent of the Senate, to make treaties provided two thirds of the Senators present concur'. However, it is the Congress which under Article 1 §8 has the power to regulate foreign commerce. This authority has been pragmatically circumscribed under the Trade Act 1974 by the so-called 'fast track' mechanism. The Congress periodically grants the President authority to negotiate an international economic agreement on the understanding that Congress will approve or reject it in its entirety and not amend it during the ratification process. Treaties which are not self-executing only become enforceable after incorporation into domestic law. Expiry of fast-track authority often draws threats from Congress not to renew. Ironically, this gives the US government added leverage in negotiations and often determines the deadline for concluding a treaty. For the first time a request for renewal was refused by Congress in 1997.

The US claims the sovereign right to protect its trade interests unilaterally, irrespective of its international commitments. Section 301 of the Trade Act 1974 empowers the President to 'respond to any act, policy, or practice of a foreign country or instrumentality that . . . is unjustifiable, unreasonable, or discriminatory and burdens or restricts United States commerce' by taking 'all appropriate and feasible action within his (sic) power to enforce such rights or obtain the elimination of such act, policy or practice' whether through discriminatory or non-discriminatory action.[57] In addition the President may suspend, withdraw or withhold the benefits of trade agreement concessions to that country or instrumentality and impose duties and other restrictions on their products or fees on their services. The Omnibus Trade and Competitiveness Act 1988 strengthened the existing 301 provisions by creating a 'super 301' authority to identify 'priority foreign countries' that displayed 'major barriers and trade distorting practices' and a 'special 301' provision to deal with violators of intellectual property rights.

The US has been particularly guarded in relation to the General Agreement on Tariffs and Trade (GATT). The President's authority to enter foreign trade agreements under the Tariff Act is explicitly 'not be construed to determine or indicate the approval or disapproval by the Congress of the executive agreement known as the General Agreement on Tariffs and Trade'.[58] The President is expected to seek information and advice from representatives of industry, agriculture and labor.[59]

The Uruguay Round Trade Agreements Act, approved after prolonged public and congressional debate, strongly reasserts US sovereignty. 'No provision of any of the Uruguay Round Agreements, nor the application of any such provision to any person or circumstance, that is inconsistent with any law of the United States shall have effect.'[60] On dispute settlement, no person can legally challenge any action of any US agency for inconsistency with the Uruguay Round agreements.[61] No state law or its application can be declared invalid for

---

57   Trade Act of 1974 §2411 (a).
58   §1351(a) 91(A).
59   §1251 (f).
60   §3512 (a)(1).
61   §3512(c).

inconsistency with the Uruguay Round agreements, except in an action brought by the Federal government for the purpose of declaring it so.[62] There are detailed procedures for notification and consultation during a dispute brought at the WTO by or against the US, including identification of the panel members and whether the US Trade Representative (USTR) agreed to them. Where a WTO dispute panel or Appellate Body finds against a US regulation or practice, a detailed process for congressional, private sector and public consultation is required before any action to amend, rescind or modify the rule. There is no requirement to make the rule conform.

Where dispute panel or Appellate Body reports involve action by the US International Trade Commission in relation to antidumping, safeguards or subsidies and countervailing measures, the Commission may be asked to report on whether the Tariff Act permits it to take steps to render its action not inconsistent with the findings.[63] If a majority believe it can be, then it must issue a determination to that effect. The USTR may, after consultation, revoke the offending duty in whole or part. The approach is stricter when an action by the administering authority under the Tariff Act is involved. Significantly, the legislation specifically retains the power of the USTR to initiate an investigation and action under section 301 *et al.*

The benefits of WTO membership are subject to ongoing review. The USTR is required to report annually to Congress in detail on the activities and implications of WTO activities for the US. A five-yearly review is mandated to analyse 'the effects of the WTO Agreement on the interests of the United States, the costs and benefits to the United States of its participation in the WTO, and the value of continued participation of the United States in the WTO'. Detailed procedures are set down for withdrawal.[64]

A major test of the US commitment to new WTO rules came with the recent interim finding of a WTO panel against a US ban on importing shrimps caught by vessels not using turtle excluder devices.[65] The US has announced its intention to appeal. However, it also maintains the right to determine whether or not to alter its policy once the WTO appeal options are exhausted. The US has more choice about this than most other countries—retaliation by the complainants (Thailand, Malaysia, India and Pakistan) is pretty meaningless. But the government still needs to balance domestic pressures, especially from environmental groups and defenders of US sovereignty, against pressures from its TNEs and the economic and strategic arguments for maintaining a credible multilateral rules-based approach to global economic activity. The outcome of such a balancing exercise is far from guaranteed. It is significant that the US Federal Court of Appeals subsequently issued a much narrower interpretation of the relevant law than applied previously, which may effectively resolve the dispute.[66]

---

[62]   §3512(2)(A).
[63]   §3538 (a)(1).
[62]   §3535.
[65]   The measure is based on Section 609 of the US Endangered Species Act.
[66]   See 'Justice wins skirmish in sea turtle war', *Journal of Commerce*, 15 June 1998, and 'Ruggiero warns against unilateral trade measures', International Centre for Trade and Sustainable Development, Feature Article, web site www.ictsd.org.

Implications for Aotearoa New Zealand

This paper has deliberately focused on overseas examples to illustrate the potential for conflicts and the factors that influence the outcomes. Aotearoa New Zealand is not immune from these tensions. There was strong opposition to the government's claims that international commitments require a move to zero tariffs. The government cited the APEC requirement for a free trade and investment regime by 2010—but failed to add that APEC commitments are non-binding and voluntary. Others have challenged the acceptance of foreign product testing and labelling, overseas qualifications and the maintenance of a virtually unfettered foreign investment regime. Government is presently considering whether foreign education companies supplying services from offshore have the right under the General Agreement on Trade in Services (GATS) to access the new tertiary student tuition vouchers.

There have been strong Maori challenges to the mandate of colonial governments to conclude international treaties which bind the Treaty partner and to confer rights on foreign actors which preclude the Crown from recognising the prior rights of Iwi and Hapu, especially over cultural knowledge and taonga.[67] Maori played a lead role in the unprecedented mobilisation of popular opposition to the proposed OECD MAI. Ironically, had the New Zealand government already signed the MAI, the foreign owners of electricity companies could have sought full market compensation for economic loss caused by the 1998 electricity company restructuring as an action having equivalent effect to an expropriation.[68] Any ICSID arbitration award would have been enforceable domestically—conferring rights not available to local investors affected in the same way and imposing a massive burden on the taxpayer. Opposition to the MAI within Aotearoa and internationally helped avert that possibility.

There are threats of dire consequences if a future New Zealand government reneges on its international commitments, fails to make new commitments or even deviates from the global economic agenda. These are almost certainly over-played. Several years ago, for example, the Alliance raised the possibility of the New Zealand government citing a serious balance of payments problem to allow temporary derogation from its GATT obligations. I was one of those who dismissed the possibility. Yet India has used the special provisions for developing countries with balance of payments difficulties to impose import restrictions despite maintaining significant foreign currency reserves.[69] New Zealand's current account deficit could certainly be considered in crisis at around seven percent of GDP.

---

[67]   *Eg.* International Conference on the Cultural and Intellectual Property Rights of Indigenous Peoples: Mataatua Declaration on Cultural and Intellectual Property Rights of Indigenous Peoples, Whakatane, Aotearoa, June 1993; Claim to the Waitangi Tribunal in Relation to Indigenous Intellectual Property (WAI-262)

[68]   *Multilateral Agreement on Investment. Consolidated Text and Commentary,* Part IV.2, DAFFE/MAI/NM(98), May 1998.

[69]   B.L. Das, 'The Diktats in the WTO', *Third World Economics*, no.170, 1-15 April 1997, p.15.

Conclusion

This argument militates against suggestions that domestic governments and courts can no longer make choices or that doing so will impose intolerable costs. It does not deny the very real pressures to integrate global economic activity and convergence of economic policy, regulation and law. It recognises that the power of global capital and threats of economic retaliation impose real constraints on state power. It also acknowledges the state as one actor in the global arena, with many other possible sites of contest over policy and law.

But the state retains considerable power. There are still choices, even for highly exposed and economically weak countries. States face a range of competing pressures—foreign and domestic, political and economic. In determining how they reconcile these there is a real potential for contesting not just what the state does, but the nature of the state itself. If governments are seen to act against the best interests of those they claim to represent, people can and do take action; some even revolt. Where courts fail to uphold domestic obligations, they too may face challenges to their legitimacy. At that stage they face the ultimate question of whether state sovereignty has any substance. These considerations have become more potent as systemic failures of the global free market have continued to emerge. The costs of pursuing such policies may become greater than the costs of rejecting them. All things are possible. Global economic policy and the new global constitutionalism are therefore far from irresistible or inevitable.

Name Index

For Product Safety Concerns and Information please contact our EU
representative GPSR@taylorandfrancis.com Taylor & Francis Verlag GmbH,
Kaufingerstraße 24, 80331 München, Germany

Printed and bound by CPI Group (UK) Ltd, Croydon, CR0 4YY

08/05/2025

01864325-0004